THE *unofficial* GUIDE®
ᵀᴼLas Vegas

2012

THE *unofficial* GUIDE®

ᴛᴏ Las Vegas

2012

BOB SEHLINGER

with LEN TESTA, MAX JACOBSON,
XANIA V. WOODMAN, CAM USHER,
and DEKE CASTLEMAN

WILEY

Please note that prices fluctuate in the course of time, and travel information changes under the impact of many factors that influence the travel industry. We therefore suggest that you write or call ahead for confirmation when making your travel plans. Every effort has been made to ensure the accuracy of information throughout this book, and the contents of this publication are believed correct at the time of printing. Nevertheless, the publishers cannot accept responsibility for errors or omissions or for changes in details given in this guide or for the consequences of any reliance on the information provided by the same. Assessments of attractions and so forth are based upon the author's own experience, and therefore descriptions given in this guide necessarily contain an element of subjective opinion, which may not reflect the publisher's opinion or dictate a reader's own experience on another occasion. Readers are invited to write the publisher with ideas, comments, and suggestions for future editions.

Published by:
John Wiley & Sons, Inc.
111 River Street
Hoboken, NJ 07030

Produced by Menasha Ridge Press

Cover design by Michael J. Freeland

Interior design by Vertigo Design

For information on our other products and services or to obtain technical support, please contact our Customer Care Department within the United States at 800-762-2974, outside the United States at 317-572-3993, or fax 317-572-4002.

John Wiley & Sons, Inc. also publishes its books in a variety of electronic formats. Some content that appears in print may not be available in electronic formats.

ISBN 978-1-1180-1230-7

Manufactured in the United States of America

5 4 3 2 1

CONTENTS

MAPS *and* ILLUSTRATIONS

ACKNOWLEDGMENTS

THE PEOPLE OF LAS VEGAS love their city and spare no effort to assist a writer trying to dig beneath the facade of flashing neon. It is important to them to communicate that Las Vegas is a city with depth, diversity, and substance. "Don't just write about our casinos," they demand; "take the time to get to know us."

We made every effort to do just that, enabled each step of the way by some of the most sincere and energetic folks a writer could hope to encounter. Thanks to Nevada expert Deke Castleman for his contributions to our entertainment, nightlife, and buffet coverage, to gambling pro Anthony Curtis for his tips on the best places to play, and to Cam Usher for her work capturing the essence of Las Vegas hotels. Xania V. Woodman, nightlife editor at *Las Vegas Weekly*, handles the nightlife scene.

Restaurant critic Max Jacobson ate his way through dozens of new restaurants. Jim McDonald of the Las Vegas Police Department shared his experiences and offered valuable suggestions for staying out of trouble. Larry Olmsted evaluated Las Vegas golf courses, Chris McBeath created our spa chapter, and forest ranger Debbie Savage assisted us in developing material on wilderness recreation. Thanks also to Fred Hazleton, who reviewed shows and inspected hotels.

Much gratitude to Steve Jones, Annie Long, Molly Merkle, Holly Cross, and Ann Cassar, the pros who turned all this effort into a book.

INTRODUCTION

ON *a* PLANE *to* LAS VEGAS

I NEVER WANTED TO GO TO LAS VEGAS. I'm not much of a gambler and have always thought of Las Vegas as a city dedicated to separating folks from their money. As it happens, however, I have some involvement with industries that hold conventions and trade shows there. For some years I was able to persuade others to go in my place. Eventually, of course, it came my turn to go, and I found myself aboard a Delta jumbo jet on my first trip to Las Vegas.

Listening to the banter of those around me, I became aware that my fellow passengers were divided into two distinct camps. Some obviously thought themselves on a nonstop flight to Nirvana and could not have been happier. Too excited to remain seated, they danced up and down the aisles, clapping one another on the back in anticipation. The other passengers, by contrast, groused and grumbled, swore under their breath, and wore expressions suggesting a steady diet of lemons. These people, as despondent as Al Capone en route to a tax audit, lamented their bad luck and cursed those who had made a trip to such a place necessary.

To my surprise, I thoroughly enjoyed Las Vegas. I had a great time without gambling and have been back many times with never a bad experience. The people are friendly, the food is good, the hotels are among the nicest in the country, it's an easy town to find your way around, and there is plenty to do (24 hours a day, if you are so inclined).

It's hard to say why so many folks have such strong feelings about Las Vegas (even those who have never been there). Among our research team, we had people willing to put their kids in boarding school for a chance to go, while others begged off to have root-canal surgery or prune their begonias. A third group wanted to go very badly but maintained the pretense of total indifference. They reminded me of people who own five TVs yet profess never to watch television; they clearly had not mustered the courage to come out of the closet.

What I discovered during my first and subsequent visits is that the nongambling public doesn't know very much about Las Vegas. Many people cannot see beyond the gambling, cannot see that there could possibly be anything of value in Las Vegas for nongamblers or those only marginally interested in gambling.

When you ask these people to describe their ideal vacation, they wax eloquent about lazy days relaxing in the sun, playing golf, enjoying the luxury of resort hotels, eating in fine restaurants, sightseeing, shopping, and going to the theater. Outdoor types speak no less enthusiastically about fishing, boating, hiking, and, in winter, skiing. As it happens, Las Vegas offers all of this. Gambling is just the tip of the iceberg in Las Vegas, but it's all many people can see.

Las Vegas is, of course, about gambling, but there's so much more. Vegas has sunny, mild weather two-thirds of the year, some of the finest hotels and restaurants in the world, the most diversified celebrity and production-show entertainment to be found, unique shopping, internationally renowned golf courses, and numerous attractions. For the outdoor enthusiast, Red Rock Canyon National Conservation Area, Lake Mead National Recreation Area, and Toiyabe National Forest offer some of the most exotic and beautiful wilderness resources in North America.

This guide is designed for those who *want* to go to Las Vegas and for those who *have* to go to Las Vegas. If you are a recreational gambler and/or an enthusiastic vacationer, we will show you ways to have more fun, make the most of your time, and spend less money. If you are one of the skeptics, unwilling spouses or companions of gamblers, business travelers, or people who think they would rather be someplace else, we will help you discover the seven-eighths of the Las Vegas iceberg that is hidden.

—*Bob Sehlinger*

LOOKING BACK, LOOKING AHEAD

IN 1946, BUGSY SIEGEL OPENED the Flamingo Hotel, kicking off the metamorphosis that changed three miles of mostly barren desert into what is now the Las Vegas Strip. The original Flamingo was an eye-popper in its day and established a baseline that all subsequent casinos had to at least match, if not improve upon.

As new hotels appeared in the neon Valhalla, each contributed something different, and occasionally something better, raising the bar incrementally. Two properties, the Desert Inn and Caesars Palace, advanced the standard significantly, but because they catered to an exclusive clientele, their competitors chose not to follow suit.

Then, in 1989, came the Mirage, a large hotel-casino offering the spectacle of Caesars and the refinement of the Desert Inn (almost) but, more importantly, targeting not the carriage trade but rather the average tourist. The Mirage was equal parts tourist attraction, hotel, and casino, and each part was executed with imagination and flair. Not many Vegas tourists could afford the Mirage's expensive guest rooms, but the place was nonetheless a must-see for every visitor.

The IMPACT of the MIRAGE

THE MIRAGE'S SUCCESS DEMONSTRATED that gamblers, contrary to prevailing opinion, actually paid attention to their gaming environment and, if given a choice, preferred an interesting, dynamic, and attractive setting to the cramped, noisy, monochromatic boiler room that was then the casino norm. Beyond a doubt, the Mirage was in a class by itself. Observers waited impatiently to see if any competitor would challenge the Mirage, but most believed the standard was impossibly high.

The answer was not long in coming. A veritable explosion of new developments was rushed from the drawing board to the construction zone. First was the Excalibur in 1990. It was big, plastic, gaudy, and certainly no direct competitor to the Mirage, but its Knights of the Round Table theme played incredibly well with the blue-collar and family markets. Next came the Class of 1993, which included the pyramid-shaped Luxor, Treasure Island (then a sister property to the Mirage), and the MGM Grand Hotel and Theme Park. Though the MGM Grand Theme Park was a bust, the hotel and casino were immediately successful. Likewise, the Luxor and Treasure Island (T. I.), with their knockout themes, rocketed up the pop chart.

In the three years before the next wave of new hotels opened in 1996, the vital signs of both the newer and older properties were monitored closely. The MGM Grand was the largest hotel-casino in the world, Excalibur was a close second, and the other new hotels offered more than 2,500 rooms each. As with the bull stock market in the late 1990s, there was endless speculation and debate about how long the building boom could last. But the preliminary data seemed to indicate that the new properties were responsible for increasing the aggregate market. Room occupancy rates remained high.

SURVIVAL of the OLDER CASINOS

THOUGH MORE VISITORS WERE COMING to Las Vegas, the lion's share of the business was going to the newer, high-profile hotels. Older properties, including some of the Strip's most established casinos, found themselves increasingly in the margins. So too, downtown Las Vegas was in a tailspin, with gaming revenues down, or flat, year after year. The new marching orders, avoided or ignored for so long, were crystal clear: if you want to play in the big league, you have to upgrade. And upgrading meant approximating the Mirage standard.

The response from downtown Las Vegas was to combine the Fremont Street casinos into a mega–gaming venue, a new Glitter Gulch, tied together by a pedestrian plaza under the canopy of the Fremont Street Experience electric light show. Back on the Strip, older properties, including Bally's, the Desert Inn, the Flamingo, the Tropicana, the Sahara, the Boardwalk, Circus Circus, and the Riviera, scrambled to upgrade. The venerable Caesars Palace alone managed to stay ahead of the game, making improvements each year to maintain its position at or near the top of the Strip food chain.

HONEY, I BLEW UP
the CASINO!

IN 1991, BOB STUPAK'S QUIRKY Vegas World was demolished to make way in 1996 for the Stratosphere Hotel and Casino, which has the tallest observation tower in the United States. The fireworks had just begun. Farther south on the Strip, the Monte Carlo hit the scene, a joint venture between then Circus Circus Enterprises and Mirage Resorts. In 1997, New York–New York opened its doors. With more than 100,000 visitors a day during its first weeks of operation, New York–New York quickly dispelled the notion that the Strip was overbuilt. In typical Las Vegas go-for-broke style, the Dunes, the Sands, El Rancho, the Boardwalk, the Hacienda, and more recently the New Frontier and the Stardust were blown up to make room for a new wave of gargantuan gambling palaces.

The boom proceeded at warp speed, with a construction frenzy that through 2001 added a whopping 28,000 new rooms to Las Vegas's inventory (now totaling roughly 149,000). Bellagio (opened in 1998) draws its inspiration from Italy's Lake Como, adding 4,000 rooms to the MGM Resorts International (MRI) galaxy and catering to the upscale market. Across the street is 2,900-room Paris Las Vegas with its own 50-story Eiffel Tower. Just south is Planet Hollywood (formerly the Aladdin), a 2,600-room complex with a Hollywood theme. On the site of the old Sands is the Venetian. An all-suite property with 3,000 suites in its first building phase and 1,013 in its second, the Venetian features a shopping complex in a Venice-canal setting complete with gondola rides. A sister hotel, the Palazzo, with 3,000-plus suites, joined the Venetian complex in 2008. At the southern end of the Strip on the old Hacienda property, the 3,300-room Mandalay Bay opened in 1999. Steve Wynn opened Wynn Las Vegas in 2005 with 2,700 rooms and premiered a second hotel, Wynn Encore, in 2008, both on the site of the fabled Desert Inn.

More and more new casinos were built around town in an effort to cater to the local population and visitors who don't want to battle the traffic of the Strip. In 2006, the Red Rock Resort opened with 400 rooms overlooking Red Rock Canyon. Also to the west of the Strip is JW Marriott, a 550-room spa and golf resort in the Summerlin area of Las Vegas that was built in 1999. To the east, Loews Lake Las Vegas (near Henderson) is surrounded by a man-made lake and a Jack Nicklaus–designed golf course.

The locals' response to Red Rock Resort demonstrated that the then-growing population of Las Vegas appreciated upscale casinos, too. M Resort, on the Strip about 12 miles south of Mandalay Bay, opened in 2009 to serve the affluent residents of the south Las Vegas valley. Similarly, Aliante Station opened in the same year to serve the suburbs of north Las Vegas.

The **GREAT MERGERS** and **ACQUISITIONS**

THEN THERE ARE THE MERGERS and acquisitions. In 2000, Steve Wynn, the visionary behind the Mirage (and the Las Vegas transformation it started), sold the Mirage, Bellagio, T. I., Golden Nugget, and half of Monte Carlo to MGM Grand for $6.4 billion. Wynn, meanwhile, purchased the Desert Inn, where he built a 2,700-room nonthemed resort called Wynn Las Vegas, stating ironically that "themes are a thing of the past." Wynn always seems to be a step ahead of the pack and might be correct about themes. Still, it's like Dr. Spock saying that children are a thing of the past.

The Mandalay Resort Group, which owned Luxor, Mandalay Bay, Excalibur, Circus Circus, and half of the Monte Carlo, was acquired in June of 2004 by MGM Grand for a whopping $6 billion, forming MGM Mirage (now MGM Resorts International) with control of 36,000 Strip hotel rooms. Only months earlier, Hilton's casino subsidiary, Park Place Entertainment, bought Caesars Palace and O'Shea's, adding them to a lineup that already included the Las Vegas Hilton, Bally's, Paris, and the Flamingo. In 2004, Park Place changed its name to Caesars Entertainment to reflect the prestige of its flagship property. In an even bigger (not to mention surprising) deal, Harrah's bought Caesars Entertainment in a $9.4 billion deal, thus becoming the largest casino-gambling company in the world. Subsequently, Harrah's also acquired the Rio, Imperial Palace, Planet Hollywood, and the Barbary Coast (renamed Bill's Gamblin' Hall and Saloon). In 2010, Harrah's changed its corporate name back to Caesars Entertainment.

GLUTTONS ARE MORE LIKELY *to* CHOKE *to* DEATH

THIS FOLKSY SAYING DESCRIBES the unbridled development of the Las Vegas Strip built precariously (some would say recklessly) on a rapidly deteriorating street-and-highway infrastructure. And it's only going to get worse.

For many years there have been sizable undeveloped parcels of land along the Strip, most conspicuously between Circus Circus and the Stratosphere. In the middle of the Strip, small retailers and second-string hotels squatted on some of the planet's most valuable real estate. No more. In a development frenzy that makes the 1990s hotel crop look like home gardening, the land has been gobbled up and giant construction cranes have redefined the Strip's skyline. High-rise mania hit Las Vegas with a vengeance. Believe it or not, this city is running out of room to develop horizontally, so it's turning vertical. Nearly 80 high-rise condominium, time-share, and condo-hotel towers have been announced in the past few years, encompassing more than 30,000 units.

The projects are not just huge hotels as in the past, but veritable self-contained cities rising above every existing resort and containing hotels (yes, plural), residential condos, restaurants, entertainment, shopping, parks, and even their own road networks. CityCenter, an MRI $9.2-billion development, was the largest construction project in the United States.

Plans for all of the combined resort and residential developments call for on-site supermarkets, pharmacies, and other services that the residents and guests will need. This is fortunate indeed because almost nothing is being done to the infrastructure to accommodate the many thousands of additional people who will live, work, and play along the Strip. We've seen model units of the condos for sale in these developments and can report that they're quite lovely, which is good, because their denizens are likely to be held hostage by surrounding traffic arteries that are already completely overwhelmed.

Sooner or later, the Strip is going to choke to death. Already the Strip is the most sclerotic traffic artery imaginable, making 45-minute slogs of a half-mile trip. Some hope of relief came in 2004 in the form of a monorail, which runs along the east side of the Strip and loops over to the Las Vegas Convention Center, then on to the Sahara. Problem is, the stations are so far removed from the Strip that only about half the riders necessary to break even are using the monorail.

OZ STUMBLES

ONCE THOUGHT TO BE RECESSION PROOF, Las Vegas was brought to its knees by the economic disasters of 2008 and 2009. The recession could not have come at a worse time. Many of the world's largest casino companies, condo developers, and hotel chains had multi-billion-dollar projects under construction and were leveraged out the proverbial wazoo. Hotel occupancy and gambling revenues plummeted. All the while, debt on the unfinished developments mounted. Industry leaders like MGM Mirage (now MGM Resorts International) and Harrah's (now Caesars Entertainment) suddenly found themselves teetering on the brink of bankruptcy. MGM Mirage, strapped with $14 billion in debt, sold Treasure Island in an effort to see CityCenter through to completion. Thousands of prospective jobs evaporated, and for the first time in decades, Las Vegas reported negative population growth.

Though condo developers held contracts on thousands of sold units, only a fraction of those managed to close. Conventions and trade shows were either called off or scaled down. Before 2009 was five months old, more than 350 Las Vegas trade show events had been cancelled, costing the local economy more than $133 million. Home values dipped precipitously, and Las Vegas still has the highest fore-closure rate in the country, topping out at seven times the national average. Gambling revenues dipped by 10%.

Hotels have dealt with decreased visitation and depressed room rates, experienced significant losses in gaming revenue, halted or postponed construction, shuttered sections, or shut down entirely. Last year, the Ritz Carlton closed its property at Lake Las Vegas, and the legendary Sahara, struggling with an increasingly isolated north Strip location, closed in May. Binion's Horseshoe on Fremont Street shuttered the hotel's 365-room tower, but the casino remains open. Downtown's room inventory has decreased from 27,100 rooms six years ago to a current count of 22,308.

Conversely, several corporations demonstrating confidence in the destination have forged ahead. Deutsche Bank's $3.9-billion invest-ment in the Cosmopolitan came to fruition when the resort unleashed 2,995 Strip-side rooms in December 2010. Dolce Resorts purchased the unoccupied Ritz Carlton at Lake Las Vegas and re-opened it as the Ravella Resort. The Golden Nugget added 500 rooms; there are 865 rooms in two new towers at the Hard Rock; and 1,200 recently com-pleted suites joined Planet Hollywood's footprint. The Tropicana underwent a complete overhaul, while Caesars Palace is finishing the long-delayed interior of the 660-room Octavius Tower. The Plaza's two towers will come online in late 2011 after a total renovation of the downtown property. Locked up since 2006, the Lady Luck's projected makeover could be complete by fall 2012. Both the MGM Grand and Wynn Resort are remodeling all guest rooms. Caesars Entertainment is contemplating a major retail, restaurant, and entertainment com-plex called Project Linq along a shortcut between the Flamingo and the Imperial Palace. The focal point will be a giant Ferris wheel.

Some resorts have been accused of luring business away from their sister properties as well as from competitors. As a result of the downturn, airlines have slashed capacity and the number of flights to Las Vegas. Another deterrent is the ever-rising price of gasoline, which will heavily impact the drive-in market and regional visitation. The higher cost of airline fuel will increase the price of airline tickets, primarily affecting the leisure traveler. Locally, the Las Vegas Monorail is in trouble with shrinking ridership, and the projected airport leg is on hold. Entire buildings of Strip-vicinity high-rise luxury condos have been revamped as apartments, and until the economy rebounds no uber-resorts are on the horizon for the next decade.

When MGM Resorts International's glamorous CityCenter urban complex with 6,000 rooms was introduced with a flourish in 2009, along with the Cosmopolitan's 2,995 suites a year later, 8,995 more accommodations were added in a down market and Las Vegas's city-wide room inventory reached a jaw-dropping 148,935 units. This year occupancy is holding its own at 80.4% but reflects a big drop over the last four years. Room rates have increased by 2%; the citywide average nightly lodging rate has inched upward by $2 to $95. However, bottom-line profits for several Las Vegas hotel corporations come not from local properties but from their Asian casinos and the establishment of their brands as nongaming retreats in Dubai, China, Abu Dhabi, and Vietnam. To stem the flood of currency away from Nevada, the state is considering the legalization of Internet gaming.

While the convention market is rebounding marginally, the business has changed with the new popularity of regional meetings overcoming corporate and nonprofit associations' previous ardor for annual megaconventions. Combined with the increased hassles of air travel and reluctance of organizations to provide more funding for business travel, the growth of this market segment is slight. While conventioneers will spend more on hotel rooms, they demonstrate lower propensity to gamble and have curbed their enthusiastic splurging for entertainment, cocktails, and luxury dining.

Some moderately priced properties have entered the youth and senior hostel market, while a few major hotels have become pet-friendly, adding a per-night surcharge for canines. Seeking additional earnings, many hotels charge unpopular resort fees ranging from $5 to $30 per night for items, such as local phone calls, Wi-Fi and Internet access, and fitness center access, that previously had been complimentary. Another source of income is personalized guest services to guarantee kings or double doubles, early check-in, or extended check-out. Ever on the bandwagon, other properties advertise themselves as "Fee-free." Hotels with showrooms have identified entertainment sales as an untapped revenue stream, offering more afternoon acts, show passes (admission to multiple shows within a limited time frame), backstage tours, meet-and-greets with performers, and dinner-show-nightclub packages. Entry-fee seasonal pool parties with concerts abound, and nightclubs have expanded poolside adding water diversions to their inventory of pleasures. Food courts have proliferated, while gourmet restaurants are closing.

Adaptation is the key to the Las Vegas resort industry's response to the recession and awareness that there is a dwindling pool of wealthy travelers. To expand their customer base, hotels are vigorously pursuing international visitors based on the strength of their currencies, an increase in direct overseas flights, a penchant for upscale shopping, and preference for longer stays. Ad campaigns focus less on the hedonistic and frivolous and embrace more conservative mass appeal. For the first time, hotels are directing ads to local residents with a staycation program. Properties are offering significantly reduced room rates, $1–$3 blackjack tables, all-you-can-eat all-day buffet passes, prix-fixe menus, dinner-show specials, extra nights free, spa combo packages, resort credits, show and concert discounts, looser slots, higher denomination gaming coupons, online rate reductions, and a smorgasbord of value-added packages. Peripheral businesses such as malls, sightseeing companies, attractions, and independent restaurants are extending coupons galore, meal deals, reduced tour prices, and two-for-one admissions. The upside of these promotions? Terrific benefits for visitors, including greater availability of hard-to-get show tickets, shorter waits for restaurant tables, less foot and vehicle traffic, lower-minimum casino games, more upgrades and amenities, closer parking, and fewer lines. Nevertheless, in many instances visitors can expect to experience somewhat higher food, beverage, and entertainment prices overall as hotels scramble to cover the loss of casino revenues for the time being.

WHAT IT MEANS *to* YOU

INTERESTINGLY, IF YOU CRUISE the Strip or downtown, everything looks pretty normal. The better shows still play to packed audiences, long queues at hotel registration desks continue to frustrate, and the casinos seem to be bustling. All of the above, however, is attributable to hotels and casinos heavily discounting, especially when it comes to rooms. Condo developers trying to generate cash flow compound the discounting by dumping empty and unsold units into the city's hotel room inventory. A quick gallop around a hotel search engine will turn up dozens of lodging options in properties that were supposed to be residences. Though Las Vegas occupancy rates were beginning to climb out of the hole as we went to press, the same could not be said of room rates, and it looks like the heavy discounting will continue unabated until late spring of 2012 at the earliest. What kind of discounts are we talking about? In April of 2011—one of the nicest months to visit Las Vegas—$350 to $450 rooms at the Bellagio and Wynn Encore were going for $169 per night. Hilton Vacation Club (time-share) condos were offered at $89 per night. More luxurious digs at Trump International were available for $95 per night. A number of hotels such as Mandalay Bay not only discounted rooms but also threw in free show tickets and other sweeteners. The Mirage promoted $85-per-night rooms packaged with a $40 dining credit and admission for four to its Secret Garden attraction. To find deals coupled with sweeteners check your favorite search engine for "name of hotel and promotions"—for example, "Caesars Palace and promotions" or "Luxor and promotions." You get the idea.

Because the larger and newer hotels have more appeal and drawing power, they can always put people in beds by discounting. Older hotels, such as the Riviera, Imperial Palace, and Circus Circus, among others, are forced to discount much more deeply to fill their rooms. This is especially true of the downtown properties and the Riviera, which count heavily on meeting attendees. Likewise, more isolated hotels are forced to offer deeper discounts. Silverton and Southpoint, both located south of Las Vegas off Interstate 15, usually represent exceptional value.

The Las Vegas entertainment scene was the last to succumb to the storms of recession. Remarkably, in 2009, the average price of undiscounted tickets for long-running shows topped $80 for the first time. 2010 and 2011, on the other hand, were another story with a succession of ticket-price reductions, twofers, dollars-off coupons in visitor mags and on the Internet, and the bundling of shows with hotel stays at bargain rates. There are still two dozen or so shows where admission tops $100, but for the first time some of these shows have become available at the local half-price ticket discounters. If you've ever wanted to see a Cirque du Soleil show on the cheap, now's the time. Nothing's guaranteed, however, and half-price tickets to premium productions may be scarce on weekends. Tickets must be purchased in person at one of the discounter locations on the same day as the performance. Higher-price VIP seating, once relegated to topless revues and celebrity headliner shows, is now ubiquitous but rarely worth the steep tariff. With attendance lagging as it is, you'll usually get a good seat buying general admission. Leave the VIP seats to myopic old coots who can't tell a nipple from a fried egg absent a telescope. If shows are too expensive, discounts notwithstanding, live music in casino lounges abounds, continuing a six-decade tradition as Las Vegas's best entertainment value.

The recession has forced many restaurants, both in and out of casinos, to close. For the most part, restaurant prices haven't come down, although some of the better restaurants now offer a fixed-price "tasting" menu at a very reasonable price to lure you in. It can be a good deal and perhaps a time-limited opportunity to try a restaurant you couldn't ordinarily afford. Just be mindful of what you order in addition to the fixed-price meal—that's where you can lose. Most of the signs of stress we're

unofficial **TIP**
A few high-quality afternoon productions offer a bargain alternative to the mortgage-the-farm-priced shows playing the major showrooms.

observing on the dining scene come in the form of a proliferation of two-for-one deals, discount coupons, free appetizers, and the like. As with hotels and casinos, restaurants know that the first step is to get you through the door, so that's where they're putting their energy.

The QUIET CONTENDER

A FEW YEARS BACK, the big buzz was Las Vegas as a family destination. Insiders understood, however, that all the talk was just that. At most, the family thing was a public relations exercise to make Las Vegas appear more wholesome. It was tacitly understood that the big dogs would never allow theme parks and other family-oriented attractions to actually compete with the casinos for a visitor's time. Lost in the backwash of this hollow debate, however, was the exponential burgeoning of theme shopping. Shopping is something that reached critical mass almost unnoticed and that keeps visitors out of the casinos. At present, the case can be made that shopping is almost as potent an attraction in Las Vegas as gambling. On the Strip are four huge themed shopping venues (Forum Shops, Grand Canal Shops, Crystals, and Miracle Mile Shops) and a comparatively white-bread mall, but one that's buttressed with every big-name department store in North America. Not to be left in the wake, downtown offers the Las Vegas Premium Outlets complex, which features 150 stores, all flogging upmarket brands. For the first time, there is something powerful enough to suck the players right out of the casinos, and it arrived on the scene as stealthily as a Trojan horse.

The impact of the economic downturn is most starkly evident among Las Vegas retailers. Where casinos appear busy, shops are anything but. Irrespective of venue, from the tony Forum Shops to hotel sundry stores, sale signs are everywhere. Sales, mind you, are relative, and even at half off, the $1,500 sport coat at Bellagio is going to cost a not-inconsiderable $750.

A TALE *of* TWO CITIES

FOR AT LEAST 30 YEARS Las Vegas has been referred to as "Disneyland for Adults." At the time this tongue-in-cheek appellation was gaining currency Las Vegas was anything but. Disneyland was systematically planned, highly polished, absolutely regimented, and totally plastic. Las Vegas, by contrast, grew like a weed, was raw, unrefined, and freewheeling, and was as real as a one-way ticket home on Greyhound with an empty wallet. Disneyland was a sanitized version of fantasy and history, Las Vegas the last vestige of the western frontier.

When we began covering Las Vegas about 20 years ago, the casinos were predominantly independent. Each had a distinct identity free of the corporate veneer that blankets Las Vegas today. Personality, or the lack thereof, was defining. As with cakes at a church fund-raiser, what was on the inside was what mattered. Now it's the icing that counts, or, expressed differently, the icon (Statue of Liberty, Sphinx, pirate ship, Eiffel Tower . . . you choose) that sits in the casino's front yard. Inside, the product is largely the same. Four casino megacorporations now run most of Las Vegas. On the Strip it's worse. Two companies—Caesars Entertainment and MGM Resorts International (MRI)—own every casino except the Tropicana, Riviera, Venetian, Stratosphere, Cosmopolitan, and Wynn resorts. Standards for restaurants, hotel rooms, entertainment, theme, and just about everything else offer all the predictability of a nice chain hotel. The maverick casinos and their rough-and-tumble owners are all but gone, and with them the gritty, boom-or-bust soul of this gambling town. Making a clichéd joke a fulfilled prophecy—Las Vegas has in fact become Disneyland.

If you'd like a taste of the old Las Vegas, now's the time. Tomorrow, or soon after, it will largely be gone. While you can, walk Glitter Gulch; enjoy a shrimp cocktail at the Golden Gate; see *Jubilee!*, the quintessential Las Vegas Parisian revue; or play craps beneath the stained-glass canopy at the Tropicana. Linger over the porterhouse special at the Redwood Bar and Grill at the California, or the duck flambé anise at Hugo's Cellar at the Four Queens. Make no mistake, this is not slumming; each example represents the best of Las Vegas in both a current and historical sense. And if you wait too long? Well, enjoy the new Las Vegas: systematically planned, highly polished, absolutely regimented, and totally plastic.

As most of you know, we also publish guides to Disneyland and Walt Disney World and have never for a moment doubted the overall quality of the Disney product. Comparing the new Las Vegas with Disneyland is a long way from a condemnation. Though we liked the sultry, wide-open, sinful feel of the old Vegas, we can't argue that corporate Las Vegas has built an Oz that no maverick dreamer could have envisioned. Whether the old Las Vegas or the new Las Vegas is better, we'll leave you to judge.

LETTERS, COMMENTS, AND QUESTIONS FROM READERS

WE EXPECT TO LEARN FROM OUR MISTAKES, as well as from the input of our readers, and to improve with each edition. Many of those who use the *Unofficial Guides* write to us to ask questions, make comments, or share their own discoveries and lessons learned in Las Vegas. We appreciate all such input, both positive and critical, and encourage our readers to continue writing. Readers' comments and observations will be frequently incorporated in revised editions of the *Unofficial Guide* and will contribute immeasurably to its improvement.

How to Write the Author:

Bob Sehlinger
The Unofficial Guide to Las Vegas

P.O. Box 43673
Birmingham, AL 35243
unofficialguides@menasharidge.com

If you write us, rest assured that we won't release your name and address to any mailing-list companies, direct-mail advertisers, or other third parties. Unless you tell us otherwise, we'll assume that you're OK with being quoted in the *Unofficial Guide*. Be sure to put your return address on both your letter and the envelope—sometimes envelopes and letters get separated. And because our work takes us out of the office for long periods of time, note that our response may be delayed.

Reader Survey

At the back of this guide, you will find a short questionnaire that you can use to express opinions concerning your Las Vegas visit. Clip the questionnaire along the dotted line and mail it to the above address.

HOW INFORMATION IS ORGANIZED: BY SUBJECT AND BY GEOGRAPHIC AREAS

TO GIVE YOU FAST ACCESS to information about the *best* of Las Vegas, we've organized material in several formats.

HOTELS Because most people visiting Las Vegas stay in one hotel for the duration of their vacation or business trip, we have summarized our coverage of hotels in charts, maps, ratings, and rankings that allow you to quickly focus your decision-making process. We do not ramble on for page after page describing lobbies and rooms which, in the final analysis, sound (and look) much the same. Instead, we concentrate our coverage on the specific variables that differentiate one hotel from another: location, size, room quality, services, amenities, and cost.

RESTAURANTS We give you a lot of detail when it comes to restaurants. Because you will probably eat a dozen or more restaurant meals during your stay, and because not even you can predict what kind of fare you might be in the mood for on, say, Saturday night, we provide detailed profiles of the very best restaurants Las Vegas has to offer.

ENTERTAINMENT AND NIGHTLIFE Visitors frequently try several different shows or clubs during their stay. Because shows and nightspots, like restaurants, are usually selected spontaneously after arriving in Las Vegas, we believe detailed descriptions are warranted. All continuously running stage shows, as well as celebrity showrooms, are profiled and reviewed in the entertainment section of this guide. The best nightspots and lounges in Las Vegas are profiled alphabetically under nightlife in the same section.

GEOGRAPHIC AREAS Though it's easy to get around in Las Vegas, you may not have a car or the inclination to venture far from your hotel. To help you locate the best restaurants, shows, nightspots, and attractions convenient to where you are staying, we have divided the city into geographic areas:

- South Strip and Environs
- Mid-Strip and Environs
- North Strip and Environs
- West of Strip
- Downtown Las Vegas
- Southeast Las Vegas–Henderson
- East of Strip

All profiles of hotels, restaurants, and nightspots include area names. For example, if you are staying at the Golden Nugget and are interested in Italian restaurants within walking distance, scanning the restaurant profiles for restaurants in Downtown Las Vegas will provide you with the most convenient choices.

COMFORT ZONES For each hotel-casino we have created a profile that describes the casino's patrons and gives you some sense of how it might feel to spend time there. The purpose of the comfort-zone section is to help you find the hotel-casino at which you will feel most welcome and at home. These comfort-zone descriptions begin on page 82 in Part One, Accommodations and Casinos.

LAS VEGAS: *An Overview*

GATHERING INFORMATION

LAS VEGAS HAS THE BEST SELECTION of complimentary visitor guides of any American tourist destination we know. Available at the front desk or concierge table at almost every hotel, the guides provide a wealth of useful information on gaming, gambling lessons, shows, lounge entertainment, sports, buffets, meal deals, tours and sightseeing, transportation, shopping, and special events. Additionally, most of the guides contain coupons for discounts on dining, shows, attractions, and tours.

Recommended publications include *Las Vegas Magazine* (**lasvegas magazine.com**), affiliated with the *Las Vegas Sun* newspaper, *Vegas2Go*, and *Where Magazine of Las Vegas* (**wheremagazine.com**). All three have much of the same information discussed above, plus feature articles. The best magazine for keeping abreast of nightlife, concerts, and happenings is *Las Vegas Weekly* (**lasvegasweekly.com**). Although all of the freebie Las Vegas visitor magazines contain valuable information, they are rah-rah rags, and their primary objective is to promote. So don't expect any critical reviews of shows, restaurants, attractions, or anything else for that matter.

The *Las Vegas Advisor* is a 12-page monthly newsletter containing some of the most useful consumer information available on gaming, dining, and entertainment, as well as deals on rooms, drinks, shows, and meals. With no advertising or promotional content, the newsletter serves its readers with objective, prescriptive, no-nonsense advice, presented with a sense of humor. The *Advisor* also operates a dynamite website at **lvahotels.com.** At a subscription rate of $50 a year, the *Las Vegas Advisor* is the best investment you can make if you plan to spend four or more days in Las Vegas each year. If you are a one-time visitor but wish to avail

Las Vegas Strip Area

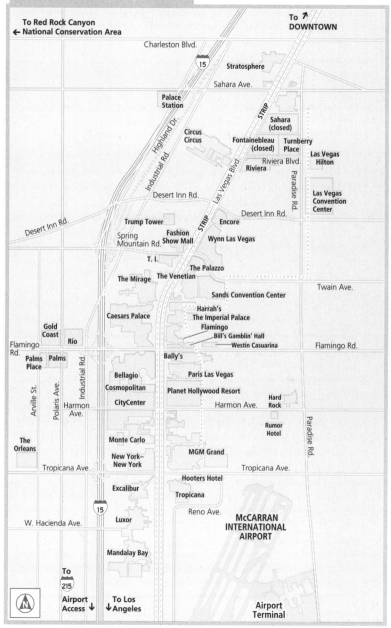

To Red Rock Canyon
← National Conservation Area

To ↗
DOWNTOWN

Charleston Blvd.

15

Stratosphere

Sahara Ave.

Palace
Station

STRIP

Sahara
(closed)

Circus
Circus

Fontainebleau
(closed)

Turnberry
Place

Highland Dr.

Industrial Rd.

Las Vegas Blvd.

Riviera Blvd.

Riviera

Las Vegas
Hilton

Paradise Rd.

Desert Inn Rd.

Desert Inn Rd.

Las Vegas
Convention
Center

Desert Inn Rd.

Trump Tower

STRIP

Encore

Spring
Mountain Rd.

Fashion
Show Mall

Wynn Las Vegas

T. I.

The Palazzo

The Mirage

The Venetian

Sands Convention Center

Twain Ave.

Caesars Palace

Harrah's
The Imperial Palace
Flamingo
Bill's Gamblin' Hall
Westin Casuarina

Gold
Coast

Rio

Flamingo
Rd.

Palms
Place

Palms

Industrial Rd.

Bally's

Flamingo Rd.

Arville St.

Polaris Ave.

Bellagio

Cosmopolitan

Paris Las Vegas

Planet Hollywood Resort

Harmon
Ave.

CityCenter

Harmon Ave.

Hard
Rock

Rumor
Hotel

Paradise Rd.

The
Orleans

Monte Carlo

New York–
New York

MGM Grand

Tropicana Ave.

Tropicana Ave.

Hooters Hotel

Excalibur

Tropicana

15

Reno Ave.

McCARRAN
INTERNATIONAL
AIRPORT

W. Hacienda Ave.

Luxor

Mandalay Bay

To
215

Airport
Access ↓

To Los
↓ Angeles

Airport
Terminal

yourself of all this wisdom, single copies of the *Las Vegas Advisor* can be purchased for $5 at the *Las Vegas Advisor* website with the other subscription options or at the Gambler's Book Club at 5473 South Eastern Avenue (☎ 702-382-7555 or 800-522-1777) or visit **gamblersbook .com.** For additional information:

Las Vegas Advisor
Huntington Press
3665 South Procyon Avenue
Las Vegas, NV 89103
☎ 702-252-0655 or 800-244-2224
lvahotels.com

Las Vegas and the Internet

The explosive growth of Las Vegas is not only physical but also virtual. The following are the best places to go on the Web to launch yourself into Las Vegas cyberspace:

The site of the *Las Vegas Advisor,* **lvahotels.com,** is a great source of information on recent and future developments, hotels, dining, entertainment, and gambling. The site features everything you need to plan your trip as well as informative blogs and podcasts. It also has a function for finding hotel deals called "Book a Room" (located in the center of the home page under "Features"). You can sort the results by price. A forum with user questions, maps, and other visitor information is also available.

The official website of the Las Vegas Convention and Visitors Authority is **visitlasvegas.com.** This site has hundreds of links to hotels, casinos, the airport, and area transportation, plus information on the convention center, sightseeing, and dining. To get started, roll over the categories (stay, play, special offers, etc.) at the top of the page.

One of the most comprehensive Las Vegas websites is **lasvegas.com.** Another big Las Vegas travel website, with an excellent listing of hotels and their dining and entertainment options, is **vegas.com.** Try *What's On* magazine's **whats-on.com** for shows and *Las Vegas Weekly*'s **lasvegas weekly.com** for nightlife. Another good site for entertainment information is *Las Vegas Magazine*'s **lasvegasmagazine.com.**

The best sites for finding discounts on hotels are **lvahotels.com,** the most reliable source for the best rates (see pages 69–71), and **kayak .com,** which allows you to compare room rates offered by a wide range of discounters.

Hotels make deals available to select markets and populations through the use of discount codes. For example, a deal targeted to San Diego, California, will be publicized in that area and a special code will be provided to obtain the discount when booking a reservation. However, for most codes, anyone who has the code can use it, even if they are not in the area or market being targeted. A good resource for finding these codes is Smarter Vegas at **smartervegas.com,** where pro-

Las Vegas Weather and Dress Chart

MONTH	POOLS O = OPEN
JANUARY average daytime temp. 57°F | average evening temp. 32°F *Recommended attire:* **coats and jackets are a must.**	–
FEBRUARY average daytime temp. 50°F | average evening temp. 37°F *Recommended attire:* **dress warmly—jackets and sweaters.**	–
MARCH average daytime temp. 69°F | average evening temp. 42°F *Recommended attire:* **sweaters for days, but a jacket at night.**	O
APRIL average daytime temp. 78°F | average evening temp. 50°F *Recommended attire:* **still cool at night—bring a jacket.**	O
MAY average daytime temp. 88°F | average evening temp. 50°F *Recommended attire:* **sweater for evening, but days are warm.**	O
JUNE average daytime temp. 99°F | average evening temp. 68°F *Recommended attire:* **days are hot; evenings are moderate.**	O
JULY average daytime temp. 105°F | average evening temp. 75°F *Recommended attire:* **bathing suits.**	O
AUGUST average daytime temp. 102°F | average evening temp. 73°F *Recommended attire:* **dress for the heat—spend time at a pool!**	O
SEPTEMBER average daytime temp. 95°F | average evening temp. 65°F *Recommended attire:* **days warm, sweater for evening.**	O
OCTOBER average daytime temp. 81°F | average evening temp. 53°F *Recommended attire:* **bring a jacket or sweater for evening.**	O
NOVEMBER average daytime temp. 67°F | average evening temp. 40°F *Recommended attire:* **sweaters and jackets for days, but coats at night.**	–
DECEMBER average daytime temp. 58°F | average evening temp. 34°F *Recommended attire:* **coats and jackets are a must—dress warmly.**	–

motional codes for the city's best hotels are routinely available. Similar sites are Vegas View at **vegasview.com,** Las Vegas Hotel Promotions at **vegas-hotels-online.com,** and Early Vegas at **earlyvegas .com.** Also see Broadway Box described below.

Find promotional tickets for Las Vegas shows, including celebrity headliners, at **lasvegasshows.com.** Note that not all tickets offered on the site are discounted. Both hotel and show discounts are available at Broadway Box at **broadwaybox.com.** Broadway Box is a Web community that shares discount codes. There are no membership fees or other costs, and no tickets are sold on the site.

Look for coupons for restaurant discounts at **citycoups.com.** Simply print the coupons for restaurants you're considering. Discount codes for rental cars are available at **mousesavers.com.** Though the site is dedicated to saving money at Walt Disney World and Disneyland, the rental car codes listed can be used anywhere.

WHEN TO GO TO LAS VEGAS

THE BEST TIME TO GO TO LAS VEGAS is in the spring or fall, when the weather is pleasant. If you plan to spend most of your time indoors, it doesn't matter what time of year you choose. If you intend to golf, play tennis, run, hike, bike, or boat, try to go in March, April, early May, October, November, or early December.

unofficial **TIP**
The winter months in Las Vegas provide an unbeatable combination of good value and choice of activities.

Because spring and fall are the nicest times of year, they are also the most popular. The best time for special deals is December (after the National Finals Rodeo in early December and excluding the week between Christmas and New Year's), January, and during the scorching summer months.

Weather in December, January, and February can vary incredibly. While high winds, cold, rain, and snow are not unheard of, chances are better that temperatures will be mild and the sun will shine. Though the weather is less dependable than in spring or fall, winter months are generally well suited to outdoor activities. We talked to people who in late February water-skied on Lake Mead in the morning and snow-skied in the afternoon at Lee Canyon. From mid-May through mid-September, however, the heat is blistering. During these months, it's best to follow the example of the gambler or the lizard—stay indoors or under a rock.

Crowd Avoidance

In general, weekends are busy and weekdays are slower. The exceptions are holiday periods and when large conventions or special events are held. Most Las Vegas hotels have a lower guest-room rate for weekdays than for weekends. Las Vegas hosts huge conventions and special events (rodeos, prize fights) that tie up hotels, restaurants, transportation, showrooms, and traffic for a week at a time. Likewise, major sporting events such as the Super Bowl, the NCAA football bowl games, the men's NCAA basketball tournament, Triple Crown horse races, the World Series, and the NBA championship fill every hotel in town on

unofficial **TIP**
For a stress-free arrival at the airport, good availability of rental cars, and a quick hotel check-in, try to arrive Monday afternoon through Thursday morning (Tuesday and Wednesday are best).

weekends. If you prefer to schedule your visit at a time when things are a little less frantic, we provide a calendar that lists the larger citywide conventions and regularly scheduled events to help you avoid the crowds. Note that two or three medium-sized conventions meeting at the same time can affect Las Vegas as much as one big citywide event.

Because conventions of more than 12,000 attendees can cause problems for the lone vacationer, the list of conventions and special events on pages 20–22 will help you plan your vacation dates. Included are the convention date, the number of people expected to attend, and the convention location (with hotel headquarters, if known at the time of publication). For a complete list of conventions scheduled during your visit, go to **lvcva.com** and click on meeting planners and then convention calendar. You can enter dates and get a full list or narrow it with different key words or search terms. Although there are usually 6 to 12 conventions being staged in Las Vegas at any given time, the effect of any convention or trade show on hotels, shows, and restaurants is negligible citywide for conventions of 10,000 or fewer, except at the host hotel or convention venue. Note that four or five concurrent conventions averaging 3,000 attendees each can impact tourism to the same extent as one large convention.

A larger Las Vegas hotel can handle small conventions without a hiccup, and the meeting or trade show might actually be an inducement to stay there . . . or not. Staying at the Rio during the International Lingerie Show in September certainly could be interesting. The annual Star Trek Convention at the Las Vegas Hilton in August is a hoot, the November National Industrial Fastener Show at Mandalay Bay less so. Those who have difficulty thinking in the abstract might enjoy the citywide World of Concrete convention in January. You get the idea. If you stay somewhere that's hosting a convention avoid arriving on the same day as the attendees.

ARRIVING *and*
GETTING ORIENTED

IF YOU DRIVE, YOU WILL HAVE TO TRAVEL through the desert to reach Las Vegas. Make sure your car is in good shape. Check your spare tire and toss a couple of gallons of water in the trunk, just in case. Once en route, pay attention to your fuel and temperature gauges.

Virtually all commercial air traffic into Las Vegas uses McCarran International Airport. At McCarran, a well-designed facility with good, clear signs, you will have no problem finding your way from the gate to the baggage-claim area, though it is often a long walk. Fast baggage handling is not the airport's strongest suit, so don't be surprised if you have to wait a long time on your checked luggage.

TAXI OPERATORS

Ace Cab Co. ☎ 702-736-8383	Nellis Cab Co. ☎ 702-248-1111
ANLV ☎ 702-643-1041	Union ☎ 702-736-8444
Henderson Taxi ☎ 702-384-2322	Western Cab ☎ 702-736-8000
Yellow Checker and Star Transportation ☎ 702-873-2000	

If you do not intend to rent a car, getting from the airport to your hotel is no problem. Shuttle services are available at a cost of $6 to $9 one-way and $12 to $16 round-trip. Sedans and "stretch" limousines

Conventions and Special Events Calendar

DATES	CONVENTION/EVENT	NUMBER OF ATTENDEES	LOCATION
2011			
Aug 3–6	AADE Annual Meeting and Exhibition	8,000	Mandalay Bay
Aug 4–7	DEF CON 19	8,000	Rio
Aug 15–20	GSA SmartPay Conference	5,000	Venetian
Aug 17–20	SendOutCards–Freedom National Conv.	5,000	Mirage
Aug 19–23	Off-Price Specialist Fall Show	10,500	Sands Expo Ctr.
Aug 22–24	MAGIC Marketplace Fall Show	75,000	LVCC
Aug 29–Sep 1	VMware–VMworld	17,500	Venetian
Aug 31–Sep 2	EMS Expo	7,500	LVCC
Sep 8–10	International Vision Expo West	14,000	Sands Expo Ctr.
Sep 8–10	Photo Marketing Association Show	27,000	LVCC
Sep 9–10	Vision Global Summer Meeting	7,500	Orleans
Sep 13–15	SuperZoo West	9,000	Mandalay Bay
Sep 14–16	Interbike Expo	18,000	Sands Expo Ctr.
Sep 16–17	2011 Mr. Olympia	30,000	LVCC
Sep 26–28	Pack Expo Las Vegas	23,000	LVCC
Oct 4–6	G2E: Global Gaming Expo	17,000	Sands Expo Ctr.
Oct 10–12	NBAA Annual Meeting and Convention	35,000	LVCC
Oct 10–13	American Dental Assoc. Annual Session	45,000	Mandalay Bay
Oct 11–13	IMEX America	8,000	Sands Expo Ctr.
Oct 19–21	National Industrial Fastener Show West	5,500	Sands Expo Ctr.
Oct 19–21	ISSA/INTERCLEAN North America	17,000	LVCC
Oct 23–25	MGMA Annual Conference	6,000	LVCC
Nov 1–4	Automotive Aftermarket Industry Week	120,000	Sands Expo Ctr.
Nov 16–19	Traders Expo Las Vegas	5,000	Caesars Palace
Nov 30–Dec 2	National Groundwater Association	6,000	LVCC
Dec 13–15	Power-Gen International Conference	20,000	LVCC
2012			
Jan 10–13	International CES	140,000	LVCC
Jan 23–26	World of Concrete	65,000	LVCC
Jan 24–27	Shooting, Hunting, and Outdoor Trade Show	45,000	Sands Expo Ctr.
Feb 2–4	International Sportsmans Expo	20,000	LVCC
Feb 4–6	Annual Winter National Convention	30,000	LVCC

DATES	CONVENTION/EVENT	NUMBER OF ATTENDEES	LOCATION
Feb 16–22	Wedding and Portrait Photographers Annual Convention and Trade Show	13,000	MGM Grand
Feb 19–23	Western Veterinary Conference	14,000	Mandalay Bay
Feb 21–24	HIMSS12 Annual Meeting	30,000	Sands Expo Ctr.
Feb 22–23	Electric West	6,000	LVCC
Feb 28–29	CaterSource/Event Solutions Annual Conference and Trade Show	7,000	LVCC
Feb 29–Mar 1	2012 Golf Course Show	20,000	LVCC
Mar 4–8	Exhibitor 2012	5,000	Mandalay Bay
Mar 7–8	Digital Signage Expo	5,000	LVCC
Mar 11–14	ASD Las Vegas	41,000	Mirage, LVCC, Sands Expo Ctr.
Mar 13–15	Annual International Pizza Expo	10,000	LVCC
Mar 14–25	MillerCoors Distributor Conference	4,000	Mandalay Bay
Mar 28–30	ISC West	15,000	Sands Expo Ctr.
Apr 11–22	Microsoft Management Corp. Summit	5,000	Venetian
Apr 23–26	Collaborate 2012	8,000	Mandalay Bay
May 1–3	National Hardware Show	35,000	LVCC
May 1–3	Waste Expo	16,000	LVCC
May 9–11	Lightfair International 2012	22,000	LVCC
May 11–12	International Garage Door Expo	5,000	LVCC
May 20–22	RECon 2012	30,000	LVCC
Jun 2–4	International Esthetics Cosmetic and Spa Conference	32,000	LVCC
June 13–15	International Communications Industries Association/Infocomm	32,000	LVCC
June 25–27	Healthcare Financial Management Assoc. Annual National Institute	5,000	Mandalay Bay
June 26–28	Food Expo Annual Meeting	22,000	LVCC
July 11–13	Associated Locksmiths of America National Convention	4,000	Mandalay Bay
Aug 1–4	UNITY Convention	8,000	Mandalay Bay
Aug 12–15	ASD Las Vegas	41,000	Mirage, LVCC, Sands Expo Ctr.
Aug 16–18	Fall Dealer Market	15,000	Sands Expo Ctr.

Conventions/Events Calendar (cont'd)

DATES	CONVENTION/EVENT	NUMBER OF ATTENDEES	LOCATION
Sep 6–10	Gay Days Las Vegas	5,000	Rio
Sep 7–8	International Vision Expo West	14,000	Sands Expo Ctr.
Sep 11–13	SuperZoo West	9,000	Mandalay Bay
Sep 24–26	MINExpo International	37,000	LVCC
Oct 2–4	G2E: Global Gaming Expo	17,000	Sands Expo Ctr.
Oct 8–10	National Assoc. of Convenience Stores, Inc. Annual Meeting and Expo	30,000	LVCC
Oct 9–12	IMEX America	8,000	Sands Expo Ctr.
Oct 18–20	Specialty Graphics Annual National Conv.	23,000	LVCC
Oct 30–Nov 2	Automotive Aftermarket Industry Week	106,000	Sands Expo Ctr./ LVCC
Nov 4–8	Society of Exploration Geophysicists Annual Convention	10,000	Mandalay Bay
Nov 11–14	Fabtech and AWS Welding Show	30,000	LVCC
Nov 14–17	DEMA Show	16,000	Sands Expo Ctr.
Nov 14–21	National Council of Teachers of English Annual Convention	7,000	MGM Grand
Dec 2–6	47th ASHP Midyear Clinical Meeting	23,000	Mandalay Bay
Dec 5–7	National Groundwater Expo and Annual Meeting	7,500	LVCC

cost about $39 to $55 one-way. For taxis, the fare is the same no matter how many passengers are traveling (maximum five). Cabs charge a $3.30 trip fee with $2.40 per mile thereafter. If a taxi ride originates at McCarran International Airport, an additional airport surcharge of $1.80 per trip is added. Cab fare to Las Vegas Strip locations ranges from $13 to $20 one-way, plus tip. One-way taxi fares to downtown run about $30. Fares are regulated and should not vary from company to company. Note that most cabs in southern Nevada do not accept credit cards. If you're going to take a taxi from the airport, it's a good idea to check out the best route on **mapquest.com** or **googlemaps.com.** Cab driver revenues have been falling since the onset of the recession, and some drivers will take a circuitous route to bump up fares. Be mindful, however, that traffic in Las Vegas is horrendous and that a route that seems circuitous may take less time than a more direct route. The most common "long-haul" route used to pad fares is traveling to Strip hotels or downtown via the airport tunnel to I-215 and I-15. The limo service counters are in the hall just outside the baggage-claim area. Cabs are at the curb. Additional information concerning ground transportation is available at the McCarran International Airport website (**mccarran.com**) and at the Nevada Taxi Cab Authority's website (**http://taxi.state.nv.us/FaresFees.htm**).

unofficial **TIP**
Any use of cell phones while driving is now against the law in Las Vegas. Keep your phone in your pocket and avoid big fines.

If you rent a car, you will need to catch the courtesy shuttle to the new consolidated McCarran Rent-A-Car Center located about two miles from the airport. The shuttle boards at the middle curb of the authorized vehicle lanes just outside terminal doors 10 and 11 on the ground level. The individual car-rental companies no longer operate shuttles of any kind, so all car-rental customers use the same shuttle.

If someone is picking you up, go to the ground level on the opposite side of the baggage-claim building (away from the main terminal) to the baggage-claim and arrivals curb. If your ride wants to park and meet you, hook up on the ground level of the baggage-claim building where the escalators descend from the main terminal.

There are two ways to exit the airport by car. You can depart via the old route, Swenson Street, which runs north–south roughly paralleling the Strip, or you can hop on the new spur of I-215. Dipping south from the airport, I-215 connects with I-15. The tunnel and I-215 will often deliver you to a point of huge congestion and delays where I-215 intersects I-15. As a general rule, exiting the airport on Swensen and then turning left (west) on the closest east–west street to your destination is the best bet for all Strip hotels. Swenson Street is also a better route if you're going to the Las Vegas Convention Center, to the University of Nevada, Las Vegas (UNLV), or to hotels on or east of the Strip.

CONVENIENCE CHART To give you an idea of your hotel's convenience to popular local destinations such as the Strip, downtown, the Las Vegas Convention Center, UNLV, and the airport, we have provided a section on getting around. Included in the next chapter is a "convenience chart" that lists estimated times by foot or cab from each hotel to the destinations outlined on pages 42–45. In the same section are tips for avoiding traffic congestion and for commuting between the Strip and downtown.

RENTAL CARS All of the rental-car companies previously located at the airport terminal, plus a few off-site companies, have moved to the huge McCarran Rent-A-Car Center situated two miles south of the airport. The airport provides large buses departing approximately every five minutes for the 7-to-12-minute commute to the facility. On arriving at the Rent-A-Car Center, you'll find all of the rental-car companies listed in the chart on page 25 on the ground floor.

When the rental-car companies were located at the airport, rental customers arrived at the rental counters in a relatively steady stream. At the new off-airport location, however, rental customers arrive by the busload, inundating the rental counters. Now, the only way to avoid a substantial wait to be processed is to join the special-customer clubs of the respective rental-car companies. These clubs (or programs) allow

Rental-car Return and Pickup

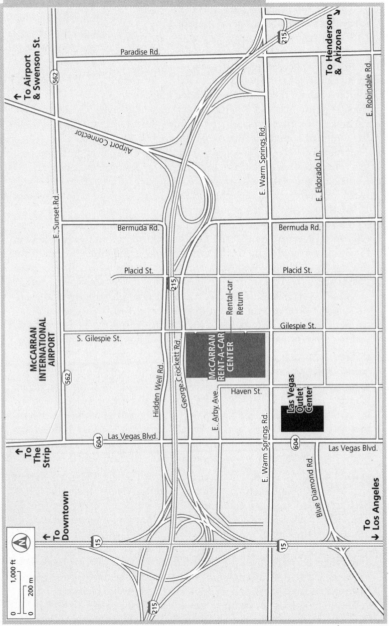

Rental-car Agencies at the McCarran Rent-A-Car Center

Advantage/US Rent A Car	800-777-9377	us-rentacar.com
Alamo	800-GO-ALAMO	alamo.com
Avis	800-331-1212	avis.com
Budget	800-922-2899	budget.com
Dollar	800-800-4000	dollar.com
Enterprise	800-RENT-A-CAR	enterprise.com
Hertz	800-654-3131	hertz.com
National Car Rental	800-CAR-RENT	nationalcar.com
Payless Car Rental	800-729-5377	paylesscarrental.com
Savmor Car Rental	800-634-6779	savmorrac.com
Thrifty	800-367-2277	thrifty.com

you to bypass the regular queue and to receive preferential processing. Just visit the website of the company of your choice and you'll see instructions for signing up. You don't have to rent cars often to join. Sign up about four weeks before you make a rental reservation so you'll have your membership number when you're ready to reserve.

All of the rental cars are under one roof. Upon completion of your paperwork you'll be directed to a specified area of the garage to pick up your car. Having picked up your car, chances are about 95% that you'll find yourself disoriented in a part of Las Vegas you've never laid eyes on. Follow the instructions below to reach your final destination.

After you pick up your rental car, you'll exit the Rent-A-Car Center onto Gilespie Street, where you'll find signs directing you to the Strip as well as to I-15 and I-215. Unfortunately, if you follow the signs, you'll end up in a traffic jam of the first order (welcome to Las Vegas!), owing to an inadequate number of right-turn lanes and a multitude of traffic signals. The exit from the Rent-A-Car Center onto Gilespie Street forces you to turn right (south), but to avoid the traffic jams you really want to be heading in the opposite direction (north) on Gilespie. From the Rent-A-Car Center exit, this can be accomplished by working your way immediately across the southbound lanes on Gilespie to a left-turn lane and then making a U-turn. Alternatively, you can go a block or so south and then get turned around less hurriedly. Once you're headed northbound on Gilespie do the following:

TO REACH THE LAS VEGAS CONVENTION CENTER, UNLV, AND HOTELS ON THE EAST SIDE OF THE STRIP, head north on Gilespie Street and turn right onto George Crockett Road. Follow signs to the airport via the Airport Connector. You'll pass through a tunnel under the runways and pop out on Swenson Street just before the intersection with Tropicana. Use the maps in this guide to reach your final destination from there.

TO REACH DOWNTOWN AND HOTELS ON THE WEST SIDE OF THE STRIP VIA I-15, head north from the Rent-A-Car Center on Gilespie, cross the bridge over I-215, and turn left on Hidden Well Road. Follow Hidden Well Road to I-15 (northbound only). Use the maps in this guide to navigate to your final destination from there.

TO ACCESS I-215 NORTHWEST TOWARD RED ROCK CANYON AND SUMMERLIN, go north on Gilespie, cross the bridge over I-215, and turn left on Hidden Well Road. Follow Hidden Well Road to the I-215 westbound ramp.

The following directions do not require going north on Gilespie:

TO ACCESS I-215 SOUTHEAST TOWARD HENDERSON, GREEN VALLEY, AND LAKE LAS VEGAS, turn right on Gilespie from the Rent-A-Car Center and turn left at the first traffic signal onto Warm Springs Road. Follow Warm Springs Road west to the intersection of I-215.

TO ACCESS LAS VEGAS BOULEVARD SOUTH OF THE I-15/I-215 INTERCHANGE, stay in the far-right lane on exiting the Rent-A-Car Center and turn right on Warm Springs Road. Warm Springs Road intersects South Las Vegas Boulevard.

TO ACCESS I-15 SOUTHBOUND TOWARD LAUGHLIN AND LOS ANGELES, turn right on Gilespie from the Rent-A-Car Center and then right on Warm Springs Road. After two blocks, turn south on South Las Vegas Boulevard, turning right on Blue Diamond Road. Follow the signs to I-15.

Fortunately, returning your rental car is much easier and there is little opportunity to become embroiled in a serious traffic jam in the environs of the Rent-A-Car Center. The same cannot be said, however, of I-15 and I-215, especially during rush hours. If you are coming from the east side of the Strip, take Paradise Road to the airport and follow the well-marked signs to the rental-car return. Likewise, as you come toward the airport on I-15 and I-215, follow the rental-car-return signs.

Because the Rent-A-Car Center shuttles run more often than buses provided by the rental-car companies under the old system, it doesn't take any longer than before to commute to the center or to get back to the airport once you've returned your car. En route to the Rent-A-Car Center, sit near a door so that you can be one of the first to disembark. If you're traveling with others, let them attend to the luggage while you sprint to the rental counter. This will ensure that you'll be ahead of your fellow bus passengers. To avoid a free-for-all of passengers trying to retrieve their bags from the onboard storage racks, most bus drivers prefer to handle luggage loading and unloading. It's about order and safety, not tips, so just go with it. Generally, after all riders have disembarked, the driver will unload the luggage via the rear doors.

Although rental cars are comparatively cheap in Las Vegas, taxes and fees are not. If you rent a car at the airport (which includes both terminal and off-terminal locations on airport property), here's what you can expect to pay:

State Sales Tax	8.1%
Nevada Rental Service Fee	10.0%
Clark County Rental Fee	2.0%
Airport Concession Recovery Fee	10.0%
Reimbursement of Registration and License Fee	Varies*
Total	30.1+%

* This fee varies among retailers and is explained further at **tax.state.nv.us/ About%20taxes%20and%20Faqs.html#short_term_lessor_tax_info.** All fees must be fully disclosed in the lease agreement.

Had enough? Powers at the airport don't think so. In addition to the above you are charged a $3 per day Consumer Facility Charge. You can avoid the 10% fee and the $3 per day by renting the car at some non-airport locations, like your hotel. Be advised, however, that it's not unusual for agencies to bump up the rental price at such locations.

In the dollar-and-cents department, prices fluctuate so much from week to week that it's anyone's guess who will offer the best deal during your visit. Usually the best deals are on the company's website, but **expedia.com, travelocity.com,** and **kayak.com** are often worth checking, especially if you're visiting during a particularly busy time, such as during a citywide convention. On rental company websites, counterintuitively, you can often get a better deal if you don't indicate that you're a member of AAA, AARP, and the like. After you get your quote, see if you can improve the deal by trying again, entering your organizational or age information.

Be aware that Las Vegas is a feast-or-famine city when it comes to rental-car availability. On many weekends, or when a citywide convention is in town, it may be impossible to get a rental car unless you reserved way in advance. If, on the other hand, you come to town when business is slow, the rental agencies will practically give you a car. We have been able to rent from the most expensive companies for as little as $22 a day under these circumstances. If you are visiting during a slow time, reserve a car in advance to cover yourself, and then, on arrival, ask each rental company to quote you its best price. If you can beat the price on your reserved car, go for it.

Improbably, one of the best places for rental-car deals is **mouse savers.com,** a site dedicated to finding deals at Disneyland and Walt Disney World. The site lists rental-car codes that you can use to get great discounts. Some of the codes are for Orlando and Southern California only, but many others apply anywhere in the United States. The site also offers some great tips on how to compare different codes and deals.

Another way to score a deal on a rental car is to bid on **priceline.com.** We've used Priceline to get cars at less than $20 per day. Understand, however, that if your bid is accepted, the entire rental cost will be non-refundably charged to your credit card. In other words, no backing out for any reason. Before placing your bid, check our conventions and special events calendar on pages 20–22. If there's a big convention in town, demand will be high and a lowball bid might not work.

When you (or your travel agent) call to reserve a rental car, ask for the smallest, least expensive car in the company's inventory, even if you ultimately intend to rent a larger vehicle. It's possible that you will be upgraded without charge when you arrive. If not, rental agencies frequently offer on-site upgrade incentives that beat any deals you can make in advance. Always compare daily and weekly rates.

If you decline insurance coverage on the rental car because of protection provided by your credit card, be aware that the coverage provided by the credit card is secondary to your regular auto insurance policy. In most situations the credit-card coverage only reimburses you the deductible on your regular policy. Happily, most car insurance covers rental cars as well as your personal vehicle. If you're not sure about your coverage, contact your insurance agent. Also be aware that some car-rental contracts require that you drive the car only in Nevada. If you, like many tourists, visit Hoover Dam or trek out to the Grand Canyon, you will cross into Arizona. Another item to check in advance, if applicable, is whether your rental agency charges for additional drivers.

When you rent your car, make sure you understand the implications of bringing it back empty of fuel. Some companies will charge $6 or more per gallon if they have to fill the tank on return. At one agency, we returned a car with between a third and a half tank of gas remaining and were charged the same as if we had coasted in with a completely empty tank at an off-site gas station. Also, beware of signs at the car-rental counters reading "Gas today—$3 per gallon" or some such. That usually applies to the price of the gas already in the car when you rent it, not the price per gallon of a fill-up should you return the car empty. The price per gallon for a fill-up on return will be somewhere in the fine print of your rental contract.

unofficial **TIP**
Before you leave the lot, inspect your rental car with care, examining every inch, and have the rental agency record anything you find.

Another rental-car problem we encountered involved a pinhead-sized chip on the windshield. Understanding the fine print of rental car contracts, and because we always decline the insurance offered by the agencies, we inspect our cars thoroughly for any damage before accepting the car and leaving the lot. In this instance, as always, we inspected the car thoroughly and did not notice any windshield flaws. When we returned the car after three days, we were requested to remain at the counter to complete an "accident report." Insisting that we were unaware of any damage, we requested that the car be retrieved for our inspection. Still unable to find the alleged damage, we asked the counter agent to identify it for us. The agent who was responsible for the accident report then had to scrutinize the windshield before she could find the mark, even though she knew its exact location from the employee who checked the car in. The conclusion to be drawn here is that if you decline coverage, the rental agency may hold you responsible for even the tiniest damage, damage so slight that you may never notice it. Check your car out well before you leave. This will not inhibit them from charging you for damage sustained while the car is in your possession, but at least you will have the peace of mind of knowing that they are not putting one over on you.

Some rental companies will charge you for "loss of use" if you have an accident that takes the car out of use. Because some car insurance policies do not pay loss-of-use charges, check your coverage with your insurance agent before you rent.

LAS VEGAS CUSTOMS AND PROTOCOL

IN A TOWN WHERE THE MOST BIZARRE behavior imaginable is routinely tolerated, it is ironic that so many visitors obsess over what constitutes proper protocol. This mentality stems mainly from the myriad customs peculiar to gaming and the *perceived* glamour of the city itself. First-timers attach a great deal of importance to "fitting in." What makes this task difficult, at least in part, is that half of the people with whom they are trying to fit in are first-timers too.

The only hard rules for being accepted downtown or on the Strip are to have a shirt on your back, shoes on your feet, some manner of clothing below the waist, and a little money in your pocket. Concerning the latter, there is no maximum. The operational minimum is bus fare back to wherever you came from.

This notwithstanding, there are three basic areas in which Las Vegas first-timers tend to feel especially insecure:

GAMBLING The various oddities of gaming protocol are described in this book under the casino games in Part Three, Gambling (page 298). Despite appearances, however, gambling is very informal. While it is intelligent not to play a game when/if you do not know how, it is unwarranted to abstain because you are uncertain of the protocol. What little protocol exists (things like holding your cards above the table and keeping your hands away from your bet once play has begun) has evolved to protect the house and honest players from cheats. Dealers (a generic term for those who conduct table games) are not under orders to be unfriendly, silent, or rigid. Observe a game that interests you before you sit down. Assure yourself that the dealer is personable and polite. Never play in a casino where the staff is surly or cold; life's too short.

EATING IN FANCY RESTAURANTS Many of these are meat-and-potatoes places with fancy names, so there is no real reason to be intimidated. Others are designer, pay-big-bucks restaurants with famous chefs. In either case, service is friendly. Men will feel more comfortable in sport coats, but ties are rarely worn. Women turn up in everything from slacks and blouses to evening wear. When you sit down, a whole platoon of waiters will attend you. Do not remove your napkin from the table; only the waiters are allowed to place napkins in the laps of patrons. After the ceremonial placement of the napkin, the senior waiter will speak. When he concludes, you may order cocktails, consider the menu, sip your water, or engage in conversation. If there are women in your party, their menus will not have prices listed. If your party includes only women, a menu with prices listed will be given to the woman who looks the oldest. When you are ready to order, even if you only want a steak and fries, do not speak until the waiter has had an opportunity to recite in French from the menu. To really please your waiters, order something that can be prepared tableside with dramatic flames and explosions. If your waiters seem stuffy or aloof, ask them to grind peppercorns or grate Parmesan cheese on something. This will usually loosen them up.

There will be enough utensils on the table to perform a triple bypass. These items are considered expendable; use a different utensil for each dish and surrender it to the waiter along with the empty plate at the end of each course.

TIPPING Because about a third of the resident population of Las Vegas are service providers in the tourist industry, there is no scarcity of people to tip. From the day you arrive until the day you depart, you will be interacting with porters, cabbies, valet-parking attendants, bellhops, waiters, maître d's, dealers, bartenders, keno runners, housekeeping personnel, room service, and others.

Tipping is an issue that makes some travelers very uncomfortable. How much? When? To whom? Not leaving a tip when one is customary makes you feel inexperienced. Not knowing how much to tip makes you feel vulnerable and out of control. Is the tip you normally leave at home appropriate in Las Vegas?

The most important thing to bear in mind is that a tip is not automatic, nor is it an obligation. A tip is a reward for good service. The suggestions in the "Tipping Guidelines" chart on the following page are based on traditional practices in Las Vegas.

STAYING TUNED IN

SURPRISINGLY, ONE OF THE MOST frequently posed questions to rental-car agents and hotel concierges is "How do I tune in NPR (National Public Radio)?" NPR station KNPR can be found at 88.9 FM.

BRINGING YOUR PET TO LAS VEGAS

FOR THE MOST PART "pet" in Las Vegas means a dog. Various restrictions apply, including weight limitations. Major hotels that welcome pets include Trump International, Westin Casuarina, Four Seasons at Mandalay Bay, and Alexis Park Hotel. The best pet programs can be found at the eight Caesars Las Vegas properties: Bally's, Caesars Palace, Flamingo, Harrah's, Imperial Palace, Paris, Planet Hollywood Resort & Casino, and Rio All-Suite Hotel & Casino. Incorporating PetStay Las Vegas (**petstaylasvegas.com**), these hotels

Tipping Guidelines

Porters A dollar a bag.

Cab drivers A lot depends on service and courtesy. For good service tip $5 or 15–20% of the total fare. If you are asking the cabbie to take you only a block or two, the fare will be small, but your tip should be large ($5) to make up for his wait in line and to partially compensate him for missing a better-paying fare. Add an extra dollar for a lot of luggage handling.

Valet parking Two dollars is correct if the valet is courteous and demon-strates some hustle. A dollar will do if the service is just OK. Only pay when you take your car out, not when you leave it. Because valet attendants pool their tips, both of the individuals who assist you (coming and going) will be taken care of. If the valet service is jammed, hand over a $10 or $20 to the person who takes your claim ticket and tell him you'd like the car brought up right away. You'll be moved to the head of the line.

Bellmen When a bellhop greets you at your car with a rolling cart and handles all of your bags, $5 is about right. The more luggage you carry yourself, of course, the less you should tip. Sometimes bellhops who handle only a small bag or two will put on a real performance when showing you your room. We had a bellhop in one hotel walk into our room, crank up the air-conditioner, turn on the TV, open the blinds, flick on the lights, flush the commode, and test the water pressure in the tub. Give us a break. We tipped the same as if he had simply opened the door and put our luggage in the room.

Waiters Whether in a coffee shop, a gourmet room, or ordering from room service, the standard gratuity for acceptable service is 15–20% of the total tab, before sales tax. At a self-serve buffet or brunch, it is customary to leave $3–$5 for the folks who bring your drinks and bus your dishes.

Cocktail waiters and bartenders Tip by the round. For two people, $1 a round; for more than two people, $2 a round. For a large group, use your judgment: Is everyone drinking beer or is the order long and complicated? In casinos where drinks are sometimes on the house, it is considered good form to tip the server $1 per round.

Dealers and slot attendants If you are winning, it is a nice gesture to tip the dealer or place a small bet for him. How much depends on your winnings and on your level of play. With slot attendants, tip when they perform a specific service or you hit a jackpot. In general, unless other services are also rendered, it is not customary to tip change makers or cashiers.

Keno runners Tip if you have a winner or if the runner provides exceptional service. How much to tip will vary with your winnings and level of play.

Showroom maître d's, captains, and servers There is more to this than you might expect. If you are planning to take in a show, see our suggestions for tipping in Part 2, Entertainment and Nightlife (see pages 203–205).

Hotel maids On checking out, leave $3–$5 for each day you stayed (more if you're really messy), providing the service was good.

have set aside specific floors and public areas that are designated as pet-friendly sections. There are on-property pathways and relief areas as well as grooming, pet sitters and pet walkers, and a directory of on-call veterinarians. Leashed canine guests must check in with their owners and weigh less than 50 pounds. A maximum of two dogs are permitted per room. An amenity package for pooches includes special dishes for food and water, doggie snacks, and comfy sleeping mats. Depending on the hotel, the rate is $25–$40 plus tax per night. Pet stays can be booked at **caesars.com** or (800) 427-7247.

A list of Las Vegas chain and proprietary hotels that welcome pets can be found at **officialpethotels.com** and **dogfriendly.com** (click on Dog Travel Guides—Nevada).

If puppies come, can cats be far behind?

LAS VEGAS *as a* FAMILY DESTINATION

OCCASIONALLY THE PUBLISHER SENDS us around to promote the *Unofficial Guide* on radio and television, and every year we are asked the same question: Is Las Vegas a good place for a family vacation?

Las Vegas is definitely *not* a family-friendly destination. Casinos are very particular about who's occupying their beds, and the least preferred customers of all are families with children. Children can't gamble, they annoy adults who come to Las Vegas to avoid kids, and they reduce or make impossible the time their parents spend in the casino. For many years, there were only two casinos that targeted the family trade: Circus Circus and Excalibur. Almost 20 years later, guess what: Circus Circus is the only one. Excalibur is making a concerted effort to ditch the family market.

However, if you don't object to being persona non grata, Las Vegas is a great place for a family vacation. Food and lodging are a good value for the dollar, and there are an extraordinary number of things, from swimming to rafting through the Black Canyon on the Colorado River, that the entire family can enjoy together. If you take your kids to Las Vegas *and forget gambling,* Las Vegas compares favorably with every family tourist destination in the United States. The rub, of course, is that gambling in Las Vegas is pretty hard to ignore.

TAKING YOUR CHILDREN TO LAS VEGAS TODAY

LAS VEGAS IS PREDOMINANTLY AN ADULT tourist destination. As a city (including the surrounding area), however, it has a lot to offer children. What this essentially means is that the Strip and downtown have not been developed with children in mind, but if you are willing to make the effort to venture away from the gambling areas, there are a lot of fun and wholesome things for families to do. As a rule, however, people do not go to Las Vegas to be continually absent from the casinos.

Persons under age 21 are not allowed to gamble, nor are they allowed to hang around while *you* gamble. If you are gambling, your children have to be somewhere else. On the Strip and downtown, the choices are limited. True, most hotels have nice swimming pools, but summer days are much too hot to stay out for long. While golf and tennis are possibilities, court or greens fees are routinely charged, and you still must contend with limitations imposed by the desert climate.

After a short time, you will discover that the current options for your children's recreation and amusement are as follows:

1. You can simply allow your children to hang out. Given this alternative, the kids will swim a little, watch some TV, eat as much as their (or your) funds allow, throw water balloons out of any hotel window that has not been hermetically sealed, and cruise up and down the Strip (or Fremont Street) on foot, ducking in and out of souvenir stores and casino lobbies.

2. If your children are a mature age 10 or older, you can turn them loose at the Adventuredome at Circus Circus. The kids, however, will probably cut bait and go cruising after about an hour or two.

3. You can hire a babysitter to come to your hotel room and tend your children. This works out pretty much like option 1, without the water balloons and the cruising.

4. You can abandon the casino (or whatever else you had in mind) and "do things" with your kids. Swimming and eating (as always) will figure prominently into the plan, as will excursions to places that have engaged the children's curiosity. You can bet that your kids will want to go to the Adventuredome at Circus Circus. The white tigers, dolphins, and exploding volcano at the Mirage; the pirate battle at T. I. (PG-13); the MGM Grand lion habitat; The Forum Shops; and the Stratosphere Tower are big hits with kids. New York–New York features a roller coaster. If you have two children and do a fraction of all this stuff in one day, you will spend $80 to $250 for the four of you, not counting meals and transportation.

If you have a car, however, there are lots of great, inexpensive places to go—enough to keep you busy for days. We recommend Red Rock Canyon and Hoover Dam, for sure. On the way to Hoover Dam, you can stop for a tour of the Ethel M. Chocolate Factory.

A great day excursion (during the spring and fall) is a guided raft trip through the Black Canyon on the Colorado River. This can easily be combined with a visit to Hoover Dam. Trips to the Valley of Fire State Park (driving, biking, hiking) are also recommended during the more temperate months.

Around Las Vegas there are a number of real museums and museums–tourist attractions. The Lied Discovery Children's Museum (just north of downtown) is worthwhile, affordable, and a big favorite with kids age 14 and younger. While you are in the neighborhood, try the Natural History Museum directly across the street.

5. You can pay someone else to take your kids on excursions. Some in-room sitters (bonded and from reputable agencies) will take your kids around as long as you foot the bill. For recommendations, check with the concierge or front desk of your hotel. If your kids are over age 12, you can pack them off on one of the guided tours advertised by the handful in the various local visitor magazines.

Hotels that Solicit Family Business

As Excalibur gets out of the family trade, Circus Circus stands alone as the only casino that welcomes children. Circus Circus actively seeks the family market with carnival game midways where children and adults can try to win stuffed animals, foam-rubber dice, and other totally dispensable objects. A great setup for the casinos, the midways turn a nice profit while innocuously introducing the youngsters to games of chance. In addition, Circus Circus operates the Adventuredome theme park and offers free circus acts each evening, starring top-notch talent, including aerialists (flying trapeze artists).

Parents traveling with children are grudgingly accepted at all of the larger hotels, though certain hotels are better equipped to deal with children than others. If your children are water puppies and enjoy being in a swimming pool all day, Mandalay Bay, Venetian, M Resort, Planet Hollywood, Flamingo, Monte Carlo, MGM Grand, Mirage, Aria, Rio, Tropicana, Caesars Palace, Wynn Las Vegas, Wynn Encore, Bellagio, Red Rock Resort, Green Valley Ranch, and T. I. have the best pools in town. The Las Vegas Hilton, the Palms, and Hard Rock Hotel, among others, also have excellent swimming facilities.

If your kids are older and into sports, the MGM Grand, Caesars Palace, the Las Vegas Hilton, and Bally's offer the most variety.

For child care and special programs, Sunset Station, Orleans, Red Rock Resort, Boulder Station, Palms, Texas Station, Santa Fe Station, and Loews Lake Las Vegas provide child-care facilities.

Our favorite hotel for a family vacation is Green Valley Ranch Resort, a Station casino and resort about 15 minutes southeast of the Strip. Its location is convenient to Lake Mead, Hoover Dam, the Black Canyon of the Colorado, and Red Rock Canyon, for starters. It has great swimming areas, good restaurants, and lovely guest rooms. And when you want to sneak into the casino or have an adults-only meal, the concierge will arrange child care for you. Best of all, Green Valley Ranch is isolated. There's no place nearby where your kids can get into trouble (right!).

Babysitting

An organization called **Nannies & Housekeepers U.S.A.** (☎ 702-451-0021; **nahusa.com**) offers 24/7 in-room babysitting. Nannies & Housekeepers, which puts their sitters through a lengthy and rigorous screening, is the exclusive babysitting agency for many Las Vegas hotels, including Wynn Las Vegas, Wynn Encore, and MGM Grand.

PART ONE

ACCOMMODATIONS *and* CASINOS

WHERE *to* STAY: *Basic Choices*

LAS VEGAS HAS AN ASTOUNDING INVENTORY of about 149,000 hotel rooms. Washington, D.C., by way of contrast, has 31,000. Before the recession, occupancy rates were over 98% on weekends and averaged 92% for the whole week, compared to a national average of 61%. Even during the slow recovery, occupancy rates for Strip hotels remain high. However, with the glut of new rooms that came online in 2009 and 2010, including unsold condo and timeshare units, expect great deals on rooms until at least late spring of 2012.

THE LAS VEGAS STRIP AND DOWNTOWN

FROM A VISITOR'S PERSPECTIVE, Las Vegas is more or less a small town that's fairly easy to navigate. Most of the major hotels and casinos are in two areas: downtown and on Las Vegas Boulevard, known as the Strip.

The downtown hotels and casinos are often characterized as older and smaller than those on the Strip. While this is true in a general sense, there are both large and elegant hotels downtown. What really differentiates downtown is the incredible concentration of casinos and hotels in a relatively small area. Along Fremont Street, downtown's main thoroughfare, the casinos present a continuous, dazzling galaxy of neon and twinkling lights for more than four city blocks. Known as Glitter Gulch, these several dozen gambling emporiums are sandwiched together in colorful profusion in an area barely larger than a parking lot at a good-sized shopping mall.

Contrast in the size, style, elegance, and presentation of the downtown casinos provides a varied mix, combining extravagant luxury and cosmopolitan sophistication with an Old West–boomtown decadence. Though not directly comparable, downtown Las Vegas has the feel of New Orleans's Bourbon Street: alluring, exotic, wicked, sultry, foreign, and, above all, diverse. It is a place where cowboy, businessperson, showgirl, and retiree mix easily. And, like Bourbon Street, it is all accessible on foot.

If downtown is the French Quarter of Las Vegas, then the Strip is Plantation Row. Here, huge resort hotel-casinos sprawl like estates along a four-mile section of South Las Vegas Boulevard. Each hotel is a vacation destination unto itself, with casino, hotel, restaurants, pools, spas, landscaped grounds, and even golf courses. While the downtown casinos are fused into a vibrant, integrated whole, the huge hotels on the Strip demand individual recognition.

Although the Strip is literally a specific length of South Las Vegas Boulevard, the large surrounding area is usually included when discussing hotels, casinos, restaurants, and attractions. East and parallel to the Strip is Paradise Road, where the Las Vegas Convention Center and several hotels are located. Also included in the Strip area are hotels and casinos on streets intersecting Las Vegas Boulevard, as well as properties to the immediate west of the Strip (on the far side of Interstate 15).

CHOOSING A HOTEL

THE VARIABLES THAT FIGURE MOST prominently in choosing a hotel are price, location, your itinerary, and your quality requirements. There is a wide selection of lodging with myriad combinations of price and value. Given this, your main criteria for selecting a hotel should be its location and your itinerary.

The Strip versus Downtown for Leisure Travelers

Though there are some excellent hotels on the Boulder Highway and elsewhere around town, the choice for most vacation travelers is whether to stay downtown or on (or near) the Strip. Downtown offers a good choice of hotels, restaurants, and gambling, but only a limited choice of entertainment and fewer amenities such as swimming pools and spas. There are no golf courses and only four tennis courts downtown. If you have a car, the Strip is an 8- to 15-minute commute from downtown via I-15. If you do not have a car, public transportation from downtown to the Strip is as efficient as Las Vegas traffic allows and quite affordable.

If you stay on the Strip, you are more likely to need a car or require some sort of transportation. There are more hotels to choose from on the Strip, but they are spread over a much wider area and are often (but not always) pricier than downtown. On the Strip, one has a sense of space and elbowroom, as many of the hotels are constructed on a grand scale. The selection of entertainment is both varied and extensive, and the Strip's recreational facilities rival those of the world's leading resorts.

Downtown is a multicultural, multilingual melting pot with an adventurous, raw, robust feel. Everything in this part of town seems intense and concentrated, an endless blur of action, movement, and light. Diversity and history combine in lending vitality and excitement to this older part of Las Vegas, an essence more tangible and real than the monumental, plastic themes and fantasies of many large Strip establishments.

Though downtown caters to every class of clientele, it is less formal and, with exceptions, more of a working man's gambling town. Here, the truck driver and welder gamble alongside the secretary and the rancher. The Strip, likewise, runs the gamut but tends to attract more high rollers, middle-class suburbanites, and business travelers going to conventions.

The Fremont Street Experience

For years, downtown casinos watched from the sidelines as Strip hotels turned into veritable tourist attractions. There was nothing downtown to rival the exploding volcano at the Mirage, the theme park at Circus Circus, the pirate battle at Treasure Island (T. I.), or the view from the Stratosphere Tower. As gambling revenue dwindled and more customers defected to the Strip, downtown casino owners finally got serious about mounting a counterattack.

The counterattack, known as the Fremont Street Experience, was launched at the end of 1995. Its basic purpose was to transform downtown into an ongoing event, a continuous party, a happening. Fremont Street through the heart of Glitter Gulch was forever closed to vehicular traffic and turned into a park, with terraces, street musicians, and landscaping. By creating an aesthetically pleasing environment, Las Vegas–style, the project united all of the casinos in a sort of diverse gambling mall.

Transformative events on the ground aside, however, the main draw of the Fremont Street Experience is up in the air. Four blocks of Fremont Street are covered by a 1,400-foot-long, 90-foot-high "space frame"—an enormous, vaulted geodesic matrix. This futuristic structure totally canopies Fremont Street. In addition to providing nominal shade from the blistering sun, the space frame serves as the stage for a nighttime attraction that has definitely improved downtown's fortune. Set into the inner surface of the space frame are 12.5 million LEDs, which come to life in a computer-driven, multisensory show. The LEDs are augmented by 40 speakers on each block, booming symphonic sound in syncopation with the lights.

We at the *Unofficial Guide* enjoy and appreciate downtown Las Vegas, and all of us hope that the Fremont Street Experience will continue to have a beneficial effect. We are amazed and appalled, however, by the city's general lack of commitment to improving its infrastructure, particularly the traffic situation. The market, in terms of aggregate number of gamblers, is undeniably located out on the Strip. To create an attraction sufficiently compelling to lure this market downtown is to fight only half the battle. The other half of the battle is to make it easy for all those folks on the Strip to get downtown.

If You Visit Las Vegas on Business

If you are going to Las Vegas for a trade show or convention, you will want to lodge as close as possible to the meeting site (ideally within easy walking distance) or, alternatively, near a monorail station. Many Strip hotel-casinos— including the Riviera, Flamingo, Venetian, Wynn Las Vegas, Paris, Bellagio, Mandalay Bay, Planet Hollywood, Las Vegas Hilton, Aria, Encore, MGM Grand, T. I., Tropicana, Mirage, Caesars Palace, Harrah's, and Bally's—host meetings from 100 to upward of 5,000 attendees, offer lodging for citywide shows and conventions held at the Las Vegas Convention Center and the Sands Expo and Convention Center, and have good track records with business travelers. Our maps should provide some assistance in determining which properties are situated near your meeting site.

unofficial **TIP**
Try to find a good deal on a room at a hotel that's not near your meeting site and commute to your meeting in a rental car. Often the savings on the room will pay for your transportation.

Because most large meetings and trade shows are headquartered at the convention center or on the Strip, lodging on the Strip is more convenient than staying downtown. Citywide conventions often provide shuttle service from the major hotels to the Las Vegas Convention Center, and, of course, cabs and the monorail are available too. Las Vegas traffic is a mess, however, particularly in the late afternoon, and there is a finite number of cabs.

LARGE HOTEL-CASINOS VERSUS SMALL HOTELS AND MOTELS

LODGING PROPERTIES IN LAS VEGAS range from tiny motels with a dozen rooms to colossal hotel-casino complexes of 5,000 rooms. As you might expect, there are advantages and drawbacks to staying in either a large or small hotel. Determining which size is better for you depends on how you plan to spend your time in Las Vegas.

If your leisure or business itinerary calls for a car and a lot of coming and going, the big hotels can be a real pain. At the Venetian, Excalibur, and MGM Grand, to name a few, it can take as long as 15 minutes to get from your room to your car if you use the self-parking lot. A young couple staying at the Las Vegas Hilton left their hotel room 40 minutes prior to their show reservations at the Mirage. After trooping to their van in the Hilton's distant self-parking lot, the couple discovered they had forgotten their show tickets. By the time the husband ran back to their room to retrieve the tickets and returned to the van, only five minutes remained to drive to the Mirage, park, and find the showroom. As it turned out, they missed the first 15 minutes of the performance.

Many large hotels have multistory, self-parking garages that require lengthy and dizzying drives down ramps. Post-9/11 security likewise has complicated coming and going at some large, multistory parking garages. If you plan to use the car frequently and do not want to deal with the hassle of remote parking lots, big garages, or the tipping associated with valet parking, we recommend staying in a smaller hotel or motel that provides quick and convenient access to your car.

Quiet and tranquility can also be reasons for choosing a smaller hotel. Many Las Vegas visitors object to passing through a casino whenever they go to or leave their room. Staying in a smaller property without a casino or a large nongaming property like the Trump Hotel Las Vegas permits an escape from the flashing lights, the never-ending noise of slot machines, and the unremitting, frenetic pace of an around-the-clock gambling town. While they may not be as exciting, smaller hotels tend to be more restful and homelike.

The ease and simplicity of checking in and out of smaller properties has its own appeal. To be able to check in or pay your bill without standing in a line, or to unload and load the car directly and conveniently, significantly diminishes the stress of arriving and departing. When we visited the registration lobby of one of the larger hotels on a Friday afternoon, for example, it reminded us of Kennedy International Airport shut down by a winter storm. Guests were stacked dozens deep in the check-in lines. Others, having abandoned any hope of registering in the near future, slept curled up around their luggage or sat reading on the floor. The whole lobby was awash in suitcases, hanging bags, and people milling about. Though hotel size and check-in efficiency are not always inversely related, the sight of a registration lobby fitted out like the queuing area of Disneyland's Jungle Cruise should be enough to make a sane person think twice.

Along similar lines, a large hotel does not ensure more comfortable or more luxurious accommodations. In Las Vegas there are exceptionally posh and well-designed rooms in both large and small hotels, just as there are threadbare and poorly designed rooms in properties of every size. A large establishment does, however, usually ensure a superior range of amenities, including on-site entertainment, room service, spas or exercise rooms, concierge services, bell services, valet parking, meeting rooms, babysitting, shoe shining, dry cleaning, shopping, 24-hour restaurants, copy and fax services, check cashing, and, of course, gambling.

> *unofficial* **TIP**
> Try a local wash-and-fold service as an affordable alternative to expensive hotel-casino laundry services.

If you spill a cosmopolitan on your khakis, however, you may want to think twice before ponying up for the hotel-casino in-house laundry service. You'll pay by the piece, and you'll pay dearly. After a couple of days' laundry pile up on the bed, do like we do and take advantage of an area wash-and-fold service. Our favorite is **Wizard of Suds** (4275 Arville Street) where the courteous staff will wash and fold your dirties for cheap. At $1.49 per pound, and with quick turnaround if you drop off before noon, you can't beat the Wizard; ☎ 702-873-1453.

If you plan to do most of your touring on foot or are attending a convention, a large hotel in a good location has advantages. There will be a variety of restaurants, entertainment, shopping, and recreation close at hand. In case you are a night owl, you will be able to eat or drink at any hour, and there will always be lots going on. Many showrooms offer 11 p.m. or midnight shows, and quite a few hotels (Sam's Town, Suncoast, Gold Coast, Orleans, South Point, Red Rock, Texas Station, Sunset Station, and Santa Fe Station) have 24-hour bowling.

For visitors who wish to immerse themselves in the atmosphere of Las Vegas, to live in the fast lane, and to be where the action is, a large hotel is recommended. These people feel they are missing something unless they stay in a big hotel-casino. For them, it is important to know that the excitement is only an elevator ride away.

GETTING AROUND:
Location and Convenience

LAS VEGAS LODGING CONVENIENCE CHART

THE CHART ON PAGES 42–45 will give you a feel for how convenient specific hotels and motels are to common Las Vegas destinations. Both walking and cab-commuting times are figured on the conservative side. You should be able to do a little better than the times indicated, particularly by cab, unless you are traveling during rush hour or attempting to navigate the Strip on a weekend evening.

Regarding the monorail, times listed include loading and unloading as well as the actual commuting time. The Strip monorail stations are located at the far rear of the host casinos, so, for example, the walk from the Strip entrance of the MGM Grand to the station is about six to eight minutes. The MGM Grand station is the closest station to the Excalibur on the west side of the Strip. From your guest room at the Excalibur it will take about 20 to 25 minutes to walk to the MGM Grand station. In our experience, because of the walking required to reach the nearest monorail station from casinos on the Strip's west side, you might want to consider a cab if you're in a hurry. Always check traffic conditions before you hop in a cab. If the Strip is gridlocked (very common), head for the monorail.

Commuting to Downtown from the Strip

Commuting to downtown from the Strip is a snap on I-15 during non–rush hours. From the Strip you can get on or off I-15 at Tropicana Avenue, Flamingo Road, Spring Mountain Road, or Sahara Avenue. Once on I-15 heading north, stay in the right lane and follow the signs for downtown and US 95 South. Exiting onto Casino Center Boulevard, you will be in the middle of downtown with several large parking garages conveniently at hand. Driving time to downtown Las Vegas varies from about 16 minutes from the south end of the Strip (I-15 via Tropicana Avenue) to about

6 minutes from the north end (I-15 via Sahara Avenue). I-15, however, is totally overwhelmed during rush hour from 7 to 9 a.m. and 3:30 to 7 p.m. During these hours you're probably better off using surface streets.

Commuting to the Strip from Downtown

If you are heading to the Strip from downtown, you can pick up US 95 North (and then I-15 South) by going north on either Fourth Street or Las Vegas Boulevard. Driving time from downtown to the Strip takes 10 to 20 minutes, depending on your destination.

Free Connections

Traffic on the Strip is so awful that the hotels, both individually and in groups, are creating new alternatives for getting around.

1. On the west side, a shuttle tram serves the Excalibur, Luxor, Mandalay Bay, Four Seasons, and THEhotel.

2. Coast Casinos operates a shuttle connecting the Gold Coast, Bill's Gamblin' Hall, and the Orleans.

3. Hard Rock Cafe offers a shuttle service to and from the MGM Grand. Note that Hard Rock Cafe is a free-standing restaurant in front of the Hard Rock Hotel.

4. M Resort provides shuttle service to and from the airport and Fashion Show Mall.

5. A "people mover" connects the Spa Tower of the Bellagio to the Monte Carlo with an intermediate stop at Crystals shopping complex at CityCenter.

6. A tram connects T. I. and the Mirage, though the hike to the tram takes more time than to commute back and forth on the Strip.

7. The Palms has a shuttle that loops to the Forum Shops and Fashion Show Mall and then back to the Palms.

8. Red Rock Resort provides shuttles to and from the airport and to Fashion Show Mall.

9. Sam's Town provides shuttles to the Strip and downtown.

10. The Silverton provides shuttles to the airport, the Forum Shops, Oasis RV Park, the Outlet Center, and Town Square.

11. There is a shuttle service between Harrah's and the Rio, and a similar service between Bally's and the Rio. Both run from 10 a.m. until 1 a.m. No luggage is allowed.

unofficial **TIP**
Because monorail stations are located at the extreme rear of the casinos served, you're better off walking to your destination if you are going less than a mile.

LAS VEGAS MONORAIL

THE LONG-AWAITED $650-MILLION Las Vegas Monorail began service in 2004 with nine trains running the four-mile route between the MGM Grand and the Sahara (now closed). The route parallels the Strip

Continued on page 44

Commuting Times in Minutes

FROM	TO				UNLV THOMAS & MACK CENTER
	LAS VEGAS STRIP	CONVENTION CENTER	DOWN-TOWN	McCARRAN AIRPORT	
Alexis Park Resort and Villas	5/cab	8/cab	15/cab	5/cab	6/cab
Aliante Station	35/cab	40/cab	25/cab	47/cab	49/cab
Ambassador Strip Travelodge	3/cab	9/cab	15/cab	4/cab	6/cab
Arizona Charlie's Boulder	12/cab	18/cab	12/cab	20/cab	22/cab
Arizona Charlie's Decatur	19/cab	18/cab	12/cab	21/cab	20/cab
Artisan Hotel and Spa	5/walk	5/cab	14/cab	14/cab	14/cab
Bally's	on Strip	8/mono	15/cab	7/cab	7/cab
Bellagio	on Strip	11/mono	15/cab	11/cab	12/cab
Best Western Mardi Gras Hotel and Casino	6/cab	10/walk	15/cab	9/cab	7/cab
Best Western McCarran Inn	6/cab	9/cab	15/cab	4/cab	7/cab
Bill's Gamblin' Hall	on Strip	7/mono	15/cab	8/cab	9/cab
Binion's Gambling Hall	14/cab	15/cab	downtown	19/cab	19/cab
Boulder Station	19/cab	18/cab	12/cab	21/cab	20/cab
Caesars Palace	on Strip	7/mono	12/cab	10/cab	10/cab
California	13/cab	15/cab	downtown	19/cab	19/cab
Candlewood Suites	5/cab	6/cab	15/cab	6/cab	6/cab
Cannery	23/cab	26/cab	20/cab	30/cab	30/cab
Casino Royale	on Strip	7/mono	14/cab	10/cab	10/cab
Circus Circus	on Strip	5/cab	13/cab	14/cab	13/cab
CityCenter Hotels	on Strip	12/cab	14/cab	15/cab	11/cab
Clarion Hotel and Casino	7/walk	5/walk	14/cab	9/cab	11/cab
Comfort Inn Paradise Road	4/cab	5/cab	15/cab	10/cab	9/cab
Cosmopolitan	on Strip	12/cab	14/cab	15/cab	11/cab
Courtyard Las Vegas South	4/cab	14/cab	15/cab	8/cab	12/cab
Courtyard Paradise Road	4/cab	5/walk	15/cab	9/cab	8/cab
Days Inn at Wild Wild West	3/cab	13/cab	14/cab	8/cab	11/cab
Eastside Cannery	20/cab	25/cab	30/cab	19/cab	18/cab
El Cortez	11/cab	15/cab	6/walk	16/cab	17/cab
El Cortez Cabana Suites	11/cab	15/cab	7/walk	16/cab	17/cab
Ellis Island	4/cab	6/cab	14/cab	8/cab	8/cab
Embassy Suites Convention Center	6/cab	10/walk	15/cab	9/cab	7/cab
Embassy Suites in Las Vegas	4/cab	6/cab	15/cab	6/cab	6/cab

FROM	TO				
	LAS VEGAS STRIP	**CONVENTION CENTER**	**DOWN-TOWN**	**McCARRAN AIRPORT**	**UNLV THOMAS & MACK CENTER**
Excalibur	on Strip	13/cab	14/cab	7/cab	8/cab
Fairfield Inn Las Vegas Airport	5/cab	5/cab	15/cab	9/cab	8/cab
Fairfield Inn and Suites Las Vegas South	4/cab	14/walk	15/cab	8/cab	12/cab
Fiesta Henderson	18/cab	17/cab	19/cab	17/cab	15/cab
Fiesta Rancho	18/cab	18/cab	10/cab	22/cab	22/cab
Fitzgeralds	14/cab	15/cab	downtown	17/cab	17/cab
Flamingo	on Strip	7/mono	13/cab	8/cab	8/cab
Four Queens	15/cab	15/cab	downtown	19/cab	17/cab
Four Seasons	on Strip	14/cab	15/cab	7/cab	13/cab
Fremont	15/cab	15/cab	downtown	19/cab	17/cab
Gold Coast	4/cab	13/cab	14/cab	10/cab	10/cab
Gold Spike	14/cab	15/cab	4/walk	18/cab	17/cab
Golden Gate	14/cab	15/cab	downtown	19/cab	18/cab
Golden Nugget	14/cab	15/cab	downtown	18/cab	19/cab
Green Valley Ranch Resort and Spa	15/cab	18/cab	16/cab	15/cab	14/cab
Hampton Inn Tropicana	10/walk	6/cab	9/cab	10/cab	6/cab
Hard Rock Hotel	4/cab	6/cab	15/cab	6/cab	6/cab
Harrah's	on Strip	5/mono	15/cab	10/cab	10/cab
Hilton Garden Inn	13/cab	23/cab	26/cab	14/cab	21/cab
Holiday Inn Express	4/cab	14/cab	15/cab	8/cab	12/cab
Hooters	5/walk	11/mono	15/cab	6/cab	8/cab
Hyatt Place	4/cab	7/walk	15/cab	10/cab	9/cab
Imperial Palace	on Strip	5/mono	15/cab	10/cab	10/cab
JW Marriott Las Vegas	18/cab	21/cab	15/cab	23/cab	24/cab
La Quinta Las Vegas Airport	5/cab	6/cab	15/cab	6/cab	6/cab
Las Vegas Club	14/cab	15/cab	downtown	19/cab	18/cab
Las Vegas Hilton*	5/mono	5/walk	13/cab	10/cab	8/cab
Las Vegas Marriott Suites	14/cab	5/walk	15/cab	10/cab	9/cab
Loews Lake Las Vegas	45/cab	49/cab	43/cab	37/cab	46/cab
Luxor	on Strip	13/cab	15/cab	8/cab	10/cab
M Resort	20/cab	27/cab	30/cab	22/cab	27/cab
Main Street Station	14/cab	15/cab	downtown	19/cab	19/cab

will cease being a Hilton after January 1, 2012

Commuting Times in Minutes (continued)

FROM	TO				UNLV THOMAS & MACK CENTER
	LAS VEGAS STRIP	CONVENTION CENTER	DOWN-TOWN	McCARRAN AIRPORT	
Mandalay Bay	on Strip	14/cab	16/cab	7/cab	13/cab
Manor Suites	10/cab	17/cab	20/cab	12/cab	17/cab
MGM Grand	on Strip	11/mono	15/cab	9/cab	9/cab
Mirage	on Strip	6/mono	15/cab	11/cab	10/cab
Monte Carlo	on Strip	11/mono	15/cab	11/cab	12/cab
Motel 6 Tropicana	3/cab	12/cab	15/cab	6/cab	8/cab
New York–New York	on Strip	11/mono	15/cab	11/cab	12/cab
Orleans	4/cab	15/cab	14/cab	11/cab	11/cab
Palace Station	5/cab	10/cab	10/cab	14/cab	15/cab
Palazzo	on Strip	6/mono	14/cab	8/cab	8/cab
Palms	5/cab	13/cab	14/cab	10/cab	10/cab
Paris	on Strip	9/mono	15/cab	8/cab	8/cab
Planet Hollywood	on Strip	8/cab	15/cab	7/cab	8/cab
Platinum Hotel	8/walk	5/cab	17/cab	7/cab	7/cab
Plaza Hotel	14/cab	15/cab	downtown	19/cab	18/cab
Quality Inn Las Vegas	5/cab	13/cab	14/cab	10/cab	10/cab
Ramada Las Vegas	5/cab	5/cab	14/cab	8/cab	10/cab
Ravella at Lake Las Vegas	45/cab	49/cab	43/cab	37/cab	46/cab
Red Rock Resort	18/cab	21/cab	15/cab	23/cab	24/cab
Renaissance Las Vegas	5/cab	10/walk	14/cab	9/cab	8/cab
Residence Inn Convention Center	4/cab	6/cab	15/cab	12/cab	12/cab
Residence Inn Las Vegas South	4/cab	14/cab	15/cab	8/cab	12/cab

Continued from page 41

between Tropicana and Sands avenues and then cuts east to the Las Vegas Convention Center and the Las Vegas Hilton before continuing to the last stop at the Sahara. Trains run approximately every ten minutes between 7 a.m. and 2 a.m. on weekdays and until 3 a.m. on weekends. From one end of the line to the other takes about 15 minutes and includes seven stops. The fare for a single one-way ride is $5. A better deal is a one-day fare (24 hours from first use) at $14 or three-day unlimited travel fare for $30. Check the website for special rates; **lvmonorail.com.** The monorail is a godsend to convention and trade-show attendees commuting from Strip hotels to the Las Vegas Convention Center and the Sands Exposition Center; ☎ 702-699-8200.

FROM	TO				
	LAS VEGAS STRIP	CONVENTION CENTER	DOWN-TOWN	McCARRAN AIRPORT	UNLV THOMAS & MACK CENTER
Rio	5/cab	14/cab	13/cab	10/cab	10/cab
Riviera	on Strip	4/cab	14/cab	11/cab	10/cab
Royal Resort	3/walk	5/cab	14/cab	13/cab	11/cab
Rumor	4/cab	6/cab	15/cab	6/cab	6/cab
Sam's Town	20/cab	25/cab	20/cab	18/cab	17/cab
Santa Fe Station	27/cab	30/cab	23/cab	33/cab	36/cab
Silverton	10/cab	17/cab	20/cab	12/cab	17/cab
South Point	16/cab	23/cab	26/cab	18/cab	23/cab
Stratosphere	3/cab	7/cab	9/cab	14/cab	14/cab
Suncoast	18/cab	21/cab	15/cab	23/cab	24/cab
Sunset Station	18/cab	17/cab	18/cab	16/cab	15/cab
Terrible's	5/cab	6/cab	15/cab	6/cab	6/cab
Texas Station	17/cab	16/cab	13/cab	22/cab	22/cab
THEhotel at Mandalay Bay	on Strip	14/cab	15/cab	7/cab	13/cab
T. I.	on Strip	6/mono	14/cab	11/cab	10/cab
Tropicana	on Strip	11/mono	15/cab	6/cab	9/cab
Trump Las Vegas	10/walk	10/cab	11/cab	13/cab	11/cab
Tuscany	5/cab	5/cab	14/cab	8/cab	10/cab
Venetian	on Strip	6/mono	14/cab	8/cab	8/cab
Westin Casuarina	4/walk	11/mono	15/cab	7/cab	7/cab
Wynn Encore	on Strip	8/cab	13/cab	10/cab	9/cab
Wynn Las Vegas	on Strip	8/cab	13/cab	10/cab	9/cab

BUSES

LAS VEGAS'S CITIZEN'S AREA TRANSIT (CAT) provides reliable bus service at reasonable rates. Although one-way fares along the Strip are $3 for the double-decker Deuce, one-way fares in residential areas are only $2. You can also purchase an all-day pass for the Strip for $7 and an all-day pass for residential areas for $5. The pass is good for 24 hours from the time of purchase. Children age 5 and under ride all routes free. All public transportation requires exact fare. All CAT buses are equipped with wheelchair lifts and bicycle racks, both of which are provided at no extra charge. Disabled persons who are certified in their home state for door-to-door service should call ☎ 702-676-1815 for reservations. People who are not certified in their home state cannot get door-to-door service in Las Vegas. For general route and fare information or to request a schedule through the mail, call ☎ 702-228-7433 or visit **rtcsouthernnevada.com/transit/route.**

COMMONLY USED PUBLIC TRANSPORTATION ROUTES				
	ROUND-TRIP FROM/TO	HOURS OF OPERATION	FREQUENCY OF SERVICE	FARE
Monorail	MGM Grand/ Sahara	7 a.m.–2 a.m. 3 a.m. weekends	Every 5 min.	$5
Citizen's Area Transit Deuce Line	South Strip Transfer Terminals/ Downtown Transportation Center	24 hours	Every 12 minutes	$3

WHAT'S *in an* ADDRESS?

DOWNTOWN

THE HEART OF THE DOWNTOWN casino area is Fremont Street between Fourth Street (on the east) and Main Street (on the west). Hotel-casinos situated along this quarter-mile four-block stretch known as Glitter Gulch include the Plaza Hotel, Golden Gate, Las Vegas Club, Binion's Gambling Hall, Golden Nugget, Fremont, Four Queens, and Fitzgeralds. Parallel to Fremont and one block north is Ogden Avenue, where the California and the Gold Spike are located. Main Street Station is situated on Main Street at the intersection of Ogden Avenue.

All of the downtown hotel-casinos are centrally positioned and convenient to the action, with the exception of the El Cortez, which sits three blocks to the east. While there is a tremendous difference in quality and price among the downtown properties, the locations of all the hotels (except the El Cortez) are excellent. When you stay downtown, everything is within a five-minute walk. By comparison, on the Strip it takes longer to walk from the entrance of Caesars Palace to the entrance of the Mirage, next door, than to cover the whole four blocks of the casino center downtown.

THE STRIP

WHILE LOCATION IS NOT A MAJOR CONCERN when choosing from among the downtown hotels, it is of paramount importance when selecting a hotel on the Strip.

We once received a flier from a Las Vegas casino proclaiming that it was located "right on the Strip." It supported the claim with a photo showing its marquee and those of several other casinos in a neat row with their neon ablaze. What recipients of this advertisement (except those familiar with Las Vegas) never would have guessed was that the photo had been taken with a lens that eliminated all sense of distance.

While the advertised casino appeared to be next door to the other casinos in the picture, it was in reality almost a mile away.

A common variation on the same pitch is "Stay Right on the Las Vegas Strip at Half the Price." Once again, the promoter is attempting to deceive by taking advantage of the recipient's ignorance of Strip geography. As it happens, the Las Vegas Strip (South Las Vegas Boulevard) starts southwest of the airport and runs all the way downtown, a distance of about seven miles. Aside from the South Point Hotel some miles south of the airport, only the four-mile section between Mandalay Bay and the Stratosphere contains the large casinos and other attractions of interest to visitors. South of Mandalay Bay "on the Strip" are the airport boundary, some small motels, discount shopping, and nice desert. North of the Stratosphere en route to downtown, the Strip runs through a commercial area sprinkled with wedding chapels, fast-food joints, and small motels.

The Best Locations on the Strip

Beware of hotels and motels claiming to be on the Strip but not located between Mandalay Bay and the Stratosphere. The Mandalay Bay basically anchors the south end of the Strip, about a quarter mile from the Luxor, its closest neighbor. Likewise, at the other end, the Stratosphere is somewhat isolated. In between, there are distinct clusters of hotels and casinos.

STRIP CLUSTER 1: THE CLUSTER OF THE GIANTS At the intersection of the Strip (South Las Vegas Boulevard) and Tropicana Avenue are five of the world's largest hotels. The MGM Grand Hotel is the third largest hotel in the world. Diagonally across the intersection from the MGM Grand is the Excalibur, the tenth largest hotel in the world. The other two corners of the intersection are occupied by New York–New York and the Tropicana. Nearby to the south are the Luxor (seventh largest) and Mandalay Bay, the Four Seasons, and THEhotel (collectively eighth largest). To the north is the Monte Carlo on the Strip. Hooters is situated on Tropicana Avenue across from the MGM Grand. From the intersection of the Strip and Tropicana Avenue, it is a half-mile walk south to Mandalay Bay. The next cluster of major hotels and casinos is at the intersection of the Strip and Harmon Avenue less than a half mile north. Including all the hotels from Mandalay Bay to Monte Carlo, Strip Cluster 1 challenges the status, at least in terms of appeal and diversity, of Strip Cluster 3 at the heart of the Strip. Progress always has its dark side, however; here it is the phenomenal increase of traffic and congestion on East Tropicana Avenue as it nears the Strip.

unofficial **TIP**
If you stay on the Strip, you want to be somewhere in the Mandalay Bay–Stratosphere stretch. Even there, though, some sections are more desirable than others.

STRIP CLUSTER 2 At Harmon Avenue and the Strip is MGM Resorts International's (MRI) CityCenter, a mammoth four-hotel lodging, dining, shopping, entertainment, and gaming complex with approximately 6,000 rooms and suites. Truly a city within a city, CityCenter came close to disaster during the credit crunch of 2009. Positioned at the northeast corner of CityCenter is the indie Cosmopolitan—a bi-towered, 2,995-suite glittering high-rise with full casino, 14 restaurants, three pools, a showroom, and much more. The Cosmo is the latest addition to Las Vegas's inventory of mid-to-high-end uber-resorts. Situated across the Strip from CityCenter and the Cosmo is Planet Hollywood, a hip, newly renovated hotel that targets younger Las Vegas visitors with its shows, nightlife, and restaurants. Planet Hollywood is attached to the Miracle Mile Shops, one of the major shopping venues on the Strip. Collectively, CityCenter, the Cosmopolitan, and Planet Hollywood compose the most exciting and avant-garde combination on the Strip.

STRIP CLUSTER 3: THE GRAND CLUSTER From Flamingo Road to Spring Mountain Road (also called Sands Avenue, and farther east, Twain Avenue) is the greatest numerical concentration of major hotels and casinos on the Strip. If you wish to stay on the Strip and prefer to walk wherever you go, this is the best location. At Flamingo Road and Las Vegas Boulevard are Bally's, Caesars Palace, Bill's Gamblin' Hall, Paris, and Bellagio. Heading east on Flamingo Road is the Westin Casuarina. Toward town on the Strip are the Flamingo, O'Shea's, Imperial Palace, Mirage, Harrah's, Casino Royale, the Palazzo and Venetian, and T. I. Also in this cluster are the Forum Shops and the Grand Canal Shoppes, Las Vegas's most distinctive shopping venues. A leisure traveler could stay a week in this section (without ever getting in a car or cab) and not run out of interesting sights, restaurants, or entertainment. On the negative side, for those with cars, traffic congestion on the Strip and at the intersection of the Strip and Flamingo Road is the worst in the city.

STRIP CLUSTER 4 Another nice section of the Strip is from Spring Mountain Road up to Wynn Encore and Wynn Las Vegas. This cluster, pretty much in the center of the Strip, is distinguished by its easy access. Visitors who prefer a major hotel on the Strip but want to avoid daily traffic snarls could not ask for a more convenient location.

unofficial **TIP**
Try Strip Cluster 4 for convenience and to escape traffic congestion.

Though Wynn Encore and Wynn Las Vegas are about a quarter mile from the nearest casino cluster in either direction, they are situated within a ten-minute walk of Fashion Show Mall, one of the most diversified upscale shopping centers in the United States. There are also some very good restaurants here, both in the hotels and in the mall. Finally, this cluster is a four-minute cab ride (or a 16-minute walk) from the Las Vegas Convention Center.

STRIP CLUSTER 5 The next cluster up the Strip is between Convention Center Drive and Riviera Boulevard. Arrayed along a stretch slightly more than a half-mile long are the Riviera and Circus Circus with its Adventuredome theme park. Casinos and hotels in this cluster are considerably less upscale than those in the other clusters but offer acceptable selections for dining and entertainment, as well as proximity to the Las

Hotel Clusters

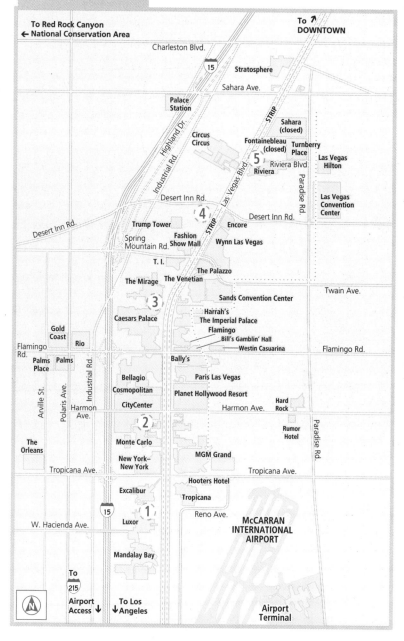

To Red Rock Canyon
← National Conservation Area

To ↗
DOWNTOWN

Charleston Blvd.

15

Stratosphere

Sahara Ave.

Palace
Station

STRIP

Sahara
(closed)

Highland Dr.

Industrial Rd.

Circus
Circus

Fontainebleau
(closed)

Turnberry
Place

Las Vegas
Hilton

5

Riviera Blvd.

Riviera

Las Vegas Blvd.

Paradise Rd.

Las Vegas
Convention
Center

Desert Inn Rd.

Desert Inn Rd.

Desert Inn Rd.

4

STRIP

Trump Tower

Encore

Spring
Mountain Rd.

Fashion
Show Mall

Wynn Las Vegas

T. I.

The Palazzo

The Mirage

The Venetian

Twain Ave.

3

Sands Convention Center

Caesars Palace

Harrah's
The Imperial Palace
Flamingo

Gold
Coast

Rio

Bill's Gamblin' Hall
Westin Casuarina

Flamingo Rd.

Flamingo
Rd.

Palms
Place

Palms

Bally's

Industrial Rd.

Arville St.

Polaris Ave.

Bellagio

Paris Las Vegas

Cosmopolitan

Planet Hollywood Resort

Harmon
Ave.

CityCenter

Harmon Ave.

Hard
Rock

Paradise Rd.

2

Rumor
Hotel

The
Orleans

Monte Carlo

MGM Grand

New York–
New York

Tropicana Ave.

Tropicana Ave.

Hooters Hotel

Excalibur

Tropicana

15

Reno Ave.

**McCARRAN
INTERNATIONAL
AIRPORT**

1

W. Hacienda Ave.

Luxor

Mandalay Bay

To
215

Airport
Access ↓

To Los
↓ Angeles

Airport
Terminal

Downtown Accommodations

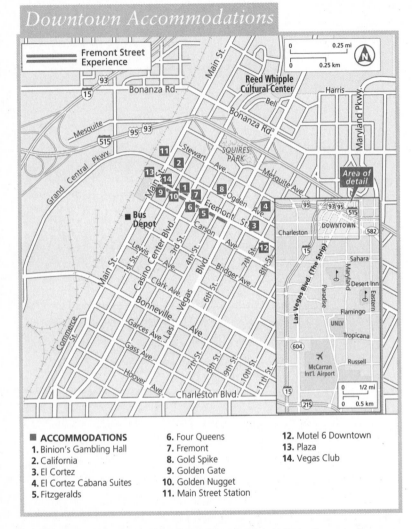

ACCOMMODATIONS
1. Binion's Gambling Hall
2. California
3. El Cortez
4. El Cortez Cabana Suites
5. Fitzgeralds
6. Four Queens
7. Fremont
8. Gold Spike
9. Golden Gate
10. Golden Nugget
11. Main Street Station
12. Motel 6 Downtown
13. Plaza
14. Vegas Club

Vegas Convention Center. Finally, about a third of a mile toward town from the intersection of Las Vegas Boulevard and Sahara Avenue is the Stratosphere. Though fairly isolated if you intend to walk, for visitors with cars or monorail riders the Stratosphere provides convenient access to the Strip, the convention center, and downtown.

JUST OFF THE STRIP

IF YOU HAVE A CAR, and if being right on the Strip is not a big deal to you, there are some excellent hotel-casinos on Paradise Road and to the east and west of the Strip on intersecting roads. The Rio, Palms, and Gold Coast on Flamingo Road, Palace Station on Sahara Avenue, and

South Strip Accommodations

■ **ACCOMMODATIONS**

1. Ambassador Strip Inn
   Travelodge
2. America's Best Value Inn
3. Courtyard by Marriott
   Las Vegas South
4. Excalibur
5. Fairfield Inn & Suites
   Las Vegas South
6. Four Seasons at
   Mandalay Bay
7. Hampton Inn Tropicana
8. Hilton Garden Inn
   Las Vegas Strip South
9. Holiday Inn Express
10. Hooters Casino Hotel
11. Luxor
12. M Resort
13. Mandalay Bay
14. Manor Suites
15. MGM Grand
16. Monte Carlo
17. New York–New York
18. Orleans
19. Quality Inn Las Vegas
20. Residence Inn by
    Marriott Las Vegas
    South
21. Silverton
22. South Point
23. THEhotel at Mandalay Bay
    (all suites)
24. Tropicana
25. Wild Wild West

Orleans on Tropicana Avenue offer exceptional value; they are less than a half mile west of the Strip and are situated at access ramps to I-15, five to ten minutes from downtown. To the east of the Strip are the Hard Rock, Rumor, and Alexis Park on Harmon Avenue; the Tuscany and the Platinum on Flamingo Road; and the Las Vegas Hilton on Paradise Road, among others.

BOULDER HIGHWAY, GREEN VALLEY, SUMMERLIN, AND NORTH LAS VEGAS

TWENTY MINUTES FROM THE STRIP in North Las Vegas are Texas Station, Fiesta Rancho, the Cannery, and, on the edge of civilization, Santa Fe Station. All four hotels have good restaurants, comfortable

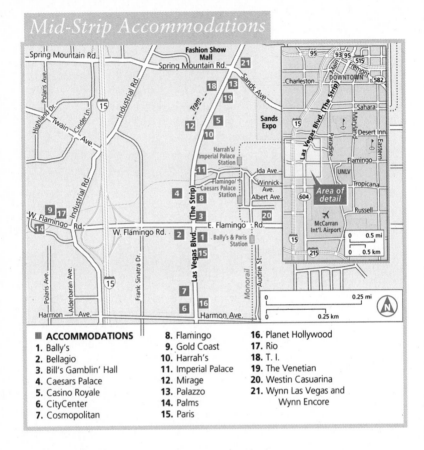

Mid-Strip Accommodations

■ **ACCOMMODATIONS**
1. Bally's
2. Bellagio
3. Bill's Gamblin' Hall
4. Caesars Palace
5. Casino Royale
6. CityCenter
7. Cosmopolitan
8. Flamingo
9. Gold Coast
10. Harrah's
11. Imperial Palace
12. Mirage
13. Palazzo
14. Palms
15. Paris
16. Planet Hollywood
17. Rio
18. T. I.
19. The Venetian
20. Westin Casuarina
21. Wynn Las Vegas and Wynn Encore

guest rooms, and lively, upbeat themes. Hotel-casinos on Boulder Highway southeast of town include Boulder Station, Sam's Town, Eastside Cannery, and Arizona Charlie's Boulder. Also to the southeast are Sunset Station, Fiesta Henderson, and Green Valley Ranch Resort and Spa. Like the North Las Vegas trio, the Boulder Highway properties cater primarily to locals. West of town is the posh JW Marriott Las Vegas, with two upscale hotels and the Tournament Player's Club (TPC) at the Canyons Golf Course. Nearby are the Suncoast and the unique Red Rock Resort. Also northwest of the Strip is Arizona Charlie's Decatur.

THE LIGHTS OF LAS VEGAS: TRAFFIC ON THE STRIP

DURING THE PAST DECADE, Las Vegas has experienced exponential growth—growth that unfortunately has not been matched with the development of necessary infrastructure. If you imagine a town designed for about 300,000 people being inundated by a million or so refugees (all with cars), you will have a sense of what's happening here.

North Strip Accommodations

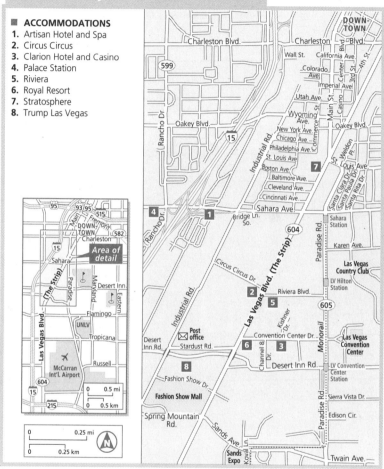

■ **ACCOMMODATIONS**
1. Artisan Hotel and Spa
2. Circus Circus
3. Clarion Hotel and Casino
4. Palace Station
5. Riviera
6. Royal Resort
7. Stratosphere
8. Trump Las Vegas

The Strip, where a huge percentage of the local population works and where more than 80% of tourists and business travelers stay, has become a clogged artery in the heart of the city. The heaviest traffic on the Strip is between Tropicana Avenue and Spring Mountain Drive, in the heart of the Strip. Throughout the day and night, local traffic combines with gawking tourists, shoppers, and cruising teenagers to create a three-mile-long, bumper-to-bumper bottleneck.

When folks discuss the "lights of Las Vegas," it used to be that they were talking about the marquees of the casinos. Today, however, the reference is to the long, multifunctional traffic lights found at virtually

East of Strip Accommodations

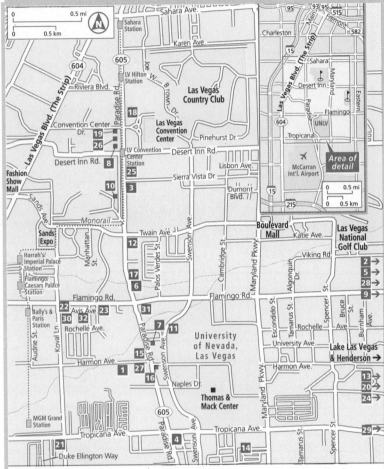

■ **ACCOMMODATIONS**

1. Alexis Park Resort and Villas
2. Arizona Charlie's Boulder
3. Best Western
   Mardi Gras Hotel
   and Casino
4. Best Western McCarran Inn
5. Boulder Station
6. Candlewood Suites
7. Comfort Inn Paradise Road
8. Courtyard by Marriott
9. Eastside Cannery
10. Embassy Suites Convention
    Center

11. Embassy Suites in
    Las Vegas
12. Fairfield Inn Las Vegas
    Airport
13. Fiesta Henderson
14. Green Valley Ranch
15. Hard Rock Hotel
16. Hyatt Place
17. La Quinta Las Vegas
    Airport North
18. Las Vegas Hilton
19. Las Vegas Marriott
20. Loews Lake Las Vegas
21. Motel 6 Tropicana

22. Platinum Hotel
23. Ramada Las Vegas
24. Ravella at Lake
    Las Vegas
25. Renaissance Las Vegas
26. Residence Inn
    by Marriott
27. Rumor
28. Sam's Town
29. Sunset Station
30. Super 8
31. Terrible's
32. Tuscany

every intersection on the Strip. These lights, which flash a different signal for every possible turn and direction, combine with an ever-increasing number of vehicles to ensure that nobody goes anywhere. The worst snarls occur at the intersection of the Strip and Flamingo Road. Trying to cross the Strip on perpendicular east-to-west-running roads is also exceedingly difficult. Desert Inn Road, which tunnels under the Strip, is the fastest way to get from one side to the other. Unfortunately, if you're heading west, Desert Inn Road is hard to access on the east side of the Strip, especially from Paradise Road. To use the tunnel from the east side, turn west on Desert Inn Road from Swenson Street.

Strip traffic is the Achilles heel of Las Vegas development and growth. It is sheer lunacy to believe you can plop a litter of megahotels on the Strip without compounding an already horrific traffic situation. While city government and the hospitality industry dance around the issue, traffic gets worse and worse. Approximately 48,000 hotel rooms were added along the Strip during the 1990s, about 30,000 more came online since the millennium, and another 10,000 or more are under construction or planned. The monorail along the east side of the Strip represents a great alternative to driving, but it has not noticeably mitigated grid-lock. Also, stations are positioned so far to the rear of the casinos that walking is faster than taking the train for distances up to one mile. In another effort, I-15 between downtown and the I-215 junction to the south has been widened and the interchanges improved. While welcome, the project has done little to alleviate traffic. Interestingly, the only initiative that has worked is the construction of elevated pedestrian bridges over the major Strip intersections. In addition to improving safety, the bridges remove pedestrians from the street, leaving the battle-field to vehicles.

Coping with Las Vegas Traffic

Even more challenging than beating the casinos in Las Vegas is beating the traffic. Las Vegas traffic is like health insurance costs in the United States. You just wonder how bad it has to get before anyone does anything about it. As it stands, there are not many good alternatives for getting around and lots of places you'll want to avoid.

We at the *Unofficial Guide* feel the impact directly when we conduct our research in Las Vegas. Where once we required about 5 to 20 minutes to go from one Strip hotel to another by car, we now allocate over an hour. If our destination is a mile or less away, we just walk.

When you plan your Las Vegas visit it's essential to get a handle on how much moving around will be necessary. The most stress-free trip is one where you can walk anywhere you need to go. Choose a hotel near the restaurants, shows, and attractions you wish to experience, or the venue for your business meeting or trade show. If you're attending a convention or trade show at the Las Vegas Convention Center, stay at a hotel within easy walking distance of the convention center, at one of the hotels on the east side of the Strip connected to the Las

North–South Roads to Know

Las Vegas Boulevard South–the Strip Connects the Strip to downtown Las Vegas. Avoid between Tropicana Avenue and Spring Mountain Road.

I-15 Avoid between the I-15/I-215 interchange and downtown.

Swensen Street (Joe W. Brown Drive) Best north–south alternative on the east side of the Strip. Runs from the airport to E. Sahara Avenue.

Paradise Road Tends to clog between the Las Vegas Convention Center and Twain Avenue. Good north–south alternative south of Twain. Leads directly to the airport.

Koval Lane Avoid between Twain and Tropicana from 3 until 8:30 p.m.

Industrial Road (Dean Martin Drive) Best north–south alternative on the west side of the Strip.

Frank Sinatra Drive Parallels I-15 and the Strip and offers easy access to some hotels on the west side of the Strip.

South Main Street Low-traffic alternative for commuting downtown from the Strip. Intersects Las Vegas Boulevard South at E. St. Louis Avenue near the Stratosphere.

Vegas Monorail, or at a hotel such as Wynn Las Vegas or Wynn Encore that provides a free shuttle service. If you're thinking you can lodge on the west side of the Strip and walk across the street to catch the monorail, think again. The average time to walk from the main elevator bank of a west-side Strip hotel to an east-side monorail station is more than 30 minutes. It takes a comparable amount of time to walk from an east-side hotel that doesn't have a monorail station to one that does.

If you're like us and need to use a car, you're probably better off at one of the hotels on the west side of the Strip or alternatively one of the off-Strip properties. Either way, you'll need to study a map of Las Vegas and familiarize yourself with the road network surrounding the Strip. As we'll discuss, there are some roads to avoid and others that will make getting around easier. If your visit centers around the Strip, here are the ones that are most important:

SOUTH LAS VEGAS BOULEVARD–THE STRIP The worst part of the Strip is from Tropicana Avenue north to Spring Mountain Road (Twain Avenue). Avoid this section whenever possible. North of Spring Mountain Road traffic on South Las Vegas Boulevard flows pretty smoothly all the way to downtown Las Vegas except for where it crosses Sahara Avenue.

I-15 I-15, the main north–south freeway, stays jammed from the I-215 interchange south of Las Vegas to the US 95 interchange near downtown. Avoid this section between 7 and 10 a.m. and from 2:45 until 7:15 p.m. Even during non-rush periods, traffic moves at a crawl, but at least

East–West Roads to Know

Sahara Avenue Usually congested at the intersection with the Strip. Otherwise fine.

Desert Inn Road Tunnels under the Strip. Best road for commuting to the west side from the east side and vice versa.

Twain Avenue (Spring Mountain Road) Crosses the Strip at one of the more efficient intersections.

Harmon Avenue Currently T-intersects the Strip and doglegs into CityCenter and then crosses over I-15 to the west side.

Flamingo Road Extreme congestion westbound at the intersection with the Strip. Avoid.

Tropicana Avenue Flows well except westbound at the intersection with the Strip.

I-215 Westbound, avoid the I-15 North exit.

it moves. Between 8:30 p.m. and 6:30 a.m. is the least-congested period of the day. If you use I-15 during daylight hours, your best bet is to stay in the right lanes so you can bail at the next exit if necessary.

INDUSTRIAL ROAD AND FRANK SINATRA DRIVE The best alternate north–south route on the west side of the strip is Industrial Road (also called Dean Martin Drive), especially between Sahara Avenue and Blue Diamond Road (a couple miles south of the I-15/I-215 interchange). Industrial Road closely parallels the Strip and I-15 and is the best choice for accessing Circus Circus, Adventuredome, Trump Las Vegas, Fashion Show Mall, CityCenter and Cosmopolitan (via Jerry Lewis Road and W. Harmon Avenue), and Excalibur, Luxor, and Mandalay Bay (including Four Seasons and THEhotel) via Aldebaran Avenue and W. Hacienda Avenue. You can likewise easily access T. I. and the Mirage by taking Spring Mountain Road east from Industrial Road, and Caesars Palace and the Forum Shops by taking Frank Sinatra Drive off Industrial Road to Jay Sarno Way. Industrial Road is also the best way to access east–west streets, including Sahara Avenue, Spring Mountain Road, Flamingo Road, and Tropicana Avenue. An easy route downtown is Industrial Road north turning east (right) on Wyoming Road and then north again on S. Main Street or South Las Vegas Boulevard. Frank Sinatra Drive can be accessed from I-15 northbound, W. Russell Road, and Industrial Drive. Running north–south directly behind hotels situated on the west side of the Strip, it provides easy access to self-parking at Mandalay Bay/THEhotel, Luxor, Excalibur, Monte Carlo, Caesars, and Fashion Show Mall. It does not provide public access to New York–New York, CityCenter, Crystals (mall), Cosmopolitan, or Bellagio. Frank Sinatra Drive is a main thoroughfare for west Strip hotel employees to access employee parking lots and becomes very congested between 7:30–9:30 a.m. and 2:30–5:30 p.m., when hotel shift changes occur.

SWENSEN STREET On the east side of the Strip the traffic situation is more complex. Although a half mile or more from the Strip, Swensen Street is the most free-flowing north–south traffic artery east of the Strip. Swensen runs from I-215 and the airport all the way north to East Sahara Avenue (the name changes to Joe W. Brown Drive after crossing Desert Inn Road). If you're driving north you can take Swensen for its full length. Going south you'll be diverted to Paradise Road, a block to the west, as Swensen becomes one-way northbound between the airport and Harmon Avenue and Paradise Road becomes one-way southbound from Harmon to the airport.

KOVAL LANE To the west and running parallel to Swensen Street and Paradise Road is Koval Lane, once a favorite for dodging Strip traffic. Now Koval is gridlocked except during non-rush periods. This is unfortunate given that Koval Lane links roads providing rear access to the parking garages of the MGM Grand, Flamingo, Imperial Palace, Harrah's, and the Venetian. Smaller streets joining Koval to the garages remain largely free of congestion, but on Koval you're likely to become gridlocked on the section from Tropicana Avenue north to Twain Avenue. Afternoons from 3 to about 8:30 p.m., Koval is especially bad. During this period, your best bet for reaching the valet or self-parking area of the hotels mentioned above is to access Harmon Avenue westbound from Swensen or Paradise, cross Koval, and then turn right on Audrie Lane. Coming out of the garages onto Audrie will frequently land you in some congestion at the Audrie–Harmon intersection, but suffering three cycles of the traffic signal is about as bad as it gets.

THE TUNNEL An extension of Paradise Road tunnels under the airport runways and connects to I-215 and beyond to the rental-car return center. The approach to the tunnel gets really jammed between 2:45 and 6:30 p.m., so if you're returning a rental car during those hours give yourself extra time. An alternative, particularly if you're coming from west of the Strip, is to take Industrial Road (Dean Martin Drive) to Warm Springs Road. Turn east (left) on Warm Springs, cross I-15, and proceed four big blocks to Gillespie Street. Go left at Gillespie to the rental car center. If you're coming west from Green Valley or Henderson on I-215, transiting the tunnel northbound to Swensen Street is a better way to reach Strip destinations than continuing to I-15 northbound.

Parking

VALET PARKING All Strip hotels offer both valet and self-parking. There is no charge to use valet parking beyond a $2 or so tip when you retrieve your car. Many hotels, including Mandalay Bay, Cosmopolitan, and Caesars Palace, provide valet service at both the front and rear entrances. As a general rule, the hotel's main entrance will be busier than the rear entrance. The problem with main-entrance valet service is that you will probably exit onto the traffic of the Strip. With rear-entrance valet you usually have the option to exit onto a side street. Though most valet services are pretty efficient, they do get swamped from time to time, such as when a show or concert has just concluded.

SELF-PARKING With the exception of the Bellagio and New York–New York, self-parking is easier at the hotels on the west side of the Strip. At any parking garage, don't park until you have located the garage entrance to the casino or the elevators leading to it. This can be tricky because some elevators deliver you to a walkway or side-walk on the ground level quite removed from the casino. Staying oriented in such large garages is challenging, but what you want to do is park as close as possible to the most direct entrance to the hotel or casino. There are always elevators, so it doesn't really matter on which level you park as long as you're near the casino entrance or the elevators that descend to it. Our experience is that close-in parking spots are most readily available on the second to highest level. If a garage has five levels, for example, you're more likely to find avail-able close-in spots on level four than on the other levels. Some of the garages are huge, so always jot down the level and row where you've parked. We should note that all of the hotels listed in the self-parking chart on pages 60–61 have Strip parking and valet entrances except Monte Carlo, New York–New York, MGM Grand, Bally's, and Bill's Gamblin' Hall. The objective of this chart is to help you avoid Strip traffic by accessing the hotels (where possible) from other streets (see chart pages 60–61).

SELF-PARKING DOWNTOWN In downtown Las Vegas we always park at Binion's garage on Casino Center Drive between Stewart and Ogden avenues. It's centrally located and rarely crowded. It's also free if you have your ticket punched at the cashier's cage in Binion's.

ROOM RESERVATIONS: *Getting a Good Room, Getting a Good Deal*

FOR DECADES LAS VEGAS had the highest room-occupancy rates in the United States, averaging 98% on weekends and 92% during the week. However, the downturn in the economy and the addition of a glut of new rooms to the city's room inventory have conspired to cre-ate a buyer's market. Some of the newly available rooms come from condo projects that were originally designed to be residences. With supply up and demand down, even the most prestigious properties are discounting. Upscale hotels are faring better than moderate and value

Self-Parking

HOTELS ON THE EAST SIDE OF THE STRIP (FROM NORTH TO SOUTH)

Riviera Use self-parking garage off Paradise Road.

Wynn Encore Use self-parking garage off the Strip. You can access the hotel elevators, casino, and showrooms from self-parking faster than by using the valet service.

Wynn Las Vegas Use self-parking garage off the Strip. Once again, you can access the hotel elevators, casino, and showrooms from self-parking faster than by using the valet service.

Palazzo/Venetian Very confusing self-parking garage. There is rear access from Koval Lane or front access from the Strip. Both are subject to considerable congestion. Park at Wynn Las Vegas or Fashion Show Mall and walk to the Venetian.

Harrah's Straightforward garage. To access it drive west on Harmon Avenue, then right on Audrie Lane and left on Winnick Avenue.

Imperial Palace Somewhat confusing but linear. To access it drive west on Harmon Avenue, then right on Audrie Lane and left on Winnick Avenue.

Flamingo Confusing garage layout. Park at Imperial Palace or Harrah's and walk to the Flamingo.

Bill's Gamblin' Hall Self-parking garage off Flamingo Road. Hard to access because traffic waiting for the light at Flamingo and the Strip blocks the entrance.

Bally's Drive east on Harmon Avenue and then left on Audrie Lane to the garage.

Paris Drive east on Harmon Avenue and then left on Audrie Lane to the garage.

Planet Hollywood Very confusing garage accessible from Harmon Avenue. After parking you must walk through the Miracle Mile Shops to reach the hotel.

MGM Grand Parking is accessible via Tropicana Avenue westbound or off Koval Lane. Very difficult to exit onto Koval Lane. Park at Hooter's, the Tropicana, or New York–New York and walk over.

Tropicana Go west on Tropicana Avenue, then left on Koval Lane and right on Reno Avenue. Large outdoor parking lot plus parking garage. Easy access by foot to Excalibur, MGM Grand, and New York–New York.

HOTELS ON THE WEST SIDE OF THE STRIP (FROM NORTH TO SOUTH)

Circus Circus Large outdoor lot and garages accessible from Industrial Road.

Fashion Show Mall Garage near the Strip is an excellent place to park if you're going to Wynn Las Vegas, Palazzo, Venetian, or T. I. Enter from Spring Mountain Road or W. Fashion Show Drive. Work your way to the southeast corner of the garage near the Neiman Marcus valet entrance. Along the wall that borders the Strip, look for a green, grassy area and stairs leading up to the Strip.

T. I. Very straightforward garage—among the most convenient on the Strip. Best access is via Spring Mountain Road.

Mirage Access also off Spring Mountain Road. It's a little convoluted, but just follow the signs.

Forum Shops From Industrial Road go south on Frank Sinatra Drive and then left on Jay Sarno Way.

Caesars Palace From Industrial Road go south on Frank Sinatra Drive and then left on Jay Sarno Way.

Bellagio The only way to access the Bellagio is via the Strip. Valet service is good here, though. Just don't get caught when half the audience from Cirque du Soleil's "O" suddenly appears at the valet claim desk.

CityCenter and Cosmopolitan From Industrial Road (Dean Martin Drive), turn west on Jerry Lewis Way, then left on West Harmon. Don't be surprised if they rename this section of West Harmon CityCenter Drive or some such.

Monte Carlo Take Frank Sinatra Drive to Rue de Monte Carlo.

New York–New York Garage is located off Tropicana Avenue.

Excalibur Excalibur has some of the most distant, far-flung parking of any hotel in Las Vegas. The closest parking is off East Reno Avenue paralleling the Strip or in the south end of the parking garage at Luxor Drive and East Reno. Luxor Drive is accessible via Dean Martin Drive, then west on Aldebaran Avenue, then right (east) on W. Hacienda Avenue (W. Mandalay Bay Drive), and finally left on Luxor Drive.

Luxor This is one of our favorite parking garages. Park on the top level. Take Dean Martin Drive, then go west on Aldebaran Avenue, then right (east) on W. Hacienda Avenue (W. Mandalay Bay Drive), and finally left on Luxor Drive.

Mandalay Bay Take Dean Martin Drive, then go west on Aldebaran Avenue, then right (east) on W. Hacienda Avenue (W. Mandalay Bay Drive), and finally right on Luxor Drive.

hotels because their clientele is more well-heeled and less price sensitive. But make no mistake, everyone is getting hit, and a number of properties may not survive.

As 2011 wore on, occupancy rates improved, but the increase was largely attributable to room rates so low that Las Vegas was inundated by legions of bargain hunters. People were in beds, but they were not spending much on dining or gambling. The city, however, can go from empty to full overnight as a consequence of a large convention or major sporting event. In general, we expect the deals to be around for a while, but you still need to scope out your specific dates.

The combination of ever-increasing hotel-room inventories and a weak economy is forcing hotels to be creative. Las Vegas hotels are limbering up deals and incentives we've not seen for almost a decade. Circus Circus, for example, offered to buy gasoline for guests who book online, and almost all hotels are flogging special packages. A "Vegas Right Now" ad campaign encourages travelers not to postpone Las Vegas travel plans. Because many of the deals require booking on the hotel's website, look there first.

THE WACKY WORLD OF LAS VEGAS HOTEL RESERVATIONS

THOUGH THERE ARE ALMOST 149,000 hotel rooms in Las Vegas, getting one is not always a simple proposition. In the large hotel-casinos, there are often five or more separate departments that have responsibility for room allocation and sales. Of the total number of rooms in any given hotel, a number are at the disposal of the casino; some are administered by the reservations department at the front desk; some are allocated to independent wholesalers for group and individual travel packages; others are blocked for special events (fights, Super Bowl weekend, and the like); and still others are at the disposal of the sales and marketing department for meetings, conventions, wedding parties, and other special groups. Hotels that are part of a large chain (Holiday Inn, Hilton, and such) have some additional rooms administered by their national reservations systems.

At most hotels, department heads meet each week and review all the room allocations. If rooms blocked for a special event, say a golf tournament, are not selling, some of those rooms will be redistributed to other departments. Since special events and large conventions are scheduled far in advance, the decision-makers have significant lead time. In most hotels, a major reallocation of rooms takes place 40 to 50 days prior to the dates for which the rooms are blocked, with minor reallocations made right up to the event in question.

If you call the reservations number at the hotel of your choice and are informed that no rooms are available for the dates that you've requested, it does not mean the hotel is sold out. What it does mean is that the front desk has no more rooms remaining in their allocation. It is a fairly safe assumption that all the rooms in a hotel have not been reserved by guests. The casino will usually hold back some rooms for high rollers, the sales department may have some rooms reserved for participants in deals they are negotiating, and some rooms will be in the hands of tour wholesalers or blocked for a city-wide convention. If any of these remaining rooms are not committed by a certain date, they will be reallocated. So a second call to the reservations department may get you the room that was unavailable when you called two weeks earlier.

THE INTERNET REVOLUTION

PURCHASING TRAVEL ON THE INTERNET has revolutionized the way both consumers and hotels do business. For you it makes shopping for a hotel and finding good deals much easier. For the hotel it makes possible a system of room inventory management often referred to as "nudging." Here's how it works. Many months in advance, hotels establish rates for each day of the coming year. In developing their rate calendar, they take into consideration all of the variables that affect occupancy in their hotel as well as in Las Vegas in general. They consider weekend versus weekday demand; additional demand stimulated by holidays, major conventions, trade shows, and sporting events; and the effect of the four seasons of the year on occupancy.

After rates for each date are determined, the rates are entered into the hotel's reservation system. Then hotel management sits back to see what happens. If the bookings for a particular date are in accord with management's expectations, no rate change is necessary. If demand is greater than management's forecast for a given date, they might raise the rate to take advantage of higher than expected bookings. If demand eases off, the hotel can revert back to the original rate.

If demand is less than expected, the hotel will begin nudging, that is, incrementally decreasing the rate for the day or days in question until booking volume increases to the desired level. Though this sort of rate manipulation has been an integral part of room inventory management for decades, the Internet has made it possible to rethink and alter room rates almost at will. A hotel can theoretically adjust rates hourly on its own website. Major Internet travel sellers (also called Online Travel Agencies or OTAs), such as Travelocity, Hotels. com, and Expedia, among others, are fast and agile and quite capable of getting a special deal (that is, a lower rate) in front of travel purchasers almost instantaneously. For the hotel, this means they can manage their inventory on almost a weekly or daily basis, nudging toward full occupancy by adjusting their rates according to demand. Of course, the hotels don't depend entirely on the Internet. Lower rates and various special deals are also communicated by e-mail to preferred travel agents, and sometimes directly to consumers (especially players-club members) via e-mail, print advertisements, or direct-mail promotions.

GETTING THE BEST DEAL ON A ROOM

COMPARED TO HOTEL RATES in other destinations, lodging in Las Vegas is so relatively inexpensive that the following cost-cutting strategies may seem gratuitous. Yes, there are $500-per-night rooms, but if you are accustomed to paying $130 a night for a hotel room, you can afford 80% of the hotels in town. You may not be inclined to wade through all the options listed below to save $20 or $30 a night. If, on the other hand, you would like to obtain top value for your dollar, read on.

ROOM RATES AND PACKAGES	SOLD OR ADMINISTERED BY
1. Gambler's rate	Casino or hotel
2. December, January, and summer specials	Hotel-room reservations or marketing department
3. Internet discounts	Internet travel vendors
4. Wholesaler packages	Independent wholesalers
5. Tour-operator packages	Tour operators
6. Reservation-service discounts	Independent wholesalers and consolidators
7. Corporate rate	Hotel-room reservations
8. Hotel standard-room rate	Hotel-room reservations
9. Convention rate	Convention sponsor

Sorting Out the Sellers and the Options

To book a room in a particular hotel for any given date, there are so many different in-house departments as well as outside tour operators and wholesalers selling rooms, that it is almost impossible to find out who is offering the best deal. This is not because the various deals are so hard to compare but because it is so difficult to identify all the sellers.

Though it is only a rough approximation, see the chart above for a list of the types of rates and packages available, ranked from the best to the worst value.

The room-rate ranking is subject to some interpretation. A gambler's rate may, at first glance, seem to be the least expensive lodging option available, next to a complimentary room. If, however, the amount of money a guest is obligated to wager (and potentially lose) is factored in, the gambler's rate might be by far the most expensive.

Complimentary and Discounted Rooms for Gamblers

Most Las Vegas visitors are at least peripherally aware that casinos provide complimentary or greatly discounted rooms to gamblers. It is not unusual, therefore, for a business traveler, a low-stakes gambler, or a nongambling tourist to attempt to take advantage of these deals. What they quickly discover is that the casino has very definite expectations of any guest whose stay is wholly or partially subsidized by the house. If you want a gambler's discount on a room, they will ask what game(s) you intend to play, the amount of your average bet, how many hours a day you usually gamble, where (at which casinos) you have played before, and how much gambling money you will have available on this trip. They may also request that you make an application for credit or provide personal information about your occupation, income, and bank account.

If you manage to bluff your way into a comp or discounted room, you can bet that your gambling (or lack thereof) will be closely monitored after you arrive. If you fail to give the casino an acceptable amount of action, you will probably be charged the nondiscounted room rate when you check out.

Even for those who expect to do a fair amount of gambling, a comp or discounted room can be a mixed blessing. By accepting the casino's hospitality, you incur a certain obligation (the more they give you, the bigger the obligation). You will be expected to do most (if not all) of your gambling in the casino where you are staying, and you will also be expected to play a certain number of hours each day. If this was your intention all along, great. On the other hand, if you thought you would like to try several casinos or take a day and run over to Hoover Dam, you may be painting yourself into a corner.

Taking Advantage of Special Deals

When you call, always ask the reservationist if the hotel has any package deals or specials. If you plan to gamble, be sure to ask about gaming specials. If you do not anticipate gambling enough to qualify for a gambling package, ask about other types of deals. On the Internet, always check the hotel's website. It's also helpful to Google the name of the hotel and the word "promotion." This sometimes turns up deals on dining and entertainment as well as room rates.

If you have a lot of lead time before your trip, call the hotel and ask about joining their players club. Though only a few hotels will send you a membership application, inquiring about the players club will get you categorized as a gambler on the hotel's mailing list. Once in Las Vegas, sign up for the players clubs of hotel-casinos that you like. This will ensure that you receive notification of special deals that you can take advantage of on subsequent visits. Being a member of a hotel's players club can also come in handy when rooms are scarce. Once, trying to book a room, we were told the hotel was sold out. When we mentioned that we had a players card, the reservationist miraculously found us a room. If you are a players-club member, it is often better to phone the club-member services desk instead of the hotel-reservations desk.

On the hotel's home page, there's invariably a "Sign our guestbook" feature, or some other way to sign up for the hotel's e-mail list. This puts you squarely on the hotel's radar and ensures that you will receive offers and news of various kinds. As far as rooms go, it's rare in our experience to find a deal on the hotel's website that's better than the ones they quote you on the phone. A reservationist on the phone knows she has a good prospect on the line and will work with you within the limits of her authority. On the Web there's no give or negotiation: it's a take-it-or-leave-it deal. Finally, most hotels, including many of the new super-properties, really haven't learned how to merchandise rooms through their website.

Having shopped the hotel for deals, start checking out Las Vegas vacation or weekend packages advertised in your local newspaper, and compare what you find with packages offered in the Sunday edition of the *Los Angeles Times*.

Timing Is Everything

Timing is everything when booking a guest room in Las Vegas. If a particular hotel has only a few rooms to sell for a specific date, it will often, as we discussed earlier, bounce up the rate for those rooms as high as it thinks the market will bear. Conversely, if the hotel has many rooms available for a certain date, it will lower the rate accordingly. The practice remains operative all year, although the likelihood of hotels having a lot of rooms available is obviously greater during off-peak periods. As an example, we checked rates at an upscale non-gaming hotel during two weeks in October. Depending on the specific dates, the rate for the suite in question ranged from $75 (an incredible bargain) to $240 (significantly overpriced) per night.

Which day of the week you check in can also save or cost you some money. At some hotels a standard room runs 20% less if you check in on a Monday through Thursday (even though you may stay through the weekend). If you check into the same room on a weekend, your rate will be higher and may not change if you keep your room into the following week. A more common practice is for the hotel to charge a lower rate during the week and a higher rate on the weekend.

NO ROOM AT THE INN (FOR REAL)   More frequently than you would imagine, Las Vegas hotels overbook their rooms. This happens when guests do not check out on time, when important casino customers arrive on short notice, and when the various departments handling room allocations get their signals crossed. When this occurs, guests who arrive holding reservations are told that their reservations have been canceled.

To protect yourself, always guarantee your first night with a major credit card (even if you do not plan to arrive late) and insist on a written confirmation of your reservation. When you arrive and check in, have your written confirmation handy.

Precautions notwithstanding, the hotel still might have canceled your reservation. When a hotel is overbooked, for whatever reason, it will take care of its serious gambling customers first, its prospective gambling customers (leisure travelers) second, and business travelers last. If you are informed that you have no room, demand that the hotel honor your reservation by finding you a room or by securing you a room at another hotel of comparable or better quality at the same rate. Should the desk clerk balk at doing this, demand to see the reservations manager. If the reservations manager stonewalls, go to the hotel's general manager. Whatever you do, do not leave until the issue has been resolved to your satisfaction.

Hotels understand their obligation to honor a confirmed reservation, but they often fail to take responsibility unless you hold their feet to the fire. We have seen convention-goers, stunned by the news that they have no room, simply turn around and walk out. Wrong. The hotel owns the problem, not you. You should not have to shop for another room. The hotel that confirmed your reservation should find you a room comparable to or better than the one you reserved, and for the same rate.

HOW TO GET THE BEST DEAL ON THE INTERNET

THE INTERNET, UNMATCHED IN TERMS OF efficient and timely distribution of information, has become the primary resource for travelers seeking to shop for and book their own air, hotels, rental cars, entertainment, and travel packages. It's by far the best direct-to-consumer distribution channel in history.

The evolution of selling travel on the Web has radically altered the way travel product producers such as airlines, hotels, cruise lines, and rental-car companies do business. Before the Internet, companies depended on travel agents or direct contact with customers via telephone. Transaction costs were high because the producers were obligated to pay commissions and fund labor-intensive in-house reservations departments.

With the advent of the Internet, inexpensive e-commerce transactions became possible. Airlines and rental-car companies were able to effectively cut travel agents out of the sales process and off-load the bulk of their booking activity to their own websites. Hotels followed suit with their own websites but also continued to sell to wholesalers and through travel agents.

It didn't take long before independent websites appeared that sold travel products from a wide assortment of travel suppliers, often at deep discounts. These sites, called Online Travel Agents or OTAs, include such familiar names as **Travelocity, Orbitz, Priceline, Expedia, Hotels.com,** and **Hotwire.** Those mentioned and others like them attract huge numbers of customers shopping for hotels.

In the beginning hotels paid the OTAs about the same commission as they paid travel agents, but then the OTAs began applying the thumbscrews, transitioning hotels from a simple commission model to what's called a merchant model. Under this model hotels provide an OTA with a deeply discounted room rate, which the OTA then marks up and sells. The difference between the marked-up price and the discounted rate provided by the hotel is the OTA's gross profit.

The merchant model, originally devised for wholesalers and tour operators, has been around since long before the Internet. Wholesalers and tour operators, then and now, must commit to a certain volume of business, commit to guaranteed room allotments, pay deposits, and bundle the discounted rates with other travel services so that the actual hotel rate remains hidden within the bundle. The merchant model costs the hotel 2–2.5 times the normal travel agent commission, considered justifiable because the wholesalers and tour operators also promote the hotel though brochures, trade shows, print ads, and events.

OTAs demand the equivalent of a wholesale commission and higher but are not subject to any of the requirements imposed on wholesalers and tour operators. The OTAs don't have to commit to a specified volume of sales or keep discounted rates opaque. Hotels give up 20–50% of gross profit and are rewarded by having their rock-bottom rates plastered all over the Internet with corresponding damage to their image and brand. The cost of a direct multiday booking on the hotel's own website is $10–$12, including website hosting, marketing costs, website analytics, and management fees. This is 10–12 times cheaper than the same booking through an OTA.

By way of example, an OTA might demand a 30% discount off the hotel's best available published rate. So if the hotel is offering rooms at $100, the rate to the OTA would be $70 ($100 less 30% = $70). The OTA then marks up the rate and posts it on its site. The OTA might sell the room for $100, the same rate advertised on the hotel's site, or it might undercut the hotel by offering the room for $95 or less. When the OTA sells the room it pays the hotel $70 and pockets whatever the mark-up is. As you can see, the hotel makes $100 if it sells the room itself but only $70 for the same room if it's sold by an OTA. For the hotel, doing business with OTAs is very expensive.

In the hotel industry, occupancy rates are important, but simply getting people in beds doesn't guarantee a profitable operation. A more critical metric is revenue per available room, or RevPAR. For a hotel full of guests who booked through an OTA, RevPAR will be 20%–50% lower than a full house of guests who booked the hotel directly (either via the hotel's website or by phone).

It's no wonder then that hotels and OTAs have a love-hate relationship. Likewise, it's perfectly understandable that it's a priority for hotels to increase direct bookings through their website and minimize OTA bookings. Current economic conditions occasioned by the recent recession, coupled in Las Vegas with a glut of rooms exceeding demand, makes this strategy difficult.

The problem is that the better-known OTAs draw a lot more website traffic than the hotel's (or even the hotel chain's) website. So the challenge for the hotel becomes how to shift room shoppers away from the OTAs and channel them to the hotel's website.

The Silver Bullet

For years we've been looking for a fast, easy way to help you find the best hotel rates in Las Vegas. Search engines such as **kayak.com** are helpful. They search large numbers of OTAs to determine which OTA has the best price for a particular hotel on a given night. Problem is, the rates that come up might not approximate the lowest obtainable, and in any event are subject to vagaries in demand the shopper might not be aware of such as conventions and sporting events.

Enter the **Las Vegas Advisor,** the newsletter and gambling book publisher that has been providing subscribers with no-nonsense consumer information and tips on Las Vegas for years. Their publications are candid, straightforward, and pull no punches. Simply put, they can be trusted to put their readers first (also a primary objective of the *Unofficial Guides*).

Like the *Las Vegas Advisor* newsletter, its **lvahotels.com** website is the most objective source of information on Las Vegas available on the Internet and is the preferred site for frequent Las Vegas visitors and especially gamblers. Assessing the needs of its readership and the needs of hotels, the Advisor developed an elegant win-win solution that would secure its readers the best room rates and at the same time provide hoteliers a powerful incentive to offer the best possible rates.

Here's how it works. Participating hotels provide the Advisor with truly exceptional deals on rooms and other services, which the Advisor lists on its website. Each deal has a code number. When you click on a specific deal you're routed to the hotel's website for additional information and booking. The hotel pays the Advisor a small commission for sending the booking its way, but only a fraction of what it would sacrifice in gross profit if the room were sold through an OTA.

The hotel's incentive for giving the Advisor the best deals available are as follows:

1. Bookings are made directly with the hotel, thus increasing both occupancy and RevPAR.
2. The Advisor website is a high-traffic site, visited exclusively (unlike OTA sites) by persons specifically interested in Las Vegas.
3. The Advisor has a longstanding record of objective consumer reporting and analysis, so the hotel knows its deals will be regarded as legitimate and trustworthy.
4. A large percentage of the Advisor's visitors and readers are gamblers, the most desirable customer for any hotel with a casino.
5. The Advisor deal program is what's called a "disintermediary" model, a fancy name for cutting out the middlemen (intermediaries) in the channels of distribution.

To check out the deals go to **lvahotels.com.** On the home page click either "LVA Hotel Deals" on the left side of the page or "Book A Room" in the center of the page under "Features." All of the hotels offering special rates will appear. You'll notice that a number of the deals listed include extras like resort credit, meals, entertainment, or other sweeteners in addition to the room. If you find a special that sounds good, an additional click will link to the hotel's website for additional information and booking.

At the insistence of the hotels, some of the best discounts are not listed on the website but can be accessed by signing up for the LVA Gold Membership. This costs nothing and can be accomplished quickly online without divulging any sensitive personal information. Special deals not available on the website are emailed to LVA Gold Members weekly. What's going on here is some legal and semantic hair-splitting. If a deal is listed on the Advisor site, it's regarded as "published" or public. Hotels have some restrictions concerning published deals. On the other hand, if deals are offered to a certain population that has requested information, in this case LVA Gold Member subscribers, then the hotel has more latitude in regard to what it can offer.

Tests

In multiday tests of the LVA program, we found that it does indeed offer incredible deals on hotel rates but that the participating hotels control the availability of those deals (and change them at their discretion, sometimes without notifying the Advisor). Such control is to be expected given that the hotels are trying to boost RevPAR for days or periods of low occupancy. Consequently, being flexible concerning your proposed dates and especially being willing to plan your stay to incorporate some weeknights (i.e., Sunday through Thursday) vastly improve your chances of getting the best deal. Searching for available dates will require some work on your part—work that you may judge well worth the effort to save $40 or $50 per night, but perhaps not so much to save only $10 or $15 a night over the best OTA rates. Sometimes also, if you don't find the quoted promotional rate for the days you want, there are frequently other deals for the same hotel on the LVA site, perhaps $10 to $20 more than the deal you wanted but still much better than OTA rates.

Many participating hotels offer availability calendars when you click through to their site, so you can determine pretty quickly when the deal you're interested in is available. Four or five months can be viewed in just a couple of seconds. Hotel sites, such as the Cosmopolitan's, that don't have availability calendars, however, are a pain in the patootie. On these you have to keep entering different dates in hopes of finding the rate listed on the Advisor's site. For the Cosmo we had to search weekday dates for four months before finding the quoted rate. If a visitor plugs away entering date after date (like we did) and finally gets to the dead of summer before he finds the advertised rate, he'll think big deal, everybody knows there are great deals in the dead of summer. There's nothing deceptive or dishonest here, but it makes you put in a lot of effort only to come away unsuccessful in the end. As an example of how screwy it can get, if you search for the lvahotels.com rate at the Cosmo, and the room isn't available for the dates you enter, the Cosmo site kicks you to a general Marriott site where the Cosmo isn't even listed.

Since LVA launched the hotel deals program it has made a lot of refinements, and recent tests have garnered better rates with less effort. As the program matures, it's hoped that hotel sites, such as the Cosmo, that don't have availability calendars will develop them, if for no other reason than to stay competitive.

If you use the LVA site, be sure to jot down the code of the deal you want before clicking through to the hotel's site for availability and booking. Sometimes the link to the hotel site will bring up a screen for the deal you're interested in. Other times, however, there's some ambiguity as to whether the site is responding to the discount code on lvahotels.com or whether you've ended up on the hotel's general central reservations screen. If the latter, you'll need to enter the discount code to bring up the deal. The LVA site works best for four- and five-star properties, though sometimes three-star hotels throw dining, shows, and room upgrades into the mix to create a really great value. As is often asked, "how much time do you spend in your room anyway?"

HOTEL-SPONSORED PACKAGES

IN ADDITION TO SELLING rooms through Internet retailers, tour operators, consolidators, and wholesalers, most hotels periodically offer exceptional deals of their own. Sometimes the packages are specialized, as with golf packages, or are offered only at certain times of the year, for instance December and January. Promotion of hotel specials tends to be limited to the hotel's primary markets, which for most properties is Southern California, Arizona, Utah, Colorado, Hawaii, and the Midwest. If you live in other parts of the country, you can take advantage of the packages but probably will not see them advertised in your local newspaper.

Some hotel packages are unbelievable deals. Once, for instance, a hotel offered three nights' free lodging, no strings attached, to any adult from Texas. On certain dates in November, December, and January, the Flamingo offered a deal that included a room for two or more nights at $35 per night (tax inclusive), with two drinks and a show thrown in for good measure. In July of 2010, 34 hotels offered rates less than $45. Look for the hotel specials in Southern California newspapers, check the promotion code sites previously listed, or call the hotel and ask.

unofficial **TIP**
Regarding hotel specials, hotel reservationists do not usually inform you of existing specials or offer them to you. In other words, you have to ask.

HOW TO EVALUATE A TRAVEL PACKAGE

HUNDREDS OF LAS VEGAS PACKAGE TRIPS and vacations are offered to the public each year. Almost all include round-trip transportation to Las Vegas and lodging. Sometimes a package will include room tax, transportation from the airport, a rental car, shows, meals, welcome parties, and/or souvenirs.

In general, because the Las Vegas market is so competitive, packages to Las Vegas are among the best travel values available. Las Vegas competes head-to-head with Atlantic City for eastern travelers and with Reno, Lake Tahoe, Laughlin, and other Nevada destinations for western visitors. Within Las Vegas, downtown competes with the Strip, and individual hotels go one-on-one to improve their share of the market. In addition to the fierce competition for the destination traveler, the extraordinary profitability of gambling also works on the consumer's behalf to keep Las Vegas travel economical. For a large number of hotels, amazing values in dining and lodging are used to lure visitors to the casino.

Packages should be a win–win proposition for both the buyer and the seller. The buyer (or travel agent) has to make only one phone call and deal with a single salesperson to set up the whole trip: transportation, lodging, rental car, show admissions, and even golf, tennis, and sightseeing. The seller, likewise, has to deal with the buyer only one time, eliminating the need for separate sales, confirmations, and billings. In addition to streamlining selling, processing, and administration, some packagers also buy airfares in bulk on contract like a broker playing the commodities market. Buying or guaranteeing a large number of airfares in advance allows the packager to buy them at a significant savings from posted fares. The same practice also applies to hotel rooms. Because selling packaged trips is an efficient way of doing business, and the packager can often buy individual components (airfare, lodging) in bulk at a discount, savings in operating expenses realized by the seller are sometimes passed on to the buyer. So the package is not only convenient but an exceptional value. In any event, that is the way it is supposed to work.

In practice, the seller occasionally realizes all of the economies and passes none of the savings along to the buyer. In some instances, packages are loaded with extras that cost the packager next to nothing but run the retail price sky-high. While this is not as common with Las Vegas packages as those to other destinations, it occurs frequently enough to warrant some comparison shopping.

When considering a package, choose one that includes features you are sure to use. Whether you use all the features or not, you will most certainly pay for them. Second, if cost is of greater concern than convenience, call or check the Internet to see what the package would cost if you booked its individual components (airfare, lodging, rental car) on your own. If the package price is less than the à la carte cost, the package is a good deal. If the costs are about the same, the package is probably worth it for the convenience.

AN EXAMPLE Bob's niece and a friend were looking at a package they found with Delta Vacations. The package included round-trip airfare (on Delta) from Atlanta, four nights' lodging (Wednesday through Saturday) at the Luxor, and about ten "bonus features," including:

- Airport parking discounts   • Discounted Lake Mead boat cruises
- Planet Hollywood $10 certificate   • $25 food and beverage credit

The price, tax included, was $777 per person, or $1,555 all together. Checking the Luxor and a number of airlines, they found the following:

Same room at the Luxor, 2 people to a room, for 4 nights with room tax included	$520
Transportation to and from the airport	$23
Subtotal	$543

Subtracting the $543 (lodging and airport transfers) from the cost of Delta's package total of $1,555, they determined that the air and "bonus features" portion of the package was worth $1,012 ($1,555 − $543 = $1,012). If they were not interested in using any of the bonus features, and they could fly to Las Vegas for less than $1,012, they would be better off turning down the package.

Scouting around, the lowest fare they could find was $469 per person on Air Tran with an advance-purchase ticket. This piece of information completed their analysis as follows:

Option A: Delta Vacation package for 2	$1,555
Option B: Booking their own air and lodging	
Lodging, including tax	$520
Airfare on Air Tran for 2	$938
Transportation to and from hotel	$23
Total	$1,481

In this example, the package costs more. Most of the two-fers and other deals bundled into the package are available through freebie Las Vegas visitor magazines if you take time to discover them. Be aware that it doesn't always work out this way. We analyze dozens of packages each year, and there are as many bad deals as good deals. The point is, always do your homework.

 # *For* BUSINESS TRAVELERS

CONVENTION RATES: HOW THE SYSTEM WORKS

BUSINESS TRAVELERS, PARTICULARLY THOSE attending trade shows or conventions, are almost always charged more for their rooms than leisure travelers. For big meetings, called citywide conventions, huge numbers of rooms are blocked in hotels all over town. These rooms are reserved for visitors attending the meeting in question and are usually requested and coordinated by the meeting's sponsoring organization in cooperation with the Las Vegas Convention and Visitors Authority.

Individual hotels negotiate a nightly rate with the convention sponsor, who then frequently sells the rooms through a central reservations system of its own. Because the hotels would rather have gamblers or leisure travelers than people attending conventions (who usually have limited time to gamble), the negotiated price tends to be high, often $10 to $50 per night above the rack rate.

Meeting sponsors, of course, blame convention rates on the hotels. Meanwhile the hotels maintain a stoic silence, not wishing to alienate meeting organizers.

To be fair, convention sponsors should be given some credit simply for having their meeting in Las Vegas. Even considering the inflated convention rates, meeting attendees will pay 15–40% less in Las Vegas for comparable lodging than in other major convention cities. As for the rest, well, let's take a look.

Sam Walton taught the average American that someone purchasing a large quantity of a particular item should be able to obtain a better price (per item) than a person buying only one or two. If anyone just walking in off the street can buy a single hotel room for $50, why then must a convention sponsor, negotiating for 900 rooms for five nights in the same hotel (4,500 room nights in hotel jargon), settle for a rate of $60 per night?

Many Las Vegas hotels take a hard-line negotiating position with meeting sponsors because (1) every room occupied by a convention-goer is one less room available for gamblers, and (2) they figure that most business travelers are on expense accounts. In addition, timing is a critical factor in negotiating room rates. The hotels do not want business travelers occupying rooms on weekends or during the more popular times of the year. Convention sponsors who want to schedule a meeting during high season (when hotels fill their rooms no matter what) can expect to pay premium rates. In addition, and regardless of the time of year, many hotels routinely charge stiff prices to convention-goers as a sort of insurance against lost opportunity. "What if we block our rooms for a trade show one year in advance," a sales manager asked, "and then a championship prize-fight is scheduled for that week? We would lose big-time."

A spokesman for the Las Vegas Convention and Visitors Authority indicated that the higher room rates for conventioneers are not unreasonable given a hotel's commitment to the sponsor to hold rooms in reserve. But reserved rooms, or room blocks as they are called, fragment a hotel's inventory of available rooms, and often make it harder, not easier, to get a room in a particular hotel. The bottom line is that convention-goers pay a premium price for the benefit of having rooms reserved for their meeting—rooms that would be cheaper, and often easier to reserve, if the sponsor had not reserved them in the first place. For a major citywide convention, it is not unusual for attendees to collectively pay in excess of $1 million for the peace of mind of having rooms reserved.

Whether room-blocking is really necessary is an interesting question. The Las Vegas Convention and Visitors Authority works with convention sponsors to ensure that there is never more than one citywide meeting in town at a time and to make sure that sponsors do not schedule their conventions at a time when Las Vegas hotels are otherwise normally sold out (National Finals Rodeo week, Super Bowl weekend, New Year's, and so on). Unfortunately for meeting planners, some major events (prizefights, tennis matches) are occasionally scheduled in Las Vegas on short notice. If a meeting planner does not block rooms and a big fight is announced for the week the meeting is in town, the attendees may be unable to find a room. This is such a nightmare to convention sponsors that they cave in to exorbitant convention rates rather than risk not having rooms. The actual likelihood of a major event being scheduled at the same time as a large convention is small, though the specter of this worst-case scenario is a powerful weapon in the bargaining arsenal of the hotels.

On balance, meeting sponsors negate their volume-buying clout by scheduling meetings during the more popular times of year or, alternatively, by caving in to the hotels' "opportunity cost" room-pricing. Conversely, hotels play unfairly on the sponsor's fear of not having enough rooms, and they charge premium rates to cover improbable, ill-defined opportunity losses. Is there collusion here? Probably not. The more likely conclusion is that both hotels and sponsors have become comfortable with an inflexible negotiating environment, but one that permits meeting sponsors to distribute the unreasonable charges pro rata to their attendees.

Working through the Maze

If you attempt to bypass the sponsoring organization and go directly through the hotel, the hotel will either refer you to the convention's central reservations number or quote you the same high price. Even if you do not identify yourself as a convention-goer, the hotel will figure it out by the dates you request. In most instances, even if you lie and insist that you are not attending the convention in question, the hotel will make you pay the higher rate or claim to be sold out.

By way of example, we tried to get reservations at the Riviera for a major trade show in the spring, a citywide convention that draws about 30,000 attendees. The show runs six days plus one day for setting up, or seven days total, Saturday through Friday. Though this example involves the Riviera, we encountered the same scenario at every hotel we called.

When we phoned reservations at the Riviera and gave them our dates, they immediately asked if we would be attending a convention or trade show. When we answered in the affirmative, they gave us the official sponsor's central reservations phone number in New York. We called the sponsor and learned that a single room at the Riviera (one person in one room) booked through them would cost $130 per night, including room tax. The same room (we found from other sources) booked directly through the Riviera would cost $98 with tax included.

We called the Riviera back and asked for the same dates, this time disavowing any association with the trade show, and were rebuffed. Obviously skeptical of our story, the hotel informed us that they were sold out for the days we requested. Unconvinced that the hotel was fully booked, we had two different members of our research team call. One attempted to make reservations from Wednesday of the preceding week through Tuesday of the trade show week, while our second caller requested a room from Wednesday of the trade show week through the following Tuesday. These respective sets of dates, we reasoned, would differ sufficiently from the show dates to convince the Riviera that we were not conventioneers. In each case we were able to make reservations for the dates desired at the $98-per-night rate.

It should be stressed that a hotel treats the convention's sponsoring organization much like a wholesaler who reserves rooms in a block for a negotiated price. What the convention, in turn, charges its attendees is out of the hotel's control. Once a hotel and convention sponsor come to terms, the hotel either refers all inquiries about reservations to the sponsor or accepts bookings at whatever nightly rate the sponsor determines. Since hotels do not want to get in the way of their convention sponsors (who are very powerful customers) or, alternatively, have convention attendees buying up rooms intended for other, nonconvention customers, the hotel reservations department carefully screens any request for a room during a convention period.

Strategies for Beating Convention Rates

1. CHECK THE INTERNET Unlike packagers and wholesalers, Internet sellers serve as a communications nexus and can often point you to a hotel you had not considered that still has rooms available, or to a property that has some last-minute rooms because of cancellations. Try the aforementioned **lvahotels.com, kayak.com,** or one of the promotion-code sites. If you link to the hotel's website through a deal on **lvahotels.com,** you'll most likely be classified as a gambler.

2. BUY A PACKAGE FROM A TOUR OPERATOR OR A WHOLESALER This tactic makes it unnecessary to deal with the convention's central reservations office or with an individual hotel's reservations department. Many packages allow you to buy extra days at a special discounted room rate if the package dates do not coincide perfectly with your meeting dates.

Packages that use air charter services operate on a fixed, inflexible schedule. As a rule these packages run three nights (depart Thursday, return Sunday; or depart Friday, return Monday) or four nights (depart Monday, return Friday; or depart Sunday, return Thursday). Two-night, five-night, and seven-night charter packages can also be found. Charter air packages offer greater savings, but usually less flexibility, than packages that use commercial carriers.

If you are able to beat the convention rate by booking a package or through the Internet, don't blow your cover when you check in. If you walk up to the registration desk in a business suit and a convention ID badge, the hotel will void your package and charge you the full convention rate. If you are supposed to be a tourist, act like one, particularly when you check in and check out.

STRIP HOTELS THAT RARELY PARTICIPATE IN ROOM BLOCKS		
Four Seasons	Bill's Gamblin' Hall	Artisan
DOWNTOWN HOTELS THAT SELDOM PARTICIPATE IN ROOM BLOCKS		
California	El Cortez	Fitzgeralds
Four Queens	Fremont	Golden Gate

3. FIND A HOTEL THAT DOES NOT PARTICIPATE IN THE CONVENTION ROOM BLOCKS Many of the downtown, North Las Vegas, and Boulder Highway hotels, as well as a few of the Strip hotels, do not make rooms available in blocks for conventions. If you wish to avoid convention rates, obtain a list of your convention's "official" hotels from the sponsoring organization and match it against the hotels listed in this guide. Any hotel listed in this book that does not appear on the list supplied by the meeting sponsors is not participating in blocking rooms for your convention. This means you can deal with the nonparticipating hotels directly and should be able to get their regular rate.

Most citywide trade shows and conventions are held at the Las Vegas Convention Center. If you stay at any of the nonparticipating hotels, you will have to commute to the convention center by shuttle, cab, or car.

4. RESERVE LATE Thirty to sixty days prior to the opening of a citywide convention or show, the front-desk room-reservations staff in a given hotel will take over the management of rooms reserved for the meeting from the hotel's sales and marketing department. "Room Res," in conjunction with the general manager, is responsible for making sure that the hotel is running at peak capacity for the dates of the show. The general manager has the authority to lower the room rate from the price negotiated with the sponsor. If rooms are not being booked for the convention in accordance with the hotel's expectations, the general manager will often lower the rate for attendees and, at the same time, return a number of reserved rooms to general inventory for sale to the public. A convention-goer who books a room at the last minute might obtain a lower rate than an attendee who booked early through the sponsor's central-housing service. Practically speaking, however, do not expect to find rooms available at the convention headquarters hotel or at most of the hotels within easy walking distance. As a rule of thumb, the farther from the convention center or headquarters a hotel is, the better the chances of finding a discounted room at the last minute.

THE LAS VEGAS CONVENTION CENTER

THE LAS VEGAS CONVENTION CENTER (LVCC) is the largest single-level convention and trade show facility in the United States and recently acquired the coveted World Trade Center site designation. This 3.2-million-square-foot facility with more than 2 million square feet of exhibit space is divided into two main buildings: the South Hall and the older North Hall. A pedestrian bridge over Desert Inn Road connects the halls. Trade shows that crowd facilities in Washington, San Francisco, and New York fit with ease in this immense Las Vegas complex. In addition to the exhibit areas, the center has a new lobby and public areas, a kitchen that can cater a banquet for 12,000 people, and 144 meeting rooms seating 20 to 7,500 delegates. Serving as headquarters for shows and conventions drawing as many as 150,000 delegates, the convention center is on Paradise Road, one very long block off the Las Vegas Strip and three miles from the airport.

For both exhibitors and attendees, the Las Vegas Convention Center is an excellent site for a meeting or trade show. Large and small exhibitors can locate and access their exhibit sites with a minimum of effort. Numerous loading docks and huge bay doors make loading and unloading quick and simple for large displays arriving by truck. Smaller displays transported in vans and cars are unloaded on the north side of the main hall and can be carried or wheeled directly to the exhibit area without climbing stairs or using elevators. The exhibit areas and meeting rooms are well marked and easy to find.

The two major restaurants in the Convention Center are **Banners** in the North Hall and the **International Food Court** in the South Hall. Throughout the complex are 18 permanent concessions with fast-food choices in sidewalk settings: a deli; two Starbucks cafes; fresh soups, sandwiches, and salads; Mexican; Asian; pasta and pizza; and burgers, hot dogs, and barbecue. Free wireless Internet access is available in all lobbies and in the two large restaurants. The center no longer provides banks of pay phones, although a few phones are scattered throughout each building. Especially helpful to business travelers is **Speed Check Advance,** the on-site baggage handler that checks luggage for five airlines from 3 to 12 hours before departure and delivers to McCarran Airport prior to flight time. Ideally, you and your gear

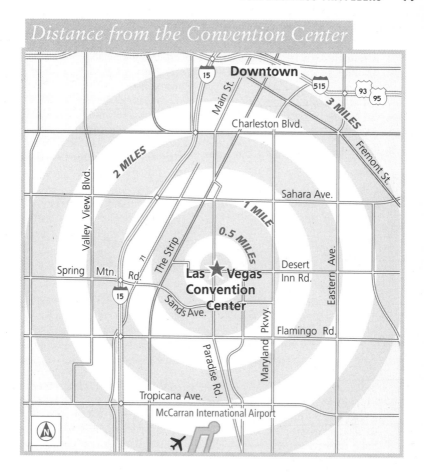

Distance from the Convention Center

will arrive together. Two on-site business centers provide a menu of services, including cable TV and voice and data services. The large Visitor Information Center sits next to the escalators at the base of the north pedestrian bridge across Paradise Road. A concierge desk handles show tickets and tours inside the main entrance. State-of-the-art Internet, data, and telephone products are available throughout the complex. The LVCC is easily navigable with a profusion of locator maps and data screens.

The Las Vegas Convention and Visitors Authority also operates Cashman Field Center, home of Las Vegas's AAA baseball team. In addition to a baseball stadium, the center contains a 1,922-seat theater and 98,100 square feet of meeting and exhibit space. For more information, call ☎ 702-892-0711 or browse **lvcva.com.**

Lodging within Walking Distance of the Las Vegas Convention Center

Although participants in citywide conventions lodge all over town, a few hotels are within easy walking distance of the LVCC. Next door, and closest, is the huge Las Vegas Hilton, with 2,950 rooms. The Hilton routinely serves as headquarters for meetings and shows in the convention center and provides, if needed, an additional 220,000 square feet of exhibit, ballroom, banquet, special event, and meeting-room space. Many smaller conventions conduct all their meetings, including exhibits, at the Hilton. The walk from the lobby of the Hilton to the LVCC is about five minutes for most people.

HOTELS WITHIN A 20-MINUTE WALK OF THE CONVENTION CENTER		
Best Western Mardi Gras Hotel	314 suites	12-minute walk
Circus Circus	3,767 rooms	15-minute walk
Courtyard (Marriott)	149 rooms	6-minute walk
Hyatt Place	202 suites	7-minute walk
Las Vegas Hilton	2,950 rooms	5-minute walk
Las Vegas Marriott Convention Center	278 suites	9-minute walk
Renaissance Las Vegas (Marriott)	548 rooms	4-minute walk
Residence Inn (Marriott)	192 suites	10-minute walk
Riviera Hotel	2,072 rooms	10-minute walk

A long half-block away is the rear entrance of the Riviera Hotel. Like the Las Vegas Hilton, the Riviera is often the headquarters for large shows and meetings at the convention center. With 150,000 square feet of meeting and banquet space, the Riviera, like the Hilton, hosts entire meetings and provides supplemental facilities for events at the convention center. The walk from the rear (eastern) entrance of the Riviera to the convention center takes about ten minutes.

Marriott International offers 1,466 rooms with a range of price points among five properties in proximity to the LVCC. Across the street on Paradise Road is Springhill Suites, which backs up to the Riviera. A half block west on Convention Center Drive is the Las Vegas Marriott with 278 guest rooms. Adjacent to the convention center on the south is the upscale Marriott Renaissance with 548 rooms, and directly across from the center on Paradise Road are two economy properties, the Marriott Residence Inn and Courtyard by Marriott.

The Royal and Clarion Hotel and Casino are inexpensive properties a half block west on Convention Center Drive. Embassy Suites is three blocks south on Paradise Road but closer to restaurants. For large conventions, the Wynn Resorts provide a shuttle bus to carry hotel guests along the resort's tree-lined golf course to the southwest corner of Paradise Road and Desert Inn Road. From there, it's just across the street to the convention center and monorail station.

Cabs and Shuttles to the Convention Center

Large citywide conventions often provide complimentary bus service from major hotels to the convention center. If you are staying at a smaller hotel and wish to use the shuttle bus, walk to the nearest large hotel on the shuttle route. Though cabs are plentiful and efficient in Las Vegas, they are sometimes in short supply at convention or trade show opening and closing times. Public transportation—CAT buses ($3)—is also available from the larger hotels. Exact fare is required. Your best bet is to stay within walking distance of the convention center. If you end up staying too far away to walk, a car is often less trouble than depending on cabs and shuttle buses.

Monorail to the Convention Center

If you are staying at a hotel in the section of the Strip between Tropicana and Sands (Spring Mountain Road) avenues, or at the Stratosphere, the best way to commute to the convention center is via the monorail. It's a no-brainer for guests in hotels on the east side of the Strip. For convention-goers who are lodging on the west side of the Strip, it's often a long walk to the nearest station. If traffic on the Strip isn't snarled, west-siders may want to take a cab. Note also that most hotels on the west side of the strip have rear or side entrances. These allow cabbies to choose an alternate route if the Strip is gridlocked.

Lunch Alternatives for Convention and Trade-show Attendees

The convention center's food service provides a better-than-average lunch and snack selection. As at most convention centers, however, prices are high. Outside of the convention center, but within walking distance, are the buffet and coffee shop at the Hilton and restaurants at the Marriott Renaissance. The better restaurants at the Las Vegas Hilton are not open for lunch.

The restaurants mentioned above provide decent food and fast service but are bustling eateries not particularly conducive to a quiet business lunch. At 3900 Paradise Road, however, **Park Center** (only three minutes from the convention center by cab and a little less than a mile by foot) offers several quiet, high-quality ethnic restaurants, including tapas, Moroccan, Brazilian, and Asian cuisines. Also located in the shopping center is a sub shop and an American steak house.

unofficial **TIP**
Take the monorail to Harrah's (about a five-minute ride), where you'll find dozens of fast-serve and full-service restaurants within a five-minute walk of Harrah's.

Café 325 in the Las Vegas Marriott on Convention Center Drive is open 6:30 a.m.–11 p.m for casual dining, as is **ENVY Steakhouse** in the Renaissance next door to the center's South Hall. Tucked away in the Clarion Hotel and Casino on Convention Center Drive is the **Bistro,** where steaks, pasta, and Continental cuisine are available for lunch.

Across the street, **Meskerem** restaurant in the Somerset Shopping Center offers Ethiopian cuisine daily, 9 a.m.–4 a.m. **The Stirling Club,** a private club in Turnbury Towers (facing the Las Vegas Hilton), will make lunch reservations for conventioneers with a minimum party of five if you call ☎ 702-732-9700 in advance; they do not accept walk-ins. One long block from the back of the convention center, heading east on Desert Inn Road, is **La Scala,** a white-tablecloth restaurant in the Mark I Tower. At the intersection of South Las Vegas Boulevard and Convention Center Drive are **Denny's, Sports World Kimchi,** and the **Peppermill,** long a locals' favorite.

Parking at the Las Vegas Convention Center

In all, there are 5,200 parking spaces for cars in nine color-coded parking lots at the LVCC. The most convenient parking is in the Silver Lots right in front of the main entrance. The largest and third-most convenient parking is in the Gold Lots across Paradise Road north of Convention Center Drive. On the east side of the convention center are the Blue, Orange, Red, and Green lots. The Blue Lot, tucked into the northeast corner of the property, is second only to the Silver Lots in convenience, but is used exclusively by convention-center employees. The Orange Lot on the southeast side is likewise convenient, but it is largely reserved for tractor-trailer parking during large trade shows. The Red Lot is adjacent to the new South Hall and is a good choice if the South Hall is where you'll spend most of your time. Finally, the Green Lot is the most remote of all, though more acceptable if your primary business is in the South Hall.

Though access to the exhibit floor varies from meeting to meeting, attendees are often required to enter through the convention center's main entrance off Paradise Road. If not parked in the Gold or Silver lots, convention-goers must hike around the complex in order to reach the front door (a seven- to ten-minute walk). For other meetings, attendees with proper credentials (that is, those with registration badges) are permitted to enter the exhibit halls by one of several doors along the sides of the convention-center halls. As a rule, getting out is not as hard as getting in, and attendees are usually permitted to exit through the side doors.

COMFORT ZONES:
Matching Guests with Hotels

WE REMEMBER A GOOD FRIEND, a 32-year-old single woman, who, in search of a little romance, decided to take a Caribbean cruise. Thinking that one cruise was pretty much like any other, she signed up for a cruise without doing much shopping around. She ended up on a boat full of retired married folks who played bingo or bridge every evening and were usually in the sack by 10:30 p.m. Our friend mistakenly assumed, as have many others, that cruises are homogeneous products. In fact, nothing could be further from the truth. Each cruise provides a tailored experience to a specific and narrowly defined market. If our friend had done her homework, she could have booked passage on a boat full of young single people and danced and romanced into the night.

In Las Vegas, it is likewise easy to assume that all the hotels and casinos are fairly similar. True, they all have guest rooms, restaurants, and the same mix of games in the casino, but each property molds its offerings to appeal to a well-defined audience. This concerted effort to please a specific population of guests creates what we call a "comfort zone." If you are among the group a hotel strives to please, you will feel comfortable and at home and will have much in common with the other guests. However, if you fail to determine the comfort zone before you go, you may end up like our friend—on the wrong boat.

Visitors come to Las Vegas to vacation and play or to attend a meeting or convention. While these reasons for coming to Las Vegas are not mutually exclusive, there is a marked difference between a recreational visitor and a business traveler. The vacationer is likely to be older (45 years and up), retired, and from the Midwest, Southern California, Arizona, Colorado, or Hawaii. The business traveler is younger on average and comes from just about anywhere. Individual hotels and casinos pay close attention to these differences and customize their atmosphere, dining, and entertainment to satisfy a specific type of traveler.

The California Hotel, downtown, for example, targets Hawaiians and maintains a food store and restaurants that supply their clientele with snacks and dishes from the islands. On the Boulder Highway, Sam's Town is geared toward cowboys and retired travelers. Entertainment at Sam's Town consists of bowling and country-western dancing. Circus Circus on the Strip attracts the RV crowd (with its own RV park) but also offers large, low-priced rooms, buffets, free circus acts, and an amusement park to lure families. Palms, Planet Hollywood, and the Hard Rock Hotel target a hip, younger audience, while the Las Vegas Hilton and the Venetian, both next door to the convention centers, go the extra mile to make business travelers feel at home.

Some hotels are posh and exclusive, while others are more spartan and intended to appeal to younger or more frugal visitors. Each property, however, from its lounge entertainment to its guest-room decor or the dishes served in its restaurants, is packaged with a certain type of guest in mind.

Because Las Vegas is basically a very informal town, you will not feel as out of place as our friend did on her cruise if you happen to end up in the wrong hotel. At any given property, there is a fairly broad range of clientele. There always will be hotels where you experience a greater comfort level than at others, however. In a place as different as Las Vegas, that added comfort can sometimes mean a lot.

DEMOCRACY IN THE CASINOS

WHILE LAS VEGAS HOTELS AND CASINOS continue to be characterized as appealing to "high rollers" or "grinds," the distinction has become increasingly blurred. High rollers, of course, are wealthy visitors who come to gamble in earnest, while grinds are less affluent folks who grudgingly bet their money a nickel or quarter at a time. For many years, the slot machine was symbolic of the grinds. Unable to join the action of the high-stakes table games, these gamblers would sit for hours pumping the arms of the slots. More recently, however, the slots are the symbol of casino profitability, contributing anywhere from 40 to 100% to a given casino's bottom line.

The popularity of the slot machine among gamblers of all types has democratized the casino. The casinos recognize that the silver-haired lady at the quarter slots is an extremely valuable customer and that it is good business to forgo the impression of exclusivity in order to make her comfortable. In Las Vegas there are casinos that maintain the illusion of catering to an upper-crust clientele while quietly practicing an egalitarianism that belies any such pretense. By virtue of its economic clout, the slot machine has broadened the comfort zone of the stuffiest casinos and made Las Vegas a friendlier, more pleasant (albeit noisier) place.

THE FEEL OF THE PLACE

LAS VEGAS'S HOTEL-CASINOS have distinctly individual personalities. While all casinos contain slot machines, craps tables, and roulette wheels, the feel of each particular place is unique, a product of the combined characteristics of management, patrons, and design. This feel, or personality, determines a hotel-casino's comfort zone, the peculiar ambience that makes one guest feel totally at home while another runs for the exit.

HOTELS *with* CASINOS

HOW TO AVOID READING THE HOTEL-CASINO DESCRIPTIONS If you don't care how a place "feels" but just want to know whether it has room service and tennis courts, or when checkout time is, you can skip to the alphabetically arranged Hotel Information Chart at the end of this chapter.

Aliante Station Casino + Hotel
(aliantecasinohotel.com)

OPENED IN NOVEMBER 2008, the classy Aliante Station Casino + Hotel in North Las Vegas is the newest relative of the Station Casinos family. The only high-rise within a nine-mile radius, the tower stands boldly against the nearby Sheep Mountain range in the northwest Las Vegas Valley. This desert chic metro-resort borders the master-planned development of Aliante (meaning "to soar"), about 20 minutes north of downtown Las Vegas via I-15, and is adjacent to the intersection of the North 215 Expressway and Aliante Parkway. Given the suburban location and distance from tourist attractions and facilities, a car is a must. The customer base is predominantly vacationers visiting family and friends, motor-sports enthusiasts, business travelers, and locals.

Designed to merge with the stark beauty of the surrounding desert, Aliante Station blends the region's neutral color palette and natural materials. The 40-acre complex includes a 202-room hotel; casino with smoke-free poker area, 170-seat sports book with individual screens, 40 table games, and more than 2,000 slot and video-poker machines; six restaurants and a food court; showroom; fitness gym; 16-screen Regal IMAX Theater; and 14,000-square-foot conference center. The layout represents the typical fine-tuned Station Casinos footprint with ample peripheral roads, lots of well-lit surface parking, four casino entrances, a separate entry to the hotel, and valet parking right outside the lobby.

The gaming area is a well-organized rectangle with restaurants, theaters, a poker room, a sports book, restrooms, and an arcade lining the perimeter. Positioned in the center are table games and slots. The casino, awash in warm hues of chocolate, taupe, and mocha, is bound by wide aisles and plenty of elbowroom at the slot carousels.

Elevating the excitement level is the vibe from E.T.A., a trendy nightclub featuring DJ entertainment and dancing. On weekends, eclectic headliner concerts at moderate prices invigorate the Access Showroom. This venue for 650 concert-goers recreates the vintage Vegas look with scarlet and gray booths and comfortable theater-style chairs.

Food seekers can choose from several brand names at the seven eateries that ring the casino. The hotel's flagship dining experience, complete with a lovely outdoor patio, is MRKT (pronounced Market) Sea & Land. A representative assortment of torrid and temperate plates accompanied by a selection of 100 tequilas is available at Camacho's Cantina with its whimsical centerpiece of 2,716 hanging Cazadoras bottles. At the foyers outside MRKT and Camacho's, electronic menus let guests savor the offerings. The Feast Buffet, a Station Casinos constant, offers Tex-Mex, American, barbecue, Asian, and Italian cooking stations, a salad board, and freshly made hand-packed ice cream at the dessert bar.

The nine-story tower houses tasteful king or double-queen rooms of approximately 400 square feet. Sustaining the rich beige-and-chocolate color scheme throughout the sleeping rooms are creamy marble, tan granite, and dark woods, again emphasizing organic textures. Sixty percent of the accommodations are configured with showers only, so if a tub is preferred, be sure to request a tub room. All rooms include flat-panel TVs and minibars and are wired for high-speed Internet and iPod docking stations. Eastward-facing rooms have a sweeping view of the Sheep Mountains and the southeast Las Vegas skyline. To the west, rooms look toward Mount Charleston and the Spring Mountains. Despite the expansive panoramas, the views are somewhat bleak—definitely not the desert at its best. The expressway's proximity notwithstanding, the tower is silent and tranquil.

Situated off the lobby, the spacious first-floor pool oasis is shaded by tall palms surrounded by seasonal bedding plants and colorful flowers. In addition to the elongated pool suitable for soaking or swimming laps, there is a corner hot tub, rentable cabanas, and an abundance of vermilion chaise longues (some doublewides). A 23-machine fitness center overlooks the pool. Just across the street is Aliante Golf Club. Joggers can enjoy a run in nearby Aliante Discovery Nature Park.

Although Aliante Station is somewhat remote, it is not isolated by any means and is a good-choice getaway for guests seeking style, value, and sophistication in a contemporary urban desert retreat.

Arizona Charlie's Boulder and Decatur (arizonacharlies.com)

PATRONIZED PRIMARILY BY LOCALS, Arizona Charlie's are working-persons' casinos with a southwestern ranch flavor. Everything is informal, a sort of shirtsleeves place. And it's busy. There is an energy, a three-ring circus feel of much going on at once—lots of slots, some table games, a sports book, burgers and beer, and a lounge. The hotel rooms are passable, but the real reason to patronize Arizona Charlie's is the video poker—they're among the best machines in town, and considering what town you're in, this means they're among the best machines anywhere. The original Arizona Charlie's is on Decatur, west of the Strip. The newer Arizona Charlie's Boulder is on the Boulder Highway.

Bally's (ballyslasvegas.com)

BALLY'S BILLS ITSELF AS "the classic Las Vegas experience." Targeted to the gamer of any age, the emphasis is clear when you step inside the main entrance from under the broad, sky-lit porte cochere. On your right, a football-field-long casino stretches beyond you. The casino is immense, open, and elegantly modern—sophisticated in a formal, understated way, like a tuxedo. Active without being claustrophobic, and classy without being stiff, Bally's captures the style of modern European casinos without sacrificing American informality. On the left of the same great room is the registration desk, along with services such as a coffee bar and a newsstand conveniently located directly in the lobby area.

Originally themed for Hollywood, now Bally's doesn't bear much of a specific visual motif. This is not at all a shortcoming. Bally's simply carries itself with a certain forthrightness, with a kind of class that says "We are confident to be who we are—timeless Las Vegas." After all, Bally's has the enduring, quintessential, top-quality topless show *Jubilee!* with which it celebrated its 29th anniversary in 2010. Million-dollar sets and Bob Mackie and Pete Menefee costumes, skimpy though they may be, hark back to the days of Sinatra and gang.

A complete resort, Bally's is blessed with exceptional restaurants, one of the better buffets in Las Vegas, and the groundbreaking Sterling Brunch. All of the north-tower wings have been renovated. Although quite spread out, Bally's is easy to navigate. Amenities include a 13,000-square-foot health club and spa and a large, diversified shopping arcade. Standard guest rooms are a generous 450 square feet and comfortable. One-bedroom grand suites have king-sized beds and a whirlpool spa. To enjoy this layout you should be physically very comfortable with your traveling partner, as most of the bathroom is exposed to the sleeping area.

For those who drive, the guest parking is all valet out front. There is limited self-parking in the back, but it is mainly for oversized vehicles. The hot tip is to park at Bally's sister property, Paris Las Vegas (the hotels are internally connected). Demonstrating legitimate concern about the traffic congestion on the Strip, Bally's joined with the MGM Grand in constructing a monorail that was the first link in the Las Vegas Monorail line. Subsequently, the monorail was extended north along the Strip, with a loop over to the Las Vegas Convention Center. Bally's also offers airport check-in shuttle service and another free shuttle every 30 minutes to take you to Caesars, Paris, Rio, and Harrah's (all Caesars Entertainment properties). In a separate project, Bally's has a series of moving walkways to transport guests from Las Vegas Boulevard into the casino. In a Las Vegas first, Bally's also offers moving walkways *out* of the casino. Maybe this is the only way, short of a forklift, that Bally's could get the bulk loaders out of the coffee shop.

Bally's caters to meetings and conventions and is one of the few hotels where you will not feel out of place in a business suit. Guests are frequently under age 40 here and come from all over, but particularly Southern California, Chicago, and elsewhere in the Midwest. Bally's also has a loyal Spanish-speaking clientele.

Bellagio (bellagio.com)

IT'S NO SECRET THAT STEVE WYNN established a new standard for Las Vegas hotel-casinos when he opened the Mirage in 1989. While it's doubtful that Wynn foresaw the impact the Mirage would have on Las Vegas, it's certain that he relishes his role as an instrument of change. Like an author trying to build on the success of an earlier work, Wynn took another shot at bumping up the standard in 1999. The vehicle for Wynn's aspirations this time was the Bellagio, on the site of the old Dunes hotel and golf course. Quite simply, Wynn intended for it to be the best hotel in the world, a hotel intended to rewrite the concept of hospitality. In 2000, however, in a move that took everyone by surprise, Wynn sold the Bellagio, along with his other casino properties, to MGM Grand (now MRI) for $6.4 billion in cash. Wynn's latest attempts to rock the Las Vegas status quo are Wynn Las Vegas and Wynn Encore, both opened on the site of the venerable Desert Inn. For now, though, back to the Bellagio.

With its main entrance off the Strip just south of Flamingo Road, the Bellagio is inspired by an Italian village overlooking Lake Como in the sub-Alpine north of Italy. The facade of the Bellagio will remind you somewhat of the themed architecture Wynn employed at T. I., only this time it's provincial Italian instead of Caribbean. The Bellagio village is arrayed along the west and north sides of a man-made lake, where dancing fountains provide allure and spectacle, albeit more dignified than the Mirage's exploding volcano or T. I.'s buccaneer carnage.

Rising behind the village facade in a gentle curve is the 3,933-room hotel, complete with casino, restaurants, shopping complex, spa, and pool. Added in late 2004 was a 33-story Spa Tower with 819 hotel rooms and 109 suites. Bundled with the tower are a restaurant, four shops, and additional convention space. Imported marble is featured throughout, even in the guest rooms and suites, as are original art, traditionally styled furnishings, and European antiques. Guest rooms and meeting rooms also feature large picture windows affording views of lushly landscaped grounds and formal gardens. In 2011, Bellagio remodeled its guest rooms to incorporate a fresh botanical feel (influenced by its beautiful conservatory) and modern touches such as iHome docking stations, media hubs, and laptop safes.

Surprisingly, the Italian village theme of Bellagio's lakefront facade is largely abandoned in the hotel's interior. Though a masterpiece of integrated colors, textures, and sight lines, the interior design reflects no strong sense of theme. In two steps, passing indoors, you go from a provincial village on a very human scale to a monumentally grand interior with proportions reminiscent of national libraries. You've heard it's lovely, and naturally it is, but somehow in a very different way than you might have anticipated. The vast spaces are exceedingly tasteful and unquestionably sophisticated, yet they fail to evoke the fun, whimsy, and curiosity so intrinsic to the Mirage and T. I.

Perhaps because Las Vegas has conditioned us to a plastic, carnival sort of stimulation, entering the Bellagio is like stepping from the midway into the basilica. The surroundings impress but do not engage our emotions—except, of course, for the art, and that is exactly the point. Seen as a rich, neutral backdrop for the extraordinary works of art displayed throughout Bellagio, the lapse of thematic continuity is understandable. No theme could compete, and none should.

The art is everywhere, even on the ceiling of the registration lobby, where a vibrant, colorful blown-glass piece by Dale Chihuly hangs. Wonderful works are showcased in the Bellagio's restaurants. Original Picassos, for example, are on exhibit in the restaurant of the same name. The Bellagio Gallery of Fine Art is touted as Las Vegas's premier art gallery. Each year the gallery presents world-class exhibitions of artworks and objects drawn from internationally acclaimed museums and private collections, such as a body of Impressionist works and the photographs of Ansel Adams.

Architecturally, Bellagio's most creative and interesting spaces are found in its signature conservatory and botanical gardens and in its restaurants. As you walk into the main entrance the primary garden is straight ahead. The opulent and oversized displays change seasonally according to the theatrical floral whimsies of the supremely accomplished botanical staff.

If you spend time at the Bellagio, visit each of the restaurants for a moment, if only to take in their stunning design. Many of Bellagio's restaurants, including a Las Vegas branch of Le Cirque, feature panoramic views. Some offer both indoor and outdoor dining experiences. In addition to the restaurants, Bellagio serves one of Las Vegas's best—and not unexpectedly one of the city's most expensive—buffets. With the exception of the buffet and coffee shop, Bellagio's restaurants require reservations, preferably made a month to six weeks before you leave home.

The Bellagio's showroom hosts a production of the justly acclaimed Cirque du Soleil. Though terribly expensive, the show is one of Cirque's most challenging productions yet, featuring a one-of-a-kind set that transforms seamlessly from hard surface to water. Like Bellagio itself, the Cirque production "O" (from the pronunciation of the French word *eau,* meaning "water") lacks the essential humor and humanness of Cirque's *Mystère* at T. I. but is nonetheless one of the hottest Cirque tickets in town.

Meant to be luxurious, the Bellagio seeks to establish itself as the prestige address of Las Vegas. Retailers in the shopping venue include Chanel, Tiffany, Prada, and Giorgio Armani. Bellagio's purported target market includes high rollers and discriminating business travelers who often eschew gaming properties. It's hard, however, to discuss exclusivity and personal service in the same breath with 3,933 rooms.

Room rates have bounced all over the place in recent years and in the future may bounce to a level that you find acceptable. If you stay at Bellagio, you will find the same basic informality typical of the rest of the Strip, and, surprisingly, you will encounter in the hotel more people like you than super-rich. Expressed more directly, Bellagio is a friendly place to stay and gamble and not at all pretentious.

Bill's Gamblin' Hall and Saloon (billslasvegas.com)

BILL'S GAMBLIN' HALL AND SALOON, formerly the Barbary Coast, is an old-fashioned casino for real gamblers. Appointed in dark wood embellished with murals in stained glass, this small hotel-casino serves a loyal clientele of locals and serious gamblers. With the feel of an exclusive and tasteful gentlemen's club, Bill's offerings are straightforward and simple. Table games still reign supreme in the casino, and its restaurant, Steakhouse at Bill's, replaced the venerable Michaels when the latter relocated to the South Point Hotel and Casino. There is no showroom, no swimming pool, no sauna or whirlpool, and many of the 196 hotel rooms (decorated in a style reminiscent of early-1900s San Francisco) are reserved by regular customers. Bill's is centrally located if you're on foot but just about the worst hotel on the Strip to get into and out of by car.

Binion's (binions.com)

BINION'S IS ONE OF THE ANCHORS OF GLITTER GULCH. The casino is large and active, with row upon row of slots clanking noisily under a suffocatingly low ceiling. The table games are less congested, occupying an extended vertical space canopied by mirrors. With an Old West theme executed in the obligatory reds and lavenders, Binion's is dark, but not dark enough to slow the enthusiasm of the locals and "real gamblers" who hang out there. One of the city's top spots for poker and craps, Binion's is famous for not having any maximum bet limitations. You can bet $1 million on a single roll of the dice if you wish.

On the lower (basement) level is the coffee shop and what may be one of the most pleasant bars in the city; it, too, is dark but for once is paneled in rich woods. Twenty or so stories up from the cellar is the Top of Binion's Steakhouse restaurant and lounge, offering a great view of the city. The recession hit downtown Las Vegas harder than the Strip. One of the casualties was the hotel at Binion's, which closed and was mothballed in 2010. Prospects for its reopening appear slim.

Boulder Station (boulderstation.com)

BOULDER STATION IS A CLONE OF PALACE STATION, sharing its railroad theme and emphasis on good food and lounge entertainment. Located on Boulder Highway not far from the Arizona Charlie's Boulder, Boulder Station features a roomy casino with a Western-town motif (more in the image of turn-of-the-century Denver than of Dodge City). Tastefully done, with much attention to detail, the casino includes one of the nicest sports books in Las Vegas. Thirty-three big-screen, high-resolution monitors make the Boulder Station sports book a superb place for spectators. Like its sister properties, Boulder Station is an oasis for the hungry, with a great buffet, several good full-service restaurants, and possibly the best selection of fast food found in any casino. Guest rooms in the 300-room hotel tower are modest but comfortable, with good views. There is a swimming pool, but it is small and stark. Clientele consists primarily of locals and Southern Californians.

Comparing Boulder Station to Palace Station, we like the casino much better at Boulder Station but prefer the guest rooms at Palace Station's tower. The buffets and restaurants run pretty much a dead heat, but Boulder Station is less crowded.

Caesars Palace (caesarspalace.com)

IF ROME IS "THE ETERNAL CITY," then its Las Vegas legacy at Caesars is a worthy, long-lived heir. Forty-five years old in 2011, Caesars Palace was the first of the themed hotels and casinos to realize fully its potential, and it is among the foremost at staying fresh through constant updating and remodeling. The perennial classic that reinvents itself, Caesars is a must-see even if you don't stay there.

An exercise in whimsical fantasy and excess, Caesars' Roman theme has been executed with astounding artistry and attention to detail. Everywhere fine mosaics, handsome statuary, mythological references, famous sculptures (including a Carrera-marble copy of Michelangelo's *David*—from Florence, not Rome—but let's not quibble) delight the eye and mind. Creating an atmosphere of informality in surroundings too pretentious to believe is hard to pull off, but that is exactly what Caesars Palace has done.

If Caesars was on a small scale it would be exquisite kitsch, but it's on a grand scale that elevates you into some kind of time machine where the bustling commerce of ancient Rome lives again. Gambling at Caesars does feel a little like pitching horseshoes in the Supreme Court, but, incredibly, it works. Everywhere the vaulted ceilings, classic statuary, and graceful arches easily accommodate the legions (pun intended) of slots, activity of the pits, shopping, dining, and lolling about in opulent pools surrounded by towering gardens. Truly, here is the grandeur that was Rome with all its desirable excesses and indulgences.

Caesars Palace provides three spacious and luxurious casinos, including a poker room with celebrity events, 26 excellent restaurants and cafes, beautiful landscaping, and top celebrity entertainment. For all of the guests who inhabit its 3,348 superb rooms, Caesars has all of the services and amenities of a world-class resort.

The pool area, expanded yet again in 2010, is arguably the most stately in Las Vegas. Framed by hotel towers, the swimming and sunbathing complex offers six different pools, all in the Roman motif, including the 10,000-square-foot pool of the Temple, which is capped by a rotunda and decorated with marble and mosaics. For lusty sinews there's the Neptune pool with 5,000 square feet for lap swimmers; and for European-style (aka topless) bathers, the Venus pool is neatly tucked away within an evergreen enclave. All the pools have cabanas available for rent with stocked refrigerators, snack and beverage service, soft lounge chairs, and a TV so you don't have to choose between the big game or the soaps and your tan.

The lobby and guest registration area has been remodeled, too, but you don't have to spend much time in its glory if you use the airport check-in/ shuttle feature that delivers you with your room key and your luggage to the hotel for $8 one-way. Or for extra ease, use the fee-based luggage concierge service that will ferry your bags from your home or office to your hotel room.

In 2003, Caesars finished a complete renovation of its original hotel towers. The year 2004 saw the opening of the Roman Plaza, a shopping, dining, and entertainment venue reaching from Caesars' Flamingo Road entrance to the hotel lobby and casino. The 26-story luxury Augustus tower opened in 2005. Besides nine-foot ceilings, these rooms feature spa tubs, TVs in the bathrooms, and great views of the Garden of the Gods pool area.

The Palace Tower, built in late 1997 and renovated in 2006, generally costs $120 more than the standard room price in the Forum, Roman, and Centurion towers. With a small sitting area in addition to the traditional marble bathroom, the standard room of 300 to 600 square feet—all with high-speed Internet access—is a great room for the price. Palace Tower rooms have 500 square feet or more, with many amenities, including marble dry bars. The Premiere Palace Tower rooms have his-and-her bathrooms that are connected by a large, sexy, glass walk-in shower. For another kind of grand experience, double-bay suites with parlors and dining tables for entertaining are available in the Forum and Roman towers.

Ever the vanguard, Caesars is currently remodeling its Centurion Tower along the Appian Way into a luxury Japanese hotel that will meld with its Roman Empire theme. By mid-2012, the interior of the Centurion Tower will be transformed into a stylish boutique hotel managed by high-end international restaurant brand Nobu Hospitality and designated Nobu Tower Las Vegas. Tapping into the global vision of Chef Nobu Matsuhisa, the tower's 180 guest rooms will feature natural materials, elegant furniture, predominantly twin beds, fine linens, robes and slippers, refrigerators well stocked with Asian snacks and spirits, as well as tubs and other amenities traditional to Japanese hospitality and service. The tower's base will have its own Nobu restaurant and lounge and a separate lobby with check-in managed by Japanese-speaking staff. On-site Nobu chefs will also provide 24-hour room service from a traditional menu. Expect a truly all-Nipponese experience. Also in 2012, Caesars plans to open some of its Octavius Tower rooms and suites.

Some say the spa is Caesars' best-kept secret. With the Roman penchant for water joys, it's logical that Caesars would have a full line of luxurious treatments and settings for men and women. Situated on the second floor of the Augustus Tower, the spa has 51 therapy rooms, signature Roman baths with hot, cold, and tepid pools, and sculpted stone chaise longues submerged in heated pools and designed as pre-massage relaxers.

Caesars is on a roll with its nightlife scene, offering four hot lounges. Pure has three luxurious rooms, including a dance club and a heated rooftop balcony overlooking the Strip. At Shadow, silhouetted dancers contort to DJ-spun hip-hop. Cleopatra's Barge, a decades-old dance club on a free-floating boat, continues to rock on. Nearby is the Seahorse Lounge, where you can watch the endangered species variety drift by in the aquarium.

For the less nocturnal, there are two shopping venues. At the Appian Way (look for the *David*) you can purchase apparel, gifts, art, and jewelry, including Caesars logo items. The extensive Forum Shops is an entirely different kind of experience. Opened in 1992 and expanded in 1997 and again in 2005, the astonishing adjoining Forum Shops give Caesars Palace the distinction of offering one of the most unusual themed shopping complexes in the United States with 160 mercantile venues and 13 restaurants and specialty food shops. Ambling through its gently cobblestoned "streets," replete with slightly sloping gutters, the sightseer and shopper alike can be delighted and charmed by full-scale fountains featuring Neptune and Bacchus and building facades topped by second-story "residences," all set against the background of a sweeping Italian sky at sunset. At every turn, you find the perfect blend of Old-World commerce and cutting-edge merchandise, including, of course, the famous Italians Versace and Armani.

Dining at Caesars has been totally revamped with the addition of Rao's, a clone of Frank Pelligrini's fabled Italian eatery in New York; Beijing Noodle No. 9; Mesa Grill; and Bradley Ogden, honored by the James Beard Foundation, that serves "farm fresh" American cuisine. Another star in the lineup is Restaurant Guy Savoy, overlooking the Roman Plaza. Headed by Parisian restaurateur Guy Savoy, recently named Chef of the Year in France, the restaurant offers one of the most singular dining experiences in town. Among other choices are authentic Chinese and Japanese (including a sushi bar) and steak and seafood. For casual dining, there's the 24-hour Lago Buffet, featuring many made-to-order specialties; Cypress Street Marketplace, an all-hours gourmet deli and food court; and Serendipity 3, another New York import specializing in burgers, dogs, stuffed sandwiches, and its signature frozen hot chocolate (don't drink too many of these before bedtime). A good antidote to the interior casino spaces, the fine buffet at Caesars is in a large sun-drenched room with a view of the pool area, also a welcome balm in counterpoint to the constant clamor of the gaming floor.

Originally designed for high rollers, from the beginning Caesars opened its arms to the world, marketing far and wide. Enjoyed by a broad range of clientele from the East, the Midwest, and Southern California, it's also popular with Asian and Hispanic visitors. Of course, it also hosts meetings and caters to business travelers in its conference center. No matter what the motivation for a visit, each guest—supported by a staff of 6,000—no doubt feels like Caesar.

California (thecal.com)

THE CALIFORNIA IS A PLEASANT, DOWNTOWN hotel-casino with excellent, moderately priced restaurants and a largely Hawaiian and Filipino clientele. It is a friendly, mellow place to stay or gamble—unpretentious, and certainly comfortable. The casino rambles but, like most downtown casinos, does not allow much elbowroom. The decor is subdued and tasteful, with wood paneling and trim. For a taste of old Las Vegas, try the porterhouse steak special at the Redwood Bar and Grill. The shops, menus, and services work to make visiting Pacific Islanders feel as much at home as visitors from Kansas City or Tampa. While some hotel-casinos are spectacles or happenings, the California is simply a nice, relaxed place to spend some time.

Cannery and Eastside Cannery
(cannerycasinos.com)

FOUR MILES NORTH OF DOWNTOWN ON CRAIG ROAD, the Cannery opened in January 2003 and expanded in 2004 with the usual locals' formula: big casino, small hotel. The theme has nothing to do with Steinbeck or fish, though the industrial, 1940s-style structure of corrugated metal and steel beams would be right at home on Cannery Row. Instead, produce, specifically vegetables and fruit, take center stage with murals and paintings of colossal berries, apples, and veggies. Even the red, patterned carpet is festooned with oranges, apples, and pears.

The roomy, uncluttered casino is roughly circular, surrounding a slightly elevated lounge decorated with World War II–era, Betty Grable–style pin-ups. Restaurants, including a good Mexican eatery, a steak house, fast-food court, and a respectable buffet, are arrayed around the periphery. For entertainment, there's a 16-screen movie theater and The Club for concerts. A recent expansion added 15,000 square feet to the casino, including a poker room and a race and sports book. Also new are a parking garage and an Italian restaurant.

Guest rooms are smallish, with oak-finish furniture and brightly colored soft goods. Views from guest-room windows are about as uninspiring as it gets.

Eastside Cannery opened in 2009 on Boulder Highway near Sam's Town. A copy of the original Cannery in many ways, Eastside offers clearly superior guest rooms in its sleek hotel tower. Each room features a 37-inch flat-panel

TV and floor-to-ceiling windows. The restaurant lineup is led by Carve, a prime-rib specialty room much in the image of Lawry's. Like the original, Eastside rounds out the dining options with a Casa Cochina Mexican restaurant, a 24-hour cafe, a buffet, and a deli. In addition to the usual table games and the locals' favorite slots, Eastside offers bingo and an active poker room. The Eastside Events Center is a venue large enough for concerts and boxing matches, while the more intimate Marilyn's Lounge showcases top Las Vegas lounge acts. Like the Cannery, Eastside targets locals, but the upscale rooms, club scene, restaurants, poker room, and lounge entertainment make it a good play for visitors as well.

Casino Royale (casinoroyalehotel.com)

LOCATED ACROSS THE STRIP FROM THE MIRAGE, the diminutive Casino Royale has about 150 guest rooms. Small, accessible, and unpretentious, Casino Royale provides bargain lodging in the Strip's high-rent district. While the crowded and slot-heavy casino will make downtown gamblers feel right at home, the Casino Royale's second-floor Outback Steakhouse offers an affordable alternative to the Strip's pricey chophouses. The property's clientele runs the gamut from tour groups to convention-goers on a tight budget to folks who could not get rooms at other hotels on the block.

Circus Circus (circuscircus.com)

CIRCUS CIRCUS IS VERY LIKELY THE ONLY hotel on the Strip that has an escalator from within the casino to a McDonald's, and that tells you pretty much what you need to know. Although most hotels do not cater to families with young children, Circus Circus is a notable exception. For parents who must bring their children, it's a good alternative and a bargain to boot.

With so many swarming, milling, and mewing short people, the lobby can sometimes remind you of a day-care center. The main casino has a second level called The Midway with good reason, as it features the simple kinds of games found at a state fair venue (wham a spring-loaded chicken into a moving pot and win a prize sort of thing). At the core of the Midway is a small grandstand that features very competent regular circus acts, also primarily for children. The entire casino affair is obviously designed as an easy hand-off platform for such directives as, "Here, honey, you take the kids for 45 minutes while I go play the quarter slots."

In 1993, Circus Circus launched what is now the Adventuredome, formerly Grand Slam Canyon, a desert-canyon-themed amusement park totally enclosed in a giant pink dome. Here guests can enjoy a roller coaster, a flume ride, robotic dinosaurs, and more. A detailed description of Adventuredome can be found in Part Five, Shopping and Seeing the Sights, on pages 422–423. The meandering hallway to the Adventuredome and the Skyrise Casino is lined with shops catering to the younger set as well. Maps and signs throughout the facility indicate the "Green Zone," where children are allowed to be (because the law against children lingering in the gaming areas is very strictly enforced in Las Vegas). Children can walk through the casino if they must, but the general atmosphere does not encourage this practice.

Perhaps because of price, in addition to families, Circus Circus also attracts some seniors and novice gamblers who don't mind dodging strollers and jacked-up kids in this ADD paradise. The labyrinthine casino has low ceilings and is frenetic, loud, and always busy, but sometimes in contrast to the main public spaces it can seem like an oasis of sanity. Nickel slots abound, as do table games, including dollar blackjack. The circus theme, both colorful and wholesome, is extended to every conceivable detail of the hotel's physical space and operation. However, most of the garish circus theme decor that once defined guest rooms at Circus Circus has happily given way to more restful, mature colors and appointments. Rooms are adequate but not luxurious.

Circus Circus has a very good steak house (one of the only escapes from the circus theme); a huge, inexpensive buffet; an RV park; and a monorail shuttle that connects the property's two main buildings. And, to give credit for great innovation, Circus Circus was the first casino to set aside a non-smoking gaming area. A hotel tower, as well as a shopping and restaurant arcade, adjoin Adventuredome. The arcade restaurants provide Circus Circus with much-needed alternatives to the steak house and the buffet. For parents with children, Circus Circus is a great alternative, but for happily child-free others, it might feel more like a zoo.

CITYCENTER (citycenter.com)

LAS VEGAS'S NEWEST DESTINATION WITHIN A DESTINATION, MRI's innovative CityCenter is truly dazzling. From glass towers reflecting sunlight by day to a skyline of crystalline pillars aglow at night, the 67-acre hotel, residence, shopping complex, and permanent public art exhibition between the Monte Carlo and Bellagio resorts transcends anything in Las Vegas or elsewhere. Designed to offer a new dimension in urban living, the complex radiates energy. The buildings are surprisingly close together, intensifying the blaze—sunglasses are recommended.

The largest privately funded commercial development in the United States, this zillion-dollar metroplex is comprised of Aria, a 61-story, 4,004-room casino resort; Vdara and Mandarin Oriental, two nongaming hotels and residences; Veer, the dual-tower residential condominium; The Harmon, a luxury boutique hotel (opening delayed by the recession); Crystals entertainment and retail district; plus interior and exterior space featuring a $40-million curated public fine-art program. Prominently fronting a quarter mile on the Las Vegas Strip, the first impression of CityCenter is visually vertical and geometric. Reminiscent of Dorothy's awestruck reaction to the Emerald City, you will be overwhelmed by yards and acres and miles of glass on the facades of seven ascending spires and the roof of Crystals. Each is distinguished by a signature hue. Facing the complex and looking left to right, the towers are the silver-blue Mandarin Oriental, white-hot Aria, lemon-tinted Veer, slate black Vdara, and cobalt Harmon (which has structural problems and may never open). In front is the multi-angled clear roof of Crystals.

For this city within a city, the elevated promenade begins at the Strip and draws visitors into the innovative development. Public art is an important element of the environment. The campus is configured with pedestrian passageways through an informal outdoor-indoor contemporary art museum. More than 15 extraordinary paintings, sculptures, and large-scale works in a variety of postmodern styles created by world-class artists are displayed. Maya Lin, Claes Oldenburg and Coosje van Bruggen, Henry Moore, Richard Long, Jenny Holzer, and Nancy Rubins are represented. Set aside at least 90 minutes for a self-conducted tour. Brochures describing the bold and eclectic collection are available on site, and small plaques detail each work. It's a must-see for art lovers! *Note:* Although The Harmon isn't open, don't miss Isa Genzken's *Rose II*, a 26-foot-tall single long-stemmed rose of stainless steel, lacquer, and aluminum (it's comprised of more than 75% recycled materials). Gracefully upright in the porte cochere at The Harmon, the piece is accessible through Crystals or from Harmon Avenue on the north side of CityCenter.

There are only two auto entrances into the development from the Strip and one from Dean Martin Drive via Jerry Lewis Road and W. Harmon Avenue. The north entrance into CityCenter is a west turn onto Harmon Avenue from the stoplight on South Las Vegas Boulevard or straight on Harmon crossing Las Vegas Boulevard. It traverses the entire north side and exits 1.5 miles to the west after crossing over the busy I-15 freeway. Midway through CityCenter on Harmon Avenue is an elevated circular drive with signage directing vehicles to Vdara, The Harmon, and the north entrance of Aria. A second street south of Harmon Avenue is named CityCenter Place, which also has a stoplight on the Strip. That west turn will put you onto CityCenter Place, which is short and becomes a semicircle passing Veer Towers, Crystals, the Aria's main entrance and returning to the Strip. The Mandarin Oriental Hotel is accessed by a left turn immediately after turning onto CityCenter Place.

Valet parking and pickup is available at both entrances to Aria, the Vdara, and at Mandarin Oriental. Valet parking for Veer and Crystals is located in the subterranean parking garage and entered via well-marked ramps. There are approximately 17,000 parking spaces. The self-parking garage is convenient to the Mandarin Oriental and Aria by foot and to Crystals, Vdara, and The Harmon via the tram. The garage itself is less confusing than most, with elevators to the hotels and tram station situated at the northeast corner of each level. On each level about 20% of available spaces are marked "no parking," presumably to accommodate modest pillars that intrude into the parking space. Practically speaking, however, most cars sedan size and smaller could fit very nicely in the verboten spaces.

CityCenter has its own tram gliding between the Bellagio and Monte Carlo resorts with an intermediate stop at Crystals. The Bellagio station serves Vdara; the Crystals station serves Aria, Veer, and Crystals; and the Monte Carlo station serves the Mandarin Oriental and Aria. Riding the tram is a hoot. It's usually full of sightseers who are totally lost. They board the tram with no idea where it's going or where they should get off, hoping it will take them someplace interesting. You'll be peppered with questions if you look like you're not lost.

For pedestrians, the Strip sidewalk is elevated from CityCenter Place to Harmon Avenue. There is also an elevated sidewalk on the latter into the complex, but only along the north side. On CityCenter Place, the walkway gradually inclines 20 feet until it reaches Aria. There is no exterior walkway diagonally across the complex, but the tram will ferry walkers. Otherwise, to reach Vdara or Nancy Rubins' colorful *Big Easy* boat sculpture from CityCenter Place, one must walk through Aria Resort and exit the north entrance, then walk along the circular section of Harmon Avenue. So immense is the complex, there is an on-site fire station and power plant.

Not to be confused with a themed destination, CityCenter is its own unique and original concept.

Aria Resort and Casino at CityCenter
(arialasvegas.com)

THE SHOWPIECE OF CITYCENTER is the ultra-modern Aria Resort and Casino, midpoint in the 67-acre complex. Just as Aria ascends to placement in the Las Vegas skyline, the name derives from an elaborate melody for a single voice rising musically. The 61-story imposing and graceful curved-glass hotel includes 4,004 rooms, an 1,800-seat showroom, nine bars and lounges, a nightclub, 16 restaurants, a spa and salon, shopping arcade, pool deck, sizeable conference center, subterranean parking, and the only casino within the CityCenter development. The structure is comprised of two high, sweeping curvilinear glass towers, two perpendicular wings, and anchored by a low-rise curved base.

The reception area, with lofty windows reaching approximately 40 feet, features a spectacular view of Crystals retail center directly east. From the lobby into the casino, restaurants, hotel rooms, hallways, and public space, natural light is filtered to inner environments via skylights, solar tubes, and sweeping vertical windows. Decor features primarily natural textures: polished and unpolished stone, reclaimed wood, and fresh greenery.

The 150,000-square-foot casino is well configured with natural light streaming through walls of angled windows. Along the edge, private salons house high-end table games and slots, while various zones divide the extensive casino floor into more intimate sections.

Guest rooms and suites are richly appointed with customized furniture. Accents of mocha, taupe, and sienna predominate. Occasional tables are chrome and glass, revealing thick, striped carpet underneath. Kings and double queens are triple sheeted with 300-thread-count sheets and feature patterned bolster pillows under padded wall-mounted headboards. Average room size is 520 square feet. These guest rooms are a techie's delight with keyless locks and one user-friendly remote controlling the temperature, drapes, lights, music, TV, wake-up calls, and other guest services. Work stations can accommodate wired, high-speed, and wireless equipment. Laptops, cameras, MP3 players, and game consoles can be connected to the 42-inch LCD high-def TV. This TV can also be programmed to wake guests through controlled lights, drapes, and music. Safes are large enough to secure a laptop and other valuables. All rooms come with stocked minibars, robes, double closets, and a dresser in the foyer dressing area. As a result of the hotel's unusual squares-on-curves architectural design, every room has front and corner views through floor-to-ceiling windows. Bathrooms feature granite double sinks, benched showers, and comfortable tubs. Ironing boards, twice-daily housekeeping, and turndown service complete the room amenities. Aria does not impose a nightly resort fee surcharge.

At the far end of the casino, escalators draw showgoers up to the elevated multilevel showroom. Still one of the most popular Las Vegas entertainers ever, Elvis has returned and is in the building at Aria. The 1,800-seat showroom presents *Viva Elvis,* a permanent Presley multimedia extravaganza by Cirque du Soleil. Presley music, film clips, live singers, dancers, acrobats, musicians, and tribute artists represent The King of Rock and Roll through the many plateaus of his too-short career. For younger fans, this show provides an excellent opportunity to experience the excitement surrounding the Elvis legacy; for more mature devotees, this is a chance to relive your youth.

International cuisines satisfying every palate abound with 16 restaurants from casual cafes and bistros to steak houses and gourmet dining. Asian cuisine includes Blossom for classic Chinese, Lemongrass for modern Thai, Bar Masa for nouvelle Japanese, and a chic dim sum room within Bar Masa. Presenting European cuisine are Sirio Ristorante for Italian, Spain's Julian Serrano tapas lounge, Jean Georges Steakhouse for steak and seafood, and Jean Philippe Maury's Patisserie Chocolate. Not to be outdone, American cuisine is well represented by Shawn McLain's Sage, Michael Mina's American Fish, Union Restaurant & Lounge, Café Vettro, Skybox Sports Bar and Grill, Roasted Bean, Sweet Chill global soda fountain, and The Buffet. Several themed bars and lounges keep the venues buzzing, while the gigantic HAZE Nightclub throbs with electricity.

At Liquid, the vast 215,000-square-foot elevated pool complex that can accommodate up to 1,500 guests, there are three oval pools, the secluded adult (topless) pool, fountains, and several hot tubs set in a tropical forest of palm, acacia, and pine trees. Fifty cabanas are interspersed among the water features and abundant foliage. Breeze Café provides all-day refreshments.

In addition to a complete menu of international beauty treatments, the 80,000-square-foot, two-level Spa at Aria, the largest in Las Vegas, includes a full-service beauty salon and barbershop, international massage and hydrotherapy treatments, redwood saunas, eucalyptus steam rooms, a salt room, heated stone beds, fitness and group exercise studios, a co-ed balcony pool, meditation rooms, and a tanning area. Spa treatments are available poolside at Liquid.

Aria is a benchmark of sustainable environmental programs. Through contemporary design, water-and-energy conservation measures, use of natural and recycled materials, indoor air filtering, on-site generated power, and extensive use of natural light, CityCenter has earned six coveted Leadership in Energy and Environmental Design (LEED) Gold certifications.

Aria is located on CityCenter Place, which is a west turn at the stoplight on South Las Vegas Boulevard. Proceeding past Crystals shopping district and the leaning towers of Veer, Aria is positioned at the end of CityCenter Place where it circles and returns to the Strip. The hotel's north valet entrance can be reached from Harmon Avenue but is not used for checking in. There is underground parking and valet service beneath the hotel via well-marked down ramps on both CityCenter Place and Harmon Avenue.

Four artists in CityCenter's $40-million public art program are displayed at Aria. At the lower north valet exit on Harmon Circle, Jenny Holzer has created *Vegas,* an elongated LED sign stretching 266 feet and incorporating scrolling text to entertain guests. Three elegant stainless steel columns by sculptor Tony Cragg welcome visitors into the self-parking lobby atrium: *Bolt,* a striking ten-foot-high stainless steel shaft of lightning twisting skyward from a narrow base; *Bent of Mind,* a six-and-a-half-foot illusory facial silhouette; and Untitled, a 15-foot sloping curve. At the mezzanine level, suspended over the Promenade, floats Antony Gormley's *Feeling Material XXVIII,* an eight-foot spiral steel bar conveying the human body and visually suggesting stillness centered in a field of energy. The reception area houses celebrated artist Maya Lin's signature work, *Silver River.* Suspended above the front desk is the 84-foot shimmering interpretation of the Colorado River cast entirely in reclaimed silver. This piece is especially appropriate to Nevada, which is the "Silver State."

Aria Resort and Casino offers an unbeatable blend of visionary architecture, cutting-edge technology, impressive dining, distinguished personalized service, high-adrenalin entertainment, lush surroundings, and environmentally conscious design.

Mandarin Oriental Las Vegas at CityCenter
(mandarinoriental.com/lasvegas)

TRULY A GLOBAL BRAND WITH HOTELS IN 25 COUNTRIES, the Mandarin Oriental Las Vegas is the newest venture of the 41-property international hospitality group. With a prime Strip-front placement, the 47-story glass pillar is the first hotel on the left when entering CityCenter via CityCenter Place. Exuding a refined Asian flavor reminiscent of its corporate origins, the 392-room nongaming boutique hotel provides Eastern hospitality in a Western setting. Half hotel and half condominium, the lower floors are transient accommodations, and the upper half are residences. In the tower's center is the spectacular 23rd-level sky lobby.

After entering the streetside porte cochere, the elevator whisks guests up to check-in on the 23rd floor. This midtower placement of lobby, bars, and restaurants is distinctive, and the skyline view from the Mandarin Bar is one of the best in Las Vegas. Oriental sculptures, pottery, baskets, prints, oil paintings, and occasional pieces are showcased in the understated public areas. Twist features classic haute cuisine with a French twist accompanied by the gorgeous cityscape. The intimate Tea Lounge serves traditional high tea along with a mix of exotic and herbal beverages. MOzen Bistro offers all-day dining with international and pan-Asian fare alongside a theater kitchen near the third-floor, glass-walled conference center. The chain-wide Amore Patisserie provides a casual menu and extravagant desserts on the Strip level.

Merging Asian decor and Western design, the 850-square-foot deluxe rooms have a contemporary look and Eastern zest with dark woods, vibrant red accents, and stylized oriental patterns. Floors are dark wood covered with deep rugs. Duvets and pillows are downy and comfortable. All rooms have walk-in closets and valet privacy closets for room deliveries. Catering to business travelers, accommodations include spacious desks, wireless Internet access, plug-and-play capabilities with room-control technologies managing the entertainment center, drapes, and lights from one component. Bathrooms highlight the skyline view through an exterior window. Another window with a retractable curtain separates the bathroom from the bedroom. Freestanding tubs are an appealing departure from the usual hotel wall-affixed bathtub configuration, and there is a separate glass shower. Flat-panel TVs are embedded in the mirrors with double sinks underneath. There is no resort fee, but the hotel charges for Internet access.

Swimmers will be keen on the two narrow lap pools, an uncommon feature of the eighth-level pool deck. The separated pools are inline: one is 66 feet in length, and the other is 75 feet. Between them is a small center island shaped like a fan—the hotel's logo. White lounges and 20 sage green private cabanas line the perimeter surrounding the pools, two hot tubs, and a plunge. The outdoor Poolside Cafe serves light meals and snacks. A wind wall shields guests from gusts. The soothing bilevel 27,000-square-foot Spa at Mandarin Oriental, located near the pool on the seventh and eighth floors, houses a beauty salon; fitness center; Kinesis body conditioning machines; a tranquility plunge with soothing mineral waters; and yoga, Pilates, and spinning studios. A business center and small conference facility assist business travelers. Cell-phone and laptop rentals are available, as well as secretarial services.

The works of two Japanese artists are prominently displayed within the hotel. The entrance showcases Masatoshi Izumi's *CACTUS Life–living with Earth,* a minutely carved 16-foot basalt lava sculpture honoring balance in nature. The lobby features three glazed ceramic monoliths by Jun Kaneko. These three rotund pieces of the *Untitled Dango Series* are five-and-a-half, six, and seven feet tall and typify their Japanese name "dumpling." Inside the Tea Lounge, Jack Goldstein's fiery eight-by-eight-foot acrylic *Untitled (Volcano)* brings vigor to the quiet setting. In the courtyard near the hotel's entrance is poised *Typewriter Eraser, Scale X.* This celebrated work by Dutch pop artists Claes Oldenburg and Coosje van Bruggen is a four-ton, 19-foot fiberglass and stainless-steel rendering of a huge red-and-blue typewriter eraser. The connecting walkway area is also a great spot to view two murals by Richard Long, which are visible through the lobby windows of Veer Towers across the street. Spectators can see both 72-by-54-foot hand-applied diluted River Avon mud wall paintings *Circle of Chance* and *Earth,* respectively, in the west and east towers. Designed to be seen from a distance, the sculptor references the land and what is seen on it.

Parking and valet service are available at the porte cochere and also beneath the hotel. When entering from the Strip onto CityCenter Place, the left turn to the Mandarin Oriental is in the center of the road and a very short distance in. Be aware that it appears very soon. Some parking is also available in the garage south of the hotel with entry from the Monte Carlo access road. Directly in front of the Mandarin Oriental on the Las Vegas Strip is a pharmacy and souvenir gift shop.

The hotel appeals to globetrotters familiar with the extensive Mandarin Oriental name, business travelers, and tourists wishing to experience the Mandarin's well-deserved reputation for refined Eastern hospitality. With the exception of the occasionally busy sky lobby, the Mandarin Oriental Las Vegas is serene and Zen-like.

Vdara Hotel at CityCenter (vdara.com)

VDARA WAS THE FIRST OF THE FOUR HOTELS at CityCenter to debut. Rising 57 floors into rarified air, the stylish all-suite nonsmoking, nongaming hotel and spa is situated in the northwest quadrant of CityCenter between Aria and Bellagio. Vdara is connected to its sister property, the Bellagio Spa Tower, by an enclosed elevated walkway. Bordering the hotel on the west side is a small park with benches. Just east of the entrance is Karim Rashid's *Seven Continents of the World* sculpture with connecting silver spheres representing the fusion of cultures among land masses. The name "Vdara" was conceived to convey a sense of international sophistication.

An art-infused property, Vdara's main entrance at Harmon Circle is dominated by *Big Edge,* Nancy Rubins' cantilevered 50-by-80-foot work of art incorporating more than 200 colorful aluminum canoes, rowboats, and other small aquatic vessels fused together to create a bouquet of boats in a desert harborage. The abstract Expressionist *Damascus Gate Variation I,* an 8-by-32-foot fluorescent resin work of linked semicircles by Frank Stella, overlooks the reception desk. Marble floors in the lobby echo the painting's semicircular designs. Two vertical stacked die-cut paper tapestries cascade on the east and west walls of the concierge lobby near the elevator bank. Titled *Day for Night, Night for Day* by Peter Wegner, together they parallel sunrise and sunset with appropriate solar and lunar colors reflecting the transition. To reflect the space, Wegner has added an original celestial light fixture suspended between the two pieces. On loan from the Bellagio, *Lucky Dream,* an 8.5-by-14-foot collage of found objects by Robert Rauschenberg, is in the lobby.

The three overlapping, crescent-shaped jet black and silver towers afford wondrous views of Las Vegas and the encompassing mountains. Corner rooms present the most panoramic sight lines. All rooms have heat-reflective horizontal windows. Imparting a residential feel, the expansive and toney 575+-square-foot suites feature king or double-queen bedrooms and a pull-out queen sofa in the living room. The furniture, carpet, and linens are predominantly brunette shades accented by cream, gold, and rust. Eye-catching mocha-and-white-striped light fixtures are wall-mounted. Large bathrooms, some with windows, continue the hotel's spa theme with large soaking tubs and separate benched showers. Low-flow faucets and showers promote water conservation. Amenities include safes, flat-screen TVs, and multiline cordless phones. There is also a media hub for cameras, DVD players, MP3 players, and game consoles. Many accommodations provide a washer-dryer unit. For guests choosing to dine in, all suites are furnished with a refrigerator, stocked minibar, microwave, cook-top stove, and dishwasher. There is 24-hour room service, a food-stocking service, and an on-site mini-mart for provisions. About 1,150 of the hotel's 1,495 suites are for nightly rental; the balance are residential condominiums. Vdara charges a per-night resort fee of $18, which covers local phone calls, newspaper, turndown service, Internet access, fitness center, and two daily bottles of water.

A focal point is Vdara Health and Beauty at levels two and three. This peaceful wood-paneled, 16,000-square-foot spa offers men's and women's salons; three relaxation lounges; eucalyptus steam, sauna, and heated plunge; holistic health treatments; a work-out room equipped with free weights, weight machines, and cardio machines with individual entertainment centers; a spa retail store; and a Champagne-and-smoothie bar with vegan and vegetarian snacks. Shimmering metallic hanging sculptures representing flowing water adorn the space. Personal trainers and fitness classes are available to guests willing to temporarily suspend relaxation.

Executive Chef Martin Heierling has moved next door from the Bellagio and oversees all food services at the property. Market Café Vdara, a gourmet mini-grocery and downsized coffee bar, offers hot and cold sandwiches, salads, crêpes, pastries, foodie snacks, organic offerings, and more. Guests will also find prepackaged fixings for easy in-room cooking and dining. Bar Vdara, the dawn-to-dawn lobby bar and coffee lounge with swings, teardrop lights, and a curved reflecting pool connecting to an outdoor garden is Vdarling.

On the second level above the porte cochere is the landscaped Sky Pool with swimming and dipping options of varying sizes and depths. Gold-and-white chaises and daybeds line the pools, while well-placed awnings shield guests from the desert sun. Among the cabanas is a semisecluded plunge. Sky Lounge on the pool deck serves specialty cocktails, tapas, and appetizers. Loungers gazing skyward have a stunning view of the surrounding urban cityscape.

Parking is valet only at the main entrance. The business center and 10,000-square-foot conference area are near the front desk.

Vdara is a smallish hotel by Las Vegas standards, yet the level of service is high with personal shoppers, a food-stocking service, and top-notch concierges. The staff has an uncanny ability to remember the names of all guests. Vdara has an air of quiet seclusion, a hideaway in the midst of a busy urban center. The resort is ideal for those who favor a more restful and exclusive Las Vegas experience yet desire proximity to CityCenter and access to its nearby action and energy.

Clarion Hotel and Casino (clarionhotel.com)

THE CLARION IS LOCATED ON CONVENTION CENTER DRIVE within five to seven minutes of the Las Vegas Convention Center by foot. Originally the Paddlewheel, it was purchased by Debbie Reynolds and completely renovated. So extensive were Debbie's improvements that she couldn't pay the mortgage and sold the place to, get this, the World Wrestling Federation (now known as World Wrestling Entertainment). WWE turned out to be (big surprise) clueless about running a hotel and sold it to the folks who turned it into the Greek Isles. In summer 2010, Choice Hotels took over the property. Operating with a small, slots-only casino, the Bistro, a pool, and a designed-by-Debbie showroom with bizarrely eclectic entertainment, the property offers nice guest rooms at great rates to convention and trade-show attendees. The Clarion is pet-friendly and a good choice if Fido is vactioning too.

Cosmopolitan of Las Vegas (cosmopolitanlasvegas.com)

THE NEW COSMOPOLITAN OF LAS VEGAS is the latest addition to Las Vegas's inventory of mid-to-high-end uber-resorts. Glittering is the word best ascribed to the unthemed, design-driven property that exudes energy, cool and heat, and an offbeat hipness, making it truly an indie hotel. The hotel's provocative ad campaign reflects its glam image with the "Just the right amount of wrong" catch phrase. Actually, the hotel is just the right amount of right—luxury with a sense of humor. Positioned at the northeast corner of the CityCenter complex, the dual-tower hotel is a 2,995-suite high-rise with a full casino, 14 restaurants, three pools, a showroom, day and night clubs, a spa, a retail arcade, two fitness centers, tennis courts, three floors of meeting space, and subterranean parking. Situated on 8.7 acres, this footprint makes the layout overwhelmingly vertical with plenty of escalators and elevators: ride more, walk less. Pedestrian overpasses along CityCenter lead into the second level, three entrances provide access from the Strip, and there are large foyers at the East and West towers from the West Harmon Road approach.

The literal and figurative centerpiece of the property, and its premier attraction, is the soaring 65-foot showcase chandelier of opulent transparent crystal drapes suspended from the 4th floor. Comprised of two million octagon-shaped crystal beads, these translucent panels enclose three cocktail lounges on three levels. Enjoy a beverage as walls of sparkling curtains shimmer around you.

Epitomizing an affluent lifestyle, the distinctive Terrace Studios, configured as 620-square-foot suites, are spacious and handsomely appointed. Each includes a den with sofa, easy chairs, and a desk separated by a low divider and a small kitchen with microwave, Sub-Zero refrigerator, wine racks, and bar stools. King rooms feature a color scheme of blue, black, brown, and white with dark contemporary furniture and thick chocolate carpet. The latest technology allows guests to book reservations for spa, restaurants, and shows and preset music, lights, heat, and air-conditioning. The suites include two flat-screen TVs and free Internet and Wi-Fi access. Black granite double-sink bathrooms have separate tubs and glassed bench showers. For a few dollars more (is Clint Eastwood in the building?), the slightly larger City Rooms are similarly configured and decorated and offer double-doubles and kings. Most rooms have sliding glass doors opening onto private open-air terraces with cozy wicker loveseats and footstools, allowing guests to relax and enjoy views of the Bellagio's lake and gardens, the close-in towers of CityCenter, the Strip's skyline, or the Las Vegas cityscape. Smoking is allowed on the terraces.

Countless glistening reflective surfaces of clear and colored glass, chrome, metal, marble, tile, crystals, bulbs, and mirrors invigorate the curved 110,000-square-foot casino. Overhead is a rampage of visually voluptuous designer lighting: jewel-like glass leis of red and white lights, square white chandeliers, interlinked chrome and glass hooks, crystal teardrops, and ribbons of gold bulbs that delineate the slot, table games, roulette, and high-limit sections. Sheer fabrics divide gaming sectors but do not minimize the size of the casino. Along the periphery are the 1950s vintage Vesper lounge adjacent the lobby, Book & Stage live entertainment venue with sports wagering, the Queue Bar (so-named for its line-up foyer for the upstairs Marquee nightclub, Henry's Scottish-themed restaurant and bar at the north entrance, and the street-level Bond Bar with high windows enabling guests to watch the mutable patterns of vivid lights and traffic flow along the Strip. Because of horizontal space constraints, the Race and Sports book is not adjacent the casino but located on the second floor. The Chelsea Showroom, booking top-flight non-traditional rock, R&B, and rap acts, is in the fourth-floor convention area.

Three distinct rooftop pools grace the property. Largest is the fourth-floor Boulevard Pool on the east side, which overlooks the Strip and is configured with an infinity pool, heated pool, and Jacuzzis. The play area offers complimentary ping pong, volleyball, croquet, a pool table, Play Station, and other kids' games for multi-generational kids. Cozy ivy-trimmed cabanas for two line the walkway. The Overlook is a six-level sunning and shading terrace with lounges, daybeds, and tables with umbrellas. A stage provides entertainment, including summer concerts, and movies can be watched on the marquee. The Overlook Bar and Grill serves alfresco small plates and blue plate specials. The Marquee Club Day Pool on the south side has four levels of lounges, tables, and umbrellas along with three-story cabana lofts. In the evening it is an extension of the nightclub. The 14th floor's permanently sunlit southern exposure houses the curving Bamboo Pool. Blue umbrellas, chaises, and daybeds line the deck. Stationary in-pool mattresses recline at the edge, and two gigantic shower heads with warm and cool water are suspended over the rim. Ten cabanas dot the perimeter. A bar with flat-screen TVs allows additional visual distractions.

The posh four-level Marquee nightclub is divided into three sections: the small Boom Box with high-tech audio and visual; the quiet (really!) Library looks like an English club with dark woods, deep leather chairs and divans, pool tables, and a library of books about Las Vegas; and the three-stage main club opens onto the private area of the Boulevard Pool.

All 14 restaurants make their Las Vegas debut at the Cosmo, and 7 are clustered on the third floor: José Andrés' Jaleo tapas bar; D.O.C.G. wine bar serving Italian comfort food; Scarpetta, offering seasonal Italian cuisine; high-end STK chop house with on-site DJ; Comme Ça, an atypical French brasserie; Estiatorio Milos with fresh Mediterranean fish and crustaceans flown in daily; and Blue Ribbon Bar and Grill for Japanese fusion. Framed menus are mounted at all host counters. The restaurant lobby lounge is embellished with historic photos of Las Vegas celebrities, a pool table, trendy easy chairs, a working record player plus hundreds of 45 rpm records, and classic books to help pass the time while awaiting your table.

The high-end, second-floor cavalcade of shops features retailers who have no brick-and-mortar stores elsewhere in Las Vegas. These include Molly Brown's (as in unsinkable) Swim Wear; Beckley women's wear; RetroSpecs & Co. eyewear; EatDrink wines and gourmet gifts; Stitched menswear; Monogram gifts and apparel; DNA 2050 denim; CRSNR sneakers; Jason of Beverly Hills jewelry; Skins beauty and fragrance products; AllSaints heritage-influenced apparel, which displays a century of sewing machines and spindles; and the automated U*tique for luxury essentials. Dining options on this floor include Va Bene café, Holstein's burgers and franks, and China Poblano with noodles and tacos to take out or eat in. Tucked away in the convention area is the Wicked Spoon buffet. For a great photo opportunity, check out the giant spike heels along the corridor.

The serene Sahra ("desert") Spa and Hammam offers holistic treatments in a 30,000-square-foot Turkish- and Moroccan-themed facility designed with native desert materials. There is a cool mist room; a monsoon cave with waterfall; a Turkish hammam providing traditional detox, steam, and cool bath therapies; rain shower, steam, hot, and cool baths; and hot tubs. The Violet Salon provides hair, nail, and other beauty services. There are 30 treatment rooms for Thai, Turkish, Swedish, Champi, or Shiatsu massages; scrubs, baths, and soaks; hot stones; and reflexology. Calming Berber music plays throughout.

Each tower has its own fitness center. The larger 5,250-square-foot 14th-floor gym in the West Tower overlooks the tennis courts and at the far end features a boxing studio with regulation ring for sparring. Both facilities provide every conceivable model of exercise machine on the market. Outdoor pilates and yoga classes or individual instruction can be scheduled. The smaller 14th-floor 2,087-square-foot East Tower gym is open 24 hours.

In the lobby, eight colossal high-def video pillars specially created for the hotel display continuous loops of video art to entertain guests waiting in the long registration lines. Too few counters and only four kiosks for automated check-in mean significant waits. To compensate, a staff of floaters with iPads monitors the area to assist guests. Concierges are stationed throughout the main floor, including the casino, to provide more accessibility and service to guests.

In keeping with CityCenter's commitment to public art, the Cosmopolitan takes it to a new level: the entire property is a gallery of non-traditional art forms or, based on one's frame of reference, an art gallery with casino. At P3 art studio visitors can observe on-site artists creating art. Cutting-edge creativity prevails in new mediums: from the aforementioned lobby columns to the commissioned garage graffiti; mounted video panels; abstract wall murals; LED displays; floating shapes suspended on slot machine screens and in elevators; the four-sided electronic rooftop marquee with revolving artwork; and faux cigarette machines dispensing diminutive original pieces of jewelry, prints, ceramics, and watercolor or oil paintings.

Vehicle entry into the hotel's expansive porte cochere is on West Harmon Road, the north entrance into CityCenter. Drivers need to pay attention because at the entry several lanes quickly converge into separate driveways for valet, guest registration, and ramps leading down to the underground garage's five floors where walls blaze with intricate graffiti art. Glass elevators at both ends whisk guests to the casino and restaurant-retail levels. Avoid the north exit, which leads to a small alley with right turn only, crossing the busy sidewalk on the Strip. Day and night, the wait to turn is interminable as pedestrians stroll by.

The target guest market for the Cosmo is sophisticated urban dwellers and travelers with a taste for the offbeat. The Cosmopolitan is fun and mildly unconventional. While the resort is a serious contender for the Las Vegas visitor, the refreshing impression imparted by the hotel is that it does not take itself too seriously and exudes a sense of fun. Adding to its popularity quotient is its no-resort-fee policy.

Days Inn at Wild Wild West (wwwesthotelcasino.com)

LOCATED JUST WEST OF THE STRIP AT Exit 37 off I-15 at Tropicana Avenue, Wild Wild West is a small, 260-room hotel and casino that is convenient to the Strip, downtown, and the airport. Its guest rooms, renovated in 2009, are cheerful and comfortable. For east-facing rooms, however, there is a lot of road noise from I-15. The casino offers mostly slots and video poker, with a few table games and a sports book thrown in to keep up appearances. There is a lounge, a pool and Jacuzzi, and in case you're packing a pig, a barbecue pit. The adjacent Wild Wild West Truck Plaza offers more than 15 acres of paved and lighted parking, security patrol, and easy access from I-15. Also available are diesel and unleaded fuel, a truck wash, convenience store, and weigh station. Wild Wild West markets to locals and truckers.

El Cortez (elcortezhotelcasino.com)

SEVERAL BLOCKS EAST OF THE CENTRAL downtown casino area, El Cortez caters to seniors, motor-coach tours, and blue-collar locals. The large, rambling casino is congested and bustling; the slots are the major draw. The oldest original casino in Las Vegas, El Cortez until 2006 had the aesthetic appeal of a garment factory, with narrow aisles, low ceilings, and slot machines packed into every conceivable crevice. The crowded aisles and low ceilings remain, but El Cortez has undergone a good plussing up, including a top-to-bottom renovation of its guest rooms. It's not the Four Seasons, but the rooms are very nice and a great bargain. Also, El Cortez just reopened the old 100-room Ogden House as the 64-room Cabana Suites, with a gym and business center. Food and drink at El Cortez are reasonably priced, and the loose slots give patrons a lot of play for their money. There is considerable Las Vegas history in El Cortez; one section of the original building appears just as it did when the casino opened in 1941.

Ellis Island Casino and Brewery (ellisislandcasino.com)

ELLIS ISLAND, ON KOVAL LANE NEAR HARMON AVENUE just minutes from the Strip, is the most modest casino imaginable, but a treasure for those in the know. Its $8 complete New York Strip–steak dinner has been among the best meal deals in town for years. Wash it down with a crafted beer from the on-site microbrewery. The casino is joined at the hip to an equally modest Super 8 hotel.

Excalibur (excalibur.com)

THE EXCALIBUR IS A HOTEL IN TRANSITION, attempting to chunk its family business for a more adult, middle-income market. Although it's difficult to transform a medieval-themed casino the size of an airplane hanger, Excalibur has succeeded to a remarkable degree. The new hotel lobby, as well as the casino, are tasteful, with dark woods and stylish lighting fixtures. Gone are the cheap plastic look rendered in a Wal-Mart color palette and the ridiculous faux Knights of the Round Table artifacts. There are still vestiges of Ozzie and Harriet's decorating touch, but the Excalibur no longer assaults the senses like it did in the good olde days.

The guest rooms likewise are in the process of a makeover. Here the medieval theme has been mercilessly exorcised and replaced by surprisingly luxurious rooms replete with 42-inch flat-panel TVs, plush bedding, dark-wood furnishings, and contemporary baths. Though the windows are not huge, the views are great.

Excalibur's restaurants and shops are on the top floor of three levels. On the lower floor is a midway-type games arcade and the showroom, where jousting tournaments are featured. Other entertainment offerings include a male strip show and a Bee Gees tribute show. A primitive motion simulator (it was the worst virtual ride in Las Vegas) has been replaced with a zippy SpongeBob SquarePants 4-D ride. The cavernous middle level contains the casino.

The Excalibur is (for the moment) the tenth-largest hotel in the world and the sixth-largest in Las Vegas, and it certainly features the world's largest hotel parking lot (so far removed from the entrance that trams are dispatched to haul in patrons). If you can get past the parking-lot commute and the fact that most guest rooms have showers only (no tubs), and you do not object to joining the masses, there is good value at the Excalibur. The food is good and economically priced, as is the entertainment. The staff is friendly and accommodating, and you won't go deaf or blind, or become claustrophobic, in the casino. A high-energy nightclub, several pools, a spa, and a workout facility round out Excalibur's product mix. If you need a change of pace, a covered walkway connects the Excalibur with the Luxor next door, pedestrian bridges provide direct access to New York–New York and the Tropicana, and an overhead train runs to Luxor and Mandalay Bay.

Fiesta Henderson (fiestahendersonlasvegas.com)

FIESTA HENDERSON'S PARENT COMPANY, Station Casinos, has stripped this property of its stuffed monkeys and lions (it was formerly The Reserve) and made it southwestern/Mexican in flavor. Located southeast of Las Vegas at the intersection of I-515 and West Lake Mead Drive, Fiesta Henderson offers a 37,000-square-foot casino, a 12-screen movie theater, three restaurants, a buffet, a food court, and three bars. As is the case with all Station casinos, the Fiesta Henderson caters primarily to locals.

Fiesta Rancho (fiestarancholasvegas.com)

THE FIESTA RANCHO WAS THE FIRST of two casinos to be situated at the intersection of Rancho Drive and Lake Mead Boulevard in North Las Vegas (the other is Texas Station). With 100 guest rooms and a video-poker-packed, 40,000-square-foot casino (including the Spin City annex), the Fiesta features an Old Mexico theme. Entertainment includes a lounge, a nightclub, and a $40-million ice arena. Restaurants specializing in southwestern food are the Fiesta's major draw. An excellent buffet features a mesquite grill. A food court and a Denny's round out the dining options. There is a very basic outdoor swimming pool and, perhaps equally enticing on a hot day, a tequila bar (20 different margaritas—*olé*!). The Fiesta depends primarily on local clientele.

Fitzgeralds (fitzgeraldslasvegas.com)

LOCATED DOWNTOWN, FITZGERALDS ANCHORS the east end of the Glitter Gulch section of Fremont Street. After filing for bankruptcy in 2002, the hotel was purchased by Don Barden, which made him Nevada's first African American casino owner. The casino is large and compartmentalized, with gold press-metal ceilings, mirrored columns, and print carpet. Completely renovated, the casino has largely abandoned its signature "luck-of-the-Irish" theme. While the new look is more consistent with the clean, polished style pioneered by the Golden Nugget, Fitzgeralds has sacrificed much of its traditional warmth and coziness.

Rooms on the upper floors of the Fitz afford some of the best views in town, and corner rooms with hot tubs are a great bargain. There's a streetside swimming pool for cooling off. The Fitz's registered guests tend to be older travelers and retirees from the Midwest. In the casino, the crowd is a mixed bag of regulars and bargain hunters lured by ads for free gifts in the local visitor guides.

Flamingo (flamingolasvegas.com)

BUILT WITH GANGSTER MONEY in the 1940s and acquired by the Hilton hotel chain in 1970, and more recently by Caesars Entertainment, the Flamingo is an oasis in the desert. When you're feeling the need for lush green other than the casino kind, head there. True to its name, the Flamingo's nature theme is in full play, especially in the public spaces. With a tropical panorama behind the registration desk, grass-themed bathroom stalls, and real plants lining the escalator, the Flamingo is an organic reprieve from the clanking slot machinery that runs the Strip. Its heart is a 15-acre Caribbean-style water playground adjacent to a large wildlife habitat that is home to Chilean flamingos, swans, ducks, koi, turtles, and foliage from around the world. Maybe best of all, you don't have to be a guest to take a stroll through this sliver of paradise.

Begun by notorious "businessman" Bugsy Siegel in 1946—once a tourist attraction in itself—this venerable hotel was the first super-resort on the Strip. Today, with its 3,300-plus rooms and suites, four towers, and prime location, it is the Queen Mother of the Strip's most prestigious block, surrounded by Bally's, Bill's Gamblin' Hall, the Imperial Palace, Caesars Palace, Harrah's, and the Bellagio. Hilton, predictably, curbed the excesses of the colorful previous owners and transformed the Flamingo from a Las Vegas exaggeration into a very dependable hotel. Today, the Flamingo is flashier than Bally's (its sister property that also caters to business travelers). It is also less formal, offering an ambience comfortable to leisure and business travelers.

Bugsy would be very proud of the newly remodeled 77,000-square-foot Caribbean-style casino with more than 1,600 slot machines, 70 gaming tables, and race and sports book broadcasting results on wide-screen TVs. The large, bustling casino's bright neon pinks, magentas, and tangerines established the Flamingo's identity more than four decades ago, but the rooms and services are standard Hilton. The Flamingo has consistent restaurants, a pretty good buffet, varied showroom productions, and truly creative lounge entertainment, in addition to boasting one of the top swimming areas in town.

The hotel's clientele comes in all colors and sizes, and from all over the country (but especially Southern California). The Flamingo actively cultivates the Japanese market and also does a strong business with tour wholesalers. Because it has one of the most diverse customer bases of any Las Vegas hotel, the Flamingo likewise has a very broad comfort zone.

Four Queens (fourqueens.com)

THE FOUR QUEENS, SITUATED IN THE HEART of downtown, offers good food, respectable hotel rooms, and a positively cheery casino. Joining its neighbor, the Golden Nugget, as a member of the "All Right to Be Bright Club," the Four Queens casino was among the first to abandon the standard brothel red in favor of a glistening, light decor offset by a tropical-print carpet. The result, as at the Golden Nugget, is a gaming area that feels fun, upbeat, and clean. Loyal Four Queens hotel guests tend to be middle-aged or older and come from Southern California, Texas, Hawaii, and the Midwest. The Four Queens also caters to the motor-coach-tour market. In the casino there is a mix of all ages and backgrounds. Locals love Hugo's Cellar restaurant, a Las Vegas landmark.

Four Seasons (fourseasons.com/lasvegas)

FOUR SEASONS HOTELS AND MANDALAY RESORT GROUP (now MRI) combined to introduce a new concept to Las Vegas: the hotel within a hotel. The Four Seasons is an exclusive 424-room, noncasino hotel contained by the greater Mandalay Bay megaresort.

You can get to Four Seasons from within Mandalay Bay, but just barely: You walk almost behind the Mandalay Bay front desk, pass through two sets of double service doors, climb down a spiral staircase, and blunder into the Four Seasons lobby. Signs are few and small. This is the "back" entrance; Four Seasons prefers you to use the main, front, valet entrance, which is right off the Strip, a little south of Mandalay Bay's entrance.

You can access Mandalay Bay from Four Seasons by backtracking or by taking the private elevator to the casino level. You can also walk up the stairs at the Four Seasons elevator bay (the elevators are a pretty long hike from the front desk).

The lobby area has a plush feel, decorated with wood, Victorian sofas and easy chairs, a grand piano, and even a fireplace—a 1930s, New York atmosphere that's very different (and pleasingly so) from Las Vegas in the new millennium. Off the lobby is a 60-seat sitting area and a second lounge that fronts the Charlie Palmer Steak gourmet room. There's also Verandah, the most exclusive coffee shop in town. Its giant French doors open onto the Four Seasons' private pool area, where you can also dine al fresco. The pool has lush foliage, a spa, and cabanas, which are kept cool and refreshing by misters.

Four Seasons' 424 rooms are on the 35th to 39th floors of the Mandalay Bay tower. Private express elevators deliver guests to the Four Seasons' floors. Housekeepers provide turndown service before bedtime.

Four Seasons will appeal to ultra-upscale travelers looking for a mini-oasis that insulates them from the hullabaloo of Las Vegas. But it doesn't come cheaply. You're paying for the "brandness" as much as the grandness, and plenty of better values are nearby (even in the same building).

Fremont (fremontcasino.com)

THE FREMONT IS ONE OF THE LANDMARKS of downtown Las Vegas. Acquired by the Boyd family in 1985, the Fremont offers good food, budget lodging, and a robust casino. Several years ago they redecorated and considerably brightened the casino, which is noisy and crowded. The table games are roomily accommodated beneath a high ceiling ringed in neon, while the slots are crammed together along narrow aisles like turkeys on their way to market. Locals love the Fremont, as do Asians, Hawaiians, and the inevitable Southern Californians. The Fremont, like all Boyd properties, is friendly, informal, and comfortable.

Gold Coast (goldcoastcasino.com)

THE GOLD COAST, A HALF MILE WEST of the strip on Flamingo Road, is a favorite hangout for locals. A casual inspection of the Gold Coast reveals nothing unique: no fantasy theme, no special decor or atmosphere. But the Gold Coast does pay attention to detail and has the local market wired. It serves one of the best breakfast specials in town, has one of the top buffets for quality and value, provides lounge entertainment at all hours of the day, offers headliners and modest production shows in its showroom, and makes sure it has the locals' favorite kind of slots. To top things off, it also has a huge bowling complex. Free transportation is provided throughout the day to the casino's sister property, the Orleans, as well as to the Strip.

Gold Spike (goldspike.com)

SITUATED DOWNTOWN AND ABOUT A four-minute walk from the heart of Fremont Street, the Gold Spike is basically a slot joint. The current owners have upgraded the casino and refurbished the hotel rooms to the tune of $3.5 million. The casino has been renovated from top to bottom, and though still diminutive, it's as pleasant a place to enjoy the slots and video poker as you'll find downtown. Guest rooms have gone from being among the seediest to among the nicest downtown. Decor and appointments are modern, and amenities include flat-panel TVs. Windows are small, and even if they weren't, there's nothing to look at. Dining is limited to the 24-hour Golden Grill.

Golden Gate (goldengatecasino.net)

THE OLDEST HOTEL IN LAS VEGAS, the Golden Gate is a vintage property with an even more vintage casino. Retaining its historical flavor, the interior is little changed since the hotel opened in 1906 as the Hotel Nevada at 1 Fremont Street directly across from the train depot. Tucked in the back by the side entrance on Main Street is the antique brass-trimmed front desk and small lobby with period furniture. Pillars, dark woods, chandeliers, carved glass, and mirrors in the low-ceilinged gaming area create the illusion that you're gambling during the Roaring Twenties. The flapper-costumed Dancing Dealers add nightly fun to this ambiance.

The aura at today's four-story Golden Gate is old is new again. The remodeled guest rooms are beyond compact, and none of the 106 rooms are similar in size and configuration, reminiscent of a time before building codes and uniformity. Rooms are decorated in a black, white, and rose red color scheme. Queens and double-doubles are available. Bathrooms are tiny with stall showers.

As the Hotel Nevada, the Golden Gate was assigned Las Vegas's first telephone number ("1") and proudly displays the town's first telephone along with old ledgers, registers, and other historical documents from the era. In the 1930s, the hotel was inanely called the Sal Sagev (Las Vegas reversed) but was rechristened the Golden Gate in 1951 when new owners from San Francisco took over. The same family has owned and managed the property ever since.

Home to the original and still famous shrimp cocktail, the casino's rear deli is dedicated to serving this honorable $1.99 snack to hundreds of customers weekly. Also on-site is Du-Par's, with old-fashioned counter service and booths from the hotel's original restaurant. One of the casino's two permanent outside bars on Fremont Street features bar-top dancers, frozen drinks, and beer, while the other refreshment stand spotlights Flair bartenders whose cocktail-creation skills are showstoppers. The hotel appeals to the budget-minded, Gen Xers interested in a historic hotel, as well as old-timers reliving Las Vegas's very early days.

Golden Nugget (goldennugget.com)

THE UNDISPUTED FLAGSHIP OF THE DOWNTOWN hotels and one of the most meticulously maintained and managed properties in Las Vegas, the Golden Nugget is smack in the middle of Glitter Gulch. The hotel offers newly renovated bright, cheery rooms, a showroom, plus lounge entertainment, excellent restaurants, a large pool, a first-rate spa, a shopping arcade, a workout room, two on-site Starbucks, and a chapel and wedding planner. The casino is clean and breezy, with white enameled walls and white lights. The feel here is definitely upscale, though comfortable and informal. There is breathing room at the Golden Nugget, and an atmosphere that suggests a happy, more fun-filled approach to gambling.

The Golden Nugget recently underwent a $200-million renovation and expansion, the first since 1973 for the perpetual AAA Four-Diamond Award winner. At the heart of the new, improved Golden Nugget are a 500-room hotel tower and the renovated 600-seat showroom. Other elements of the makeover include a new covered porte cochere, a new VIP lounge, Vic and Anthony's steak house, and Lillie's Asian Cuisine specializing in Cantonese and Szechuan fare. Plus, the spa and fitness center has been modernized and expanded. The most intriguing touch is the reconfiguration of the swimming complex to surround a 30-foot-deep shark aquarium. (More on that below.) Overlooking the aquarium is a revamped buffet, and integrated into the shark tank and pool is Grotto, a trattoria-style Italian restaurant.

The Golden Nugget's recently opened 25-floor smoke-free [Gold] Rush Tower brings Strip-scene energy to Downtown's premium property. Located on the west side of the hotel's footprint, where First Street right-angles Carson Avenue, the hotel facade on both streets (along with the parking garage opposite) have been repainted russet and gold. Beautifying the Carson Avenue entrance, medians are landscaped with palms, and the new tower has a separate porte cochere with valet parking. The 500 Rush rooms are 20% larger than the rest of the hotel's inventory, with a marginally higher rate. Boasting a brown, orange, and gold palette with cream down comforters and linens, beige carpet, a dark leather sectional and ottoman, and a desk, the rooms resemble an upscale condo and impart a southwestern Zen flavor. Original oil paintings created by the hotel's artists soften the bronze walls. Each unit includes a DVD player, iPod docking station, Internet access, and flat-panel TV. The sizable bathrooms feature parquet floors, oversize tub–glass shower combos, double raised sinks, and stylish brushed chrome fixtures. A separate make-up vanity adjoins the bathroom. King rooms make up 95% of the tower's inventory.

Snaking through the Rush lobby is a dazzling white, umber, and yellow crystal chandelier, which coils above the registration counter. The area includes two new restaurants: Red Sushi and Chart House, housing a 75-gallon coral reef fish tank surrounded by turquoise walls and floors. Upstairs is Gold Diggers nightclub with an above-bar stage where guests can strut their above-average stuff. There's also a splendid outdoor patio overlooking the Fremont Street Experience. Popular impressionist and comedian Gordie Brown impresses Tuesday through Saturday in the reconfigured showroom.

The updated three-level Tank aquatorium was voted among the "Top Ten Extreme Pools" by the Travel Channel. The focal point is a 30-foot-deep 200,000-gallon carnivorous fish aquarium, which sharks call home. A three-story yellow tube shoots thrill seekers down an elongated chute that becomes clear acrylic straight through the shark habitat...all the better to see you with, my dear. The property's signature colors of goldenrod and orange overtake every striped chaise, daybed, awning, and lounge. H2O offers drinks and snacks amid a fire pit with multi-pillowed seating. Blackjack is available at shaded gaming tables. The circular second level includes seven private cabanas; the third level features the Hideout, with a bar and lounge, warm-water infinity pool, and six more cabanas. Tank hours are 10 a.m.–5 p.m., and the Hideout is open until 2 a.m.

In the lobby near the hotel's display of authentic golden nuggets, you can purchase gold from an untraditional ATM Machine. GOLD-to-go dispenses 24-karat gold bars in seven weight choices from one gram to 250 grams. With spot pricing, the price can fluctuate every 10 minutes depending on the gold market. Gold coins and Golden Nugget souvenir pieces are also available. Each is presented in a gift box. Cash only!

Though the Golden Nugget has always been downtown's prestige address, the new hotel tower and top-to-bottom makeover will catapult the Nugget into the rarified atmosphere of the premiere Strip resorts. More, the Golden Nugget's renovation and expansion may well be the investment gamble that triggers the metamorphosis of all of downtown Las Vegas.

The Golden Nugget is popular with Hawaiians and Pacific Islanders and also appeals to Texans and the Southern California drive-in market. Younger travelers (ages 28 to 39) like the Golden Nugget, as do older tourists and retirees, many of whom arrive on motor-coach tours.

Green Valley Ranch Resort, Spa, and Casino (greenvalleyranchresort.com)

IF YOU LIKE PAMPERING AND FRESH AIR with your gambling and dining, you'll love Green Valley Ranch. This Mediterranean-Mission–style, indulgent retreat, perched on a hill overlooking the distant Strip and the mountains, is in an upscale residential area about 15 minutes southeast of the Strip at the intersection of Green Valley Parkway and the I-215 Beltway. The property offers a 490-room hotel, a casino with 55 table games and more than 2,650 slot and video-poker machines, eight restaurants (including a buffet), a spa, and a ten-screen cinema complex. Like all Station casinos, Green Valley Ranch provides locals with high-pay slots, good dining value, an excellent players club, and high-quality lounge entertainment.

Unlike most Station casinos, however, Green Valley Ranch is very upscale. The restaurants are trendy, featuring some of Las Vegas's best-known chefs. Watering holes include the elegant Drop Bar, the Lobby Bar, and Quinn's Irish Pub. The hotel and its enfolding guest rooms are truly luxurious. Many of the guest rooms feature great views of the pool and spa areas and/or the desert and Strip beyond.

The eight-acre pool complex is lovely, more resembling a country-club setting than that of a Las Vegas hotel. Features include vanishing-edge pools near the spa and a large, centrally located swimming pool that has a sandy beach at one end, perfect for the kids. There is also a small grassy playground area for children.

Dining options abound. Hank's is a plush, masculine chophouse and martini bar. Other fine-dining options include Terra Verde and the ultra-hip Sushi + Sake. The Feast Buffet is one of Las Vegas's best, and for those who like their carbs served with butter and maple syrup, there's an Original Pancake House. An informal Chinese bistro and a food court complete the culinary collage.

The 30,000-square-foot spa is a real star. The curving path from the hotel proper to the relaxation center is lined by a small vineyard offset by red roses. In addition to a wonderful array of treatments, the soothing architectural aesthetics at Green Valley do their part in providing a higher-quality experience. For example, the gym here is filled with light that pours in through a window wall. On the treadmills you can meditate on the Zen sculpture arising from the three-lane lap pool or contemplate the Spring Mountains. The steam room has an outdoor view. Pilates and yoga classes are held in a perfect wood, glass, and mirrored high-ceilinged studio.

Located within easy striking distance of Lake Mead, Hoover Dam, the Black Canyon of the Colorado, and Red Rock Canyon, Green Valley Ranch offers a super option for families, the outdoor-oriented traveler, and for those who believe in the healing powers of being pampered.

Hard Rock Hotel (hardrockhotel.com)

HARD ROCK HOTEL AND CASINO, living up to its name, honestly rocks around the clock. Here the heart of rock and roll beats 24/7. The hotel is fun, comfortable, and informal. Powerful music elevates the energy level with a constant percussive in-your-ears din.

After a $750-million expansion, the Hard Rock tops out at 1,506 rooms. The addition of a 40,000-square-foot casino, three restaurants, an upgraded spa, Harmon Avenue porte cochere and parking garage, and two new towers of power repositions the small property to medium size and provides more pampering and amenities. HRH has become a major player in the quest for tourists and casino guests.

The 18-floor Paradise Tower, the larger of the two towers, presents 490 tribal tattoo rock-and-roll decadent rooms. Each guest room features dark wood furniture; a maroon leather headboard; and black, brown, and cream accessories. Red or chocolate wallpaper with a matching carpet design distinguishes each room, and all the high-tech bells and whistles are included. Dual armoires with smoky mirrors replace the closets. Bathrooms are spacious but offer showers only. This tower is convenient to the conference area. Request a poolside room for a voyeur's view overlooking the tropical gardens..

The all-suite HRH Tower, with a higher level of service, appeals to an older, more affluent demographic. The tower's subdued lobby with blond marble counters and leather couches provides guests with a private registration area. A Kiss photo montage tapestry, a gigantic hologram of Jimi Hendrix, and Michael Jackson's $50,000 sequined white glove grace the lobby's black walls.

The guest rooms maintain a clean, contemporary look in muted beige, white, and black with parquet floors at the entry. In the bathrooms, dark tile walls and walk-in showers contrast with light tile floors and white bathtubs. A glass wall divides the bedroom and bath, with an optional curtain providing privacy. Every room features a wet bar and photos and lithographs of iconic rock stars. A detached wall with back-to-back wide-screen TVs divides the sitting area and bedroom. No closets again, but armoires suffice. Guests will want to rock out all night to the in-room Sound Matters Sound Bar jukebox with 2,000 songs available at a touch. You can choose a genre, artist, or decade and download songs to your own iPod.

The Hard Rock's expansion includes a 40,000-square-foot casino extension where The Joint (Las Vegas's first rock venue) used to be. This ancillary casino is more spacious and features an international pit offering Asian-preferred games: pai gow, baccarat, mini- and midi-baccarat, slots, and a high-limit room. Both casinos exhibit museum-quality rock memorabilia. The upsized Joint showroom, which presents legendary guitarist Carlos Santana in residence, seats 4,000 and features top rock artists. While the sound system is state-of-the-art, the floor-seating configuration is not inclined, so sight lines are poor from the middle and rear of the showroom.

The 25,000-square-foot Reliquary Water Sanctuary & Spa creates a luxurious experience in spartan surroundings. Patterned tile floors and walls are the only trim—no plants or *objets d'art* soften the pristine look. Although there are detached areas for men and women, the high-decibel bathhouse and lounge are co-ed, so fraternizing is encouraged. Twenty-one treatment rooms include an area for couples massage with a tub and four-person party rooms with treatment beds and TVs for bachelor and bachelorette groups. The spa's signature treatment is the Ancient Cane Ritual, combining sugar exfoliation with a deep-pressure bamboo reed body rollover to rebalance energy flow. Atypical is the pole-dance studio with group lessons for bachelorette parties. The small fitness center has 26 machines and an adjoining hair salon. With the opening of Reliquary, the downstairs Rock Spa is now a well-equipped fitness center with a 53-machine gym, steam room, and Jacuzzi (open 6 a.m–9 p.m.).

The extensive Beach Club pool complex is notorious for its televised anything goes Rehab parties. Five pools are divided into two sections, with the walled Rehab zone imposing a cover charge on afternoons when a TV crew is filming. An elevated infinity pool adjoins the Skybar and Restaurant and overlooks the shallow dish pool. The complex features island-themed evening concerts. Avoid the Rehab side on summertime Sundays if you're seeking solitude and the sounds of silence.

The 14,000-square-foot Vanity Nightclub (formerly Body English), open Friday–Sunday, is adorned with antique mirrors, crystals, pearl light fixtures, diamond patterns, and shiny copper walls pierced with metallic gold threads. Above the dance floor is the centerpiece $1-million cyclone chandelier comprised of 20,000 LED lights that can produce a technicolor image, text, or movies. Unlike other clubs, Vanity boasts open seating. A fire pit dominates the casual outdoor patio overlooking the Beach Club.

Along the casino perimeter and in the shopping arcade are restaurants Ago (Italian), Nobu, Pink Taco, Rare 120 Steakhouse, Mr. Lucky's cafe, and Starbucks. The Espumoso coffee and smoothie bar in the Paradise Tower lobby offers light Latin snacks. Boutiques include Rocks (jewelry), Love Jones (lingerie), Affliction (trendwear), Fuel (sundries), Hart & Huntington Tattoo Co., and John Varvatos (men's clothing with a bandstand and musical instrument array where shoppers can jam or be jammed). Adjacent to the hotel in front of the property is the legendary Hard Rock Cafe; although it's separately owned and operated, the two Hard Rock enterprises maintain a cordial relationship.

Situated three-quarters of a mile east of the Strip, the Hard Rock's Paradise Road at Harmon Avenue location eliminates many of the traffic hassles confronting Strip visitors and gives guests excellent access to the airport, Las Vegas Convention Center, and major freeways I-15, I-215, and I-95. HRH caters to all ages but targets the hip and wannabes primarily from Southern California, the Midwest, Canada, and Asia. Lots of satisfaction here, but it's not for the faint of heart or hard of hearing. If you're a rock fan from any era, this is rock and roll heaven if you don't mind the constant ear-numbing wall of sound.

Harrah's (harrahslasvegas.com)

A LAS VEGAS STAPLE, JAZZY HARRAH'S occupies the middle of the Strip's most prestigious block and is within easy walking distance of Bally's, the Flamingo, the Mirage, Caesars Palace, Paris, Bellagio, the Venetian, and T. I. Unpretentious and upbeat, Harrah's offers 2,652 guest rooms as well as a beautiful showroom, a comedy club, above-average restaurants, a buffet alongside the casino, a dance club, a pool, an exercise room, and a spa.

Harrah's theme celebrating carnival and Mardi Gras is evident in the two giant gold-leaf court jesters hefting a ten-ton, 22-foot-diameter globe that first welcome you on either side of the main hotel entrance, and a gold-swirled ceiling above the registration area continues the theme. The casino is decorated with brightly colored confetti-patterned carpet, ceiling murals, and fiber-optic lighting. Although the theme treatment is bright, it sports a somewhat tired feeling, rather like a Mardi Gras dawn.

The L-shaped casino of 87,000 square feet is loud beyond average. It can be entered directly from the Strip alongside an open-air lounge with very talented "show" bartenders and a stage that hosts mostly rock music. This covered amphitheater adds to the raucous, let-loose feeling of Harrah's, but might interrupt the sleep of some guests.

Though it is hard to imagine anyone not feeling comfortable at Harrah's, its clientele tends to be older visitors from the Midwest and Southern California, as well as business and convention travelers.

Other enticements include a large but otherwise unremarkable swimming area where you get sound bleed from the outdoor stage, a cozy upscale steak house with a view of the Strip, and an outdoor plaza with fountains. With its "Let the good times roll" spirit, Harrah's is an interesting blend of modern and vintage Las Vegas.

Hooters Casino Hotel (hooterscasinohotel.com)

LET'S GET ONE THING SETTLED AT THE BEGINNING. If you like Hooters—the chain of restaurants featuring hot wings and other pub grub served by waitresses in tight T-shirts and hot pants—then you will love the Hooters Casino Hotel. If you don't like Hooters restaurants, you won't much care for this place either, as the Hooters "mystique" is omnipresent from the casino floor to the hotel rooms (the latter even replaces typical hotel chairs with Hooters-style barstools). However, if you're not constitutionally averse to the brand, you might be surprised at how well the restaurateurs transformed the darkly dank San Remo into this bright, happening, and admittedly fun place. The casino floor looks remarkably like a Hooters restaurant, with the same light blonde wood, cheerful lighting, and simple orange accents. A large Hooters-like square bar greets you at the front door. At the gaming tables, rotating shifts of dealers are often attired in full Hooters uniform, right down to the orange hot pants. In addition to a pleasant lounge and coffee shop, there's an actual Hooters restaurant inside as well, and it draws huge lines of eager diners at peak times. A decent-sized pool dominates the back of the hotel, complete with waterfall, pool bar, and stage for live music. The reasonable room rates, utter lack of pretension or attitude, and party-hearty atmosphere draw a mix of middle-aged patrons and college kids, with a few families thrown in for good measure. Rooms have a vaguely Florida-tropical decor and are trimmed in Hooters orange, with moderate-budget amenities (bathrooms are a little on the cheap side). Although Hooters has been a breakout hit, the company tried to sell it to Hedwigs, a California investment group. Plans fell through, however, and Hooters is now looking for a new suitor.

Imperial Palace (imperialpalace.com)

IMPERIAL PALACE OWNER RALPH ENGELSTAD died in November of 2003. Though most Vegas watchers expected the then-27-year-old resort to go on the auction block, Engelstad's plucky wife, Betty, not only decided to keep plugging away but also ordered a major renovation. Though Betty's intentions were good, she sold the property to Harrah's (now Caesars Entertainment) before much of the renovation was completed.

From the Strip, access to the Imperial Palace casino is by way of a shallow reception area that immediately feeds up an escalator. Although you almost have to hunt for the architectural grace amidst the large, active casino, it's still there. Massive wooden beams and carved dragons crowning the ceiling supports whisper a once-grand Eastern elegance.

The dining scene at the I.P. has been a work in progress since Harrah's acquired the property. Except for Embers Steakhouse, the I.P.'s gourmet room during the Engelstad years, and the Emperor's Buffet, all of the restaurants were swapped out in the past couple of years. Headliners include Hash House A Go Go, where "Indiana home-style favorites meet the excess of the Strip" (I promise we're not making this up); the 24-hour Burger Palace; the 24-hour Ginseng 3, specializing in Korean, Japanese, and Chinese fare; and Quesadilla, serving Mexican dishes.

The casino has a "Geisha Bar," but the burly bartender will definitely be omitted from the memoirs. The attraction on the casino floor is the dealers, who are fair-to-poor celebrity impersonators, including the likes of Stevie Wonder (would a blind dealer be a good thing?), Reba McEntire, Dolly Parton, Little Richard, and the perennial Elvis. It's a fun gimmick, even when it's weakly executed. These players are a nod to the excellent impersonators of *Legends in Concert,* one of the hottest shows in Las Vegas that played nightly at the Imperial Palace's showroom before moving to Harrah's in 2009. The Imperial Palace casino is full of action, and its intensity is multiplied by the unusual number of mirrored surfaces that nearly pay homage to Orson Welles's famous classic reflection on life's enigmas, *The Lady from Shanghai.*

The small bank of elevators to the guest rooms is at the back of the casino, and this same narrow hallway feeds the modest shopping area, monorail, and casino-level restaurant. There are several classifications of rooms. Classic, Capri, and Deluxe rooms, accounting for the bulk of the guest-room inventory, offer a color palate and mix of furniture and appointments that is decidedly feminine. Though of recent vintage, the rooms remind me of my sister's bedroom growing up in the 1960s (sans bulletin board and pictures of Elvis). More upscale rooms are pretty wild, especially the Deluxe Luv Tub Room that features a mirror on the ceiling over the bed in addition to, of course, the Luv Tub. High-speed wireless Internet service is available in the rooms, as is a small refrigerator, but both add to the standard room rate.

The single swimming pool and sunbathing area are large but unremarkable by Las Vegas standards. The exercise (two treadmills, two exercise bikes, and so on) and spa spaces (two massage rooms) are small but adequate for the traveler who wants basic service. Attractions at the I.P. include an excellent vintage auto museum and The King's Ransom Museum, featuring an extensive collection of Elvis memorabilia and artifacts.

The ambitious renovation, on hold for the moment, calls for a new facade for the building, a sidewalk cafe, a glass-walled upscale restaurant, and a pedestrian corridor for monorail passengers. Many Las Vegas insiders, however, maintain that the renovation will never happen, citing the size and value of the real estate the Imperial Palace sits on. In their opinion, the Imperial Palace's future will more likely involve a lot of dynamite.

JW Marriott Las Vegas/Rampart Casino
(jwlasvegasresort.com; rampartcasino.com)

THE JW MARRIOTT LAS VEGAS WAS THE FIRST of several upscale properties to offer a Scottsdale–Palm Beach resort experience as an alternative to the madness of the Strip. Situated west of town near Red Rock Canyon, the JW Marriott Las Vegas consists of two southwestern-style hotels built around the Tournament Players Club (TPC) golf course. The JW Marriott officially opened as The Resort at Summerlin in 1999, and a year or so later changed its name to The Regent Las Vegas. Marriott acquired the property in late 2001, and the name changed again. As an added twist, the classy, circular casino has yet another name, Rampart Casino (after the road on which the casino is located). The JW Marriott operates primarily as a meeting venue with a secondary emphasis on golf and the resort's exceptional spa. The casino, operated by an independent contractor, targets the local market.

Standard hotel rooms are huge at 560 square feet. In many rooms, French doors open onto a balustrade overlooking the pools and gardens (11 acres of palms and pines tower over the winding pools, waterfalls, and walkways), or better yet, the mountains to the west, a stirring alternative to the usual neon. Baths feature a whirlpool tub, separate shower, bathrobes, and telephone.

Restaurants serve Italian, Continental, Japanese, Irish, and American fare. The buffet here is one of the better spreads in town. Although the lounges, including the Irish pub, offer live entertainment, there is no showroom. The JW Marriott is pricey but perfect for those who come to enjoy the beauty and recreational resources of the mountains and valleys west of Las Vegas. Only minutes away are world-class hiking, rock climbing, mountain biking, and road biking.

Las Vegas Club (vegasclubcasino.net)

LAS VEGAS CLUB IS A DOWNTOWN hotel-casino with a sports theme. The corridor linking the casino with the sports bar is a veritable sports museum and has dozens of vintage photos of boxing, baseball, and basketball legends. The casino itself, with its high, mirrored ceilings, is modest but feels uncrowded. It also has some of the more player-friendly blackjack rules around. If you plan to stay at the Las Vegas Club, ask for a room in the North Tower. The Great Moments Room, one of the last few Las Vegas gourmet rooms, closed in 2009 and is considered a great loss. Current dining options include Tinoco's Kitchen and Tinoco's Express, both serving eclectic fare. Though the Las Vegas Club doesn't have a pool, its guests have privileges at the rooftop pool of the Plaza Hotel across the street. The Las Vegas Club draws visitors from Hawaii and the Midwest but also does a big business with bus groups and seniors.

Las Vegas Hilton (lvhilton.com)

IN SOME WAYS LIKE BALLY'S, the Las Vegas Hilton bills itself as a classic, straightforward Vegas experience with comfortable lodging, good restaurants, a strong casino, and headliner entertainment, but no exotic theme. Lacking a theme hook, the Hilton has the advantage of being adjacent to the Las Vegas Convention Center. What it lacks in convenient access to the Strip (a 10- to 12-minute walk or 5-minute monorail ride away), it makes up for in one-stop partying for the conventioneer who can go to sessions via a hall connecting the hotel and convention center. Consequently, this hotel does more meeting, trade-show, and convention business than any other hotel in town.

There are days at the Hilton when it's rare to see someone not wearing a convention badge. Operating under the valid assumption that many of its guests may never leave the hotel during their Las Vegas stay (except to go to the convention center), the Hilton is an oasis of self-sufficiency. It boasts lounges, a huge pool, an exercise room, a shopping arcade, a buffet, and a coffee shop. It is also next door to a golf course.

Architecture is vintage high-rise—bland, smooth, and unmemorable, but not unpleasant. Rooms are more than adequate—accommodating but not glitzy, with a comfortable, neutral environment for the business clientele.

The Las Vegas Hilton has a decent buffet and some excellent fine-dining options with enough ethnic and culinary variety to keep most guests happy. The main showroom hosts big-name headliners, while the intimate Shimmer Cabaret hosts musical acts and small production shows.

The casino is moderate in size by Las Vegas standards and, like the hotel, tastefully businesslike in its presentation, but by no means formal or intimidating. The Hilton sports book is one of the largest in Las Vegas.

The Hilton is the most convenient place to stay in town if you are attending a trade show or convention at the Las Vegas Convention Center. If, however, you are in Las Vegas for pleasure, staying at the Hilton is like being in exile. Anywhere you go you will need a cab, a car, or the monorail with a station right at the hotel. If you park in one of the Hilton's far-flung, self-parking lots, it will take you as long as 15 minutes to reach your car from your guest room. At press time, the Hilton hotel chain announced that it intends to terminate its license agreement with the Las Vegas Hilton by the end of 2011. The property expects to announce an affiliation with another major hotel chain before year's end.

Luxor (luxor.com)

THE LUXOR IS ON THE STRIP south of Tropicana Avenue next to the Excalibur. Representing Mandalay Resort Group's (now MRI) first serious effort to attract a more upscale, less family-oriented clientele, the Luxor is among the more tasteful of Las Vegas's themed hotels. Though originally not believed to be on a par with T. I. and the MGM Grand, the Luxor may well be the most distinguished graduate of the much-publicized hotel class of 1993. While the MGM Grand is larger and T. I. originally more ostentatious, the Luxor demonstrates an unmatched creativity and architectural appeal.

Rising 30 stories, the Luxor is a huge pyramid with guest rooms situated around the outside perimeter from base to apex. Guest-room hallways circumscribe a hollow core containing the world's largest atrium. Inside the atrium, inclinators rise at a 39-degree angle from the pyramid's corners to access the guest floors. While the perspective from inside the pyramid is stunning, it is easy to get disoriented. Stories about hotel guests wandering around in search of their rooms are legend. After reviewing many complaints from readers, we seriously recommend carrying a small pocket compass.

The Luxor's main entrance is from the Strip via a massive sphinx. From the sphinx, guests are diverted into small entryways designed to resemble the interior passages of an actual pyramid. From these tunnels, guests emerge into the dramatic openness of the Luxor's towering atrium. Rising imposingly within the atrium is an exotic cityscape. The Luxor has succumbed to the let's-nuke-our-theme contagion and is merrily spending $300 million to drive the Egyptians back to Egypt.

Proceeding straight ahead at ground level from the main entrance brings you into the casino. Open and attractive, the 120,000-square-foot casino is tasteful by any standard.

One level below the casino and the main entrance is the Luxor's main showroom. One floor above entry level, on a mezzanine of sorts, is an array of structures that reach high into the atrium. These dramatic buildings and facades transform the atrium. The atrium is home to two exceptional exhibits. Bodies—The Exhibition is an extraordinary and riveting introduction to human anatomy through authentic, preserved human bodies. It takes you stepwise through every part of the human body explaining its many systems. The second exhibit is Titanic: The Artifact Exhibition, which takes guests on a chronological odyssey from the design and building of the ocean liner to life on board to its sinking. Luxor's 26,000-square-foot LAX nightclub is one of the hottest late-night venues in the city, and Cathouse is a combination restaurant, ultra lounge, and dance club with a bordello theme.

Flanking the pyramid are two hotel towers that were part of an expansion completed in 1997; the expansion included a new health spa and fitness center and additional meeting and conference space.

Soft goods play off the mixed wood tones of the furniture to create some of the warmest and most visually appealing guest rooms in Las Vegas. In all, the Luxor offers 4,450 guest rooms.

Entertainment includes a topless revue, a magic-themed production show, a comedy headliner, and an off-Broadway musical.

The Luxor's large, attractive pool complex, surrounded by private cabanas, desperately needs some additional plants and trees. Self-parking is not as much a problem at the Luxor as at most large properties. Valet parking is quick and efficient, however, and well worth the $2 tip. The Luxor is within a 5- to 12-minute walk of the Excalibur, the Tropicana, and the MGM Grand. A moving walkway connects the Luxor to the Excalibur and an overhead "cable liner" (a monorail propelled by a cable à la San Francisco cable cars) connects it with Mandalay Bay.

M Resort (themresort.com)

REPLACING SOUTH POINT AS THE MOST UPSCALE RESORT south of the Strip, M Resort opened in March 2009 at South Las Vegas Boulevard and Saint Rose Parkway, about 10 miles from Mandalay Bay. The "M" of M Resort could easily stand for "mirage," given how it rises all by itself, shimmering in the desert. "M," however, is actually from the family name Marnell in honor of founder and CEO, Anthony Marnell III. Active in Las Vegas hospitality and gaming for decades, the Marnells previously built and operated the Rio, establishing a reputation for style and innovation. The Marnells have always produced a high-quality product geared to the local population. With a refreshing lack of spectacle and abundance of modern elegance, M Resort is specifically located to serve the affluent residential developments in the south Las Vegas Valley.

The hotel's glass-ceiling lobby is wide and bright with high ceilings. Behind the registration desk and across the foyer are four 15-foot spills of water sliding down beige walls of unpolished marble. Plants and dark leather furniture create comfortable seating. Softening the ceiling is a center panel with fabric waves of red and cream. Imparting a sense of timelessness, rows of identical glass vases display fresh lilies. The hotel's iconic M logo is inlaid in copper in the marble floor. Stand to the left side and the M becomes a stylized martini glass in keeping with the hotel's hip aura. A piano bar is at the north end, with elongated windows that reveal an extraordinary sight line encompassing the entire Las Vegas Valley.

A delineating feature of M's public areas is the abundance of striking molded back-lit pillars, lights, ceiling fixtures, chandeliers, and bar tables seen throughout the space. Each piece has a distinctive design of brown waves brightened by amber, orange, red, or gold.

The well-configured casino with spacious aisles groups similar slots together with ample playing room. Blackjack, pai gow, mini-baccarat, roulette, and craps are arranged in small groups of eight tables. Dealers are assigned to the same table for an entire month, so players partial to a lucky dealer can return to his table. The race and sports book is intimate, seating just 50 people, but absolutely cutting edge. The Jewelry Box slots, 124 slot machines in the center of the casino, feature payoffs based on precious-stone images and randomly reward players up to $5,000. Above all, 30,000 square feet of mother-of-pearl material covers the gaming area in long sweeps of shell tile separated by dark wood. A centerpiece shower of connected glass discs cascades over the gaming tables.

The 110,000-square-foot Villagio Del Sole and Entertainment Piazza is expansive. Bamboo and palm trees line the left side of the marble entry staircase where running water tumbles over large marble cubes along the steps. Private cabanas line the perimeter of the grounds, and two hot tubs are positioned at each rear corner along with a fire pit and tall metal torches. Also at the far end are two walled, elevated enclosures for sunning on grass turf. Tucked away on the west side is the Daydream pool for adults. The infinity pool is divided along the center by a walkway scattered with orange daybeds. The tile in each half pool traces the footprint of the M hotel tower. There is a shallow in-pool ledge for lounge chairs. An outdoor stage at the north end of the pool features concerts regularly. You can score the best seats in the house by dining on the terrace of the Hash House A Go Go, which directly overlooks the concert stage. During normal operations, with just 390 rooms at the M, the 2.3-acre pool area is seldom congested.

Dining options include the Studio B buffet, which includes unlimited beer and wine for dinner and adds special seafood dishes to the usual lineup on weekends. With the exception of the Studio B buffet and Vig Deli, the restaurants have terraces and outdoor dining to take advantage of the breathtaking view of Las Vegas, enhanced by the hotel's elevation (400 feet higher than the Strip). To better control the quality and price point of meat offerings, the resort maintains a butcher shop on the premises with fresh beef, pork, and lamb flown in from its own Montana ranch. The hotel's own filtration system creates water not only for drinking but also for baking pastries, breads, and desserts. The system can duplicate water in France for baguettes or Italian water for focaccia.

Fine-dining options include Terzetto, specializing in chops and seafood; Marinelli's for regional Italian cuisine and homemade pastas; and Veloce Cibo for dining and nightlife high above the Strip.

Lounges are stylish and feature some of the best free entertainment anywhere. Check out the Ravello lounge for high-energy music that includes all the classics of rock, pop, and jazz as well as modern favorites. If you crave a taste of the grape or the fruit of the barley, M has you covered. 32° Draft offers 96 different beers on tap. More novel but just as interesting is Hostile Grape, a chic and cozy wine cellar where you can sample 160 different wines by the glass. Wine is available from a one-ounce taste to a full glass and priced accordingly. Vintages from all the great wine-producing areas of the world are represented. Oh yeah, cola and soft-drink fans have their oasis too with a free soft-drink dispenser just off the casino, a first in any casino.

Guest rooms feature floor-to-ceiling windows with electric drapes, Bose radios, high-speed Internet, iPod docking stations, and 42-inch flat-panel TVs as well as bathroom TVs embedded in the mirrors. Standard rooms are large at 420 square feet, and views can be either of the Nevada desert landscape to the south or the Strip to the north, overlooking the pool. The luxury bath has a glass wall that faces the center of the room and the window.

Though it feels incredibly remote, M Resort is only a 10- to 12-minute drive on I-15 from the heart of the Strip. One caution, however: do not miss the Saint Rose Parkway exit when you're driving southbound. It's 23 miles to the next exit.

Main Street Station (mainstreetcasino.com)

SITUATED ON MAIN STREET BETWEEN OGDEN and Stewart avenues in downtown Las Vegas, Main Street Station originally opened in 1992 as a paid-admission nighttime entertainment complex with a casino on the side. Owned and managed by an Orlando, Florida, entrepreneur with no casino experience, it took Main Street Station less than a year to go belly-up. The property was acquired several years later by Boyd Gaming, which used Main Street Station's hotel to accommodate overflow guests from the California across the street. In 1997, the Boyds reopened the casino, restaurants, and shops, adding a brewpub in the process.

The casino is one of the most unusual in town (thanks largely to the concept of the original owner), with the feel of a turn-of-the-20th-century gentlemen's club. Though not as splendid now as in its original incarnation, the casino still contains enough antiques, original art, and oddities to furnish a museum. With its refurbished guest rooms, brewpub, excellent buffet, and unusual casino, Main Street Station is both interesting and fun, adding some welcome diversity to the downtown hospitality mix.

Mandalay Bay (mandalaybay.com)

MANDALAY BAY OPENED ON MARCH 2, 1999, on the site of the old Hacienda, imploded on New Year's Day 1998. It completes the Mandalay Bay "Miracle Mile," which stretches along the Strip south from the Bellagio and includes CityCenter, the Monte Carlo, New York–New York, the Excalibur, Luxor, and finally Mandalay Bay. A cable liner connects Excalibur, Luxor, and Mandalay Bay every 15 minutes, 24 hours a day (it stops at Luxor on the northbound leg only).

Mandalay Bay, with 4,756 rooms (including the on-site Four Seasons Hotel and THEhotel), is a megaresort in the true sense of the overworked word. Within the sprawling complex are the 43-story, three-wing tower; a 12,000-seat arena; a 1,600-seat theater; an 1,800-seat House of Blues concert venue; two dozen restaurants; an 11-acre water park; three large lounges; and the third-largest convention facility in Las Vegas. Mandalay Bay had Las Vegas's first hotel-within-a-hotel on the property: the 424-room Four Seasons. The whole schmear cost a cool billion plus. Adjoining the main casino is a second on-site hotel, THEhotel at Mandalay Bay, with 1,120 suites. Both the Four Seasons and THEhotel are profiled in this section under their own names.

But that's not the half of it, because Mandalay Bay isn't your standard mega-resort. It's clear that the planners and designers set out to take a few risks and appeal to a young, hip, fun-seeking market—as opposed to Bellagio, which targets a more refined, sophisticated, older clientele. If Bellagio is the crowning culmination of 20th-century Las Vegas, Mandalay Bay might be Las Vegas's first foray into the 21st. All the different ideas jammed into Mandalay Bay might not always add up to a cohesive whole, but so many parts of the sum are unique that you can't help being intrigued.

The signature spectacle is the four-story wine tower at Manhattan celebrity chef Charlie Palmer's restaurant, Aureole. This nearly 50-foot-tall glass-and-stainless-steel structure stores about 10,000 bottles of wine. Lovely, athletic women dressed all in black—spandex tights, racing gloves, hard hats—manipulate the motorized cable, one on each of the four sides, that raises them up to retrieve a selected bottle and lowers them back down to deliver it.

Red Square Russian restaurant has a one-of-a-kind refrigerated walk-in showcase, open to the public, which stores 200 different varieties of vodka at 15°F. Drinks are served on a long bar top that has a thick strip of ice running its length. Rumjungle, a Polynesian dining and nightclub combo, is fronted by a huge "wall of fire": 80 small gas-fed flames surround two big flames at the entrance. The House of Blues restaurant and entertainment complex serves food (Southern-style and Creole-Cajun) and has the world's largest collection of Deep South folk art, as well as a strange dark bar with a crucifix theme. House of Blues also puts on a Sunday gospel brunch and holds rock and pop concerts in its 1,800-seat theater. China Grill (serving Asian-inspired dishes), Wolfgang Puck's Lupo (serving Italian fare), Michael Mina's STRIPSTEAK, Fleur by Hubert Keller (serving globally inspired small plates), Rick Moonen's RM Seafood, Shanghai Lilly (serving Cantonese and Szechuan specialties), Mix (an Alain Ducasse French eatery with midcentury modern furniture and knockout views of the Strip), a Mexican restaurant, a noodle room, a coffee shop, a somewhat disappointing buffet, and ice-cream and coffee counters round out the dining possibilities at Mandalay Bay.

A main attraction at Mandalay Bay is Shark Reef, a 90,000-square-foot aquarium exhibit with a walk-through acrylic tunnel. The aquarium is home to about 2,000 marine species, including Nile crocodiles, moray eels, stingrays, and, of course, sharks.

In the nightlife department, Mix is one of the hottest clubs in town and is described on page 284. Eyecandy Sound Lounge & Bar, a sprawling DJ dance venue that's nicer than most ultralounges, makes clubbing hassle-free. There are no queues, no VIP line, no cover or admission charges, no minimum drink purchase, no bottle-service requirement, and almost no reserved seating. Enter at will through any of several entrances and boogie as long as you like.

Speaking of acreage, the casino is typically monumental, with plenty of elbowroom between machines and tables. The race and sports book boasts the largest screen in town, which is only right, since the book is so big the screen must be seen from long distances. The 80-seat (each one an oversized, velour-covered easy chair) lounge and the large poker room are connected.

The pool area is also imaginative. The 11-acre Mandalay Bay Beach has a lazy river, a placid pool, a beachfront cafe and bar, and a wedding chapel. The centerpiece, however, is a huge wave pool. The surf can be cranked up from one to six feet.

The Shoppes at Mandalay Place, in the pedestrian passage that connects Mandalay Bay with the Luxor, features more than 35 boutiques and restaurants, including a burger joint where you can purchase a $60 hamburger.

All in all, Mandalay Bay accomplishes what every mega-casino-hotel sets out to do—deliver an inventive and hip experience that sets a standard for all the megajoints that follow.

MGM Grand (mgmgrand.com)

MGM GRAND CLAIMS THE DISTINCTION of having Vegas's largest casino. Within the 112-acre complex, there is a 16,800-seat special-events arena, 380,000 square feet of convention space, 171,500 square feet of casino space, and a multilevel parking facility. There's also a small casino outside the lobby of the Mansion, MGM's ultra-upscale whale digs. Finally, a 6.6-acre pool-and-spa complex took over a chunk of the now-defunct amusement park along with the dedicated convention center.

The MGM Grand is on the northeast corner of Tropicana Avenue and the Strip. The Strip entrance passes beneath a 45-foot-tall MGM Lion atop a 25-foot pedestal, all surrounded by three immense digital displays. The lion entrance leads to a domed rotunda with table games and a Rainforest Cafe, and from there to the MGM Grand's four larger casinos. All of the casinos are roomy and plush, with high ceilings and a comfortable feeling of openness.

A second entrance, with a porte cochere 15 lanes wide, serves vehicular traffic from Tropicana Avenue. For all practical purposes, this is the main entrance to the MGM Grand, permitting you to go directly to the hotel lobby and its 53 check-in windows without lugging your belongings through the casinos. Just beyond the registration area is the elevator core, with 35 elevators servicing 30 guest floors.

Beyond the elevator core, a wide passageway leads toward five of the MGM Grand's many restaurants. The MGM Grand's supernova restaurant is Joël Robuchon, which serves a French culinary feast of the highest quality and greatest exclusivity. Other fine-dining stars in the hotel's galaxy include L'Atelier de Joël Robuchon, serving more fine French cuisine via counter service (dishes are prepared in front of you); Tom Colicchio's Craftsteak, offering beef and seafood; Nobhill Tavern, serving California-style cuisine; Diego, a Mexican restaurant; SeaBlue, a Mediterranean tapas restaurant; Fiamma, an Italian trattoria; Shibuya, a Japanese restaurant; Emeril's, offering Creole-Cajun dishes; and The Grand Wok and Sushi Bar, featuring Asian specialties from a half-dozen countries. More informal dining is available at the Rainforest Cafe and the Studio Café. MGM Grand's buffet (disappointing) and pizza kitchen adjoin the casinos between the porte cochere and lion entrances. For fast food there is a food court including McDonald's, Mamma Ilardo's, and Hamada's Oriental Express.

There are three showrooms at the MGM Grand. The 740-seat Hollywood Theater features headliners, the larger KÀ Theatre is home to Cirque du Soleil's KÀ, and the Crazy Horse Cabaret is home to the saucy Frenchy show of the same name. Entertainment is also offered in the casino's four lounges. In addition, the MGM Grand's special-events arena can accommodate boxing, tournament tennis, rodeo, and basketball, as well as major exhibitions.

Amenities at the MGM Grand, not unexpectedly, are among the best in Las Vegas. The swimming complex is huge—23,000 square feet of pool area, with five interconnected pools graced with bridges, fountains, and waterfalls. Other highlights of the complex include an artificial stream to float in, a poolside bar, and luxury cabanas. Adjoining the swimming area is a complete health club and spa. For those to whom recreation means pumping quarters into a machine, there is an electronic games arcade supplemented by a "games-of-skill" midway. The most exotic addition to the entertainment mix is Lion Habitat, where you can watch live lions. In the transportation department, the MGM Grand is the southern terminus of the Las Vegas Monorail.

Guest rooms at the MGM Grand are comfortable, with large baths. Almost all of the rooms have a small sitting area positioned by a large window. Rooms on the higher floors have exceptional views. Part of the old MGM Marina Hotel was incorporated into the new MGM Grand. Rooms in the old structure have been renovated but are not comparable in size or quality to the newer rooms. In 2012 MGM Grand will remodel 4,300 deluxe guest rooms and suites in its main tower with rich, jewel-like colors and modern conveniences such as flat-screen TVs and media hubs.

A rare enclave of peace and privacy are MGM Grand's Signature condo-hotel towers, which opened in 2007. Located a five-to-seven-minute walk east of the main casino, the towers offer suite accommodations with floor-to-ceiling windows, full kitchens, flat-panel TVs, Jacuzzi tubs, and high-speed

Internet connections. Conspicuous by its absence is on-site gambling. Signature's suites are not especially large but are beautifully appointed, and some units have private balconies. Each tower has its own pool, 24-hour concierge service, and a private entrance with valet parking. The private entrance makes for easy coming and going if you have a car.

Drawing from a wide cross section of the leisure market, the MGM Grand gets the majority of its business from individual travelers and tour and travel groups, but with a rising percentage coming from trade-show and convention attendees. Midrange room rates make the MGM Grand accessible to a broad population. Geographically, the MGM Grand targets Southern California, Phoenix, Denver, Dallas, Houston, Chicago, and the Midwest.

Mirage (mirage.com)

THE MIRAGE HAS HAD AN IMPACT ON THE LAS VEGAS tourist industry that will be felt for years to come. By challenging all the old rules and setting new standards for design, ambience, and entertainment, the Mirage precipitated the development of a class of super-hotels in Las Vegas, redefining the thematic appeal and hospitality standard of hotel-casinos.

Exciting and compelling without being whimsical or silly, the Mirage has demonstrated that the public will respond enthusiastically to a well-executed concept. Blending the stateliness of marble with the exotic luxury of tropical greenery and the straightforward lines of polished bamboo, the Mirage has created a spectacular environment that artfully integrates casino, showroom, shopping, restaurants, and lounges. Both lavish and colorful, inviting and awe-inspiring, the Mirage has avoided cliché. Not designed to replicate a famous palace or be the hotel version of "Goofy Golf," the Mirage makes an original statement.

An atrium rain forest serves as a central hub from which guests can proceed to all areas of the hotel and casino. Behind the hotel's front desk, a 60-foot-long aquarium contains small and colorful tropical fish. Outside, instead of blinking neon, the Mirage has a 55-foot-tall erupting volcano that disrupts traffic on the Strip every hour on the hour (6–11 p.m.). There is also a live dolphin exhibit and a modern showroom that is among the most well designed and technologically advanced in Las Vegas.

The Mirage boasts several fine-dining opportunities, including Japonais, a concept restaurant featuring Japanese and "old-style" European cuisine; Fin, serving contemporary Chinese; Kokomo's, a chop, seafood, and lobster house; STACK, an American grill; Samba, a Brazilian *churrascuria;* and Onda, one of the city's better Italian restaurants. For bulk eaters, there is an excellent and affordable buffet. *LOVE,* a Cirque du Soleil production based on the music of the Beatles, plays in one of two showrooms. Amenities include a swimming and sunning complex with waterfalls, inlets, and an interconnected series of lagoons; a shopping arcade; and a spa with exercise equipment and aerobics instruction. The casino is huge and magnificently appointed, yet informal, with its tropical motif and piped-in Jimmy Buffett music. Guest rooms at the Mirage have been completely renovated and are now among the nicest in town.

Though registered guests pay premium prices for the privilege of staying at the Mirage, the hotel is not an exclusive retreat of the wealthy. With its indoor jungle and traffic-snarling volcano, the Mirage remains one of Clark County's top tourist attractions. Whether by foot, bus, cab, or bicycle, every Las Vegas visitor makes at least one pilgrimage. The Mirage has become the Strip's melting pot and hosts the most incredible variety of humanity imaginable.

Monte Carlo (montecarlo.com)

THE MONTE CARLO OPENED IN 1996. With 3,006 guest rooms, the Monte Carlo ranks as one of the larger hotels in Las Vegas. The megaresort is modeled after the Place du Casino in Monte Carlo, Monaco, with ornate arches and fountains, marble floors, and a Gothic, glass registration area. If the Monte Carlo fails as a resort, the building will be a perfect place to relocate the Nevada State Capitol.

In an effort to pep things up, however, the resort hatched an idea that turned the dull Monte Carlo theme on its head. Astonishingly, they tacked a Diablo's Cantina restaurant onto the south corner of the resort, with a wildly colorful Strip-side exterior complete with an eye-popping, scantily clad she-devil statue straddling the roof. The cantina effectively drains the stuffiness of the namesake theme and achieves a contrast (or dissonance) that could only be matched by grazing yaks in the casino.

On the surface, it's yet another huge hotel in the Las Vegas Age of the Megaresort. But scratch the surface just a little and you glimpse the future of Monopoly-board Las Vegas and the gambling business in general.

The guest rooms, furnished with marble entryways and French-period wall art, are mid- to upper-priced. In 2009, the Monte Carlo opened Hotel 32 on the 32nd and highest floor of the hotel. The idea (they say) is to provide a high-roller, VIP experience at an affordable price. Five different configurations of studios and suites are available. Extras include a "suite assistant" (butler?) and a private lounge, among others.

There is an elaborate swimming complex with slides, a wave pool, and a man-made stream. There is also an exceptional health and fitness center, an interesting shopping arcade, and a brewpub with a DJ on Friday and Saturday nights. The casino, about a football field long and similarly shaped, is capped with simulated skylights and domes. The showroom features comedy from impressionist Frank Caliendo and the dance group Jabbawockeez. Restaurants cover the usual bases, offering steak, Italian, and Asian specialties, with the brewpub thrown in for good measure. The signature restaurant is Andre's (after chef André Rochat), serving traditional French cuisine and offering a wine list with 1,500 selections.

Compared to the powerful themes of New York–New York and the Luxor, the Monte Carlo's turn-of-the-century Monegasque theme fails to stimulate much excitement or anticipation. Besides being beyond the average tourist's frame of reference, the theme lacks any real visceral dimension. The word *grand* comes to mind, but more in the context of a federal courthouse or the New York Public Library.

New York–New York (newyorknewyork.com)

WHEN IT OPENED IN JANUARY 1997, this architecturally imaginative hotel-casino set a new standard for the realization of Las Vegas mega-resort themes. It's a small joint by megaresort standards ("only" around 2,000 rooms), but the triumph is in the details. The guest rooms are in a series of distinct towers reminiscent of a mini–Big Apple skyline, including the Empire State, Chrysler, and Seagram buildings. Though the buildings are connected, each offers a somewhat different decor and ambience.

A half-size Statue of Liberty and a replica of Grand Central Station lead visitors to one entrance, while the Brooklyn Bridge leads to another. The interior of the property is broken into themed areas such as Greenwich Village, Wall Street, and Times Square. The casino, one of the most visually interesting in Las Vegas, looks like an elaborate movie set. Table games and slots are sandwiched between shops, restaurants, and a jumble of street facades.

The street scenes are well executed, conveying both a sense of urban style and tough grittiness. New York–New York sacrificed much of its visual impact, however, by not putting in an imitation sky. At Sunset Station, by way of contrast, the Spanish architecture is augmented significantly by vaulted ceilings, realistically lighted and painted with clouds. This sort of finishing touch could have done wonders for New York–New York.

Like its namesake, New York–New York is congested to the extreme, awash day and night with curious sightseers. There are so many people just wandering around gawking that there's little room left for hotel guests and folks who actually came to gamble. Because aisles and indoor paths are far too narrow to accommodate the crowds, New York–New York succumbs periodically to a sort of pedestrian gridlock.

Manhattan rules, however, do not apply at New York–New York: it's OK here to make eye contact and decidedly rude to shove people out of the way to get where you want to go. If you find yourself longing for the thrill of a New York cab ride, go hop on the roller coaster. New York–New York's coaster isn't the only one on the Strip, but it's the only one where you can stand on the street and hear the riders scream.

The showroom features Cirque du Soleil's *Zumanity*. Lounges include a raucous Irish pub, a dueling pianos bar, a high-energy dance club, and a Coyote Ugly bar. Based on the movie of the same name, the bar features a platoon of dancing female bartenders with enough attitude to stop a real New Yorker dead in his tracks. Nine Fine Irishmen, the pub with live Irish music, is the *Unofficial* research team's favorite Las Vegas hangout.

Guest rooms at New York–New York have been renovated and upgraded. However, the swimming area and health and fitness center are just average. Full-service restaurants are a little better than average, though Gallagher's Steakhouse, a real Big Apple import, can hold its own with any beef place, in or out of Las Vegas. Counter-service fast food is quite interesting, if not altogether authentic New York.

Orleans (orleanscasino.com)

OPENED IN 1997, ORLEANS IS JUST WEST of I-15 on Tropicana Avenue. Marketed primarily to locals, Orleans has a New Orleans–bayou theme executed in a hulking cavern of a building. The casino is festive with bright carpets, high ceilings, a two-story replication of a French Quarter street flanking the table games, and a couple of nifty bars. Orleans has a celebrity showroom that attracts great talent (Air Supply, The Pointer Sisters, Gin Blossoms, Norm Macdonald) and several restaurants that have little to do with the Louisiana theme. The buffet, which does serve Creole-Cajun dishes, is good but can't quite match Louisiana standards. Upstairs, over the slots and buffet area, is a 70-lane bowling complex. The Orleans Arena is a 9,000-seat facility and home to the Las Vegas Wranglers pro hockey team. Two hotel towers with a total of 1,886 large guest rooms complete the package.

Orleans has expanded steadily since its first year, adding restaurants, an 18-screen movie complex, more casino space, the arena, a games arcade, bowling, and a child-care center.

Palace Station (palacestation.com)

LOCATED FOUR MINUTES OFF THE STRIP on West Sahara Avenue, Palace Station is a local favorite that also attracts tourists. With great lounge acts, a first-rate buffet, dependable restaurants that continuously offer amazing specials, a tower of Holiday Inn–caliber guest rooms, good prices, and a location that permits access to both downtown and the Strip in less than ten minutes, Palace Station is a standard setter for locals' casinos. Decorated in a railroad theme, the casino is large and busy with a heavy emphasis on slots (which are supposedly loose—that is, having a high rate of payoff). There is also Louie Anderson's comedy club and a showroom.

Palms (palms.com)

LOCATED WEST OF THE STRIP ON FLAMINGO ROAD, the Palms is one of the primo hangouts for well-heeled youth. Consisting of two high-rise hotel towers and a 50-story luxury hotel-condo, the Palms offers solid four-star guest rooms with floor-to-ceiling windows and fantastic views of the Strip.

Though the casino is roomy, at 95,000 square feet, it's the Palms' nightlife mix that sets the hotel apart. Atop the 55-story original tower is Ghostbar with panoramic views of the entire Las Vegas Valley. On the ground level of the same tower is Rain, a high-energy dance club with pulsing fountains and high-tech special effects. Small and intimate is Moon at the top of the newer Fantasy Tower (so called because of the tower's fantastic high-roller suites, featuring such amenities as basketball courts). Like Ghostbar, Moon offers incredible views. Unlike Ghostbar, Moon has a retractable roof. One floor down from Moon is the Playboy Club, the only such club in existence and the first new Playboy Club to open in decades. The club features table games, knockout views, and a lot of cleavage. A show lounge, a 14-screen cinema, and Pearl—a very cool concert venue—complete the mix. All of the clubs, as well as Pearl, attract a hip under-30 crowd that keeps the Palms jumping until the wee hours.

Also very cool is the two-acre pool complex featuring three bars, including one situated beneath a glass-bottom pool. Strong drinks relieve the pain of sprained necks. At the pools you can swim, of course, but mostly they're used as a party or concert venue or as an additional nightspot.

The restaurant lineup, equally impressive, leads off with Alizé, serving gourmet French cuisine and stunning views from the top story; N9NE, a steak house imported from Chicago; and Nove Italiano, an elegant room graced by topiaries in the form of classic nudes. Rounding out the dining mix are an Asian-fusion restaurant, a Mexican restaurant, a good buffet, a 24-hour coffee shop, and a food court.

Palms is too far from the Strip for most guests to feel comfortable walking. For those with a car, however, the coming and going is easy, and the hotel location on West Flamingo Road facilitates accessing Strip casinos via alternate routes rather than joining the gridlock on Las Vegas Boulevard. Both in design and target market, Palms is very much like the Hard Rock Hotel. You can bet that the two will compete head-to-head for the trend-conscious, affluent, young-adult market. Older guests may feel like relics at Palms' nightspots but will otherwise find the property friendly, accessible, and convenient.

Paris (parislasvegas.com)

ON THE STRIP NEXT TO BALLY'S AND ACROSS from Bellagio, Paris trots out a French-Parisian theme in much the same way New York–New York caricatures the Big Apple. Paris has its own 50-story Eiffel Tower (with a restaurant halfway up) and an Arc de Triomphe. Thrown in for good measure are the Champs-Elysées, Parc Monceau, and the Paris Opera House.

Like New York–New York, Paris presents its iconography in a whimsical way, contrasting with the more realistic Venetian or the Forum Shops at Caesars Palace. The casino resides in a parklike setting roughly arrayed around the base of the Eiffel Tower, three legs of which protrude through the roof of the casino. The video-poker schedules are lackluster, but the casino offers all of the usual table games.

Flanking the tower and branching off from the casino are dining and shopping venues designed to re-create Parisian and rural *petit village* street scenes. Though spacious, the casino and other public areas at Paris are exceedingly busy, bombarding the senses with color, sound, and activity. While at the Venetian you have the sense of entering a grand space, at Paris the feeling is more of envelopment.

The hotel towers, with almost 3,000 guest rooms, rise in an L shape framing the Eiffel Tower. The rooms are quite stunning and rank along with the dining as one of Paris's most outstanding features.

Like at the Venetian, the pool complex is on the roof. The facility is spacious but rather plain and underdeveloped in comparison with the rest of the property. One of the better spas and health clubs in Las Vegas connects both to the pool area and to the hotel.

The dining scene at Paris is a work in progress, with the homogenization mandated by the parent company, Caesars Entertainment, adversely impacting the quality of Paris's better restaurants. The flagship Eiffel Tower Restaurant is situated 11 stories above the Strip in the, of course, Eiffel Tower. Several other restaurants, closer to the ground, and including the buffet, also feature French cuisine. Options include the Italian-French Le Provençal; Les Artistes Steakhouse; Mon Ami Gabi, serving French bistro fare on an outdoor terrace overlooking the Strip; Le Café Île St. Louis, a sidewalk cafe serving classic French and American cuisine 24/7; and Sugar Factory American Brasserie, serving a wide array of sweet treats as well as salads, sandwiches, and more.

In the entertainment department, Paris features headliner Barry Manilow and hypnotist Anthony Cools.

You'll find two shopping venues. The Paris-Bally's Promenade offers French jewelry, women's accessories, an art gallery of French and French-inspired work, and more. Le Boulevard houses boutiques, a home-and-garden store, a gourmet food shop, and a newsstand, among other shops. And, of course, if you don't mind a little waiting, you can take an elevator to the top of the Eiffel Tower for a knockout view of the Strip.

Paris and its next-door neighbor, Bally's, share a monorail station, making both hotels a very convenient choice if you're attending a convention at the Las Vegas Convention Center.

Planet Hollywood
(planethollywoodresort.com)

PLANET HOLLYWOOD IS THE LATEST AND BEST INCARNATION of the Aladdin. The Aladdin opened in 1963 as the Tally Ho but was renamed the King's Crown in 1964. In 1966, the King's Crown was purchased by Milton Prell, who gave the property a $3-million face-lift with an Arabian Nights theme and dubbed it the Aladdin. For the next 30 years, the Aladdin changed ownership many times, which resulted in an eclectic, constantly changing identity. Each new owner of the Aladdin tacked on a wing, changed the carpeting, or removed the wall art inherited from the previous owner.

While the Aladdin was choking on its own mixed metaphors, the real estate it occupied became increasingly valuable. In the late 1990s, the Aladdin was once more acquired and promptly blown up to make way for a brand-new Aladdin, where the exotic Arabian Nights theme could realize its full potential and where there was room for a Middle Eastern bazaar–themed mall to compete with Caesars' Forum Shops and the Venetian's Grand Canal Shops. Though the vision of the new Aladdin was executed with flair and imagination, it failed to attract enough patrons to offset the considerable debt. After passing into receivership, the Aladdin was sold in 2003 to Planet Hollywood and Starwood Hotels, and then again in 2010 to Caesars Entertainment.

From the beginning, Planet Hollywood, or PH as it bills itself now, was committed to throwing the exhausted Arabian Nights under the bus in favor of a youthful, upscale, Hollywood look. PH, however, took its own sweet time in making the change, and it wasn't until fall of 2007 that the casino and all of the public spaces were completed. Guest-room renovations were completed in 2009.

The new look, clubby and masculine with dark woods and rich textiles, is drop-dead gorgeous. Carpet patterns and stone works capture the feel and beauty of a desert canyon and integrate them into a whole that is both sophisticated and relaxing. Face it, there are dozens of casinos that awe and overwhelm the senses, but only a handful that are artful and soothing.

Placement of the hotel lobby separates quite distinctly the bustle of guests and baggage from the casino, eliminating the flow of almost all transitory traffic in the casino. The casino floor, at almost three acres, offers the usual slots and table games but feels more exclusive. In fact, the whole casino has the ambience of sequestered high-roller gaming areas in other hotels. As for theme, there are some strictly Hollywood touches, but in the public areas it's very much understated.

The new guest rooms are created around a focal object of Hollywood memorabilia and a room-long combination wardrobe and entertainment center with a flat-panel TV. The furniture is a little large and plentiful for the size of the room, but the distinctly masculine overall effect is one of luxury and great attention to ergonomic detail.

Additional accommodations are available in the PH Towers Westgate, a nongaming, all-suite timeshare property positioned over the Miracle Mile shopping mall. For additional information on PH Towers Wesgate, see page 160.

Planet Hollywood has three showrooms, including the 7,000-seat Theatre for the Performing Arts. An additional two showrooms in the adjoining Miracle Mile Shops (formerly Desert Passage) make PH one of the most happening entertainment venues in Las Vegas. Speaking of the shopping venue, it has undergone a multimillion-dollar makeover, which converted the original Middle Eastern Bazaar design to a more contemporary look.

Retained from the Aladdin is the highly acclaimed Spice Market Buffet. Fine-dining options include KOI, serving a sort of Japanese-California fusion fare, and a clone of New York City's Strip House restaurant. PH has a rooftop pool.

Paris Las Vegas is only an eight-minute walk to the north, but the closest hotel to the south is the MGM Grand about a third of a mile away. The new CityCenter resort, however, is right across the street. Self-parking at Planet Hollywood is very confusing, and you must troop through the Miracle Mile Shops to reach the hotel or casino. If you are a hotel guest, definitely plan on using valet parking. If you're going to hit the shops, self-parking is fine.

PH targets an under-50 market from the southwestern United States and is also active in the European, Asian, and Latin American markets.

Plaza (plazahotelcasino.com)

THE PLAZA HAS THE DISTINCTION of being the only hotel in Las Vegas with its own railroad station (though passenger trains no longer run on this stretch of track). Occupying the historic site of the Union Pacific train depot midway between Los Angeles and Salt Lake City, the iconic Plaza Hotel and Casino at 1 Main Street presides at the west entrance to the Fremont Street Experience. The 1,037-room property has been completely renovated, and its two 24-floor towers, casino, and public space resumed providing downtown hospitality in September of 2011. With tower elevators nearby, the front desk and lobby are just steps from the 10,000-light porte cochere. The lively adjacent Aqua Lounge beckons guests with happy-hour and drink specials.

The spacious remodeled guest rooms are configured with queens or double-doubles plus a loveseat and coffee table in the sitting area. Blending contemporary décor are umber patterned carpet and blonde woods with dark, light brown, and cream fabrics accented with mixed shades of blue. Small bathrooms have tub-shower combos. The only closet is a small doorless box in the bathroom. All rooms provide safes and portable refrigerators. Coffeemakers are available on request. Every room is adorned with an imposing 1970s photo of the original Union Plaza. There is a desk with 32-inch TV and computer hook-up. Panoramic views from both towers sweep above downtown and the surrounding commercial area, neighboring rail yards, the architecturally idiosyncratic Cleveland Clinic Ruvo Brain Center, the soon-to-open Smith Center for the Performing Arts, and suburban Las Vegas.

The casino features 820 of the latest and greatest video poker machines and slots, a full pit of popular casino games, and a private pit where groups can gamble and party together. Bingo, now a rarity in most downtown casinos, is also available. Twenty-six TV screens of monolithic proportions are the prominent décor of Lucky's Race and Sports Book, Bar, and TV lounge. Individual screens also dominate its 40 counter desks.

All new restaurants include the diner, steakhouse, buffet, food court, and the signature restaurant at the all-glass second-floor Center Stage with an unparalleled sight line down Glitter Gulch. Adjoining the lobby are a coffee bar, video arcade, and gift and sundries shop. Entertainment includes rotating afternoon shows and a Rat Pack revue at 7:30 p.m. followed by an adult show at 10:30.

The expansive sports deck features a small pool with chaises and cabanas and a snack and cocktail bar. A wedding chapel is nestled among the meeting rooms on the second floor. The parking garage at the property's south entrance charges $5 per in and out, but that cost is reimbursed to hotel guests. Hotel customers are drive-ins from surrounding states and Texas. The property is considering a return to its original name, the Union Plaza, so stay tuned.

Ravella at Lake Las Vegas (ravellavegas.com)

THE NEW NONGAMING 349-room Ravella at Lake Las Vegas is the former Ritz-Carlton reincarnated. After the latter closed in May 2010, the property was acquired by Dolce Hotels and Resorts, an international boutique hotel operator, which rebranded the complex to reflect the style and urban sophistication of its new corporate owner. Within tranquil surroundings, the Tuscan-themed 15-acre lakefront property is approximately 22 miles from McCarran Airport and 25 miles from the Las Vegas Strip.

The redesigned rectangular lobby is furnished in gleaming dark woods and rich area rugs over tile and wood floors and divided into three sections: a business networking lounge with handsome library tables and complimentary Wi-Fi hookups, a center social lounge, and the Firenze Bar serving breakfast, lunch, small plates, and light dinners from 6 a.m. until 1 a.m. Cocktails are served on the outdoor terrace overlooking the formal Florentine garden and fire pit, an ice-skating rink, the marina, and the lake. Downstairs, Café Medici creates new menus every few weeks and is open when conventions are in the hotel.

Situated on eight floors, the 486-square-foot guest rooms with kings or double-doubles are serenely decorated in a pale Mediterranean palate of mint, butter, and beige. Luxurious 350-count linens cover feather beds. Furniture combines light and dark woods and includes a desk, settee tables, and occasional chairs. All rooms have a 42-inch flat-panel TVs, dual-line cordless phone, free Wi-Fi and high-speed internet, in-room coffee service, and complimentary daily newspaper. Marble bathrooms are oversized with a two-sink vanity, weight scale (ouch!), and separate tub and glassed-in shower.

Stretching across the west lip of the lake is the three-story 375-foot Ponte Vecchio Bridge over untroubled waters. Sailboats and kayaks glide underneath the bridge. This wing of the hotel houses guest rooms facing east toward the lake or west toward the stark desert hillsides. An additional parking lot lies at the north end of the span.

The peaceful 30,000-square-foot two-story Spa at Ravella is a separate building across from the hotel's circular drive and sits atop a sandy beach and waterfall with handsome heated pool adjacent at water's edge. A fitness center with 25 machines and weights; hair, skin, nail, and other salon services; a variety of European massages; and 24 holistic treatment rooms are available along with an indoor plunge, Jacuzzi with waterfall, and relaxation rooms. The facility includes a private garden proffering outdoor yoga classes, exercise sessions, and a meditation area. A restful terrace overlooks the pool, gardens, and the lagoon. During summer, a grill and bar provide sustenance poolside. For guests relishing the outdoors, hiking and biking trails hug the lake, and paddle boats, canoes, and kayaks are available for rental.

Valet parking is accessible and convenient. The parking garage near the southside meeting rooms is a distant stroll from the hotel lobby and elevators.

A wedding chapel, wedding planner, and florist are also on-site. The business center is in the conference area. With limited merchandising and meal service at the hotel, the Ravella has partnered with the adjacent Aston MonteLago Village Resort, a waterfront boutique retail and restaurant complex that allows hotel guests a variety of dining options with preferred reservations and the ability to charge meals to their hotel bill at the Ravella. The reopened Casino MonteLago offers 275 slot machines and electronic table games. Golf is available at the nearby Southshore Golf Club, the first Jack Nicklaus Signature Course in Nevada. The hotel can arrange airport transfers, but most guests prefer to rent a car for flexibility. Pets are accepted.

Red Rock Casino Resort Spa (redrocklasvegas.com)

CONTINUING THE UPSCALE EVOLUTION begun with Green Valley Ranch Resort and Spa, Station Casinos created a very similar and even tonier property in the Red Rock Casino Resort Spa. Set about ten miles west of the Strip on Charleston Boulevard and isolated from any other property of similar stature, Red Rock attempts to make itself a destination worth the trip. It's an impressive place, with a low, curving, monolithic roofline meant to echo the desert landscape and slopes of the nearby Red Rock Canyon. Inside, the decor and layout represent the continuing Station mission to fuse the "wow" factor with the practical desires of their local fan base. Stone, wood, and glass predominate; again, forms and colors are often meant to echo the surrounding geography. The overall impression is reminiscent of an accessible, upscale desert spa hotel, as opposed to the more glitzy palaces on the Strip. The casino's arrangement is similar to that of Green Valley Ranch—wide alleys between banks of slots and rings of table games—and the two casinos even share some of the same restaurants. Swarovski crystal is a favorite design element, with the finer restaurants and bars sporting hundreds or even thousands of individual crystals built into light fixtures or chandeliers. Several of the restaurants open onto the pool area, which, while not staggeringly huge, is quite elegant. Tiers of outdoor lounges and patios look over smaller wading pools and rentable cabanas, plus the inevitable pool bar. As you proceed further through the casino, the feel gets more and more "local"; the entrance on the far end is in fact specifically geared to locals, with close parking on the outside and local-friendly assortments of games right inside the door. This is also where you find the attached movie theater and Kids Quest children's complex, making it convenient to drop off the offspring en route to the casino.

Red Rock Resort takes advantage of its location by offering a number of outdoor adventure programs, including guided rock climbing, hiking, and mountain biking outings, among others. The spa at Red Rock Resort can hold its own with any on the Strip in variety of treatments and amenities offered.

Rooms and suites are extremely mod in appearance and in amenities, mixing chocolate browns and other earth tones with high-tech gadgetry and high-end appointments. Best of all, however, are the guest-room views. West-facing rooms look out onto Red Rock Canyon while east-facing rooms peer down the valley to the Las Vegas Strip.

Dining at Red Rock Resort is predominantly casual, except for T-Bones Chophouse. Other options include Terra Rossa for Italian cuisine, Cabo Mexican Restaurant, Hachi for Japanese fare, a top-notch buffet, a cafe, and sandwich shops. In the entertainment department, Rocks Lounge is the place for wee-hour dancing, while Onyx Bar and Lucky Bar provide stunning settings for a drink. For the sedentary there's a 16-screen cinema, and for the more active a 72-lane bowling complex.

Finally, a navigation note. Although Red Rock Resort is located at the West Charleston Boulevard exit off I-215, it's faster to commute to the Strip and downtown on West Charleston. Under most circumstances, it's about a 25-minute trip.

Rio (riolasvegas.com)

THE RIO IS ONE OF LAS VEGAS'S GREAT TREASURES. Vibrantly decorated in a Latin American carnival theme, the Rio offers resort luxury at local prices. The guest rooms (all plush one-room suites) offer exceptional views and can be had for the price of a regular room at many other Las

Vegas hotels. The combination of view, luxury, and price makes the Rio a great choice for couples on romantic getaways or honeymoons.

On Flamingo Road, three minutes west of the Strip, the Rio also allows easy access to downtown via I-15. The Rio's dining scene is headed by Búzio's Seafood Restaurant and Martorano's, an Italian eatery under the direction of Fort Lauderdale legend Steve Martorano. Unique is Gaylord India Restaurant, the only Indian restaurant located in a casino-hotel. VooDoo Steak & Lounge and the more casual All-American Bar Grille are the Rio's chophouses, and McFadden's Restaurant and Saloon (a famous New York City Irish pub) specializes in traditional Irish fare. The Rio has two buffets that are perennially at the top of everyone's hit parade. The Carnival World Buffet offers 300 dishes from a dozen cuisines prepared fresh daily, while the Village Seafood Buffet is one of the best seafood buffets in Las Vegas.

With five showrooms plus the free *Masquerade Show in the Sky* pageant and a high-energy stage show in the casino, the Rio's entertainment mix is one of the most varied and extensive in Las Vegas. Long-running shows include the *Penn & Teller* comedy-magic show and the *Chippendales* beefcake revue. Nightspots include the rooftop VooDoo Lounge, one of the city's most dynamic and enduring clubs, and Flirt Lounge, where guys can flirt with women warmed up by a just-concluded *Chippendales* show. Factoring in an extensive shopping arcade, a workout room, and an elaborate swimming area, the Rio offers exceptional quality in every respect. Festive and bright without being tacky or overdone, the casino is so large that it's easy to get disoriented.

Masquerade Village—a retail, restaurant, and specialty shopping venue that rings the casino—is home to *Show in the Sky,* a parade featuring floats and performers suspended from tracks high above the casino floor. Embracing the maxim that sex sells, the Rio has turned up the heat on *Show in the Sky,* with emphasis less on carnival than lingerie.

In a phased expansion over the past decade, the Rio has quadrupled its guest-room inventory, doubled the size of its swimming complex, beefed up its lineup of restaurants, and in the process turned into a true destination resort.

The Rio staff ranks very high in terms of hospitality, warmth, and an eagerness to please. The Rio is one of the few casinos to successfully target both locals and out-of-towners, particularly Southern Californians.

If you want to spend time on the Strip, the Rio offers a complimentary shuttle service with departures every 30 minutes to Harrah's and Bally's.

Riviera (rivierahotel.com)

EXTENDING FROM THE STRIP HALFWAY TO PARADISE ROAD (and the Las Vegas Convention Center), the Riviera is well positioned to accommodate both leisure and business travelers. The Riviera provides a complete package of gambling, entertainment, and amenities and has more longrunning shows (seven) than any other hotel in Las Vegas. These include a comedy club, a topless revue, a production show, a hypnotist, and celebrity entertainers and lounge acts.

Guests on the move can choose from a number of fast-food restaurants in the food court or go for the Riviera's buffet. More upscale restaurants round out the package and supply ethnic diversity. As for amenities, the Riviera provides a spacious pool and sunbathing area, a shopping arcade, and a wedding chapel. Guest rooms, particularly in the towers, are more comfortable than the public areas suggest. The guest rooms were modernized and renovated in 2009. It's possible, however, owing to the credit crunch in 2009 and 2010, that there may still be a few unrenovated rooms. If you book, insist on a renovated room.

The casino is large (big enough you can get lost on the way to the restroom) and somewhat of a maze. There is always a lot of noise and light, and a busy, unremitting flurry of activity. Walk-in traffic mixes with convention-goers, retirees on "gambling sprees," and tourists on wholesaler packages. Asians, Asian Americans, and Southern Californians also patronize the Riviera.

Rumor (rumorvegas.com)

"RUMOR—SPREAD IT!" is the catchphrase of Rumor, an all-suite boutique hotel directly across from the Hard Rock Hotel and Casino. Formerly the St. Tropez, the newly remodeled property is swathed in black, silver, and white with plum and metal accents creating a crisp mid-century techno look and feel. Like its boisterous neighbor, the hotel is geared toward a youthful market with low-decibel Euro-techno music on the sound system providing a permanent back-beat. Tucked into a corner of the lobby is the airy Addiction restaurant open daily, 7 a.m.–11 p.m. Alongside a small bar, the restaurant spills outside into the firepit lounge furnished with white leather couches shaded by mature palms and a white canopy.

The 150 suites, like the public areas, are a juxtaposition of dark and light. Charcoal walls and dark gray carpet envelop the kings or double queens, which sport cream colored bedding and plum accents. Most accommodations feature an elevated triangular hot tub alongside the bed. The living room includes a love seat, metal-latticed coffee table, and a side chair. All rooms have garden-view patios or balconies with chairs and side table.

The three-pool "Gossip" complex offers cabanas and daybeds and a plush lawn for hammocks and chaises. With the property's circular configuration, self-parking is limited, but free valet parking is available. Since the property has no gym, Rumors has a reciprocal agreement with the Hard Rock, so guests are invited to use the fitness facilities across the street. The $11.99 resort fee covers wireless Internet, in-room bottled water, pool party admission, and daybed rentals.

Sam's Town (samstownlv.com)

ABOUT 20 MINUTES EAST OF THE STRIP on Boulder Highway, Sam's Town is a long, rambling set of connected buildings with an Old West mining-town motif. In addition to the hotel and casino, there is a bowling complex, a very good buffet, one of Las Vegas's better Mexican eateries, a steak house, a cafe, and two RV parks. Roxy's lounge is popular with both locals and visitors and features an eclectic mix of live music and dancing. Sam's Town Live is the

Boulder Strip's first real concert venue, hosting acts such as Kenny Loggins, Tracy Lawrence, Lynyrd Skynyrd, and CCR.

Other pluses include a free-form pool, a sand volleyball court, and a spa. Joining the "let's be an attraction" movement, Sam's Town offers an atrium featuring plants, trees, footpaths, waterfalls, and even a "mountain." A waterfall in the atrium is the site of a free but very well-done fountains-and-light show (keep your eye on the robotic wolf). Frequent customers, besides the locals, include seniors and cowboys.

Santa Fe Station (santafestationlasvegas.com)

SANTA FE STATION IS ABOUT 20 minutes northwest of Las Vegas, just off US 95. Like Sam's Town, the Rio, and the Suncoast, Santa Fe Station targets both locals and tourists. Bright and airy, with a warm southwestern decor, Santa Fe Station is one of the more livable hotel-casinos in Las Vegas.

Santa Fe Station offers a spacious casino with a poker room and sports book. Restaurants include the upscale Charcoal Room steak house, as well as a Mexican restaurant and Station Casino's signature Feast buffet. The Chrome showroom features an eclectic mix of country and rock headliners, and there is also entertainment in the lounge. In addition to a pool, there is a bowling complex and a movie theater. Guest rooms, also decorated in a southwestern style, are nice and a good value.

Silverton (silvertoncasino.com)

SOUTHWEST OF LAS VEGAS at the Blue Diamond Road exit off I-15, Silverton opened in 1994 as Boomtown, with a nicely executed Old West mining-town theme. The casino has since removed or replaced much of the mining paraphernalia, however. The Silverton just might be the best-kept secret in Las Vegas. Its luxurious guest rooms feature dark hardwood furniture, leather couches, pillow-top mattresses, and tile bathrooms. Thick drapes and good soundproofing insulate the rooms from highway noise. At rack rates of about $60, Silverton hotel rooms are among the best values.

As concerns dining, the Twin Creeks Steakhouse can hold its own with any chophouse in town, and the 24-hour Sundance Grill, aside from serving excellent food, is a gorgeous room, reminiscent in décor of the celebrity chef restaurants at Bellagio or Mandalay Bay. On the quirky side is the Shady Grove Lounge, with a 1967 Airstream trailer and a couple of bowling lanes worked into the theme. There's also a Mexican restaurant and an excellent buffet. And good lounge entertainment is a Silverton's tradition.

In 2004, the casino was doubled in size and designed around $5-million worth of freshwater and saltwater aquariums. And speaking of fish, an adjacent retail development includes a 165,000-square-foot Bass Pro Shops Outdoor World megastore with indoor archery, a putting range, a driving range, and a stuffed specimen of every mammal on Earth. There are whales, dolphins, and game fish dangling from the ceiling, and earthbound creatures from every continent placed fetchingly around the store. There's probably more dead stuff in the Bass Pro Shops than in many cemeteries. Even if you're not outdoorsy, this veritable natural history museum is worth a visit.

In 2008, Silverton expanded the casino again and added a parking garage. Ten minutes from the Strip, Silverton is in a great position to snag Southern Californians. It also targets the RV crowd with a large, full-service RV park.

South Point (southpointcasino.com)

ACQUIRED BY MICHAEL GAUGHAN, THE SOUTH POINT sits almost alone in a huge desert plot off the south end of Las Vegas Boulevard, well away from the Strip. Rising up with nothing of comparable size anywhere nearby, South Point looks gigantic. This isn't just a trick of perspective, as South Point contains 2,163 large guest rooms, an 80,000-square-foot casino, two lounges, an enormous bingo auditorium, and a unique equestrian center. The latter, already being touted as one of the better indoor horse facilities in the country, includes a 4,600-seat arena and 1,200 climate-controlled horse stalls. The equestrian center hosts a number of prestigious equestrian events each year. For those without a horse, there's a 64-lane bowling complex, a 500-seat showroom that doubles as a dance club, a spa and fitness center, and a manicured swimming pool complex. Restaurants include Michael's Gourmet Room, a longtime Las Vegas culinary standard setter, relocated from Bill's Gamblin' Hall; the Silverado Steakhouse; an Italian bistro; an oyster bar; Primarily Prime Rib; Baja Miguel's Mexican; and a better-than-average buffet.

The decor of public spaces is ostensibly inspired by design accents from Southern California and the Pacific Coast, but the overriding visual theme is lots and lots and lots of yellow—deep golds to light wheats to every other shade in the crayon box. It's attractive and soothing, though not particularly memorable or interesting. Locals and regional guests are much beloved, and the roomy casino floor is a vast, open rectangle designed for their enjoyment. You only need walk along the walls to find the restaurants and lounges; the bowling lanes and bingo hall are up an escalator. The South Point rooms are quite large and have nicer-than-average beds, plus a few tech treats like big flat-panel TVs and high-speed Internet.

Stratosphere (stratospherehotel.com)

KNOWN PRIMARILY FOR ITS HIGH-ALTITUDE THRILL RIDES at the top of the "tallest (1,149 feet) free-standing observation tower in the United States," the Stratosphere has decanted money into its guest rooms and casino and emerges crisp, bright, and a more significant player in the mid-priced competition for tourists. The main entrance has been moved directly on the Strip, xerescape landscaping added, and an impressive port cochere replaces the original side-street entry. The hotel has created 909 "Stratosphere Select"–grade accommodations, which are $10–$20 more than a standard room. And the standard rooms are worthy, with a comfortable color scheme of cream and taupe bedding, dark furniture, and rust carpet. Bathrooms are tub-shower combos with one sink. Flat-panel TVs are in all rooms. The upgrade to the "Select" level is the similar king or double-double configuration with more attention to décor. White duvets with red, rust, and brown pillows and bolsters, plus a headboard and striped carpet share the same fall color mix. An armoire is included, plus the rooms sport a flashy red chair. Laminate bathroom counters have been exchanged for black marble, and linoleum floors are replaced with white tile. These rooms also include a safe and MP3 alarm clock. A resort fee covers Wi-Fi and Internet service.

The 80,000-square-foot casino meanders, the result of consecutive additions to the property over the last 15 years. New spectral cove lighting along the ceiling changes hues throughout the hours and is engaging to watch. Offering the standard mix of table games and slots, the casino is primarily a home for 21, slots, and video games, although roulette, crapless craps, poker, mini-baccarat, and Pai Gow Progressive are offered as well. The Double-Down Pit Girls add glamour and fun. The property has aligned itself with NASCAR and the Dale Earnhardt brand and displays Earnhardt memorabilia, collectibles, and slots. Along the perimeter are Starbucks, the C (circular) Bar, Images Lounge, and the decidedly garage-like Back Alley Bar. The sports book telecasts daily sports events and horse racing on nine screens in the second-floor showroom.

The huge eighth-floor pool deck faces south and west for enough or more than enough sun. Blue lounges and chartreuse umbrellas provide color and cover alongside two free-form pools and several white cabanas. There's a store for pool necessities, and bikini-clad Blackjack dealers provide eye candy during the summer months. For great food, a well-kept secret is the pool's Café Bar at Level 8, offering unique sandwiches at attractive prices. The multiple-choice mojito and margarita menu entices as well. A 24-hour fitness center is outfitted with weights and exercise machines and is free to hotel guests. The Roni James Salon and Spa provides beauty treatments and massages daily, 9 a.m.–8 p.m. Both amenities are in the second-floor Tower Shops arcade. Restaurants include the Top of the World, Plate Buffet, 24-hour Roxy's 50s Diner, Tower Pizzeria, and Fellini's Italian cuisine.

The property's crown jewel is the four-floor Observation Deck at levels 106 through 109 offering unsurpassed *National Geographic*–quality views of Las Vegas, the surrounding desert, mountains, and beyond. Level 106 boasts the rotating haute cuisine Top of the World restaurant, open for lunch and dinner. The Level 107 Lounge, Las Vegas's highest bar, is the focal point of the 107th floor. Level 108 features the indoor observation deck and Air Bar nightclub. The outdoor observation deck and entrance to three thrill rides are on Level 109. X-Scream is a roller coaster hurtling riders on a track over the top side of the tower. It stops and goes abruptly and dangles interminably. Insanity is a merry-go-round-like apparatus that swings riders in metal baskets over the edge at speeds of three g's. Most popular is the Big Shot, a gravity thrill experience that rockets riders up and down the tower's needle with a force of four g's. Day passes can be purchased for unlimited rides on these three attractions. The most recent addition is the Sky Jump, a controlled free fall from the 108th floor. Riders are suited up in special coveralls with cables attached to a high-speed Descender and then plunge 855 feet at 40 mph down the side of the tower. Those in the three top-floor restaurants, bars, and decks can watch these over-the-edge exploits.

The vast parking garage is on the west side of the property. At the bottom of the garage, escalators whisk guests into the casino, where the friendly information staff is spot-on providing assistance. Clients are primarily auto sports fans, regional drive- and fly-ins, and adrenaline junkies seeking an airborne rush.

Suncoast (suncoastcasino.com)

LIKE MOST OF THE COAST CASINOS, SUNCOAST is designed to attract locals. Located west of Las Vegas in Summerlin near some of the area's best golf courses, Suncoast offers high-return slots and video poker, a surprisingly good (for a locals joint) fitness center, 64 lanes of bowling, and a 16-screen movie complex. In the food department, the clubby SC Prime Steakhouse tops the roster. There's also a decent buffet, as well as a T.G.I. Friday's and restaurants serving Italian and Mexican. The casino is open and uncrowded, rendered in a southwestern-Mission style. A 500-seat showroom featuring name bands and a pool round out the offerings. For its size (427 rooms and an 80,000-square-foot casino), Suncoast offers a pretty amazing array of attractions and amenities. Perhaps Suncoast's most extraordinary yet unheralded feature is the breathtaking view of the mountains to the west as seen through floor-to-ceiling windows in every guest room. And, speaking of mountains, the Suncoast is a perfect location for anyone interested in hiking, rock climbing, mountain biking, or road biking in the nearby canyons and valleys.

Sunset Station (sunsetstation.com)

SUNSET STATION OPENED IN JUNE 1997, the fourth Station Casino (after Palace, Boulder, and Texas), just off I-215 in far southeast Las Vegas Valley about a 20-minute drive from the Strip (depending on traffic). Known as the "Henderson high-rise," the 21-story tower presides over a fast-growing residential neighborhood; with 457 rooms, Sunset is large for a locals' casino. It's also one of the classiest, most highly themed, and architecturally realized of the Station Casinos, decorated to replicate a Spanish village. The casino's centerpiece is the Gaudí Bar; with its tiled floors and stained-glass ceilings, it reflects the eccentric vision of Barcelona architect Antoni Gaudí.

Station's formula of good food, lounge entertainment and movies, child care, and extra touches prevails. It boasts a steak house, Italian and Mexican restaurants, as well as a Hooters, the Feast Buffet, a 24-hour coffee shop, and fast food galore. There's also a Kids Quest child-care center, the 500-seat Club Madrid lounge, a 13-screen movie theater, and a $26-million bowling center—the largest in Las Vegas. Extras include a pool and plaza area featuring two sand volleyball courts, a badminton court, and a 5,000-seat amphitheater.

All in all, it's worth staying in the slightly oversized and moderately priced rooms at Sunset Station if you're visiting friends and relatives in Henderson or want to be close to Hoover Dam, Lake Mead, or Valley of Fire.

Terrible's (terriblescasinos.com)

TERRIBLE'S IS THE PRODUCT OF A WELL-DONE $65-million renovation of the dilapidated old Continental Hotel and Casino. Located a couple of blocks off the Strip at the intersection of Paradise and Flamingo roads,

Terrible's offers excellent value with totally refurbished guest rooms, a good buffet, and a modest casino that's clean, bright, and busy. Terrible, by the way, is a person, Terrible Herbst to be exact. The Herbst family is well known locally for their gas stations and for auto racing. Terrible's targets locals but is a good choice, by virtue of its location and easy parking, for anyone who has a car and intends to use it.

Texas Station (texasstation.com)

OWNED BY STATION CASINOS, WHICH ALSO OWNS and operates Palace Station, Sunset Station, Boulder Station, Green Valley Ranch, the two Fiestas, and Red Rock Resort, Texas Station has a single-story full-service casino with 91,000 square feet of gaming space, decorated with black carpet sporting cowboy designs such as gold, boots, ropes, revolvers, covered wagons, and such. The atmosphere is contemporary Western, a subtle blend of Texas ranch culture and Spanish architecture. This property offers four full-service restaurants, a good buffet, plenty of fast-food options, two bars, a dance hall, a 60-lane bowling center, child-care facilities, and an 18-screen theater showing first-run movies. Texas Station caters to locals and cowboys and is at the intersection of Rancho Drive and Lake Mead Boulevard in North Las Vegas.

THEhotel at Mandalay Bay (mandalaybay.com)

LIKE THE FOUR SEASONS AT MANDALAY BAY, THEhotel is another "hotel within a hotel." Situated on the west side of the main casino, THEhotel can be accessed through a connecting corridor or through a dedicated porte cochere. While the Four Seasons is designed to blend with and reinforce the general style of Mandalay Bay, THEhotel, very much a boutique property, offers a starkly contrasting experience. THEhotel is clubby and masculine, with rich dark woods, modern furnishings, and a style that mixes empire, Art Deco, and Asian influences. The public areas achieve a feeling of both spaciousness and intimacy, while the suites are cozy in the way of a private library or reading room. Elegant and sophisticated—descriptors often applied indiscriminately—are words that fit THEhotel perfectly.

Though multibedroom suites are available, the standard one-bedroom suite at 725 square feet is the largest of any hotel in Las Vegas. The suites offer a separate sitting room with slate-colored walls and oversized upholstered couch and side chair. These are complemented by a polished-wood contemporary desk and side tables. The overall effect is totally congruent and extremely striking. A large flat-panel TV, a wet bar, and simple yet arresting Asian wall art complete the picture. The bedroom is more conventional with earth-toned soft goods but includes a dark-colored accent wall behind the bed. The bathrooms, appointed in granite, marble, and chrome, are large, with a separate glass-enclosed tub and shower. Because THEhotel targets business travelers, all suites are equipped with high-speed Internet connections and a fax/printer/copier.

On the top, 43rd floor of the hotel tower is Mix, offering fine dining and panoramic views of the Strip. Adjoining the restaurant is a lounge. An informal 24-hour restaurant on the ground floor rounds out the dining options. Also on the ground floor is THEbar. One floor up is a full-service spa and a fitness center.

T. I. (treasureisland.com)

ONE OF THREE MEGACASINO RESORTS that opened during the fall of 1993, Treasure Island is now the hipper T. I. On the southwest corner of the Strip at Spring Mountain Road next door to the Mirage, T. I. is Caribbean in style. Management thought the original buccaneer theme was juvenile and Disneyesque, and further believed that it was responsible for luring thousands of unwanted families with children to the resort. So down came all the pirate hats, sabers, skulls, crossbones, and all the other grisly skeletal parts that were the, shall we say, backbone of the joint's décor. The new adult version is fine but a little dull by comparison. The only vestige of the buccaneer days is the streetside battle where pirates now fight very adult, full-bosomed "sirens" instead of the frumpy English Navy. As you would expect, all the cleavage and leg ensures about twice as many kids in the audience as before. Though similar in amenities and services, T. I. targets a younger, more middle-class clientele than the Mirage.

T. I. is an attraction as well as a hotel and casino. Crossing the Sirens' Cove from the Strip on a plank bridge, guests enter a seaside village. Colorful and detailed, the village (which serves as the main entrance to the hotel and casino) is sandwiched between rocky cliffs and landscaped with palms. Every 90 minutes a pirate ship sails into the harbor and engages the sirens in a raging battle (firing over the heads of tourists on the bridge). Exceptional special effects, pyrotechnics, and a cast of almost two dozen pirates and sirens per show ensure that any Strip traffic not snarled by the Mirage's volcano (next door) will most certainly be stopped dead by T. I.'s battle of the sexes. The pirates are always defeated, of course, but have a lot more fun losing to the sirens than they ever did beating the British.

Passing through the main sally port, you enter the commercial and residential area of the village, with shops, restaurants, and, of course, the casino. The casino continues the old Caribbean theme, with carved panels and whitewashed, beamed ceilings over a black carpet, punctuated with fuchsia, sapphire blue, and emerald green. The overall impression is one of tropical comfort: exciting, but easy on the eye and spirit. In addition to the usual slots and table games, a comfortable sports book is provided.

The main interior passageway leads to a shopping arcade, restaurants, and the buffet. Dining selections include Isla, thought by many to be the best Mexican restaurant in Las Vegas; Khotan, serving Pan-Asian cuisine in a beautiful room; Pizzeria Francesco's; Phil's Italian Steak House; and Kahunaville, a sort of Parrot-Head joint serving Bahamian and Caribbean dishes.

T. I. amenities include a beautifully landscaped swimming area. The Caribbean theme gives way to luxury and practicality in the well-equipped health club and spa. Larger than that of the Mirage, the facility features weight machines, free weights, a variety of aerobic workout equipment, large whirlpools, steam rooms, and saunas.

T. I. is home to Cirque du Soleil's extraordinary *Mystère,* which is performed in a custom-designed 1,629-seat theater. Nightlife options include Kahunaville, a Jimmy Buffet Margaritaville clone, and a Gilley's Saloon.

Guest rooms at T. I. are situated in a Y-shaped, coral-colored tower that rises directly behind the pirate village. Decorated in soft, earth-toned colors, the rooms provide a restful retreat from the bustling casino. Additionally, the rooms feature large windows affording a good view of the Strip or (on the east side) of the mountains and sunset. The balconies that are visible in photos of T. I. are strictly decorative and cannot be accessed from the guest rooms. Self-parking is easier at T. I. than at most Strip hotels. Valet parking is fast and efficient. An elevated tram connects T. I. to the Mirage next door.

Tropicana (troplv.com)

THE SOUTHERNMOST HOTEL ON THE EAST SIDE OF THE STRIP, the new Tropicana is well located at the intersection of Tropicana Avenue and the Strip across from the MGM Grand, New York–New York, and the Excalibur. Once the "Tiffany of the Strip," the completely renovated Tropicana has been reinvented with a South Beach theme incorporating Miami's Nikki Beach brand. Vibrant tropical colors and music, natural light, and equatorial fibers and florals percolate throughout the property. The upgrades have created a fun-and-sun laidback lifestyle in the mid-price market. With the deconstruction of an entire wing and a phalanx of rooms enlarged as lofts, inventory has decreased to a cozy 1,658 rooms, almost placing the Trop in Las Vegas's boutique class of properties.

The guest rooms feel like a comfortable oasis in a rain forest with light hardwood, bamboo, and rattan trim throughout. Beige and gold patterned carpet, pillows, and walls accentuate the henna, cream, and warm brown tones that diffuse the rooms. The oversized standard rooms feature kings or double queens with 300-count linens, jungle red-and-white spreads, a desk console, and a russet cushioned daybed. Instead of drapes, plantation shutters cover the windows, and even more unusual—the windows open! All rooms include wireless access, 42-inch TV, dual-line phone, and a safe. Coffeemakers and refrigerators are available on request for a small fee. Bathrooms are standard tub-shower combos with a single-sink vanity and colorful decorative wall and floor file. Hair dryers are included. For an additional $75 per night, larger triangular corner rooms with a sitting area and a dramatic view of one of the Strip's major intersections are available. The room rate includes a per-night resort fee.

The reconfigured oblong casino offers 21 tables, midi and mini-baccarat, roulette, and craps. Overhead remains the hotel's original Art Nouveau stained glass ceiling. A poker room, slots, video poker, and the high-limit area dominate the casino's sidelines. The large Sports Book and Pub near the front desk has been updated and conveniently has an outside entrance. The Rotunda has become a party pit gaming area next to the Ambhar Lounge.

The Trop's luxuriant pool gardens are some of the most famous in Las Vegas, with 4.2 acres of mature palms and lawn embracing two pools, waterfalls, a lagoon cave, and two heated Jacuzzis all surrounded by white chaises. Nikki Beach outdoor café and bar features swim-up blackjack, sand volleyball, champagne beds, lounges, cabanas, misters, bottle service with hors d'ouvres, outdoor concerts, and a private island at pool center.

All restaurants have been remodeled with new menus and themes. On the main floor are the 24-hour Café Nikki bar, buffet, and café overlooking the pool. Close by are the Tropical Beach Deli and South Beach food court offering yogurt, pizza, sandwiches, Starbucks, and Asian fast food. On the second floor are the spare and elegant Biscayne Steak Sea & Wine, with a pool view and adjacent wine bar, and an upscale Italian kitchen.

In the Convention Pavilion are the wedding chapel, business center, a second Starbucks, and the Tropics Lounge. Retail stores scattered throughout the property include sundries, souvenirs, clothing, shoes, and several branded kiosks along the Palm Way overlooking both sides of the pool. The new Las Vegas Mob Experience interactive attraction and exhibit memorializes the rise and fall of organized crime and several of its prominent members. The Comedy Club features established and on-the-rise comedians, while the showroom presents a South Beach–themed headliner musical. For non-stop partying, Club Nikki is a 15,000-square-foot ultralounge and nightclub famous for its all-white décor and exotic cocktails. Included in the complex is Club Nikki Beach with a private pool open in the evenings.

The three-level Mandira Spa overlooks the lush pool greens from the south side with each floor specializing in a specific fitness and spa component: exercise room, an esthetician salon and barber shop, and massage treatment rooms.

The hotel's original main entrance at the corner of the Strip and Tropicana remains, but for easier access, use the new entrance on Tropicana Avenue east of the stoplight. This entrance also brings you closer to Club Nikki. Covered parking is on the Strip side just south of the main entrance.

Tuscany (tuscanylasvegas.com)

THE TUSCANY'S LODGING FOOTPRINT is 15 three-story buildings spread over several acres with an abundance of drive-up parking. Mature landscaping of tall shade trees and extensive grass is vigilantly maintained, and the complex feels like a large residential compound. Off the lobby near the fireplace are Tuscany Garden Italian restaurant and the Piazza lounge, which features nightly live music or a DJ and dancing. Beachfront Coffee displays luscious pastries, sandwiches, and drinks for poolside snacks. Although connected by a passageway, the lobby and the casino are separate wings. The Cantina and Marilyn's Café with take-out counter are in the casino, along with the games typical of a full casino—mostly slots but also craps, blackjack, roulette, a sports book, and a poker room—but all are downsized.

An all-suite property, the Tuscany's mid-size studio suites have been remodeled but still have a neutral look with a brown and cream color scheme. Rooms are kings or double-doubles. Cherry wood furniture includes headboard, desk, two bedside tables, and a coffee table in front of a gold loveseat and easy chair. Walls display stereotypical watercolor prints of Italian villages. The 25-inch TV is dated (no flat panels here) and sits on a bureau against the window, creating a glare if you're watching daytime TV. Tiny kitchens include a round table with two chairs, a wet bar, a small fridge, and a coffeemaker; microwaves can be requested. Bathrooms are serviceable with a separate tub and glass-door shower and one sink.

Amenities include two fenced pools (one is a lap pool) and a fitness center with Laundromat. Internet is free in the public areas; there is a charge for in-room connections. A resort fee applies but includes two free cocktails, 2 for 1 or a food credit, and a casino match play.

The Venetian (venetian.com) and The Palazzo (palazzo.com)

THE VENETIAN On the site of the fabled Sands hotel across the Strip from T. I., the Venetian is a gargantuan development constructed in two phases. The first phase, the Venetian, drawing its theme from the plazas, architecture, and canals of Venice, Italy, opened in spring 1999. The second phase, including a 1,000-guest-room tower, opened in the summer of 2003. The Venetian follows the example of New York–New York, Mandalay Bay, Luxor, and Paris Las Vegas in bringing the icons of world travel to Las Vegas.

Visiting the Venetian is like taking a trip back to the artistic, architectural, and commercial center of the world in the 16th century. You cross a 585,000-gallon canal on the steep-pitched Rialto Bridge, shadowed by the Campanile Bell Tower, to enter the Doge's Palace. Inside, reproductions of famous frescoes, framed by 24-karat-gold molding, adorn the 65-foot domed ceiling at the casino entrance. The geometric design of the flat-marble lobby floor provides an M. C. Escher–like optical illusion that gives the sensation of climbing stairs—a unique touch. Behind the front desk is a large illustrated map of the island city, complete with buildings, landmarks, gondolas, and ships. Characters in period costumes from the 12th to 17th centuries roam the public areas, singing opera, performing mime, and jesting.

Although the Venetian claims that its bread-and-butter customers are business travelers and shoppers, it hasn't neglected to include a casino in its product mix. In fact, the Venetian casino, at 116,000 square feet, is larger than that of most Strip competitors. When the Lido Casino came online with the completion of phase two, the overall resort topped out at more than 200,000 square feet of casino. The Venetian casino is styled to resemble a Venetian palace with architecture and decor representative of the city's Renaissance era. Period frescoes on recessed ceilings over the table games depict Italian villas and palaces. The huge and stupefyingly ornate casino offers 139 table games and 1,700 slot and video-poker machines. The perimeter of the casino houses a fast-food court, along with French, Italian, and southwestern restaurants, and one of the fanciest coffee shops in town.

Upstairs are the Grand Canal Shoppes, with 64 stores, mostly small boutiques. The Escher-like floor design continues throughout the shopping venue, with different colors and shapes providing variations on the theme. The centerpiece of the mall is the quarter-mile Grand Canal itself, enclosed by brick walls and wrought-iron fencing and cobbled with small change.

Gondolas ply the waterway, steered and powered by gondoliers who serenade their passengers ($16 per ride). Passing beneath arched bridges, the canal ends at a colossal reproduction of St. Marks Square. Like The Forum Shops, the Grand Canal Shoppes are arranged beneath a vaulted ceiling painted and lighted to simulate the sky. The Venetian adjoins its sister property, The Palazzo, via a shopping mall that connects the Grand Canal Shoppes to the Shoppes at Palazzo, which offer an additional 49 stores and six restaurants.

The Venetian's 18 restaurants, most designed by well-known chefs, provide a wide range of dining environments and culinary choice. Wolfgang Puck's Postrio, Joachim Splichal's Pinot Brasserie, Emeril Lagasse's Delmonico Steakhouse, Piero Selvaggio's Valentino, Thomas Keller's Bouchon, Tom Moloney's AquaKnox, Zefferino Belloni's Zefferino, and Mario Batali's B&B Ristorante are some of the culinary power-hitters represented.

An all-suite hotel, the Venetian offers guest accommodations averaging 700 square feet and divided into sleeping and adjoining sunken living areas. The living-room areas provide adequate space for meetings or entertaining.

The five-acre swimming complex and spa area are situated on the rooftop over the shopping venue and are well insulated from the bustle of the Strip. You'll find two standard pools, one lounge pool, and a hot tub. One of the largest of its kind in the country, the ultra-upscale bilevel Canyon Ranch Spa offers fitness equipment and classes, therapies, and sauna and steam rooms, as well as a 40-foot indoor rock-climbing wall, medical center, beauty salon, and cafe.

The Venetian targets the convention market with its mix of high-end business lodging, power restaurants, unique shopping, and proximity to Sands Expo and Convention Center (second in size only to the Las Vegas Convention Center). The Venetian certainly welcomes tourists and gamblers, who come mostly on the weekend, but the other five days are largely monopolized by the trade-show crowds.

THE PALAZZO It's a testament to the Palazzo's designers to see tourists who've already walked past replica pyramids, New York City skyscrapers, and million-dollar fountain displays still whip out their cell-phone cameras the first time they see the Palazzo's lobby. Much more pedestrian-friendly than the neighboring (and similarly ultra-luxe) Wynn or down-the-Strip Bellagio, the Palazzo is arguably the best combination of shopping, dining, and lodging in Las Vegas.

Opened in December 2007, the Palazzo is owned by the same parent company as the Venetian and is connected to the Venetian by walkways and the Grand Canal waterway. Like the Venetian, the architecture of Palazzo's public spaces employs arched passageways, Doric columns, fountains, and painted ceilings in neutral beige, yellow, and brown hues. Even with a three-story lobby, however, the Palazzo's decor is more subtle than that of the Venetian. That subtlety extends to the Palazzo's 105,000-square-foot casino, where the tables and slots seem to have slightly more walking room between them than at, say, the Bellagio. The net effect is a quieter, more relaxed feel. Depending on your preference (and your luck), you might consider this either a welcome relief or boring beyond words.

The Palazzo has 15 restaurants covering everything from Italian to Peruvian, including three steak houses associated with celebrity chefs: Mario Batali's Carnevino, Wolfgang Puck's CUT, and Eric Bauer's Morel's French Steakhouse and Bistro. Asian restaurants are also well represented with Zine Noodles Dim Sum and Sushisamba. If you're in the mood for Italian, LAVO is the fancy place, and Espressamente Illy is the cafe. Emeril Lagasse's Table 10 holds down the fine-dining category for American cuisine. In-room dining has an equally wide variety of choices and isn't as expensive as one might think, given the setting.

Shopping options abound at The Shoppes at Palazzo, with 49 upscale stores, including Barneys New York and Michael Kors. Shoe aficionados can debate the merits of Jimmy Choo and Christian Louboutin at their namesake stores, and there's no lack of jewelry and other designer-clothing options, especially for women. Slightly more affordable options are available at the Venetian's Grand Canal Shoppes, which connect to the Palazzo's stores and together provide hours of window-shopping opportunities.

A Canyon Ranch Spa provides everything from massages, facials, and a full health club to simple haircuts. While reservations for all-day treatments are recommended, we didn't have any trouble getting a walk-in hair appointment on 15 minutes' notice during one of the busier times of the year.

The Palazzo's 3,066 rooms are all suites. Rooms come in 720-, 940-, or 1,280-square-foot configurations. All have sunken living rooms and two flat-panel TVs; most have a single king bed, but some 940-square-foot rooms also have two queen beds. Bathrooms are spacious, with marble tile, another TV (with remote), a dressing table, plenty of counter space, and a separate bathtub and glass-door shower. The shower boasts multiple massage heads with enough water pressure to work out the knots in your spine after a long day hunched over the slots; it's one of the best showers we've had in any hotel in the United States. If you can't decide whether you're in the mood for that or a bath, a consultant is available to help you decide and provide options such as a rubber-ducky theme, a chocolate option, a rose-petal motif, and so on.

Service at the Palazzo is excellent: the staff is prompt and easy to find, without giving the impression that you're being watched. When we asked for directions, more often than not an employee walked us to our destination rather than describe how to get there.

Westin Casuarina (starwoodhotels.com/westin)

TALK ABOUT PHOENIX RISING. Westin acquired the old Maxim hotel, a place where business travelers reluctantly stayed when they couldn't get into Bally's, and transformed it into a high-end boutique hotel. Both the casino and showroom are modest by Las Vegas standards, but the guest rooms, though small, are exceptionally nice. The Westin caters to business travelers, so each room is equipped with dual-line telephones and a cordless phone, but you'll have to pay for high-speed Internet access. There is ample meeting space for small meetings and conventions. If you travel with

Fido, he's welcome at the Westin (they even supply a special dog bed), though you will have to pay a $35 cleaning fee and a $150 pet deposit. Travelers with some downtime can enjoy the pool, full-service spa, and fitness center. As for dining, the Westin offers Suede, which serves an excellent breakfast buffet. Situated about a block from the heart of the Strip, the Westin is within easy walking distance of dozens of shows and hundreds of restaurants. If you have a car, the Westin has ample parking and is easy to enter and exit. Finally, in case you're interested, a casuarina is a type of tree that is native to the Cayman Islands. If you want to see one, the Cayman Islands is where you'll have to go: there are no casuarina trees at the Casuarina.

WYNN RESORTS
Wynn Las Vegas (wynnlasvegas.com)

WITH EACH PROPERTY HE DEVELOPS on the Las Vegas Strip, Wynn's vision for the ultimate megaresort-casino becomes more sophisticated. Wynn Las Vegas opened in May 2005 and did so without whumping volcanoes, jets of water undulating to Frank Sinatra tunes, or pirate-versus-siren skirmishes. The handsome swoosh of the sunlit-copper glass facade stands in stark contrast to the immediate, raucous fun of traditional Las Vegas hotel-casinos. Up close, the building positively looms, and there's no attraction, no show, no kitsch visible to the passerby from any vantage point. That is the point. This megahotel-casino wasn't designed to lure visitors in from the sidewalk. Instead, it is internally focused, stylish, and mysterious. It's grown-up, and it's for grown-ups in the best sense of the word.

Wynn Las Vegas is all about exclusivity. The resort was ostensibly designed to bring to mind the exclusive boutique hotels of New York City, but with 2,716 rooms, 200,000 square feet of meeting space, a 111,000-square-foot casino, 76,000 square feet of shopping, an 18-hole golf course, an art gallery, and 22 places to have a meal or whet your whistle, that's one hell of a boutique. The trick, and it's done well, is to create intimate spaces within the larger whole. If Wynn's Bellagio is an ocean with one sweeping vista all the way to the horizon, then Wynn Las Vegas is a mountain river with a delightful surprise and changing view around every turn.

This is also the resort that bears Steve Wynn's name, and the man's flourish of a signature is on absolutely everything—from the building itself to the poker chips to the mini-bar snacks in guest rooms. It took two years of collaboration between a New York design firm and the Wynns to come up with the branding concept, and it includes everything from color palette (warm browns, rusty reds, amber yellow, and the occasional shock of chartreuse green) to typography to the logo and crest. Each thoughtfully considered detail has been approved by Steve Wynn, whose reach extends from personally testing mattresses for comfort to designing 18 holes of golf with Tom Fazio so that no tee-off faces into the sun. Longtime collaborator and interior designer Roger Thomas was on board here, too, creating with Wynn the immensely comfortable and well-appointed rooms.

But don't think that the exclusivity means that tourists and visitors aren't welcome at Wynn Las Vegas. Just the opposite. We found the staff to be one of the most courteous and helpful of any major resort on the Strip. The cocktail servers make frequent passes on the casino floor, the front desk and concierge are pleased to answer questions, and the security staff monitoring who goes where is kind and not in the least condescending.

One of the most remarkable aspects of this resort is that entering visitors aren't immediately shunted through a brain-rattling casino cavern, as is typical in most hotel-casinos. This adds to the impression that WLV is a resort first and a casino second. From both the main entrance, off the Strip, and the south entrance, off Sands Avenue, visitors are welcomed with a spacious, verdant atrium lobby. The ceiling is a high, domed skylight above an elaborate indoor garden where balls of flowers dangle like oversize Christmas ornaments from the branches of trees overhead. In addition to these two main entrances, the South Tower entrance, reserved for guests staying in the Tower, shares a drive with the south entrance.

In the casino proper, just to the left of the lobby, ceilings are raised over aisles and walkways and lowered over the gaming tables, instead of the other way around, as is common in many casino designs. We at the *Unofficial Guide* have lamented for years the suffocating atmosphere in most casinos and are pleased as punch to find a casino that provides gamblers with natural light and room to breathe. Another gaming amenity at WLV is a poolside casino (guests only) where you can work on your tan while you empty your wallet. Of course, there is the usual run of slots and gaming tables in the casino area, a 26-table poker room, sports book, keno, baccarat, and so on. The poker area is just across from the Ferrari–Maserati dealership, should you win really, really big.

The resort is loaded with exclusive brands like Ferrari and nowhere-else-in-Vegas shopping, most positioned along the shopping Esplanade, which begins across the main entrance lobby from the casino. Boutiques include couturier Chanel, Manolo Blahnik for the serious shoe diva, and the requisite Louis Vuitton, Cartier, and many others. Then there are the shops exclusive to WLV: Wynn & Company Jewelry; Wynn & Company Watches; and the Wynn Signature Shop. By all means check out the shopping on the Esplanade, but be aware that there aren't any retailers here you're likely to find in the mall at home. If you're prepared to drop $500 (and up) for a pair of fabulous heels, this is your place. If you need an extra pair of khakis or flip-flops, head across the street to the Fashion Show Mall.

There are many upscale options for a drink or a meal at WLV, all under the guidance of executive chef David Snyder. But even at the (comparatively) modest Zoozacrackers, a Reuben sandwich runs $10.95 plus tax. It was outstanding, but it smarted to part with such a sum for a sandwich. Both Wynn Las Vegas and sister resort Wynn Encore have their share of celebrity chefs. At Wynn, however, the chefs do more than lend their name to the restaurant—they actually prepare your meal. Steve Wynn insists that his chefs take full responsibility, and that includes being present. Standouts include Tableau for American cuisine, Okada Japanese

(AAA Four-Diamond winner), Bartolotta for Mediterranean seafood and shellfish (AAA Four-Diamond winner), SW Steakhouse, Wing Lei for French-influenced Shanghai specialties, La Cave for small plates, and Lakeside for nouvelle American cuisine (and a spectacular view overlooking the Lake of Dreams).

"Water features" are an integral part of creating intimate spaces at Wynn Las Vegas. The five different water features are keyed to various viewing areas such as registration, nightclubs, and restaurants. Probably the ultimate WLV water feature is *Le Rêve*. Under the creative direction of Franco Dragone, creator of Cirque du Soleil's watery *"O,"* *Le Rêve* is an aquatic Cirque-style show performed in the round. The claim is that no seat is more than 40 feet from the performance, which may be true. On the Wynn Las Vegas website, this warning is issued: "You will get wet in rows A through C of every section. In row A you may get soaked."

If *Le Rêve* inspires you to get wet, wade into the dog bone–shaped swimming pool, the long stretch of which will give lap swimmers just about 100 yards for stroking. The water is kept at a constant 82°F, and the landscaping surrounding you will delight and soothe when you come up for air. There is a complete spa, and the gym has Cybex equipment with plenty of amenities, such as one of the best free-weight training areas we've seen.

Aim high, if you can, in your choice of rooms, for the elevators are speedy, gentle, and quiet. Your reward will be an exhilarating view of the Strip, the golf course, or the mountains through your room's floor-to-ceiling window wall. When it's finally time to rest, you can leave on the gentle glow of the soft lights installed *under* the bathroom vanities—the perfect solution for a kind orientation in the middle of the night.

Barely six years old, the entire inventory of guest rooms and suites is being renovated at a cost of $99 million, in keeping with Steve Wynn's continual crusade for perfectionism.

Unexpected pluses include the self-parking garage that is closer to the guest elevators than valet parking. There's not a large hotel in Las Vegas that matches it for convenience. An unexpected minus was the signature nightclub Tryst, where we found it impossible to get in without proffering a serious bribe to the gatekeepers.

Steve Wynn has again definitely raised the bar with WLV. Overall, critics notwithstanding, WLV delivers, as promised, the innovative touches the city has come to expect from Steve Wynn. It's a resort for the 21st century, and its neighbors are going to have to get busy if they intend to keep up with the Wynns.

Wynn Encore (wynnlasvegas.com)

WYNN LAUNCHED CONSTRUCTION ON A SECOND HOTEL on the first anniversary of Wynn Las Vegas. The new 2,034-suite hotel, called Wynn Encore, is similar in size and design to the original hotel. More than an expansion of Wynn Las Vegas, Encore is a full-scale resort with a 74,000-square-foot casino, an elaborate pool complex, five fine-dining venues, a half dozen lounges and bars (including a hot and très-chic nightclub), a showroom, an upscale shopping venue, and, of course, a spa and fitness center. Standard accommodations at Encore are 700-square-foot suites with separate sleeping and sitting areas. According to Steve Wynn, the casino is modeled on Wynn's Macau casino (**wynnmacau.com**).

The signature components of Encore's environment are the color red, flowers, natural sunlight, and butterflies. Each is featured throughout the hotel with subtle and obvious flair. The rich, vibrant reds signify luck—appropriate for a gaming establishment—and the whimsical, beautiful, and colorful butterflies denote evolution and change. The most distinctive use of red is in the numerous hand-blown Murano chandeliers above the casino's gaming tables, the single largest order of Murano glass on record. The design of the fixtures represents the twirling of a woman's skirt, evoking fluid movement. The flowers too, predominantly red roses and red chrysanthemums, are effusive throughout. The two images abound in the red carpeting throughout the hotel and also prevail in the wallpaper and Venetian-glass tile floors of the atria, the casino, and the Esplanade at Encore shopping arcade. The poolside fountain near the indoor-outdoor Eastside lounge bar displays more red flowers, butterflies, and a dragonfly among red vases.

The Oriental influence at Encore is apparent from the moment you arrive at the hotel's dual porte cocheres, where two bronze sculptures greet arrivals. The Foo Dogs are replicas of large canines that historically guarded Asian palaces and temples by thwarting evil spirits. One dog sitting over a ball representing earth symbolizes power, and the other straddling a baby is the symbol of good fortune. Guests are invited to rub the paws of each dog.

The entire hotel feels open and airy. A deluge of sunlight flows though vaulted translucent ceilings and vertical windows at the main entrance atrium, as well as in the casino, conference center, shopping area, and nooks overlooking the pool. Those same windows transmit radiant moonlight as well. Affecting the light are lustrous white-and-beige marble floors and walls, which reflect the glow. At the main entrance beneath the vaulted ceiling is a suspended lattice treatment softening the austere upward view.

Encore restaurants include Sinatra, serving classical Italian cuisine; Botero, a chophouse; Society Café Encore, serving American cuisine; Wazuzu, featuring pan-Asian preparations; Switch, specializing in seafood and beef presented in ways that amaze; and the Lobby Bar and Café, a more casual venue. All Encore restaurants offer a sophisticated and visually exciting environment.

Sinatra, devoted to the memory of iconic entertainer Frank Sinatra (a longtime friend of Encore owner Steve Wynn), is decorated with Sinatra memorabilia, including photos, record albums, and Sinatra's Emmy and Oscar. Wynn, seeking the same dining spot Sinatra might have chosen, has selected the first booth on the right for his permanent table and is in residence many evenings.

The largest water features are the two oval plunges immediately outside the casino. The pools impart a San Tropez vibe with white cabanas, lily pods (reclining cushions surrounding umbrellas), and in-pool daybeds. The

Resort pool is bordered by a formal garden of slender amphora vases, flowering plants, palms, and evergreen magnolia trees. The European pool's island bar encourages guests to dip their feet while enjoying cocktails. Several blackjack tables are positioned poolside. Adjacent to XS nightclub, this lounge area merges with the nightclub's festive and sultry environment after dark.

Unlike many casinos that are an enormous spread of tables and slots, the Encore gaming floor is sectioned by columns and drapery to suggest intimacy and privacy. In addition to the standard casino games, Encore offers both pai gow and pai gow tiles. Roulette slots are included among the 1,600 slot and video-poker machines. For gaming comfort, there are low- and high-rise blackjack tables. The sentinels at the High Limit baccarat lounge are two life-size peacocks. These sparkling, long-plumed fowl are covered with crystals. The pocket doors at the lounge are embroidered in metallic gold thread on green-and-gold silk.

The second floor of the 61,000-square-foot Spa and Salon at Encore combines marble, flowing water, sunlight, and huge windows to provide an opulent indoor-outdoor feeling while you are beautified and pampered. Inside are more vaulted ceilings and tile floors. The hammered metal occasional tables, deep-cushioned couches and chairs, and sandalwood scent in the glass-enclosed courtyard impart a sense of India. The wow factor occurs at the entry to the 51 treatment rooms housed along two dimly lit extended passages featuring water silently sliding down cylindrical urns. At the far end is an inscrutable Buddha. The spa offers not just mere treatments but "transformational rituals." I wanted my waistline transformed, but none of the rituals evidently last long enough for that to be accomplished. A well-equipped fitness center adjoins the spa.

The Esplanade shopping arcade is well placed and leads to not only the Encore Theater but also completes a seamless transition from Encore into the Wynn Las Vegas casino. At the southwest end of the Esplanade is the Le Rêve Theater at Wynn Las Vegas. At the northeast end of the Esplanade are Botero restaurant and XS nightclub. Between these entertainment, dining, and nightlife venues are 27,000 square feet of shopping with 11 boutiques beneath a vaulted glass ceiling etched with a botanical pattern. High-end retailers include Hermès, Chanel, In Step, Shades, Mojitos (resort wear), Homestore, Nite Life Shop, and Wynn & Company.

Encore nightlife centers around XS (as in "excess"), a plush lounge arranged around lighted pools in a design that emulates the curves of the female body. Because XS is contiguous with Encore's outdoor pool, there is limited complimentary seating at the pool's lounge tables. If you're fortunate enough to score a complimentary seat, maybe you can make up for it by ordering an Ono—a Champagne-cognac mix that sells for $10,000 and is served with XS-logo silver cufflinks for men or a black-pearl pendant necklace for women (I promise I'm not making this up).

Guest rooms at Encore offer lovely views of the Strip or downtown through floor-to-ceiling, wall-to-wall windows with electric-powered drapes and sheers. The sleeping area is separated from the living area by a three-foot partition crowned by a high-definition TV on a swivel base. Seating in the living room is oriented to enjoying the vistas, with no furniture of any kind blocking the windows. Baths offer a separate tub and shower, as well as a private toilet with a locking door. Room lighting is high-tech with multiple control panels. With a lot of head-scratching you can figure it out on your own, but we recommend having someone from the bell staff or housekeeping give you a lesson. Signature suites are located at the west end of the hotel tower and have their own private reception area and elevators. Views are superior there (though not by much), and the suites are a bit wider than the standard suites.

Wynn Encore and Wynn Las Vegas each have a self-parking garage. The Wynn LV parking garage, placed between the Encore and Wynn LV resorts and entered from the Strip, is more convenient for those heading toward the Encore casino, Esplanade arcade, XS nightclub, and the Encore and Wynn LV showrooms. A subtle door in the northeast corner on the garage's second level provides an almost-covert entry into the Esplanade. The larger Encore parking garage is on the property's east side and is accessed from the Strip and an extended drive on the north side of the property. That entry is handier to the front desk, conference area, spa, and hotel elevators. Like the Wynn LV garage, an LED sign at each level indicates the number of spots still available.

Coming and going is easy at Encore. The main entrance is on the Strip, but in a section that's rarely congested. You can exit Encore onto the Strip in either direction or onto eastbound Desert Inn Road. Both Wynn LV and Encore provide complimentary shuttle service to the Las Vegas Convention Center and the Convention Center monorail station.

The client base at Encore is Wynn Resort customers eager to experience the newest famed Wynn hospitality and Asian visitors familiar with the Wynn casino in Macau. International visitors are plentiful since the Wynn brand is synonymous worldwide with classic grace, style, and service.

In addition to Wynn Encore, plans are afoot to develop the land occupied by the Wynn Golf Club. On tap are a 1.5-million-square-foot convention center flanked by two additional hotels with a total of 5,200 guest rooms. The new hotels and convention center would be situated closer to Paradise Road and be separated from Wynn Las Vegas and Wynn Encore by a 20-acre lake similar to that of Bellagio. At last word, construction was delayed by economic conditions in Las Vegas.

NAVIGATING *the* LAND *of the* GIANTS

GRAND HOTELS OF LAS VEGAS are celebrated on television, in film, and, of course, in countless advertisements. These are the prestige properties in a town that counts more hotel rooms than any other city in the world. Located along the center and southern end of the Strip, these mammoths beckon with their glamour and luxury. Specifically we're talking about:

Aria	Monte Carlo
Bellagio	New York–New York
Caesars Palace	Paris Las Vegas
Cosmopolitan	Planet Hollywood
Luxor	T. I.
Mandalay Bay/Four Seasons/	Venetian/Palazzo
THEhotel	Wynn Encore
MGM Grand	Wynn Las Vegas
Mirage	

But can so many hotels actually mean less choice? From a certain perspective, the answer is yes. The Strip, you see, is suffering a paroxysm of homogeneity. After you've chosen your preferred icon (Statue of Liberty, Eiffel Tower, pyramid, pirate ship, volcano, and so on), you've done the heavy lifting. Aside from theme, or lack thereof, the big new hotels are pretty much the same. First, they're all so large that walking to the self-park garage is like taking a hike. Second, there are high-quality guest rooms in all of the new properties, as well as at Caesars Palace, an older hotel that has kept pace. This is a far cry from 15 years ago, say, when only a handful of hotels offered rooms comparable to what you'd find at a garden-variety Hyatt or Marriott. Third, all of the megahotels are distinguished by designer restaurants, each with its big-name chef, that are too expensive for the average guest to afford. Ditto for most of the showrooms.

So let's say you're a person of average means and you want to stay in one of the new, glitzy super-hotels. Location is not important to you as long as it's on the Strip. How do you choose? If you have a clear preference for gondolas over pirate ships, or sphinx over lions, simply select the hotel with the theme that fires your fantasies. If, however, you're pretty much indifferent when it comes to the various themes, make your selection on the basis of price. Using the Internet, your travel agent, and the resources provided in this guide, find the colossus that offers the best deal. Stay there and venture out on foot to check out all the other hotels. Believe us, once you're ensconced, having the Empire State Building outside your window instead of a statue of Caesar won't make any difference.

As it happens, there are also a number of livable but more moderately priced hotels mixed in among the giants, specifically:

Bally's	Excalibur	Imperial Palace
Bill's Gamblin' Hall	Flamingo	Tropicana
Casino Royale	Harrah's	

Many of these hotels were the prestige addresses of the Strip before the building boom of the past two decades. They are still great places, however, and properties where you can afford to eat in the restaurants and enjoy a show. Best of all, they are located right in the heart of the action. It's cool, of course, to come home and say that you stayed at Wynn Las Vegas, but you could camp at the Excalibur for a week for what a Wynn Las Vegas weekend would cost.

BUSINESS HOTELS

MOST BUSINESS TRAVELERS stay in hotels with casinos or in all-suite hotels. There is one nongaming hotel, however, that merits special mention by virtue of its proximity to the Las Vegas Convention Center.

Renaissance Las Vegas Hotel
(renaissancelasvegas.com)

NEIGHBORING THE LAS VEGAS CONVENTION CENTER sits the Renaissance Las Vegas, a haven of tranquility amid the buzz and traffic surrounding the vast meeting complex next door. This 15-floor property on Paradise Road is a 548-room, nonsmoking, nongaming sanctuary. The oversized sleeping rooms have restful sage, apricot, and beige accents with light cherry furniture. Well suited for business travelers, accommodations include a lounge chair with ottoman, an ergonomic chair and rectangular work desk, an armoire, coffeemaker, clock radio, stereo and CD player, dual-line phone, dataport, Internet access, flat-panel TV, mini-fridge, safe, hairdryer, ironing board, and complimentary newspaper. Bathrooms feature glass showers, separate tubs, marble floors, and granite counters. Configured primarily with kings, there are also 180 twin queen rooms. Guests with platinum and gold membership status can access the Club Lounge (located on the 15th floor), which provides complimentary breakfast and evening cocktails and appetizers, a boarding-pass station, a flat-panel TV, and concierge service.

Through the main lobby, the large center courtyard has windows on three sides. A cozy outdoor area includes black-and-red tables, lounges, daybeds, and circle beds. Patio heaters warm the space on cool evenings. Food and beverage service is available. A small heated swimming pool and detached whirlpool are at the opposite end of the courtyard. The area is protected on all sides by the hotel's high walls—a welcome feature on Las Vegas's perennially windy days.

Award-winning ENVY Steakhouse, with a unique red marble floor, is open daily, 6:30 a.m.–2 a.m. There is also a glass-enclosed Wine Room, with more than 400 vintages and seating for 20. An abbreviated menu is available in the adjoining bar, and a popular Jazz Brunch is offered Sunday, 10 a.m.–3 p.m.

Services include a business center, 24-hour in-room dining, a health club, an activities concierge, valet parking, a coffee cafe, and a sundries shop. The rear parking garage has easy ingress for 400 vehicles. The property is close to the monorail stop at the convention center but is four lengthy blocks to the Strip—better to cab it.

SUITE HOTELS

SUITES

THE TERM *SUITE* IN LAS VEGAS covers a broad range of accommodations. The vast majority of suites are studio suites consisting of a larger-than-average room with a conversation area (couch, chair, and coffee table) and a refrigerator added to the usual inventory of basic furnishings. In a one-bedroom suite, the conversation area is normally in a second room separate from the sleeping area. One-bedroom suites are not necessarily larger than studio suites in terms of square footage but are more versatile. Studio and one-bedroom suites are often available in Las Vegas for about the same rate as a standard hotel room.

Larger hotels, with or without casinos, usually offer roomier, more luxurious multiroom suites. Floor plans and rates for these premium suites can usually be obtained on the hotel's website.

There are some suite hotels that do not have casinos. Patronized primarily by business travelers and nongamblers, these properties offer a quiet alternative to the glitz and frenetic pace of the hotel-casinos. Because there is no gambling to subsidize operations, however, suites at properties without casinos are usually (but not always) more expensive than suites at hotels with casinos.

While most hotels with casinos offer suites, only the Rio, Cosmopolitan, Tuscany, Signature at MGM Grand, Vdara at CityCenter, THEhotel at Mandalay Bay, Wynn Encore, and the Venetian/Palazzo are all-suite properties. The basic studio suite is a plush, one-room affair with a wet bar and a sitting area but no kitchen facilities. The Rio sometimes makes its suites available at $49 per night and is one of the best lodging values in town. In addition, Signature and Tuscany are by far the easiest to get in and out of if you have a car.

Many thousands of condos and timeshares, some stand-alone nongaming properties and others associated with established casinos, were being developed when the bottom fell out of the economy. The majority of these condos were pre-sold and under contract but for obvious reasons never closed. Now developers are trying to stay afloat by making these units available to the general public. If you check the travel search engine **kayak.com** or **lvahotels.com,** a number of these properties will pop up, usually at extremely attractive rates. As a corollary, developers dumping condos and timeshares into the city's room inventory has put downward pressure on hotel rates across the board.

SUITE HOTELS *without* CASINOS

Alexis Park Resort Hotel (alexispark.com)

THIS 496-SUITE NONGAMING PROPERTY was one of the first in Las Vegas to create this concept in the 1980s. Situated on 16 acres, the 19 buildings house a variety of suites ranging in size from bedroom-parlor combos to large two-level lofts. Front to back, all are being renovated. The standard junior suite is one room with king or double-double sharing space with a hide-a-bed loveseat, two side chairs, and a desk. All rooms have a 32-inch flat-panel TV, Wi-Fi availability, and dual-line phones. A corner wet bar with granite counters encloses a fridge, coffeemaker, and storage cabinets. Microwaves are available on request. Two doors open into the bathroom, which has a tub-shower combo. In the larger one-bedroom suites, a Jacuzzi tub and glass-enclosed shower are alongside the king-size bed. There is a separate large living room with easy chairs and a sofa, more kitchen space, and a small powder room. Architectural prints line the walls. Ice machines are nearby.

The property features three medium-sized fenced pools and mature lawns and landscaping. Buildings are freshly painted, but the passageways underneath stairwells are underlit and all walkways are in need of resurfacing. The exterior of the complex appears fatigued. Along with a comedy club, the lobby includes an Internet station, poolside Alexis Gardens restaurant, and Pegasus lounge to the right of the comfortable leather couch groupings and grand piano. Other amenities include a men's and women's hair salon, business center, and a downsized fitness center with limited equipment. Room service is available, and pets are accepted.

Best Western Mardi Gras Hotel and Casino (mardigrasinn.com)

THE MARDI GRAS OFFERS SPARTAN SUITES at good rates. Quiet, with a well-manicured courtyard and a pool, the Mardi Gras is only a short walk from the Las Vegas Convention Center. There is a coffee shop on the property, and a number of good restaurants are less than half a mile away. Though a sign in front of the property advertises a casino, there is only a small collection of slot machines.

Hyatt Place Las Vegas (lasvegas.place.hyatt.com)

AT PARADISE ROAD AND HARMON AVENUE, Hyatt Place Las Vegas offers contemporary one-room suites at good prices. In addition to a small fitness center, an outdoor pool, and a few small meeting rooms, Hyatt Place serves a complimentary Continental breakfast. By taxi, Hyatt Place is about four minutes from the Strip and five minutes from the Las Vegas Convention Center. The hotel offers a complimentary airport shuttle.

SpringHill Suites Las Vegas Convention Center (marriott.com)

WITH AN OUTDOOR POOL AND HOT TUB, a fitness center, a full-service restaurant, and room service, SpringHill Suites offers the amenities you would expect from a Marriott. And the small building and easy access to parking make the property easy to navigate. Suites are tastefully decorated, though not as plush as some Marriott properties. SpringHill Suites is directly across from the convention center, with a monorail station adjacent, and two blocks from the Strip.

PH Towers Westgate (phtowers.com)

IF YOUR IDEA OF NIRVANA IS A LUXURY HOTEL atop a cosmopolitan shopping center, the PH Towers (opened in 2010) is a good choice. The hotel is positioned over the 170-boutique Miracle Mile shopping arcade and is an upscale satellite of the Planet Hollywood Resort & Casino. Accessible from East Harmon Avenue, the 52-story all-suite red-and-blue tower offers several suite combinations to a maximum of four bedrooms with a parlor. The top five floors are residential condos, and the lower 47 are vacation-ownership hotel suites. All units feature high-tech components along with fully equipped granite and stainless-steel kitchens. Bathrooms provide a tub-shower and double sinks. Next to the king bed in the spacious sleeping room is a zebra-striped chaise and mirrored whirlpool tub. There are four flat-panel TVs throughout. Photos of Marilyn Monroe, the hotel's muse, can be found in all suites. A spectacular rectangular pool, framed by tall palms, faces south for all-day rays and no sun blockage by vertical buildings. Other amenities include room service, a business center, a gift shop, a gym, Starbucks, and 24-hour concierge service. PH Towers Westgate is about a five-minute stroll through the mall's south wing to reach the hotel's nucleus. This is a plus and a minus for guests: The plus is nongaming serenity with immediate access to eclectic shopping, and the minus is the significant distance to all Planet Hollywood venues. Guests preferring to stay towerside can sample the 15 culinary offerings within the Miracle Mile. The property offers front-door valet parking, but self-parking is only available in the Miracle Mile garage.

Platinum Hotel (theplatinumhotel.com)

THIS TRICOLOR, 17-STORY METROTOWER is one mega block from the famed Four Corners intersection of the Strip. An intimate all-suite, casino-less retreat, it's a non-Vegas hotel in the middle of Las Vegas. This property is a sleeper. The lobby looks and feels like a high-end high-rise. The Platinum's standard one-bedroom, the 910-square-foot Solitaire Suite, is huge in comparison to similar accommodations elsewhere. At the entry is a good-sized fully equipped kitchen. All bathrooms boast large Jacuzzi tubs, double sinks, and a separate glass shower. The celadon-and-tan bedrooms easily handle two double queens or one king plus an easy chair or loveseat. In the parlor are a queen sofa sleeper, side chair, coffee table, desk, and Bose radio. High-speed wireless Internet access and overnight laundry are available. Both the bedroom and parlor are furnished with 42-inch flat-panel TVs. The even larger 1,150-square-foot Princess Suite contains the aforementioned accoutrements plus a washer and dryer and show fireplace in the bedroom and living room. All units feature balconies. West-facing rooms oversee the center Strip area, while east-facing rooms reveal suburban Las Vegas and Sunrise Mountain. Extended stays are welcome. Amenities include a year-round, heated indoor-outdoor pool; KIL@ watt restaurant (open for breakfast and lunch); the ground-floor STIR lounge (open at 5 p.m. daily for happy hour with a limited dinner menu served 5–10 p.m. in the adjoining diminutive bistro); WELL Spa; and a fitness center.

Residence Inn (residenceinn.com)

ACROSS FROM THE LAS VEGAS CONVENTION CENTER, the Residence Inn by Marriott offers comfortable one- and two-bedroom suites with full kitchens. Patronized primarily by business travelers on extended stays, the Residence Inn provides a more homelike atmosphere than most other suite properties. While there is no restaurant at the hotel, there is an excellent selection within a half-mile radius. Amenities include a pool, hot tubs, and a coin laundry. A second Residence Inn is about a mile away at the Hughes Center.

The Signature at MGM Grand
(signaturemgmgrand.com)

THE SIGNATURE CONDO-HOTEL TOWERS OPENED in 2007. Located a five-to-seven-minute walk east of MGM's main casino, the towers provide a welcome respite from the frantic action of Las Vegas yet still offer proximity to the bustle and the endless amenities and entertainment options at MGM Grand. Suite accommodations feature floor-to-ceiling windows, full kitchens, flat-panel TVs, Jacuzzi tubs, and high-speed Internet connections. Signature's suites are not especially large but are beautifully appointed, and many units have private balconies. Each tower has its own pool, 24-hour concierge service, lounge, deli, fitness center, business center, and a private entrance with valet parking. The private entrance on Harmon Avenue makes for easy coming and going if you have a car. And it's only a five-minute walk to the MGM Grand monorail station.

Trump International Hotel and Tower Las Vegas
(trumplasvegashotel.com)

OPENED IN 2008, TRUMP LAS VEGAS is a nongaming all-suite hotel located on Fashion Show Drive about 600 yards west of the Strip. It's a hotel, not a tourist attraction, offering studios and one-, two-, and three-bedroom suites. Its 64-story tower is situated to provide good views in every direction through floor-to-ceiling windows. While there is no showroom or nightclub, there is gourmet dining at the DJT (Donald J. Trump) restaurant, libations at the H2(eau) lounge, an adequate pool, and an excellent spa and fitness center. When we inspected Trump Las Vegas we were immediately struck by the quiet of the place. From the lobby to the restaurants to the guest suites, it was restful and relaxing. The suites provide all the connectivity a business traveler could want, as well as full kitchens in the one- to three-bedroom units. Furnishings are Scandinavian contemporary, mixing dark and blond wood tones and restful pastel soft goods. Though it's a ten-minute walk to the Strip, Trump is directly across Fashion Show Drive from the Fashion Show Mall, Las Vegas's largest shopping venue. The Las Vegas Convention Center is about ten minutes away by cab, and the Sands Convention Center is about ten minutes distant by foot.

LAS VEGAS MOTELS

BECAUSE THEY MUST COMPETE with the huge hotel-casinos, many Las Vegas motels offer great rates or provide special amenities, such as a complimentary breakfast. Like the resorts, motels often have a very specific clientele. La Quinta Inn, for instance, caters to government employees, while the Best Western on Craig Road primarily serves folks visiting Nellis Air Force Base.

For the most part, national motel chains are well represented in Las Vegas. We have included enough chain and independent motels in the following ratings-and-rankings section to give you a sense of how these properties compare with hotel-casinos and all-suite hotels. Because chain hotels are known entities to most travelers, no descriptions are provided beyond the room-quality ratings. After all, a Comfort Inn in Las Vegas is pretty much like a Comfort Inn in Louisville, and we are all aware by now that Motel 6 leaves the light on for you. ·

RV CAMPING *in* LAS VEGAS

MANY CASINOS, including Main Street Station, Circus Circus, Silverton, Sam's Town, and Arizona Charlie's (Boulder), operate RV campgrounds with full facilities. There are also quite a few KOA or independent campgrounds. Of these, we prefer the **Las Vegas RV Resort** (**lasvegasrvresort.com**, ☎ 866-846-5432), one of the largest in town with 398 sites. Limited to adults, this palm tree–lined RV complex is located two blocks north of Sam's Town on Boulder Highway at 3890 South Nellis Boulevard. The 18-acre resort offers full hookups for pull-thrus and multiple slide-outs. Standard, deluxe, and premium sites are available. Each site includes a picnic table. Among the park's amenities are a heated pool and hot tub, a clubhouse with lounge seating and big-screen TV, two Laundromats, multiple shower and restroom facilities, free wireless Internet, and two pet runs. A small fitness facility is open daily, 8 a.m.–11 p.m. Every Thursday evening, a computer expert assists with laptop and desktop problems. Propane deliveries can be preordered. Daily, weekly, or monthly rentals are available.

ACCOMMODATIONS:
Rated and Ranked

WHAT'S IN A ROOM?

EXCEPT FOR CLEANLINESS, state of repair, and decor, most travelers do not pay much attention to hotel rooms. There is, of course, a discernible standard of quality and luxury that differentiates Motel 6 from Holiday Inn, Holiday Inn from Marriott, and so on. In general, however, most hotel guests fail to appreciate that some rooms are better engineered than other rooms.

Contrary to what you might suppose, designing a hotel room is (or should be) a lot more complex than picking a bedspread to match the carpet and drapes. Making the room usable to its occupants is an art, a planning discipline that combines both form and function.

Decor and taste are important, certainly. No one wants to spend several days in a room where the furnishings are dated, garish, or even ugly. But beyond the decor, there are variables that determine how "livable" a hotel room is. In Las Vegas, for example, we have seen some beautifully appointed rooms that are simply not well designed for human habitation. The next time you stay in a hotel, pay attention to the details and design elements of your room. Even more than decor, these are the things that will make you feel comfortable and at home.

ROOM RATINGS

TO SEPARATE PROPERTIES according to the relative quality, tastefulness, state of repair, cleanliness, and size of their standard rooms, we have grouped the hotels and motels into classifications denoted by stars. Star ratings in this guide apply to Las Vegas properties only and do not necessarily correspond to ratings awarded by Mobil, AAA, or other travel critics. Because stars have little relevance when awarded in the absence of commonly recognized standards of comparison, we have tied our ratings to expected levels of quality established by specific American hotel corporations.

Star ratings apply to *room quality only* and describe the property's standard accommodations. For almost all hotels and motels, a "standard accommodation" is a hotel room with either one king bed or two queen beds. In an all-suite property, the standard accommodation is either a studio or one-bedroom suite. Also, in addition to standard accommodations, many hotels offer luxury rooms and special suites, which are not rated in this guide. Star ratings for rooms are assigned without regard to whether a property has a casino, restaurant(s), recreational facilities, entertainment, or other extras.

In addition to stars (which delineate broad categories), we also employ a numerical rating system. Our rating scale is 0 to 100, with 100 as the best possible rating and zero (0) as the worst. Numerical ratings are presented to show the difference we perceive between one property and another. Rooms at the Riviera, Monte Carlo, and Orleans, for instance, are all rated as ★★★½ (three-and-a-half stars). In the supplemental numerical ratings, the Riviera and the Monte Carlo are rated 79 and 82, respectively, while the Orleans is rated 75. This means that within the three-and-a-half-star category, the Riviera and the Monte Carlo are comparable, and both have somewhat nicer rooms than the Orleans.

HOW THE HOTELS COMPARE

ON PAGES 170–173 IS A COMPARISON of hotel rooms in town. We've focused on room quality only and excluded any consideration of location, services, recreation, or amenities. In some instances, a one- or two-room suite can be had for the same price or less than that of a hotel room.

If you used an earlier edition of this guide, you will notice that many of the ratings and rankings have changed. These changes are occasioned by such positive developments as guest-room renovation, improved maintenance, and improved housekeeping. Failure to properly maintain guest rooms and poor housekeeping affect the ratings negatively. Finally, some ratings change as a result of enlarging our sample size. Because we cannot check every room in a hotel, we inspect a number of randomly chosen rooms. The more rooms we inspect in a particular hotel, the more representative our sample is of the property as a whole. Some of the ratings in this edition have changed as a result of extended sampling.

The guest rooms in many Las Vegas hotels can vary widely in quality. In most hotels the better rooms are situated in high-rise structures known locally as "towers." More modest accommodations, called "garden rooms," are routinely found in one- and two-story outbuildings. It is important to understand that not all rooms in a particular hotel are the same. When you make inquiries or reservations, always define the type of room you are talking about.

Finally, before you begin to shop for a hotel, take a hard look at this letter we received from a couple in Hot Springs, Arkansas:

> We canceled our room reservations to follow the advice in your book [and reserved a hotel room highly ranked by the Unofficial Guide]. We wanted inexpensive, but clean and cheerful. We got inexpensive, but [also] dirty, grim, and depressing. I really felt disappointed in your advice and the room. It was the pits. That was the one real piece of information I needed from your book! The room spoiled the holiday for me aside from our touring.

Needless to say, this letter was as unsettling to us as the bad room was to our reader. Our integrity as travel journalists, after all, is based on the quality of the information we provide to our readers. Even with the best of intentions and the most conscientious research, however, we cannot inspect every room in every hotel. What we do, in statistical terms, is take a sample: we check out several rooms selected at random in each hotel and base our ratings and rankings on those rooms. The inspections are conducted anonymously and without the knowledge of the management. Although it would be unusual, it is certainly possible that the rooms we randomly inspect are not representative of the majority of rooms at a particular hotel. Another possibility is that the rooms we inspect in a given hotel are representative but that by bad luck a reader is assigned a room that is inferior. When we rechecked the hotel our reader disliked, we discovered that our rating was correctly representative, but that he and his wife had unfortunately been assigned to one of a small number of threadbare rooms scheduled for renovation.

The key to avoiding disappointment is to snoop around in advance. We recommend that you check out the hotel's website before you book. Be forewarned, however, that some hotel chains use the same guest room photo for all hotels in the chain; a specific guest room may not resemble the brochure photo. When you or your travel agent call, ask how old the property is and when your guest room was last renovated. If you arrive and are assigned a room inferior to that which you had been led to expect, demand to be moved to another room deserving of your expectations.

Cost estimates are based on the hotel's published rack rates for standard rooms, averaged between weekday and weekend prices. Rack rates during the recession, as you can imagine, are in a continual state of flux, so with a little effort you should be able to significantly beat the rates listed. Each "$" represents $50. Thus a cost symbol of "$$$" means a room (or suite) at that hotel will cost about $150 a night.

THE TOP 30 BEST DEALS IN LAS VEGAS

HAVING LISTED THE NICEST ROOMS in town, we also reorder the list to rank the best combinations of quality and value in a room. As before, the rankings are made without consideration of location or the availability of restaurants, recreational facilities, entertainment, and/ or amenities.

A reader recently complained to us that he had booked one of our top-ranked rooms in terms of value and had been very disappointed in the room. We noticed that the room the reader occupied had a quality rating of ★★½. We would remind you that the value ratings are intended to give you some sense of value received for dollars spent. A ★★½ room at $30 may have the same value rating as a ★★★★ room at $85, but that does not mean the rooms will be of comparable quality. Regardless of whether it's a good deal or not, a ★★½ room is still a ★★½ room.

Listed on the following page are the best room buys for the money, regardless of location or star classification, based on averaged rack rates. Note that sometimes a suite can cost less than a hotel room.

WHEN ONLY THE BEST WILL DO

THE TROUBLE WITH PROFILES is that details and distinctions are sacrificed in the interest of brevity and information accessibility. For example, while dozens of properties are listed as having swimming pools, we've made no qualitative discriminations. In the alphabetized profiles, a pool is a pool.

Top 30 Best Deals

HOTEL	STAR RATING	ROOM RATING	COST ($=$50)	LOCATION
1. Eastside Cannery	★★★★	83	$+	Boulder Highway
2. Terrible's	★★★½	78	$+	East of Strip
3. Fitzgeralds	★★★½	76	$+	Downtown
4. Sunset Station	★★★★	87	$$−	Henderson
5. Las Vegas Club (north tower)	★★★	73	$+	Downtown
6. El Cortez	★★★	72	$+	Downtown
7. Days Inn at Wild Wild West	★★★	68	$+	South Strip
8. Artisan Hotel and Spa	★★★½	78	$$−	North Strip
9. Fiesta Henderson	★★★	72	$+	Henderson
10. Silverton	★★★★	88	$$+	South of Las Vegas
11. Gold Spike	★★½	64	$	Downtown
12. Royal Resort	★★★	73	$+	North Strip
13. Las Vegas Hilton	★★★★	85	$$+	East of Strip
14. Boulder Station	★★★½	76	$$−	Boulder Highway
15. South Point	★★★½	81	$$	South of Las Vegas
16. Main Street Station	★★★½	75	$$−	Downtown
17. Rumor	★★★½	78	$$	East of Strip
18. Santa Fe Station	★★★	73	$$−	Rancho Drive
19. Aliante Station	★★★★	88	$$$−	North Las Vegas
20. Circus Circus (tower rooms)	★★★½	81	$$	North Strip
21. Fremont	★★★	70	$$−	Downtown
22. Riviera	★★★½	79	$$	North Strip
23. Renaissance Las Vegas	★★★★½	90	$$$	East of Strip
24. El Cortez Cabana Suites	★★★	72	$$−	Downtown
25. Las Vegas Club (south tower)	★★½	58	$	Downtown
26. Sam's Town	★★★½	79	$$	Boulder Highway
27. Palace Station (tower rooms)	★★★½	81	$$+	North Strip
28. Texas Station	★★★	70	$$−	Rancho Drive Area
29. Red Rock Resort	★★★★½	91	$$$+	Summerlin
30. Manor Suites	★★★	67	$$−	South of Las Vegas

In actuality, of course, though most pools are quite basic and ordinary, some (Wynn Las Vegas, Wynn Encore, Mirage, Tropicana, Flamingo, Monte Carlo, MGM Grand, Planet Hollywood, Mandalay Bay, Bellagio, Caesars Palace, M Resort, Venetian, JW Marriott Las Vegas, Aria at CityCenter, and the Rio) are pretty spectacular. To distinguish the exceptional from the average in a number of categories, we provide a best-of list below.

BEST DINING (Expense No Issue)

1. Cosmopolitan
2. Wynn Las Vegas/Wynn Encore
3. Venetian/Palazzo
4. CityCenter
5. Bellagio
6. Caesars Palace
7. MGM Grand
8. Mandalay Bay
9. Mirage

BEST DINING (For Great Value)

1. Orleans
2. Suncoast
3. California
4. Main Street Station
5. Gold Coast
6. Palace Station
7. South Point
8. Fiesta Rancho
9. Boulder Station
10. Sam's Town

BEST SUNDAY BRUNCHES (listed alphabetically

Cookin' with Jazz Brunch, Wynn Las Vegas
Gospel Brunch, House of Blues at Mandalay Bay
Jasmine, Bellagio
Simon Brunch, Palms Place
Sterling Brunch, Bally's

BEST BUFFETS

1. Cosmopolitan Wicked Spoon Buffet
2. Wynn Buffet
3. Bellagio Buffet
4. M Resort Studio B Buffet
5. Planet Hollywood Spice Market Buffet
6. Mirage Cravings
7. Aria Buffet
8. Buffet at T. I.
9. Red Rock Feast
10. Rio Carnival World

MOST VISUALLY INTERESTING HOTELS

1. Venetian
2. Caesars Palace
3. Wynn Las Vegas/Wynn Encore
4. Bellagio
5. Mandalay Bay
6. Luxor
7. Red Rock Resort
8. Mirage
9. New York–New York
10. Paris Las Vegas
11. M Resort
12. Aria at CityCenter
13. Rio
14. Cosmopolitan
15. Planet Hollywood

BEST FOR BOWLING (listed alphabetically)

Gold Coast
Orleans
Red Rock Resort
Sam's Town
Sante Fe Station
South Point
Sunset Station
Texas Station

BEST SPAS (listed alphabetically)

Bellagio
Caesars Palace
CityCenter: Aria, Mandarin Oriental, Vdara
Cosmopolitan
Green Valley Ranch Resort and Spa
Mandalay Bay/THEhotel/Four Seasons
MGM Grand
Mirage
Monte Carlo
Palazzo
Paris Las Vegas
Red Rock Resort
T. I.
Trump Las Vegas
Venetian
Wynn Encore
Wynn Las Vegas

BEST FOR GOLF (listed alphabetically)

Aliante Station
JW Marriott Las Vegas
Las Vegas Hilton
Ravella
Suncoast
Wynn Las Vegas

BEST FOR TENNIS (listed alphabetically)

Bally's
Cosmopolitan
Flamingo
JW Marriott Las Vegas
Las Vegas Hilton
Monte Carlo
Paris Las Vegas
Plaza
Riviera

BEST FOR SHOPPING ON-SITE OR WITHIN AN EIGHT-MINUTE WALK

1. Caesars Palace
2. Venetian
3. Mirage
4. Wynn Las Vegas/Wynn Encore
5. T. I.
6. Planet Hollywood
7. CityCenter
8. Trump Las Vegas
9. Cosmopolitan

How the Hotels Compare in Las Vegas

HOTEL	STAR RATING	ROOM RATING	COST ($ = $50)	LOCATION
Mandarin Oriental at CityCenter	★★★★★	96	$$$$$$–	Mid Strip
Signature at MGM Grand (all suites)	★★★★★	96	$$$$+	East of Strip
THEhotel at Mandalay Bay (all suites)	★★★★★	96	$$$$$	South Strip
Wynn Encore	★★★★★	96	$$$$$$–	Mid Strip
Aria at CityCenter	★★★★½	95	$$$$$$	Mid Strip
Bellagio	★★★★½	95	$$$$$$$+	Mid Strip
Caesars Palace	★★★★½	95	$$$$$$–	Mid Strip
Four Seasons at Mandalay Bay	★★★★½	95	$$$$$$$–	South Strip
Hard Rock Hotel	★★★★½	95	$$$$–	East of Strip
The Palazzo (all suites)	★★★★½	95	$$$$$$–	Mid Strip
Palms (Palms Tower)	★★★★½	95	$$$$$$–	West of Strip
Trump International Hotel & Tower Las Vegas (all suites)	★★★★½	95	$$$+	West of Strip
Vdara at CityCenter	★★★★½	95	$$$$$$–	Mid Strip
Wynn Las Vegas	★★★★½	95	$$$$$$–	Mid Strip
Cosmopolitan	★★★★½	94	$$$$$$$–	Mid Strip
The Venetian	★★★★½	94	$$$$$$–	Mid Strip
JW Marriott Las Vegas	★★★★½	93	$$$$	Summerlin
PH Towers Westgate	★★★★½	93	$$$$$	Mid Strip
Mandalay Bay	★★★★½	92	$$$$$+	South Strip
Paris	★★★★½	91	$$$$$$–	Mid Strip
Red Rock Resort	★★★★½	91	$$$+	Summerlin
Golden Nugget (Rush Tower)	★★★★½	90	$$$+	Downtown
M Resort	★★★★½	90	$$$+	South of Las Vegas
Mirage	★★★★½	90	$$$$–	Mid Strip
Renaissance Las Vegas	★★★★½	90	$$$	East of Strip
Palms (Fantasy Tower)	★★★★	89	$$$$	West of Strip
Tropicana	★★★★	89	$$$+	South Strip
Aliante Station	★★★★	88	$$$–	North Las Vegas
Loews Lake Las Vegas	★★★★	88	$$$$	Henderson
Platinum Hotel	★★★★	88	$$$$+	East of Strip

HOTEL	STAR RATING	ROOM RATING	COST ($ = $50)	LOCATION
Ravella at Lake Las Vegas	★★★★	88	$$$	Henderson
Silverton	★★★★	88	$$+	South of Las Vegas
Embassy Suites Convention Center	★★★★	87	$$$+	East of Strip
Flamingo	★★★★	87	$$$	Mid Strip
Green Valley Ranch Resort and Spa	★★★★	87	$$$	Henderson
Luxor	★★★★	87	$$$+	South Strip
MGM Grand	★★★★	87	$$$$$	South Strip
Planet Hollywood	★★★★	87	$$$$$−	Mid Strip
Sunset Station	★★★★	87	$$−	Henderson
Embassy Suites in Las Vegas	★★★★	86	$$$−	East of Strip
Residence Inn by Marriott Las Vegas South	★★★★	86	$$$−	South Strip
Rio	★★★★	86	$$$+	Mid Strip
Bally's	★★★★	85	$$$$+	Mid Strip
Las Vegas Hilton	★★★★	85	$$+	East of Strip
New York–New York	★★★★	85	$$$$	South Strip
Las Vegas Marriott	★★★★	84	$$$$−	East of Strip
Treasure Island (T.I.)	★★★★	84	$$$$+	Mid Strip
Eastside Cannery	★★★★	83	$+	Boulder Highway
Residence Inn by Marriott Las Vegas Convention Center	★★★★	83	$$$	East of Strip
Westin Casuarina	★★★★	83	$$$+	East of Strip
Monte Carlo	★★★½	82	$$$	Mid Strip
Suncoast	★★★½	82	$$$+	Summerlin
Circus Circus (tower rooms)	★★★½	81	$$	North Strip
Harrah's	★★★½	81	$$$	Mid Strip
Palace Station (tower rooms)	★★★½	81	$$+	North Strip
South Point	★★★½	81	$$	South of Las Vegas
Candlewood Suites	★★★½	79	$$+	East of Strip
Courtyard by Marriott LV Convention Center	★★★½	79	$$$	East of Strip
Plaza	★★★½	79	$$+	Downtown
Riviera	★★★½	79	$$	North Strip

How the Hotels Compare (continued)

HOTEL	STAR RATING	ROOM RATING	COST ($ = $50)	LOCATION
Sam's Town	★★★½	79	$$	Boulder Highway
Stratosphere	★★★½	79	$$+	North Strip
Artisan Hotel and Spa	★★★½	78	$$−	North Strip
Golden Nugget	★★★½	78	$$$−	Downtown
Rumor	★★★½	78	$$	East of Strip
Terrible's	★★★½	78	$+	East of Strip
Bill's Gamblin' Hall and Saloon	★★★½	76	$$$	Mid Strip
Boulder Station	★★★½	76	$$−	Boulder Highway
Excalibur	★★★½	76	$$$	South Strip
Fitzgeralds	★★★½	76	$+	Downtown
Courtyard by Marriott Las Vegas South	★★★½	75	$$$	South Strip
Fairfield Inn & Suites Las Vegas South	★★★½	75	$$$	South Strip
Holiday Inn Express	★★★½	75	$$$	South Strip
Main Street Station	★★★½	75	$$−	Downtown
Orleans	★★★½	75	$$$	South Strip
Arizona Charlie's Boulder	★★★	74	$$$+	Boulder Highway
Palace Station (courtyard)	★★★	74	$$−	North Strip
Best Western Mardi Gras Hotel and Casino	★★★	73	$$	East of Strip
Hooters Casino Hotel	★★★	73	$$$+	South Strip
Royal Resort	★★★	73	$+	North Strip
Santa Fe Station	★★★	73	$$−	Rancho Drive
Las Vegas Club (north tower)	★★★	73	$+	Downtown
El Cortez	★★★	72	$+	Downtown
El Cortez Cabana Suites	★★★	72	$$−	Downtown
Fairfield Inn Las Vegas Airport	★★★	72	$$$−	East of Strip
Fiesta Henderson	★★★	72	$+	Henderson
Hampton Inn Tropicana	★★★	72	$$$−	South Strip
Hilton Garden Inn Las Vegas Strip South	★★★	72	$$$−	South of Las Vegas

HOTEL	STAR RATING	ROOM RATING	COST ($ = $50)	LOCATION
Hyatt Place	★★★	72	$$$+	East of Strip
Alexis Park Resort and Villas	★★★	71	$$	East of Strip
Best Western McCarran Inn	★★★	71	$$+	East of Strip
Four Queens	★★★	70	$$−	Downtown
Fremont	★★★	70	$$−	Downtown
Texas Station	★★★	70	$$−	Rancho Drive Area
Tuscany	★★★	70	$$$−	East of Strip
La Quinta Las Vegas Airport North	★★★	69	$$+	East of Strip
Comfort Inn Paradise Road	★★★	68	$$−	East of Strip
Days Inn at Wild Wild West	★★★	68	$+	South Strip
Imperial Palace	★★★	68	$$$+	Mid Strip
Ramada Las Vegas	★★★	68	$$+	East of Strip
California	★★★	67	$$	Downtown
Manor Suites	★★★	67	$$−	South of Las Vegas
Arizona Charlie's Decatur	★★★	66	$$$−	West Las Vegas
Clarion Hotel and Casino	★★★	65	$$+	North Strip
Cannery	★★½	64	$$−	North Las Vegas
Casino Royale	★★½	64	$$+	Mid Strip
Gold Spike	★★½	64	$	Downtown
Quality Inn Las Vegas	★★½	64	$$	South Strip
Fiesta Rancho	★★½	62	$$−	Rancho Drive
Circus Circus (manor rooms)	★★½	59	$$−	North Strip
Gold Coast	★★½	58	$$$−	Mid Strip
Las Vegas Club (south tower)	★★½	58	$	Downtown
Motel 6	★★	53	$$−	Downtown
Motel 6 Tropicana	★★	53	$$−	East of Strip
Golden Gate	★★	52	$$−	Downtown
Super 8	★★	52	$$	East of Strip
Ambassador Strip Inn Travelodge	★½	43	$$$	South Strip
America's Best Value Inn	★	33	$$$−	South Strip

Hotel Information Chart

Alexis Park Resort and Villas ★★★	
375 E. Harmon Ave.	
Las Vegas, NV 89169	
☎ 702-796-3300	
FAX 702-796-4334	
TOLL FREE 800-453-8000	
alexispark.com	
RACK RATE	$$
ROOM QUALITY	71
LOCATION	East of Strip
DISCOUNTS	Gov't, military, AAA, AARP
NO. OF ROOMS	495
CHECKOUT TIME	11
NONSMOKING	•
CONCIERGE	•
CONVENTION FACIL.	•
MEETING ROOMS	•
VALET PARKING	•
RV PARK	Limited
ROOM SERVICE	•
FREE BREAKFAST	—
FINE DINING/TYPES	Continental
COFFEE SHOP	•
24-HOUR CAFE	—
BUFFET	Breakfast
CASINO	—
LOUNGE	•
SHOWROOM	—
GIFTS/DRUGS/NEWS	—
POOL	•
EXERCISE ROOM	•
TENNIS & RACKET	—

Aliante Station ★★★★	
7300 Aliante Pkwy.	
North Las Vegas, NV 89084	
☎ 702-692-7777	
TOLL FREE 877-477-7627	
aliantecasinohotel.com	
RACK RATE	$$$–
ROOM QUALITY	88
LOCATION	North Las Vegas
DISCOUNTS	AAA, AARP, military
NO. OF ROOMS	202
CHECKOUT TIME	11
NONSMOKING	•
CONCIERGE	•
CONVENTION FACIL.	•
MEETING ROOMS	•
VALET PARKING	•
RV PARK	—
ROOM SERVICE	•
FREE BREAKFAST	—
FINE DINING/TYPES	Steak, seafood, Italian, Mexican
COFFEE SHOP	•
24-HOUR CAFE	• (Johnny Rocket's)
BUFFET	•
CASINO	•
LOUNGE	•
SHOWROOM	•
GIFTS/DRUGS/NEWS	•
POOL	•
TENNIS & RACKET	—

Aria at CityCenter ★★★★½	
3730 S. Las Vegas Blvd.	
Las Vegas, NV 89109	
☎ 702-590-7111	
FAX 702-590-7112	
TOLL FREE 866-359-7757	
arialasvegas.com	
RACK RATE	$$$$$$
ROOM QUALITY	95
LOCATION	Mid-Strip
DISCOUNTS	AAA, AARP
NO. OF ROOMS	4,004
CHECKOUT TIME	Noon
NONSMOKING	•
CONCIERGE	•
CONVENTION FACIL.	•
MEETING ROOMS	•
VALET PARKING	•
RV PARK	•
ROOM SERVICE	•
FREE BREAKFAST	—
FINE DINING/TYPES	Steak, Italian, Chinese, Thai, Japanese, American
COFFEE SHOP	•
24-HOUR CAFE	•
BUFFET	•
CASINO	•
LOUNGE	•
SHOWROOM	•
GIFTS/DRUGS/NEWS	•
POOL	•
EXERCISE ROOM	Health spa
TENNIS & RACKET	—

Bally's ★★★★	
3645 S. Las Vegas Blvd.	
Las Vegas, NV 89109	
☎ 702-739-4111	
FAX 702-967-4405	
TOLL FREE 800-634-3434	
ballyslasvegas.com	
RACK RATE	$$$$+
ROOM QUALITY	85
LOCATION	Mid-Strip
DISCOUNTS	AAA, senior
NO. OF ROOMS	2,814
CHECKOUT TIME	11
NONSMOKING	Floors
CONCIERGE	•
CONVENTION FACIL.	•
MEETING ROOMS	•
VALET PARKING	•
RV PARK	•
ROOM SERVICE	•
FREE BREAKFAST	—
FINE DINING/TYPES	Continental, steak, sushi, Italian
COFFEE SHOP	•
24-HOUR CAFE	•
BUFFET	•
CASINO	•
LOUNGE	•
SHOWROOM	Production show, celebrity headliners
GIFTS/DRUGS/NEWS	•
POOL	•
EXERCISE ROOM	Health spa
TENNIS & RACKET	Tennis

Bellagio ★★★★½	
3600 S. Las Vegas Blvd.	
Las Vegas, NV 89109	
☎ 702-693-7444	
FAX 702-693-8585	
TOLL FREE 888-987-6667	
bellagio.com	
RACK RATE	$$$$$$$+
ROOM QUALITY	95
LOCATION	Mid-Strip
DISCOUNTS	AAA
NO. OF ROOMS	3,933
CHECKOUT TIME	Noon
NONSMOKING	•
CONCIERGE	•
CONVENTION FACIL.	•
MEETING ROOMS	•
VALET PARKING	•
RV PARK	•
ROOM SERVICE	•
FREE BREAKFAST	—
FINE DINING/TYPES	Continental
COFFEE SHOP	•
24-HOUR CAFE	•
BUFFET	•
CASINO	•
LOUNGE	•
SHOWROOM	Production show
GIFTS/DRUGS/NEWS	•
POOL	•
EXERCISE ROOM	Health spa
TENNIS & RACKET	—

Best Western Mardi Gras Hotel and Casino ★★★	
3500 Paradise Rd.	
Las Vegas, NV 89169	
☎ 702-731-2020	
FAX 702-731-3981	
TOLL FREE 800-634-6501	
bestwestern.com	
RACK RATE	$$
ROOM QUALITY	73
LOCATION	East of Strip
DISCOUNTS	AAA, AARP, military, senior
NO. OF ROOMS	314
CHECKOUT TIME	11
NONSMOKING	•
CONCIERGE	—
CONVENTION FACIL.	—
MEETING ROOMS	—
VALET PARKING	—
RV PARK	—
ROOM SERVICE	—
FREE BREAKFAST	—
FINE DINING/TYPES	American
COFFEE SHOP	—
24-HOUR CAFE	—
BUFFET	—
CASINO	Slots
LOUNGE	•
SHOWROOM	—
GIFTS/DRUGS/NEWS	—
POOL	•
EXERCISE ROOM	—
TENNIS & RACKET	—

Arizona Charlie's Boulder
★★★
4575 Boulder Hwy.
Las Vegas, NV 89121
☎ 702-951-9000
FAX 702-951-1046
TOLL FREE 888-236-9066
arizonacharliesboulder.com

RACK RATE	$$$+
ROOM QUALITY	74
LOCATION	Boulder Hwy.
DISCOUNTS	AAA, AARP
NO. OF ROOMS	301
CHECKOUT TIME	11
NONSMOKING	•
CONCIERGE	−
CONVENTION FACIL.	•
MEETING ROOMS	•
VALET PARKING	−
RV PARK	•
ROOM SERVICE	•
FREE BREAKFAST	−
FINE DINING/TYPES	American, steak
COFFEE SHOP	•
24-HOUR CAFE	•
BUFFET	•
CASINO	•
LOUNGE	•
SHOWROOM	Live music
GIFTS/DRUGS/NEWS	•
POOL	•
EXERCISE ROOM	−
TENNIS & RACKET	−

Arizona Charlie's Decatur ★★★
740 S. Decatur Blvd.
Las Vegas, NV 89107
☎ 702-258-5111
FAX 702-258-5192
TOLL FREE 888-236-8645
arizonacharliesdecatur.com

RACK RATE	$$$−
ROOM QUALITY	66
LOCATION	West Las Vegas
DISCOUNTS	AAA, AARP, military
NO. OF ROOMS	258
CHECKOUT TIME	11
NONSMOKING	•
CONCIERGE	−
CONVENTION FACIL.	−
MEETING ROOMS	−
VALET PARKING	•
RV PARK	−
ROOM SERVICE	−
FREE BREAKFAST	−
FINE DINING/TYPES	American, steak
COFFEE SHOP	•
24-HOUR CAFE	•
BUFFET	•
CASINO	•
LOUNGE	•
SHOWROOM	Local bands
GIFTS/DRUGS/NEWS	•
POOL	•
EXERCISE ROOM	−
TENNIS & RACKET	−

Artisan Hotel and Spa ★★★½
1501 W. Sahara Ave.
Las Vegas, NV 89102
☎ 702-214-4000
FAX 702-733-1571
TOLL FREE 800-554-4092
theartisanhotel.com

RACK RATE	$$−
ROOM QUALITY	78
LOCATION	North Strip
DISCOUNTS	AAA, AARP, corp.
NO. OF ROOMS	64
CHECKOUT TIME	11
NONSMOKING	•
CONCIERGE	•
CONVENTION FACIL.	−
MEETING ROOMS	•
VALET PARKING	•
RV PARK	−
ROOM SERVICE	•
FREE BREAKFAST	−
FINE DINING/TYPES	Italian
COFFEE SHOP	−
24-HOUR CAFE	−
BUFFET	−
CASINO	−
LOUNGE	•
SHOWROOM	−
GIFTS/DRUGS/NEWS	−
POOL	•
EXERCISE ROOM	•
TENNIS & RACKET	−

Best Western McCarran Inn ★★★
4970 Paradise Rd.
Las Vegas, NV 89119
☎ 702-798-5530
FAX 702-798-7627
TOLL FREE 800-528-1234
bestwestern.com

RACK RATE	$$+
ROOM QUALITY	71
LOCATION	East of Strip
DISCOUNTS	Gov't, military, senior
NO. OF ROOMS	100
CHECKOUT TIME	Noon
NONSMOKING	•
CONCIERGE	−
CONVENTION FACIL.	−
MEETING ROOMS	−
VALET PARKING	−
RV PARK	•
ROOM SERVICE	−
FREE BREAKFAST	•
FINE DINING/TYPES	−
COFFEE SHOP	−
24-HOUR CAFE	−
BUFFET	−
CASINO	−
LOUNGE	−
SHOWROOM	−
GIFTS/DRUGS/NEWS	−
POOL	•
EXERCISE ROOM	−
TENNIS & RACKET	−

Bill's Gamblin' Hall and Saloon ★★★½
3595 S. Las Vegas Blvd.
Las Vegas, NV 89109
☎ 702-737-2100
FAX 702-894-9954
TOLL FREE 866-245-5745
billslasvegas.com

RACK RATE	$$$
ROOM QUALITY	76
LOCATION	Mid-Strip
DISCOUNTS	AAA, AARP
NO. OF ROOMS	200
CHECKOUT TIME	Noon
NONSMOKING	•
CONCIERGE	−
CONVENTION FACIL.	−
MEETING ROOMS	−
VALET PARKING	•
RV PARK	−
ROOM SERVICE	•
FREE BREAKFAST	−
FINE DINING/TYPES	Continental
COFFEE SHOP	•
24-HOUR CAFE	•
BUFFET	−
CASINO	•
LOUNGE	•
SHOWROOM	Live music
GIFTS/DRUGS/NEWS	−
POOL	−
EXERCISE ROOM	−
TENNIS & RACKET	−

Boulder Station ★★★½
4111 Boulder Hwy.
Las Vegas, NV 89121
☎ 702-432-7777
FAX 702-432-7730
TOLL FREE 800-683-7777
boulderstation.com

RACK RATE	$$−
ROOM QUALITY	76
LOCATION	Boulder Hwy.
DISCOUNTS	AARP, AAA, corp., military, gov't
NO. OF ROOMS	300
CHECKOUT TIME	Noon
NONSMOKING	•
CONCIERGE	•
CONVENTION FACIL.	•
MEETING ROOMS	•
VALET PARKING	•
RV PARK	•
ROOM SERVICE	•
FREE BREAKFAST	−
FINE DINING/TYPES	Steak, seafood, Italian, Mexican
COFFEE SHOP	•
24-HOUR CAFE	•
BUFFET	•
CASINO	•
LOUNGE	•
SHOWROOM	Live music
GIFTS/DRUGS/NEWS	•
POOL	•
EXERCISE ROOM	•
TENNIS & RACKET	−

Hotel Information Chart (continued)

	Caesars Palace ★★★★½	California ★★★	Candlewood Suites ★★★½
	3570 S. Las Vegas Blvd.	12 E. Ogden Ave.	4034 S. Paradise Rd.
	Las Vegas, NV 89109	Las Vegas, NV 89101	Las Vegas, NV 89109
	☎ 702-731-7110	☎ 702-385-1222	☎ 702-836-3660
	FAX 702-866-1700	FAX 702-388-2670	FAX 702-836-3661
	TOLL FREE 800-634-6661	TOLL FREE 800-634-6255	TOLL FREE 877-226-3539
	caesarspalace.com	thecal.com	candlewoodsuites.com
RACK RATE	$$$$$$–	$$	$$+
ROOM QUALITY	95	67	79
LOCATION	Mid-Strip	Downtown	East of Strip
DISCOUNTS	AAA, senior, gov't	Military	AAA, AARP, gov't, military
NO. OF ROOMS	3,348	781	276
CHECKOUT TIME	11	Noon	Noon
NONSMOKING	Floors	•	•
CONCIERGE	•	—	—
CONVENTION FACIL.	•	—	—
MEETING ROOMS	•	—	—
VALET PARKING	•	•	—
RV PARK	—	—	—
ROOM SERVICE	•	•	—
FREE BREAKFAST	—	—	—
FINE DINING/TYPES	Asian, French, Japanese, Italian, steak	Pasta, seafood, steak, Hawaiian	—
COFFEE SHOP	•	•	—
24-HOUR CAFE	•	•	•
BUFFET	•	•	—
CASINO	•	•	—
LOUNGE	•	•	—
SHOWROOM	Celebrity headliners	—	—
GIFTS/DRUGS/NEWS	•	•	—
POOL	•	•	—
EXERCISE ROOM	Health spa	•	•
TENNIS & RACKET	—	—	—

	Clarion Hotel and Casino ★★★	Comfort Inn Paradise Road ★★★	Cosmopolitan ★★★★½
	305 Convention Center Dr.	4350 Paradise Rd.	3708 S. Las Vegas Blvd.
	Las Vegas, NV 89109	Las Vegas, NV 89169	Las Vegas NV 89109
	☎ 702-952-8000	☎ 702-938-2000	☎ 702-698-7000
	FAX 702-952-8100	FAX 702-938-2001	FAX 702-698-7007
	TOLL FREE 800-633-1777	TOLL FREE 866-847-2001	TOLL FREE 877-551-7778
	clarionhotel.com	comfortinn.com	cosmopolitanlasvegas.com
RACK RATE	$$+	$$–	$$$$$$$–
ROOM QUALITY	65	68	94
LOCATION	North Strip	East of Strip	Mid-Strip
DISCOUNTS	AAA, AARP, corp.	AAA, AARP, military, gov't	—
NO. OF ROOMS	202	199	2,995
CHECKOUT TIME	11	11	11
NONSMOKING	•	•	•
CONCIERGE	•	—	•
CONVENTION FACIL.	—	—	•
MEETING ROOMS	•	—	•
VALET PARKING	—	•	•
RV PARK	—	—	—
ROOM SERVICE	•	—	•
FREE BREAKFAST	—	•	—
FINE DINING/TYPES	—	Continental	American, Italian, Mediterranean, French, Asian
COFFEE SHOP	•	—	•
24-HOUR CAFE	—	—	•
BUFFET	—	—	•
CASINO	•	—	•
LOUNGE	•	—	•
SHOWROOM	•	—	•
GIFTS/DRUGS/NEWS	•	—	•
POOL	•	•	•
EXERCISE ROOM	•	—	Health spa
TENNIS & RACKET	—	—	•

Cannery ★★½
2121 E. Craig Rd.
Las Vegas, NV 89030
☎ 702-507-5700
FAX 702-507-5750
TOLL FREE 866-999-4899
cannerycasinos.com

RACK RATE	$$–
ROOM QUALITY	64
LOCATION	North Las Vegas
DISCOUNTS	AAA, AARP, gov't
NO. OF ROOMS	201
CHECKOUT TIME	Noon
NONSMOKING	•
CONCIERGE	—
CONVENTION FACIL.	—
MEETING ROOMS	•
VALET PARKING	•
RV PARK	•
ROOM SERVICE	•
FREE BREAKFAST	—
FINE DINING/TYPES	American, Italian Mexican, steak
COFFEE SHOP	•
24-HOUR CAFE	•
BUFFET	•
CASINO	•
LOUNGE	•
SHOWROOM	Live music
GIFTS/DRUGS/NEWS	•
POOL	•
EXERCISE ROOM	—
TENNIS & RACKET	—

Casino Royale ★★½
3411 S. Las Vegas Blvd.
Las Vegas, NV 89109
☎ 702-737-3500
FAX 702-650-4743
TOLL FREE 800-854-7666
casinoroyalehotel.com

RACK RATE	$$+
ROOM QUALITY	64
LOCATION	Mid-Strip
DISCOUNTS	AAA
NO. OF ROOMS	151
CHECKOUT TIME	Noon
NONSMOKING	•
CONCIERGE	—
CONVENTION FACIL.	—
MEETING ROOMS	•
VALET PARKING	•
RV PARK	—
ROOM SERVICE	—
FREE BREAKFAST	—
FINE DINING/TYPES	American, Italian
COFFEE SHOP	•
24-HOUR CAFE	•
BUFFET	•
CASINO	•
LOUNGE	•
SHOWROOM	—
GIFTS/DRUGS/NEWS	•
POOL	•
EXERCISE ROOM	—
TENNIS & RACKET	—

Circus Circus ★★★½/★★½*
2880 S. Las Vegas Blvd.
Las Vegas, NV 89109
☎ 702-734-0410
FAX 702-794-3896
TOLL FREE 800-634-3450
circuscircus.com

RACK RATE	$$/$$–
ROOM QUALITY	81/59*
LOCATION	North Strip
DISCOUNTS	AAA, military, senior
NO. OF ROOMS	3,773
CHECKOUT TIME	11
NONSMOKING	Floors
CONCIERGE	—
CONVENTION FACIL.	•
MEETING ROOMS	•
VALET PARKING	•
RV PARK	•
ROOM SERVICE	•
FREE BREAKFAST	—
FINE DINING/TYPES	Steak, Italian, Mexican
COFFEE SHOP	•
24-HOUR CAFE	•
BUFFET	•
CASINO	•
LOUNGE	•
SHOWROOM	Circus acts, free theme park
GIFTS/DRUGS/NEWS	•
POOL	•
EXERCISE ROOM	•
TENNIS & RACKET	—
*tower rooms/manor rooms	

Courtyard by Marriott Las Vegas South ★★★½
5845 Dean Martin Dr.
Las Vegas, NV 89118
☎ 702-895-7519
FAX 702-895-7568
TOLL FREE 800-321-2211
marriott.com

RACK RATE	$$$
ROOM QUALITY	75
LOCATION	South Strip
DISCOUNTS	AAA, gov't, military, corp.
NO. OF ROOMS	146
CHECKOUT TIME	Noon
NONSMOKING	•
CONCIERGE	—
CONVENTION FACIL.	—
MEETING ROOMS	•
VALET PARKING	—
RV PARK	•
ROOM SERVICE	—
FREE BREAKFAST	—
FINE DINING/TYPES	American
COFFEE SHOP	—
24-HOUR CAFE	—
BUFFET	• (Breakfast only)
CASINO	—
LOUNGE	•
SHOWROOM	—
GIFTS/DRUGS/NEWS	—
POOL	•
EXERCISE ROOM	•
TENNIS & RACKET	—

Courtyard by Marriott Las Vegas Convention Center ★★★½
3275 Paradise Rd.
Las Vegas, NV 89109
☎ 702-791-3600
FAX 702-736-7981
TOLL FREE 800-321-2211
marriott.com

RACK RATE	$$$
ROOM QUALITY	79
LOCATION	East of Strip
DISCOUNTS	AAA, gov't, military, senior
NO. OF ROOMS	149
CHECKOUT TIME	Noon
NONSMOKING	•
CONCIERGE	•
CONVENTION FACIL.	—
MEETING ROOMS	•
VALET PARKING	—
RV PARK	•
ROOM SERVICE	—
FREE BREAKFAST	—
FINE DINING/TYPES	American
COFFEE SHOP	—
24-HOUR CAFE	—
BUFFET	• (Breakfast only)
CASINO	—
LOUNGE	•
SHOWROOM	—
GIFTS/DRUGS/NEWS	—
POOL	•
EXERCISE ROOM	•
TENNIS & RACKET	—

Days Inn at Wild Wild West ★★★
3330 W. Tropicana Ave.
Las Vegas, NV 89103
☎ 702-739-5003
FAX 702-736-7106
TOLL FREE 800-777-1514
wwwesthotelcasino.com

RACK RATE	$+
ROOM QUALITY	68
LOCATION	South Strip
DISCOUNTS	AAA
NO. OF ROOMS	260
CHECKOUT TIME	Noon
NONSMOKING	•
CONCIERGE	—
CONVENTION FACIL.	—
MEETING ROOMS	—
VALET PARKING	—
RV PARK	—
ROOM SERVICE	—
FREE BREAKFAST	—
FINE DINING/TYPES	American
COFFEE SHOP	—
24-HOUR CAFE	•
BUFFET	—
CASINO	•
LOUNGE	•
SHOWROOM	—
GIFTS/DRUGS/NEWS	•
POOL	•
EXERCISE ROOM	—
TENNIS & RACKET	—

Hotel Information Chart (continued)

	Eastside Cannery ★★★★
	5255 Boulder Hwy.
	Las Vegas, NV 89122
	☎ 702-856-5300
	eastsidecannery.com

RACK RATE	$+
ROOM QUALITY	83
LOCATION	Boulder Hwy.
DISCOUNTS	AAA, AARP
NO. OF ROOMS	300
CHECKOUT TIME	Noon
NONSMOKING	•
CONCIERGE	•
CONVENTION FACIL.	•
MEETING ROOMS	•
VALET PARKING	•
RV PARK	—
ROOM SERVICE	•
FREE BREAKFAST	—
FINE DINING/TYPES	Steak, Mexican
COFFEE SHOP	•
24-HOUR CAFE	•
BUFFET	•
CASINO	•
LOUNGE	•
SHOWROOM	•
GIFTS/DRUGS/NEWS	•
POOL	•
EXERCISE ROOM	•
TENNIS & RACKET	—

	El Cortez ★★★
	600 E. Fremont St.
	Las Vegas, NV 89101
	☎ 702-385-5200
	FAX 702-474-3726
	TOLL FREE 800-634-6703
	elcortezhotelcasino.com

RACK RATE	$+
ROOM QUALITY	72
LOCATION	Downtown
DISCOUNTS	—
NO. OF ROOMS	300
CHECKOUT TIME	Noon
NONSMOKING	•
CONCIERGE	—
CONVENTION FACIL.	•
MEETING ROOMS	•
VALET PARKING	•
RV PARK	•
ROOM SERVICE	•
FREE BREAKFAST	—
FINE DINING/TYPES	Family, steak, Chinese
COFFEE SHOP	—
24-HOUR CAFE	•
BUFFET	•
CASINO	•
LOUNGE	•
SHOWROOM	—
GIFTS/DRUGS/NEWS	•
POOL	—
EXERCISE ROOM	—
TENNIS & RACKET	—

	El Cortez Cabana Suites ★★★
	651 E. Ogden Ave.
	Las Vegas, NV 89101
	☎ 702-385-5200
	FAX 702-474-3726
	TOLL FREE 800-634-6703
	elcortezcabanasuites.com

RACK RATE	$$−
ROOM QUALITY	72
LOCATION	Downtown
DISCOUNTS	—
NO. OF ROOMS	64
CHECKOUT TIME	Noon
NONSMOKING	—
CONCIERGE	—
CONVENTION FACIL.	—
MEETING ROOMS	—
VALET PARKING	• (at El Cortez)
RV PARK	• (at El Cortez)
ROOM SERVICE	—
FREE BREAKFAST	•
FINE DINING/TYPES	—
COFFEE SHOP	—
24-HOUR CAFE	—
BUFFET	—
CASINO	—
LOUNGE	•
SHOWROOM	—
GIFTS/DRUGS/NEWS	—
POOL	—
EXERCISE ROOM	•
TENNIS & RACKET	—

	Fairfield Inn & Suites Las Vegas South ★★★½
	5775 Dean Martin Dr.
	Las Vegas, NV 89118
	☎ 702-895-9810
	FAX 702-895-9310
	TOLL FREE 800-228-2800
	marriott.com

RACK RATE	$$$
ROOM QUALITY	75
LOCATION	South Strip
DISCOUNTS	AAA, AARP, gov't, military
NO. OF ROOMS	142
CHECKOUT TIME	Noon
NONSMOKING	•
CONCIERGE	—
CONVENTION FACIL.	—
MEETING ROOMS	—
VALET PARKING	—
RV PARK	•
ROOM SERVICE	•
FREE BREAKFAST	•
FINE DINING/TYPES	—
COFFEE SHOP	—
24-HOUR CAFE	—
BUFFET	—
CASINO	—
LOUNGE	—
SHOWROOM	—
GIFTS/DRUGS/NEWS	•
POOL	•
EXERCISE ROOM	•
TENNIS & RACKET	—

	Fairfield Inn Las Vegas Airport ★★★
	3850 Paradise Rd.
	Las Vegas, NV 89169
	☎ 702-791-0899
	FAX 702-791-2705
	TOLL FREE 800-228-2800
	marriott.com

RACK RATE	$$$−
ROOM QUALITY	72
LOCATION	East of Strip
DISCOUNTS	AAA, gov't, military
NO. OF ROOMS	129
CHECKOUT TIME	Noon
NONSMOKING	•
CONCIERGE	—
CONVENTION FACIL.	—
MEETING ROOMS	—
VALET PARKING	—
RV PARK	—
ROOM SERVICE	—
FREE BREAKFAST	•
FINE DINING/TYPES	—
COFFEE SHOP	—
24-HOUR CAFE	—
BUFFET	—
CASINO	—
LOUNGE	—
SHOWROOM	—
GIFTS/DRUGS/NEWS	—
POOL	•
EXERCISE ROOM	•
TENNIS & RACKET	—

	Fiesta Henderson ★★★
	777 W. Lake Mead Pkwy.
	Henderson, NV 89015
	☎ 702-558-7000
	FAX 702-567-7373
	TOLL FREE 888-899-7770
	fiestahendersonlasvegas.com

RACK RATE	$+
ROOM QUALITY	72
LOCATION	Henderson
DISCOUNTS	AAA, AARP
NO. OF ROOMS	224
CHECKOUT TIME	Noon
NONSMOKING	Floors
CONCIERGE	•
CONVENTION FACIL.	—
MEETING ROOMS	•
VALET PARKING	•
RV PARK	—
ROOM SERVICE	• (Breakfast only)
FREE BREAKFAST	—
FINE DINING/TYPES	Steak, Mexican
COFFEE SHOP	•
24-HOUR CAFE	•
BUFFET	•
CASINO	•
LOUNGE	•
SHOWROOM	Live music
GIFTS/DRUGS/NEWS	•
POOL	•
EXERCISE ROOM	—
TENNIS & RACKET	—

Embassy Suites Convention Center ★★★★
3600 S. Paradise Rd.
Las Vegas, NV 89169
☎ 702-893-8000
FAX 702-893-0378
TOLL FREE 800-EMBASSY
embassysuites1.hilton.com

RACK RATE	$$$+
ROOM QUALITY	87
LOCATION	East of Strip
DISCOUNTS	AAA, gov't, senior
NO. OF ROOMS	286
CHECKOUT TIME	Noon
NONSMOKING	•
CONCIERGE	—
CONVENTION FACIL.	•
MEETING ROOMS	•
VALET PARKING	—
RV PARK	•
ROOM SERVICE	•
FREE BREAKFAST	•
FINE DINING/TYPES	American
COFFEE SHOP	—
24-HOUR CAFE	—
BUFFET	—
CASINO	—
LOUNGE	•
SHOWROOM	—
GIFTS/DRUGS/NEWS	—
POOL	•
EXERCISE ROOM	•
TENNIS & RACKET	—

Embassy Suites in Las Vegas ★★★★
4315 Swenson St.
Las Vegas, NV 89119
☎ 702-795-2800
FAX 702-795-1520
TOLL FREE 800-EMBASSY
embassysuites1.hilton.com

RACK RATE	$$$–
ROOM QUALITY	86
LOCATION	East of Strip
DISCOUNTS	AAA, gov't, senior
NO. OF ROOMS	220
CHECKOUT TIME	Noon
NONSMOKING	•
CONCIERGE	•
CONVENTION FACIL.	—
MEETING ROOMS	•
VALET PARKING	•
RV PARK	—
ROOM SERVICE	•
FREE BREAKFAST	•
FINE DINING/TYPES	American
COFFEE SHOP	—
24-HOUR CAFE	—
BUFFET	—
CASINO	—
LOUNGE	•
SHOWROOM	—
GIFTS/DRUGS/NEWS	•
POOL	•
EXERCISE ROOM	•
TENNIS & RACKET	—

Excalibur ★★★½
3850 S. Las Vegas Blvd.
Las Vegas, NV 89109
☎ 702-597-7777
FAX 702-597-7163
TOLL FREE 800-937-7777
excalibur.com

RACK RATE	$$$
ROOM QUALITY	76
LOCATION	South Strip
DISCOUNTS	AAA, AARP, military
NO. OF ROOMS	3,991
CHECKOUT TIME	11
NONSMOKING	Floors
CONCIERGE	—
CONVENTION FACIL.	•
MEETING ROOMS	•
VALET PARKING	•
RV PARK	—
ROOM SERVICE	•
FREE BREAKFAST	—
FINE DINING/TYPES	Continental, steak, Italian, Asian
COFFEE SHOP	•
24-HOUR CAFE	•
BUFFET	•
CASINO	•
LOUNGE	•
SHOWROOM	Production show, King Arthur's Tournament
GIFTS/DRUGS/NEWS	•
POOL	•
EXERCISE ROOM	•
TENNIS & RACKET	—

Fiesta Rancho ★★½
2400 N. Rancho Dr.
Las Vegas, NV 89130
☎ 702-631-7000
FAX 702-638-3605
TOLL FREE 888-899-7770
fiestaranchoslasvegas.com

RACK RATE	$$–
ROOM QUALITY	62
LOCATION	Rancho Drive
DISCOUNTS	AAA, AARP
NO. OF ROOMS	100
CHECKOUT TIME	Noon
NONSMOKING	•
CONCIERGE	—
CONVENTION FACIL.	—
MEETING ROOMS	•
VALET PARKING	•
RV PARK	—
ROOM SERVICE	•
FREE BREAKFAST	—
FINE DINING/TYPES	Mexican, Italian, steak, Chinese
COFFEE SHOP	•
24-HOUR CAFE	•
BUFFET	•
CASINO	•
LOUNGE	•
SHOWROOM	—
GIFTS/DRUGS/NEWS	•
POOL	•
EXERCISE ROOM	—
TENNIS & RACKET	—

Fitzgeralds ★★★½
301 Fremont St.
Las Vegas, NV 89101
☎ 702-388-2400
FAX 702-388-2181
TOLL FREE 800-274-LUCK
fitzgeraldslasvegas.com

RACK RATE	$+
ROOM QUALITY	76
LOCATION	Downtown
DISCOUNTS	AAA, senior
NO. OF ROOMS	634
CHECKOUT TIME	Noon
NONSMOKING	Floors
CONCIERGE	•
CONVENTION FACIL.	—
MEETING ROOMS	•
VALET PARKING	•
RV PARK	—
ROOM SERVICE	—
FREE BREAKFAST	—
FINE DINING/TYPES	Steak, American
COFFEE SHOP	•
24-HOUR CAFE	•
BUFFET	—
CASINO	•
LOUNGE	•
SHOWROOM	•
GIFTS/DRUGS/NEWS	•
POOL	•
EXERCISE ROOM	—
TENNIS & RACKET	—

Flamingo ★★★★
3555 S. Las Vegas Blvd.
Las Vegas, NV 89109
☎ 702-733-3111
FAX 702-733-3285
TOLL FREE 888-902-9929
flamingolasvegas.com

RACK RATE	$$$
ROOM QUALITY	87
LOCATION	Mid-Strip
DISCOUNTS	AAA, AARP
NO. OF ROOMS	3,352
CHECKOUT TIME	Noon
NONSMOKING	Floors, part of casino
CONCIERGE	•
CONVENTION FACIL.	•
MEETING ROOMS	•
VALET PARKING	•
RV PARK	•
ROOM SERVICE	•
FREE BREAKFAST	—
FINE DINING/TYPES	Italian, Asian, seafood, Continental
COFFEE SHOP	•
24-HOUR CAFE	•
BUFFET	•
CASINO	•
LOUNGE	•
SHOWROOM	Production show, musical comedy
GIFTS/DRUGS/NEWS	•
POOL	•
EXERCISE ROOM	Health spa
TENNIS & RACKET	Tennis

Hotel Information Chart (continued)

	Four Queens ★★★	Four Seasons at Mandalay Bay ★★★★½	Fremont ★★★
	202 Fremont St.	3960 S. Las Vegas Blvd.	200 E. Fremont St.
	Las Vegas, NV 89101	Las Vegas, NV 89119	Las Vegas, NV 89101
	☎ 702-385-4011	☎ 702-632-5000	☎ 702-385-3232
	FAX 702-387-5160	FAX 702-632-5195	FAX 702-385-6270
	TOLL FREE 800-634-6045	TOLL FREE 877-632-5000	TOLL FREE 800-634-6182
	fourqueens.com	fourseasons.com/lasvegas	fremontcasino.com
RACK RATE	$$–	$$$$$$$–	$$–
ROOM QUALITY	70	95	70
LOCATION	Downtown	South Strip	Downtown
DISCOUNTS	Senior, military	—	—
NO. OF ROOMS	690	424	447
CHECKOUT TIME	Noon	Noon	Noon
NONSMOKING	Floors	•	•
CONCIERGE	—	•	•
CONVENTION FACIL.	—	•	•
MEETING ROOMS	•	•	•
VALET PARKING	•	•	•
RV PARK	—	•	—
ROOM SERVICE	•	•	—
FREE BREAKFAST	—	•	—
FINE DINING/TYPES	American	American, Continental	Ribs, Chinese, American
COFFEE SHOP	•	—	•
24-HOUR CAFE	•	—	•
BUFFET	—	—	•
CASINO	•	—	•
LOUNGE	•	—	•
SHOWROOM	•	—	—
GIFTS/DRUGS/NEWS	•	•	•
POOL	—	•	•
EXERCISE ROOM	—	Health and fitness spa	—
TENNIS & RACKET	—	—	—

	Golden Nugget ★★★★½/★★★½	Green Valley Ranch Resort and Spa ★★★★	Hampton Inn Tropicana ★★★
	129 E. Fremont St.	2300 Paseo Verde Pkwy.	4975 S. Dean Martin Dr.
	Las Vegas, NV 89101	Henderson, NV 89052	Las Vegas, NV 89118
	☎ 702-385-7111	☎ 702-617-7777	☎ 702-948-8100
	FAX 702-387-4422	FAX 702-617-7778	FAX 702-948-8101
	TOLL FREE 800-634-3454	TOLL FREE 866-782-9487	TOLL FREE 800-426-7866
	goldennugget.com	greenvalleyranchresort.com	hamptoninntropicana.com
RACK RATE	$$$+/$$$–	$$$	$$$–
ROOM QUALITY	90/78	87	72
LOCATION	Downtown	Henderson	South Strip
DISCOUNTS	AAA	AAA, AARP, military	AAA, AARP, corp., gov't
NO. OF ROOMS	1,900	490	322
CHECKOUT TIME	Noon	Noon	Noon
NONSMOKING	Floors	•	•
CONCIERGE	•	•	—
CONVENTION FACIL.	•	•	•
MEETING ROOMS	•	•	•
VALET PARKING	•	•	—
RV PARK	—	•	—
ROOM SERVICE	•	•	—
FREE BREAKFAST	—	—	•
FINE DINING/TYPES	Italian, Chinese, Continental, steak	Italian, steak, seafood, Asian	—
COFFEE SHOP	•	•	—
24-HOUR CAFE	•	•	—
BUFFET	•	•	—
CASINO	•	•	—
LOUNGE	•	•	—
SHOWROOM	Headliners	Headliners	—
GIFTS/DRUGS/NEWS	•	•	—
POOL	•	•	•
EXERCISE ROOM	•	•	•
TENNIS & RACKET	—	—	—

Gold Coast ★★½
4000 W. Flamingo Rd.
Las Vegas, NV 89103
☎ 702-367-7111
FAX 702-367-8575
TOLL FREE 800-331-5334
goldcoastcasino.com

RACK RATE	$$$
ROOM QUALITY	58
LOCATION	Mid-Strip
DISCOUNTS	AAA, senior
NO. OF ROOMS	711
CHECKOUT TIME	Noon
NONSMOKING	Floors
CONCIERGE	—
CONVENTION FACIL.	•
MEETING ROOMS	•
VALET PARKING	•
RV PARK	—
ROOM SERVICE	•
FREE BREAKFAST	—
FINE DINING/TYPES	Steak, Chinese, American
COFFEE SHOP	•
24-HOUR CAFE	—
BUFFET	•
CASINO	•
LOUNGE	•
SHOWROOM	Dancing
GIFTS/DRUGS/NEWS	•
POOL	•
EXERCISE ROOM	•
TENNIS & RACKET	—

Gold Spike ★★½
400 E. Ogden Ave.
Las Vegas, NV 89101
☎ 702-384-8444
FAX 702-382-6248
TOLL FREE 866-600-8600
goldspike.com

RACK RATE	$
ROOM QUALITY	64
LOCATION	Downtown
DISCOUNTS	—
NO. OF ROOMS	110
CHECKOUT TIME	11
NONSMOKING	•
CONCIERGE	—
CONVENTION FACIL.	—
MEETING ROOMS	—
VALET PARKING	—
RV PARK	—
ROOM SERVICE	—
FREE BREAKFAST	—
FINE DINING/TYPES	—
COFFEE SHOP	—
24-HOUR CAFE	•
BUFFET	—
CASINO	•
LOUNGE	•
SHOWROOM	—
GIFTS/DRUGS/NEWS	•
POOL	•
EXERCISE ROOM	—
TENNIS & RACKET	—

Golden Gate ★★
1 Fremont Street
Las Vegas, NV 89101
☎ 702-385-1906
TOLL FREE 800-426-1906
goldengatecasino.com

RACK RATE	$$–
ROOM QUALITY	52
LOCATION	Downtown
DISCOUNTS	—
NO. OF ROOMS	106
CHECKOUT TIME	11
NONSMOKING	•
CONCIERGE	—
CONVENTION FACIL.	—
MEETING ROOMS	—
VALET PARKING	—
RV PARK	—
ROOM SERVICE	—
FREE BREAKFAST	—
FINE DINING/TYPES	—
COFFEE SHOP	•
24-HOUR CAFE	—
BUFFET	—
CASINO	•
LOUNGE	—
SHOWROOM	—
GIFTS/DRUGS/NEWS	•
POOL	—
EXERCISE ROOM	—
TENNIS & RACKET	—

Hard Rock Hotel ★★★★½
4455 Paradise Rd.
Las Vegas, NV 89109
☎ 702-693-5000
FAX 702-693-5021
TOLL FREE 800-HRD-ROCK
hardrockhotel.com

RACK RATE	$$$$–
ROOM QUALITY	95
LOCATION	East of Strip
DISCOUNTS	—
NO. OF ROOMS	1,506
CHECKOUT TIME	11
NONSMOKING	Floors
CONCIERGE	•
CONVENTION FACIL.	•
MEETING ROOMS	•
VALET PARKING	•
RV PARK	—
ROOM SERVICE	•
FREE BREAKFAST	—
FINE DINING/TYPES	Steak, Japanese, Continental, Mexican
COFFEE SHOP	•
24-HOUR CAFE	•
BUFFET	—
CASINO	•
LOUNGE	•
SHOWROOM	Live music
GIFTS/DRUGS/NEWS	•
POOL	•
EXERCISE ROOM	Health spa
TENNIS & RACKET	—

Harmon Hotel at CityCenter
3176 S. Las Vegas Blvd.
Las Vegas, NV 89109
☎ 702-590-6888
FAX 702-590-6889
TOLL FREE 877-590-6888
theharmon.com

RACK RATE	n/a
ROOM QUALITY	n/a
LOCATION	Mid-Strip
DISCOUNTS	—
NO. OF ROOMS	400
CHECKOUT TIME	Noon
NONSMOKING	•
CONCIERGE	•
CONVENTION FACIL.	•
MEETING ROOMS	•
VALET PARKING	•
RV PARK	—
ROOM SERVICE	•
FREE BREAKFAST	—
FINE DINING/TYPES	Chinese
COFFEE SHOP	—
24-HOUR CAFE	—
BUFFET	—
CASINO	—
LOUNGE	•
SHOWROOM	—
GIFTS/DRUGS/NEWS	•
POOL	•
EXERCISE ROOM	Health spa
TENNIS & RACKET	—

Harrah's ★★★½
3475 S. Las Vegas Blvd.
Las Vegas, NV 89109
☎ 702-369-5000
FAX 702-369-6014
TOLL FREE 800-214-9110
harrahslasvegas.com

RACK RATE	$$$
ROOM QUALITY	81
LOCATION	Mid-Strip
DISCOUNTS	AAA, corp., senior
NO. OF ROOMS	2,652
CHECKOUT TIME	11
NONSMOKING	•
CONCIERGE	•
CONVENTION FACIL.	•
MEETING ROOMS	•
VALET PARKING	•
RV PARK	—
ROOM SERVICE	•
FREE BREAKFAST	—
FINE DINING/TYPES	Steak, seafood, Italian, Asian
COFFEE SHOP	•
24-HOUR CAFE	•
BUFFET	•
CASINO	•
LOUNGE	•
SHOWROOM	Production show, comedy show, magic show
GIFTS/DRUGS/NEWS	•
POOL	•
EXERCISE ROOM	Health spa
TENNIS & RACKET	—

Hotel Information Chart (continued)

Hilton Garden Inn Las Vegas Strip South ★★★
7830 S. Las Vegas Blvd.
Las Vegas, NV 89123
☎ 702-453-7830
FAX 702-453-7850
TOLL FREE 877-STAY-HGI
hiltongardeninn.com

RACK RATE	$$$–
ROOM QUALITY	72
LOCATION	South of Las Vegas Corp.
DISCOUNTS	
NO. OF ROOMS	155
CHECKOUT TIME	Noon
NONSMOKING	—
CONCIERGE	—
CONVENTION FACIL.	—
MEETING ROOMS	•
VALET PARKING	—
RV PARK	—
ROOM SERVICE	• (Evening only)
FREE BREAKFAST	—
FINE DINING/TYPES	American
COFFEE SHOP	—
24-HOUR CAFE	—
BUFFET	• (Breakfast only)
CASINO	—
LOUNGE	•
SHOWROOM	—
GIFTS/DRUGS/NEWS	—
POOL	•
EXERCISE ROOM	•
TENNIS & RACKET	—

Holiday Inn Express ★★★½
5760 Polaris Ave.
Las Vegas, NV 89118
☎ 702-736-0098
FAX 702-736-0084
TOLL FREE 888-465-4329
hiexpress.com

RACK RATE	$$$
ROOM QUALITY	75
LOCATION	South Strip
DISCOUNTS	AAA, AARP, corp., gov't
NO. OF ROOMS	139
CHECKOUT TIME	Noon
NONSMOKING	•
CONCIERGE	—
CONVENTION FACIL.	—
MEETING ROOMS	•
VALET PARKING	—
RV PARK	—
ROOM SERVICE	—
FREE BREAKFAST	•
FINE DINING/TYPES	—
COFFEE SHOP	—
24-HOUR CAFE	—
BUFFET	—
CASINO	—
LOUNGE	—
SHOWROOM	—
GIFTS/DRUGS/NEWS	—
POOL	•
EXERCISE ROOM	•
TENNIS & RACKET	—

Hooters Casino Hotel ★★★
115 E. Tropicana Ave.
Las Vegas, NV 89109
☎ 702-739-9000
FAX 702-736-1120
TOLL FREE 866-LV-HOOTS
hooterscasinohotel.com

RACK RATE	$$$+
ROOM QUALITY	73
LOCATION	South Strip
DISCOUNTS	AAA, gov't, military
NO. OF ROOMS	689
CHECKOUT TIME	Noon
NONSMOKING	Floors
CONCIERGE	•
CONVENTION FACIL.	•
MEETING ROOMS	•
VALET PARKING	•
RV PARK	—
ROOM SERVICE	•
FREE BREAKFAST	—
FINE DINING/TYPES	American, steak, seafood, wings
COFFEE SHOP	•
24-HOUR CAFE	•
BUFFET	•
CASINO	•
LOUNGE	•
SHOWROOM	•
GIFTS/DRUGS/NEWS	•
POOL	•
EXERCISE ROOM	•
TENNIS & RACKET	—

La Quinta Las Vegas Airport North ★★★
3970 Paradise Rd.
Las Vegas, NV 89109
☎ 702-796-9000
FAX 702-796-3537
TOLL FREE 800-753-3757
lq.com

RACK RATE	$$+
ROOM QUALITY	69
LOCATION	East of Strip
DISCOUNTS	AAA, AARP, corp., gov't, senior
NO. OF ROOMS	252
CHECKOUT TIME	Noon
NONSMOKING	•
CONCIERGE	—
CONVENTION FACIL.	—
MEETING ROOMS	•
VALET PARKING	—
RV PARK	—
ROOM SERVICE	—
FREE BREAKFAST	•
FINE DINING/TYPES	American
COFFEE SHOP	—
24-HOUR CAFE	—
BUFFET	—
CASINO	—
LOUNGE	—
SHOWROOM	—
GIFTS/DRUGS/NEWS	—
POOL	•
EXERCISE ROOM	•
TENNIS & RACKET	—

Las Vegas Club ★★★/★★½*
18 E. Fremont St.
Las Vegas, NV 89101
☎ 702-385-1664
FAX 702-380-5715
TOLL FREE 800-634-6532
vegasclubcasino.net

RACK RATE	$+/$
ROOM QUALITY	73/58*
LOCATION	Downtown
DISCOUNTS	AAA, AARP, military
NO. OF ROOMS	410
CHECKOUT TIME	11
NONSMOKING	•
CONCIERGE	—
CONVENTION FACIL.	—
MEETING ROOMS	•
VALET PARKING	•
RV PARK	—
ROOM SERVICE	—
FREE BREAKFAST	—
FINE DINING/TYPES	American, Italian
COFFEE SHOP	—
24-HOUR CAFE	—
BUFFET	—
CASINO	•
LOUNGE	•
SHOWROOM	Occasional lounge entertainment
GIFTS/DRUGS/NEWS	•
POOL	•
EXERCISE ROOM	•
TENNIS & RACKET	Tennis

*north tower/south tower

Las Vegas Hilton ★★★★
3000 Paradise Rd.
Las Vegas, NV 89109
☎ 702-732-5111
FAX 702-262-5089
TOLL FREE 888-732-7117
lvhilton.com

RACK RATE	$$+
ROOM QUALITY	85
LOCATION	East of Strip
DISCOUNTS	AAA, AARP, gov't, military, senior
NO. OF ROOMS	2,950
CHECKOUT TIME	Noon
NONSMOKING	•
CONCIERGE	•
CONVENTION FACIL.	•
MEETING ROOMS	•
VALET PARKING	•
RV PARK	—
ROOM SERVICE	•
FREE BREAKFAST	—
FINE DINING/TYPES	Steak, Asian, Mexican, Italian, deli
COFFEE SHOP	•
24-HOUR CAFE	•
BUFFET	•
CASINO	•
LOUNGE	•
SHOWROOM	Production show
GIFTS/DRUGS/NEWS	•
POOL	•
EXERCISE ROOM	Health spa
TENNIS & RACKET	Tennis

Hyatt Place ★★★	
4520 Paradise Rd.	
Las Vegas, NV 89169	
☎ 702-369-3366	
FAX 702-369-0009	
TOLL FREE 888-492-8847	
lasvegas.place.hyatt.com	
RACK RATE	$$$+
ROOM QUALITY	72
LOCATION	East of Strip
DISCOUNTS	AAA, gov't, military, senior
NO. OF ROOMS	202
CHECKOUT TIME	Noon
NONSMOKING	•
CONCIERGE	—
CONVENTION FACIL.	—
MEETING ROOMS	•
VALET PARKING	—
RV PARK	•
ROOM SERVICE	—
FREE BREAKFAST	•
FINE DINING/TYPES	—
COFFEE SHOP	—
24-HOUR CAFE	—
BUFFET	—
CASINO	—
LOUNGE	—
SHOWROOM	—
GIFTS/DRUGS/NEWS	—
POOL	•
EXERCISE ROOM	•
TENNIS & RACKET	—

Imperial Palace ★★★	
3535 S. Las Vegas Blvd.	
Las Vegas, NV 89109	
☎ 702-731-3311	
FAX 702-731-3063	
TOLL FREE 800-351-7400	
imperialpalace.com	
RACK RATE	$$$+
ROOM QUALITY	68
LOCATION	Mid-Strip
DISCOUNTS	Gov't, military, senior
NO. OF ROOMS	2,640
CHECKOUT TIME	11
NONSMOKING	•
CONCIERGE	•
CONVENTION FACIL.	•
MEETING ROOMS	•
VALET PARKING	•
RV PARK	—
ROOM SERVICE	•
FREE BREAKFAST	—
FINE DINING/TYPES	Steak, seafood, Chinese, ribs, southwestern
COFFEE SHOP	•
24-HOUR CAFE	•
BUFFET	•
CASINO	•
LOUNGE	•
SHOWROOM	•
GIFTS/DRUGS/NEWS	•
POOL	•
EXERCISE ROOM	•
TENNIS & RACKET	—

JW Marriott Las Vegas ★★★★½	
221 N. Rampart Blvd.	
Las Vegas, NV 89145	
☎ 702-869-7777	
FAX 702-869-7339	
TOLL FREE 877-869-8777	
marriott.com	
RACK RATE	$$$$
ROOM QUALITY	93
LOCATION	Summerlin
DISCOUNTS	AAA, gov't, military, senior
NO. OF ROOMS	548
CHECKOUT TIME	Noon
NONSMOKING	•
CONCIERGE	•
CONVENTION FACIL.	•
MEETING ROOMS	—
VALET PARKING	•
RV PARK	—
ROOM SERVICE	•
FREE BREAKFAST	—
FINE DINING/TYPES	Health food, Irish, Italian, Japanese
COFFEE SHOP	•
24-HOUR CAFE	•
BUFFET	•
CASINO	•
LOUNGE	•
SHOWROOM	—
GIFTS/DRUGS/NEWS	•
POOL	•
EXERCISE ROOM	Health spa
TENNIS & RACKET	—

Las Vegas Marriott ★★★★	
325 Convention Center Dr.	
Las Vegas, NV 89109	
☎ 702-650-2000	
FAX 702-650-9466	
TOLL FREE 800-228-9290	
marriott.com	
RACK RATE	$$$$–
ROOM QUALITY	84
LOCATION	East of Strip
DISCOUNTS	AAA, senior
NO. OF ROOMS	277
CHECKOUT TIME	Noon
NONSMOKING	•
CONCIERGE	—
CONVENTION FACIL.	•
MEETING ROOMS	•
VALET PARKING	—
RV PARK	—
ROOM SERVICE	•
FREE BREAKFAST	—
FINE DINING/TYPES	American
COFFEE SHOP	—
24-HOUR CAFE	—
BUFFET	—
CASINO	—
LOUNGE	•
SHOWROOM	—
GIFTS/DRUGS/NEWS	—
POOL	•
EXERCISE ROOM	•
TENNIS & RACKET	—

Loews Lake Las Vegas ★★★★	
101 Montelago Blvd.	
Henderson, NV 89011	
☎ 702-567-6000	
FAX 702-567-6067	
TOLL FREE 877-386-6397	
loewshotels.com	
RACK RATE	$$$$
ROOM QUALITY	88
LOCATION	Henderson
DISCOUNTS	AAA, corp., gov't, senior
NO. OF ROOMS	493
CHECKOUT TIME	Noon
NONSMOKING	•
CONCIERGE	•
CONVENTION FACIL.	•
MEETING ROOMS	•
VALET PARKING	•
RV PARK	—
ROOM SERVICE	•
FREE BREAKFAST	—
FINE DINING/TYPES	American, Pacific, Asian, Mediterranean
COFFEE SHOP	•
24-HOUR CAFE	•
BUFFET	—
CASINO	—
LOUNGE	•
SHOWROOM	—
GIFTS/DRUGS/NEWS	•
POOL	•
EXERCISE ROOM	•
TENNIS & RACKET	•

Luxor ★★★★	
3900 S. Las Vegas Blvd.	
Las Vegas, NV 89119	
☎ 702-262-4444	
FAX 702-262-4137	
TOLL FREE 877-386-4658	
luxor.com	
RACK RATE	$$$+
ROOM QUALITY	87
LOCATION	South Strip
DISCOUNTS	Military
NO. OF ROOMS	4,450
CHECKOUT TIME	11
NONSMOKING	•
CONCIERGE	—
CONVENTION FACIL.	•
MEETING ROOMS	•
VALET PARKING	•
RV PARK	—
ROOM SERVICE	•
FREE BREAKFAST	—
FINE DINING/TYPES	American, seafood, steak, Asian, Mexican
COFFEE SHOP	•
24-HOUR CAFE	•
BUFFET	•
CASINO	•
LOUNGE	•
SHOWROOM	Production show
GIFTS/DRUGS/NEWS	•
POOL	•
EXERCISE ROOM	Health spa
TENNIS & RACKET	—

Hotel Information Chart (continued)

	M Resort ★★★★½	**Main Street Station** ★★★½	**Mandalay Bay** ★★★★½
	12300 S. Las Vegas Blvd.	200 N. Main St.	3950 S. Las Vegas Blvd.
	Henderson, NV 89044	Las Vegas, NV 89101	Las Vegas, NV 89119
	☎ 702-797-1000	☎ 702-387-1896	☎ 702-632-7777
	TOLL FREE 877-673-7678	FAX 702-386-4421	FAX 702-632-7234
	themresort.com	TOLL FREE 800-713-8933	TOLL FREE 877-632-7800
		mainstreetcasino.com	mandalaybay.com
RACK RATE	$$$+	$$–	$$$$$+
ROOM QUALITY	90	75	92
LOCATION	Henderson	Downtown	South Strip
DISCOUNTS	–	–	–
NO. OF ROOMS	390	406	4,756
CHECKOUT TIME	11	Noon	11
NONSMOKING	•	•	Floors
CONCIERGE	•	•	•
CONVENTION FACIL.	•	–	•
MEETING ROOMS	•	•	•
VALET PARKING	•	•	•
RV PARK	–	•	–
ROOM SERVICE	•	–	•
FREE BREAKFAST	–	–	–
FINE DINING/TYPES	Steak, seafood, Italian	Steak, brewery	Russian, French, Italian, Mexican
COFFEE SHOP	•	•	•
24-HOUR CAFE	•	•	•
BUFFET	•	•	•
CASINO	•	•	•
LOUNGE	•	–	•
SHOWROOM	•	–	Headliners, live music, sports
GIFTS/DRUGS/NEWS	•	•	
POOL	•	•	•
EXERCISE ROOM	Health spa	–	Health spa
TENNIS & RACKET	–	–	–

	Mirage ★★★★½	**Monte Carlo** ★★★½	**New York–New York** ★★★★
	3400 S. Las Vegas Blvd.	3770 S. Las Vegas Blvd.	3790 S. Las Vegas Blvd.
	Las Vegas, NV 89109	Las Vegas, NV 89109	Las Vegas, NV 89109
	☎ 702-791-7111	☎ 702-730-7777	☎ 702-740-6969
	FAX 702-792-7632	FAX 702-730-7250	FAX 702-740-6700
	TOLL FREE 800-627-6667	TOLL FREE 800-311-8999	TOLL FREE 866-815-4365
	mirage.com	montecarlo.com	newyorknewyork.com
RACK RATE	$$$$–	$$$	$$$$
ROOM QUALITY	90	82	85
LOCATION	Mid-Strip	South Strip	South Strip
DISCOUNTS	AAA	AAA, military	Gov't, military
NO. OF ROOMS	3,044	3,006	2,024
CHECKOUT TIME	Noon	11	11
NONSMOKING	Floors	Floors	Floors
CONCIERGE	•	–	•
CONVENTION FACIL.	•	•	•
MEETING ROOMS	•	•	•
VALET PARKING	•	•	•
RV PARK	–	–	–
ROOM SERVICE	•	•	•
FREE BREAKFAST	–	–	–
FINE DINING/TYPES	Asian, seafood, Italian, Brazilian	Steak, Asian, Italian, French, seafood	Steak, Chinese, Italian, Mexican, Irish, deli
COFFEE SHOP	•	•	•
24-HOUR CAFE	•	•	•
BUFFET	•	•	• (Breakfast only)
CASINO	•	•	•
LOUNGE	•	•	•
SHOWROOM	Production show, celebrity headliner	Magic show, comedy	Production show, comedy
GIFTS/DRUGS/NEWS	•	•	•
POOL	•	•	•
EXERCISE ROOM	Health spa	Health spa	Health spa
TENNIS & RACKET	–	–	–

Mandarin Oriental at CityCenter ★★★★★
3752 S. Las Vegas Blvd.
Las Vegas, NV 89109
☎ 702-590-8888
FAX 702-590-8880
TOLL FREE 888-881-9578
mandarinoriental.com/
lasvegas

RACK RATE	$$$$$$–
ROOM QUALITY	96
LOCATION	Mid-Strip
DISCOUNTS	–
NO. OF ROOMS	392
CHECKOUT TIME	Noon
NONSMOKING	•
CONCIERGE	•
CONVENTION FACIL.	•
MEETING ROOMS	•
VALET PARKING	•
RV PARK	–
ROOM SERVICE	•
FREE BREAKFAST	–
FINE DINING/TYPES	French
COFFEE SHOP	•
24-HOUR CAFE	–
BUFFET	–
CASINO	• (Adjacent)
LOUNGE	•
SHOWROOM	–
GIFTS/DRUGS/NEWS	• (Adjacent)
POOL	•
EXERCISE ROOM	Health spa
TENNIS & RACKET	–

Manor Suites ★★★
7230 S. Las Vegas Blvd.
Las Vegas, NV 89119
☎ 702-939-9000
FAX 702-939-9014
TOLL FREE 800-691-7169
manorsuites.com

RACK RATE	$$–
ROOM QUALITY	67
LOCATION	South of Las Vegas
DISCOUNTS	–
NO. OF ROOMS	260
CHECKOUT TIME	11
NONSMOKING	•
CONCIERGE	–
CONVENTION FACIL.	–
MEETING ROOMS	–
VALET PARKING	–
RV PARK	–
ROOM SERVICE	–
FREE BREAKFAST	–
FINE DINING/TYPES	–
COFFEE SHOP	–
24-HOUR CAFE	–
BUFFET	–
CASINO	–
LOUNGE	–
SHOWROOM	–
GIFTS/DRUGS/NEWS	–
POOL	•
EXERCISE ROOM	–
TENNIS & RACKET	–

MGM Grand ★★★★
3799 S. Las Vegas Blvd.
Las Vegas, NV 89109
☎ 702-891-1111
FAX 702-891-3036
TOLL FREE 877-880-0880
mgmgrand.com

RACK RATE	$$$$$
ROOM QUALITY	87
LOCATION	South Strip
DISCOUNTS	–
NO. OF ROOMS	5,044
CHECKOUT TIME	11
NONSMOKING	Floors
CONCIERGE	•
CONVENTION FACIL.	•
MEETING ROOMS	•
VALET PARKING	•
RV PARK	–
ROOM SERVICE	•
FREE BREAKFAST	–
FINE DINING/TYPES	Steak, seafood, Cajun, Italian, Chinese, French
COFFEE SHOP	•
24-HOUR CAFE	•
BUFFET	•
CASINO	•
LOUNGE	•
SHOWROOM	Production show, visiting headliners
GIFTS/DRUGS/NEWS	•
POOL	•
EXERCISE ROOM	Health spa
TENNIS & RACKET	•

Orleans ★★★½
4500 W. Tropicana Ave.
Las Vegas, NV 89103
☎ 702-365-7111
FAX 702-365-7500
TOLL FREE 800-ORLEANS
orleanscasino.com

RACK RATE	$$$
ROOM QUALITY	75
LOCATION	South Strip
DISCOUNTS	AAA, AARP
NO. OF ROOMS	1,886
CHECKOUT TIME	Noon
NONSMOKING	•
CONCIERGE	•
CONVENTION FACIL.	•
MEETING ROOMS	•
VALET PARKING	•
RV PARK	–
ROOM SERVICE	•
FREE BREAKFAST	–
FINE DINING/TYPES	Italian, steak, Cajun, Chinese, Mexican, Asian
COFFEE SHOP	•
24-HOUR CAFE	•
BUFFET	•
CASINO	•
LOUNGE	Pub
SHOWROOM	Celebrity headliners on weekends, sports
GIFTS/DRUGS/NEWS	•
POOL	•
EXERCISE ROOM	Health spa
TENNIS & RACKET	–

Palace Station ★★★½/★★★★*
2411 W. Sahara Ave.
Las Vegas, NV 89102
☎ 702-367-2411
FAX 702-367-2478
TOLL FREE 800-6-STATIONS
palacestation.com

RACK RATE	$$+/$$–
ROOM QUALITY	81/74*
LOCATION	North Strip
DISCOUNTS	AAA
NO. OF ROOMS	1,028
CHECKOUT TIME	Noon
NONSMOKING	Floors
CONCIERGE	•
CONVENTION FACIL.	•
MEETING ROOMS	•
VALET PARKING	•
RV PARK	–
ROOM SERVICE	•
FREE BREAKFAST	–
FINE DINING/TYPES	Seafood, Chinese, Mexican, Italian
COFFEE SHOP	•
24-HOUR CAFE	•
BUFFET	•
CASINO	•
LOUNGE	•
SHOWROOM	Comedy, music
GIFTS/DRUGS/NEWS	•
POOL	•
EXERCISE ROOM	•
TENNIS & RACKET	•

*tower rooms/courtyard rooms

The Palazzo ★★★★½
3355 S. Las Vegas Blvd.
Las Vegas, NV 89109
☎ 702-607-1000
FAX 702-414-1100
TOLL FREE 877-263-3001
palazzo.com

RACK RATE	$$$$$$–
ROOM QUALITY	95
LOCATION	Mid-Strip
DISCOUNTS	–
NO. OF ROOMS	3,066
CHECKOUT TIME	11
NONSMOKING	•
CONCIERGE	•
CONVENTION FACIL.	•
MEETING ROOMS	•
VALET PARKING	•
RV PARK	–
ROOM SERVICE	•
FREE BREAKFAST	–
FINE DINING/TYPES	Steak, Italian, Asian, French, Mexican, Japanese
COFFEE SHOP	•
24-HOUR CAFE	•
BUFFET	•
CASINO	•
LOUNGE	•
SHOWROOM	Production show
GIFTS/DRUGS/NEWS	•
POOL	•
EXERCISE ROOM	Health spa
TENNIS & RACKET	–

Hotel Information Chart (continued)

	Palms ★★★★½/★★★★*	Paris ★★★★½	Planet Hollywood ★★★★½/★★★★*
	4321 W. Flamingo Rd.	3655 S. Las Vegas Blvd.	3667 S. Las Vegas Blvd.
	Las Vegas, NV 89103	Las Vegas, NV 89109	Las Vegas, NV 89109
	☎ 702-942-7777	☎ 702-946-7000	☎ 702-785-5555
	FAX 702-942-6999	FAX 702-946-4405	FAX 702-785-5558
	TOLL FREE 866-942-7777	TOLL FREE 888-266-5687	TOLL FREE 877-333-9474
	palms.com	parislasvegas.com	planethollywoodresort.com
RACK RATE	$$$$$$–/$$$$	$$$$$$–	$$$$$/$$$$$–
ROOM QUALITY	95/89	91	93/87
LOCATION	Mid-Strip	Mid-Strip	Mid-Strip
DISCOUNTS	–	AAA, senior, gov't	–
NO. OF ROOMS	1,303	2,916	2,567
CHECKOUT TIME	11	11	11
NONSMOKING	Floors	Floors	•
CONCIERGE	•	•	•
CONVENTION FACIL.	•	•	•
MEETING ROOMS	•	•	•
VALET PARKING	•	•	•
RV PARK	–	–	Large
ROOM SERVICE	•	•	•
FREE BREAKFAST	–	–	–
FINE DINING/TYPES	Asian, French, steak, Mexican	French, Asian, Caribbean, Italian	Asian, steak
COFFEE SHOP	•	•	•
24-HOUR CAFE	•	•	•
BUFFET	•	•	•
CASINO	•	•	•
LOUNGE	•	•	•
SHOWROOM	Headliners	Dancing	Headliners
GIFTS/DRUGS/NEWS	•	•	•
POOL	•	•	•
EXERCISE ROOM	•	Health spa	•
TENNIS & RACKET	–	•	–
	*Palms Tower/Fantasy Tower		*PH Towers Wesgate/Planet Hollywood

	Ramada Las Vegas ★★★	Ravella at Lake Las Vegas ★★★★	Red Rock Resort ★★★★½
	325 E. Flamingo Rd.	1610 Lake Las Vegas Pkwy.	11011 W. Charleston Blvd.
	Las Vegas, NV 89109	Henderson, NV 89011	Las Vegas, NV 89135
	☎ 702-732-9100	☎ 702-567-4700	☎ 702-797-7777
	FAX 702-731-9784	FAX 702-567-4777	FAX 702-797-7745
	TOLL FREE 888-288-4982	TOLL FREE 888-810-0440	TOLL FREE 866-767-7773
	ramada.com	ravellavegas.com	redrocklasvegas.com
RACK RATE	$$+	$$$	$$$+
ROOM QUALITY	68	88	91
LOCATION	East of Strip	Henderson	Summerlin
DISCOUNTS	AAA, AARP, gov't, military	AAA, corp., gov't, senior	AAA, AARP
NO. OF ROOMS	150	349	816
CHECKOUT TIME	Noon	Noon	Noon
NONSMOKING	•	•	Floors
CONCIERGE	–	•	•
CONVENTION FACIL.	•	•	•
MEETING ROOMS	•	•	•
VALET PARKING	–	•	•
RV PARK	–	–	–
ROOM SERVICE	–	•	•
FREE BREAKFAST	–	–	–
FINE DINING/TYPES	–	American, Italian	American, steak, Mexican, Italian
COFFEE SHOP	•	•	•
24-HOUR CAFE	–	–	•
BUFFET	–	–	•
CASINO	–	–	•
LOUNGE	–	•	•
SHOWROOM	–	•	Piano bar, live entertainment, dancing
GIFTS/DRUGS/NEWS	–	•	
POOL	•	•	•
EXERCISE ROOM	•	Health spa	Health spa
TENNIS & RACKET	–	•	–

Platinum Hotel ★★★★
211 E. Flamingo Rd.
Las Vegas, NV 89169
☎ 702-365-5000
FAX 702-636-2500
TOLL FREE 877-211-9211
theplatinumhotel.com

RACK RATE	$$$$+
ROOM QUALITY	88
LOCATION	East of Strip
DISCOUNTS	—
NO. OF ROOMS	255
CHECKOUT TIME	11
NONSMOKING	•
CONCIERGE	•
CONVENTION FACIL.	•
MEETING ROOMS	•
VALET PARKING	•
RV PARK	—
ROOM SERVICE	•
FREE BREAKFAST	—
FINE DINING/TYPES	American
COFFEE SHOP	•
24-HOUR CAFE	—
BUFFET	—
CASINO	—
LOUNGE	—
SHOWROOM	—
GIFTS/DRUGS/NEWS	•
POOL	•
EXERCISE ROOM	•
TENNIS & RACKET	—

Plaza ★★★½
1 Main St.
Las Vegas, NV 89101
☎ 702-386-2110
FAX 702-382-8281
TOLL FREE 800-634-6575
plazahotelcasino.com

RACK RATE	$$+
ROOM QUALITY	79
LOCATION	Downtown
DISCOUNTS	AAA, AARP, military
NO. OF ROOMS	1,052
CHECKOUT TIME	11
NONSMOKING	Floors
CONCIERGE	•
CONVENTION FACIL.	•
MEETING ROOMS	•
VALET PARKING	•
RV PARK	—
ROOM SERVICE	•
FREE BREAKFAST	—
FINE DINING/TYPES	American, Continental
COFFEE SHOP	•
24-HOUR CAFE	—
BUFFET	•
CASINO	•
LOUNGE	•
SHOWROOM	Production show, comedy
GIFTS/DRUGS/NEWS	•
POOL	• (Rooftop)
EXERCISE ROOM	—
TENNIS & RACKET	—

Quality Inn Las Vegas ★★½
4975 S. Valley View Blvd.
Las Vegas, NV 89118
☎ 702-798-7736
FAX 702-798-5951
TOLL FREE 888-798-7736
qualityinn.com

RACK RATE	$$
ROOM QUALITY	64
LOCATION	South Strip
DISCOUNTS	AAA, AARP, corp., gov't, senior
NO. OF ROOMS	59
CHECKOUT TIME	Noon
NONSMOKING	•
CONCIERGE	—
CONVENTION FACIL.	—
MEETING ROOMS	•
VALET PARKING	—
RV PARK	—
ROOM SERVICE	—
FREE BREAKFAST	—
FINE DINING/TYPES	—
COFFEE SHOP	—
24-HOUR CAFE	—
BUFFET	—
CASINO	—
LOUNGE	—
SHOWROOM	—
GIFTS/DRUGS/NEWS	—
POOL	•
EXERCISE ROOM	•
TENNIS & RACKET	—

Renaissance Las Vegas ★★★★½
3400 Paradise Rd.
Las Vegas, NV 89169
☎ 702-784-5700
FAX 702-735-3130
TOLL FREE 800-750-0980
renaissancelasvegas.com

RACK RATE	$$$
ROOM QUALITY	90
LOCATION	East of Strip
DISCOUNTS	AAA, gov't, military, senior
NO. OF ROOMS	548
CHECKOUT TIME	Noon
NONSMOKING	Floors
CONCIERGE	•
CONVENTION FACIL.	•
MEETING ROOMS	•
VALET PARKING	•
RV PARK	—
ROOM SERVICE	•
FREE BREAKFAST	—
FINE DINING/TYPES	Steak
COFFEE SHOP	•
24-HOUR CAFE	—
BUFFET	—
CASINO	—
LOUNGE	•
SHOWROOM	—
GIFTS/DRUGS/NEWS	•
POOL	•
EXERCISE ROOM	•
TENNIS & RACKET	—

Residence Inn by Marriott Las Vegas Convention Center ★★★★
3225 Paradise Rd.
Las Vegas, NV 89109
☎ 702-796-9300
FAX 702-796-9562
TOLL FREE 800-677-8328
marriott.com

RACK RATE	$$$
ROOM QUALITY	83
LOCATION	East of Strip
DISCOUNTS	AAA, corp., gov't, military, senior
NO. OF ROOMS	192
CHECKOUT TIME	Noon
NONSMOKING	Floors
CONCIERGE	—
CONVENTION FACIL.	—
MEETING ROOMS	•
VALET PARKING	—
RV PARK	—
ROOM SERVICE	—
FREE BREAKFAST	•
FINE DINING/TYPES	—
COFFEE SHOP	—
24-HOUR CAFE	—
BUFFET	—
CASINO	—
LOUNGE	—
SHOWROOM	—
GIFTS/DRUGS/NEWS	—
POOL	•
EXERCISE ROOM	•
TENNIS & RACKET	•

Residence Inn by Marriott Las Vegas South ★★★★
5875 Dean Martin Dr.
Las Vegas, NV 89118
☎ 702-795-7378
FAX 702-795-3288
TOLL FREE 800-677-8328
marriott.com

RACK RATE	$$$–
ROOM QUALITY	86
LOCATION	South Strip
DISCOUNTS	AAA, corp., gov't, military, senior
NO. OF ROOMS	160
CHECKOUT TIME	Noon
NONSMOKING	—
CONCIERGE	—
CONVENTION FACIL.	—
MEETING ROOMS	•
VALET PARKING	—
RV PARK	—
ROOM SERVICE	(Dinner from local restaurant)
FREE BREAKFAST	•
FINE DINING/TYPES	American
COFFEE SHOP	—
24-HOUR CAFE	—
BUFFET	• (Breakfast only)
CASINO	—
LOUNGE	—
SHOWROOM	—
GIFTS/DRUGS/NEWS	•
POOL	•
EXERCISE ROOM	•
TENNIS & RACKET	Tennis

Hotel Information Chart (continued)

	Rio ★★★★	Riviera ★★★½	Royal Resort ★★★
	3700 W. Flamingo Rd.	2901 S. Las Vegas Blvd.	99 Convention Center Dr.
	Las Vegas, NV 89103	Las Vegas, NV 89109	Las Vegas, NV 89109
	☎ 702-252-7777	☎ 702-734-5110	☎ 702-735-6117
	FAX 702-967-3890	FAX 702-794-9451	FAX 702-735-2546
	TOLL FREE 800-PLAYRIO	TOLL FREE 800-634-3420	TOLL FREE 800-634-6118
	riolasvegas.com	rivierahotel.com	royalhotelvegas.com
RACK RATE	$$$+	$$	$+
ROOM QUALITY	86	79	73
LOCATION	Mid-Strip	North Strip	North Strip
DISCOUNTS	AAA, gov't, senior	AAA	AAA, AARP, corp., gov't, military
NO. OF ROOMS	2,563	2,076	191
CHECKOUT TIME	11	Noon	11
NONSMOKING	Floors		Floors
CONCIERGE	•	•	•
CONVENTION FACIL.	•	•	—
MEETING ROOMS	•	•	•
VALET PARKING	•	•	—
RV PARK	—	—	—
ROOM SERVICE	•	•	•
FREE BREAKFAST	—	—	—
FINE DINING/TYPES	Italian, Chinese, southwestern, Indian, French	Steak, seafood, Chinese, deli	Italian
COFFEE SHOP	•	•	•
24-HOUR CAFE	•	•	—
BUFFET	•	•	—
CASINO	•	•	—
LOUNGE	•	•	—
SHOWROOM	Live entertainment, headliners	Production show, female impersonators, comedy club	—
GIFTS/DRUGS/NEWS	•	•	•
POOL	•	•	•
EXERCISE ROOM	Health spa	•	•
TENNIS & RACKET	—	Tennis	—

	Signature at MGM Grand ★★★★★	Silverton ★★★★	South Point ★★★½
	145 E. Harmon Ave.	3333 Blue Diamond Rd.	9777 S. Las Vegas Blvd.
	Las Vegas, NV 89109	Las Vegas, NV 89139	Las Vegas, NV 89123
	☎ 702-797-6000	☎ 702-263-7777	☎ 702-796-7111
	FAX 702-797-6150	FAX 702-893-7405	FAX 702-797-8041
	TOLL FREE 877-612-2121	TOLL FREE 800-588-7711	TOLL FREE 866-796-7111
	signaturemgmgrand.com	silvertoncasino.com	southpointcasino.com
RACK RATE	$$$$+	$$+	$$
ROOM QUALITY	96	88	81
LOCATION	East of Strip	South of Las Vegas	South of Las Vegas
DISCOUNTS	—	AAA, AARP, military	AAA, AARP
NO. OF ROOMS	1,734	300	2,163
CHECKOUT TIME	11	Noon	Noon
NONSMOKING	•	Floors	•
CONCIERGE	•	•	•
CONVENTION FACIL.	—	—	•
MEETING ROOMS	•	—	•
VALET PARKING	•	•	•
RV PARK	—	•	•
ROOM SERVICE	•	•	•
FREE BREAKFAST	—	—	—
FINE DINING/TYPES	Steak, seafood, Cajun, Italian, Chinese, French	Seafood, steak	Italian, seafood, steak, Mexican
COFFEE SHOP	•	•	•
24-HOUR CAFE	•	•	•
BUFFET	—	•	•
CASINO	•	•	•
LOUNGE	•	•	•
SHOWROOM	—	—	Live music
GIFTS/DRUGS/NEWS	•	•	•
POOL	•	•	•
EXERCISE ROOM	•	•	•
TENNIS & RACKET	—	—	—

Rumor ★★★½
455 East Harmon Ave.
Las Vegas, NV 89169
☎ 702-369-5400
TOLL FREE 877-997-8667
rumorvegas.com

RACK RATE	$$
ROOM QUALITY	78
LOCATION	East of Strip
DISCOUNTS	—
NO. OF ROOMS	150
CHECKOUT TIME	11
NONSMOKING	•
CONCIERGE	•
CONVENTION FACIL.	—
MEETING ROOMS	—
VALET PARKING	—
RV PARK	—
ROOM SERVICE	•
FREE BREAKFAST	—
FINE DINING/TYPES	Eclectic
COFFEE SHOP	—
24-HOUR CAFE	—
BUFFET	—
CASINO	—
LOUNGE	•
SHOWROOM	—
GIFTS/DRUGS/NEWS	•
POOL	•
EXERCISE ROOM	—
TENNIS & RACKET	—

Sam's Town ★★★½
5111 Boulder Hwy.
Las Vegas, NV 89122
☎ 702-456-7777
FAX 702-454-8014
TOLL FREE 800-897-8696
samstownlv.com

RACK RATE	$$
ROOM QUALITY	79
LOCATION	Boulder Highway
DISCOUNTS	AAA, AARP
NO. OF ROOMS	648
CHECKOUT TIME	Noon
NONSMOKING	•
CONCIERGE	•
CONVENTION FACIL.	—
MEETING ROOMS	•
VALET PARKING	•
RV PARK	•
ROOM SERVICE	—
FREE BREAKFAST	—
FINE DINING/TYPES	Steak, American, Mexican
COFFEE SHOP	•
24-HOUR CAFE	—
BUFFET	•
CASINO	•
LOUNGE	•
SHOWROOM	•
GIFTS/DRUGS/NEWS	•
POOL	•
EXERCISE ROOM	—
TENNIS & RACKET	—

Santa Fe Station ★★★
4949 N. Rancho Dr.
Las Vegas, NV 89130
☎ 702-658-4900
FAX 702-658-4919
TOLL FREE 866-767-7771
santafestationlasvegas.com

RACK RATE	$$–
ROOM QUALITY	73
LOCATION	Rancho Drive
DISCOUNTS	AAA, AARP
NO. OF ROOMS	200
CHECKOUT TIME	Noon
NONSMOKING	•
CONCIERGE	•
CONVENTION FACIL.	•
MEETING ROOMS	•
VALET PARKING	•
RV PARK	—
ROOM SERVICE	—
FREE BREAKFAST	—
FINE DINING/TYPES	Mexican, steak, seafood, American
COFFEE SHOP	•
24-HOUR CAFE	•
BUFFET	•
CASINO	•
LOUNGE	•
SHOWROOM	Live music, tribute show
GIFTS/DRUGS/NEWS	•
POOL	•
EXERCISE ROOM	•
TENNIS & RACKET	—

Stratosphere ★★★½
2000 S. Las Vegas Blvd.
Las Vegas, NV 89104
☎ 702-380-7777
FAX 702-380-7732
TOLL FREE 800-998-6937
stratospherehotel.com

RACK RATE	$$+
ROOM QUALITY	79
LOCATION	North Strip
DISCOUNTS	AAA, military, senior
NO. OF ROOMS	2,444
CHECKOUT TIME	11
NONSMOKING	Floors
CONCIERGE	•
CONVENTION FACIL.	•
MEETING ROOMS	•
VALET PARKING	•
RV PARK	•
ROOM SERVICE	•
FREE BREAKFAST	—
FINE DINING/TYPES	Seafood, steak, Italian, American
COFFEE SHOP	•
24-HOUR CAFE	•
BUFFET	•
CASINO	•
LOUNGE	•
SHOWROOM	Production show
GIFTS/DRUGS/NEWS	•
POOL	•
EXERCISE ROOM	Health spa
TENNIS & RACKET	—

Suncoast ★★★½
9090 Alta Dr.
Las Vegas, NV 89145
☎ 702-636-7111
FAX 702-636-7288
TOLL FREE 877-677-7111
suncoastcasino.com

RACK RATE	$$$+
ROOM QUALITY	82
LOCATION	Summerlin
DISCOUNTS	AAA, senior
NO. OF ROOMS	427
CHECKOUT TIME	Noon
NONSMOKING	•
CONCIERGE	—
CONVENTION FACIL.	•
MEETING ROOMS	•
VALET PARKING	•
RV PARK	—
ROOM SERVICE	—
FREE BREAKFAST	—
FINE DINING/TYPES	Italian, Chinese, American, seafood, Mexican
COFFEE SHOP	•
24-HOUR CAFE	•
BUFFET	•
CASINO	•
LOUNGE	•
SHOWROOM	Headliners
GIFTS/DRUGS/NEWS	•
POOL	•
EXERCISE ROOM	•
TENNIS & RACKET	—

Sunset Station ★★★★
1301 Sunset Rd.
Henderson, NV 89014
☎ 702-547-7777
FAX 702-547-7744
TOLL FREE 800-6-STATIONS
sunsetstation.com

RACK RATE	$$–
ROOM QUALITY	87
LOCATION	Henderson
DISCOUNTS	AAA
NO. OF ROOMS	457
CHECKOUT TIME	Noon
NONSMOKING	Floors
CONCIERGE	•
CONVENTION FACIL.	—
MEETING ROOMS	•
VALET PARKING	•
RV PARK	—
ROOM SERVICE	—
FREE BREAKFAST	—
FINE DINING/TYPES	American, Italian, steak, seafood, Mexican
COFFEE SHOP	•
24-HOUR CAFE	•
BUFFET	•
CASINO	•
LOUNGE	•
SHOWROOM	Concerts, live entertainment
GIFTS/DRUGS/NEWS	•
POOL	•
EXERCISE ROOM	•
TENNIS & RACKET	—

Hotel Information Chart (continued)

Terrible's ★★★½
4100 S. Paradise Rd.
Las Vegas, NV 89109
☎ 702-733-7000
FAX 702-791-2423
TOLL FREE 800-640-9777
terriblescasinos.com

RACK RATE	$+
ROOM QUALITY	78
LOCATION	East of Strip
DISCOUNTS	AAA
NO. OF ROOMS	330
CHECKOUT TIME	11
NONSMOKING	•
CONCIERGE	•
CONVENTION FACIL.	—
MEETING ROOMS	•
VALET PARKING	—
RV PARK	•
ROOM SERVICE	•
FREE BREAKFAST	—
FINE DINING/TYPES	American, Chinese, Mexican
COFFEE SHOP	•
24-HOUR CAFE	•
BUFFET	•
CASINO	•
LOUNGE	•
SHOWROOM	—
GIFTS/DRUGS/NEWS	•
POOL	•
EXERCISE ROOM	•
TENNIS & RACKET	—

Texas Station ★★★
2101 Texas Star Ln.
Las Vegas, NV 89030
☎ 702-631-1000
FAX 702-631-8120
TOLL FREE 800-654-8888
texasstation.com

RACK RATE	$$–
ROOM QUALITY	70
LOCATION	Rancho Drive Area
DISCOUNTS	AAA
NO. OF ROOMS	200
CHECKOUT TIME	Noon
NONSMOKING	Floors
CONCIERGE	—
CONVENTION FACIL.	—
MEETING ROOMS	•
VALET PARKING	•
RV PARK	—
ROOM SERVICE	•
FREE BREAKFAST	—
FINE DINING/TYPES	Seafood, Italian, Mexican, steak
COFFEE SHOP	•
24-HOUR CAFE	•
BUFFET	•
CASINO	•
LOUNGE	•
SHOWROOM	Live entertainment nightly
GIFTS/DRUGS/NEWS	•
POOL	•
EXERCISE ROOM	—
TENNIS & RACKET	—

THEhotel at Mandalay Bay
(all suites) ★★★★★
3950 S. Las Vegas Blvd.
Las Vegas, NV 89119
☎ 702-632-7777
FAX 702-632-7228
TOLL FREE 877-632-7800
mandalaybay.com

RACK RATE	$$$$$
ROOM QUALITY	96
LOCATION	South Strip
DISCOUNTS	AAA, AARP
NO. OF ROOMS	1,117
CHECKOUT TIME	11
NONSMOKING	Floors
CONCIERGE	•
CONVENTION FACIL.	•
MEETING ROOMS	•
VALET PARKING	•
RV PARK	—
ROOM SERVICE	•
FREE BREAKFAST	—
FINE DINING/TYPES	French, Asian, American
COFFEE SHOP	•
24-HOUR CAFE	Nearby
BUFFET	Nearby
CASINO	Nearby
LOUNGE	•
SHOWROOM	Production show, live music
GIFTS/DRUGS/NEWS	•
POOL	•
EXERCISE ROOM	Health spa
TENNIS & RACKET	—

Tuscany ★★★
255 E. Flamingo Rd.
Las Vegas, NV 89169
☎ 702-893-8933
FAX 702-947-5994
TOLL FREE 877-TUSCAN-1
tuscanylv.com

RACK RATE	$$$–
ROOM QUALITY	70
LOCATION	East of Strip
DISCOUNTS	AAA, AARP
NO. OF ROOMS	716
CHECKOUT TIME	11
NONSMOKING	Floors
CONCIERGE	•
CONVENTION FACIL.	•
MEETING ROOMS	•
VALET PARKING	•
RV PARK	—
ROOM SERVICE	•
FREE BREAKFAST	—
FINE DINING/TYPES	Italian, Mexican
COFFEE SHOP	•
24-HOUR CAFE	•
BUFFET	—
CASINO	•
LOUNGE	•
SHOWROOM	—
GIFTS/DRUGS/NEWS	•
POOL	•
EXERCISE ROOM	•
TENNIS & RACKET	—

Vdara at CityCenter ★★★★½
2600 W. Harmon Ave.
Las Vegas, NV 89109
☎ 702-590-2111
FAX 702-590-2112
TOLL FREE 866-745-7767
vdara.com

RACK RATE	$$$$$$–
ROOM QUALITY	95
LOCATION	Mid-Strip
DISCOUNTS	—
NO. OF ROOMS	1,495
CHECKOUT TIME	Noon
NONSMOKING	•
CONCIERGE	•
CONVENTION FACIL.	•
MEETING ROOMS	•
VALET PARKING	•
RV PARK	—
ROOM SERVICE	•
FREE BREAKFAST	—
FINE DINING/TYPES	—
COFFEE SHOP	—
24-HOUR CAFE	—
BUFFET	—
CASINO	• (adjacent)
LOUNGE	—
SHOWROOM	—
GIFTS/DRUGS/NEWS	—
POOL	•
EXERCISE ROOM	Health spa
TENNIS & RACKET	—

The Venetian ★★★★½
3355 S. Las Vegas Blvd.
Las Vegas, NV 89109
☎ 702-414-1000
FAX 702-414-1100
TOLL FREE 866-659-9643
venetian.com

RACK RATE	$$$$$$–
ROOM QUALITY	94
LOCATION	Mid-Strip
DISCOUNTS	—
NO. OF ROOMS	4,027
CHECKOUT TIME	11
NONSMOKING	Floors
CONCIERGE	•
CONVENTION FACIL.	•
MEETING ROOMS	•
VALET PARKING	•
RV PARK	—
ROOM SERVICE	•
FREE BREAKFAST	—
FINE DINING/TYPES	Italian, French, Asian, gourmet
COFFEE SHOP	•
24-HOUR CAFE	•
BUFFET	•
CASINO	•
LOUNGE	•
SHOWROOM	Headliners, live music, production show
GIFTS/DRUGS/NEWS	•
POOL	•
EXERCISE ROOM	Health spa
TENNIS & RACKET	—

T. I. ★★★★
3300 S. Las Vegas Blvd.
Las Vegas, NV 89109
☎ 702-894-7111
FAX 702-894-7414
TOLL FREE 800-288-7206
treasureisland.com

RACK RATE	$$$$+
ROOM QUALITY	84
LOCATION	Mid-Strip
DISCOUNTS	AAA, gov't
NO. OF ROOMS	2,885
CHECKOUT TIME	Noon
NONSMOKING	Floors
CONCIERGE	–
CONVENTION FACIL.	•
MEETING ROOMS	•
VALET PARKING	•
RV PARK	–
ROOM SERVICE	•
FREE BREAKFAST	–
FINE DINING/TYPES	Seafood, steak, American, Caribbean, Japanese
COFFEE SHOP	•
24-HOUR CAFE	•
BUFFET	•
CASINO	•
LOUNGE	•
SHOWROOM	Production show
GIFTS/DRUGS/NEWS	•
POOL	•
EXERCISE ROOM	Health spa
TENNIS & RACKET	–

Tropicana ★★★★
3801 S. Las Vegas Blvd.
Las Vegas, NV 89109
☎ 702-739-2222
FAX 702-739-3648
TOLL FREE 888-826-8767
troplv.com

RACK RATE	$$$+
ROOM QUALITY	89
LOCATION	South Strip
DISCOUNTS	–
NO. OF ROOMS	1,658
CHECKOUT TIME	Noon
NONSMOKING	Floors
CONCIERGE	•
CONVENTION FACIL.	–
MEETING ROOMS	•
VALET PARKING	•
RV PARK	–
ROOM SERVICE	•
FREE BREAKFAST	–
FINE DINING/TYPES	Steak, Caribbean, Japanese, Italian
COFFEE SHOP	•
24-HOUR CAFE	•
BUFFET	•
CASINO	•
LOUNGE	•
SHOWROOM	Production show, comedy club, magic
GIFTS/DRUGS/NEWS	•
POOL	•
EXERCISE ROOM	Health spa
TENNIS & RACKET	–

Trump Int'l Hotel and Tower Las Vegas ★★★★½
2000 Fashion Show Dr.
Las Vegas, NV 89109
☎ 702-982-0000
FAX 702-476-8450
TOLL FREE 866-939-8786
trumplasvegashotel.com

RACK RATE	$$$+
ROOM QUALITY	95
LOCATION	North Strip
DISCOUNTS	–
NO. OF ROOMS	1,282
CHECKOUT TIME	11
NONSMOKING	•
CONCIERGE	•
CONVENTION FACIL.	•
MEETING ROOMS	•
VALET PARKING	•
RV PARK	–
ROOM SERVICE	•
FREE BREAKFAST	–
FINE DINING/TYPES	American, Mediterranean
COFFEE SHOP	•
24-HOUR CAFE	24-hour in-suite dining
BUFFET	–
CASINO	–
LOUNGE	•
SHOWROOM	–
GIFTS/DRUGS/NEWS	•
POOL	•
EXERCISE ROOM	Health spa
TENNIS & RACKET	–

Westin Casuarina ★★★★
160 E. Flamingo Rd.
Las Vegas, NV 89109
☎ 702-836-5900
FAX 702-836-9776
TOLL FREE 866-716-8132
starwoodhotels.com/westin

RACK RATE	$$$+
ROOM QUALITY	83
LOCATION	Mid-Strip
DISCOUNTS	AAA
NO. OF ROOMS	826
CHECKOUT TIME	11
NONSMOKING	•
CONCIERGE	•
CONVENTION FACIL.	•
MEETING ROOMS	•
VALET PARKING	•
RV PARK	–
ROOM SERVICE	•
FREE BREAKFAST	–
FINE DINING/TYPES	American
COFFEE SHOP	•
24-HOUR CAFE	•
BUFFET	• (Breakfast only)
CASINO	•
LOUNGE	•
SHOWROOM	–
GIFTS/DRUGS/NEWS	•
POOL	•
EXERCISE ROOM	Health spa
TENNIS & RACKET	–

Wynn Encore ★★★★★
3121 S. Las Vegas Blvd.
Las Vegas, NV 89109
☎ 702-770-8000
FAX 702-770-1500
TOLL FREE 888-320-7123
wynnlasvegas.com

RACK RATE	$$$$$$–
ROOM QUALITY	96
LOCATION	Mid-Strip
DISCOUNTS	–
NO. OF ROOMS	2,034
CHECKOUT TIME	Noon
NONSMOKING	•
CONCIERGE	•
CONVENTION FACIL.	•
MEETING ROOMS	•
VALET PARKING	•
RV PARK	–
ROOM SERVICE	•
FREE BREAKFAST	–
FINE DINING/TYPES	Italian, steak, seafood, Asian
COFFEE SHOP	•
24-HOUR CAFE	•
BUFFET	•
CASINO	•
LOUNGE	•
SHOWROOM	•
GIFTS/DRUGS/NEWS	•
POOL	•
EXERCISE ROOM	Health spa
TENNIS & RACKET	–

Wynn Las Vegas ★★★★½
3131 S. Las Vegas Blvd.
Las Vegas, NV 89109
☎ 702-770-7000
FAX 702-770-1500
TOLL FREE 877-321-WYNN
wynnlasvegas.com

RACK RATE	$$$$$$–
ROOM QUALITY	95
LOCATION	Mid-Strip
DISCOUNTS	–
NO. OF ROOMS	2,716
CHECKOUT TIME	Noon
NONSMOKING	Floors
CONCIERGE	•
CONVENTION FACIL.	•
MEETING ROOMS	•
VALET PARKING	•
RV PARK	–
ROOM SERVICE	•
FREE BREAKFAST	–
FINE DINING/TYPES	French, Italian, seafood, Asian
COFFEE SHOP	•
24-HOUR CAFE	•
BUFFET	•
CASINO	•
LOUNGE	•
SHOWROOM	Production show
GIFTS/DRUGS/NEWS	•
POOL	•
EXERCISE ROOM	Health spa
TENNIS & RACKET	–

PART TWO

ENTERTAINMENT *and* NIGHTLIFE

LAS VEGAS SHOWS *and* ENTERTAINMENT

LAS VEGAS CALLS ITSELF the "Entertainment Capital of the World." This is arguably true, particularly in terms of the sheer number of live entertainment productions staged daily. On any given day in Las Vegas, a visitor can select from dozens of presentations, ranging from major production spectaculars to celebrity headliners, from comedy clubs to live music in lounges. The standard of professionalism and value for your entertainment dollar is very high. There is no other place where you can buy so much top-quality entertainment for so little money.

 Jubilee!, a full-blown Las Vegas production show, is one of the best buys in town, with tickets as low as $60 plus tax.

But here's the bad news: The average price of a ticket to one of the major production shows has topped $80. However, the standard of quality for shows has likewise soared. And variety, well, there's now literally something for everyone, from traditional Las Vegas feathers and butts to real Broadway musicals. And believe it or not, the value is still there—maybe not in the grand showrooms and incessantly hyped productions, but in the smaller showrooms and lounges and in the main theaters of off-Strip hotels. There's more of everything now, including both overpriced shows and bargains. Regarding the former, you'll be numbed and blinded by their billboards all over town. As concerns the latter, you'll have to scout around, but you'll be rewarded with some great shows at dynamite prices. And there are always discount coupons floating around.

CHOICES, CHOICES, CHOICES

MOST LAS VEGAS LIVE ENTERTAINMENT offerings can be lumped into one of several broad categories:

- Celebrity headliners
- Long-term engagements
- Broadway and off-Broadway shows
- Production shows
- Impersonator shows
- Comedy clubs
- Lounge entertainment

CELEBRITY HEADLINERS As the name implies, these are concerts or shows featuring big-name entertainers on a limited-engagement basis, usually one to four weeks, but sometimes for a one-night stand. Headliners are usually backed up by a medium-sized orchestra, and the stage sets and special production effects are either very minimal or completely over the top. Performers such as David Copperfield and Jay Leno play Las Vegas regularly. Some even work on a rotation with other performers, returning to the same showroom for several engagements each year. Other stars, such as Barbra Streisand, Paul McCartney, and the Rolling Stones, play Las Vegas only rarely, transforming each appearance into a truly special event. While there are exceptions, the superstars are regularly found at the MGM Grand, the Mirage, Mandalay Bay, Caesars Palace, Planet Hollywood, Las Vegas Hilton, Bally's, Wynn Encore, and the Hard Rock. Big-name performers in the city's top showrooms command premium admission prices. Headliners of slightly lesser stature play at various other showrooms.

LONG-TERM ENGAGEMENTS These are shows by the famous and once-famous who have come to Las Vegas to stay. Comic Rita Rudner is making a go of it at the Venetian. Barry Manilow holds court at Paris Las Vegas, Garth Brooks has settled in at Encore, and Celine Dion is back and better than ever at Caesars Palace.

BROADWAY AND OFF-BROADWAY SHOWS Las Vegas showrooms have dallied with Broadway shows for a long time. Some caught on, but most didn't, and many were signed for limited engagements. The tide has turned, however, and there are now a goodly number of shows that originated on Broadway or in London playing long-term engagements in Las Vegas. As of this writing, these include *Blue Man Group, The Lion King, Phantom—The Las Vegas Spectacular, Jersey Boys, Defending the Caveman,* and *Tony 'n' Tina's Wedding.*

PRODUCTION SHOWS These are continuously running, Broadway-style theatrical and musical productions. Cast sizes run from a dozen performers to more than 100, with costumes, sets, and special effects spanning a comparable range. Costing hundreds of thousands, if not millions, to produce, the shows feature elaborate choreography and great spectacle. Sometimes playing twice a night, six or seven days a week, production shows often run for years.

Production shows generally have a central theme to which a more or less standard mix of choreography and variety acts (also called specialty acts) are added. Favorite central themes are magic and illusion and "best of Broadway," a theme that figures prominently in several current shows. Defying categorization, Cirque du Soleil now offers seven shows.

Las Vegas puts its own distinctive imprint on all this entertainment, imparting a great deal of homogeneity and redundancy to the mix of productions. The quality of Las Vegas entertainment is quite high, even excellent, but most production shows seem to operate according to a formula that fosters a numbing sameness. Particularly pronounced in the magic/illusion shows and the Broadway-style musical productions, this sameness discourages sampling more than one show from each genre. While it is not totally accurate to say that "if you've seen one Las Vegas production or magic show, you've seen them all," the statement comes closer to the truth than one would hope.

We should mention that only one show, *Jubilee!* at Bally's, carries on the tradition of the Ziegfeld Follies–inspired, Las Vegas grand production show. As recently as 1990, these immense productions dominated Las Vegas showrooms. They even spawned a new genre of musical theater, the "Las Vegas–Style Musical Revue," that is alive and well in a much-scaled-down form on cruise ships and elsewhere throughout the Western world. The Parisian *Folies Bergere* went dark permanently in 2009 after a 49-year run at the Tropicana, leaving only *Jubilee!* to represent the genre. When *Jubilee!* ends its decades-long run, a fabled piece of Las Vegas history will die with it.

In the magic/illusion shows, the rage is to put unlikely creatures or objects into boxes or behind curtains and make them disappear. Some featured magicians repeat this sort of tiresome illusion more than a dozen times in a single performance, with nothing really changing except the size of the box and the object placed into it. Into these boxes go doves, ducks, dwarfs, showgirls, lions, tigers, panthers, motorcycles (with riders), TV cameras (with cameramen), and even elephants. Sometimes the illusionist himself gets into a box and disappears, reappearing moments later in the audience. Generally the elephants and other animals don't reappear until the next performance. These box illusions are amazing the first time or two, but become less compelling after that. After they had seen all of the illusion shows in Las Vegas, our reviewers commented that they had witnessed the disappearance in a box of everything except their mortgages. Food for thought.

While they share a common format, production shows, regardless of theme, can be differentiated by the size of the cast and by the elaborateness of the production. Other discriminating factors include the creativity of the choreography, the attractiveness of the performers, the pace and continuity of the presentation, and its ability to build to a crescendo. Strength in these last-mentioned areas sometimes allows a relatively simple, lower-budget show to provide a more satisfying evening of entertainment than a lavish, long-running spectacular.

IMPERSONATOR SHOWS These are usually long-running production shows, complete with dancers, that feature the impersonation of celebrities, both living (Joan Rivers, Cher, Neil Diamond, Tina Turner, Madonna) and deceased (Marilyn Monroe, Elvis Presley, Liberace,

Blues Brother John Belushi). In shows such as Harrah's *Legends in Concert,* the emphasis is on the detail and exactness of the impersonation. In general, men impersonate male stars and women impersonate female stars (as you might expect). There have been several productions over the years, however, featuring males impersonating female celebrities. But no one—dead or alive, male or female—is impersonated as frequently as The King. The Las Vegas Convention and Visitors Authority says there are at least 260 Elvis impersonators locally. We'd love to see them all in the same show. Wouldn't *that* be "a hunk-a hunk-a burnin' love"!

COMEDY CLUBS Stand-up comedy has long been a tradition in Las Vegas entertainment. With the success of comedy clubs around the country and the comedy-club format on network and cable television, stand-up comedy in Las Vegas was elevated from lounges and production shows to its own specialized venue. Las Vegas comedy clubs are small- to medium-sized showrooms featuring anywhere from two to five comedians per show. As a rule, the shows change completely each week, with a new group of comics rotating in. Each showroom has its own source of talent, so there is no swapping of comics from club to club. Comedy clubs are one of the few Las Vegas entertainments that draw equally from both the tourist and local populations. While most production shows and many celebrity-headliner shows are packaged for the over-40 market, comedy clubs represent a concession to youth. Many of the comics are young, and the humor is often raw and scatological, and almost always irreverent.

unofficial **TIP**
In general, if you find a casino with lounge entertainment that suits your tastes, you will probably be comfortable lodging, dining, and gambling there also.

LOUNGE ENTERTAINMENT Many casinos offer exceptional entertainment at all hours of the day and night in their lounges. For the most part, lounges feature musical groups. On a given day almost any type of music, from oldies rock to country to jazz to folk, can be found in Las Vegas lounges. Unlike the production and headliner showrooms and comedy clubs, no reservations are required to take advantage of most lounge entertainment. If you like what you hear, just walk in. Sometimes there is a one- or two-drink minimum for sitting in the lounge during a show, but just as often there are no restrictions at all. You may or may not be familiar with the lounge entertainers by name, but you can trust that they will be highly talented and very enjoyable. To find the type of music you prefer, consult one of the local visitor guides available free from the front desk or concierge at your hotel. Lounge entertainment is a great barometer of a particular casino's marketing program; bands are specifically chosen to attract a certain type of customer.

As an alternative to high ticket prices in Las Vegas showrooms (more than a dozen shows now cost upward of $100), several casinos have turned their nightclubs and lounges into alternative show venues with ticket prices in the $30 to $60 range. We've seen a number of marginal or unsuccessful clubs turned into showrooms over the years, but this is the first time we've observed highly successful nightspots converted. In the main, we don't care for this trend. True, it offers some low-price shows, but at the cost of sacrificing some of the city's best lounges and nightclubs.

THEY COME AND THEY GO

LAS VEGAS SHOWS COME AND GO all the time. Sometimes a particular production will close in one Las Vegas showroom and open weeks later in another. Some shows actually pack up and take their presentations to other cities, usually Reno/Lake Tahoe or Atlantic City. Other shows, of course, close permanently. The bottom line: It's hard to keep up with all this coming and going. Do not be surprised if some of the shows reviewed in this guide have bitten the dust before you arrive. Also do not be surprised if the enduring shows have changed or moved to another casino.

LEARN WHO IS PLAYING BEFORE YOU LEAVE HOME

ON THE INTERNET, CHECK OUT **vegas.com/shows.** The site also provides information and reviews on long-run headliners and production shows. The *Las Vegas Advisor* (see page 14) offers a complete listing of shows on its website **lvahotels.com,** along with pretty good discounts on tickets. The Las Vegas Convention and Visitors Authority publishes a free Official Visitors Guide that lists shows alphabetically according to host hotel, tells who is playing, provides appearance dates, and lists information and reservation numbers. You can view this publication at **visitlasvegas.com.**

SHOW PRICES AND TAXES

ADMISSION PRICES FOR LAS VEGAS shows range from around $12 all the way up to $265 per person. Usually show prices are quoted exclusive of entertainment and sales taxes. Also not included are server gratuities.

Once, there was no such thing as a reserved seat at a Las Vegas show. If you wanted to see a show, you would make a reservation (usually by phone) and then arrive well in advance to be assigned a seat by the showroom maître d'. Slipping the maître d' a nice tip ensured a better seat. Typically, the price of the show included two drinks, or there would be waitstaff service and you would pay at your table after you were served. While this arrangement is still practiced in a few showrooms, the prevailing system is reserved seating. With reserved seating, you purchase your tickets at the casino box office (or by phone or online in advance with your credit card). As at a concert or a Broadway play, your seats are designated and preassigned at the time of purchase, and your section, aisle, and seat number will be printed on your ticket. When you arrive at the showroom, an usher will guide you to your assigned seat. Reserved seating, also known as "hard" or "box-office" seating, sometimes includes drinks but usually does not.

If there are two performances per night, the early show is often (but not always) more expensive than the late show. In addition, some shows add a surcharge on Saturdays and holidays. If you tip your server a couple of bucks and slip the maître d' or captain some currency for a good seat (in a showroom without reserved seating), you can easily end up paying $47 or more for a $40 list-price show and $63 or more for a $50 list-price show.

unofficial **TIP**
Avoid buying show tickets from independent brokers. They tack on extra surcharges.

BUYING TICKETS

AS WITH MANY OTHER THINGS, the Internet has revolutionized how Las Vegas show tickets are sold. For the first time you can purchase all of your show tickets well in advance online before you leave home. Many sites have a seating chart of the theater to help choose where to sit. Sellers include the host casino's website; the Las Vegas Visitor and Convention Authority's **visitlasvegas.com;** sites offering discounts and special deals (seat upgrades, free drinks, etc.) such as **lasvegasshows .com** and **vegas.com/shows;** and national event and ticket-selling sites such as **ticketmaster.com.**

Buying in advance is definitely recommended if you want to see a popular show or celebrity headliner on a weekend. As an example, tickets went on sale in March 2010 for Celine Dion's new show that didn't premiere until March 2011. Every show for the first several months sold out in just a couple of days.

Many of the online ticket vendors sell only at full retail, while others offer modest discounts on some but not all shows. None of the online discounts come close to matching those of half-price ticket outlets in Las Vegas described below, but with the latter you have to buy your ticket in person on the day of the show.

You can also purchase tickets in advance at the show's box office, either in person or by phoning and using your credit card. The main advantage of phoning or going to the box office is that you're able to discuss seating options with a live person. The main disadvantage is that the box offices are usually understaffed. Because each buyer takes up a lot of agent time asking questions and going over seating charts, your chances of being stuck on hold or in a long line are about 80%. We were once in line at the MGM Grand box office behind a tour operator who purchased show tickets for a group of 60 people—can't begin to tell you how long that took.

HOW TO SAVE BIG BUCKS ON SHOW TICKETS

THE EASIEST WAY TO SAVE is to see *Dr. Naughty X-Rated Hypnosis* instead of *Viva ELVIS.* OK, just kidding. Here are some practical tips:

1. Most of the high-price shows are in new, state-of-the-art theaters, which often have several classifications of seats. You can see Celine Dion at Caesars Palace from a second-level mezzanine seat for far less than in a front orchestra seat at the same show.

TIX4TONIGHT TICKET OUTLET LOCATIONS	
Bill's Gamblin' Hall (Mid-Strip)	Hawaiian Marketplace (Mid-Strip)
Casino Royale (Mid-Strip)	Showcase Mall (South Strip)
Circus Circus (North Strip)	Slots-A-Fun (Mid-Strip)
Fashion Show Mall (North Strip; ground floor by Neiman Marcus)	Town Square Shopping Center (South Strip)
Four Queens (Downtown)	

2. Half-price ticket outlets. The preeminent half-price ticket seller in Las Vegas is **Tix4Tonight (tix4tonight.com),** with nine locations (see location chart above). Box offices open at 10 a.m., though show postings are available at 9:30 a.m. Each morning shows with unsold seats make some of those seats available to the half-price sellers. Sometimes it's a lot of seats, and other times it's just a handful, depending on the show. The sellers post the available shows for customers to choose from. Before the recession, tickets to the most popular productions, such as the Cirque du Soleil shows, *Lion King, Phantom,* and most major celebrity headliners, were almost never available. Now, however, it's possible to find discounted tickets for just about any show in town, though the number of tickets for sale may be quite limited, or on weekends nonexistent.

You have to go in person to one of the box offices the day of the show to purchase your tickets. If you're staying on the Strip, there's usually a discounter within a 15-minute walk. If you're driving, parking can be a hassle for the Strip locations but is usually not a problem for off-Strip box offices. Instead of an actual ticket, discounters will issue you a voucher that you can exchange for a ticket at the official box office of the show. If it's not terribly inconvenient, we recommend exchanging your voucher sometime during the day instead of waiting until just before showtime.

You can blow a fair amount of time buying half-price tickets. Strip discounter locations are almost invariably understaffed. This coupled with each purchaser asking untold questions can combine for a long, slow-moving queue. For this reason, and for convenient parking, we usually purchase our discounted tickets at off-Strip locations such as the Town Square Shopping Center.

It's helpful to have one of the local freebie visitor magazines with you when shopping. These publications always list the non-discounted price for show tickets. If you know the non-discounted price, you can calculate what a half-price ticket should cost. It's not uncommon in Las Vegas today for shows to offer VIP seating at a premium price. Often discounters will sell you a VIP seat without letting you know if there are less expensive seats available. For almost all shows, paying extra for a VIP seat is a waste of money. Tix4Tonight charges a service fee of $4 per ticket for processing your purchase. Coupons for $2 off this charge are available on the Tix4Tonight website and also in freebie magazines.

We found that after buying tickets, the discounters tell you to arrive at the show much earlier than necessary. True, you might encounter a logjam at the box office when you show up to exchange your vouchers, but arriving an hour in advance should be more than sufficient.

We're often asked whether the seats you're assigned when exchanging your voucher are inferior to those not sold at discount. The answer is often, but not always, yes. As discussed above, you can improve your assigned seating somewhat by exchanging your voucher well in advance of showtime. If seats at a showroom are first-come, first-served, or assigned on the spot by a maître' d, your chances of scoring a primo seat are as good as anyone else's.

3. The drawback of Tix4Tonight, discussed above, is having to go to one of their locations to find out what's available and purchase tickets. An alternative is **goldstar.com,** an Internet seller with a growing list of Las Vegas shows. Discounts range from 20% to more than 50%, and you can buy tickets for dates in advance (but not very far in advance). Ticket availability for the major shows is slim, but the site is very strong on stand-up comedy shows, both male and female skin shows, celebrity impersonator shows, and hypnosis shows. You have to become a Gold Star member (easily accomplished online) to obtain the discounts. For each show listed you can read ratings and reviews from Gold Star members.

4. Showrooms, like other Las Vegas hotel and casino operations, sometimes offer special deals. Sometimes free or discounted shows are offered with lodging packages. Likewise, coupons from complimentary local tourist magazines or casino "fun books" (see pages 14–17) provide discounts or two-for-one options. Since these specials come and go, your best bet is to inquire about currently operating deals and discounts when you call for show reservations. If you plan to lodge at a hotel-casino where there is a show you want to see, ask about room-show combo specials when you make your room reservations. When you arrive in Las Vegas, pick up copies of the many visitor magazines distributed in rental-car agencies and at hotels. Scour the show ads for discount coupons.

DINNER SHOWS

SOME DINNER SHOWS REPRESENT GOOD DEALS, others less so. Be aware that with all dinner shows, your drinks will be extra, and invariably expensive. Food quality at dinner shows varies. In general, it can be characterized as acceptable, but certainly not exceptional. What you are buying is limited-menu banquet service for 300 to 500 people. Whenever a hotel kitchen tries to feed that many people at once, it is at some cost in terms of the quality of the meal and the service.

At *Tournament of Kings,* all shows include a dinner of Cornish hen with soup, potatoes, vegetable, dessert, and choice of nonalcoholic beverage for about $57 per person, plus taxes and gratuities. *Tournament of Kings* is described in detail later in the chapter. *Tony 'n' Tina's*

Wedding at the V Theater integrates the meal into the unfolding story line of the show. At *Tony 'n' Tina's,* you're a wedding guest. You're sucked into the story and expected to role-play as the show demands.

Several casinos offer show-and-dinner combos where you get dinner and a show for a special price, but dinner is served in one of the casinos' restaurants instead of in the showrooms. Many restaurants provide only coffee-shop ambience, but the food is palatable and a good deal for the money. At each casino, you can eat either before or after the early show.

Early versus Late Shows

If you attend a late show, you'll have time for a leisurely dinner before the performance. For those who prefer to eat late, the early show followed by dinner works best. Both shows are identical, except that for some topless revues the early show is covered and the late show is topless. On weekdays, late shows are usually more lightly attended. On weekends, particularly at the most popular shows, the opposite is often the case.

PRACTICAL MATTERS

What to Wear to the Show

While it is by no means required, guests tend to dress up a bit when they go to a show. For a performance in the main showrooms at Bellagio, Caesars Palace, Mandalay Bay, Wynn Las Vegas, Wynn Encore, Aria, Venetian, Palazzo, or the Mirage, gentlemen will feel more comfortable in sport coats, with or without neckties. Women generally wear suits, dresses, skirt-and-blouse/sweater combinations, and even semiformal attire. That having been said, however, you'll find a third to a half of the audience at any of these casinos dressed more casually than described.

Showrooms at the Luxor, Stratosphere, Monte Carlo, New York–New York, Treasure Island (T. I.), the MGM Grand, Harrah's, Rio, Flamingo, Las Vegas Hilton, Paris Las Vegas, Tropicana, Planet Hollywood, and Riviera are a bit less dressy (sport coats are fine, but slacks and sweaters or sport shirts are equally acceptable for men), while showrooms at the Excalibur, Imperial Palace, Orleans, Sam's Town, Suncoast, Sunset Station, Texas Station, House of Blues at Mandalay Bay, Golden Nugget, and Hard Rock are the least formal of all (come as you are). All of the comedy clubs are informal, though you would not feel out of place in a sport coat or, for women, a dress.

Getting to and from the Show

When you make your reservations, always ask what time you need to arrive for seating, and whether you should proceed directly to the showroom or stop first at the box office. You are normally asked to arrive one hour before the curtain rises, though a half hour or even less will do if you already have your reserved-seat tickets (ticket will show a designated row and seat number). If you are driving to another hotel for a show and do not wish to avail yourself of valet parking, be forewarned that many casinos' self-parking lots are quite distant from the showroom. Give yourself an extra 15 minutes or more to park, walk to the casino, and find the showroom. If you decide to use valet parking, be advised that the valet service may be swamped immediately following the show.

A show with a large seating capacity in one of the major casinos can make for some no-win situations when it comes to parking. At all of the megahotels except Wynn Las Vegas and Wynn Encore, self-parking is either way off in the boonies or in a dizzying multistory garage, so your inclination may be to use valet parking. After the show, however, 1,000 to 1,650 patrons head for home, inundating the valets, particularly after a late show.

unofficial **TIP**
After shows, patrons flood the valets. To avoid delays, your best bet is to use self-parking and give yourself some extra time, or use valet parking and plan to stick around the casino for a while after the show.

Invited Guests and Line Passes

Having arrived at the casino and found the showroom, you will normally join other show-goers waiting to be seated. If the showroom assigns reserved seats, the process is simple: just show your tickets to an usher and you will be directed to your seats. At showrooms without reserved seating, you will normally encounter two lines. One line, usually quite long, is where you will queue up unless you are an "invited guest." There is a separate line for these privileged folks that allows them to be seated without waiting in line or coming an hour early. Most invited guests are gamblers who are staying at the host casino. Some have been provided with "comps" (complimentary admission) to the show. These are usually regular casino customers or high rollers. If you are giving the casino a lot of action, do not be shy about requesting a comp to the show.

unofficial **TIP**
If you are an invited guest under any circumstances, always arrive to be seated for a show at least 30 minutes early.

Gamblers or casino-hotel guests of more modest means are frequently given line passes. These guests pay the same price as anyone else for the show but are admitted without waiting via the Invited-Guest line. To obtain a line pass, approach a floorman or pit boss (casino supervisory personnel are usually distinguished from dealers by their suits and ties) and explain that you have been doing a fair amount of gambling in their casino. Tell him or her that you have reservations for that evening's show and ask if you can have a line pass. Particularly if you ask on Sunday through Thursday, your chances of being accommodated are good.

Reservations, Tickets, and Maître d' Seating

If, like most guests, you do not have a line pass, you will have to go through the process of entering the showroom and being seated. A dwindling number of showrooms practice what is known as maître d' seating. This means that, except in the case of certain invited guests, no seats are reserved. If you called previously and made a reservation, that will have been duly noted and the showroom will have your party listed on the reservations roster, but you will not actually be assigned a seat until you appear before the maître d'. At some showrooms with maître d' seating, you are asked to pay your waiter for everything (show, taxes, drinks, and so on) once you have been seated and served.

At the comedy clubs and an increasing number of major showrooms, you will be directed to a booth variously labeled "Tickets," "Reservations," "Box Office," or "Guest Services." The attendant will verify your reservation and ask you to go ahead and pay. Once paid, you will receive a ticket to show the maître d' upon entering the showroom. This arrangement eliminates any requirement for paying the tab at your table (unless drinks are not included), thus simplifying service once you are seated. The ticket does not reserve you any specific seat; you still need to see the maître d' about that. Also, the ticket does not include gratuities for your server in the showroom unless specifically stated.

As discussed earlier, most showrooms have discarded maître d' seating in favor of "box office" or "hard" seating. Specific reserved-seat assignments are printed on each ticket sold, as at a football game or on Broadway.

Where to Sit

When it comes to show seating, there are two primary considerations: visibility and comfort. The newer main showrooms at Caesars Palace, Mandalay Bay, Bellagio, Mirage, T. I., MGM Grand, Venetian, Palazzo, Paris, Luxor, Wynn Las Vegas, Wynn Encore, Aria, Planet Hollywood, Monte Carlo, New York–New York, Stratosphere, and the Las Vegas Hilton provide plush theater seats, many with drink holders in the arms. The best accommodations in older showrooms are roomy booths, which provide an unencumbered view of the show. The vast majority of seats in these showrooms, however, and all in some, will be at banquet tables—a euphemism for very long, narrow tables where a dozen or more guests are squeezed together so tightly they can hardly move much less eat. When the show starts, guests seated at the banquet tables must turn their chairs around in order to see. This requires no small degree of timing and cooperation, since every person on the same side of the table must move in unison.

Showrooms generally will have banquet-table seating right in front of the stage. Next, on a tier that rises a step or two, will be a row of plush booths. These booths are often reserved for the casino's best customers (and sometimes for big tippers). Many maître d's would rather see these booths go unoccupied than have high rollers come to the door at the last minute and not be able to give them good seats. Behind the booths and up a step will be more banquet tables. Moving away from the stage and up additional levels, the configuration of booths and banquet tables is repeated on each tier.

For a big production show on a wide stage like *Jubilee!*, Cirque du Soleil shows, *The Lion King*, or *Jersey Boys*, you want to sit in the middle and back a little. Being too close makes it difficult to see everything without wagging your head back and forth as if you were at a tennis match. Likewise, at a concert by a band or musical celebrity headliner (such as Tom Jones, Al Jarreau, or B. B. King), partway back and in the center is best. This positioning provides good visibility and removes you from the direct line of fire of amplifiers and lights. This advice, of course, does not apply to avid fans who want to fling their underwear or room keys at the star. For smaller production shows on medium-sized stages (*Penn & Teller, Legends in Concert,* and such), right up front is great. This is also true for headliners like Rita Rudner and Garth Brooks. For female impersonators the illusion is more effective if you are back a little bit.

> Be aware that comedians often single out unwary guests sitting down front for harassment, or worse, incorporate them into the act.

At comedy clubs and smaller shows, there are really no bad seats.

Getting a Good Seat at Showrooms with Maître d' Seating

1. ARRIVE EARLY No maître d' can assign you a seat that's already taken. This is particularly important for Friday and Saturday shows. We have seen comped invited guests (the casino's better customers) get lousy seats because they waited until the last minute to show up.

2. TRY TO GO ON AN OFF NIGHT (that is, Sunday through Thursday) Your chances of getting a good seat are always better on weeknights, when there is less demand. If a citywide convention is in town, weekdays also may be crowded.

3. TRY TO KNOW WHERE (AS PRECISELY AS POSSIBLE) YOU WOULD LIKE TO SIT. In showrooms with maître d' seating, it is always to your advantage to specifically state your seating preferences.

4. UNDERSTAND YOUR TIPPING ALTERNATIVES Basically, you have three options:
- Don't tip.
- Tip the maître d'.
- Tip the captain instead of the maître d'.

DON'T TIP Politely request a good seat instead of tipping. This option actually works better than you would imagine in all but a few showrooms, particularly Sunday through Thursday. If the showroom is not sold out and you arrive early, simply request a seat in a certain area. Tell the maître d', "We would like something down front in the center." Then allow the captain (the showroom staff person who actually takes you to your seat) to show you the seats the maître d' has assigned. If the assigned seat is not to your liking, ask to be seated somewhere else of your choosing. The captain almost always has the authority to make the seat-assignment change without consulting the maître d'.

On slower nights, the maître d' will often "dress the showroom." This means that the maître d', not expecting a full house, will distribute patrons pretty equally throughout the showroom, especially nearer the stage. This procedure, which makes the audience look larger than it really is, is done for the morale of the performers and for various practical reasons, such as ensuring a near-equal number of guests at each server station. On these nights, you have a pretty good shot at getting the seats you want simply by asking.

TIP THE MAÎTRE D' When you tip the maître d', it is helpful to know with whom you are dealing. First, the maître d' is the man or woman in charge of the showroom. The showrooms are their domain, and they rule as surely as battalion commanders. Maître d's in the better showrooms are powerful and wealthy people, with some maître d's taking in as much as $1,650 a night. Even though these tips are pooled and shared in some proportion with the captains, it's still a lot of money.

When you tip a maître d', especially in the better showrooms, you can assume it will take a fairly hefty tip to impress him, especially on a busy night. The bottom line, however, is that you are not out to impress anyone; you just want a good seat. Somebody has to sit in the good seats, and those who do not tip, or tip small, have to be seated regardless. So, if you arrive early and tip $15 to $20 (for a couple) in the major showrooms, and $5 to $10 in the smaller rooms, you should get decent seats. If it is a weekend or you know the show is extremely popular or sold out, bump the tip up a little. If you arrive late on a busy night, ask the maître d' if there are any good seats left before you proffer the tip.

Have your tip in hand when you reach the maître d'. Don't fool around with your wallet or purse as if you are buying hot dogs and beer at the ball park. Fold the money and hold it in the palm of your hand, arranged so that the maître d' can see exactly how big the tip is without unfolding and counting the bills. State your preference for seating at the same time you inconspicuously place the bills in the palm of his hand. If you think all this protocol is pretty ridiculous, we agree. But style counts, and observing the local customs may help get you a better seat.

A variation is to tip with some appropriate denomination of the casino's own chips. Chips are as good as currency to the maître d' and implicitly suggest that you have been gambling with that denomination of chips in his casino. This single gesture, which costs you nothing more than your cash tip, makes you an insider and a more valued customer in the eyes of the maître d'.

Many maître d's are warm and friendly and treat you in a way that shows they appreciate your business. These maître d's are approachable and reasonable, and they will go out of their way to make you comfortable. There are also a number of maître d's and captains, unfortunately, who are extremely cold, formal, and arrogant. Mostly older men dressed in tuxedos, they usually have gray hair and an imperious bearing and can seem rather imposing or hostile. Do not be awed or intimidated. Be forthright and, if necessary, assertive; you will usually be accommodated.

TIP THE CAPTAIN Using this strategy, tell the maître d' where you would like to sit, but do not offer a tip. Then follow the captain to your assigned seats. If your seats are good, you have not spent an extra nickel. If the assigned seats are less than satisfactory, slip the captain a tip and ask if there might be something better. If you see seats you would like to have that are unoccupied, point them out to the captain. Remember, however, that the first row of booths is usually held in reserve.

Before the Show Begins

Some showrooms serve drinks, while others offer self-service. A few of the variations you will encounter: A cash bar and no table service; if you want a drink before the show, you walk to the bar and buy it. Drinks are included, but there is no table service; you take a receipt stub to the bar and exchange it for drinks. In most other showrooms there is table service where you can obtain drinks from a server.

In showrooms with table service, the servers run around like crazy trying to get everybody served before the show. Because all the people at a given table are not necessarily seated at the same time, the server responsible for that table may make five or more passes before everyone is taken care of. If your party is one of the last to be seated at a table, stay cool. You *will* be noticed and you *will* be served.

BLADDER MATTERS Be forewarned that in most showrooms there is no restroom, and that the nearest restroom is invariably a long way off, reachable only via a convoluted trail through the casino. Since the majority of show-goers arrive early and consume drinks, it is not uncommon to start feeling a little pressure on the bladder minutes before showtime. If you assume that you can slip out to the restroom and come right back, think again. If you are at the Las Vegas Hilton or the Tropicana, give yourself more than ten minutes for the round-trip, and prepare for a quest. If you get to the can and back without getting lost, consider yourself lucky.

At most other showrooms, restrooms are somewhat closer but certainly not convenient. The Riviera, Imperial Palace, Luxor, Planet Hollywood, Harrah's, New York–New York, MGM Grand, Stratosphere, Venetian, Palazzo, Wynn Las Vegas, Aria, and Mirage, however, seem to have considered that show guests may not wish to combine emptying their bladders with a five-mile hike. Showrooms in these casinos are situated in close and much-appreciated proximity to the restrooms.

▌ SELECTING *a* SHOW

SELECTING A LAS VEGAS SHOW is a matter of timing, budget, taste, and schedule. Celebrity headliners are booked long in advance but may play only for a couple of days or weeks. If seeing Elton John or Jerry Seinfeld in concert is a big priority for your Las Vegas trip, you will have to schedule your visit to coincide with their appearances. If the timing of your visit is not flexible, as in the case of conventioneers, you will be relegated to picking from those stars playing when you are in town. To find out which shows and headliners are playing before you leave home, call the Las Vegas Convention and Visitors Authority at ☎ 702-892-7576 (**lvcva.com**). On the Internet, go to **visitlasvegas.com** or **lvahotels.com.**

Older visitors are often more affluent than younger visitors. It is no accident that most celebrity headliners are chosen, and most production shows created, to appeal to the 40-and-over crowd. If we say a Las Vegas production show is designed for a mature audience, we mean that the theme, music, variety acts, and humor appeal primarily to older guests. Most Las Vegas production shows target patrons 40 to 50 years old and up, while a few appeal to audiences 55 years of age and older.

As the post–World War II baby boomers have become older and more affluent, they have become a primary market for Las Vegas. Stars from the "golden days" of rock and roll, as well as folk singers from the 1960s, are turning up in the main showrooms all across town. On one occasion, Paul Revere and the Raiders, the Coasters, the Platters, the Temptations, the Four Tops, B. J. Thomas, and Arlo Guthrie were playing in different showrooms on the same night.

The hippest, avant-garde show in town is *Blue Man Group* (Venetian), which targets younger audiences and is wild, loud, and conceptually quite different from anything else in Las Vegas. A close runner-up is *MÜS.I.C,* a rap and hip-hop production popularly called JABBA-WOCKEEZ after its featured dance crew.

If you are younger than 35 years old you will also enjoy the Las Vegas production shows, though for you their cultural orientation (and usually their music) will seem a generation or two removed. Several production shows, however, have broken the mold, in the process achieving a more youthful presentation while maintaining the loyalty of older patrons. Cirque du Soleil's *Mystère* (T. I.) is an uproarious yet poignant odyssey in the European tradition, brimming over with unforgettable characters. Ditto for Cirque's "*O*" at Bellagio, *KÀ* at MGM Grand, *LOVE* at Mirage, and *Zumanity* at New York–New York. And, again, the comedy clubs have a more youthful orientation.

LAS VEGAS SHOWS FOR THE UNDER-21 CROWD

AN EVER-INCREASING NUMBER OF SHOWROOMS offer productions appropriate for younger viewers. Circus Circus provides complimentary high-quality circus acts about once every half hour, and *Tournament of Kings* at the Excalibur is a family dinner show featuring jousting and other benign medieval entertainments. Other family candidates include *Disney's The Lion King* at Mandalay Bay; *Legends in Concert,* a celebrity impersonation show at Harrah's; and Cirque du Soleil's *Mystère* at T. I., *LOVE* at the Mirage, and "*O*" at Bellagio.

Many of the celebrity-headliner shows are fine for children, and a few of the production shows offer a covered early show to accommodate families. Of the topless production shows, some operate on the basis of parental discretion while others do not admit anyone under age 21. Comedy clubs and comedy theater usually will admit teenage children accompanied by an adult. All continuously running shows are profiled later in this section. The profile will tell you whether the show is topless or particularly racy. If you have questions about a given showroom's policy for those under age 21, call the showroom's reservation and information number listed in the profile.

CELEBRITY-HEADLINER ROOMS

CHOOSING WHICH CELEBRITY HEADLINER to see is a matter of personal taste, though stars like Cher and David Copperfield seem to have the ability to rev up any audience. We talked to people who, under duress, were essentially dragged along by a friend or family member to see Wayne Newton. Many of these folks walked into the showroom prepared to hate Wayne Newton. Yet despite their negative attitude, Newton delighted and amazed them.

Our point is not to hype Wayne Newton but to suggest that the talent, presence, drive, and showmanship of many Las Vegas headliners often exceed all expectations, and that adhering to the limitations of your preferences may prevent you from seeing many truly extraordinary performers. Las Vegas is about gambling, after all. Do not be reluctant to take a chance on a headliner who is not familiar to you.

Most of the major headliners play at a relatively small number of showrooms. Profiles of the major celebrity showrooms and their regular headliners follow. The list is not intended to be all-inclusive but rather to give you an idea of where to call if you are interested in a certain headliner. Long-running (that is, a year or more) celebrity-headliner shows, including *Celine Dion, Garth Brooks, Barry Manilow, Rita Rudner,* and so on, are reviewed in depth in our coverage of continuously running production shows later in this chapter.

Hard Rock Hotel—The Joint

RESERVATIONS AND INFORMATION ☎ 702-693-5000 or 800-693-7625; hardrockhotel.com

---

Frequent headliners Top current and oldies rock, pop, blues, folk, electronic, and world music stars. **Usual showtimes** 8 p.m. **Dark** Varies. **Approximate admission price** $25–$600. **Drinks included** None. **Showroom size** 4,000 persons.

DESCRIPTION AND COMMENTS The Joint, once an intimate concert venue, has been redesigned and more than doubled in size with a new, larger stage and cutting-edge lighting and video effects. The main floor of the multi-level venue can be configured for theater-type seating, lounge seating (two to four chairs around a small cocktail table), or for standing only. So versatile is The Joint that it can set up for professional prize fights. Lines of sight are super, as is the sound system. For bands with a video dimension, there are 36 monitors, including a huge high-definition screen on each side of the stage. Paul McCartney, one of the first to perform in the expanded facility, said, "It's good in here, isn't it?" The upper levels of The Joint provide standing-room-only balcony viewing as well as seating and

VIP accommodations. Acoustics are excellent with a felt-like material covering the walls to minimize echo and sound bleeds.

CONSUMER TIPS If you don't want to be put in balcony Siberia where you can hear well enough but see nothing, or pinned against the stage for the whole show by a crush of sweaty rowdies, don't buy standing-room tickets. Book early for reserved seating—or shrug and say, "Oh well."

The Hard Rock Hotel box office sells reserved seats to shows at The Joint. You can purchase tickets via phone using your credit card or in person at the box office. Shows at The Joint are hot tickets in Las Vegas and sell out quickly, so buy your tickets as far in advance as possible.

Mandalay Bay—House of Blues
RESERVATIONS AND INFORMATION ☎ 702-632-7600 or 877-632-7600; hob.com

Frequent headliners Current and former pop, rock, R & B, reggae, folk, and country stars. **Usual showtimes** Varies. **Dark** Varies. **Approximate admission price** $12–$100. **Drinks included** None. **Showroom size** 1,800 seats.

DESCRIPTION AND COMMENTS House of Blues is a newer Las Vegas concert hall, very different from The Joint at the Hard Rock, with which it competes head-on for performers and concertgoers. The House of Blues is more like an opera house than the high school gym–like Joint: low-ceilinged, multi-tiered, and split-leveled, which gets the audience as close to the act as possible. To that end, the acoustics are much better than The Joint's, but the House of Blues can get claustrophobic. Also, the sight lines are highly variable, even bizarre, especially for a modern room—it's almost as if the designers were modifying an old theater. And it doesn't seem to have much to do with how much you pay for a seat: some bad seats (in the nosebleed section and on the sides of the stage) don't cost much less than the best seats or much more than the cheapest tickets.

Live music is presented almost every night of the year. Major headliners appear once or twice a week at 8 p.m.; for these shows you must be 21 years old to attend. Performers have included Ted Nugent, Rusted Root, Violent Femmes, Al Green, and Frank Zappa. Filling in the booking gaps are minor shows; check the hotline and website. You must be 18 years or older for most of them (the few others are designated "all ages").

CONSUMER TIPS The box office is open 10 a.m.–7 p.m. The headliner shows sell out extremely fast, though you can usually pick up standing-room-only tickets, where you'll be sardined in front of the stage (watch your wallet). If money is no object, try to get a VIP seat front and center in the balcony. If you can't, you might as well just opt for the cheap standing room, as the upper balcony and many of the loge seats aren't worth the extra money. Indeed, many people give up their bad reserved seats to move down to the floor where they can see the whole stage!

MGM Grand—Grand Garden Arena
RESERVATIONS AND INFORMATION ☎ 702-891-7777 or 800-929-1111; mgmgrand.com

Frequent headliners National acts, superstars, televised boxing, wrestling, and other sporting events. **Usual showtimes** Varies. **Dark** Varies. **Approximate admission price** $20–$1,250. **Drinks included** None. **Showroom size** 16,800 seats.

DESCRIPTION AND COMMENTS This 275,000-square-foot special-events center is designed to accommodate everything from sporting events and concerts to major trade exhibitions. The venue also offers auxiliary meeting rooms and ballrooms adjacent to the entertainment center. Barbra Streisand christened this venue with her first concert in more than 20 years on New Year's Eve 1993. Championship boxing events are favorite attractions at the Grand Garden Arena, as are the many big-name musical concerts.

CONSUMER TIPS Reserved-seat tickets can be purchased one to two months in advance with your credit card online or by calling the MGM Grand main reservations number or Ticketmaster outlets (☎ 800-745-3000), for most but not all shows. If you are not staying at the MGM Grand, either arrive by cab or give yourself plenty of extra time to park and make your way to the arena.

MGM Grand—Hollywood Theatre

RESERVATIONS AND INFORMATION ☎ **702-891-7777 or 800-929-1111; mgmgrand.com**

Frequent headliners David Copperfield, Howie Mandel, and Tom Jones. **Usual showtimes** Varies. **Dark** Varies. **Approximate admission price** $70–$100. **Drinks included** None. **Showroom size** 740 seats.

DESCRIPTION AND COMMENTS A modern and comfortable showroom, with all front-facing seats, the Hollywood Theatre hosts a wide range of musical and celebrity-headliner productions for one- to three-week engagements.

CONSUMER TIPS Reserved-seat tickets can be purchased one to two months in advance with your credit card online or by calling the MGM Grand's main reservations number. Children are allowed at most presentations (check first). If you are not staying at the MGM Grand, either arrive by cab or give yourself of extra time to park and make your way to the showroom.

Orleans—Orleans Showroom

RESERVATIONS AND INFORMATION ☎ **702-365-7075 or 888-365-7111; orleanscasino.com**

Frequent headliners Clint Black, Michael Bolton, Air Supply, Four Tops, Kenny G, Bill Maher, Etta James, Dennis Miller, and Don Rickles. **Usual showtimes** Varies. **Dark** Varies. **Approximate admission price** $35–$40. **Drinks included** None. **Showroom size** 850 seats.

DESCRIPTION AND COMMENTS This small but comfortable showroom offers tiered theater seats arranged in a crescent around the stage. Designed for solo performers and bands, the Orleans Showroom is an intimate venue for concerts with good visibility from anywhere in the house. The star lineup runs the gamut with a concentration on country-and-western singer celebrities.

CONSUMER TIPS This showroom features some great talent at bargain prices. All seats are reserved. Tickets can be purchased at the box office to the left of the showroom or over the phone using your credit card.

PRODUCTION SHOWS

LAS VEGAS PREMIER PRODUCTION SHOWS: COMPARING APPLES AND ORANGES

WHILE WE ACKNOWLEDGE THAT LAS VEGAS production shows are difficult to compare and that audiences of differing tastes and ages have different preferences, we have nevertheless ranked the continuously running shows to give you an idea of our favorites. This is definitely an apples-and-oranges comparison (how can you compare *Zumanity* to *Blue Man Group?*), but one based on each show's impact, vitality, originality, pace, continuity, crescendo, and ability to entertain.

We would hasten to add that even the continuously running shows change acts and revise their focus periodically. Expect our list, therefore, to change from year to year. Also, be comforted by the knowledge that while some shows are better than others, there are only one or two real dogs. The quality of entertainment among the continuously running production shows is exceptional. By way of analogy, we could rank baseball players according to their performance in a given All-Star game, but the entire list, from top to bottom, would still be All-Stars. You get the idea.

A Word about Small Showrooms

During the past couple of years, we have seen a number of casinos convert their lounge into a small showroom. Though the stage in these showrooms is routinely about the size of a beach towel, productions are mounted that include complex choreography, animal acts, and, in one notable demonstration, an illusionist catching bullets in his teeth. In the case of musical revues, as many as four very thin or three average-sized hula dancers can fit comfortably on the stage at one time.

A real problem with some smaller shows is that they often cost as much as productions in Las Vegas's major showrooms. Another problem is that small shows often play to even smaller crowds. We saw a performance of *That's Magic* at O'Shea's where the cast outnumbered the audience. Though the show featured talented illusionists, a good ventriloquist, and some dancers, the small facility made the production seem amateurish. It was heartrending to see professional entertainers work so hard for such a tiny audience. We felt self-conscious and uncomfortable ourselves, as well as embarrassed for the performers.

When it comes to smaller showrooms, simpler is better. That's why *Mac King* and *Crazy Girls* work so well: both shows take a minimalist approach. Additionally, both shows play in casinos large enough to draw an audience. Little showrooms in smaller casinos that attempt to mount big productions create only parody and end up looking foolish. Better that they revert to offering lounge shows.

We've given up trying to cover the productions that play in these small showrooms, mostly because the shows are very short-lived. If a small-showroom production is exceptionally good and demonstrates staying power, however, we sometimes review it right along with the full-scale shows. In this edition, for example, we provide full reviews of seven small-room productions. (This discussion, by the way, does not apply to comedy clubs, which work best in small rooms.)

Gotta Keep on Movin'

If every player in major-league baseball were a free agent, the willy-nilly team-hopping would bear a close resemblance to the Las Vegas entertainment scene. If, after reading our show reviews, you discover that your preferred performer or production has disappeared from the listed showroom, don't despair. Chances are good that the show has moved to a different venue. Melinda, "The First Lady of Magic" (now retired after years of being impaled nightly on the giant screw of death), holds the all-time record, having played at almost a dozen different casinos during her career.

LAS VEGAS SHOW HIT PARADE

SIMPLY BASED ON EXCELLENCE, we rank the continuously running productions playing the showrooms of Las Vegas. (See pages 214–215.) We have apples, oranges, artichokes, and even pomegranates here, so we're not making any direct comparisons. For each show listed, all we're saying is that, in our opinion, that show is a better night's entertainment than those ranking below it.

Excluded from the list are short-run engagements. Falling into this category are limited-engagement celebrity headliners and hypnosis shows. We also exclude comedy clubs (because the comedians change nightly) and afternoon shows, though both are covered in some detail later in this section. We further decided to rank the straight-up skin shows, for both men and women, separately.

HYPNOSIS SHOWS

IN HYPNOSIS SHOWS, volunteers from the audience are invited onto the stage to be hypnotized. The volunteers really do get hypnotized. We have had medical clinicians who use hypnosis in their practice review the shows and verify the authenticity of the trance. Folks that fake being under hypnosis or for whom the hypnotic state is marginal are quickly identified by the hypnotist and returned to their seats. To the best of our knowledge, there are no plants or ringers.

Most if not all of the Las Vegas hypnosis shows are very blue. In practice, this means that volunteers may end up doing things which after the fact may embarrass them immensely. We've seen volunteers attempt to have sex with a folding chair, perform fellatio on imaginary objects, enjoy orgasms, and audition for a job as an exotic dancer. One fellow was induced to have an erection every time a certain word was mentioned. We should make it clear that the contestants do all of this fully clothed. Most showrooms record each performance and make a DVD available for sale after the show.

The quality(?) and relative outrageousness of any given performance depends on the number of volunteers and their susceptibility to hypnosis. So if you prefer to be a voyeur instead of a volunteer, your best chance for a really wild spectacle is to choose a show in a big hotel where the size of the audience is likely to be large. We profile only the Anthony Cools hypnosis show at Paris Las Vegas, but his review is pretty representative of the genre.

LAS VEGAS SHOW PROFILES

FOLLOWING IS A PROFILE OF EACH of the continuously running production shows, listed alphabetically by the name of the show. If you are not sure of the name of a show, consult the previous section. Comedy clubs, afternoon shows, and limited-engagement celebrity-headliner showrooms are profiled in separate sections. Prices are approximate and fluctuate about as often as you brush your teeth.

Absinthe ★★

APPEAL BY AGE	18–21 ★★★	21–37 ★★	38–50 ★	51+ ★

HOST CASINO AND SHOWROOM **Caesars Palace—Spiegeltent on the Roman Plaza; ☎ 800-745-3000; ticketmaster.com or absinthevegas.com**

Type of show Low-tech, low-brow circus. **Admission** $76–$109. **Cast size** 23. **Night of lowest attendance** Wednesday. **Usual showtimes** Tuesday–Sunday, 7:30 p.m.; Tuesday and Thursday–Saturday, 9:30 p.m. **Dark** Monday. **Special comments** No one under 18 admitted. **Topless** Yes (male), almost (female). **Duration of presentation** 90 minutes.

DESCRIPTION AND COMMENTS It's a silly, sultry, risqué interactive and participatory experience. Equal parts cabaret, burlesque, circus, and midway sideshow, *Absinthe* incorporates an impudent cast of slick professionals. The aerial and acrobatic performances are separated by repartee, tomfoolery, and other shtick hosted by an in-your-face ringmaster and his ditzy female assistant. Among the rotating acts are a quartet of tubby aerialists, an acrobat balancing on a tower of chairs, a chanteuse who sings and strips while surrounded by four guys in drag, an erotic roller-skating pas de deux, a limber lady on ropes, two musclemen with exceptional equilibrium, and a trio of highly focused low-wire tightrope walkers. While the performers are skilled and execute wonders on a miniscule circular stage, without fail each act features the artists disrobing, which gives you an idea of the general tenor of the goings-on.

Occasionally, celebrity guests are featured. The show includes some audience participation. Expect raunch and lots of dirty jokes as the MC comments on the dress, physical attributes, proclivities, and vulnerabilities of the performers and audience members in the front rows and on the aisles. A libation or three will help you decide whether this is a clever lampoon of big-ticket gymnastic-infused performance art, a bawdy tour de farce, or a below-the-belt satire with little to redeem it. No offense to Wisconsin, but the show is cheesy.

CONSUMER TIPS Pre- and postshow, food vendors offer treats in the adjacent beer garden. The 600-seat venue is a round European wooden tent with air-conditioning. Be prepared to sit on uncomfortable folding chairs. There is no reserved seating except for those purchasing the VIP package. Leave your inhibitions, good taste, and sense of propriety on the plaza.

The Amazing Johnathan ★★★★

APPEAL BY AGE   UNDER 21 −   21–37 ★★★★   38–50 ★★★★   51+ ★★★½

HOST CASINO AND SHOWROOM **Miracle Mile Shops at Planet Hollywood— Harmon Theater; ☎ 702-836-0836; harmontheater.com**

Type of show Comedy. Admission $60–$70 plus fee. Cast size 2. Night of lowest attendance Wednesday. Usual showtimes Tuesday–Saturday, 9 p.m. Dark Sunday and Monday. Special comments No one under 18 admitted. Topless No. Duration of presentation 90 minutes.

DESCRIPTION AND COMMENTS The Amazing Johnathan, known as John Szeles to his family, is one of Las Vegas entertainment's great characters. He is very blue and also incredibly funny. Playing to a sold-out house every night, Johnathan went from a trial-balloon production to a fixture at the Golden Nugget in less than half a year before moving to the Sahara and then to the Harmon Theater at the Miracle Mile Shops. As a character, Johnathan is eerily appealing and totally frightening (if you're conscripted from the audience to help out on stage, you'll know what we mean). Naturally, he's supposed to do some tricks, but most are never completed, and in any case the magic merely serves as the glue that binds the gags. Johnathan has an assistant, a lovable ditzy blond, who almost steals the show. The two of them in combination are a comedic tour de force unparalleled in our view by any two comics that we've seen in Las Vegas for 15 years. If you can stand some rough language and blue humor (or if you can suspend your moral rectitude and political correctness for just 90 minutes), this show is a must-see.

CONSUMER TIPS If you're looking for magic and illusion, forget Johnathan. If you want a PG version of Johnathan, the closest thing is Mac King at Harrah's. If you decide to go, buy your admission in advance: tickets to Johnathan are among the hottest in town. To avoid being part of the show, ask for seats a row or two back.

American Storm ★★★

APPEAL BY AGE   UNDER 21 ★★★★★   21–37 ★★★★   38–50 ★★★   51+ ★★★

HOST CASINO AND SHOWROOM **Miracle Mile Shops at Planet Hollywood— V Theater; ☎ 702-932-1818 or 866-932-1818; varietytheater.com**

Type of show Stud-puppy strip show. Admission $30–$40 plus tax. Cast size 6. Night of lowest attendance Friday. Usual showtimes Friday, 10 p.m. and Saturday, 11:30 p.m. Dark Monday–Thursday and Sunday. Topless Buff pecs. Duration of presentation 75 minutes.

DESCRIPTION AND COMMENTS Judging by audience reaction, *American Storm* might well be called *The Mighty Clouds of Joy*. Although this oiled-up

Las Vegas Show Hit Parade

SHOW	LOCATION
1. Cirque du Soleil's *Mystère*	Treasure Island
2. Cirque du Soleil's *LOVE*	Mirage
3. *Jersey Boys*	Palazzo
4. Cirque du Soleil's *KA*	MGM Grand
5. Celine Dion	Caesars Palace
6. Cirque du Soleil's "*O*"	Bellagio
7. *The Lion King*	Mandalay Bay
8. Garth Brooks	Encore
9. *Blue Man Group*	Venetian
10. Terry Fator	Mirage
11. Cirque du Soleil's *Viva ELVIS*	Aria at CityCenter
12. *Phantom: The Las Vegas Spectacular*	Venetian
13. *Le Rêve*	Wynn Las Vegas
14. Cirque du Soleil's *Zumanity*	New York–New York
15. *Peepshow*	Planet Hollywood
16. David Copperfield	MGM Grand
17. *Jubilee!*	Bally's
18. *Menopause: The Musical*	Luxor
19. Donny & Marie	Flamingo
20. *MÜS.I.C*	Monte Carlo
21. Penn & Teller	Rio
22. The Amazing Johnathan	Harmon Theater
23. Barry Manilow	Paris Las Vegas
24. *Human Nature*	Imperial Palace
25. Gordie Brown	Golden Nugget
26. *Defending the Caveman*	Harrah's
27. Anthony Cools	Paris Las Vegas
28. *Legends In Concert*	Harrah's

male-nudity show doesn't offer the "full Monty" (by law no Las Vegas establishment can show complete nudity and serve alcohol), that didn't seem to matter to the howling, whooping, screaming audience made up of almost entirely women. Anyone who is laboring under the notion that women are dainty creatures, foresworn of raucous sexuality, should be a fly on the wall for the 70 minutes of *American Storm,* where piercing chants of "Touch it!" can sometimes be heard over the fray.

The half-dozen men, roughly 25 years old, are gorgeous, with rippling physiques, and they are fair dancers, too. Their choreography in lightly themed numbers featuring cowboys, gangsters, soldiers, and the like, however, definitely takes a back seat to general prancing, gyrating, grinding, and skipping about on stage and through the audience. Several women

SHOW	LOCATION
29. *The Rat Pack Is Back*	Plaza
30. *Sandy Hackett's Rat Pack Show*	Sahara
31. Rita Rudner	Harrah's
32. Cirque du Soleil's *CRISS ANGEL Believe*	Luxor
33. Frank Caliendo	Monte Carlo
34. George Wallace	Flamingo
35. *V: The Ultimate Variety Show*	Miracle Mile Shops
36. *Steve Wyrick: Ultra Magician*	Las Vegas Hilton
37. Matt Goss Live	Caesars Palace
38. *Tony 'n' Tina's Wedding*	Miracle Mile Shops
39. Carrot Top	Luxor
40. *Tournament of Kings*	Excalibur
41. Frank Marino's *Divas Las Vegas*	Imperial Palace
42. *Absinthe*	Caesars Palace
43. *BeatleShow!*	Miracle Mile Shops
44. Vinnie Favorito	Flamingo

TOPLESS REVUES*

1. *Crazy Horse Paris* **(good for couples)**	MGM Grand
2. *Bite*	Stratosphere
3. *Crazy Girls*	Riviera
4. *Fantasy* **(good for couples)**	Luxor
5. *X Burlesque*	Flamingo

*Does not include major production shows such as *Jubilee!* and *Peepshow* that are also topless but are targeted at a more general audience.

MALE STRIPPER SHOWS

1. *Chippendales*	Rio
2. *Thunder from Down Under*	Excalibur
3. *American Storm*	Miracle Mile Shops

of various body types and ages were drafted to mount the stage to participate in transparently configured sex acts, which makes the evening sound lurid, but it seemed to be great fun for all involved. The cast members, selected from the VH1 reality show *Strip Search,* have an almost embarrassed sweetness about them, which makes the show seem even more like innocent, albeit wild, excess.

American Storm's men were approved in part by *Thunder from Down Under* creator Billy Cross, so the shows are relatively comparable.

CONSUMER TIPS Arrive early to get in line and sit in the front. Don't expect dazzling costumes. During the show, there is quite a bit of dancing and it actually takes these guys a while to get their clothes off. If the typical routine was anywhere from seven to ten minutes, you're looking at a good five minutes of dancing before the guys even start stripping. After the show, everyone is invited to pose for a free Polaroid with the cast.

Anthony Cools ★★★½

APPEAL BY AGE	UNDER 21 –	21–37 ★★★★	38–50 ★★	51+ ★

HOST CASINO AND SHOWROOM **Paris—Anthony Cools Theater;**
☎ **702-946-7000 or 877-374-7469; parislasvegas.com or anthonycools.com**

Type of show Uncensored hypnosis comedy. **Admission** $53 and $76 plus tax. **Cast size** 3 (+12 volunteers). **Night of lowest attendance** Tuesday. **Usual showtimes** Thursday–Sunday and Tuesday, 9 p.m. **Dark** Monday and Wednesday. **Topless** No. **Special comments** Must be 18 or older to attend. **Duration of presentation** 90 minutes.

DESCRIPTION AND COMMENTS   If you must see a hypnotist show—and you don't mind incessant cursing and dirty talking—then this is the show. Unlike his thematic predecessor, the late and unlamented "Dr. Naughty," Anthony Cools is a slick, adroit manipulator and a truly devious creator of setups for his hypnotized zombie minions. As with any hypnotist show, you (and the audience, and the volunteers) have to buy into the idea that the volunteers really are hypnotized and unconsciously obeying the bizarre suggestions by Cools. But that suspension of disbelief gets easier when the skits are so funny—his volunteers are afflicted with burning nether regions, must deal with uncontrollably vocal genitals, or make sweet love to a chair, among other torments. The young and enthusiastic crowd really gets into it, and that juice motivates the performing volunteers to greater heights of debauchery. Ultimately, you really won't care if they're hypnotized or not, as long as the hot chick on stage is really good at screaming out fake orgasms.

CONSUMER TIPS   Obviously, this is not a show for the easily offended or intimidated. Salacious humor is the order of the day, and it's one of the bawdiest productions in town. Get in early if you want a seat near the front, and feel free to volunteer (or volunteer your friends) if you'd like to get into the hypnosis thing. Note that taking photos during the show is encouraged; also, an instantly produced DVD of the show you just saw is available after it's over. Grade-A blackmail material.

Barry Manilow ★★★½

APPEAL BY AGE	UNDER 21 ★★	21–37 ★★★	38–50 ★★★½	51+ ★★★½

HOST CASINO AND SHOWROOM **Paris Las Vegas—Paris Theatre;**
☎ **800-745-3000; parislasvegas.com**

Type of show Celebrity headliner. **Admission cost** $95–$299. **Cast size** 13. **Night of lowest attendance** Sunday. **Usual showtimes** Friday–Sunday, 7:30 p.m. **Dark** Monday–Thursday. **Topless** No. **Special comments** Show is scheduled on selected weekend nights; visit parislasvegas.com for dates. **Duration of presentation** 90 minutes.

DESCRIPTION AND COMMENTS   Long-standing pop icon Barry Manilow, supported by excellent backup vocalists and a ten-piece band, delivers 90 well-paced minutes of the music that made him famous. Staging is creative and incorporates some high-tech gimmicks. The show really doesn't have a weakness, BUT, it definitely helps to be a Barry Manilow fan.

While Elton John or Gladys Knight can effortlessly turn on an audience who has little knowledge of their music, Manilow tends to stall for the uninitiated. Fortunately for Manilow, most of his audience are fans, and gushing fans at that.

CONSUMER TIPS The Paris Theatre is a perfect size for celebrity headliners, offering exceptional intimacy for a large showroom and excellent lines of sight. Because the stage is quite wide, we recommend requesting seats at least eight rows or more from the front. The best bet if you're coming from the Strip is to take the Las Vegas Monorail.

BeatleShow! ★★★

APPEAL BY AGE	UNDER 21 ★★	21–37 ★★★	38–50 ★★★½	51+ ★★★½

HOST CASINO AND SHOWROOM **Miracle Mile Shops at Planet Hollywood— V Theater; ☎ 702-260-7200 or 866-932-1818; fabfourlive.com**

Type of show Musical impressionist and tribute act. Admission $50–$80. Cast size 5 (4 Beatles, 1 Ed Sullivan impersonator). Night of lowest attendance Tuesday. Usual showtimes Nightly, 5:30 p.m. Dark None. Topless No. Duration of presentation 90 minutes.

DESCRIPTION AND COMMENTS It's immediately obvious that the performers in this Beatles tribute group have honed their craft to expertise. The chief draw here is the music, as the four artists actually play all their own instruments on stage—no backing tapes or synthesized tracks. Vocally they are dead-on, and the audience gets especially charged up and rowdy during sing-alongs like "Twist and Shout." The costumes and musical selections follow the Beatles' career, from the early 1960s through psychedelia and into the 1970s. Film clips of fans from relevant eras form interludes, and "John" and "Paul" each get a chance to solo. The Beatle-esque mannerisms and speech patterns are there, even if the physical resemblance falls more into the category we call the "haircut impression." Fans of the lads from Liverpool and their music will have an absolute blast.

CONSUMER TIPS The V Theater is located in the Miracle Mile Shops at Planet Hollywood. Self-parking at Planet Hollywood funnels you directly into the Miracle Mile Shops not far from the theater. Arrive 40 minutes or more before showtime if you are buying or picking up tickets or redeeming ticket vouchers.

Bite ★★★

APPEAL BY AGE	UNDER 21 ★★★	21–37 ★★★½	38–50 ★★★	51+ ★★½

HOST CASINO AND SHOWROOM **Stratosphere—Stratosphere Theater; ☎ 702-382-4446 or 800-998-6937; stratospherehotel.com**

Type of show Erotic rock-and-roll vampires. Admission $50. Cast size 12. Night of lowest attendance Wednesday. Usual showtimes Friday–Wednesday, 10:30 p.m. Dark Thursday. Topless Yes. Special comments Must be 18 or older to attend. Duration of presentation 80 minutes.

DESCRIPTION AND COMMENTS *Bite,* a campy skin revue featuring buff women with really weird dentition, has a big-kahuna vampire, played by Mike Tyson (just kidding), on the prowl for his long-lost and now reincarnated lover. The plot, such as it is, is told through rock music of the 1970s, 1980s, and 1990s, and gets in the way as much as it binds the show together. The music, on the other hand, drives the show with a vengeance. The pace is furious, the choreography above average, and the showgirls hardworking and easy on the eyes. The vampire thing adds a *Rocky Horror Picture Show* gestalt to the show. Every production has to have its gimmick.

Your reaction to *Bite* will revolve around one factor: your ability to take vampires seriously when they groove to classic rock. Perhaps we've been culturally indoctrinated to think bloodsuckers either prefer orchestral dirges or dark-Goth punk, but it's still weird to see the Vampire Lord mooning around to the strains of the Eagles' "Desperado." Thankfully, there are no speaking parts, other than an occasional voice-over. The dancing, singing, and performing talent on display is mostly genuine, but the hokey quotient is very high.

CONSUMER TIPS This is edgier than most of the other T&A revues, with a dance style more at home in a strip club than in a casino showroom. Ziegfeld it ain't. Also, it really helps to like Guns N' Roses, ZZ Top, and Ted Nugent. Seats on the extreme left-front and right-front by the stage are at too severe an angle to afford much of a view.

Blue Man Group ★★★★½

APPEAL BY AGE	UNDER 21 ★★★★½	21–37 ★★★★½	38–50 ★★★★	51+ ★★★

HOST CASINO AND SHOWROOM **Venetian—Blue Man Group Theatre;**
☎ **702-414-7469 or 800-BLUE-MAN; blueman.com or venetian.com**

Type of show Performance-art production show. **Admission** $75–$159. **Cast size** 3 plus a 15-piece band. **Nights of lowest attendance** Sunday and Monday. **Usual showtimes** Nightly, 7 p.m. and 10 p.m. **Dark** None. **Topless** No. **Special comments** Teenagers will really like this show, but the blue guys, loud music, and dark colors could scare small children (we suggest 5 years as the minimum age). **Duration of presentation** 1 hour and 45 minutes.

DESCRIPTION AND COMMENTS What could demonstrate more mainstream cultural success than your own custom-designed 1,760-seat theater in Las Vegas? What could be more hip than to be a mystical, magical, and mute hero and clown and be blue? If you watch *Blue Man Group* at their Venetian venue with its immense stage area, you may well come up with the answer that nothing is more befuddlingly mainstream or cooler.

Blue Man Group gives Las Vegas its first large-scale introduction to that nebulous genre called "performance art." If the designation "performance art" confuses you, relax—it won't hurt a bit. *Blue Man Group* serves up a stunning show that all kinds of folks ages 8 to 80 can appreciate. Younger children may be frightened by the silent, wide-eyed, blue men.

The three blue men are just that—blue—and bald and mute. Wearing black clothing and skullcaps slathered with bright-blue greasepaint, their fast-paced show uses music (mostly percussion) and multimedia effects to make light of contemporary art and life in the information age. The Vegas act is just one expression of a franchise that started with three friends in New York's East Village. Now you can catch their zany, wacky, smart stuff in New York, Boston, Chicago, Berlin, and Toronto.

Funny, sometimes poignant, and always compelling, *Blue Man Group* hooks the audience even before the show begins with digital messages that ultimately spin performers and audience alike into a mutual act of joyous complicity. The trio pounds out vital, visceral tribal rhythms on complex instruments (made of PVC pipes) and makes seemingly spontaneous eruptions of visual art rendered with marshmallows and a mysterious goo. Their weekly supplies include 25.5 pounds of Cap'n Crunch, 60 Twinkies, 75 gallons of Jell-O, 996 marshmallows, 9.5 gallons of paint, and 185 miles, yes, miles, of rolled recycled paper. If all this sounds silly, it is, but it's also strangely thought-provoking about such various topics as the value of modern art, DNA, the way rock music moves you, and how we are all connected. (*Hint:* It's not the Internet.)

A 15-piece percussion band backs the Blue Man Group with a relentless and totally engrossing industrial dance riff. The band resides in long dark alcoves above the stage. At just the right moments, their lofts are lit to reveal a group of neon-colored pulsating skeletons.

Audience participation completes the Blue Man experience. The blue men often move into the audience to bring audience members on stage. At the end of the show, the entire audience is involved in an effort to move a sea of paper across the theater. And a lot of folks can't help standing up to dance—and laugh. Magicians for the creative spirit that resides in us all, *Blue Man Group* makes everyone a coconspirator in a culminating joyous explosion.

CONSUMER TIPS This show is decidedly different and requires an open mind to be appreciated. It also helps to be a little loose, because everybody gets sucked into the production and leaves the theater a little bit lighter in spirit, judging by the rousing standing ovations. If you don't want to be pulled onstage to become a part of the improvisation, don't sit in the first half dozen or so rows. If you drive, give yourself lots of extra time to park and make it to the showroom. The Venetian showrooms are toward the rear of the property around the corner from the V Bar nightspot.

Carrot Top ★★★

APPEAL BY AGE   UNDER 21 ★★★★   21–37 ★★★★   38–50 ★★★   51+ ★★

HOST CASINO AND SHOWROOM **Luxor—Atrium Showroom; ☎ 702-262-4400 or 800-557-7428; luxor.com**

Type of show Stand-up comedy. **Admission** $50–$66, $78–$89 with dinner buffet. **Cast size** 1. **Night of lowest attendance** Thursday. **Usual showtimes** Wednesday–Monday, 8:30 p.m. **Dark** Tuesday. **Topless** Only Carrot Top. **Special comments** Must be 18 or older to attend. **Duration of presentation** 1 hour 40 minutes.

DESCRIPTION AND COMMENTS Fans of comedian Carrot Top will love this fast-paced, high-energy, quick-spurting comedy orgy that strikes many mature themes. The redhead makes extensive use of the special effects (including fog, smoke, and strobe), lighting, and sound capabilities of the room. These heighten the experience far beyond the boundaries of standard nightclub stand-up fare. Pulling from large crates and even a washing machine, Carrot Top relies heavily on "homemade" props. His basic routine runs to "look at this" as he pulls strange thing after strange thing from the containers.

His humor is highly topical: rednecks, rock musicians, NASCAR, etc. Many of his quips are tasteless and offensive to various groups and persuasions, but the delivery is so fast and so brief that it's hard to take offense. In fact, his full-tilt boogie onslaught makes it difficult to stay with him, and you find yourself tuning out just to give your brain a respite. The pacing may prompt recall of the comedic delirium of Robin Williams. But whereas Williams explores our common humanity, Carrot Top fires bullets past the head that never touch the heart. His routines could be described as quick-witted, but not brainy. The 100-minute show includes a 15-minute opening act with another comedian. Dedicated fans will be delighted, but the uninitiated may find that Carrot Top's comedy degenerates too quickly to the bottom drawer.

CONSUMER TIPS Alcohol is not served in the theater. The theater is tiered, and seats (all with good sight lines) are preassigned. Bring along a couple of aspirins—you'll need them for your headache after the show.

Celine Dion ★★★★★

APPEAL BY AGE UNDER 21 ★★★ 21–37 ★★★★★ 38–50 ★★★★★ 51+ ★★★★★

HOST CASINO AND SHOWROOM **Caesars Palace–Colosseum; ☎ 702-731-7110 or 877-423-5463; caesarspalace.com or online reservations at ticketmaster.com/celinedion**

Type of show Celebrity headliner. Admission $55–$250 plus tax. Cast size 1 plus 31-piece orchestra and 4 back-up singers. Night of lowest attendance Midweek. Usual Showtimes Tuesday–Sunday, 7:30 p.m. Dark Sunday and Monday. Topless No. Duration of presentation 90 minutes.

DESCRIPTION AND COMMENTS It takes a big voice and a bigger personality to fill the 4,300-seat Colosseum at Caesars Palace. Celine Dion is blessed with both, which she amply demonstrates in her return to Las Vegas. She is emotional and energetic, graceful and glamorous, exquisitely gowned, and at the top of her very sophisticated game. Celine's show is dazzling, with an extravagance of spectacular visuals, lights, and music surrounding her versatile five-octave range. She leads with "Open Arms" while a video clip updates the audience on her life during the three years since she left Caesars Palace. Like a vertical tsunami, a massive white drape billows then drops to the titanic 250-foot stage revealing the orchestra. After an abridged trip through her hits and a virtuoso pageant of power ballads, she heads for the path not taken: tributes to the music of James Bond, Michael Jackson, and subdued renderings of a lullaby by Billy Joel and a Carole King melody written for her. Celine alone is more than enough, but she also duets with her on-screen self then duets again with a holographic Stevie Wonder. The powerful 31-piece orchestra and four back-up singers sit on five separate mobile stages that reconfigure contingent upon the requisite of the music. Sometimes it's just the horns, other times just the strings, a quartet, or a quintet as accompaniment. Light panels beneath the orchestra change color depending on mood or theme. On the sides of the stage and extending over the audience are screens that depict family scenes or blaze with vibrant patterns of fire and fireworks, flowers, stardust, and hundreds of other 3-D images exploding toward the audience. The set list is 20 songs followed by a wildly popular encore about an enduring heart. Visually gorgeous and aurally breathtaking, this upbeat and refined event is a class act from initial downbeat to final note.

CONSUMER TIPS Celine's engagement runs for three years, and she is contracted for 70 shows per year. She performs for 3–4 weeks, goes on hiatus for a short interlude, then returns again. Check with Caesars Palace or **celineinvegas.com** for show dates. Tickets are available up to one year in advance. Concerning seat selection, there are good sight lines from every seat. Plus, the enormity of the stage and scope of the production make sitting close to the stage less than desirable unless you intend to chat up Celine on potato-pancake recipes or some such. If you drive to Caesars, use the valet parking at the adjoining Forum Shops rather than the hotel-casino valet service at Caesars' main entrance. There is also valet service, as well as self-parking, at the rear of the hotel, with an entrance convenient to the theater. Give yourself lots of extra time to process through the metal detectors and bag-purse search at the entrance to the theater.

Chippendales ★★★★

APPEAL BY AGE 18–20 ★★★★ 21–37 ★★★★ 38–50 ★★★★ 51+ ★★★½

HOST CASINO AND SHOWROOM **Rio—The Chippendales Theatre;**
☎ **702-777-7776 or 888-746-7784; riolasvegas.com**

Type of show Male revue. Admission $40–$50. Cast size 12. Night of lowest attendance Monday. Usual showtimes Sunday–Tuesday and Thursday, 8 p.m.; Friday and Saturday, 8 and 10:30 p.m. Dark Wednesday. Topless Yes (male). Duration of presentation 75 minutes.

DESCRIPTION AND COMMENTS *Chippendales* strives to be the ultimate ladies' night out and succeeds. The show, which originated in Los Angeles and celebrated its 30th anniversary in 2008, is a mesmerizing erotic exploration of female fantasies. Performed by a cast of one dozen flawless model types, the men of *Chippendales* exude sex appeal while acting out a sequence of 11 vignettes. Most of the tightly synchronized dance routines are performed to contemporary R & B slow jams, creating a seductive and sensual atmosphere. Unlike the comparatively tame *Thunder from Down Under*, the *Chippendales* dancers feign sex acts and remove their G-strings entirely at several times during the show (albeit only when the guys have their backs turned to the audience). Large video screens surround the 600-or-more-person showroom, offering a close-up view of the dancers, who can be difficult to see at times from the general-admission seating. The dancers also venture out into the audience at various points throughout the performance, although not as much as the *Thunder* cast. After the show, the men of *Chippendales* host a meet-and-greet session.

CONSUMER TIPS No smoking is allowed during the show. On weekends, tables are removed from the VIP/floor section to provide more seating, requiring guests to hold their drinks (which can be pricey, so be careful not to spill). The bathroom is located next to the Masquerade Bar, diagonally across the casino. Paying extra for floor seats is well worth it for ladies seeking the best view. A seating chart is available online.

CIRQUE DU SOLEIL SHOWS

CIRQUE DU SOLEIL HAS TAKEN LAS VEGAS by frontal assault. There are now seven Cirque du Soleil productions playing Las Vegas showrooms. First to open was *Mystère* at T. I., followed some years later by *"O"* at the Bellagio. The third show to premier was *Zumanity* at New York–New York, with *KÀ* at the MGM Grand following close on its heels in 2005. Cirque's production *LOVE,* based on the music of the Beatles, opened in June of 2006; *CRISS ANGEL Believe* opened in September of 2008; and Cirque's latest effort, *Viva ELVIS,* opened in February of 2010.

KÀ, Mystère, LOVE, and *"O"* are representative of Cirque shows everywhere, albeit on a grand scale, and are appropriate for all ages. *Zumanity,* an in-your-face celebration of everything sexual, is much different from the other productions. *CRISS ANGEL Believe* likewise breaks the mold but has more in common with the original four shows than with *Zumanity. Viva ELVIS* is the most hard-driving of the Cirque shows and the least transcendent. All Cirque shows except *CRISS ANGEL* provide an awe-inspiring evening of entertainment, so you really can't go too wrong (assuming in the case of *Zumanity* that you're comfortable with the sexual content).

If you've never seen a Cirque du Soleil show, we suggest you start with *KÀ* or *Mystère.* Tickets for *Mystère* sell at $25 to $45 less than for *KÀ* and *"O,"* making *Mystère* by far the best value. Below you will find reviews of all the Las Vegas Cirque du Soleil shows. This information will help you make your choice of productions.

Cirque du Soleil's *CRISS ANGEL Believe* ★★★

APPEAL BY AGE UNDER 21 ★★★½ 21–37 ★★★ 38–50 ★★★ 51+ ★★★

HOST CASINO AND SHOWROOM **Luxor–Luxor Showroom; ☎ 702-262-4400 or 800-557-7428; luxor.com/entertainment**

Type of show Magic and illusion. **Admission** $60–$176 plus tax. **Cast size** Not available. **Night of lowest attendance** Wednesday. **Usual showtimes** Tuesday–Saturday, 7 and 9:30 p.m. **Dark** Sunday and Monday. **Topless** No. **Special comments** Not suitable for those under 12 years of age. **Duration of Presentation** 90 minutes.

DESCRIPTION AND COMMENTS Criss Angel is an illusionist who as an adolescent studied mysticism, music, martial arts, and dance and was inspired by Aldo Richiardi and especially Harry Houdini. In honor of Harry Houdini, Angel chose "Believe" as the title for his grand collaboration with Cirque du Soleil. On his death bed, reportedly, legendary magician and escape artist Harry Houdini told his wife: "After my death, many people will claim that they are still able to communicate with me. If their claims are valid, they will be able to tell you a code word—that word is 'Believe.'"

Angel made his prime-time television debut in the ABC special "Secrets." His surreal and critically acclaimed *Criss Angel Mindfreak* brought a new kind of entertainment to Broadway. He is currently the star and creator of the A&E Network series *Criss Angel Mindfreak*.

I had been mountain biking during the afternoon before I (Bob) reviewed *CRISS ANGEL*. Arriving at the showroom only minutes before the curtain rose, I hadn't had time to eat and was also parched and dehydrated. When I explained why I was running late to the Cirque publicist who met me, she immediately ran off and brought me back a Coke. I was both extremely embarrassed and eternally grateful. As it turned out, that coke was the best part of my evening with Criss Angel.

Believe is about a dream that takes the form of a nice little morality play, the standard good-versus-evil thing except that the bad guys are bunnies (I'm not making this up). Criss enters this dream state after being gruesomely electrocuted trying to perform a stunt his mom (on a video screen) tells him not to do. If you mess with mom you'll pay the consequences, and that's pretty much the only object lesson of the show.

But wait, I forgot about the preamble. Criss's warm-up act is Criss, strutting around the stage and down into the audience inviting adulation. He's pretty in your face about this, "What? I can't hear you! Louder! I want to hear you really make some noise!" This goes on interminably with nothing more than his august presence to cheer about. After milking it for all it's worth (and falling short of canonization), he shows some video clips of himself with famous people and performing the illusions that put him on the map. This all leads to mom and the electrocution, and finally we're underway.

As with all Cirque shows, the imagery, the music, the costumes, the choreography, the sets, and the special effects are magnificent. Nobody, after all, can create and furnish a dream like Cirque du Soleil. The showroom is exceptional too and was specially designed for *Believe*. However, wrapping your mind around those menacing dark-furred evil bunnies is a challenge. You don't so much get over it as wall it off.

Though *Believe* has its moments, such as when the train of a wedding dress expands to cover an entire wall, the show generally limps along. There are enough bright spots to grasp the potential of a Cirque du Soleil production centering on magic and illusion, but loud, brash Criss Angel is the absolute antithesis of Cirque's trademark subtlety and grace. It's almost an oil-and-water thing. Cirque and Criss Angel simply clash. You have to wonder how good this concept could have been if Cirque had teamed up with Lance Burton or David Copperfield.

Criss Angel has created some pretty amazing illusions in his time, but they're not on display in *Believe*. In fact, a number of illusions in the show are very transparent. Angel specializes in levitation, floating, and wall-walking illusions, for example. After each such illusion you can see assistants moving behind him to unfasten his harness. I've always enjoyed seeing an illusion break new ground, but *Believe* does not deliver on this score either. As evidenced by his adroit sleight of hand, Angel is a talented magician, and *Believe* could have been a better show if the emphasis was magic and illusion. As it is, the show is about Criss, who demands the sort of hysteria and fan worship Celine elicits, but without delivering the goods.

Many comments about the show on Internet discussion boards crack me up. Here are two that hit the nail on the head:

Don't waste your time or money. Buy Terry Fator (ventriloquist/puppeteer) tickets instead. He makes his turtle levitate at half the cost.

And

One of his doves pooped on my friend's leg, and that about sums up the show.

CONSUMER TIPS   Like all Cirque productions, *CRISS ANGEL Believe* makes use of the entire showroom. Consequently, sitting near the stage requires that you turn in your seat to see things going on overhead or behind you. The Luxor Theater is split into a front section and a rear section separated by a broad aisle. The best seats are in the first ten rows of the rear section. Owing to the location of the showroom, it's just as convenient to park in Luxor's self-parking lot as to use valet.

Cirque du Soleil's *KÀ*   ★★★★½

APPEAL BY AGE   UNDER 21 ★★★★   21–37 ★★★★★   38–50 ★★★★★   51+ ★★★★★

HOST CASINO AND SHOWROOM   **MGM Grand—KÀ Theater; ☎ 702-891-7777 or 866-774-7117; mgmgrand.com/ka**

Type of show   Fearsome ballet as epic journey. Admission cost   Adults, $76–$165; children, $35–$75 (no tax or fees included). *Note:* Wheelchair-accessible seating available at all ticket levels. Cast size   80. Night of lowest attendance   Wednesday. Usual showtimes   Tuesday–Saturday, 7 and 9:30 p.m. Dark   Sunday and Monday. Topless   No. Special comments   Guests age 12 and under permitted only if accompanied by an adult; no children under age 5. Duration of presentation   90 minutes.

DESCRIPTION AND COMMENTS   *KÀ* is a departure for Cirque du Soleil in many ways. Most striking is the menacing atmosphere of KÀ theater. It has the look of an enchanted Asian foundry from space complete with 30-foot bursts of flame, performers hanging batlike from girders and scampering along catwalks, and industrial clangs reverberating as you find your seat. You are shown to your seat by one of many hair-raising Gatekeepers, who also serve as security during the show. (This reviewer would not advise breaking theater rules; it will be a Gatekeeper who sees to your punishment.) At the center of the theater, a gaping pit lurks where the stage would rightfully be.

The overall effect, while chilling, isn't off-putting, but the proscription against very young children makes good sense.

KÀ is also unique in that it is the first Cirque production that attempts to tell a linear story. That story follows twins who have been separated and must each make a journey to meet their destiny. That journey is the focus of the show, and the twins travel through beaches, mountains, forests, and blizzards, face warriors and whimsical sea and forest creatures, and witness remarkable feats of strength and agility. All these, of course, completely overshadow the storytelling and relegate the story to something you're vaguely conscious of from time to time, but nothing more.

If there is a single star of *KÀ*, it is the gantry stage. From the pit emerges a large deck, supported by a boom, that is manipulated with computer precision to spin, tilt, raise, and lower throughout the show, all with surprising fluidity and speed. Not to knock the performers, who are as lithe and powerful as any cast of humans has a right to be, but the stage is an incredible industrial achievement. In one of the most breathtaking scenes, the stage tilts fully vertical as warriors loose arrows toward it and their intended victims scramble to find purchase. The arrows appear to stick in the stage, giving the "attacked" performers the handholds they need to dance and spin and flip their way up the vertical wall. As the performers ascend the wall, the "arrows" (which are actually 80 retractable pegs built into the stage) retract and the stage appears to shrug off the performers like so much detritus—an effect that is both unforgettable and disturbing.

In short, *KÀ* is a spectacle, and arguably the most technologically complex show in Las Vegas. The story line fails, but the production as a whole doesn't suffer from the loss. *KÀ* is a new breed of Cirque show, though it still contains the elements of all Cirque productions: elaborate costumes, haunting scores, physical prowess and beauty, and acrobatic feats. If you've already fallen hard for *Mystère*, KÀ may not be quite what you expect of a Cirque performance. While *KÀ* does display some of the whimsy of *Mystère,* the overall impression is shock, awe, and menacing power. If you are in a show-going mood, you can easily see both *KÀ* and *Mystère* in a single vacation without feeling over-Cirqued. In fact, we recommend it. *KÀ* is a fearsome production, and an elegant foil for the playful *Mystère*.

CONSUMER TIPS *KÀ* is a fine show—as virile and stirring as anything on the Strip—but the tariff is steep. Comparatively, though, the mid-priced seats are a better deal than similar seats at *"O,"* because *KÀ* Theater was thoughtfully designed without "limited-visibility" seats. *Note:* there are wheelchair-accessible seats in all three of the theater's ticketed sections.

If you do see *KÀ* and if you can manage to remember this tip with menacing creatures dangling overhead, arrows zipping at the performers, and a stage that's come shouldering to life in front of you, try to spot the three "performers" on stage who are actually technicians in costume.

Cirque du Soleil's *LOVE* ★★★★½

APPEAL BY AGE UNDER 21 ★★★ 21–37 ★★★★ 38–50 ★★★★ 51+ ★★★★★

HOST CASINO AND SHOWROOM **Mirage—LOVE Theater; ☎ 702-792-7777 or 800-963-9634; mirage.com or cirquedusoleil.com/love**

Type of show Circus based on music of the Beatles. **Admission** $93.50–$150.
Cast size 60. **Night of lowest attendance** Monday. **Usual showtimes** Thursday–
Monday, 7 and 9:30 p.m. **Dark** Tuesday and Wednesday. **Topless** No. **Duration
of presentation** 90 minutes.

DESCRIPTION AND COMMENTS *LOVE,* like most Cirque du Soleil shows, is nothing if not an overwhelming spectacle. But this latest Cirque extravaganza
is a definite departure from what might be loosely called the norm. First,
it's heavily multimedia, combining extensive video effects projected onto
a variety of screens with dancers, acrobats, and aerialists in outlandish
costumes and bizarre props, all driven by the most powerful soundtrack
ever, perhaps, produced. And because music, especially familiar music, is
the force behind the visuals and theatrics, *LOVE* is grounded in a reality
that the audience shares, which renders this show unified and accessible
in a way that *Mystère* approximates, but that *"O," Believe,* and even *KÀ*
with its loose plot line, can never be.

That's not to imply, however, that *LOVE* doesn't have its extreme
flights of fancy. The teaming of Cirque and the Beatles is, simply put, a
marriage made in psychedelic heaven. Only Cirque could so effectively
choreograph, costume, and showcase the characters, images, themes,
humor, whimsicality, and all-around 1960s optimism, exuberance, and
magic that the Beatles continue, 40 years later, to embody.

The show opens with a rousing rendition of "Get Back." Then it flashes
back to begin a loose retrospective based on the Beatles' meteoric rise to
become the most influential rock-and-roll band in history. "Eleanor Rigby"
is set to theatrical scenes of the devastation that World War II wrought
on the Beatles' Liverpool. "I Want to Hold Your Hand" introduces the
collective planetary hysteria of Beatlemania. By now you know what
you're in for. The stage, in pieces controlled by individual hydraulics, rises
and falls as necessary. Visuals range from actual Beatles concerts and appearances to paisleys and spirals guaranteed to give (some of) you flash-
backs. The music, which has been digitized and remixed by Sir George
Martin (the fifth Beatle) and his son Giles, isn't exactly the same as on the
LPs, as you might expect, and it's fun to listen for the little differences. The
soundtrack consists of full songs, medleys, snippets of tunes down to a bar
or two that disappear as soon as you recognize them, along with Beatles
banter and fragments from recording sessions, plus suitably surreal tran-
sitions holding it all together. One thing's for sure: The acoustics are outstanding. More than 6,000 speakers surround you, with one installed in
the backrest of every seat in the house.

Song after timeless song parades by. "Something in the Way She
Moves" is accompanied by an aerial ballet; "Lucy in the Sky with Diamonds" is similar. The skit around "Blackbird" is hilarious, with spastic
birds learning to fly. For "Strawberry Fields," big bubbles are blown from
the top of a grand piano. "Octopus's Garden" has airborne squids and
anemones. If you pay close attention, you'll catch new lyrics at the end of
"While My Guitar Gently Weeps." Four skaters perform acrobatics on
steep ramps to "Help," "Lady Madonna," "Here Comes the Sun," "Come
Together," "Revolution Number Nine," "Back in the USSR," and "A Day

in the Life"—ultimately, *LOVE* passes the true test of psychedelia: it doesn't matter if your eyes are open or closed.

For the finale, umbrellas spread confetti all over the room to "Hey Jude" and predictably, the show ends on "Sgt. Pepper's Lonely Hearts Club Band": "We hope you have enjoyed the show and we're sorry but it's time to go." The audience is sorry too. An encore of "All You Need Is Love" caps the evening.

CONSUMER TIPS *LOVE* plays in the space where Siegfried and Roy used to perform, but the new theater underwent a mere $120-million worth of renovations. There's not a bad seat in the new 2,000-seat theater-in-the-round, but the top $150 ticket might be too close. Since all the action occurs on the elevated stages and above, the eye-level mid-priced seats are better. You can't see *LOVE* anywhere else on the planet, folks, so be sure to buy your tickets by phone or online (**cirquedusoleil .com**) as far in advance as possible. The concession stand sells bottled water, beer, wine, and popcorn.

Cirque du Soleil's *Mystère*   ★★★★★

APPEAL BY AGE UNDER 21 ★★★★ 21–37 ★★★★★ 38–50 ★★★★★ 51+ ★★★★½

HOST CASINO AND SHOWROOM **T. I.—*Mystère* Theater; ☎ 702-894-7722 or 800-392-1999; treasureisland.com**

Type of show Circus as theater. **Admission** $60–$109, limited seats. **Cast size** 72. **Night of lowest attendance** Tuesday. **Usual showtimes** Saturday–Wednesday, 7 and 9:30 p.m. **Dark** Thursday and Friday. **Special comments** No table service (no tables!). **Topless** No. **Duration of presentation** 90 minutes.

DESCRIPTION AND COMMENTS *Mystère* is a far cry from a traditional circus but retains all of the fun and excitement. It is whimsical, mystical, and sophisticated, yet pleasing to all ages. The action takes place on an elaborate stage that incorporates almost every part of the theater. The original musical score is exotic, like the show.

Mystère is the most difficult show in Las Vegas to describe. To categorize it as a circus does not begin to cover its depth, though its performers could perform with distinction in any circus on earth. Cirque du Soleil is much more than a circus. It combines elements of classic Greek theater, mime, the English morality play, Dali surrealism, Fellini characterization, and Chaplin comedy. *Mystère* is at once an odyssey, a symphony, and an exploration of human emotions. The show pivots on its humor, which is sometimes black, and engages the audience with its unforgettable characters. Though light and uplifting, it is also poignant and dark. Simple in its presentation, it is extraordinarily intricate, always operating on multiple levels of meaning. As you laugh and watch the amazingly talented cast, you become aware that your mind has entered a dimension seldom encountered in a waking state. The presentation begins to register in your consciousness more as a seamless dream than as a stage production. You are moved, lulled, and soothed as well as excited and entertained. The sensitive, the imaginative, the literate, and those who love good theater and art will find no show in Las Vegas that compares with *Mystère* except Cirque's sister productions.

CONSUMER TIPS Be forewarned that the audience is an integral part of *Mystère* and that at almost any time you might be plucked from your seat to participate. Our advice is to loosen up and roll with it. If you are too rigid, repressed, hungover, or whatever to get involved, politely but firmly decline to be conscripted.

Because *Mystère* is presented in its own customized showroom, there are no tables and, consequently, no drink service. In keeping with the show's circus theme, however, spectators may purchase refreshments at nearby concession stands. Tickets for reserved seats can be purchased seven days in advance at the Cirque's box office or over the phone, using your credit card.

Cirque du Soleil's "O" ★★★★

APPEAL BY AGE UNDER 21 ★★★★ 21–37 ★★★★★ 38–50 ★★★★★ 51+★★★★½

HOST CASINO AND SHOWROOM **Bellagio—"O" Theater; ☎ 702-693-7722 or 888-488-7111; bellagio.com**

Type of show Circus and aquatic ballet as theater. **Admission** $93.50–$150 plus tax and $7.50 processing fee. **Cast size** 74. **Night of lowest attendance** Sunday. **Usual showtimes** Wednesday–Sunday, 7:30 and 10 p.m. **Dark** Monday and Tuesday. **Topless** No. **Special comments** Guests age 18 and under permitted only if accompanied by an adult. **Duration of presentation** 1 hour and 45 minutes.

DESCRIPTION AND COMMENTS The title "O" is a play on words derived from the concept of infinity, with 0 (zero) as its purest expression, and from the phonetic pronunciation of *eau,* the French word for water. Both symbols are appropriate, for the production (like all Cirque shows) creates a timeless dream state and (for the first time in a Cirque show) also incorporates an aquatic dimension that figuratively and literally evokes all of the meanings, from baptism to boat passage, that water holds for us. The foundation for the spectacle that is "O" resides in a set (more properly an aquatic theater) that is no less than a technological triumph. Before your eyes, in mere seconds, the hard, varnished surface of the stage transforms seamlessly into anything from a fountain to a puddle to a vast pool. Where only moments ago acrobats tumbled, now graceful water ballerinas surface and make way for divers somersaulting down from above. The combined effect of artists and environment is so complete and yet so transforming that it's almost impossible to focus on specific characters, details, or movements. Rather there is a global impact that envelops you and holds you suspended. In the end you have a definite sense that you *felt* what transpired rather than having merely seen it.

Though "O" is brilliant by any standard and pregnant with beauty and expression, it lacks just a bit of the humor, accessibility, and poignancy of Cirque's *Mystère* at T. I. Where "O" crashes over you like a breaking wave, *Mystère* is more personal, like a lover's arrow to the heart. If you enjoyed *Mystère*, however, you will also like "O," and vice versa. What's more, the productions, while sharing stylistic similarities, are quite different. Though you might not want (or be able to afford) to see them both on the same Las Vegas visit, you wouldn't feel like you saw the same show twice if you did.

CONSUMER TIPS If you've never seen any of the Las Vegas Cirque du Soleil productions, we recommend catching *Mystère, LOVE,* or *KÀ* first. *Mystère* is more representative of Cirque du Soleil's hallmark presentation and tradition, in *LOVE* the real star is the music, while *KÀ* is a brilliant example of the Cirque concept evolved to full technological potential.

If you want to go, buy tickets via credit card over the phone before you leave home. If you decide to see *"O"* at the spur of the moment, try the box office about 30 minutes before showtime. Sometimes seats reserved for comped gamblers will be released for sale.

Cirque du Soleil's *Viva ELVIS* ★★★★

APPEAL BY AGE UNDER 21 ★★★★ 21–37 ★★★★ 38–50 ★★★★½ 51+ ★★★★½

HOST CASINO AND SHOWROOM **Aria at CityCenter—Viva ELVIS Theater;**
☎ **877-25-ELVIS or 702-590-7760; arialasvegas.com;**
online reservations at ticketmaster.com

Type of show Rock nostalgia musical about the life of Elvis Presley. **Admission** $69–$175 plus tax and $7.50 fee. Cast size 75 including musicians and dancers. **Night of lowest attendance** Monday. Usual showtimes Tuesday–Saturday, 7 and 9:30 p.m. Dark Sunday and Monday. Topless No. Duration of presentation 90 minutes.

DESCRIPTION AND COMMENTS *Viva ELVIS* is a musical tribute to Elvis Presley, both the man and his music. His life story, chronologically presented and somewhat sanitized, provides the framework for the 90-minute production.

The emphasis in early rock was on the beat and the instrumental revolution occasioned by the invention of the electric guitar. Lyrics were the icing on the cake, and no one demanded sophistication. It was all about teen romance, dancing, and having a good time. In short, it was feel-good music. In contrast to the Beatles, Elvis didn't write his own music, so his songs never expressed his worldview or personal feelings. Rather, Elvis caught fire because of his good looks, sensual style, remarkable voice, and, most of all, his bold embrace of a musical genre that was an offspring of black R&B. Elvis was controversial, and teens were rebellious. As an icon, he became the white standard bearer for a new genre of music that would eventually transcend race.

Viva ELVIS, through Elvis's music, delivers a totally cranked rampage through rock's nascent years. From saddle oxfords and poodle skirts to leather jackets and greased hair, it captures nostalgically the halcyon teen scene of the period, later moving to Elvis's military service, the reestablishment of his career, and becoming a Hollywood celeb.

A dynamite band with a bari sax and two drummers, usually working on stage, belts out the hits—19 full-blown and an equal number of snippets. Some are familiar rock classics such as "Hound Dog," "Heartbreak Hotel," and "All Shook Up"; some, such as "King Creole," "Love Me Tender," and "Viva Las Vegas," come from movies, while a few, such as "Mystery Train" and "Follow That Dream," may be new except to the Elvis cognoscenti.

There's a decided nod to choreography in *Viva ELVIS* with the circus-acrobatic element taking a slightly subordinate role, augmenting rather than competing with the music. There are myriad subtleties that you'll appreciate artistically but really won't understand unless you have an in-depth knowledge of Elvis's life. In the "One Night" number, for example, two acrobats represent Elvis and his twin brother Jesse who was stillborn. Staging is straightforward but highly imaginative. The backdrop to "Return to Sender" is a giant American flag fashioned from boxer shorts and long johns. Other sets feature oversized sculptures of Elvis as a cinema cowboy and a 1,500-pound blue suede shoe. The most haunting visual is the silver outline of a giant guitar floating translucent in a galaxy of stars. Though the production is punctuated by ballads and some intimate moments, in the main *Viva ELVIS* is a hard-driving hurricane of a show. It was designed to be fun and it is.

CONSUMER TIPS   If you're trying to decide between seeing *Viva ELVIS* and *LOVE,* featuring the music of the Beatles, *LOVE* is more poignant and more nuanced, bringing to life the evocative lyrics that so distinguish Beatles music. In *LOVE* all the music is recorded, whereas in *Viva ELVIS* all the music is live. Choreography is stronger in *Viva ELVIS*, while acrobatics and circus skills are preeminent in *LOVE*. You really can't go wrong with either.

The custom-designed *Viva ELVIS* Theater is a perfect venue, with excellent sight lines from every seat. Speaking of which, the up-close, high-priced seats are on sofas; all others are plush theater seats with armrests and drink holders. Because the stage is very wide, you really need to be back about 20 rows or so to take it all in without a lot of head wagging. Ticketmaster.com has a seating diagram of the theater. There's a cash bar outside the showroom and convenient restrooms at both ends of the theater lobby.

CityCenter in general is a little confusing. If you want to valet park, use the Aria north valet rather than the front valet that serves the hotel reception area. Drive west on Harmon Avenue and follow the signs to Vdara and Aria. The self-parking garage is accessible from CityCenter Place, a west turn off South Las Vegas Boulevard. Once parked, take the escalator down to the southern entrance of Aria. Inside Aria, turn left and continue until you see the escalators serving the buffet and showroom. Signage is good in the casino, and you shouldn't have any difficulty finding the theater whichever Aria entrance you use.

Cirque du Soleil's *Zumanity*   ★★★★

APPEAL BY AGE	UNDER 21—	21–37 ★★★★	38–50 ★★★★	51+ ★★★½

HOST CASINO AND SHOWROOM   **New York–New York–*Zumanity* Theatre;**
☎ **702-740-6815 or 866-606-7111; newyorknewyork.com or zumanity.com**

Type of show A risqué Cirque du Soleil. **Admission** $69–$142; duo sofas also available at $129 (sold in pairs). **Cast size** 50. **Night of lowest attendance** Wednesday. **Usual showtimes** Tuesday, Wednesday, and Friday–Sunday, 7:30 and 10:30 p.m. **Dark** Monday and Thursday. **Topless** Yes. **Special comments** For ages 18 and over due to adult themes and nudity. **Duration of presentation** 90 minutes.

DESCRIPTION AND COMMENTS *Zumanity* is about love, emotional and physical, in all its unrequited, sated, comedic, tender, and lunatic dimensions. It is also the first Cirque production to chart a decidedly adult course. As it turns out, Cirque does love and sex as well as it does everything else, and *Zumanity* is a hell of a ride.

Zumanity is zany, raucous, and decidedly outrageous. It is lovable in its humor and insightful in its understanding of sex. The visually rich production blends its challenging theme with Cirque du Soleil's signature music, color, acrobatics, and dance. *Zumanity* is sometimes very tender but at other moments hard-edged. It urges us to look at how we define human beauty and makes a plea for the acceptance of differences. *Zumanity* delivers a powerful message.

Like all Cirque productions, *Zumanity* is hauntingly dreamlike. But where other Cirque shows operate on multiple levels of meaning and interpretation, *Zumanity* tells us in unambiguous terms that sex is amazing, infinitely varied, and wonderful. As the production unfolds, you witness an artful sequence of sexual vignettes celebrating heterosexual sex, gay sex, masturbation, sex between obese lovers, sex with midgets, group sex, sadomasochistic sex, and sex enjoyed by the very old. As the name *Zumanity* implies, sex (and the varied emotions we bring to it) is a defining element of our humanity. Sex is happy, sex is sad, sex is of the moment, sex is transcendent, sex is funny, sex is bewildering. And as *Zumanity* so ably demonstrates, sex is a window into our essential being.

Now, after digesting the above, you might be thinking that's one window you're uncomfortable peering into, that you really don't need to know all that much about our essential being. But there's also this nagging impulse to take a little peek. You might even want to take a big peek, but aren't sure it's a good idea with your wife, mother, or father-in-law sitting beside you. That's the genius of *Zumanity*: it forces you to confront your own sexuality, including your hangups—all in the presence of your friends, family, and possibly your own lover (plus, of course, 1,200 strangers). For some it's very disquieting, even frightening. Tension is palpable. Some shift continuously in their seats. They laugh a bit too loud at the jokes, try to appear unaffected by the orgasmic groaning, pretend they're quite accustomed to leather and whips, and attempt to will themselves not to be aroused. Most people, however, will find *Zumanity* to be exhilarating, and more than a few find it absolutely liberating.

CONSUMER TIPS *Zumanity* is brilliant, but clearly not for everyone. Certainly, it's not for prudes, the sexually repressed (probably half of America), or the sexually phobic. Equally, it's not for the "gentlemen's club" set. *Zumanity* is altogether too complex, cerebral, and theatrical for their taste. Give some thought to who you see *Zumanity* with and make sure they know what they're getting into. Many readers have reported being so preoccupied with the reaction of their companion that they couldn't enjoy the show.

The production is staged in a 1,256-custom-seat, custom-designed showroom that facilitates a performer–audience intimacy remarkable for a theater so large and for a production of *Zumanity*'s scope. With the exception of some first-floor seats (under the balcony outcropping) that make viewing aerial acts impossible, sight lines are excellent. The best seats are on the lower-floor center and about 12 rows or more back. As with all Cirque du Soleil shows, audience members are at risk of being hauled into the performance.

Crazy Girls ★★★½

| APPEAL BY AGE | UNDER 21 – | 21–37 ★★★½ | 38–50 ★★★½ | 51+ ★★★½ |

HOST CASINO AND SHOWROOM **Riviera—Crazy Girls Showroom;**
☎ **702-794-9301 or 800-634-3420; rivierahotel.com**

Type of show Erotic dance and adult comedy. **Admission** $45–$73. **Cast size** 8. **Nights of lowest attendance** Wednesday and Monday. **Usual showtimes** Wednesday–Monday, 9:30 p.m. **Dark** Tuesday. **Topless**. Yes. **Duration of presentation** 75 minutes.

DESCRIPTION AND COMMENTS *Crazy Girls* gets right to the point. This is a no-nonsense show for men who do not want to sit through jugglers, magicians, and half the score from *Oklahoma!* before they see naked women. The focus is on eight engaging, talented, and athletically built young ladies who bump and grind through more than an hour of exotic dance and comedy. The choreography (for anyone who cares) is pretty creative, and the whole performance is highly charged and quickly paced, though most vocals are lip-synched. The dancers are supported by a zany comedienne who doesn't shy away from X-rated humor. Solo routines (which may be dancing or just sexy writhing) are shown in close-up on large video screens, but the videos are from previous performances, creating an odd disconnect when the video and the onstage performer get out of sync.

CONSUMER TIPS The show is not really as risqué as the Riviera would lead you to believe, and the nudity does not go beyond topless and G-strings (how could it?). While designed for men, there is not much of anything in the show that would make women or couples uncomfortable. Men looking for total nudity might try the Palomino Club in North Las Vegas or Talk of the Town on Las Vegas Boulevard just south of Charleston Boulevard.

Tickets may be reserved up to 21 days in advance at the Riviera box office or over the phone with a credit card up to ten days in advance. Up-close VIP seating, available for old farts who forgot their glasses, includes a line pass.

Crazy Horse Paris ★★★★

| APPEAL BY AGE | UNDER 21 – | 21–37 ★★★★ | 38–50 ★★★½ | 51+ ★★★ |

HOST CASINO AND SHOWROOM **MGM Grand—*Crazy Horse* Cabaret;**
☎ **702-891-7777 or 877-880-0880; mgmgrand.com**

Type of show Artsy topless dance performance from France. **Admission** $51, $61. **Cast size** 12. **Night of lowest attendance** Sunday. **Usual showtimes** Wednesday–Monday, 8 and 10:30 p.m. **Dark** Tuesday. **Topless** Yes. **Duration of presentation** 75 minutes.

DESCRIPTION AND COMMENTS Imported from the legendary Crazy Horse club in Paris, *Crazy Horse Paris* is something of an oddity. The showroom is quite beautiful, done up in plush reds that call to mind an upscale bordello. Most of the dancers are Parisian imports as well, and they must not only be in excellent physical condition, they also are not allowed surgical enhancements. So what you see is *au naturel.* There's a wide variety of musical and dance numbers, and these are mixed with the odd comedy interlude or a bit of historical footage from the original Crazy Horse. The show's erotic routines are decidedly European, relying on arty lighting, sensuous music, and a lot of writhing. There's not anything else like it in Vegas. On the whole, *Crazy Horse Paris* is diverting, cool, and sexy.

CONSUMER TIPS   The stage for *Crazy Horse Paris* is very small for such a large room, so seats in the rear may result in eyestrain. Tickets can be purchased in person at the box office, on the phone at the number above, or online at the MGM Grand website.

David Copperfield   ★★★★

APPEAL BY AGE   UNDER 21 ★★★★   21–37 ★★★★   38–50 ★★★★   51+ ★★★★

HOST CASINO AND SHOWROOM   **MGM Grand—Hollywood Theatre;**
☎ **702 891-7777; mgmgrand.com**

Type of show Illusion and magic. **Admission** $89 and $116 plus tax. **Cast size** 1. **Night of lowest attendance** Thursday. **Usual showtimes** Nightly, 7:30 and 10 p.m. **Dark** None. **Topless** No. **Duration of presentation** 90 minutes.

DESCRIPTION AND COMMENTS   David Copperfield has been the preeminent illusionist in Las Vegas for decades, including the Siegfried & Roy era. Lance Burton could give Copperfield a run for his money when it came to showmanship and sleight of hand, but Copperfield has always set the standard for originality and creativity. Magic and illusion shows in Las Vegas wrote the book on redundancy. Regardless whose name was on the marquee, one magic show was pretty much like the next. Production values varied wildly, ranging from Siegfried and Roy's extravaganzas to the modest Showgirls of Magic (whose show could fit on a 12-x-12-foot stage), but the content was largely the same. There were trends, of course, and for a while it was embarrassing to perform without a lion, tiger, leopard, or panther. Impaling devices were likewise all the rage for a time. We reviewed show after show and could barely keep them straight. That is, except for Copperfield.

Copperfield performs as a celebrity headliner, so he isn't in town all the time. Whenever we review him, however, we know we're seeing the illusions that the other magicians will try to emulate a year or two down the road. Like the other guys, Copperfield puts things in boxes or behind curtains and makes them disappear. But jaded reviewers aside, audiences still love that stuff, and even here Copperfield tops the competition. In one such illusion he selects 13 audience members at random and puts them in what looks like a suspended jury box and then makes them vanish. If you're wondering about animals that eat people, Copperfield eschews them in favor of a modest white duck.

Another Copperfield trademark is making use of his audience, as many as 40 of them in a given performance! Sometimes he selects them individually, and sometimes he tosses a number of large inflatable balls into the audience—if you catch one consider yourself conscripted. Illusions range from passing through a steel plate, to making a vintage auto appear, to sleight of hand only inches from an audience volunteer. Elaborate illusions, including walking through an industrial fan and guessing a lottery number, are punctuated with simpler, less prop-dependent illusions. Copperfield works alone (except for a crew who moves his heavy contraptions) and engages the audience in a nearly continuous repartee and chatter. The pace is measured and includes several illusions with lengthy (and sometimes schmaltzy) narratives, including the story of how a butterfly inspires a little girl imprisoned by the Nazis.

CONSUMER TIPS Copperfield works hard cranking out a full 90-minute show, including encores. The Hollywood Theatre, located along the south wall of the main casino, is a perfect venue for Copperfield with good sight lines supplemented by large LED screens showing all the action. Except for cushy high-roller booths, seating is cramped at banquet tables and little round four-tops. Waitstaff take orders for an extensive and expensive selection of drinks before the show. The nearest restroom is in another zip code away and gone in the casino.

Defending the Caveman ★★★½

APPEAL BY AGE	UNDER 21 ★★	21–37 ★★★★	38–50 ★★★★	51+ ★★★★

HOST CASINO AND SHOWROOM **Harrah's; ☎ 702-369-5111; harrahslasvegas.com**

Type of show Stand-up comedy. **Admission** $40–$66. **Cast size** 1. **Night of lowest attendance** Monday. **Usual showtimes** Daily, 7 p.m. plus 3 p.m. Sunday and Monday. **Dark** None. **Topless** No. **Duration of presentation** 80 minutes.

DESCRIPTION AND COMMENTS Veteran stand-up comic Kevin Burke stars in this insightful and clever exploration of how men and women relate. Written by Rob Becker, *Defending the Caveman* was the longest-running solo play in the history of Broadway. In addition to the ongoing gig at Harrah's, eight other comics take the production on the road all across the country. Great material coupled with flawless timing and super delivery make for an excellent evening's entertainment. Dealing with sexuality, contemporary feminism, masculine sensitivity, and why women have more shoes than men, it's *Men Are from Mars, Women Are from Venus* on laughing gas.

CONSUMER TIPS The show is a rare bargain among Las Vegas productions these days. Be forewarned that the show is pretty blue. If you're easily offended, you're better off with Donny and Marie. One detractor posted a comment on the Internet that "Cave Man is a one-man show and all he does is talk about relationships." Well, hello? We can't think of another topic that offers a comedian more grist for the mill. Also, you will discover that your gender-influenced behaviors are not unique to you and will be trotted out in all their embarrassing dimensions. Throughout the show you'll hear people whisper, "George, that's exactly what you do!" or "Sally, he absolutely has you nailed."

Donny & Marie ★★★★

HOST CASINO AND SHOWROOM   **Flamingo—Flamingo Showroom;**
☎ **702-733-3333 or 800-221-7299; flamingolasvegas.com**

Type of show Celebrity headliner. **Admission** $95, $109, $125, and $260 plus tax. **Cast size** 19. **Night of lowest attendance** Wednesday. **Usual showtimes** Tuesday–Saturday, 7:30 p.m. **Dark** Sunday and Monday. **Topless** No. **Duration of presentation** 90 minutes.

DESCRIPTION AND COMMENTS   Donny and Marie Osmond demonstrate the same chemistry that made them irresistible on TV in the 1970s and late 1990s—and both still have their chops. The production showcases their hits (mostly Donny's) like "Puppy Love," "Soldier of Love," and "Go Away, Little Girl," but also includes enough contemporary and Broadway tunes that you don't founder on Memory Lane. Marie provides the most surprises, strutting her stuff with torch songs and revealing her sensual side as she vamps around the stage. She even tosses in a little opera. There are lots of duets, but each also performs alone, and yes, they still do that brother-sister ribbing and arguing thing, and their fans still eat it up. They're backed by a nine-piece live band and eight very modestly attired dancers. Production values are high with compelling sets and a lot of nostalgic video footage.

CONSUMER TIPS   The Flamingo Showroom is a good venue for this production, offering good sight lines and the kind of intimacy desirable in a celebrity headliner show. The showroom has always had a hard time getting people in and seated expeditiously, so come prepared to wait in line to enter. As with Wayne Newton and several other performers over the years, we've had readers recount being dragged to Donny and Marie by their spouse or friend and being blown away by the quality and energy of the performance. Finally, as you'd expect, Donny and Marie put on as squeaky clean a show as you'll find in Las Vegas, making it a great choice for the under-21 crowd.

Fantasy ★★★

HOST CASINO AND SHOWROOM   **Luxor—Atrium Showroom;** ☎ **702-262-4400 or 800-557-7428; luxor.com**

Type of show Topless dance-and-comedy revue. **Admission cost** $39–$65. **Cast size** 12. **Night of lowest attendance** Tuesday. **Usual showtimes** Nightly, 10:30 p.m. **Dark** None. **Topless** Yes. **Special comments** Must be age 18 or older to attend. **Duration of presentation** 90 minutes.

DESCRIPTION AND COMMENTS   Speculate on the anthropological reasons why the American appetite for female breasts is a cultural staple. *Fantasy,* possibly the Strip's most artistic topless show, satisfies this hunger in a tasteful, glamorous way in this smorgasbord of sexual scenarios. Angelica

Bridges of *Baywatch* fame is the auburn beauty featured among the cast of eight very adept dancers, a male singer, and a comedian who very ably channels Tina Turner, Sammy Davis Jr., and James Brown. Rubber bondage, dominatrix office-politics, and light lesbianism are a few of the erotic offerings, none of which ever reach raunchy, which is perhaps why the audience includes many women. Breasts are indeed revealed early on in the show, but not every number is topless. The office scene, for example, is performed chiefly in men's business suits. The Vegas feeling of high production values with sets, lights, smoke, and bass-filled sound is certainly there to support the well-executed Bob Fosse–style choreography. While the sexually suggestive theme runs strongly throughout, most of the numbers could stand on their own without the topless element.

CONSUMER TIPS Staged in the same fairly intimate house as Carrot Top's show, you can be pulled on stage if you are a man sitting in the first row or two. Row D offers the most leg room.

Frank Caliendo ★★★½

APPEAL BY AGE	UNDER 21 ★★½	21–37 ★★★½	38–50 ★★★½	51+ ★★★

HOST CASINO AND SHOWROOM **Monte Carlo—Monte Carlo Theatre;**
☎ **702-730-7160 or 877-386-8224; montecarlo.com**

Type of show Impressions and stand-up comedy. **Admission** $48.64, $64.54, $72.73, $81.36 plus tax. **Cast size** 5 including 3-piece band and a warm-up comedian. **Night of lowest attendance** Tuesday. **Usual showtimes** Tuesday–Saturday, 7:30 p.m. **Dark** Sunday and Monday. **Topless** No. **Duration of presentation** 90 minutes.

DESCRIPTION AND COMMENTS Made famous by the Fox series *MADtv* and by numerous appearances on the *Tonight Show* and *Late Night with David Letterman*, Frank Caliendo now is known mostly for his appearances on Fox NFL Sunday. You might wonder how a comedian gets a seat behind the desk of a football show (with apologies to Dennis Miller) until you hear him do his spot-on impression of John Madden, the former NFL coach and broadcaster. Although the Madden impression put him on the map, Caliendo does dozens of other impressions, especially nailing George W. Bush, Charles Barkley, Robin Williams, Jay Leno, Bill Clinton, and Jerry Seinfeld. The show loses some steam during the last act but ends on a high note with an improvised montage of his impressions.

CONSUMER TIPS The best way to judge an impressionist is to close your eyes and try to picture the personality being presented. If the voice you are hearing matches the image in your mind, you know the impressionist has done his job well. Caliendo is right on with his impressions but needs to add more recognizable personalities to his repertoire. Some of the best moments are when he interacts with the band. You are introduced to the band as you enter the theater while they play quirky numbers like TV theme songs and ditties from commercials. The band remains on stage to add the occasional background music to bits by the warm-up comedian and the main show. There isn't really a bad seat in the house, though those somewhat distant from the stage will appreciate the large video screen that shows a zoomed-in projection of Caliendo's facial expressions. The theater is located on the left at the front of the casino.

Frank Marino's *Divas Las Vegas* ★★★

APPEAL BY AGE   **UNDER 21** ★★½   **21–37** ★★★½   **38–50** ★★★½   **51+** ★★★

HOST CASINO AND SHOWROOM **Imperial Palace—Main Showroom;**
☎ **702-731-3311 or 888-777-7664; imperialpalace.com**

Type of show Cross-dressing celebrity impersonator show. **Admission** $39, $69, $79 VIP plus tax. **Cast size** 14. **Night of lowest attendance** Monday. **Usual showtimes** Saturday–Thursday, 10 p.m. **Dark** Friday. **Topless** No. **Duration of presentation** 75 minutes.

DESCRIPTION AND COMMENTS Frank Marino, who ages at the same rate as Dick Clark, has been heading boys-will-be-girls shows in Las Vegas for decades. Doing his signature impression of Joan Rivers (who unhappily has aged much more rapidly than he), Marino presides over a high-tempo revue where the guys impersonate such stars as Cher, Diana Ross, Beyonce, Britney Spears, Madonna, and Dolly Parton. A crew of dancers, also men playing dress-up, give the presentation the feel of a quirky production show.

Some of the impersonators are convincing and pretty enough to fool just about anyone. Their costumes reveal slender, feminine arms and legs and hourglass figures. Others, however, look like who they are—men in drag. The cast performs with great self-effacement and gives the impression that nobody is expected to take things too seriously. As one impersonator quipped, "This is a hell of a way for a 40-year-old man to earn a living."

Divas is kinky yet solid entertainment. It is also pretty popular and plays to appreciative heterosexual audiences. If you are curious, broadminded, and looking for something different, give it a try. If the idea of a bunch of guys traipsing around in fishnet stockings and feather boas gives you the willies, opt for something more conventional.

CONSUMER TIPS This is definitely a show where you want to pass on VIP seats—the illusion is much more effective if you are back a little. The Imperial Palace Showroom is a little large for this type of production, but the big stage facilitates a more fully realized presentation. The showroom is at the top of the escalator behind the hotel check-in desk.

Garth Brooks ★★★★½

APPEAL BY AGE   **18–20** ★★★★   **21–37** ★★★★   **38–50** ★★★★½   **51+** ★★★★

HOST CASINO AND SHOWROOM **Wynn Resort—Encore Theater;**
☎ **702-770-7000 or 877-654-2784; wynnlasvegas.com**

Type of show Celebrity headliner. **Admission** $253. **Cast size** 1. **Night of lowest attendance** Friday. **Usual Showtimes** Friday and Saturday, 8 and 10:30 p.m. **Dark** Sunday–Thursday. **Topless** No. **Special comments** Brooks usually appears one weekend a month. **Duration of presentation** 120 minutes or longer.

DESCRIPTION AND COMMENTS Casino impresario Steve Wynn offered Garth Brooks a jetful of legal tender to abandon an eight-year retirement and perform at Wynn Resorts. Promised that this engagement could be anything he wanted, the top-selling country virtuoso chose a playlist primarily of other artists' songs with his own guitar as the only accompaniment. There's no band, props, back-up singers, elaborate lighting, or stage decor: just the talent of a solitary man and his music on an empty stage. Brooks is witty, engaging, and, like much of the audience, comfortably attired in jeans, workboots, and a baseball cap. The theme throughout the show is influences; Brooks pays tribute to the music and the artists who inspired him. From Merle Haggard and George Jones through Otis Redding, Bob Dylan, James Taylor, Bob Seeger, Billy Joel, Randy Travis, Jim Croce, and other performers too numerous to recount, he runs chronologically through more than 20 songs over four decades in each artist's style and voice. The set list changes depending on his mood, and he decides in the moment what he wants to sing. There's also time for his own hits and several impromptu sing-alongs, including the wildly popular "Friends in Low Places." Midway through the show, wife Tricia Yearwood, a star in her own right, joins her husband for marital repartee and two of her top-five singles; this terrific interlude should be a permanent segment. During requests, the audience enthusiastically shouts out more of their favorite tunes, and Brooks happily obliges. Known for his affinity to play all night, after a 100-plus-minute show, he delivers a 30-minute encore. Conversational, versatile, and charismatic, Garth Brooks charms and awes audiences simply by singing alone with an acoustic guitar. Less is the most.

CONSUMER TIPS This open-ended commitment could run as long as five years. Show dates are announced every quarter to coordinate with Brooks's real-life schedule back home in Oklahoma. The show has been sold out since the instant Wynn's coup was announced; however, patient ticket seekers can line up at the resort's theater counter one hour before showtime. By then, uncollected tickets are released for resale. The line is long.

George Wallace ★★★½

APPEAL BY AGE   UNDER 21 ★★★   21–37 ★★★★   38–50 ★★★★   51+ ★★★½

HOST CASINO AND SHOWROOM **Flamingo—Flamingo Showroom;**
☎ **702-733-3333 or 800-221-7299; flamingolasvegas.com**

Type of show Stand-up comedy. **Admission** $50 (balcony), $60 (main floor), $75 (Golden Circle) plus tax and fees. **Cast size** 2. **Night of lowest attendance** Tuesday. **Usual showtimes** Tuesday–Saturday, 10 p.m. **Dark** Sunday and Monday. **Topless** No. **Duration of presentation** 90 minutes.

Description and comments George Wallace is a big man in his 50s with a gruff, acerbic, Redd Foxx–style stage persona. Following a warm-up comic, Wallace grouses and rails through 80 minutes of first-rate stand-up comedy. Unlike Rita Rudner, who presents as sweet and empathetic, Wallace stakes out his turf as the only sensible person in a world of idiots. Working the room with ease, Wallace moves from one topic to the next on a current of sharp one-liners delivered at a furious pace. Slipping in and out of Ebonics ("I be thinkin' "), he lampoons both black and white stereotypes en route to settling down to such favorite subjects as young people and Las Vegas traffic.

CONSUMER TIPS Wallace plays equally well across age and color lines. He keeps things moving and connects with his audience, and his commanding stage presence tells you immediately that you're in the hands of a pro. As the only black stand-up comic playing a major showroom, he delivers edgy, race-related humor and a certain hipness that's largely absent elsewhere. The Flamingo Showroom, with maître d' seating, is not the most efficient.

Gordie Brown ★★★½

APPEAL BY AGE   UNDER 21 ★★★   21–37 ★★★½   38–50 ★★★½   51+ ★★★½

HOST CASINO AND SHOWROOM **Golden Nugget—The Showroom;**
☎ **702-386-8100; goldennugget.com**

Type of show Impressions with music and comedy. Admission $25, $30, $50, and $65. Cast size 8. Night of lowest attendance Wednesday. Usual showtimes Tuesday–Saturday, 7:30 p.m. Dark Sunday and Monday. Topless No. Duration of presentation 90 minutes.

DESCRIPTION AND COMMENTS Impressionists are almost as ubiquitous as show-girls in Las Vegas, so we weren't expecting anything special from Gordie Brown. *Wrong!* His is the sleeper show of Las Vegas. Brown sets the house on fire with his impressions, musicianship, and humor. Backed by a turbo-energized live band consisting of lead guitar, bass, two keyboard players, two drummers, and sax, Brown moves along at a gallop impersonating such artists as Travis Tritt, Roy Orbison, Willie Nelson, Paul Simon, Billy Joel, Henry Fonda, MC Hammer, and Frank Sinatra. Aside from nailing the voices and mannerisms of his celebrity subjects, Brown has an uncanny chameleon-like ability to change his countenance to actually look like them. Brown is at his best when he's moving quickly. Unfortunately, he has a pronounced tendency, particularly with his comedy, to drive a rou-tine into the ground. As you would expect, trying to ride a horse that's been dead for ten minutes isn't good for a show's momentum. Sooner or later though, Brown will plug the holes in his act.

CONSUMER TIPS Gordie Brown earned his stripes at the Golden Nugget and after gigs at the V Theater and the Venetian has come back. The Golden Nugget Showroom can be accessed via escalators located on the casino level just off the long pedestrian promenade that leads to the hotel lobby.

Human Nature ★★★★

APPEAL BY AGE   UNDER 21 ★★★½   21–37 ★★★★   38–50 ★★★★   51+ ★★★★

HOST CASINO AND SHOWROOM **Imperial Palace—Imperial Palace Showroom;**
☎ **702-731-3311; imperialpalace.com**

Type of show Motown musical tribute. Admission $50–$60 plus tax. Cast size 10 including the band. Night of lowest attendance Monday. Usual showtimes Saturday–Wednesday, 7:30 p.m. Dark Thursday and Friday. Topless No. Dura-tion of presentation 80 minutes.

Description and comments *Human Nature* is an Australian vocal group, produced by legendary Motown vocalist Smokey Robinson. Hugely popular down under, the group has racked up a number of multi-platinum albums and charted 17 Top-40 hits and 5 Top-10 singles in wallaby land. Their first American album was released in 2009. Featuring the harmonies of Toby Allen, Phil Burton, Andrew Tierney, and Michael Tierney, *Human Nature* presents a high-energy musical field trip down Motown's Memory Lane. They nail the Motown sound as well as the smooth moves (their showmanship was honed opening for Celine Dion and Michael Jackson, respectively), a singular accomplishment for four white guys from Australia. They are backed by a live band.

CONSUMER TIPS The IP Showroom, longtime home of the celebrity impersonator show, *Legends in Concert,* underwent an extreme makeover in 2009, including the installation of a cutting-edge sound system. To access the showroom, take the escalator to the right of the hotel registration desk.

JABBAWOCKEEZ *MÜS.I.C* ★★★★

APPEAL BY AGE   UNDER 21 ★★★★   21–37 ★★★★   38–50 ★★★½   51+ ★★½

HOST CASINO AND SHOWROOM **Monte Carlo—Monte Carlo Theatre;**
☎ **702-873-7160 or 877-386-8224; montecarlo.com**

Type of show Ultra-hip-hop dance production. **Admission** $59–$92 plus tax. **Cast size** 12. **Night of lowest attendance** Thursday. **Usual showtimes** Nightly, 7:30 p.m. with 9:30 p.m. show Thursday–Saturday. **Dark** None. **Topless** No. **Duration of presentation** 75 minutes.

Description and comments JABBAWOCKEEZ is an all-male modern-dance troupe disguised, or more correctly, rendered indistinguishable by white masks and loose-fitting clothes. The frenetic production features some of the best break and robotic dancing around. Sprinkle in some mime, humor, and a pulsing hip-hop score and you have one of the freshest and most energetic shows to hit Las Vegas in a long time.

The crew was introduced to a national audience on *America's Got Talent* and later won Season 1 of *America's Best Dance Crew.* The white masks create an overall homogeneous appearance, more or less forcing you to zero in on the choreography as a whole as opposed to being seduced by the looks and talents of any individual performer. The troupe's name is derived from the nonsense-verse poem "Jabberwocky" by Lewis Carroll. Interestingly, as per the JABBAWOCKEEZ name, if you don't understand the show, then by George, you've got it! That's the idea, as expressed by the Lewis Carroll character Alice (from *Through the Looking Glass*) after reading "Jabberwocky."

"'It seems very pretty,' she said when she had finished it, 'but it's rather hard to understand!' (You see she didn't like to confess, even to herself, that she couldn't make it out at all.) 'Somehow it seems to fill my head with ideas—only I don't exactly know what they are!'"

Bottom line, don't burn out your circuits trying to make sense of JABBAWOCKEEZ, just enjoy.

CONSUMER TIPS Anyone who enjoys modern dance will like JABBAWOCK-EEZ. Beyond that, however, appreciation divides along chronological lines, with those under 40 wildly enthusiastic and those older than 40 pretty much mystified. The Monte Carlo Theatre is located near the Strip entrance to the casino and is a perfect match for JABBAWOCK-EEZ with excellent acoustics and unimpeded sight lines. The box office is next to the showroom.

Jersey Boys ★★★½

APPEAL BY AGE UNDER 21 ★★★★ 21–37 ★★★★½ 38–50 ★★★★½ 51+ ★★★★★

HOST CASINO AND SHOWROOM **Palazzo—Jersey Boys Theater;**
☎ **702-414-9000 or 866-641-7469; jerseyboysinfo.com**

Type of show Broadway musical. **Admission** $72–$259. **Cast size** 20. **Night of lowest attendance** Monday. **Usual showtimes** Monday, Tuesday, Thursday, and Friday, 7 p.m.; Saturday, 6:30 and 9:30 p.m.; Sunday, 3 and 7 p.m. **Dark** Wednesday. **Topless** No. **Duration of presentation** 2 hours and 10 minutes (including a 10-minute intermission).

DESCRIPTION AND COMMENTS The Palazzo is the permanent home for the Las Vegas production of *Jersey Boys,* Tony Award winner of Best Musical in 2006. In addition to the Las Vegas show, *Jersey Boys* also plays on Broadway and in London, Melbourne, and Chicago.

Jersey Boys is the story of four blue-collar kids from Newark trying to escape the mean streets through their music. More in context, it's the compelling tale of Frankie Valli and the Four Seasons. If ever a musical group had an interesting history, it's this one: crazy managers, the mob, jail time, band and marriage make-ups and breakups—it's all there. And the music, well, as one audience member put it, "I can't believe one group had all those hits!" From the breakout "Sherry," through "Walk Like a Man," "Dawn," "Big Girls Don't Cry," "Let's Hang On," to "Oh What a Night," there are 30 songs and chances are you'll remember almost all of them. The arrangements and choreography are incredibly tight. The cast is so perfect that you can't imagine how they found enough talent to field five city-based productions plus a traveling road show. Likewise, the staging is some of the best we've seen in an entertainment scene that's known worldwide for pulling out all the stops.

CONSUMER TIPS *Jersey Boys* satisfies all age groups. If you weren't familiar with the music when you went in, you'll be a fan when you come out. The custom-built theater is huge, but the sight lines are all good. You'll be able to see fine if you go for the cheaper mezzanine seats. A short ten-minute intermission is strictly enforced, so don't dally in the restroom or buying drinks at the cash bar.

Jubilee! ★★★★

APPEAL BY AGE UNDER 21 – 21–37 ★★★ 38–50 ★★★½ 51+ ★★★★

HOST CASINO AND SHOWROOM **Bally's—Jubilee! Theater;** ☎ **702-967-4567 or 800-237-SHOW; ballyslasvegas.com**

Type of show Grand-scale musical and variety production show. **Admission** $57.50–$117.50. **Cast size** 100. **Nights of lowest attendance** Sunday, Thursday. **Usual showtimes** Saturday–Thursday, 7:30 and 10:30 p.m. **Dark** Friday. **Topless** Yes. **Duration of presentation** 90 minutes.

DESCRIPTION AND COMMENTS *Jubilee!* is the quintessential, traditional Las Vegas production show, and with the closing of *Folies Bergere* in 2009, the last of its genre. Faithfully following a successful decades-old formula, *Jubilee!* has elaborate musical production numbers, extravagant sets, beautiful topless showgirls, and quality variety acts.

   With a cast of 100, an enormous stage, and some of the most colossal and extraordinary sets found in theater anywhere, *Jubilee!* is much larger than life. Running one hour and 30 minutes each performance, the show is lavish, sexy, and well performed but redundant to the point of numbness.

   Two multiscene production extravaganzas top the list of *Jubilee!* highlights. The first is the sultry saga of Samson and Delilah, climaxing with Samson's destruction of the temple. Not exactly biblical, but certainly awe-inspiring. The second super-drama is the story of the *Titanic,* from launch to sinking. Once again, sets and special effects on a grand scale combine with nicely integrated music and choreography to provide an incredible spectacle.

   Jubilee!'s opening act kicks things off in a big way. Based on a popular song by Jerry Herman, "Hundreds of Girls," it showcases 75 singers, dancers, and showgirls multiplied by gargantuan mirrors. The opening is said to have cost $3 million to produce. The above-average specialty acts include an illusionist executing big-stage tricks, a juggler-acrobat couple whose main prop is a giant aluminum cube, and a strongman who performs mostly upside-down. The production concludes with "The Jubilee Walk," a parade of elaborately costumed showgirls patterned after the grand finale of the *Ziegfeld Follies.*

CONSUMER TIPS The 1,035-seat Jubilee Theater, with its high, wide stage and multitiered auditorium, is one of the best-designed showrooms in town. It underwent a complete $2.5-million renovation in the late 1990s. It now consists of seating at banquet tables at the foot of the stage (too close and cramped); a row of booths above the tables (more expensive but worth it); and 789 theater-style seats. The table and booth seats come with cocktail service; the theater-seat audience has to carry in their own drinks.

   Jubilee! is restricted to persons 18 years or older except for the 7:30 p.m. Saturday show, which is not topless. Ages 13 and older are welcome for this performance.

   Jubilee! offers a backstage tour on Monday, Wednesday, and Saturday at 11 a.m. at a cost of $17 per person ($12 with a ticket). A *Jubilee!* dancer serves as tour guide and demonstrates how costumes, make-up, lighting, and elaborate sets combine to produce one of Las Vegas's most historic stage spectaculars. Although the tour is not physically challenging, you must climb stairs. Call ☎ 702-946-4567 for additional information.

Le Rêve ★★★★

HOST CASINO AND SHOWROOM **Wynn Las Vegas—Wynn Theater;**
☎ **702-770-9966 or 888-320-7110; wynnlasvegas.com/le-reve**

Type of show Aquatic theater in the round. **Admission** $99–$195. **Cast size** 85.
Nights of lowest attendance Sunday and Monday. **Usual showtimes** Friday–
Tuesday, 7 and 9:30 p.m. **Dark** Wednesday and Thursday. **Topless** No. **Special
comments** No seat is more than 42 feet from the stage. **Duration of presentation** 90 minutes.

DESCRIPTION AND COMMENTS Imagine a wet concoction of someone else's
dreams. The anchoring image is a nocturnal voyager in a red dress who
explores from her own bed of dreams. Her journey recalls images from
the swirling dark psychology of the fantastical movie *Brazil;* Busby
Berkeley's dance routines; swamp things with long tails; the rescuing
flights from *Angels in America;* "Baby Elephant Walk" from *Daktari;*
dancing flowers from *Fantasia;* the deft touch of Gene Kelly's *Singin' in
the Rain,* with a setting undercurrent of *Mad Max: Beyond Thunderdome.*
All this is a taste of the theatrical pastiche of Franco Dragone's specialty
production *Le Rêve* at Wynn Las Vegas.

  The collaboration of hands-on Steve Wynn and Belgian Dragone,
who logged ten years with Cirque du Soleil, including designing their
watery world of *"O,"* was highly anticipated. *Le Rêve* (French for "the
dream") requires a specially constructed amphitheater seating 2,100
where no seat is more than 42 feet from the action (audience members
in the front rows are given water-protective clothing). Performed in
the round, the cast of more than 70 internationally assembled gym-
nasts, acrobats, synchronized swimmers, and dancers execute their
impressive routines within an expansive, mysterious tank of water.
Mechanical lifts hoist various configurations of the stage out of the
seemingly bottomless reservoir. The set is heightened by fire, smoke,
and dripping skin. At times the performers are atop a rising column,
and at other times they appear to walk on water with the "beach" platform, as they call it, just below the water's surface. Sometimes they are
hoisted straight up into the dome's opening. Sometimes they swing on
trapezes or they dangle in suspended contortions like a Michelangelo
version of hell. Yet none of these descriptions can do justice to the
physical display that arises everywhere before your eyes.

  Roman in its level of spectacle and operatic in its reach, *Le Rêve* is
indeed long on sensuality and short on narrative. Perhaps its only
defense of weak, illogical storytelling is its very title, for who can make
true sense of another's dream? Another criticism is that the water and
Cirque-style elements have been seen before and done better in *"O."* As
with the comparable Cirque du Soleil shows, the concepts and especially the physical feats invite a thinking person to reconsider the
possibilities of what it is to be human. While some may have a definite
preference for *"O,"* *Le Rêve* is an inspiring treat for the eye and ear.

CONSUMER TIPS Parking in Wynn's self-parking garage is more convenient than using valet parking, if you drive. In our opinion, the first 15 rows are too close and too low to take in the whole of this expansive production that makes use of the entire theater.

Legends in Concert ★★★½

APPEAL BY AGE   UNDER 21 ★★★   21–37 ★★★½   38–50 ★★★★   51+ ★★★★

HOST CASINO AND SHOWROOM **Harrah's; ☎ 702-369-5111 or 888-777-7664; harrahslasvegas.com**

Type of show Celebrity-impersonator and musical-production show. **Admission** $55.45, $65.45 plus tax. **Cast size** Approximately 20. **Night of lowest attendance** Tuesday. **Usual showtimes** For a current list of showtimes, visit Harrah's website listed above. **Topless** No. **Duration of presentation** 90 minutes.

DESCRIPTION AND COMMENTS *Legends in Concert* is a musical-production show featuring a highly talented cast of impersonators who re-create the stage performances of such celebrities as Elvis, Cher, Jay Leno, Michael Jackson, and Aretha Franklin. Impersonators actually sing and/or play their own instruments, so there's no lip-synching or faking. In addition to the impersonators, *Legends* features an unusually hot and creative company of dancers, much in the style of TV's *Solid Gold* dancers of old. There are no variety acts.

The impersonations are extremely effective, replicating the physical appearances, costumes, mannerisms, and voices of the celebrities with remarkable likeness. While each show features the work of about eight stars, with a roster that ensures something for patrons of every age, certain celebrities (most notably Elvis) are always included. Regardless of the stars impersonated, *Legends in Concert* is fun, happy, and upbeat. It's a show that establishes rapport with the audience.

CONSUMER TIPS In addition to the Las Vegas production, *Legends in Concert* also fields a road show. The second show makes possible a continuing exchange of performers between the productions, so that the shows are always changing.

The Lion King ★★★★½

APPEAL BY AGE   UNDER 21 ★★★★½   21–37 ★★★★½   38–50 ★★★★★   51+ ★★★★½

HOST CASINO AND SHOWROOM **Mandalay Bay–Mandalay Bay Theatre; ☎ 702-632-7580; mandalaybay.com or lionkinglasvegas.com**

Type of show Broadway musical based on the Disney animated feature film. **Admission** $64, $86, $113.50, and $168.50 plus tax. **Cast size** 79. **Night of lowest attendance** Tuesday. **Usual showtimes** Monday–Thursday, 7:30 p.m.; Saturday and Sunday, 4 and 8 p.m. **Dark** Friday. **Topless** No. **Duration of presentation** 2 hours and 45 minutes plus 20-minute intermission.

DESCRIPTION AND COMMENTS Despite the spotty success record of Broadway productions transplanted to Las Vegas, *The Lion King* seems poised to beat the odds. Combining Disney Imagineering with Vegas spectacle in a custom-designed theater creates a very special show indeed.

Anyone with children and most of those without are familiar with the story from the 1994 Disney animated feature film. An infant son, Simba, is born to the philosophical lion king Mufasa, who presents his heir to the assembled animals of the Pridelands. Scar, Simba's uncle, seeks to attain the lion-king throne and plots against his brother Mufasa as well as against Simba and his lioness sweetheart, Nala. Other characters who play key roles in the epic are Simba's friends Timon (a meercat) and Pumbaa (a warthog), the hornbill Zazu whom Mufasa calls on to ride herd on the mischievous youngsters, and Rafiki, an aged baboon who serves as medicine man and sage to the animals of the lion kingdom.

Unlike most Broadway imports, which are truncated to 90 minutes so as not to test the attention span and bladder capacity of Las Vegas audiences, *The Lion King* arrives full blown at 2 hours and 45 minutes with a 20-minute intermission. Its scale is impressive, being comparable to that of the largest Cirque du Soleil productions. Like the Cirque du Soleil shows, *The Lion King* is distinguished by its phenomenal costuming, its inventive and beautiful staging, its kinetic energy, and its abundantly colorful pageantry. The choreography incorporates the motions and rhythms of the animals portrayed, while the main characters come to life in the form of exquisitely manipulated puppets.

And then there's the music, songs that stay with you for a long time, many written by Elton John and augmented with African harmonies and rhythms. A 22-piece orchestra in the pit is aided by hand percussionists flanking the stage with congas and kotos. Like the film, the stage production moves at a crisp pace. The story line, leavened by humor, tugs persistently at your emotions before reaching its triumphant conclusion. In the end, you'll be surprised by how powerfully *The Lion King* affects you.

CONSUMER TIPS Because of the scale of *The Lion King* and its use of the entire theater, you don't want to sit too close to the stage. Self-parking at Mandalay Bay is relatively convenient to the showroom. From the rear entrance to the casino, bear left past several restaurants and then continue left, passing the sports book en route. Although there are restrooms just outside the theater and a bar in the theater lobby, you'll save time, especially during intermission, by using the restroom and bar facilities in the main casino. Hold onto your ticket stub—you'll need it to get back into the theater. Finally, if you happen to visit New York, see *The Lion King* on Broadway—tickets are less expensive there.

Matt Goss Live ★★

APPEAL BY AGE	UNDER 21 ★★½	21–37 ★★	38–50 ★★½	51+ ★★½

HOST CASINO AND SHOWROOM **Caesars Palace—Cleopatra's Barge**
☎ **702-731-7110 or 800-745-3000; caesarspalace.com**

Type of show New-fashioned lounge show. **Admission** $40 plus tax. **Cast size** 13. **Usual showtimes** Friday and Saturday, 9:30 p.m. **Dark** Sunday–Thursday. **Topless** No. **Special comments** Must be 21 or older to attend. **Duration of presentation** 90 minutes.

DESCRIPTION AND COMMENTS A 1980s UK pop star, hunky Brit Matt Goss is an excellent singer who covers rock, standards, R&B, and his own compositions in this ten-tune, high-energy show. Not quite a Sinatra clone but mirroring his style, Goss sings just two from Ol' Blue Eyes' repertoire but in homage strives to re-create the spirit of a cozy retro-Vegas lounge. He channels Sinatra's appearance too: a slim, blue-eyed guy in tux and fedora. Wedged into a corner of glossy Cleopatra's Barge, Goss is cool and self-possessed while surrounded by the frenzied activity of six musicians, two back-up singers, and four so-so go-go dancers crowding the miniscule stage. Distracting rear-screen projection loops Rat Pack and James Bond clips, scenes from *Rebel without a Cause,* Marilyn Monroe, vintage Vegas footage, flowers, and kaleidoscope patterns. There is too much going on to focus on the deserving Goss and his music, and the show is cluttered by the black-sequined dancers who are pushed to boogie among the stage-side front tables. The four dancers are two too many and not enough eye candy for what they contribute, but the show's producer is *Pussycat Dolls* creator Robin Antin, so these ladies are a permanent addition. The backup band is blazing hot with smokin' arrangements, but the show lacks the spontaneity of the old days. It's fun, but nowhere near what the Vegas lounge shows were like in the day. But of course, it's not supposed to be.

CONSUMER TIPS The classic 1970s-era Cleopatra's Barge bar has been refurbished to accommodate this show. Old-timers will remember when lounge shows were free. This one is pricy at $40-plus without drinks, but younger audiences probably won't mind. If you're not familiar with Caesars Palace, you'll probably need to ask directions to the barge.

Menopause: The Musical ★★★★

APPEAL BY AGE   UNDER 21 ★★   21–37 ★★★   38–50 ★★★★★   51+ ★★★★★

HOST CASINO AND SHOWROOM **Luxor—Atrium Showroom; ☎ 702-262-4000 or 800-557-7428; luxor.com or menopausethemusical.com**

Type of show Off-Broadway musical comedy. **Admission** $50, $65. **Cast size** 4. **Night of lowest attendance** Wednesday. **Usual showtimes** Wednesday– Monday, 5:30 p.m.; Tuesday, 8 p.m. **Dark** None. **Topless** No. **Duration of presentation** 90 minutes.

DESCRIPTION AND COMMENTS This cabaret-style jewel was first launched in a 76-seat theater in Orlando in 2001. Only five years later it is a rollicking frolic, packing in people in 15 major American cities, plus in Canada, Italy, Korea, and Australia. Yes, it really is about "the change," and, yes, about 10% of the audience were unabashed men who were also having an uproariously good time. But hands down and hot flashes up, this is a show for anyone approaching, in, or past menopause.

Many of the heads in the audience are silver, but the punch of estrogen is still palpable upon entering the theater. There was a preponderance of red and purple clothing in the house, perhaps because members of the Red Hat Society, the Red Hot Mamas, Heart Truth, and Minnie Pauz frequently attend the show in groups. Creator Jeanie Linders summed up the crux of the production: "Four women meet at a Bloomingdale's lingerie sale with nothing in common but a black lace bra, hot flashes, night sweats, memory loss, chocolate binges, not enough sex, too much sex, and more." The soap star, the earth mama, the power woman, and the Iowa housewife are each skillfully drawn and wonderfully executed. It would be hard to imagine how to improve upon the show we saw—the cast was perfect in physical style, comedic timing, and song-and-dance delivery.

The 90-minute production moves along by lyrically parodying 24 wonderful songs of the past, especially of the 1960s. For example, Aretha Franklin's "Chain of Fools" becomes "Change, Change, Change"; Irving Berlin's "Heat Wave" becomes "Tropical Hot Flash"; and "Looking for Love in All the Wrong Places" becomes "Looking for Food . . . ," with a chorus that begins "Now I'm packin' on pounds where I don't have spaces, / Looking for food in too many places . . . ." You get the idea.

You must be 14 years of age to attend, for some of the content is deemed "mature." It's basically a clean, if anatomically forthright show, but if the idea of mechanical "Good Vibrations" paired with "What's Love Got to Do with It?" bothers you, maybe it's time to hit the nickel slots again instead. That would be something of a shame, however, because *Menopause: The Musical* is clever, tons of fun, and very self-affirming. The synergy cycling in the room between the cast and the audience is a jubilant intoxicant that you shouldn't miss imbibing.

Finally for men, this show is a total hoot, especially if you've been married or close to a menopausal woman.

CONSUMER TIPS Alcohol is not served in the theater. The theater is tiered, and seats (all with good sight lines) are preassigned.

Peepshow ★★★★

APPEAL BY AGE UNDER 21 ★★★½ 21–37 ★★★★ 38–50 ★★★★ 51+ ★★★★

HOST CASINO AND SHOWROOM **Planet Hollywood—Chi Showroom;**
☎ **702-785-5555; lasvegaspeepshow.com**

Type of show Large-scale topless production show. Admission $65, $75, $100, and $125 plus tax. Cast size 23 plus live band. Night of lowest attendance Monday. Usual showtimes Sunday–Tuesday, Thursday, and Friday, 9 p.m.; Saturday, 8 and 10:30 p.m. Dark Wednesday. Topless Yes. Special comments Must be 18 or older to attend. Duration of presentation 85 minutes.

DESCRIPTION AND COMMENTS *Peepshow* is a topless revue, but much more. In terms of scale it doesn't approach the Ziegfeld grand spectacle of *Jubilee!* but nonetheless represents a quantum leap up from topless productions like *Crazy Girls, Fantasy,* and *Crazy Horse Paris* that play medium and small showrooms. Replacing *Stomp,* the all-percussion tour de force, *Peepshow* inherited one of the most comfortable and modern showrooms in the city, allowing the show to expand way beyond the norm for its genre. The production was created by Jerry Mitchell, Tony Award–winning director and choreographer, who sought to combine star headliners with a gifted dance troupe in an allegorical story of women taking charge of their lives, their sexuality, and yes, their men.

Peepshow features Holly Madison from *The Girls Next Door* television show. Madison plays Bo Peep, an innocent young woman trying to get in touch with her sexuality. Peep Diva, a mistress of ceremonies with a big attitude, guides Bo Peep in her transformation into a confident, sensual woman. Madison is backed by three female and two male vocalists, 14 lithe and athletic dancers, a couple of stud muffins, and an all-girl band.

The selection of music works well but is all over the map, with the Commodores' "She's a Brick House," Aerosmith's "Pink (Is the Color of Passion)," Dionne Warwick's "You'll Never Get to Heaven," Nina Simone's "It's a New Day," Connie Francis's "Teddy," Madonna's "Hung Up," and Kelis' rap hit "Milkshake."

Peepshow is major eye candy for men, a sugar coating that does little to disguise the theme of sexual empowerment for women. Peep Diva coaches Bo Peep through a series of vignettes based on children's stories such as *The Three Little Pigs,* but with naughty, playful twists. In the best tradition of burlesque, *Peepshow* relies on teasing more than nudity. Yes, it's topless, but for some reason the dancers wear pasties during most numbers, something abhorred by men, and bruising and abrasive to the breasts of performers who wear them. Staging is wild and steamy, making use of a giant pumpkin, a milk-filled aquarium, a VW, and stripper poles, among other devices.

CONSUMER TIPS *Peepshow* is expensive if you regard it as just another T&A show, but if you give it its props as a major showroom production, admission costs are in line with presentations of equal scope and scale. The more-power-to-women theme makes *Peepshow* attractive to women and compatible to couples. The night we reviewed *Peepshow,* we were astonished by the number of women in the audience, including more than a few bachelorette parties.

The Chi Showroom is located on the mezzanine level just up the escalator from the north end of the casino. Showroom management was dismal during our visit, with ticket sales and will call painfully slow and understaffed. Like problems were experienced at the drink concessions. All of this bungling resulted in the performance starting 20 minutes late.

Penn & Teller ★★★½

APPEAL BY AGE   UNDER 21 ★★★½   21–37 ★★★½   38–50 ★★★★   51+ ★★★★

HOST CASINO AND SHOWROOM **Rio—Penn & Teller Theater; ☎ 702-777-7776 or 888-746-7784; riolasvegas.com or pennandteller.com**

Type of show Magic and comedy. **Admission** $75, $85, $95. **Cast size** 4. **Night of lowest attendance** Wednesday. **Usual showtimes** Saturday–Wednesday, 9 p.m. **Dark** Thursday and Friday. **Topless** No. **Special comments** Sometimes they reveal secrets to their tricks. **Duration of presentation** 90 minutes.

DESCRIPTION AND COMMENTS OK, for starters, Penn is the big, loud one and Teller is the cute, passive little guy. They've been together for more than 30 years. The show is great fun, but long on talk (Penn's endless digressions tend to numb after five minutes or so), and short on magic. Well, not short actually. It's just that the setup for every illusion takes so much time that only a handful of tricks will fit in the allocated 90 minutes. But that's part of the show and provides the backdrop for Penn & Teller's playful tension and hallmark onstage chemistry. The illusions vary from the simple to the elaborate, with Penn & Teller sometimes sharing magician secrets of the trade along the way. Though most of the stuff, including Penn's occasionally blue monologues and the majority of the magic, is old hat to Penn & Teller followers, it works fine for the uninitiated. Plus, the duo always offer an illusion or two that you won't see in any of the other magic shows around town.

CONSUMER TIPS   Strictly speaking, this show is about two parts comedy to one part magic. If you're hot primarily for magic, you'll be happier at one of the other magic productions in town. Penn & Teller don't perform any illusions on the order of Siegfried and Roy of old or Steve Wyrick, so sitting up front is fine. Be aware that Penn & Teller are the whole show. There are no showgirls, singing, dancing, or warm-up acts: just the big guy and the little guy.

Phantom: The Las Vegas Spectacular   ★★★★

APPEAL BY AGE   UNDER 21 ★★★★   21–37 ★★★★   38–50 ★★★★   51+ ★★★★

HOST CASINO AND SHOWROOM   **Venetian—*Phantom* Theatre;**
☎ **702-414-9000; venetian.com or phantomlasvegas.com**

Type of show Adapted Broadway musical. **Admission cost** $79–$175 plus tax. **Night of lowest attendance** Thursday. **Usual showtimes** Tuesday–Friday, 7 p.m.; Monday and Saturday, 7 and 9:30 p.m. **Dark** Sunday. **Topless** No. **Duration of presentation** 95 minutes.

DESCRIPTION AND COMMENTS   The longest-running show in Broadway history has finally descended upon Las Vegas, but with a face-lift. The show has been shortened to a mere 95 minutes, but *Phantom* fans need not be too alarmed. Andrew Lloyd Webber and Hal Prince have personally revamped the show, and all of Webber's songs are sung and the story line remains the same. The Venetian built a custom theater to house the show, and enhanced illusions, expanded set designs, and more spectacular effects differentiate the Las Vegas version from its Broadway cousin.

   Phantom: The Las Vegas Spectacular is based on the novel *Le Fantôme de l'Opéra* by Gaston Leroux. The Paris Opera House is haunted not by a ghost, but by a masked man residing beneath the catacombs of the opera house. While spreading havoc and terror over all those associated with the opera house, the Phantom falls madly in love with the soprano singer Christine and vows to transform her into a star.

CONSUMER TIPS   If you drive, give yourself lots of extra time to park and make it to the showroom.

The Rat Pack Is Back   ★★★½

APPEAL BY AGE   UNDER 21 –   21–37 ★★★   38–50 ★★★½   51+ ★★★½

HOST CASINO AND SHOWROOM   **Plaza—Copa Room;** ☎ **702-386-2444 or 800-634-6575; ratpackisback.com**

Type of show Celebrity impersonation. **Admission** $59, show only; $73, dinner show; $76, VIP show only; $90, VIP dinner show. **Cast size** 17, including 12-piece band. **Night of lowest attendance** Wednesday. **Usual showtimes** Nightly, 7:30 p.m. **Dark** None. **Topless** No. **Duration of presentation** 75 minutes.

DESCRIPTION AND COMMENTS The heart and soul of the original Rat Pack were crooners Frank Sinatra, Dean Martin, and Sammy Davis Jr., and comedian Joey Bishop. They all worked the Las Vegas showrooms of the 1960s, sometimes dropping in on each other's shows and sometimes working together. Their late-night antics at the old Sands, particularly, are among the richest of Las Vegas showroom legends.

The Rat Pack Is Back re-creates a night when the acerbic Bishop and hard-drinking Martin team up with Davis and Sinatra. Backed by piano, bass, drums, along with, get this, a nine-piece horn section, four talented impersonators take you back to a night at the Sands Copa Room in 1963. The impressionists are excellent: each impersonator captures his character's voice, singing style, and body language. The performers playing Bishop and Davis bear strong physical resemblances to the originals, and the Sinatra impressionist more or less squeaks by, but the Martin character looks more like an Elvis impersonator.

The casual interplay among the four effectively transports you back to the 1960s, and what you see is pretty much how it was. The humor was racist, sexist, and politically incorrect, the showroom packed and smoky, and the music, well . . . drop-dead brilliant.

The Rat Pack Is Back producers had a falling out in 2009 that resulted in Sandy Hackett pulling up stakes and opening a nearly identical show most recently at the Riviera called *Sandy Hackett's Rat Pack Show.* Though the split diluted the talent pool somewhat, both versions are well done. See the one most convenient to where you're staying. Both productions cost roughly the same. In fact, the productions are so similar we have elected not to profile Sandy Hackett's show, but it is rated in our Hit Parade on pages 214–215.

CONSUMER TIPS There are usually discount coupons for *The Rat Pack Is Back* in the local tourists mags.

Rita Rudner   ★★★½

APPEAL BY AGE   UNDER 21 ★★   21–37 ★★★★   38–50 ★★★★   51+ ★★★★

HOST CASINO AND SHOWROOM **Venetian—Main Showroom; ☎ 702-414-9000 or 866-641-7469; venetian.com**

Type of show Stand-up comedy. **Admission** $49, $69 VIP plus tax. **Cast size** 1. **Night of lowest attendance** Wednesday. **Usual showtimes** Monday and Wednesday, 8:30 p.m.; Saturday, 6 p.m. **Dark** Sunday, Tuesday, Thursday, and Friday. **Topless** No. **Duration of presentation** 90 minutes.

DESCRIPTION AND COMMENTS Rita Rudner walks onto the stage and holds forth for almost 90 minutes. No band, no singers or dancers, just Rita. And even if you've never heard of Rita Rudner, those 90 minutes will seem like 10. Her topics—male–female relationships, shopping, Las Vegas—are worn, but her perspective is fresh and her humor is sharp, very sharp. Like a good elementary-school teacher, she monitors her room, stopping to connect personally with a look, a smile, or even a question. In the end, we're all Miss Rudner's students and we find ourselves trying to file away some of her stories and zippy one-liners to repeat later to friends.

CONSUMER TIPS Rita Rudner has to be the cleanest stand-up comic working in Las Vegas. You forget that it's possible to be uproarious in PG mode.

Steve Wyrick: Ultra Magician ★★★½

APPEAL BY AGE UNDER 21 ★★★★ 21–37 ★★★½ 38–50 ★★★½ 51+ ★★★½

HOST CASINO AND SHOWROOM **Las Vegas Hilton—Las Vegas Hilton Theater;**
☎ **888-732-7117; lvhilton.com**

Type of show Magic and illusion production show. **Admission** $40–$125 plus tax and service charges. **Cast size** 1. **Nights of lowest attendance** Monday and Tuesday. **Usual showtimes** Nightly, 7:30 p.m. **Special comments** No drinks included. **Topless** No. **Duration of presentation** 90 minutes.

DESCRIPTION AND COMMENTS *Steve Wyrick: Ultra Magician* is the Las Vegas show scene's version of "We try harder." With four or five magic-themed production shows playing in town at any given time, it takes a fair amount of creativity to be different. Steve Wyrick digs deep and delivers some great illusion and sleight of hand that you won't see in other showrooms. While his style and presentation, particularly his ability to connect with his audience, are reminiscent of David Copperfield, each illusion has a special twist that makes it unique. The Las Vegas Hilton Theater is a big showroom, perfect for Wyrick's big prop illusions and Siegfried and Roy–style eye-poppers. If you go for the magic, you won't be disappointed. Expect lots of flash and thunder—pyrotechnics, roaring engines, and a pounding soundtrack.

CONSUMER TIPS The Las Vegas Hilton Theater seats 1,700 with no seat more than 87 feet from the stage. The Hilton can be accessed by monorail but is otherwise not convenient to guests of Strip hotels. If you drive, the easiest and closest parking is to the rear of the Hilton off Joe W. Brown Drive. The Hilton box office is located on the right side of the hotel registration desk. The Wyrick box office is usually staffed by only one or two persons, so give yourself a little extra time to purchase or pick up tickets.

Terry Fator ★★★★

APPEAL BY AGE UNDER 21 ★★★★ 21–37 ★★★★ 38–50 ★★★★ 51+ ★★★★

HOST CASINO AND SHOWROOM **Mirage—Terry Fator Showroom;**
☎ **702-792-7777; mirage.com and terryfator.com**

Type of show Voice-impersonation ventriloquism. **Admission** $59, $79, $99, and $129 plus tax. **Cast size** 2 plus live band. **Night of lowest attendance** Wednesday. **Usual showtimes** Tuesday–Saturday, 7:30 p.m. **Dark** Sunday and Monday. **Topless** No. **Duration of presentation** 90 minutes.

DESCRIPTION AND COMMENTS As stated on Fator's website, it took him "32 years to become an overnight sensation." The catalyst was taking first place (and a million bucks) in the *America's Got Talent* television show. Though the talent-show win was long in coming, Fator's arrival in one of Las Vegas's most prestigious showrooms was near meteoric.

Terry Fator brings so many talents to the Mirage that his show is tough to categorize. He's a superb and versatile vocalist, a consummate comedian, a world-class ventriloquist, and an imaginative puppeteer. Fator can mimic virtually any voice, male or female, and during his ventriloquism routines, pulls it off with his mouth closed. His quirky puppet costars are what you might have expected from Jim Hensen had he designed puppets for adults. Topping the list is Winston, the Impersonating Turtle, inspired by Hensen's Kermit the Frog. Winston sings a duet of "Wonderful World" with Satchmo—one of the most magical moments in the show. Other puppet characters include Walter T. Airedale, a country singer; lovable and sassy Emma Taylor; Maynard Thomkins, an Elvis impersonator who doesn't know any Elvis songs; Julius, an African American soul singer who nails Marvin Gaye; Johnny Vegas, a lounge singer who impersonates the likes of Dean Martin and Tony Bennett; and Dougie Scott Walker, a hippy dippy heavy-metal dude who cranks on AC/DC and Guns n' Roses among others. The latest addition is Vikki "The Cougar," a cut-up with a big mouth and plenty of attitude.

Ventriloquism isn't what usually comes to mind when you're shopping for a Las Vegas show, but ventriloquism is only the tip of Terry Fator's iceberg. Consider his ventriloquism and puppets as icing on some of the best voice impersonation and edgy humor you're likely to find. When he trots out a perfect duet between Garth Brooks and Michael Jackson, you won't believe what you're hearing. Never mind that he's belting it out with his mouth closed! Fator is backed by a seven-piece live band and a comely assistant. The show has great energy throughout and runs the gamut from zany to poignant. The puppets are a little hard to see from the seats in back, but large LED screens flanking the stage monitor the action. The main problem we'd like to see corrected is that of the band overwhelming the vocals.

CONSUMER TIPS Terry Fator's humor is definitely adult but not often blue, so the show is OK for those under 18, though they might not dig the music. Because of the location of the showroom, you're better off using Mirage self-parking rather than valet parking.

Thunder from Down Under ★★★

APPEAL BY AGE	UNDER 21 ★★★	21–37 ★★★	38–50 ★★★	51+ ★★★

HOST CASINO AND SHOWROOM **Excalibur—Thunder from Down Under Showroom; ☎ 702-597-7600; excalibur.com or thunderfromdownunder.com**

Type of show Male revue. Admission $41–$51. Cast size 10. Night of lowest attendance Monday. Usual showtimes Sunday–Thursday, 9 p.m.; Friday and Saturday, 9 and 11 p.m. Dark None. Topless Yes (male). Duration of presentation 75 minutes.

DESCRIPTION AND COMMENTS *Thunder from Down Under* offers a naughty night of ladies' fun—a girls' night out that won't cause complete embarrassment for the conservative set. These Aussies are the guys next door—friendly and cute, but not the *Chippendales* dancers. *Thunder* is suggestive but not explicit, much tamer, in fact, than its American-based competitor. The scantily clad cast performs upbeat dance, acrobatics, and martial-arts routines, with a few comedy sketches tossed in (including one done in drag). Acts are performed to a varied soundtrack, resulting in a fast-paced, high-energy—but not always sexy—show.

There's lots of audience interaction as the Thundermen constantly pull girls out of the crowd and onto the stage. If you're shy and want to remain inconspicuous, try sitting in the back, where the lighting is also softer (our reviewer experienced light-blindness a few times from harsh overheads above her front-center seat in the 400-person showroom). After the show, cast members stick around to mingle with guests and offer photo opportunities.

Although there's lots of teasing and suggestion, the Thundermen never fully remove their G-strings (unlike the *Chippendales* guys). *Thunder* seemingly presumes that women can't appreciate blatantly risqué entertainment. Our female reviewer also got the distinct impression that the guys of *Thunder* would be more interested in each other than any of the hundreds of girls in the audience, which for some may diminish the show's sex appeal.

CONSUMER TIPS No smoking is allowed in the Thunder from Down Under Showroom, located on the "Medieval" level, above the casino. Conveniently, there's a bathroom within the showroom. Drinks must be purchased directly from the bar (no at-the-table cocktail service).

Tony 'n' Tina's Wedding ★★★½

APPEAL BY AGE	UNDER 21 ★	21–37 ★★★½	38–50 ★★★½	51+ ★★★

HOST CASINO AND SHOWROOM **Miracle Mile Shops at Planet Hollywood— V Theater; ☎ 702-892-7790; tonylovestina.com**

Type of show Interactive dinner theater. **Admission** $90, $140 VIP. **Cast size** 20. **Night of lowest attendance** Tuesday. **Usual showtimes** Friday–Wednesday, 7:30 p.m. **Dark** Thursday. **Topless** No. **Duration of presentation** 2 hours.

DESCRIPTION AND COMMENTS Have you ever been to a wedding or wedding reception where you really didn't know anyone? Well, that's the premise for *Tony 'n' Tina's Wedding.* You're a wedding guest, welcomed into a large banquet hall and seated at a dinner table with total strangers. There you sit befuddled and somewhat uncomfortable as members of the bride's family (actors) stop to say hello and reminisce about Tony and Tina. And this is just the beginning. If you thought you could sit passively and watch a show, you're quite mistaken. During the course of a panicky few minutes, you become acutely aware that you are being sucked into the cast of this strange piece of theater, or if you can suspend your disbelief, this wedding. First there's the ceremony, then obligatory toasts, then dancing, then dinner followed by more toasts, and the tossing of the bouquet and the garter. As it unfolds, you are taken back to all those weddings in your life where one of the bridesmaids gets drunk, where an uninvited guest makes a five-minute toast, and where the best man wants to sing with the band. Inevitably it's you that the inebriated bridesmaid wants to spin around the dance floor, you who are pushed into the conga line, and you who are pulled into the throng to vie for the bouquet or garter.

There's a story line, of course, plus enough subplots to give Robert Ludlum a run for his money. The families don't get along well, and each in its own way tries to monopolize the reception. The strain is almost too much for the happy couple and for a while their minutes-old marriage hangs in the balance.

CONSUMER TIPS Is this fun? At the show we attended, we observed a pretty diverse range of audience reaction (if you can call it that). Some really got into it, danced to every tune, and role-played right along with cast. Others kept as much as possible to themselves, refusing to the extent possible to be drawn in. With some difficulty, we warmed to the proceedings but nonetheless kept a wary lookout for the sloshed bridesmaid. It was impossible not to admire how exactly the production nailed every wedding cliché, and how, if you weren't familiar with the family members as individuals, you had met their characters at similar events dozens of times in real life. If it helps you make up your mind, we'll tell you that the dinner was passable, sort of a pasta buffet, and that you had one chance to go through the line and load up your plate. The only alcohol served was a splash of Champagne for one of the toasts, though there was a cash bar (where we spent a goodly sum trying to improve our attitude).

Tournament of Kings ★★★

APPEAL BY AGE   UNDER 21 ★★★★   21–37 ★★★★   38–50 ★★★★   51+ ★★★★

HOST CASINO AND SHOWROOM **Excalibur–King Arthur's Arena;**
☎ **702-597-7600 or 877-750-5464; excalibur.com**

Type of show Jousting and medieval pageant. **Admission** $57, includes dinner. **Cast size** 35 (with 38 horses). **Night of lowest attendance** Monday. **Usual showtimes** Monday–Wednesday, 6 p.m.; Thursday–Sunday, 6 and 8:30 p.m. **Dark** None. **Topless** No. **Duration of presentation** 75 minutes.

DESCRIPTION AND COMMENTS *Tournament of Kings* is a retooled version of *King Arthur's Tournament,* which logged 6,000 performances (from Excalibur's opening night in June 1990 till late 1998). It's basically the same show, with a slightly different plot twist. If you saw one, the other will come as no surprise.

The idea is that Arthur summons the kings of eight European countries to a sporting competition in honor of his son Christopher. Guests view the arena from dinner tables divided into sections; a king is designated to represent each section in the competition. Ladies-in-waiting and various court attendants double as cheerleaders, doing their best to whip the audience into a frenzy of cheering for their section's king. The audience, which doesn't require much encouragement, responds by hooting, huzzahing, and pounding on the dinner tables. Watch your drinks—all the pounding can knock them over.

Soup is served to the strains of the opening march. The kings enter on horseback. Precisely when the King of Hungary is introduced, dinner arrives (big Cornish hen, small twice-baked potato, bush of broccoli, dinner roll, and dessert turnover). The kings engage in contests with flags, dummy heads, javelins, swords, and maces and shields and joust a while, too. The horse work, fighting, and especially the jousting are exciting, and the music (by a three-man band) and sound effects are well executed.

Right on cue, Mordred the Evil One crashes the party, accompanied by his Dragon Enforcers. Arthur is mortally slain and all the kings are knocked out, leaving Christopher to battle the forces of evil and emerge—surprise!—victorious in the end.

Except that . . . it's not over. The coronation is the culmination, after some acrobatics and human-tower stunts from a specialty act. Finally, the handsome new king goes out in a (literal) blaze of glory. It's a bit anticlimactic and bogged down, which helps hurry you out so the crew can quickly set up for the second show or clean up and go home.

CONSUMER TIPS One of the few Las Vegas shows suitable for the whole family, and one of the fewer dinner shows, *Tournament of Kings* enjoys great popularity and often plays to a full house. Reserved seats can be purchased with a credit card up to five days in advance by calling the number listed on the previous page (there's an extra $2 charge if you order by phone). Or you can show up at the Excalibur box office, which opens at 8 a.m., up to five days ahead.

No matter where you sit, you're close to the action—and the dust and stage smoke. The air-conditioning system is steroidal, so you might consider bringing a wrap. Seating is reserved, so you can walk in at the last minute and don't have to tip any greeters or seaters.

Dinner is served without utensils and eaten with the hands, so you might want to wash up beforehand. Eating a big meal is a bit awkward with the show going on and all the cheering duties, so you might consider bringing some aluminum foil and a bag to take out the leftover bird. Beverage is limited to soda with dinner, but the food server will bring you water, and a cocktail waitress will bring you anything else. Service is adequate; no one tips, so you'll be a hero if you do.

V: The Ultimate Variety Show ★★★★

APPEAL BY AGE   UNDER 21 ★★½   21–37 ★★★   38–50 ★★★   51+ ★★½

HOST CASINO AND SHOWROOM **Miracle Mile Shops at Planet Hollywood— V Theater; ☎ 702-892-7790; vtheshow.com**

Type of show A hodgepodge of variety acts. **Admission** $66, $86 with dinner, $101 VIP plus tax and fees. **Cast size** About 12 (varies). **Nights of lowest attendance** Monday and Wednesday. **Usual showtimes** Nightly, 7 and 8:30 p.m. **Special comments** Some of Las Vegas's quirkiest acts; great fun. **Topless** No. **Duration of presentation** 75 minutes.

DESCRIPTION AND COMMENTS In quite a few headlining Las Vegas shows, old and new, intermissions are handled by variety acts—comics, jugglers, acrobats, magicians, ventriloquists, and more. And in several of these cases (particularly the older ones), these variety acts become more entertaining than the headliners. The advantage of V is that the cast consists of a rotating stable of variety acts culled from Vegas and elsewhere. This means that no act lasts longer than a few minutes; it's the show for the short-attention-span set. Most of the acts are quite good. The emcee is a hilariously flamboyant and aggressive comic-magician, and when we visited, there was also an amusingly abusive juggler, a few species of acrobats, and a bizarre ventriloquist who uses audience volunteers as his "dummies," among others.

CONSUMER TIPS The V Theater is located in the Miracle Mile Shops at Planet Hollywood. Self-parking at Planet Hollywood funnels you directly into the Miracle Mile Shops not far from the theater. Because there are only a couple of windows at the box office, arrive 40 minutes or more before showtime if you are buying or picking up tickets, or redeeming ticket vouchers. The split-level showroom has a bar on a mezzanine floor and most seating on ground level. Because the V Theater is a multifunctional facility, there's no vertical rise from front to back for the seating. If you sit behind someone tall, in other words, your line of sight will be majorly obstructed. Also be aware that the available restrooms are totally inadequate for the size of the audience.

Vinnie Favorito ★★★

APPEAL BY AGE   UNDER 21 ★★★   21–37 ★★★½   38–50 ★★★½   51+ ★★½

HOST CASINO AND SHOWROOM **Flamingo—Bugsy's Cabaret; ☎ 702-733-3333 or 800-221-7299; flamingolasvegas.com**

Type of show Stand-up comedy. **Admission** $54.95–$65.95 plus tax. **Cast size** 1. **Nights of lowest attendance** Tuesday and Wednesday. **Usual showtimes** Nightly, 8 p.m. **Dark** None. **Topless** No. **Duration of presentation** 70 minutes.

DESCRIPTION AND COMMENTS Italian "shock"-comic Vinnie Favorito occupies Bugsy's Cabaret for the early show nightly at the Flamingo. Las Vegas has its fair share of blue comics, but this guy takes it to the next level. No ethnicity is safe as he works the room blasting every race with equal abandon. His humor is packed with stereotypes interrupted only by the occasional raunchy sex joke. The initial shock wanes as the audience realizes that everyone is picked on equally. His attempts at tempering the offensiveness with an occasional apology are transparent, but his real genius is his ability to build quips around the interactions with the audience. Eventually, it sinks in that he is getting laughs without prepared material. Before the set is through, he will have spoken to nearly a third of the audience, remembering each individual by name, occupation, and race. No small feat.

CONSUMER TIPS Vinnie Favorito is one offensive comic. If you have a gentle spirit or are easily offended, look elsewhere. Bugsy's Cabaret is an intimate venue with good sight lines, so you won't have any difficulty hearing or seeing. Favorito is likely to find and lampoon you no matter where you sit, though being up front makes you more of a target. Cocktails are served ($9 mixed drinks, $7 beer) before and during the show if your ruffled feathers need a little pain relief. You will hear as many groans as laughs—there are plenty of both. To enjoy Vinnie Favorito, try to go with the flow and recognize his point that we all sometimes take ourselves too seriously. Digital audio copies of the live show are made every night, and guests can wait outside the show to purchase a signed copy. Take it home and show ma and pa the new words you learned in Vegas.

X Burlesque ★★★

APPEAL BY AGE	UNDER 21 –	21–37 ★★	38–50 ★★½	51+ ★★½

HOST CASINO AND SHOWROOM **Flamingo–Bugsy's Cabaret;**
☎ **702-733-3333 or 800-221-7299; flamingolasvegas.com**

Type of show Topless revue. **Admission** $45, $56 plus tax. **Cast size** 8. **Night of lowest attendance** Tuesday. **Usual showtimes** Nightly, 10 p.m. **Dark** None. **Topless** Yes. **Duration of presentation** 90 minutes.

DESCRIPTION AND COMMENTS Less erotic than athletic, *X Burlesque* presents a half-dozen skilled dancers performing highly choreographed routines to songs ranging from Broadway standards to techno. Some numbers feature all the dancers, while others involve only one or two. The dancers wear tops as often as not, and their bodies are lithe and toned rather than top-heavy, so guys looking for a hot and juicy T&A show may want to look elsewhere. Those seeking more subtle eroticism won't be disappointed. The audience sits at round tables, nightclub-style, and the comely dancers strut on and off the stage and through the tables, sometimes taking a swing on a pole near the back of the room. The variety of music, the lights and costumes, and the sensual images flashing on large screens at either side of the small stage give the show a charged energy that captures the crowd. Given the general tone of the show, the appearance of the stand-up comics Nancy Ryan or Jane Bean constitutes a real interruption. In *X*'s defense, however, it should be pointed out that a bit of stand-up comedy is pretty routine in topless revues as well as in many strip joints.

CONSUMER TIPS Bugsy's Cabaret is small, giving the show an appropriate intimacy, and most of the tables are set up near the stage. The music is loud, the images bright and quick, and the choreography often frenetic, so expect a full sensory experience.

AFTERNOON SHOWS

AFTERNOON SHOWS HAVE BECOME an affordable alternative to the high-priced productions playing in the major showrooms at night. Most cost under $50, and many can be enjoyed for even less by taking advantage of coupons and special offers found in the local freebie visitor magazines.

Below is a list of the profiled afternoon shows, ranked in terms of overall excellence. There's been a numbing proliferation of afternoon shows recently, and as you might expect, the shows vary immensely in quality. Finding the good ones and avoiding the bad ones is not unlike threading your way through a minefield. The good ones are better than a lot of the high-ticket productions holding down stages around town at night. But the bad ones—heaven help us.

AFTERNOON SHOWS

RANK AND SHOW	LOCATION
1. *The Mac King Comedy Magic Show*	**Harrah's**
2. *The Price Is Right—Live!*	**Bally's**
3. *Matsuri*	**Imperial Palace**
4. *Nathan Burton Comedy Magic*	**Flamingo**

Unfortunately, because afternoon shows erupt like wildflowers (or weeds) and disappear just as fast, we can't cover all of them in the *Unofficial Guide*. What we can do, however, is to provide a short profile of those afternoon shows that have demonstrated staying power. Showtimes for specific afternoon productions are usually in the 2-to-4:30-p.m. range but change almost weekly. Call the information and reservations number provided for performance times during your visit. The following profiles are arranged alphabetically.

The Mac King Comedy Magic Show ★★★★

APPEAL BY AGE   UNDER 21 ★★★★   21–37 ★★★★   38–50 ★★★★   51+ ★★★★

HOST CASINO AND SHOWROOM **Harrah's—Harrah's Theater;**
☎ **702-369-5111; harrahs.com or mackingshow.com**

Type of show Mostly comedy with some magic thrown in. **Admission** $25 plus tax and fees. **Cast size** 1. **Usual showtimes** Monday–Friday, 1 and 3 p.m. **Dark** Saturday and Sunday. **Appropriate for children** Yes. **Duration of presentation** 1 hour.

DESCRIPTION AND COMMENTS Our pick for the best afternoon show in town, Mac King uses magic and illusion as a platform for his unique brand of comedy. His humor pokes fun at Las Vegas, other Vegas magicians, and at himself. The presentation is fresh and imaginative, and the illusions are good. But it's King's ability to work an audience, coupled with his sheer insanity, that keeps audiences rolling. If it's really magic you crave (as opposed to comedy), then *Nathan Burton*, described below, is a better choice.

CONSUMER TIPS Harrah's runs two-fer and discount specials on *Mac King*, but they come and go. Unique among afternoon shows, *Mac King* frequently sells out. So purchase tickets in advance if possible.

Matsuri ★★★

HOST CASINO AND SHOWROOM **Imperial Palace–Imperial Showroom;**
☎ **702-731-3311 or 888-777-7664; imperialpalace.com**

Type of show Acrobatic revue. **Admission** $50 and $60 VIP plus tax. **Cast size** 20.
Day of lowest attendance Tuesday. **Usual showtimes** Saturday–Thursday, 4
p.m.; Friday, 8 p.m. **Dark** None. **Appropriate for children** Yes. **Duration of presentation** 75 minutes.

DESCRIPTION AND COMMENTS *Matsuri,* sometimes referred to as a "muscle musical," is a fast-paced presentation of gymnastics as entertainment. All of the
Olympic disciplines, from the vault, to parallel bars, to tumbling, are creatively combined with music, dance, and exotic costuming to produce an
action-packed, yet nuanced, tour de force. In addition to gymnastics, Matsuri also draws on the martial arts, traditional oriental ribbon dancing,
baton twirling, and even rope skipping. One memorable routine has the
whole cast drumming in unison on their bodies. As a whole, Matsuri comes
off as a fusion of Cirque du Soleil and the celebrated percussion production, *Stomp.*

CONSUMER TIPS *Matsuri* is one of the few afternoon shows that also performs one day each week in the evening. Half-price tickets are almost
always available from Tix4Tonight locations. To reach the Imperial
Showroom, take the escalator behind the hotel front desk.

Nathan Burton Comedy Magic   ★★★

HOST CASINO AND SHOWROOM **Flamingo–Flamingo Showroom;**
☎ **702-733-3333; flamingolasvegas.com or nathanburton.com**

Type of show Comedy magic (duh!). **Admission** $34–$44. **Cast size** 6. **Usual
showtimes** Tuesday–Sunday, 4 p.m. **Dark** Monday. **Appropriate for children**
Yes. **Duration of presentation** 1 hour.

DESCRIPTION AND COMMENTS The show begins with a collection of video clips
on two large video screens flanking the stage (you may recognize Burton
from his appearance on TV's *America's Got Talent,* which brought him a
lot of attention). From there, he runs the magical gamut, from some
baffling gimmick illusions to classic magic tricks. Burton doesn't break
any new ground, but his illusions are current and represent the genre
well. With a nod to magic's history, he performs Houdini's straitjacket
escape with a modern twist—it's completely see through—and a levitation trick with what must be the world's largest hair dryer. High-energy
(and very loud) music augments the upbeat pace of the show. Burton
smiles his way through a production that is longer on magic than on
comedy, but still, it all works well. If your primary interest is magic and
illusion, Nathan Burton does a good job. If it's more comedy you crave,
try Mac King at Harrah's.

CONSUMER TIPS The Flamingo Showroom is an old-fashioned showroom with crowded banquet tables and plush booths on each of five levels. Seating is by the maitre'd. Afternoon performances rarely sell out, so getting a good seat should not be a problem, even without a tip.

The Price Is Right—Live!   ★★★½

APPEAL BY AGE	UNDER 21 ★★½	21–37 ★★★½	38–50 ★★★★	51+ ★★★★

HOST CASINO AND SHOWROOM **Bally's—*Jubilee!* Theater; ☎ 702-967-4567 or 800-237-7469; ballyslasvegas.com**

Type of show Game show with prizes. **Admission cost** $56.25. **Cast size** 7. **Day of lowest attendance** Wednesday. **Usual showtimes** Tuesday–Thursday and Saturday, 2:30 p.m.; Friday, 7:30 p.m. **Dark** Sunday and Monday. **Appropriate for children** Yes, but must be 21 to play. **Duration of presentation** 90 minutes.

DESCRIPTION AND COMMENTS This is a reprise of the classic TV game show. Contestants, who must be 21 or older, compete for thousands of dollars in cash and prizes. Interactive keypads attached to seats allow audience members to vie for a chance to be the next contestant. *The Price Is Right* draws the largest and most excitable audiences of any afternoon show we've ever reviewed. For the uninitiated, it's like going to a cheerleader camp. In fact, the first 20 minutes of the show are devoted to teaching the audience how to scream, applaud, and jump around. You're even instructed in the art of ooh-ing and aah-ing when the prizes are shown, as well as sighing "Awww!" when a contestant goes down in flames. If you're called upon to "come on down," you are pressed to hurl yourself down the aisle with the greatest weirdness you can manage. Videos of bizarre contestants from the TV show "coming on down" are shown to inspire you and give you an idea of what's expected. The audience is so lathered up when the day's host is introduced, you'd think the angel Gabriel had just arrived on a lightning bolt. Whatever the hoopla, however, the prizes are very good, ranging from cash to cruise vacations and cars.

CONSUMER TIPS Before entering, you must check in at the registration desk just to the right of the theater entrance. Here, your seat number will be recorded and you'll be issued a giant name tag. This process gets you listed in the show computer, from which contestant names are chosen at random. *Jubilee!* Theater is one of the grand dames of the Las Vegas show scene. For a glimpse of Las Vegas history, come back in the evening and see *Jubilee!*

COMEDY CLUBS

THERE IS A LOT OF STAND-UP COMEDY in Las Vegas, and several of the large production shows feature comedians as specialty acts. In addition, there is usually at least one comedy headliner playing in town. Big names who regularly play Las Vegas include Jerry Seinfeld, Jay Leno, Rita Rudner, Tim Conway, the Smothers Brothers, Joan Rivers, and Don Rickles. Finally, there are the comedy clubs.

A comedy club is usually a smaller showroom with a simple stage and two to five stand-up comics. In most Las Vegas comedy show-rooms, a new show with different comedians rotates in each week. There are six bona fide Las Vegas comedy clubs:

Brad Garret's Comedy Club: Tropicana
Improv at Harrah's: Harrah's
LA Comedy Club: Four Queens
Louie LOL: Palace Station
Playboy Comedy: Palms
Riviera Comedy Club: Riviera

Comedy clubs, unlike production showrooms, are almost never dark. There are usually two shows each night, seven days a week. The humor at the comedy clubs, as well as the audience, tends to be young and ir-reverent. A favorite and affordable entertainment for locals as well as for tourists, comedy clubs enjoy great popularity in Las Vegas.

The comedy-club format is simple and straightforward. Comedi-ans perform sequentially, and what you get depends on who is performing. The range of humor runs from slapstick to obscene to ethnic to topical to just about anything. Some comics are better than others, but all of the talent is solid and professional. There is no way to predict which club will have the best show in a given week. In fact, there may not be a "best" show, since response to comedy is a matter of individual sense of humor.

Brad Garrett's Comedy Club

HOST CASINO AND SHOWROOM **Tropicana—Brad Garrett's Comedy Club;**
☎ **702-739-2222 and 800-829-9034; troplv.com**

Type of show Stand-up comedy. Admission $39–$59 plus tax. Cast size 2. Night of lowest attendance Thursday. Usual showtimes Nightly, 8 p.m. with 10 p.m. show Friday and Saturday. Dark None. Duration of presentation 70 minutes.

DESCRIPTION AND COMMENTS Brad Garrett is an actor and comedian best know for playing Robert Barone in the television series *Everybody Loves Raymond*. Garrett appears for a 2- or 3-night stand once each month. Between Garrett appearances, various stand-up comics play 6-night gigs. There are various specials, usually two-fers, for locals and military.

The Improv

HOST CASINO AND SHOWROOM **Harrah's—The Improv;** ☎ **702-369-5111; harrahs.com**

Type of show Stand-up comedy. Admission $31.95, $49.95 VIP plus tax and fees. Cast size 3–4. Nights of lowest attendance Wednesday and Thursday. Usual showtimes Tuesday–Sunday, 8:30 and 10:30 p.m. Dark Monday. Duration of presentation 70 minutes.

DESCRIPTION AND COMMENTS Comedians at the Improv are usually up-and-comers who do set routines as well as improvisation. Drinks are not included, but there is a cash bar. The showroom is on the second floor at the top of the escalator from the main casino.

LA Comedy Club

HOST CASINO AND SHOWROOM **Four Queens—Canyon Club; ☎ 702-385-4011; thelacomedyclub.com**

Type of show Stand-up comedy. Admission $18.65 and up plus tax. Cast size 2. Night of lowest attendance Wednesday. Usual showtimes Tuesday–Sunday, 9 p.m. Dark Monday. Duration of presentation 70 minutes.

DESCRIPTION AND COMMENTS Formerly at Trader Vic's, the LA Comedy Club features two veteran comics a night for four- or five-day engagements. Schedule headliners and their bios can be found on the LA Comedy website. General admission includes all-you-can-drink draft beer and well drinks. VIP admission includes all-you-can drink beer and well or call drinks. The VIP admission includes a line pass, which is not a big deal at the Canyon Club. There is also a $15 general admission option, which includes no drinks.

Louie LOL

HOST CASINO AND SHOWROOM **Palace Station—Louie Anderson Theater; ☎ 702-547-5300; palacestation.com**

Type of show Stand-up comedy. Admission $50 plus tax. Cast size Usually 2. Night of lowest attendance Thursday. Usual showtimes Tuesday–Saturday, 8:30 p.m.; Sunday, 8:30 p.m. (Bonkers Comedy Jam). Dark None. Duration of presentation 75 minutes.

DESCRIPTION AND COMMENTS Seasoned stand-up comedian Louie Anderson is the resident headliner. LOL also hosts acts such as The Irish Comedy Tour, Pam Matteson, Tony Esposito, Ron Shock, and Jack Mayberry. Name comics like Jerry Seinfeld and Larry the Cable Guy have been known to drop in. All shows are restricted to those age 21 and over.

Playboy Comedy

HOST CASINO AND SHOWROOM **Palms—The Lounge at the Pearl; ☎ 702-944-3200; ticketmaster.com**

Type of show Stand-up comedy. Admission $40 plus tax. Cast size 1–2. Night of lowest attendance Thursday. Usual showtimes Thursday and Friday, 9:30 p.m.; Saturday, 7:30 and 9:30 p.m. Dark Sunday–Wednesday. Duration of presentation 70 minutes.

DESCRIPTION AND COMMENTS Contrary to what you might expect, Playboy Comedy is staged at The Lounge at the Pearl near the Pearl Concert Theater rather than in the Playboy Club. Name comics play three-night stands. For additional info and scheduled acts, see **lvahotels.com** or **ticketmaster.com.**

Riviera Comedy Club

HOST CASINO AND SHOWROOM **Riviera—Mardi Gras Showrooms, second floor;**
☎ **702-794-9433; rivierahotel.com**

Type of show Stand-up comedy. **Admission** $25, $35 VIP. **Cast size** Approximately 4. **Nights of lowest attendance** Sunday–Wednesday. **Usual showtimes** Nightly, 9 p.m. **Duration of presentation** 75 minutes.

DESCRIPTION AND COMMENTS Venues for the Riviera Comedy Club and the *Crazy Girls* show are on the second and third floors above the Riviera casino in what are called the Mardi Gras Showrooms. The club is unique in that it features ventriloquists, hypnotists, and "shock" comedians in addition to stand-up comics.

Sin City Comedy Show

HOST CASINO AND SHOWROOM **Miracle Mile Shops—V Theater;**
☎ **702-932-1818; vtheaterboxoffice.com**

Type of show Stand-up comedy and burlesque. **Admission** $49.50 and $60.50 plus tax. **Cast size** 6. **Night of lowest attendance** Thursday. **Usual showtimes** Nightly, 9 p.m. **Special comments** Must be 18 or older to attend. **Duration of presentation** 75 minutes.

DESCRIPTION AND COMMENTS We just tossed this in for good measure. This is more of a production show than anything resembling a comedy club. Stand-up comedy alternates with strip tease and modest production numbers. Admission discounts are available on the V Theater website, and half-price tickets are usually available at Tix4Tonight box offices. The more expensive ticket option provides a line pass, preferred seating, and a drink. The split-level showroom has a bar on a mezzanine floor and most seating on ground level. The V Theater has a flat floor, so if someone taller sits in front of you your view will be compromised.

LAS VEGAS NIGHTLIFE

AT FIRST BLUSH, LAS VEGAS'S NIGHTLIFE SCENE closely resembles the city's many buffets—amid the chaos, there's something for everybody. Vegas makes billions as America's go-to city for dining and entertainment, not to mention its long history of gaming, but this was not always the case.

In the Rat-Pack era, it was gaming that raked in the big bucks, with steak houses and 99-cent breakfasts batting for the food-and-beverage teams. Entertainment took the form of big-room shows with Elvis, Liberace, and Sinatra and the boys, and smoky dives where the booze flowed endlessly. Disco wasn't even a twinkle in anyone's eye. Cut to 1988, when local bars Tramps and the Shark Club began—gasp—charging cover. The 1990s brought the rise and subsequent fall of rave music and parties (much of which centered around Vegas's electronic-music trailblazer, Utopia nightclub), but by the Millennium the casinos were creating nightlife worth getting off the couch for: Club Rio, Studio 54, C2K, Ra. . . .

Today, creating fulfilling party opportunities for tourists, locals, and everyone in between is big business for the casinos. And it's only intensifying. New York, Chicago, Miami, and L.A. all have their flag planted somewhere on the Strip or just slightly off-Strip. Electronic music and internationally jet-setting DJs dominate the club scene, with Top 40 and hip-hop occupying what vacancy remains. Celebrity nightclub appearances are at an all-time high. The annual spate of trendy new venues means that Vegas is currently a buyer's market, with more clubs than tourists to fill all of them. If it's true that the Great Recession is technically behind us now, word of this development has yet to reach Vegas; every visitor is ravenous for a deal, and every club wants to sell you something, anything to get you into *their* VIP booth rather than their neighbor's. Call it the upside. So keep your wits about you, and we'll show you how to reap the many benefits of the nightlife buffet.

*un***official TIP**
For a post-clubbing dining experience that doesn't involve a grubby casino coffee shop, hit First Food & Bar, a trendy late-night dining concept located between the Venetian and the Shoppes at the Palazzo, right where the gondola rides begin.

LAS VEGAS NIGHTLIFE BESTIARY

THE KEY TO UNLOCKING LAS VEGAS'S bewildering club scene is to do your homework *before* you arrive. You're already reading this handy guide, so that puts you light years beyond those who show up clueless, only to be preyed upon for being so unsavvy. But don't be discouraged if you de-plane at McCarran with little more of a clue than when you left home. Here's a quick-and-dirty rundown of just some of the categories of nightlife activity available to you.

CASINO BAR Casino bars, lobby bars and lounges, and center bars are generally open 24/7. These watering holes take their titles from whatever they are located nearest (hence, lobby bar) and generally have one thing in common: accessibility to a good drink. Some even count among the city's finest beverage programs. (Insert puns here about the proverbial bar having been raised.) Requirements for entry? A valid ID, a pulse, and a penchant for cocktails. One need never wander too far in Vegas sober.

Ones to try: Throw a rock and you'll hit one. Every casino has a bar, and most have several. But try Fusion Mixology Bar and Laguna Champagne Bar (Palazzo), Bond and Vesper (Cosmopolitan), Aurora and Flight (Luxor), Rouge, Zuri, and Centrifuge (MGM Grand), Eyecandy (Mandalay Bay), Center Bar (Hard Rock), The Mint (The Palms), and Rojo (Palms Place).

BARS AND PUBS Separated from the casino by actual walls, or perhaps even as freestanding structures, bars and pubs occupy the gap between the too-casual casino bar and the martini-slinging lounges. Since they're less stringent about dress code than lounges and clubs, and often feature a bar menu and light entertainment, bars and pubs are a perfect place for large groups. Cover charges here are rare, and speed of entry is usually gauged by capacity.

Ones to try: Hussong's Cantina (Mandalay Place), BB King's Blues Club (The Mirage), Coyote Ugly and Nine Fine Irishmen (New York–New York), Book & Stage (Cosmopolitan), Diablo's Cantina and The Pub (Monte Carlo), McFadden's (Rio), Todd English P.U.B. (Aria), and Yard House (Town Square and Red Rock).

LOUNGE Whether Downtown, Center Strip, or off-Strip, lounges offer a heavy dose of class and ambience, forgoing the velvet rope dance in favor of getting you inside with a drink in your hand. Plush, oversized, open seating, elegant lighting, generous cocktails, and a possible bar menu are the calling cards of a proper lounge. The town being so spread out, Vegas locals are accustomed to having to come together in the middle; lounges being so plentiful and accessible, they are at the heart of the "meet market" singles scene. Locals love the happy hours (which usually last two to four hours), so expect an after-work crowd early and a pre-club party later. Ease of entry is generally dependent upon the day of the week, big conventions, and holidays; sometimes, cover charges appear for special events.

Ones to try: Mandarin Bar (Mandarin Oriental), The Deuce (Aria), Parasol Up and Down (Wynn), Eastside Lounge (Encore), Chandelier (Cosmopolitan), Downtown Cocktail Room (Downtown), Blue Martini (Town Square), Caramel (Bellagio), and Rocks Lounge (Red Rock).

ULTRALOUNGE This was a specious marketing term invented by Vegas promoters a few years back, but "ultralounge" serves as well as anything to describe high-end venues that charge dearly both at the door and at the bar. Such places are immaculately designed and furnished, staffed with gorgeous servers (and ogrelike security), and policed to ensure compliance with a snappy dress code. "Bottle service"—that is, paying hundreds of dollars for a bottle of booze—is typically the only way to reserve a table. Clientele tends toward the well-heeled and supercool, though if you don't mind standing, even the modestly loaded can pay the cover and drink à la carte. Space here is limited and therefore sold at a premium for cover charges rivaling those of full-scale nightclubs.

Ones to try: Gold Lounge (Aria), Tabu (MGM), Revolution Lounge (Mirage), Playboy Club and Ghostbar (The Palms), and the members-only mixology lounge, Savile Row, which replaces Noir Bar beneath the LAX entrance tunnel (Luxor; entry at doorman's discretion).

BOUTIQUE/INTIMATE Fed up with being pigeonholed as fashions trended toward smaller size, clubs have within the last year or two become "intimate" and "boutique" to differentiate themselves, taking advantage of hot hotel and travel buzzwords and thumbing their noses at the ever-swelling megaclub.

Ones to try: Surrender (Encore), Blush (Wynn), Lavo (Palazzo), The Bank (Bellagio), and the new Pussycat Dolls Burlesque Saloon (Planet Hollywood).

COUNTRY AND COUNTRY-CROSSOVER A whole new subcategory! Line dancing to today's Top-40 hits? VIP bottle service and Stetsons? The latest trend to take root is the country-crossover nightclub, where you might find yourself two-stepping to the Black Eyed Peas, Kenny Chesney, and Justin Timberlake, then riding a mechanical bull to the sounds of crossover artists Taylor Swift, Keith Urban, and Carrie Underwood.

Ones to try: Revolver (Texas Station), Stoney's Rockin' Country (South Strip) and Stoney's North 40 (Northwest), Back Alley Bar (Stratosphere), PBR Bar (Miracle Mile Shops), and Gilley's (T. I.).

NIGHTCLUB/MEGACLUB Resorts now customarily spend multiple millions on nightlife, so you can expect the best in everything from the attractive staff and the digs to the internationally renown DJs and the celebrity contingent. These sprawling labyrinths may cover several floors and include dance room(s), side lounges, bars, a restaurant, uncountable VIP rooms, and possible access to a pool. They might even have multiple entrances. Count on long lines at every entrance regardless; more than anything else, the success of megaclubs have brought the era of door bribes to Vegas. Palm $20 at least (per person in your party) to the doorman, and you'll find your names appearing mysteriously (and invisibly) on his list; VIP host tips are now practically mandatory for the privilege of making a table reservation at the tonier spots. Otherwise, expect to wait an hour or more to get in, if ever. Inside, you'll find massive crowds of beautiful people, dressed to the nines and ready to party, plus a half-dozen ways to entertain yourself—DJs, dance troupes, novelty performers, live "mannequins," you name it. The time and expense effectively kills the idea of club-hopping, but with all this on offer, you probably won't need anything else—unless it's a cup of coffee at dawn. Promoters use every trick in the books to assemble the most attractive clientele in one place. Bottle service is king, and everyone else is there to merely fill in the spaces between the most valuable real estate. Check your ego at the door unless you intend to spend heavily to keep up with the wealthiest of the Joneses, and that means both once you are inside the ropes as well as just to make it through

unofficial **TIP**
Trend Alert! Sunday Brunch is back: Hot people, cool music, bottomless drinks. Sounds like a nightclub, but it's brunch. Try First Food & Bar at the Palazzo and Simon at Palms Place for a party. Prefer traditional? Bouchon at the Venetian and chef Carlos Guia's Jazz Brunch at the Wynn Country Club scratch that itch. Also consider heading to the pools—Marquee Dayclub, Liquid, Bare, Wet Republic, and Tao Beach all serve up exceptional poolside fare.

them—at the door, tip (or offer to tip) anything in a suit.

Ones to try: XS (Encore), Tao (Venetian), Vanity (Hard Rock), Pure (Caesars), Haze (Aria), Studio 54 (MGM), Moon and Rain (The Palms), House of Blues (Mandalay Bay), Jet (Mirage), LAX (Luxor), and newcomers Chateau (Paris) and Gallery (Planet Hollywood).

AFTERHOURS When the clubs close, the staff doesn't exactly rush home and go to bed, nor does the party crowd. Those wishing to test the limits of their endurance can do so at one of a few dedicated late-night joints offering after-hours parties. Doors may open as early as midnight or as late as 4 a.m., but all keep the music and drinks flowing till dawn, and often well beyond that. These days, afterhours is the near-exclusive domain of the gentlemen's clubs, which are generally open during the wee-est hours regardless. Music usually tends toward house, trance, and electronica, but Drai's also offers a hip-hop room. While there is almost always a cover charge, lines are not so much a problem here as parking. But at 6 a.m., should you really be driving anyway?

Ones to try: Discreet Gentlemen's Club, Déjà vu Erotic Ultralounge, Posh at The Playground, The Artisan (all West Side), and Drai's (Bill's Gamblin' Hall & Saloon).

POOL PARTIES Incredible to think that only eight years ago such an animal didn't exist. That is, until Rehab came on the scene turning day into nightlife. Two years ago, Wet Republic introduced the term "daylife" into the party lexicon. Just about every casino these days invests in the holy trinity of nightclub, ultra-lounge, and the hip dining experience loosely called "dining with a scene." All are run like battleships by a staff of pretty young things, the restaurants and lounges operating much the same as the nightclubs. But during the summer—roughly from March into October—adults-only pools pop up, joining the trinity and boasting every amenity the clubs do, only without the roof: bottle service, VIP hosts, cocktail servers, DJ music. Just add water, cabanas, hot tubs, and, in some cases, European bathing (read: topless). Admittance to this kind of flesh parade is at the doorman's discretion and is very much determined by appearance and the maintenance of a healthy female-to-male ratio.

> *un*official **TIP**
> Topless pools and pool parties have taken Las Vegas by storm. **Arnold Snyder,** who's seen more breasts than Colonel Sanders, describes these happenings in detail in his book *Topless Vegas,* published by Huntington Press.

Ones to try: The Naked Pool (Artisan), Azure (Palazzo), Bare (Mirage), Daydream (M Resort), Encore Beach Club (Encore), Liquid (Aria), Marquee Dayclub (Cosmopolitan), Moorea (Mandalay Bay), Nikki Beach Club (The Tropicana), Palms Pool & Bungalows (Palms), Red Rock Cabana Club (Red Rock Resort), Rehab Pool and Relax Bar (Hard Rock), Rumor (Rumor Boutique Resort), Tao Beach (Venetian), Venus (Caesars Palace), Voodoo Beach and The Voo (Rio), and Wet Republic (MGM Grand).

What NOT to bring to a pool party:

- Large backpacks: Small purses and bags are ok but will likely be searched.
- Valuables: Unless you have a cabana with a safe, take only what you need.
- Liquids: All beverages must be purchased after going through security.
- Medications: Paramedics are almost always on hand, so leave all pills, potions, and inhalers behind. You can argue for insulin syringes and epi pens, but be prepared for a fight.
- Weapons of any and all kinds.
- Glass: Duh.

CELEBRITIES

THEY'RE EVERYWHERE, and it isn't by happenstance. Celebrity sightings are more than just common occurrences; more often than not, they are arranged in advance by ambitious nightclubs, promoters, and sponsors. Stars of film, music, and TV are regularly booked to tip their hat, make a toast, celebrate a birthday, or belt out a tune or two. For a club to bill a star as a "guest performer" is to subject itself to a mandatory live-entertainment tax (LET) or casino-entertainment tax (CET). Many do this, but just as many do not, and prefer instead to keep a live mic on hand, you know, *just in case*. Often billed as a host or as making a special guest appearance, some of today's hottest artists can be seen performing a quick two- or three-song set. If you're fortunate enough to cross paths with actor-singer Jamie Foxx, clear your night—his visits are legendary.

INSIDER ADVICE

VEGAS—NOT JUST FOR WEEKENDS ANYMORE Vegas was, is, and always will be a weekend destination—one that hits its stride at about 8 p.m. on Friday and doesn't slow down until early Monday morning. It's a given that the town's bars, lounges, and clubs will be filled to the brim on Friday and Saturday nights. But what all locals (and few tourists) know is that Sunday through Thursday the clubs don't close their doors; they just refocus. The secret to midweek partying is finding out which night each club holds its local-industry night, thus avoiding the tourist traps that will take anyone off the street—Birkenstocks, shorts, and all. Expect gratuitous contests, costumes, gimmicky promotions, and hordes of locals and cognoscenti partying like it's Mardi Gras. While there, get on everyone's email list, bring business cards, and if someone says they're a VIP host from another venue (as many will on industry nights), buy him a shot—he's your new best friend.

unofficial **TIP**
Mandalay Place—located between Luxor and Mandalay Bay—has about the fastest valet on the Strip and offers access to all the Luxor and Mandalay Bay clubs. Just tell them you're going shopping.

Ones to try: Industry Sundays (The Bank and XS) and Sin Sundays (Vanity); Mondays at Marquee (Cosmopolitan); Tuesdays at Chateau (Paris) and Pure (Caesars); Wednesdays at Haze; Worship Thursdays (Tao).

GETTING IN Showing up is half the battle, so do so—nice and early. For any party size or gender mix other than two attractive young ladies by themselves, save yourself and your guests the agonizing, soul-crushing velvet-rope experience by doing some of the work ahead of time. At the rope, the uninitiated and uninformed can expect a long wait (30 minutes to upward of two hours), a complete lack of eye contact, and even possible ridicule. Sometimes doormen employ intimidation and humiliation to pressure a group's point man into investing his life savings in bottle service or huge tips to pass through the pearly gates. Or worse, a doorman might keep you in line for an eternity only to finally grant you entry . . . into an empty club. The most notorious providers of an ego-crushing entry experience include Haze, The Bank, Pure, LAX, Tao, Rain, XS, and Moon/Playboy. Marquee is the newest proving ground, rivaling airport security lines, at the Cosmopolitan. Consider yourself warned.

Your best bet for getting into your club of choice is to contact the club directly (consult **JackColton.com** for the lead VIP hosts' actual email and cell numbers) or work with an independent VIP hosting company such as **Red Carpet VIP** (**VIPNite.com**) and **VegasHotSpots.com.** For a small fee, these companies and individuals can walk you directly into the club of your choice or book you a table for bottle service. And yes, there is an app for that—hundreds of 'em actually.

TIME IS MONEY Ah yes, bottle service. If the dutifully paying customers who line the bars and walls of a club are the meat and potatoes of the industry, bottle-service patrons are the dessert. But nightclubs like to have dessert first, so you will see bottle-service patrons waiting far less time to get in. But remember that these patrons are paying a great deal more for that privilege. The bottom line is you will spend time or money. In other words, if you want to spend very little money, you can get in for just the cover charge, but you might wait a long time. Or, consider investing in bottle service (that is, buying a bottle—or, likely, multiple bottles—of liquor to get a VIP table or booth) to bypass the line entirely, thus spending very little time outside the club. Bottles can go up to the high hundreds, even into the thousands for rare Champagnes or Cognacs. The industry benchmark is Grey Goose vodka, a liter of which will cost you $250 at Downtown Cocktail Room, $475 at Tao, and $495 at Tryst and XS. But $100 bottles of Skyy vodka are becoming more prevalent, too.

While a liter of Goose is obtainable at any neighborhood liquor store for about $35, it's not what's inside the bottle you're paying for. It's the valuable real estate of having a private booth or table, the attention of an attractive cocktail server, a busser to clean up spills and refresh ice, and likely even a neighboring thug of a security guard to keep an eye on your prize. Bottle service is unique to each club: one table's price might be determined by location, while another's is by the number of people (usually three to four people per bottle). Be prepared for a possible shakedown; you might find yourself being walked to an undesirable table, past better ones, only to be told that those tables cost extra—cash preferably, payable right now to your host. If this happens, stand firm and ask to see other available tables within your price range. Once you have the table, take your time with your bottles and resist your server's offers to pour you shots, as you may find yourself required to order more bottles or else shove off to make room for another party. You will find this is more prevalent in clubs than lounges.

COMFORT ZONES A place for everyone, and everyone in their place. Vegas has it. Just as there are clubs, bars, and lounges where everyone can feel comfortable, there are some where not everyone would. The top clubs target a 21-to-35 age range, and though guests of any age (over 21) are welcome to try their luck at the rope or make a reservation, they may find that it's the other patrons who might make a club unfriendly to someone over that hump. Tight confines, loud music, inebriated neighbors, and little to no elbowroom might make for an uncomfortable evening.

But some venues make it easier for patrons of any age to enjoy themselves. The **Beatles Revolution Lounge** at the Mirage is situated just a stone's throw from Cirque du Soleil's show *LOVE*. It's Beatles-driven in design, though chic and young in music and live entertainment, making it a hot spot for any demographic early in the evening; as the hour grows late, it gives way to a younger, hipper crowd. Open seating helps too. The city's many dueling piano bars, such as Pete's at Town Square and Napoleon's at Paris, play everything from the best of the 1980s to today in a convivial environment that is inclusive rather than exclusive. **Downtown Cocktail Room** and **Sidebar** will appeal to the sophisticated imbiber from any age bracket, while **Studio 54** might just be the "big-club" experience for someone who remembers the heydays of the original 54. Even from Light Group—who have Haze and The Bank, two of Vegas's hottest clubs—**Gold Lounge** and **Caramel** are small and approachable without giving up the Vegas excitement you came for. Just about every casino has something that will appeal to the 35-and-over set; they want to keep you on property and will do just about anything to satisfy, and that includes providing nightlife venues for every age group.

DRESS CODES Inside every club you will witness flagrant violations of dress code—hats, sneakers, T-shirts, ripped jeans, and more. Attempt to emulate this behavior and you may find yourself left on the wrong side of the ropes. The only people who can get away with this sort of rebellion are celebrities, well-known local socialites, and the DJ. Even if you think you are on close, personal terms with a doorman or VIP host, you might see him blanch and go cold when you show up in tennis shoes and a ball cap. Gentlemen, pack dress shoes, a nice pair of jeans, and remember that a sport coat (thrown over anything) cures most ills. Ladies, you pretty much have carte blanche, but think practical—comfiest heels, smallest purse.

TIPPING Keep plenty of small bills handy for tipping purposes. Aside from the valet and the coat-check girl, tip anyone who goes out of their way for you. The doorman who looked the other way about your scuzzy loafers, the VIP host who walked you past the line, the bathroom attendant who got the cranberry juice out of your shirt . . . all are deserving of your monetary thanks. Bartenders and cocktail servers can usually be tipped on a bill if you're charging your round. Otherwise, cash tips are highly recommended lest you should find yourself high and dry the rest of the night.

If your line situation is looking hopeless, you can try to encourage (read: tip, grease, bribe) a doorman or VIP host to expedite the process. A good rule of thumb is $20 per head, but with so many trying the same thing, it's not so much the amount as the ease of his slipping you through that will help or hurt the situation. A doorman letting in ten guys will get a stern look from his boss, while a doorman letting in six ladies and four guys might get a mere eyebrow raise. Gentlemen, pad your group heavily with women and keep the guy count low. Be discreet (don't wave money around), but make your presence and your willingness to play (pay) known.

THE DOWNTOWN RENAISSANCE Fremont Street is the original Las Vegas Strip. Now called Downtown Las Vegas, it caps off the current or "New" Strip like a T, with a covered pedestrian entertainment zone called The Fremont Street Experience to the west of Las Vegas Boulevard and the Fremont East Entertainment District to the east. Tourists are generally drawn to the bright lights of "The Old Strip" like moths to the Luxor light, but savvy travelers are finally beginning to follow the locals' example and venture into Fremont East territory. There you will find the sophisticated and cocktail-centric **Downtown Cocktail Room,** the cavelike hipster haven **The Griffin,** ultracool **Vanguard Lounge,** barcade **Insert Coin(s),** young and irreverent live music spot **Beauty Bar,** and piano bar **Don't Tell Mama.** For coffee, vinyl records, and an eyeful of modern art, visit **Emergency Arts** and **The Beat Coffeehouse** on East Fremont at Sixth Street, and then venture just north of the Fremont Street Experience to find **Triple George Restaurant** and its sister bar, **Sidebar,** before letting your hair down and perhaps donating a bra to the impressive collection found at **Hogs & Heifers,** the iconic biker-friendly bar. Newest to the area is the trio of Urban Taverns in the 18 blocks that make up Vegas's Arts District: **Bar + Bistro,** the **Lady Silvia,** and **Artifice.**

NIGHTCLUB PROFILES

Aurora

The Luxor, 3900 South Las Vegas Boulevard; ☎ 702-262-4591; luxor.com South Strip and Environs

Cover None. **Mixed drinks** $10 and up. **Wine** $7 and up. **Beer** $6 and up. **Dress** Casual. **Food available** None. **Hours** 24/7.

WHO GOES THERE 21 and older. Broad mix of ages, tends toward 30+. With little to make it a destination spot, it attracts mostly guests at the Luxor, Excalibur, and Mandalay Bay.

WHAT GOES ON Aurora provides a break from the rapidly retreating Egyptian theme at the Luxor. Named to evoke the aurora borealis or northern lights, it's decorated in rich blues and greens and has a hip-yet-casual elegance. Aurora offers European bottle-and-wine service as well as tableside martinis. Though not stuffy, it's not a party place either. It's where you go to plan the next move or to take a break from shopping or the casinos. Aurora offers live lounge entertainment on Friday and Saturday, 7 p.m. to 2 a.m.

SETTING AND ATMOSPHERE From the rich colors and comfortable chairs to the smooth jazz on the sound system, Aurora offers a mellow, sophisticated atmosphere. With a capacity of more than 150 customers, it's spacious—easily enough room between tables to allow privacy and relaxation. Though the lounge juts into the main walking area, it's raised a couple of steps above the passersby, giving it a self-contained ambience.

IF YOU GO There's not enough here to warrant hanging out for long, and the crowd seems to turn over regularly, so there's no need to hit the scene early to beat the rush.

ALSO TRY Liquidity and Flight Casino Bars at the Luxor; **luxor.com.**

The Bank

Bellagio, 3600 South Las Vegas Boulevard, ☎ 702-693-8300; lightgroup.com Mid-Strip and Environs

Cover $30 men and women, locals free on Thursdays and Sundays. **Mixed drinks** $9–$15. **Wine** $9–$15. **Beer** $6–$8. **Dress** Fashionably chic; no sunglasses, shorts, tank tops, flip-flops, jerseys, athletic war, sneakers, and hats. **Specials** Industry and locals nights on Thursday and Sunday. **Food available** None. **Hours** Thursday–Sunday, 10:30 p.m.–4 a.m.

WHO GOES THERE Many will remember—and perhaps miss—the triumphant, late Light Nightclub, which reigned in this space since 2001. Those who do not will still be impressed by the quality of the party Light Group still puts on for longtime patrons, locals, and stars of sport and screen.

WHAT GOES ON Celebrities, sports figures, and foreign magnates eagerly mix with tourists and locals to create a party that does not see its peak until at least 2 a.m.

SETTING AND ATMOSPHERE The intimate, elevated, square-shaped club welcomes you via the original escalators and through the Cristal Champagne–lined anteroom, to the main room, which unfolds down to the mezzanine and dance-floor levels. Understated 1950s-style, Atomic Era designs in gold stand out bravely against a backdrop of black dotted with pricey chandeliers and blessed with a booming sound system.

IF YOU GO Party with the professionals. Consider saving this one for a Sunday night, when the top echelons of the local nightlife set turn out in droves.

ALSO TRY For a bigger experience, winding, multilevel Haze at Aria well satisfies; for something smaller, nearby Caramel Lounge at the Bellagio is an ideal spot in which to convene after dinner and before joining the fray. (For more information on both, call ☎ 702-693-8300 or visit **lightgroup.com.**)

Blue Martini Lounge

CASUAL, ACCESSIBLE, SPRAWLING AFTER-WORK DATE SPOT

6593 South Las Vegas Boulevard; ☎ 702-949-2583; bluemartinilounge.com   South Strip and Environs

Cover Wednesday–Saturday, beginning at 11 p.m.: women always free; men $20 Wednesday and Saturday, $5 Thursday and Friday. **Mixed drinks** $11 and up. **Wine** $9 and up. **Beer** $6 and up. **Dress** Business casual. **Specials** Discounted food and drinks daily, 4–8 p.m. **Food available** Large-portion tapas. **Hours** Wednesday–Saturday, 4 p.m.–4 a.m.; Sunday–Tuesday, 4 p.m.–3 a.m.

WHO GOES THERE Everyone. Locals and visitors with a car have no trouble journeying to the far south end of the Strip for this gem hidden within the Town Square Mall, above Yard House.

WHAT GOES ON As a popular pre/post locale, Blue Martini catches all the after-work, premovie, preparty action and is also a destination unto itself. With live music nightly and four bars (three inside, one out), everyone seems to find their place, although the hottest action usually revolves around the outside bar.

SETTING AND ATMOSPHERE Surprisingly, the place is not overdone. In red, blue, and black, with generous additions of warm wood and subtle lighting, Blue Martini achieves its attractiveness without the use of props, themes, or much artwork. Unsurprisingly, the attractive staff is decoration enough.

IF YOU GO Flying solo, you might find it difficult to strike up a conversation here, as almost everyone here comes with at least one friend. Bring a group of any size to create an instant party.

ALSO TRY Double Helix Wine & Whiskey Lounge, Caña Latin Kitchen, Yard House, The Grape, Cadillac Ranch, and Nu Sanctuary, all at Town Square Mall (**townsquarelasvegas.com**).

Las Vegas Nightclubs

CLUB	TYPE OF CLUB
Aurora	Place to decompress
The Bank	Reincarnation of Light, Vegas's original jewel-box nightclub
Blue Martini	Casual, accessible, sprawling after-work date spot
Blush	Vegas's first boutique nightclub
Center Bar	The original catch-all casino bar
Chandelier Bar	Pre-post at the heart of the Strip's newest casino
Chateau Nightclub and Gardens	Terraced indoor-outdoor nightlife
Coyote Ugly	Drink-slinging barmaids stomp and holler above the crowd
Diablo's Cantina	Spring break happening nightly
Double Helix Wine & Whiskey Bar	Secluded yet central power stop
Downtown Cocktail Room	Bohemian-chic speakeasy
Drai's	Vegas's enduring after-hour power
Gallery Nightclub	Newest nightclub complex on the Strip
Haze	The latest from Light Group
House of Blues	Cover bands, live rock, headliners

Blush

VEGAS'S FIRST BOUTIQUE NIGHTCLUB

Wynn Las Vegas, 3131 South Las Vegas Boulevard; ☎ 702-770-7300; blushlasvegas.com **Mid-Strip and Environs**

Cover Men $30, women $20, local women always free. **Mixed drinks** $15 and up. **Wine** $15 and up. **Beer** $9 and up. **Dress** Casual chic; no baggy clothing, sandals, hats, shorts, or athletic footwear. **Specials** Most nights, women on the guest list enjoy free champagne 11 p.m.–midnight. **Food available** None. **Hours** Monday–Saturday, 9 p.m.–4 a.m.

WHO GOES THERE 25–40; socialites, local industry members, off-duty cocktail servers, and on-duty models.

WHAT GOES ON Though the doors open early, the party hits its stride at midnight. Throughout the week, Blush presents elaborately themed promotions and events. On weekends guest hosts and celebrities populate the choicest tables at the dance floor (those closest to the patio). Resident DJ Mighty Mi keeps it lively with an endless mix of rock, house, and hip-hop.

SETTING AND ATMOSPHERE Formerly Lure Ultralounge, partner-owner Sean Christie's baby is a pretty one. Designed by women, with women in

CLUB	TYPE OF CLUB
Marquee Nightclub & Dayclub	Glamorous megaclub from Tao Group
Mix Lounge	Vegas's most beautiful vantage point
Pete's Dueling Pianos	Raucous sing-along fun
Playboy Club	Cleavage, table games, and nostalgia
Posh	The intersection of nightclub and gents club
Pure Nightclub	Massive, expensive, upscale nightclub
Rí Rá	Fine Irish pub grub and authentic Irish music and *craic*
Stoney's Rockin' Country	Line dancing, two-stepping, and live country bands
Studio 54	Dance and top 40, paying slight homage to the original
Surrender	Party outside under the stars and inside with them
Tabu	The ultralounge that launched a thousand others
Tao	Super-giant-megaclub, restaurant, and lounge
Vanity	Attractive midsize club at the Hard Rock
XS	Excessively beautiful, inside and out
Yard House	Modern sports bar–meets–brew pub

mind, Blush mixes the decidedly fashionable with fashionably playful—banquettes in soft, sable brown velvet, an interactive ceiling made of sculptured silk lanterns, *Basquiat*-inspired art, Barbie and Ken shadow-boxes gracing the disco ball–like bathrooms.

IF YOU GO Dress the part and don't skimp on the shoes. The club is small, so little escapes the notice of Blush's team of hawk-eyed VIP hosts and doormen.

ALSO TRY Surrender at Encore; ☎ 702-770-7300; **SurrenderNight club.com.**

Center Bar

THE ORIGINAL CATCH-ALL CASINO BAR

Hard Rock, 4455 Paradise Road; ☎ 702-693-5000; hardrockhotel.com   East of Strip

Cover None. Mixed drinks $8–$13. Wine $8–$10. Beer $5–$6. Dress Casual. Specials Happy hour daily, 4–8 p.m. Food available None. Hours 24/7.

WHO GOES THERE 21–60; more subject to its surroundings than anywhere else, Center Bar—the original and eponymous item—gets its crowd from The Joint's most current concert, from gamers taking a breather, and from sheer centrifugal force; as the name implies, Center Bar is the nucleus of a circularly constructed casino, so everyone just seems to end up there.

WHAT GOES ON If standing around and drinking were sport, Center Bar would be the Olympics. As there is little else to focus on—there are no walls, no art, and no distractions to speak of—patrons tend to turn their focus to one another and drink heavily. Bartenders struggle to keep pace with the relentless orders.

SETTING AND ATMOSPHERE Center Bar draws crowds into the light-maple wood space with gaming at the 360-degree and trippy, psychedelic dome lit up overhead. On occasion dealers will man the surrounding table games, which have been hoisted up onto the platform bar so as not to waste a second of a dedicated gamer's time.

IF YOU GO As this is technically a casino bar, glassware (and therefore your cocktail) is laughably tiny. The wait for drinks being eternal, you should order doubles every round and keep it simple.

Chandelier Bar

PRE–POST AT THE HEART OF THE STRIP'S NEWEST CASINO

Cosmopolitan, 3708 South Las Vegas Boulevard; ☎ 702-698-7000; cosmopolitanlasvegas.com Mid-Strip and Environs

Cover None. **Mixed drinks** $9 and up. **Wine** $9 and up. **Beer** $6 and up. **Dress** Casual. **Food available** None. **Hours** 24/7.

WHO GOES THERE 21–50; couples grabbing cocktails before or after dinner, groups fueling up before (or instead of) heading to the clubs.

WHAT GOES ON Whether for sheer convenience and location's sake, or because they heard there was a top-notch beverage program to be sampled, bodies pile up at the Chandelier Bar by evening time, when everyone kind of just joins together as one giant party.

SETTING AND ATMOSPHERE A thing of certain beauty: Multiple bar levels are stacked vertically within a massive three-story chandelier constructed of more than two million glass crystals, which dominates the center of the casino. Stairs and elevators connect Levels 1, 1.5, and 2, which cumulatively serve as a center bar, a stand-alone hot spot, and a central meeting point for Marquee Nightclub's VIP hosts and their would-be patrons.

IF YOU GO Find seats first, then either send emissaries to the bar or send up flares to attract the attention of a cocktail server. Off the menus, go for classics and award-winning cocktails on Level 1, flirty and feminine notions on Level 2, and avant-garde (read: experimental) mixology in between on Level 1.5.

ALSO TRY The Cosmopolitan's other fine jewels: Vesper Bar just off the lobby and Bond by the Strip entrance; **cosmopolitanlasvegas.com.**

Chateau Nightclub

TERRACED INDOOR–OUTDOOR NIGHTLIFE

Paris, 3655 South Las Vegas Boulevard; ☎ 702-776-7770; chateaunightclublv.com Mid-Strip and Environs

Cover $30 men, $20 women. **Mixed drinks** $11 and up. **Wine** $12 and up. **Beer** $9 and up. **Dress** Upscale casual; men must wear dress shoes and collared shirts; no shorts or shredded jeans. **Specials** Locals free on Tuesday industry night. **Food available** Sandwiches, salads, pizzas, and appetizers in the Beer Garden, daily 10 a.m.–sunset. **Hours** Tuesday and Friday–Sunday, 10:30 p.m.–4 a.m.

WHO GOES THERE 21–40; tourists from all over, overjoyed to partake in the mass gawking at the usual suspects from this group's stable of celebrities, including the Kardashian clan, hot hip-hoppers, and young Hollywood.

WHAT GOES ON While there is a good party to be had inside the former Risqué nightclub space, this new incarnation has more going for it outdoors. When the sun goes down, the beer garden joins up with the nightclub to become Chateau Terrace, and Chateau Garden, which is perched directly beneath the Eiffel Tower Restaurant, hosts private affairs and an outdoor concert series. For all its many bars, the best cocktails (thanks to mixologist Ken Hall) can be had in the Sugar Factory bar downstairs.

SETTING AND ATMOSPHERE Think *Alice in Wonderland,* assuming Wonderland was located in France. Here, nightlife coexists with its host casino in theme-y cooperation: oversized gilt and silver mirrors, exaggerated furniture, cocktail staff in French maid unis, one DJ booth atop a fireplace, another atop a bar, and so on. But implied Francophilia gives way to out-n-out luxury outside, where private VIP cabanas overlook the Strip and directly oppose the Bellagio fountains.

IF YOU GO Begin the evening downstairs with dinner at the Sugar Factory American Brasserie or, better yet, with chocolate fondue in the Chocolate Lounge. Steal a quick look at the inside of the club but then make an immediate beeline straight for the outdoors. Preferably with a Swedish Fish cocktail from the brasserie.

ALSO TRY Gallery Nightclub at Planet Hollywood; ☎ 702-818-3700; **gallerylv.com.**

Coyote Ugly

DRINK-SLINGING BARMAIDS STOMP AND HOLLER ABOVE THE CROWD

New York–New York, 3790 South Las Vegas Boulevard; ☎ 702-740-6330; coyoteuglysaloon.com South Strip and Environs

Cover $10 after 9 p.m. **Mixed drinks** $8 and up. **Wine** None. **Beer** $7 and up. **Dress** Casual. **Specials** Happy hour daily, 6–9 p.m. with 2-for-1 drinks. **Food available** None. **Hours** Daily, 6 p.m.–until; Daiquiri Bar: daily, 6 p.m.–3 a.m.

WHO GOES THERE 21–45; curious passersby and booze-crazed barflies.

WHAT GOES ON An imported concept from New York City (and made famous by the eponymous movie), Coyote Ugly is a rootin'-tootin' saloon whose main attractions are the slinky female bartenders who leap atop the bars and stomp, clog, sing, dance, and generally whip the crowd into a drunken frenzy (sometimes literally pouring shots into the mouths of the howling masses). The crowd is an almost immobile press, broken only by the occasional scuffle as the security thugs eject a too-rowdy patron.

SETTING AND ATMOSPHERE Vaguely reminiscent of a wood-floored honky-tonk, the surprisingly small room has two bars on opposite walls. That's where you'll find the strutting barmaids doing their stuff. If you can make it through the packed gawkers, an even smaller room in back is only slightly more subdued.

IF YOU GO Forget having a conversation and get ready for some serious, protracted yee-haws. If ogling the barmaids and standing in a crowd are not your bag, you should probably go elsewhere for the evening.

ALSO TRY Pussycat Dolls Burlesque Saloon at Planet Hollywood (☎ 702-818-5700) or, for the real deal, Hogs & Heifers downtown (201 North 3rd Street; ☎ 702-676-1457; **hogsandheifers.com**).

Diablo's Cantina

SPRING BREAK HAPPENING NIGHTLY

Monte Carlo, 3770 South Las Vegas Boulevard; ☎ 702-730-7979; lightgroup.com South Strip and Environs

Cover No cover Sunday–Thursday; Friday and Saturday, free until midnight, then $10. **Mixed drinks** $12 and up. **Wine** $9 and up. **Beer** $6 and up. **Dress** No hats or flip-flops for men. **Specials** Happy hour daily, 3–7 p.m.; $3 drinks change every 30 minutes according to a spin on the "Wheel of Sin." **Food available** Mexican with American twist, served 11 a.m–11 p.m. **Hours** Sunday–Wednesday, 11 a.m.–1 a.m.; Thursday, 11 a.m.–2 a.m.; Friday and Saturday, 11 a.m.–4 a.m.

WHO GOES THERE 21–40; college kids and thirsty pedestrian passersby.

WHAT GOES ON Diablo's has that same voyeuristic temptation you feel when strolling New Orleans's streets during Mardi Gras and looking up at all the lively balcony parties. College kids and former college kids with fond memories of spring breaks past just can't seem to help themselves and get sucked in by Diablo's shabby-shack look, faux-Mexican finishes, strands of party lights, and, of course, the balcony. Local bands perform for free on Thursday nights. On Friday and Saturday nights, you'll find a DJ.

SETTING AND ATMOSPHERE Industrial materials and adobe walls along with vintage-looking tequila signs together look about as authentic as the Indiana Jones ride at Disneyland, but they also tug at the heartstrings while you down nachos and dive headlong into a scary-big margarita.

IF YOU GO If you're looking for elegant modern Mexican dining, keep looking. Though the food is certainly tasty and innovative, Diablo's might not suit a date or a family vacation. Know your audience before giving them the full-on Cabo San Lucas experience.

ALSO TRY Rockhouse Bar & Nightclub outside Imperial Palace at 3535 South Las Vegas Boulevard (☎ 702-691-2909; **therockhousebar.com**) and Cabo Wabo Cantina in the Miracle Mile Shops at Planet Hollywood at 3663 South Las Vegas Boulevard (☎ 702-385-2226; **cabowabo cantina.com**).

Double Helix Wine & Whiskey Bar

SECLUDED YET CENTRAL POWER STOP

Palazzo, 3327 South Las Vegas Boulevard; ☎ 702-735-9463; doublehelixwine.com Mid-Strip and Environs

Cover None. Mixed drinks $12 and up. Wine $7 and up. Beer $3 and up. Dress Casual. Specials Weekly wine tastings every Friday, 5–7 p.m.; happy hour daily, 3–6 p.m. Food available Salads, sandwiches, cheese and fruit delicacy plates, desserts. Hours Sunday–Thursday, 10 a.m.–11 p.m.; Friday and Saturday, 11 a.m.–midnight.

WHO GOES THERE 21–65; sommeliers and restaurateurs, wine aficionados and those they wish to impress.

WHAT GOES ON Close to the action at the Venetian and Palazzo, across the way from Fashion Show mall, and not far from Wynn and Encore, Double Helix wine bar is ideally situated for casual meetings, engaging refreshment breaks, and entertaining a group before or after dinner.

SETTING AND ATMOSPHERE At the crossroads of four wide indoor avenues of high-end shops and boutiques (ladies: Laboutin!), a circular enclosure offers comfortable open seating, high-boy tables, and a full bar. Here, espresso drinks and liquor flow (especially the new addition of a whiskey menu), but the main attraction is the wine, available in tasting portions, by the glass, and as flights. Next door, Double Helix's retail wine shop offers wine by the bottle, wine products (including wine brownies), and accessories. Owner Ray Nisi's passion for wine education and experimentation is observable in the menu—try a winetail!

IF YOU GO If it is possible, time your visit during the daily happy hour, 3–6 p.m., for half off the featured beer, wine, and flights, or 5–7 p.m. Fridays for the weekly $5 wine tasting.

ALSO TRY Double Helix Wine & Whiskey Lounge in Town Square at 6599 South Las Vegas Boulevard Suite 150B (☎ 702-735-9463; **doublehelix wine.com**); Bottles and Burgers by Double Helix in Tivoli Village at 450 S. Rampart Boulevard Suite 120 (☎ 702-735-9463; **doublehelixwine .com**); La Cave Wine & Food Hideaway at Wynn (☎ 702-248-3463; **wynnlasvegas.com**); or Hostile Grape at M Resort (☎ 702-797-1000; **themresort.com**).

Downtown Cocktail Room

BOHEMIAN-CHIC SPEAKEASY

111 Las Vegas Boulevard; ☎ 702-880-3696; thedowntownlv.com Downtown

Cover None. Mixed drinks $7 and up. Wine $5 and up. Beer $3 and up. Dress Casual. Specials Happy hour Monday–Friday, 4–8 p.m. with reduced drinks. Food

available Upscale bar hors d'oeuvres during happy hour. **Hours** Monday–Friday, 4 p.m.–2 a.m.; Saturday, 7 p.m.–2 a.m.

WHO GOES THERE   25–50; artists, musicians, writers, and dilettantes.

WHAT GOES ON   With the arrival of Downtown Cocktail Room, Vegas was made nearly whole. What has long been missing was an oasis to draw in the artists, writers, cognoscenti, and whiskey-bottle philosophers. Small-time filmmakers, big-time DJs, and those who just like to be in a creative atmosphere flock to the corner of Las Vegas Boulevard and Fremont East (opposite the pedestrian-only, covered Fremont Street Experience). The parking validation is a huge bonus.

SETTING AND ATMOSPHERE   Showing up is half the battle, especially when faced with a puzzle at the door. The first hurdle here is locating the door. Inside, regulars chuckle as tourists and first-timers attempt to manipulate the glass panels to get in, completely ignoring the scuffed metal sheet that is the actual door; just push. Once inside, darkness pervades except for pin spotlights and flickering red candles. Partake of the open seating on chaises and leather-couch groupings, at the cement bar, or in the back room—called The Speakeasy—with its high-backed leather booths, tinkling chandeliers, and exposed pipes overhead.

IF YOU GO   Keep an open mind. Classic cocktails and absinthe (now legal in the United States) are a specialty, as is the seasonal cocktail list. Get your Red Bull and Jägermeister fixes elsewhere. Soak up the groovy vibes, listen to a live singer-songwriter, or just strike up a conversation with the bleary-eyed Hunter S. Thompson–looking fellow on the next barstool. He probably painted the art you were so admiring on the walls.

ALSO TRY   Vanguard Lounge at 516 Fremont Street (☎ 702-868-7800; **vanguardlv. com**) or Savile Row at the Luxor (☎ 702-222-1500; **savile rowlv.com.**

Drai's Afterhours

VEGAS'S ENDURING AFTER-HOUR POWER

Bill's Gamblin' Hall and Saloon, 3595 South Las Vegas Boulevard;
☎ **702-737-0555; lasvegas.drais.net**   **Mid-Strip and Environs**

Cover Thursday and Sunday, $20 and $10 for locals; Friday and Saturday, $30 and $20 for locals. **Mixed drinks** $12 and up. **Wine** $18 and up. **Beer** $12 and up. **Dress** Dress to impress; no hats, oversized jeans, baggy clothing, tennis shoes, athletic wear, or excessive jewelry. **Food available** None. **Hours** Thursday–Monday, 1 a.m.–until.

WHO GOES THERE   21–40; a hodgepodge of DJs, local industry movers and shakers, and an older European contingency.

WHAT GOES ON   The extreme in late-night party shifts, this one really gets rollicking around 3 a.m. The booths and dance floor are home to professional partiers and Continental playboys wearing shades and blasé attitudes. With a door presided over by some of nightlife history's most infamous thugs and notorious femme fatales, you must be on your "A" game or on the arm of an NFL star to vault to the front of the line when there is one. But as with ultralounges, some nights, and especially early on, one can often walk right in with little to no hassle. Most tables are available for seating until the reservation party arrives.

SETTING AND ATMOSPHERE   Two things stand out as the signatures of Hollywood producer–turned–restaurateur–turned–nightlife impresario Victor Drai: superb lighting and red, red, red everywhere. In the library, deep couches and cushions nestle fireside in front of bookcases entirely shellacked in red, including the books, picture frames, and busts of composers. Animal-print booths, gaudy mirrors, and forests of ferns dot the large subterranean space, formerly Drai's restaurant. House and trance music dominate the main rooms, while hip-hop emanates from the back room.

IF YOU GO   Drink sizes and prices are shockingly large. Cocktails arrive in heavy pint glasses topped with plastic beverage lids (ostensibly to prevent spills, but locals know that afterhours as a concept comes with an unfortunate history in illicit substances and the like; the lids supposedly stave off unwanted additives). There is a $50 minimum tab for credit card charges, and the ATM also charges more than anywhere else, so bring all the cash you think you will need for the night or be prepared to be taken one way or another.

ALSO TRY   Posh at The Playground (3525 West Russell Road; ☎ 702-673-1700; **poshlasvegas.com**) or The Artisan Lounge in the Artisan Hotel (☎ 702-214-4000; **artisanhotel.com**).

Gallery Nightclub

NEWEST NIGHTCLUB COMPLEX ON THE STRIP

Planet Hollywood, 3667 South Las Vegas Boulevard; ☎ 702-818-3700; gallerylv.com   Mid-Strip and Environs

Cover $20 men, $10 women. **Mixed drinks** $12 and up. **Wine** $12 and up. **Beer** $9 and up. **Dress** Upscale nightclub; men must wear collared, button-up shirt and dress shoes. **Specials** Locals free on Industry Wednesdays. **Food available** None. **Hours** Wednesday–Saturday, 10 p.m.–4 a.m.

WHO GOES THERE   Hot coeds, voyeurs, star-stalkers, people who didn't get the memo that Privé closed down.

WHAT GOES ON   Planet Hollywood gets heavy tourist traffic, what with the Miracle Mile Shops, nearby Koi Restaurant, and Peepshow. Gallery throws a high-energy fête for an energetic young crowd that truly appreciates the little design elements that make a night there more comfortable than at some of the larger party factories. Events bounce between hipster heroes and electronic music stars.

SETTING AND ATMOSPHERE   Sexy from top to bottom: Above, entertainers writhe and creep around in suspended nets; below, butter-soft booths flank dance platforms that invite the lither of the crown to kick off their heels and dance like everyone is watching; and all around, provocative black-and-white photos (hot masked woman playing the cello? Yes.) seem to pop out from the photo-wrapped walls and grace the bar tops. Candlelit hallways, women dancing in alcoves, chandeliers, fireplaces. . . . Forget *Eyes Wide Shut;* you'll want to keep 'em wide open.

IF YOU GO Make sure to go on a night when the Pussycat Dolls Burlesque Saloon is open next door. Yes, those Pussycat Dolls of Robin Antin–choreographed fame perform routines on stage, on the catwalk, and on bejeweled carousel horses. The petite, attractive lounge is attached to the larger club, so bouncing back and forth is encouraged.

ALSO TRY Chateau Nightclub at Paris Las Vegas; ☎ 702-776-7770; **chateaunightclublv.com.**

Haze Nightclub

BIG NEW BEAUTY—THE LATEST FROM LIGHT GROUP

Aria, 730 South Las Vegas Boulevard; ☎ 702-693-8300; hazenightclub.com Mid-Strip and Environs

---

Cover $40, women $30. **Mixed drinks** $10 and up. **Wine** $10 and up. **Beer** $6 and up. **Dress** Trendy chic; no hats. **Food available** None. **Hours** Thursday–Saturday, 10:30 p.m.–4 a.m.

WHO GOES THERE 25–45; magnates, heirs and heiresses, impresarios and the people who gawk at them and then Twitter about it.

WHAT GOES ON Today's hottest singers, DJs, and actors are imported nightly to tip their hat or ply their trade for the crowds. Bartenders churn and burn despite their requisite corsets; partiers travel from all over the world to see top electronic DJs and just to say they were there. It's a must-see on any avid clubber's list.

SETTING AND ATMOSPHERE A bit on the warehouse side (Studio 54 meets Ra; remember Ra?!), but a chic, well-decorated converted warehouse. And where better to house the top tier of Vegas's hottest partiers? Music is loud, crowds are densely packed, and security is typically gruff with a hair-trigger temper.

IF YOU GO Like sister club Jet, Haze tends to become one giant traffic jam; during high tide, all movement grinds to a certain halt. Make right for the bar, spring for a double, find a comfy spot with a view, and plan to stay there for the night. There's a nice little balcony and bar overlooking the dance floor that is ideal for this.

ALSO TRY Moon Nightclub at the Palms; ☎ 702-942-6832; **n9negroup.com.**

House of Blues

COVER BANDS, LIVE ROCK, HEADLINERS

Mandalay Bay, 3950 South Las Vegas Boulevard; ☎ 702-632-7605; houseofblues.com/lasvegas South Strip and Environs

---

Cover Cover for most shows; cost varies. **Mixed drinks** $8 and up. **Wine** $9 and up. **Beer** $6 and up. **Dress** Clothes. **Food available** Daily lunch and dinner; Sunday gospel brunch; Southern-inspired dining. **Hours** Restaurant: Sunday–Thursday, 8 a.m.–midnight; Friday and Saturday, 8 a.m.–1 a.m. Music hall: daily, 8 p.m.–midnight or 1 a.m. (depending on event).

WHO GOES THERE 21–60; locals, tourists, music lovers.

WHAT GOES ON House of Blues sports two venues: the 1,800-seat concert auditorium downstairs and the restaurant-bar upstairs (casino level). In this review, we're talking about the live music that takes place in the restaurant Thursday–Saturday, 10:30 p.m.–1 a.m., when blues and R & B performers take the stage under lights that spell out "Have Mercy, Las Vegas." It's a cool, casual, and not-too-cacophonous scene, with an eclectic audience mix all grooving to some hot licks.

SETTING AND ATMOSPHERE House of Blues is one of the more evocative dining rooms in town, set to resemble an outdoor courtyard in the middle of a small bayou village, with a huge tree in the middle and tables on a stone floor under and around it, as well as up on patio-type wooden decks. Wrought-iron railings, stone walls, etched and stained glass, and the facades of swamp shacks extend the theme, all under dim lighting. (They also account for the good acoustics.) The only incongruity is the collection of TV monitors on various walls throughout.

IF YOU GO Anything seems to go here during the music: big tables of beer-drinking college kids; couples (and singles) dancing all around the room; unreconstructed barefoot hippies in peasant blouses and patchouli perfume praising the Lord; lead singers or guitarists roaming the room wireless and interacting directly with the audience. It's best on Thursday nights when there's no concert downstairs and only those in the know are upstairs, enjoying some of the best bargain (free) entertainment in town.

ALSO TRY BB King's Blues Club at the Mirage (☎ 702-242-5464; **bbkingclubs .com**) or Crown Theater and Nightclub at the Rio (☎ 888-727-6966; **thecrownvegas.com**).

Marquee Nightclub & Dayclub

GLAMOROUS MEGACLUB FROM TAO GROUP

Cosmopolitan, 3708 South Las Vegas Boulevard; ☎ 702-333-9000; marqueelasvegas.com   Mid-Strip and Environs

Cover Monday: men $30, women $20, locals free; Friday: men $30, women, $20, local ladies free; Saturday: men $50, women $20, local ladies free. **Mixed drinks** $11 and up. **Wine** $12 and up. **Beer** $8 and up. **Dress** Stylish nightlife attire required; collared shirts for men. **Specials** Locals free on Marquee Mondays. **Food available** None. **Hours** Monday, Friday, and Saturday; one Thursday monthly.

WHO GOES THERE Everyone. No, seriously—everyone.

WHAT GOES ON Vegas's newest mega-club is the mega-ist. Marquee dominates the Strip in all aspects. The scene at the door is a cattle call of unthinkable proportions, the dance floor a sea of beautiful bodies, the stairwells connecting the main room to the Boom Box Room and The Library surging arteries. So, why would you want to throw yourself into such a mix? Please refer back to "Who goes there" above.

SETTING AND ATMOSPHERE Featuring similar attention to detail as big sisters Tao and Lavo (though without the Asian or Italian themey-ness), Marquee makes luxury its theme. The circular main room is a well-appointed house music amphitheater, perfectly arranged so that even someone in the back can see the DJ jump up on his rig and feel the rush of wind as confetti cannons fire off overhead. The Boom Box Room packs bodies in around the DJ and bar like a subway car, so New Yorkers should feel right at home. Upstairs in The Library, a fire roars, sexy librarians serve serious cocktails, and a vintage pool table awaits your attention.

IF YOU GO Strategy is a must. Dine nearby at Holsteins or China Poblano. From there you can keep an eye on the velvet ropes. When the bodies begin to stack up, get the check and a to-go cocktail, and get in line. Among the first through the door that night, you will have the rare opportunity to see how beautiful the rooms are (and get to the bar) before all hell breaks loose. Don't miss out on the pool deck, which goes strong all day and all night on the 17th floor of the Cosmo.

ALSO TRY Haze at Aria (☎ 702-693-8300; **lightgroup.com**) and Tao at the Venetian (☎ 702-388-8588; **taolasvegas.com**).

Mix Lounge

VEGAS'S MOST BEAUTIFUL VANTAGE POINT

THEhotel, Mandalay Bay, 3950 South Las Vegas Boulevard;
☎ **702-632-9500; mandalaybay.com** South Strip and Environs

Cover Sunday–Wednesday, no cover; Thursday–Saturday, $15–$25; local ladies and THEhotel guests, always free. **Mixed drinks** $16 and up. **Wine** $12 and up. **Beer** $8 and up. **Dress** Business casual; no shorts, sandals, or athletic wear. **Food available** Appetizers available 5–9:30 p.m., until 10:30 p.m. on weekends. **Hours** Lounge: Sunday–Wednesday, 5 p.m.–midnight; Thursday–Saturday, 5 p.m.–3 a.m.

WHO GOES THERE 21–60; the moneyed, the curious, design aficionados.

WHAT GOES ON A glass elevator in the passage connecting THEhotel to the rest of Mandalay Bay elevates guests to Mix, the lounge attached to the Alain Ducasse restaurant of the same name. Once there, prepare to spend about half an hour gasping at the stunning view of the Strip, directly north over the point of the Luxor pyramid. Then spend some time gasping at the room itself. Then go gasp at the restaurant next door, with its 15,000-glass-bulb, half-million-dollar chandelier. Then realize that you're surrounded by a youngish but still loungey crowd intent on conversation, cocktails, and periodic stares out the windows. If there's a better place in Vegas to start your night, we're not aware of it. As far as ending your night here—or never leaving—you could do a lot worse.

SETTING AND ATMOSPHERE Did we mention the view? About 15 feet of floor-to-ceiling glass sheaths Mix on both sides of the lounge. There's an outdoor observation area railed with clear glass, as well. Inside, it's all deep reds and sleek blacks. An oversized main bar dominates, with two ranks of tables facing the windows. A diminutive dance floor and some seating in the round don't hurt either. DJs play light house and pop on busy nights, but it's not intrusive—this is a lounge, after all, not a club.

IF YOU GO The lounge opens earlier than other high-end nightspots, and you can sometimes get a break on the cover charge if they're looking to fill up the room a bit. Also an obvious choice for drinks before or after a meal at the attached restaurant, though bring your gold card. The bathrooms boast spectacular views as well.

ALSO TRY Chandelier Bar at the Cosmopolitan (☎ 702-698-7000; **cosmo politanlasvegas.com**) and the Mandarin Bar at Mandarin Oriental Hotel (☎ 888-881-9367; **mandarinoriental.com.**)

Pete's Dueling Piano Bar

RAUCOUS, SING-ALONG FUN

6551 South Las Vegas Boulevard; ☎ 702-220 7383; petesduelingpianobar.com   South Strip and Environs

Cover None. **Mixed drinks** $7.50 and up. **Wine** $7.50 and up. **Beer** $5.50 and up. **Dress** Casual. **Food available** None. **Hours** Wednesday–Saturday, 7 p.m.–2 a.m.

WHO GOES THERE College students, tourists, southerners, and anyone looking for a night out that can still include flip-flops and a ball cap.

WHAT GOES ON Talented singers wail away on pianos like impassioned, well-tipped Jerry-Lee Lewises. Bachelorettes, birthday boys and girls, and creepy, out-of-place older men are herded on stage and forced to sing, dance, and generally mock themselves for the amusement of a howling, boozed-up crowd. The Pete's songbook spans the 1960s to today, as well as country and odd hip-hop arrangements. Request "The Piano Man" and expect a rain of projectiles.

SETTING AND ATMOSPHERE What might normally be used as a dance floor is crowded with tiny cabaret tables and lots of chairs. Cocktail servers weave in and out delivering rounds of beer and cocktails, while every inch of standing room quickly fills up around them. The no-nonsense bars are sturdy and sizeable, the walls decorated with liquor- and beer-branded mirrors and—what else?—photos of patrons enjoying themselves at Pete's!

IF YOU GO Arrive early, meaning as soon as doors open at 7 p.m., to claim a table on the dance floor. Once the shows begin at 8 p.m. there is very little turnover, and groups seem to expand exponentially over the night, grandfathering tables out to friends arriving later rather than making them available to newcomers.

ALSO TRY The Eastside Lounge at Encore (☎ 702-770-8000; **wynnlasvegas .com**); Napoleon's at Paris (☎ 877-603-4386; parislasvegas.com); the Bar at Times Square at New York–New York (☎ 702-740-6466; **newyorknewyork.com**); and Don't Tell Mama (☎ 702-207-0788).

Playboy Club

CLEAVAGE, TABLE GAMES, AND NOSTALGIA

Palms Hotel, 4321 West Flamingo Road; ☎ 702-942-6900; playboyclub.com   Mid-Strip and Environs

Cover $20 men, ladies free; cover also grants admission to Moon nightclub. **Mixed drinks** $8 and up. **Wine** $8 and up. **Beer** $8 and up. **Dress** Nightlife attire; no tennis shoes, flip-flops, or baseball hats. **Specials** Local-industry night Sunday. **Food available** None. **Hours** Daily, 9 p.m.–4 a.m.

WHO GOES THERE Beautiful under-40s and graying Playboy nostalgics.

WHAT GOES ON Admiring the views of Las Vegas, and table-game gambling dealt by those queens of cleavage, the fabled Playboy Bunnies (and you thought they were extinct).

SETTING AND ATMOSPHERE Situated one floor below the Moon rooftop nightclub in the Fantasy Tower of the Palms, the Playboy Club is an intimate venue with floor-to-ceiling windows on three sides and, on the fourth, cushy lounge seating beneath a display of vintage *Playboy* covers and memorabilia. In the middle of the club, and taking up most of the floor space, are the gaming tables and black Baccarat chandeliers, as well as a relatively new dance floor. A cozy lounge (to the left as you enter the club) features leather chairs, vintage Playboy pinball machines, and a chic modern gas-fed hearth but no views.

IF YOU GO Your cover charge includes admission to Moon, one floor up, with its retractable roof and stunning views of the Las Vegas Valley. If you eat at Nove, the Italian restaurant below the Playboy Club, you can enter the clubs from there. You'll still have to cough up the cover, but you'll avoid the ground-floor line.

Posh Boutique Nightclub

THE INTERSECTION OF NIGHTCLUB AND GENTS CLUB

3525 West Russell Road; ☎ 702-673-1700; poshlasvegas.com
South Strip and Environs

Cover Two-drink minimum for men, ladies free. **Mixed drinks** $8 and up. **Wine** None. **Beer** $7 and up. **Dress** Fashionable; no shorts, sandals, or baseball caps. **Specials** Ladies Night every Friday. **Food available** Sushi and bar food. **Hours** Friday and Saturday, midnight–7 a.m.

WHO GOES THERE Vampires, partymonsters, nightcrawlers, and off-duty industry members blowing off steam before (and even after) the next day dawns.

WHAT GOES ON When the restaurants close and the clubs are already hitting their stride, the evening is just getting started at Posh. Locals enjoy bottle specials, ladies enjoy an open bar from midnight until 2 a.m., and everyone enjoys the luxe surroundings, sexy staff, and top-tier DJ imports.

SETTING AND ATMOSPHERE Formerly the Rock Room, this corner of The Playground nightlife complex was without distinction until Posh opened its doors, moving in with fresh and, well, posh furnishings. Luxurious dark woods and warm chocolate and gold fabrics let you know you're in a club; the peek-a-boo wall reminds you that the club's neighbor is the Crazy Horse III gentlemen's club.

IF YOU GO Go late. Why not? There are plenty of clubs that will help you see 4 a.m., maybe 5 a.m., but few—outside of the traditional gentleman's club—that can see you through till the dawn. If you are determined to go the distance, Posh has a hookah lounge, sushi restaurant, and even a strip club close by to get you to the finish line.

ALSO TRY Drai's Afterhours (☎ 702-737-0555; **afterhours.drais.net**) and Déjà Vu Erotic Afterhours (☎ 702-227-5200; **dejavuvegas.com**).

Pure Nightclub

MASSIVE, EXPENSIVE, UPSCALE NIGHTCLUB

Caesars Palace, 3570 South Las Vegas Boulevard; ☎ 702-731-7873; caesarspalace.com   Mid-Strip and Environs

Cover Men $30, women $20; locals free on Tuesday. **Mixed drinks** $15 and up. **Wine** $15 and up. **Beer** $9 and up. **Dress** No shorts, sneakers, jerseys, hats, or baggy pants. **Specials** Tuesday local-industry night. **Food available** None. **Hours** Tuesday and Thursday–Sunday, 10 p.m.–4 a.m.

WHO GOES THERE 21–50; tourists, high rollers, wannabes, bachelors and bachelorettes in droves.

WHAT GOES ON Dancing, drinking, and exploring the three rooms downstairs is the main gig, but many go for the rooftop view of the Strip. Then there's the exclusivity thing, the celebrity thing, the impress-or-be-impressed thing, the we're-here-and-you're-not thing, and the curiosity thing. You get the idea.

SETTING AND ATMOSPHERE Basically four clubs within a club—the Main Room decorated in shades of white; the Red Room decorated (obviously) in red with upholstered walls and private booths; the Terrace, up one floor with fabulous outdoor views of the Strip; and the now-defunct Pussycat Dolls Lounge (look for the Dolls at their new Planet Hollywood burlesque saloon). Each area has its own bars, decor, dance floor, and music, so you can experience completely different atmospheres in each.

IF YOU GO A pilgrimage for bachelor and bachelorette parties, expect large groups, lots of little white veils, and long bathroom lines. While much of the A-list has moved on, because of sheer volume, reservations are a must. Independent VIP-hosting companies come in mighty handy here.

ALSO TRY LAX at Luxor; ☎ 702-262-4529; **laxthenightclub.com.**

Rí Rá Las Vegas

FINE IRISH PUB GRUB AND AUTHENTIC IRISH MUSIC AND CRAIC

The Shoppes at Mandalay Place, 3930 South Las Vegas Boulevard; ☎ 702-632-7771; rira.com/rira/las_vegas   South Strip and Environs

Cover None. **Mixed drinks** $5 and up. **Wine** $5 and up. **Beer** $5 and up. **Dress** Casual. **Food available** Authentic Irish cuisine with a hint of American flair; a wide selection of appetizers, sandwiches, lunch fare, and entrées 7 days a week. **Hours** Monday–Thursday, 11 a.m.–3 a.m.; Friday, 11 a.m.–4 a.m.; Saturday, 9 a.m.–4 a.m.; Sunday, 9 a.m.–3 a.m.

WHO GOES THERE Eireophiles, Celtic music fans, and footie fiends.

WHAT GOES ON Deceiving from the outside, the seemingly endless interior of this lively, casual gastropub and bar is actually a buzzing hive of nearly constant activity. Bands Irish and beyond play for the exuberant crowd, those that are not entranced by a football game (soccer to the rest of us) showing on one of the infinitesimal flat-screen TVs that dot the space.

The food is tasty and interesting, especially the generous fish and chips and the house-made soda bread; here, every Guinness is well poured.

SETTING AND ATMOSPHERE No expense was spared in bringing a whole lotta Ireland to Sin City. Professional pickers salvaged authentic 19th-century materials, millwork, and statuary from all over the Emerald Isle, including artifacts dating back to 1890 from the Olympia Theater in Dublin.

IF YOU GO Try not to be in a hurry; so much of pub life is about leaving the world out on the doorstep, or in this case, in the mall. Take the time to experience and appreciate the individual personality of each room as well as the entertainment—this can mean the live music variety as well as the stars of sport and the friendly Irish staff.

ALSO TRY McFadden's at the Rio (☎ 702-270-6200; **mcfaddensvegas .com**); Nine Fine Irishmen at New York–New York (☎ 702-740-6463; **ninefineirishmen.com**); and Queen Victoria Pub at The Riviera (☎ 800-634-3420; **rivierahotel.com**).

Stoney's Rockin' Country

LINE DANCING, TWO-STEPPING, AND LIVE COUNTRY BANDS

9151 South Las Vegas Boulevard, #300; ☎ 702-435-2855; stoneysrockincountry.com South Strip and Environs

Cover Locals $5; nonlocals $10; Thursday, $1 for ladies. **Mixed drinks** $7 and up. **Wine** $7 and up. **Beer** $4 and up. **Dress** No beanies, bandanas, do-rags, jerseys, or cutoff sleeves. Think Levis, ten-gallon hats, and truly massive belt buckles. **Specials** Visit their website for a current list. **Food available** Chips, candy, and assorted snacks. **Hours** Thursday–Saturday, 7 p.m.–5 a.m.; Sunday, 9 p.m.–5 a.m.

WHO GOES THERE 21–60+; country-music fans, cowboys, and ladies who like cowboys.

WHAT GOES ON Whether it's NASCAR, PBR, or just a Tim McGraw after-concert party, the dance floor is teeming on Saturday nights with two-stepping and boot-scootin' cowboys and the women who love them. Manners prevail as men still ask ladies to dance, let them pass, and take sloooow rides on the mechanical bull ahead of them.

SETTING AND ATMOSPHERE Mechanical bull? Check. Sawdust on the floor? Check. A VIP section, mile-long bars, and 2,500 square feet of slick-pine dance floor housed within 20,000 square feet of pure country? Check. There's no mistaking owner Stoney Gray's intentions when he built his Rockin' Country nightclub, a follow-up to Gilley's at the since-imploded New Frontier Hotel. A cowboy arcade of games, mini-bowling, darts, and pool complete the experience.

IF YOU GO Arrive early, not so much to beat the lines (and there are indeed lines) but rather to avail yourself of the complimentary line-dancing lessons at 7:30 p.m. (most nights the club is open).

ALSO TRY Revolver at 4949 North Rancho (☎ 702-658-4900; **nightlife station.com**) and the new Gilley's at T. I. (☎ 702-894-7111; **treasure island.com**).

Studio 54

DANCE AND TOP 40, PAYING SLIGHT HOMAGE TO THE ORIGINAL

MGM Grand, 3799 South Las Vegas Boulevard; ☎ 702-891-7254; mgmgrand.com   **South Strip and Environs**

Cover Tuesday–Thursday, men $20, women $10; Friday, men and women $20; Saturday, men $30, women $20; locals always free. **Mixed drinks** $10 and up. **Wine** $10 and up. **Beer** $8 and up. **Dress** Clubwear; no baggy jeans, shorts, tennis shoes, or work boots. **Specials** Local-industry night Tuesday. **Food available** None. **Hours** Tuesday–Saturday, 10 p.m.–4 a.m.

WHO GOES THERE   25–40; local regulars, returning tourists, and the unapologetically nostalgic.

WHAT GOES ON   The New York club that set the standard during disco's heyday in the 1970s comes to Las Vegas. Stylish, beautiful people gather for a night of high energy, music, dance, and socializing. Friday nights bring DJ Loczi's Electric Dream, a wild night of dance music, impressive visuals, and surprise guest acts.

SETTING AND ATMOSPHERE   It's two stories tall with dance floors, bars, VIP booths, and conversation areas on each level. The black-girder-and-steel-grate flooring and exposed elevator lifts (really just go-go cages) give the club an industrial, high-tech feel. Black-and-white photographs of celebrities and trendsetters visiting New York's venerable Studio 54 of yesteryear line the walls on the second floor.

IF YOU GO   If you know anything about the original Studio 54, then you know about the concept's history of drama at the door. On big nights (fight weekends, concerts), Vegas's installment is no different. Though club management and hotel presidents have changed over the years, the attitude at the door remains constant. While locals and regulars are greeted with smiles and open ropes, others find themselves embarking on a long wait. Arrive early and keep a Zenlike calm.

ALSO TRY   Rain at the Palms; ☎ 702-942-6832; **n9negroup.com.**

Surrender Nightclub

PARTY OUTSIDE UNDER THE STARS AND INSIDE WITH THEM

Wynn Encore, 3131 South Las Vegas Boulevard; ☎ 702-770-7300; EncoreBeachClub.com or SurrenderNightclub.com   **Mid-Strip and Environs**

Cover Men $40, women $30. **Mixed drinks** $15 and up. **Wine** $15 and up. **Beer** $9 and up. **Dress** Resort casual and nightclub chic; no athletic gear or street clothes. **Food available** None. **Hours** Wednesday, Friday, and Saturday, 10:30 p.m.– 4 a.m.

WHO GOES THERE   25–45; local tastemakers, casino guests, tourists with the wherewithal to try anything Steve Wynn is backing.

WHAT GOES ON   By day, the Encore Beach Club offers 60,000 square feet of lush oasis with three tiered pools, daybeds, 26 cabanas, and a walk-up grill (daily, 11 a.m.–7 p.m.), but by night the smallish club (about 5,000 square feet) envelops the Beach Club into its embrace and offers a unique, climate-controlled combined 65,000 square feet of party acreage—Vegas's largest party spot at present. Fans of European-style electronic music and DJs will definitely want to make a pilgrimage, as Encore Beach Club keeps an impressive stable of renowned resident DJs as well as fresh talent on tap.

SETTING AND ATMOSPHERE High ceilings, 20-foot-tall windows, wide-open spaces, and dramatic views of the pool deck create the "wow" factor. Playing on the theme of original sin, fabric and feature colors are eye-popping yellows, chrome is abundant, and the carpets leopard print—subtlety is for wusses. Statues hang from the walls, and sculptures hold lighting fixtures.

IF YOU GO Consider making the Beach Club your stop during the day and make a point of introducing yourself to some VIP host–looking fellows (they'll be the ones with furrowed brows and barking into a Blackberry) who will likely offer to help you out in returning that night.

ALSO TRY Marquee Nightclub & Dayclub at the Cosmopolitan; ☎ 702-333-9000; **marqueelasvegas.com.**

Tabu

THE ULTRALOUNGE THAT LAUNCHED A THOUSAND OTHERS

MGM Grand, 3799 South Las Vegas Boulevard; ☎ 702-891-7183; mgmgrand.com or tabulv.com   South Strip and Environs

Cover Friday and Saturday, $20; Sunday and Monday, men $20, women $10; locals always free. **Mixed drinks** $10 and up. **Wine** $10 and up. **Beer** $8 and up. **Dress** Fashionable upscale. **Food available** None. **Hours** Friday–Monday, 10 p.m.–5 a.m.

WHO GOES THERE 30–50; high rollers and hotties of all persuasions.

WHAT GOES ON Hyped as an ultralounge, Tabu may come close to whatever that means. Once inside (only very occasionally a hassle; interest has waned over time), you'll be rewarded with some excellent eye candy via both the space and its inhabitants. The staff are dressed to kill and seem to be cloned from a diverse assortment of supermodels and porn stars; the patrons do their best to rise to that standard. If you've had a great day in the casino and want to really test your meat-market mettle, this is the place.

SETTING AND ATMOSPHERE The main room is plushly decorated with frosted glass and subtle lighting, and there are plenty of tables and chairs for the daring (since all are reservable, you'll be sitting on borrowed time unless you ante up). Three tables in the main room project images onto their surface that ripple or change color in reaction to your presence and motion. There's a second, smaller room off to the side that's a little more intimate, and it has its own bar as well. Last is the oval Tundra Room (also called the Igloo Room or The Egg) with a view to the vodka locker and done up in appropriate whites with a central table and cushions.

IF YOU GO Despite their attempts to organize a general admission line to the left of the door, would-be patrons directly address the VIP host stand instead. However, on a weekday night, you might also walk straight in without a glance or a cover. In addition, early birds can often sit at reserved VIP tables until kicked out by those who have paid for the space (check with staff about which tables to avoid).

ALSO TRY Ghostbar at Palms; ☎ 702-938-2666; **n9negroup.com.**

Tao

SUPER-GIANT-MEGACLUB, RESTAURANT, AND LOUNGE

Venetian, 3377 South Las Vegas Boulevard; ☎ 702-388-8588; taolasvegas.com Mid-Strip and Environs

Cover Thursday, ladies $10, men $20; Friday, local women free, men and non-local women $20; Saturday, local ladies free, nonlocal ladies $20, men $30. **Mixed drinks** $14 and up. **Wine** $12 and up. **Beer** $8 and up. **Dress** Upscale casual (collared shirts or blazers for men). **Specials** Local-industry night Thursday. **Food available** Asian cuisine and sushi available in the restaurant, Sunday–Thursday, 5 p.m.–midnight; Friday and Saturday, 5 p.m.–1 a.m. **Hours** Lounge: daily, 5 p.m.–5 a.m.; nightclub: Thursday–Saturday, 10 p.m.–4 a.m.

WHO GOES THERE 21–45; Hard-core clubcrawlers, pretty people, sexpots, the scantily clad, hedonists.

WHAT GOES ON The Venetian finally hit the jackpot with Tao, after misfiring with several nightlife venues since the property opened. A huge combination of restaurant, lounge, and nightclub, Tao offers highly sought-after dinner reservations, a cool lounge space, and a labyrinthine club that packs 'em in from the moment the velvet rope drops. Hordes of casino patrons and Strip-walkers swarm all of Tao's parts, so it's a good thing the place is so large. The music is keyed to the hottest dance mixes and meant to move the most flesh as quickly as possible, en masse. It's meat-market central for the young, sweaty, and on the make.

SETTING AND ATMOSPHERE The pretty but minimally decorated lounge serves mainly as an air lock and chill-out space for the upstairs club space, which includes several bars, two levels of VIP cells, a recessed dance floor, several dancer showcase platforms, and a tiny bit of Strip-side balcony. Various Buddhas sit in nooks and crannies or in placid groups, while barely clad living models do the "human statue" thing in gauzy boudoirs. Vaguely exotic and certainly sexy, Tao's look and feel is downright aphrodisiacal when the crowd is right.

IF YOU GO Go early, or go with your celebrity friends. The line will be long, but it does move, and everyone really does get a chance to get in eventually. Front-of-line passes available from various websites or other sources would come in handy here, and if you have (or are) a group of attractive females, your chances of skipping the line or portions thereof will be dramatically improved.

ALSO TRY Lavo at Palazzo; ☎ 702-791-1818; **lavolv.com.**

Vanity Nightclub

ATTRACTIVE MIDSIZE CLUB AT THE HARD ROCK

Hard Rock Hotel, 4455 Paradise Road; ☎ 702-693-5557; vanitylv.com East of Strip

Cover $40 men, $20 ladies; local ladies free; local men free Sunday. **Mixed drinks** $13 and up. **Wine** $15 and up. **Beer** $9 and up. **Dress** Upscale casual/nightclub attire required. **Food available** None. **Hours** Friday–Sunday, 10:30 p.m.–4 a.m.

WHO GOES THERE 21–40; hardcore house-heads, other DJs, post-Rehab partiers, off-duty club promoters, and locals a-plenty.

WHAT GOES ON On Fridays, Vanity presents DJ Eric D-Lux, and Sundays are for Sin, the local-industry night. If anyone asks, you live in "Green Valley" or "Summerlin" and you just arrived, haven't visited the DMV just yet.

SETTING AND ATMOSPHERE Don't feel vain for checking yourself out in almost every reflective surface; Vanity is all about You. A magnificent cyclone of an LED chandelier whips up from the floor to illuminate the dance floor from above. A VIP stage overlooks the club with its two large bars, ample and varying VIP seating arrangements, a catwalk with brass street lamps (well, stripper poles really), and a patio with fire pit, cabanas, and access to neighboring Relax Bar.

IF YOU GO Preparty at Relax Bar from 6 p.m. to midnight and catch a beautiful desert sunset before heading inside; by the time you emerge, it might be near sunrise . . . almost time for a day at the Rehab pool.

XS

EXCESSIVELY BEAUTIFUL, INSIDE AND OUT

Wynn Encore, 3131 South Las Vegas Boulevard; ☎ 702-770-5350; xslasvegas.com Mid-Strip and Environs

Cover Men $30, women $20; men $50 on Saturday. **Mixed drinks** $15 and up. **Wine** $20 and up. **Beer** $10. **Dress** Casual chic; no hats, oversized jeans, or athletic wear. **Food available** None. **Hours** Friday–Monday, 10 p.m.–4 a.m.

WHO GOES THERE With 13,000 square feet of indoor space for bars, a dance floor, and VIP seating, and 27,000 square feet of exterior space for more bars, 95 additional VIP tables, an illuminated pool, a blackjack pit, and 30 poolside cabanas, XS is naturally a magnet for the well-heeled and wannabe-well-heeled.

WHAT GOES ON No gimmicks, cheesy hosts, or costume parties here; there's no need. Supernatural beauty is rewarded by XS's cast of beautiful servers and VIP hosts. Guests are encouraged to make use of the VIP table backs for elevated seating—all the better to view and be viewed—and to put the stripper poles to good use.

SETTING AND ATMOSPHERE Vegas's most beautiful nightclub was inspired by the sexy curves of the human body and boasts more than 10,000 individual light sources, including a disco chandelier and 16 stripper poles thinly disguised as lamps. Focal features include gold-leaf body forms, an illuminated outdoor pool (open summer Sunday nights), and a large circular dance floor surrounded by VIP tables.

IF YOU GO Bring your A-game and break out the good shoes. Long before you pass through XS's gilded gates, you will have to navigate a maze of admission lines and pass through multiple sets of eyes critical of your attitude, dress, comportment, and entourage. A Darwinian process ensues, culling the herd down to the haves and the have-nots. Leave embarrassing in-laws, cousins, and friends in the casino, and expect to throw down a mortgage payment for a table and more bottles than your group could ever realistically consume.

Yard House

MODERN SPORTS BAR–MEETS–BREW PUB

6593 South Las Vegas Boulevard; ☎ 702-734-9273; yardhouse.com
South Strip and Environs

Cover None. **Mixed drinks** $8.75 and up. **Wine** $5.25 and up. **Beer** $4.25 and up. **Dress** No dress code. **Specials** Daily happy hour 3–6 p.m., reverse happy hour Sunday–Wednesday, 10 p.m.–close; drink discounts and half-off select appetizers. **Food available** American fusion; PF Changs–meets–Cheesecake Factory. **Hours** Sunday–Thursday, 11 a.m.–2 a.m.; Friday and Saturday, 11 a.m.–3 a.m.

WHO GOES THERE   21–35; former college rugby players, current pick-up basketball lovers, and cheerleaders. "Frat boy utopia," it has been called.

WHAT GOES ON   When there's an important game on, all attention is on two things: the multiple flat-screen TVs throughout the restaurant and the eye-crossing draft-beer selection. In between major sporting events, the primary focus blurs a little to include eating casual American bistro-style cuisine and picking up dates.

SETTING AND ATMOSPHERE   A chain found in ten states, Yard House consistently provides a modern brew-pub look with a bright, upbeat party vibe. Massive metal tubes overhead bring beer from the keg room to 160 taps that pour out 140 types of beer to all manner of patrons, though the young and sporty tend to dominate.

IF YOU GO   If your wallet can stand it, avoid happy hour unless you enjoy standing at the bar eating and rubbing elbows with strange men. Periodic cheers and jeers reflect the progress of the sporting event du jour and can wreak havoc on intense conversation; head upstairs to Blue Martini for that. If beer is not your cup of tea, Yard House also boasts 23 martinis and more than 44 wines.

ALSO TRY   Freakin' Frog (4700 South Maryland Parkway; ☎ 702-597-9702; **freakinfrog.com**) or The Pub at Monte Carlo (☎ 702-730-7777; **montecarlo.com**).

LAS VEGAS *below the* BELT

DON'T WORRY, BE HAPPY

IN MANY WAYS, LAS VEGAS IS A BASTION of hedonism. Simply being there contributes to a loosening of inhibitions and a partial discarding of the rules that apply at home. Las Vegas exults in its permissiveness and makes every effort to live up to its image and to bestow upon its visitors the freedom to have fun. Las Vegas has a steaminess, a cosmopolitan excitement born of superabundance, an aura of risk and reward, a sense of libertine excess. The rules are different here; it's all right to let go.

Behind the illusion, however, is a community, and more particularly, a police department that puts a lot of effort into making it safe for visitors to experience the liberation of Las Vegas. It is hard to imagine another city where travelers can carry such large sums of money so safely. A tourist can get robbed or worked over in Las Vegas, but it is comparatively rare, and more often than not is due to the visitor's own carelessness or naivete. The Strip and downtown, especially, are well patrolled, and most hotels have very professional in-house security forces.

In general, a tourist who stays either on the Strip or downtown will be very safe. Police patrol in cars, on foot, and, interestingly, on mountain bikes. The bikes allow the police to quickly catch pickpockets or purse snatchers attempting to make their escape down sidewalks or through parking lots. Cross-streets that connect the Strip with Paradise Road and the Las Vegas Convention Center are also lighted and safe. When tourists get robbed, they are commonly far from downtown or the Strip and often in pursuit of drugs or sex.

ORGANIZED CRIME AND CHEATING

VERY FEW VISITORS WALK THROUGH a casino without wondering if the games are rigged or if the place is owned by the Mafia. During the early days of legalized gambling, few people outside of organized crime had any real experience in managing gaming operations. Hence, a fair number of characters fresh from eastern gangs and crime families came to work in Nevada. Since they constituted the resource pool for experienced gambling operators, the state suffered their presence as a necessary evil. In 1950, Tennessee senator Estes Kefauver initiated an attack on organized crime that led (indirectly) to the formation of the Nevada Gaming Commission and the State Gaming Control Board. These agencies, in conjunction with federal efforts, were ultimately able to purge organized crime from Las Vegas. This ouster, coupled with the Nevada Corporate Gaming Acts of 1967 and 1969 (allowing publicly held corporations such as Hilton, Holiday Inn, Bally, and MGM to own casinos), at last brought a mantle of respectability to Las Vegas gambling.

Today the Gaming Control Board oversees the activities of all Nevada gaming establishments, maintaining tight control through frequent unannounced inspections of gambling personnel and equipment. If you ever have reason to doubt the activity or clout of the Gaming Control Board, try walking around the Strip or downtown in a dark business suit and plain black shoes. You will attract more attention from the casino management than if you entered with a parrot on your head.

Ostensibly, cheating exists in Las Vegas gambling to a limited degree. But a case of a Nevada casino cheating customers hasn't been publicized for decades. "Gaffing" the games is seldom perpetrated by the house itself. In fact, most cheating is done at the expense of the house, though honest players at the cheater's table may also get burned. Sometimes a dealer, working alone or with an accomplice (posing as a player), will cheat, and there are always con artists, grab-and-run rip-off artists, and rail thieves ready to take advantage of the house and legitimate players.

SKIN GAMES—SEX IN LAS VEGAS Though nudity, prostitution, and pornography are regulated more tightly in Las Vegas than in many Bible-Belt cities, the town exudes an air of sexual freedom and promiscuity. Las Vegas offers a near-perfect environment for marketing sex. More than 50% of all visitors are men, most ages 21–59. Some come to party, and many, particularly convention-goers, are alone and ready for action. Almost all have time and money on their hands.

Las Vegas evolved as a gambler's city, projecting the image of a trail town where a man could be comfortable and just about anything could be had for a price. It was not until strong competition developed for the gambling dollar that hotels sought to enlarge their market by targeting women and meetings. Today, though there is something for everyone in Las Vegas, its male orientation remains unusually strong.

Las Vegas, perhaps more than any other American city, has objectified women. A number of Las Vegas production shows continue to feature topless showgirls and erotic dance, even though audiences are mostly couples. Lounge servers and keno runners are almost exclusively women, invariably attired in revealing outfits. Video marquees, highway billboards, taxi banners, magazine ads, and tabloids in curbside newspaper vending machines all tout naked women to some degree. Showroom comedians, after 30 years, persist in describing Las Vegas as an adult Disneyland.

STRIPPING ON THE STRIP Compared to the live adult entertainment in many cities, "girlie" (and "boy-ie") shows in Las Vegas, both downtown and on the Las Vegas Strip, are fairly tame. In some of the larger showrooms, this is an accommodation to the ever-growing percentage of women in the audience. More often, however, it is a matter of economics rather than taste, the result of a curious City of Las Vegas law that stipulates that you can offer totally nude entertainment or you can serve alcoholic beverages, but not both.

MALE STRIPPERS Economics and the market have begun to redress (or undress) the inequality of women's erotic entertainment in Las Vegas. Spearheaded by the Rio, which features (*Chippendales*) male strippers for lengthy engagements, and empowered by the ever-growing number of professional women visiting Las Vegas for trade shows and conventions, the rules for sexual objectification are being rewritten. Today in Las Vegas, if watching a young stud flex his buns is a woman's idea of a good time, that experience is usually available. In addition to the Rio, male strippers perform at the Palomino Club (the only fully nude male revue in the United States). *Thunder from Down Under,* the Australian male revue, plays at the Excalibur and *American Storm* is at the Miracle Mile Shops.

WHERE THE GIRLS ARE

BELOW WE DESCRIBE A FEW of the better-known strip joints. If you want the whole scoop, buy a copy of *Sin City Advisor's Topless Vegas,* by Arnold Snyder. The book is available in both print and e-book format at **lvahotels.com** (☎ 800-244-2224). In a city where it's relatively easy to spend $400 at a topless club, Snyder's guide is a real bargain. It tells you where the most beautiful dancers are and where they're not; how to have a great strip club experience for $30 or less; topless club etiquette (there's a lot more to this than you might imagine); lap dancing A to Z; and how to avoid taxi scams and scams at the clubs. There are detailed rankings and reviews of all nude clubs and topless clubs, all topless shows playing at the casinos, and, for good measure, all of the city's topless pools. Straight talk is Snyder's trademark, so you can count on him to address just about any question you can think of, including those you'd be too embarrassed to ask.

On the Internet

Try **vegas-after-dark.com** for reviews of the clubs and ratings of the attractiveness of the dancers, among other things. The site also provides links to the individual club websites and offers discussion boards where visitors discuss such topics as the relative merits of fully nude versus topless clubs. One poster thought topless clubs superior because, as he put it, "I've never had anything contagious leap off a boobie at me." All righty, then.

THE PALOMINO CLUB (☎ 702-642-2984) At the Palomino Club, ten minutes from downtown, the customer can have it all. The Palomino Club is not inexpensive, but at least they're up front about what they're selling. As competition has heated up in the Las Vegas nude trade, Palomino's previously high prices have come down. Before 9 p.m. admission is free; after 9 it's $10 Sunday–Thursday and $20 on Friday and Saturday. Things don't heat up till around 11 p.m., so you'll have to do a lot of sitting (and drinking) to beat the entrance fee. Still, though you have to be 21 to get in, dancers have to be only 18 to work there, so the scenery, if you're into youngish girls, is easy on the eyes.

An average of seven professionals dance nightly, performing in rotation and stripping nude. Most of the women are attractive and athletic. The Palomino is without pretense. It delivers some of the best erotic dancing in town for about the same cost as a production show on the Strip.

LITTLE DARLINGS (☎ 702-366-1141, 1514 Western Avenue, **dejavu .com**) If you can do without alcohol, Little Darlings is our pick for the best nude stage show in the state. Not only are the dancers stunningly gorgeous, but many of them are extremely athletic. Unlike many topless and nude shows where the performers pretty much clamber around the stage, Little Darlings' showgirls can dance. Beverage service is limited to non-alcoholic drinks. Cover is $30 for nonlocals, $10 for locals.

TOPLESS BARS The main difference between a topless bar and a totally nude nightclub (aside from the alcohol regulations) is a G-string. Unless you're a gynecology intern, you might be satisfied with a topless bar. If you have more than a few drinks, the topless bars aren't less expensive than the Palomino but are often more conveniently located. Downtown, on Fremont Street, is the **Girls of Glitter Gulch** (☎ 702-385-4774; **glittergulchlv.com**). There's no cover charge, but drinks average a stiff (no pun intended) $10 each, with a two-drink minimum. Clientele is almost all tourists, so the pressure to buy a lap dance and overpriced drinks is intense. There are exceptions, but by and large the dancers are a bit overweight and long in the tooth.

The **Sapphire Club** (**sapphirelasvegas.com**) claims 6,000 women in its lineup of strippers (insiders say it's closer to 2,000, which is still plenty). By observation, the later you arrive in the evening, the better-looking the dancers. Though the club claims to be the largest of its kind in the world, much of the space is allocated to private rooms and VIP areas. For the average patron, Sapphire is upscale but doesn't seem all that big. The admission charge of $30, though, seems big.

An equally upscale venue is **OG** (formerly Olympic Garden) at 1531 Las Vegas Boulevard; **ogvegas.com.** OG is the only strip club on the Strip (right across from Stratosphere). Given its location, it caters to out-of-town men, and its prices are a dead giveaway: a $30 cover charge and $380 for a half hour in the VIP room.

Crazy Horse III (3525 West Russell Road; ☎ 702-673-1700; **ch3lv .com**) replaced The Penthouse Club in mid-2009 after a major overhaul. Admission is $30. The usual $9 beers and $20 lap dances are available. The venue is sprawling and swanky, and thanks to free-drink and other promotions, locals show up in droves, which attracts the hot dancers. They also have good deals on sushi (which is served all night), a hookah lounge, and Obsession afterhours club opening at 2 a.m.

Note: Be aware that taxi drivers get a kickback for delivering you to a particular gentlemen's club. Do not let a taxi driver talk you out of your chosen destination and take you someplace he recommends.

EROTIC HERITAGE MUSEUM (☎ 702-369-6442; 3275 Industrial Road; **eroticheritage.org**) Located just north of Desert Inn Road next door to the Déjà Vu all-nude club, this 17,000-square-foot museum exhibits a small part of the erotic art of two collectors who between them own whole warehouses full of the stuff. The permanent collection includes all the mid- to late 20th-century films that launched the sexual revolution; bondage paraphernalia from the famous bondage inventor Gord; arcade peep machines and other fetish equipment; a display devoted to Larry Flynt and the First Amendment; the work of urban sex artists (muralists, cartoonists, sculptors, photo-realists, and the like) celebrating mostly low-brow public art; and much more. The boutique sells reproductions and posters of erotic art, classic erotic DVDs, books, T-shirts, and the like. Admission is a $15 donation, $10 for locals and students.

PART THREE

GAMBLING

 ## The **WAY IT IS**

GAMBLING IS THE REASON LAS VEGAS (in its modern incarnation) exists. It is the industry that fuels the local economy, paves the roads, and gives the city its identity. To visitors and tourists, gambling may be a game. To those who derive their livelihood from gambling, however, it is serious business.

There is an extraordinary and interesting dichotomy in the ways gambling is perceived. To the tourist and the gambler, gambling is all about luck. To those in the business, gambling is about mathematics. To the visitor, gambling is a few hours a day, while to the casinos, gambling is 24 hours a day, every day. The gambler *hopes* to walk away with a fortune, but the casinos *know* that in the long run that fortune will belong to the house. To visitors, gambling is recreation combined with risk and chance. To the casinos, gambling is business combined with near-certainty.

The casino takes no risk in the games themselves. In almost all cases, in the long run the house will always win. The games, the odds, and the payoffs are all carefully designed to ensure this outcome. Yet the casino does take a chance and is at risk. The casino's bet is this: that it can entice enough people to play.

Imagine a casino costing hundreds of millions of dollars, with a staff numbering in the thousands. Before a nickel of profit can be set aside, all the bills must be paid, and the payroll must be met. Regardless of its overwhelming advantage at the tables, the house cannot stay in business unless a lot of people come to play. The larger the casino, the more gamblers are required. If the casino can fill the tables with players, the operation will succeed and be profitable, perhaps spectacularly so. On the other hand, if the tables sit empty, the casino will fail.

The gambling business is competition personified. All casinos sell the exact same product. Every owner knows how absolutely critical it is to get customers (gamblers) through the door. It is literally the *sine qua non:* no players, no profit. The casinos are aggressive and creative when it comes to luring customers, offering low-cost buffets, $2 shrimp cocktails, stage shows, lounge entertainment, free drinks, gambling tournaments, and players clubs.

The most common tactic for getting customers through the door is to package the casino as a tourist attraction in its own right. Take the Mirage. There are exploding volcanoes in the front yard, palm trees in the living room, and live sharks in the parlor. Who, after all, wants to sip their free drink in a dingy, red-Naugahyde-upholstered catacomb when they can be luxuriating in such a resplendent tropical atrium?

THE SHORT RUN

ASK A MATHEMATICIAN OR A CASINO OWNER if you can win gambling in a casino, and the truthful answer is yes, but almost always only in the short run. Unless you're a professional player who only plays with the long-term edge on your side, the longer you play, the more certain it is that you will lose.

I (Bob here) learned about the short run (and the long run) on a road trip when I was in the fifth grade. My family lived in Kentucky, and every year we were fortunate enough to take a vacation to Florida. This particular year I was allowed to invite a schoolmate, Glenn, along.

As the long drive progressed, we became fidgety and bored. To pass the time, we began counting cars traveling in the opposite direction. Before many miles had passed, our counting evolved into a betting game. We each selected a color and counted the cars of that color. Whoever counted the most cars of his chosen color would win.

Glenn chose blue as his color. I was considering red (my favorite), when I recalled a conversation between my mother and a car salesman. The salesman told my mother that white was by far the most popular color "these days." If this were true, I reasoned, there should be more white cars on the road than blue cars. I chose white.

As we rumbled through the hilly Kentucky countryside between Bowling Green and Elizabethtown, my friend edged ahead. This puzzled me and I began to doubt the word of the car salesman. By the time we made it to Bowling Green, Glenn was ahead by seven cars. Because I was losing, I offered to call it quits and pay up (a nickel for each car he was ahead). Glenn, not unexpectedly, was having a high time and insisted we continue playing.

By the time we crossed the Tennessee line I had pulled even. Once again I suggested we quit. Glenn would have none of it. Gloating enormously, he regained a three-car lead halfway to Nashville. Slowly, however, I overtook him, and by Nashville I was ahead by four cars. Tired of the game, I tried once more to end it. Since he was behind, Glenn adamantly demanded that we play all the way to Atlanta. We did, and by the time we got there, Glenn owed me almost $4.

After a night in Atlanta and a great deal of sulking on Glenn's part, we resumed our travels. To my amazement, Glenn insisted—demanded, in fact—the opportunity to win back his previous day's losses. There would be one great "do-or-die battle, blues against whites," he said, all the way to our destination (St. Augustine, Florida). As we drove south, I went ahead by a couple of cars, and then Glenn regained the lead by a small margin. By the time we reached St. Augustine, however, Glenn owed me another $5.40.

Outraged (and broke), Glenn exercised the only option remaining—he complained to my parents. Shaking his head, my father said, "Give Glenn his money back. Everybody knows that there are more white cars than blue cars." Not so. Glenn didn't.

While Glenn's behavior is not particularly unusual for a preadolescent, you would assume that adults have better sense. Everybody knows there are more white cars than blue cars, remember? In Las Vegas, however, the casinos are full of Glenns, all over age 21, and all betting on blue cars.

I nailed Glenn on the cars because I knew something that he didn't. In casino games, patrons either do not understand what they are up against, or alternatively (and more intelligently), they do understand, but chalk up their losses as a fair price to pay for an evening's entertainment. Besides, in the short run, there's a chance they might actually win.

Glenn's actions on our trip mirrored almost exactly the behavior of many unfortunate casino gamblers:

1. He did not understand that the game was biased against him.

2. He did not take his winnings and quit when he was ahead in the short run.

3. On losing, he continued playing and redoubled his efforts to pull even or win, ultimately (in the long run) compounding his losses.

EAGLES AND ROBINS

IF ON OUR DRIVE I HAD SAID, "Let's count birds. You take eagles and I'll take robins," Glenn would have laughed in my face, instantly recognizing that the likelihood of spotting an eagle was insanely remote. While the casinos will not offer a fair game (like betting even money on the flip of a coin), they do offer something a bit more equitable than eagles and robins.

I had another friend growing up who was big for his age. Whenever I went to his house to play, he would beat me up. I was not a masochist, so I finally stopped going to his house. After a few days, however, he asked me to come back, offering me ice cream and other incentives. After righteously spurning his overtures for a time, I gave in and resumed playing at his house. True to his word, he gave me ice cream and generously shared his best toys, and from that time forward he beat me up only once a week.

This is exactly how the casinos operate, and why they give you a better deal than eagles versus robins. The casinos know that if they hammer you every time you come to play, sooner or later you will quit coming. Better to offer you little incentives and let you win every once in a while. Like with my big friend, they still get to beat you up, but not as often.

THE BATTLE AND THE WAR

IN CASINO GAMBLING, the short run is like a battle, and either player or casino can win. However, the casino almost always wins the war. The American Indians never had a chance against the continuing encroachment of white settlers. There were just too many settlers and too few Indians for the outcome ever to be in doubt. Losing the war, however, did not keep the Indians from winning a few big battles. So it goes in casino gambling. The player struggles in the face of overwhelming odds. If he keeps slugging it out, he is certain to lose. If, on the other hand, he hits and runs, he may come away a winner.

Gambling is like a commando raid: the gambler must get in, do some damage, and get out. Hanging around too long in the presence of superior forces can be fatal.

To say that this takes discipline is an understatement. It's hard to withdraw when you are winning, and maybe even harder to call it quits when you are losing. Glenn couldn't do either, and a lot of gamblers are just like Glenn.

THE HOUSE ADVANTAGE

IF CASINOS DID ENGAGE IN FAIR BETS, they would win about half the bets and lose about half the bets. In other words, the casino (and you), on average, would break even, or at least come close to breaking even. While this arrangement would be more equitable, it would not, as a rule, generate enough money for the casino to pay its mortgage, much less foot the bill for the dancing waters, pirate battles, lounge shows, $8 steaks, and free drinks.

To ensure sufficient income to meet their obligations and show a profit, casinos establish rules and payoffs for each game to give the

HOUSE ADVANTAGES

Baccarat	1.17% on bank bets, 1.36% on player bets
Blackjack	0.5% to 5.9% for most games
Craps	1.4% to almost 17%, depending on the bet
Keno	20% to 35%
Roulette	5.26% to 7.89%, depending on the bet
Slots	2% to 25% (average 4% to 14%)
Video poker	0.2% to 12% (average 4% to 8%)
Wheel of fortune	11% to 24%

house an advantage. While the house advantage is not strictly fair, it is what makes bargain rates on guest rooms, meals, and entertainment possible.

There are three basic ways in which the house establishes its advantage:

1. THE RULES OF THE GAME ARE TAILORED TO THE HOUSE'S ADVANTAGE In blackjack, for instance, the dealer by rule always plays his own hand last. If any player busts (attains a point total over 21), the dealer wins by default before having to play out his hand.

2. THE HOUSE PAYS OFF AT LESS THAN THE ACTUAL ODDS Imagine a carnival wheel with ten numbers. When the wheel is spun, each number has an equal chance of coming up. If you bet a dollar on number six, there is a one in ten chance that you will win and a nine in ten chance that you will lose. Gamblers express odds by comparing the likelihood of losing to the likelihood of winning. In this case, nine chances to lose and one to win, or nine to one. If the game paid off at the correct odds, you would get $9 every time you won (plus the dollar you bet). Each time you lost you would lose a dollar.

Let's say you start with $10 and do not win until your tenth try, betting your last dollar. If the game paid off at the correct odds, you would break even. Starting with $10, you would lose a dollar on each of your first nine attempts. In other words, you would be down $9. Betting your one remaining dollar, you win. At nine to one, you would receive $9 and get to keep the dollar you bet. You would have exactly the $10 you started with.

As we have seen, there is no way for a casino to play you even-up and still pay the bills. If, therefore, a casino owner decided to install a wheel with ten numbers, he would decrease the payoff. Instead of paying at the correct odds (nine to one), he might pay at eight to one. If you won on your last bet and got paid at eight to one (instead of nine to one), you would have lost $1 overall. Starting with $10, you lose your first nine bets (so you are out $9) and on your last winning bet you receive $8 and get to keep the dollar you bet. Having played ten times at the eight-to-one payoff, you have $9 left, for a total loss of $1. Thus the house's advantage in this game is 10% (one-tenth).

The house advantage for actual casino games ranges from less than 1% for certain betting situations in blackjack to 35% on keno. Although 1% doesn't sound like much of an advantage, it will get you if you play long enough. Plus, for the house it adds up.

Because of variations in game rules, the house advantage for a particular game in one casino may be greater than the house advantage for the same game in another casino. In most Las Vegas casinos, for instance, the house has a 5.26% advantage in roulette. At European casinos, however, because of the elimination of 00 (double zero) on certain roulette wheels, the house advantage is pared down to about 2.7%.

The rule variations in blackjack swing the house advantage from almost zero in single-deck games (surrender, doubling on any number of cards, dealer stands on soft 17, etc.) to more than 6% in multiple-deck games with draconian rules, such as a recent wrinkle at blackjack, where a natural 21 pays off at 6 to 5 rather than the age-old 3 to 2. Quite a few mathematicians have taken a crack at computing the house's advantage in blackjack. Some suggest that the player can gain an advantage over the house by keeping track of cards played. Others claim that without counting cards, a player utilizing a decision guide known as "basic strategy" can play the house nearly even. The reality for 95% of all blackjack players, however, is a house advantage of between 0.5% and 5.9%, depending on rule variations and the number of decks used.

Getting to the meat of the matter: blackjack and some video poker played competently, baccarat, and certain bets in craps minimize the house advantage and give the player the best opportunity to win. Keno and wheel of fortune are outright sucker games. Slots, other video poker, and roulette are only marginally better.

How the house advantage works in practice causes much misunderstanding. In most roulette bets, for example, the house holds a 5.26% advantage. If you place a dollar on black each time the wheel is spun, the house advantage predicts that, on average, you will lose 5.26 cents per dollar bet. Now, in actual play you will either lose one whole dollar or win one whole dollar, so it's not like somebody is making small change or keeping track of fractional losses. The longer you play, however, the greater the likelihood that the percentage of your losses will approximate the house advantage. If you played for a couple of hours and bet $1,000, your expected loss would be about $53.

All right, you think, that doesn't sound too bad. Plus, you're thinking: I would never bet as much as $1,000. Oh, yeah? If you approach the table with $200 and make 20 consecutive $10 bets, it is not very likely that you will lose every bet. When you take money from your winning bets and wager it, you are adding to your original stake. This is known as "action" in gambling parlance, and it is very different from bankroll. Money that you win is just as much yours as the stake with which you began. When you choose to risk your winnings by making additional bets, you are giving the house a crack at a much larger amount than your original $200. If you start with $200, win some and lose some, and keep playing your winnings in addition to your original stake until you have lost everything, you will have given the house (on average) about $3,800 worth of action. You may want to believe you lost only $200, but every penny of that $3,800 was yours.

3. THE HOUSE TAKES A COMMISSION In all casino poker games and in certain betting situations in table games, the house will collect a commission on a player's winnings.

Sometimes the house combines its various advantages. In baccarat, for instance, rules favor the house; payoffs are less than the true odds; and in certain betting situations, the house collects a commission on the player's winnings.

GAMES OF CHANCE AND THE LAW OF AVERAGES

PEOPLE GET FUNNY IDEAS ABOUT the way gambling works. In casinos there are games of chance (roulette, craps, keno, bingo, slots, baccarat) and games of chance *and* skill (poker, blackjack, video poker).

A game of chance is like flipping a coin or spinning a wheel with ten numbers. What happens is what happens. A player can guess what the outcome will be but cannot influence it. Games of chance operate according to the law of averages. If you have a fair coin and flip it ten times, the law of averages leads you to expect that approximately half of the tosses will come up heads and the other half tails. If a roulette wheel has 38 slots, the law of averages suggests that the ball will fall into a particular slot one time in 38 spins.

The coin, the roulette ball, and the dice, however, have no memory. They just keep doing their thing. If you toss a coin and come up with heads nine times in a row, what are your chances of getting heads on the tenth toss? The answer is 50%, the same chance as getting heads on any toss. Each toss is completely independent of any other toss. When the coin goes up in the air that tenth time, it doesn't know that tails has not come up for a while, and certainly has no obligation to try to get the law of averages back into whack.

Though most gamblers are familiar with the law of averages, not all of them understand how it works. The operative word, as it turns out, is "averages," not "law." If you flip a coin a million times, there is nothing that says you will get 500,000 heads and 500,000 tails, no more than there is any assurance you will get five heads and five tails if you flip a coin ten times. What the law of averages *does* say is that, *in percentage terms,* the more times you toss the coin, the closer you will come to approximating the predicted average.

If you tossed a coin ten times, for example, you would not be surprised to get six tails and four heads. Six tails is only one flip off the five tails and five heads that the law of averages tells you is the probable outcome. By percentage, however, tails came up 60% (six of ten) of the time, while heads came up only 40% (four of ten) of the time. If you continued flipping the coin for a million tries, would you be surprised to get 503,750 tails and only 496,250 heads, a difference of 7,500 more tails than heads? The law of averages stipulates that the more we toss (and a million tosses are certainly a lot more than ten tosses) the closer we should come to approximating the average, but here we are with a huge difference of 7,500 more tails. What went wrong?

Nothing went wrong. True, after ten flips, we had only two more tails than heads, while after a million flips we had 7,500 more tails

The Intelligence Test

If you have been paying attention, here is what you should understand by now:

1. That all gambling games are designed to favor the house, and that in the long run the house will always win.
2. That it costs a lot to build, staff, and operate a casino, and that a casino must attract many players in order to pay the bills and still make a profit.
3. That casinos compete fiercely for available customers and offer incentives ranging from 99-cent hot dogs to free guest rooms to get the right customers to their gaming tables.

Question: Given the above, what kind of customer gets the best deal?

Answer: The person who takes advantage of all the incentives without gambling.

Question: What kind of customer gets the next best deal?

Answer: The customer who sees gambling as recreation, gambles knowledgeably, makes sensible bets, sets limits on the amount he or she is prepared to wager, and enjoys all of the perks and amenities, but stays in control.

Question: What kind of customer gets the worst deal?

Answer: The person who thinks he or she can win. This person will foot the bill for everyone else.

than heads. But in terms of percentage, 503,750 tails is 50.375% of one million, only about one-third of a measly percent from what the law of averages predicts. The law of averages is about percentages. Gambling is about dollars out of your pocket. If you had bet a dollar on heads each toss, you would have lost $2 after ten flips. After a million flips you would have lost $7,500. The law of averages behaved just as mathematical theory predicted.

Games of Chance and Skill

Blackjack, poker, and video poker are games of chance and skill, meaning that the knowledge, experience, and skill of the player can have some influence on the outcome. All avid poker players or bridge players can recall nights when they played for hours without being dealt a good hand. That's the chance part. In order to win, you need good cards. There is usually not much you can do if you are dealt a bad hand. As the Nevada mule drivers say, "You can't polish a turd."

If you are dealt something to work with, however, you can bring your skill into play and try to make your good hand even better. In casino poker, players compete against each other in the same way they do at Uncle Bert's house back home. The only difference is that in the casino the house takes a small percentage of each winning pot as compensation for hosting the game (are you listening, Uncle Bert?). Although not every casino poker player is an expert, your chances of coming up against an expert in a particular game are good.

Our advice on casino poker: if you're not a tough fish, better not try to swim with the sharks.

Blackjack likewise combines chance and skill. In blackjack, however, players compete against the house (the dealer). Players have certain choices and options in blackjack, but the dealer's play is completely bound by rules. Much has been written about winning at blackjack. It's been said that by keeping track of cards played (and thereby knowing which cards remain undealt in the deck), a player can raise his or her bets when the deck contains a higher-than-usual percentage of aces, tens, and picture cards. In practice, however, the casino confounds efforts to count cards by combining several decks together, "burning" cards (removing undisclosed cards from play), and keeping the game moving at a fast pace. If an experienced gambler with extraordinary memory and power of concentration is able to overcome these obstacles, the casino will simply throw out this person.

In blackjack, as in every other casino game, it is ludicrous to suggest that the house is going to surrender its advantage. Incidentally, a super-gambler playing flawlessly and keeping track of every card will gain only a nominal and temporary advantage over the house. On top of playing perfectly and being dealt good cards, the super-gambler must also disguise his play and camouflage his betting so the house won't know what he's up to. It's not impossible, but very few players who try ever pull it off successfully.

Playing It Smart

Experienced, noncompulsive, recreational gamblers typically play in a disciplined and structured manner. Here's what they recommend:

1. **Never gamble when you are** tired, depressed, or sick. Also, watch the drinking. Alcohol impairs judgment (you play badly) and lowers inhibitions (you exceed prudent limits).

2. **Set a limit before you leave home** on the total amount you are willing to lose gambling. No matter what happens, do not exceed this limit.

3. **Decide which game(s) interest you and get the rules down before you play.** If you are a first-timer at craps or baccarat, take lessons (offered free at the casinos most days). If you are a virgin blackjack player, buy a good book and learn basic strategy. For all three games, spend an hour or two observing games in progress before buying in. Stay away from games like keno and wheel of fortune, in which the house advantage is overwhelming.

4. **Decide how long you want to play** and work out a gambling itinerary consistent with the funds you set aside for wagering. Let's say you plan to be in Las Vegas for two days and want to play about five hours each day. If you have $500 in gambling money available for the trip, that's $250 a day. Dividing the $250 a day by five hours, you come up with $50 an hour.

Now, forget time. Think of your gambling in terms of playing individual sessions instead of hours. You are going to play five sessions a day with $50 available to wager at each session.

5. **Observe a strategy for winning and losing.** On buying in, place your session allocation by your left hand. Play your allotted session money only once during a given session. Anytime you win, return your original bet to the session-allocation stack (left hand), and place your winnings in a stack by your right hand. Never play any chips or coins you have won. When you have gone through your original allocation once, pick up the chips or coins in your winning stack (right hand) and quit. The difference between your original allocation and what you walk away with is your net win or loss for the session.

During the session, bet consistently. If you have been making $1 bets and have lost $10, do not chase your losses by upping your bets to $10 in an effort to get even in a hurry.

If you were fortunate and doubled your allocated stake during the session (in this case, walked away with $100 or more), take everything in excess of $100 and put it aside as winnings, not to be touched for the remainder of your trip. If you won, but did not double your money, or if you had a net loss (quit with less than $50 in your win stack), use this money in your next playing session.

6. **Take a break between sessions.** Relax for a while after each session. Grab a bite to eat, enjoy a nap, or go for a swim.

7. **When you complete** the number of sessions scheduled for the day, stop gambling. **Period.**

GAMING INSTRUCTION AND RESOURCES

MOST CASINO GAMES ARE ACTUALLY FAIRLY SIMPLE once you know what's going on. A great way to replace inexperience and awkwardness with knowledge and confidence is to take the free gaming lessons offered by the casinos. Going slowly and easily, the instructors take you step by step through the play and the betting without you actually wagering any money. Many casinos feature low-minimum-bet "live games" following the instruction. We also recommend the lessons to nonplaying companions of gamblers. For folks who usually spend a fair amount of time as spectators, casino games, like all other games, are more interesting if you know what is going on.

We highly recommend the free gaming lessons offered by casinos. They introduce you not only to the rules but also to the customs and etiquette of the respective games.

No matter how many books you have read, take a lesson in craps before you try to play in a casino. You don't need to know much to play baccarat, but *understanding* it is a different story. Once again, we strongly recommend lessons. Though you can learn to play blackjack by reading a book and practicing at home, lessons will make you feel more comfortable.

When "new games" are added to the traditional selection, casinos often offer instruction for a limited time. The latest rages are poker and a whole bunch of poker derivatives: Texas Hold 'Em, Let It Ride, Caribbean Stud, Three Card poker, Crazy 4 poker, 3-5-7 poker, along with Casino War, and, owing to the increasing number of Asian gamblers, Pai Gow and Pai Gow poker. Lessons are also available in traditional poker. A list of free gambling lessons currently offered in Las Vegas can be found at **lvahotels.com.** Click on "Gambling Advisor" at the top right of the page.

WRITTEN REFERENCES AND THE GAMBLER'S BOOK CLUB Most libraries and bookstores offer basic reference works on casino gambling. If you cannot find what you need at home, call the Gambler's Book Shop at ☎ 800-522-1777 for a free catalog. If you would like to stop in and browse while you are in Las Vegas, the club's store is located at 5473 S. Eastern Avenue. The local phone is ☎ 702-382-7555. Gambler's Book Shop, incidentally, sells single issues of the *Las Vegas Advisor,* quoted above.

WHERE TO PLAY

WE RECEIVE A LOT OF MAIL FROM READERS asking which casino has the loosest slots, the most favorable rules for blackjack, and the best odds on craps. We directed the questions to veteran gambler and tournament player Anthony Curtis, publisher of the *Las Vegas Advisor.* Here's Anthony's reply:

> *Where's the best casino in Las Vegas to play blackjack, video poker, and the rest of the gambling games? It could be almost any place on any given day due to spot promotions and changing management philosophies. A few casinos, however, have established reliable track records in specific areas. Absent a special promotion or change in policy, I recommend the casinos in the chart on pages 310–311 as the best places for the games listed.*

CHANGES IN ATTITUDE, CHANGES IN LATITUDE

MOST PEOPLE WHO LOVE TO GAMBLE are not motivated solely by greed. Usually it is the tension, excitement, and anticipation of the game that they enjoy. Misunderstanding this reality has led many naive and innocent people into the nightmare of addictive gambling.

Ed was attending a convention on his first visit to Las Vegas. One evening, he decided to try his luck at roulette. Approaching the table, Ed expected to lose ("I'm not stupid, after all"). His intentions were typical. He wanted to "try" gambling while in Nevada, and he was looking for an adventure, a new experience. What Ed never anticipated was the emotional impact gambling would have on him. It transcended winning and losing. In fact, it wasn't about winning or losing at all. It was the *playing* that mattered. The "action" made him feel alive, involved, and terribly sophisticated. It also made him crazy.

The "high" described by the compulsive gambler closely parallels the experience of drug and alcohol abusers. In fact, there is a tendency for chemical addiction and gambling compulsion to overlap. The compulsive gambler attempts to use "the action" as a cure for a variety of ills, in much the same way that people use alcohol and drugs to lift them out of depression, stem anxiety or boredom, and make them feel more "in control."

Some people cannot handle gambling, just as some people cannot handle alcohol. The problem, unfortunately, is compounded by the attitude of our society. As we profess to admire the drinker who can "hold his liquor," we reinforce the gambler who beats the odds in Las Vegas. By glamorizing these behaviors we enable afflicted individuals to remain in denial about the destructive nature of their problem. The compulsive gambler blames circumstances and other people for the suffering occasioned by his or her affliction. One may hear excuses like: "I didn't get enough sleep; I couldn't concentrate with all the noise; I lost track of the time; I'm jinxed at this casino."

If this sounds like you or someone you love, get help. In Las Vegas there is a meeting of Gamblers Anonymous almost every night. Call ☎ 888-442-2110 or check the Web at **gamblersanonymous.org.** If, like Ed, you catch something in Las Vegas and take it home with you, Gamblers Anonymous is listed in your local *White Pages*.

▐ **RULES** *of the* **GAMES**

SLOT MACHINES

SLOT MACHINES, INCLUDING VIDEO POKER, have eclipsed table games in patron popularity. Few Las Vegas casinos remain that have not allocated more than half of their available floor space to various types of slot machines.

The popularity of slots is not difficult to understand. First, slots allow a person to enjoy casino gambling at low or high stakes. Except at the oldest and lowest-tier casinos, all slot machines are now multi-denominational, meaning you can play them for a penny, nickel, dime, quarter, and, perhaps, dollar and up. You don't need change to do so; slot machines no longer have slots. You load them up with bills, then play at your chosen denomination. Higher-stakes players can find machines that accept bets of $1 to $500 ($2,500 to load up a $500 video poker machine).

Second, many people like the slots because no human interaction is required. Absent in slot play is the adversarial atmosphere of the table games. Machines are less intimidating—at least more neutral—than dealers and pit bosses. A patron can sit at a machine for as long as his stamina and money last and never be bothered by a soul.

Finally, slot machines are simple, or at least ostensibly so. Although there are a number of things you should know before you

Anthony's Recommended Best Places to Play

BLACKJACK EL CORTEZ

El Cortez steadfastly continues to offer the 3-2 payoff for naturals on single-deck games, and at low ($5) stakes. Add in the good promotions here and you've got the best place in town for low-stakes blackjack.

QUARTER SLOTS GOLDEN GATE

Since you can't tell definitively whose slots pay best (they can't be analyzed like video-poker machines), picking a casino with strong player benefits is as good a way to choose as any. In 2011 the Golden Gate made a bold move by raising its players club rebate for slot machine play to 5X its prior level. At 1% ($100 in play earns $1 in free-play), it's now the highest in town and by a fairly large margin.

DOLLAR SLOTS PALMS

Evidence still points to the Palms as being loosest for slots in general. Lots of promotions and a good players club make it the best of the bunch and the pick at the dollar level.

CRAPS CASINO ROYALE

Casino Royale, the little casino located smack at the center of the Strip, still deals 100X odds on its crap games. This generous odds multiple makes it the best in all of Las Vegas in this category.

QUARTER VIDEO POKER PALMS

Lots of high-return schedules, led by a bank of Full Pay Deuces Wild with a progressive royal flush. Add in players-club benefits and you're playing with a return of better than 101% here. The Palms also has at least a few full-pay machines in Double Bonus, Double Double Bonus, Loose Deuces, and Joker Wild that all return more than 100%, as well as 9/6 Jacks or Better in denoms from 25¢ to $2.

DOLLAR VIDEO POKER SOUTH POINT

Hundreds of machines here pay at the 9/6 Jacks or Better level (99.54%) or better. Add on the generous South Point players club and other benefits and you're almost always playing dollars at the 100% and above level. Plus, whereas many casinos now lower players club benefits on machines with the best schedules, South Point pays full benefits on all machines, regardless of the schedule.

ROULETTE MIRAGE

The best you can hope for with this game is a wheel with a single zero (as opposed to the standard two zeros). There are several in town, but almost all

play the slots, the only thing you have to know is how to put money (mostly bills) into the machine and press the spin button (it's the rare slot machine that still has a handle).

What You Need to Know before You Play Slot Machines

Starting at the beginning: All slot machines have a slot for inserting either coins, bills, or machine tickets, a button to push to activate the machine, a visual display where you can see the reels spin and stop or are in the high-limit rooms. The Mirage is one of the few casinos with a double-zero game on the main floor 24 hours.

BACCARAT PALACE STATION
Action around the clock at oversized mini baccarat tables. Minimums are low.

KENO EL CORTEZ
Better-than-average returns and promotions for keno players. Plus, the casino has spruced up tremendously over the past few years.

BINGO GOLD COAST
The upstairs room at the Gold Coast has been one of Las Vegas's busiest for years. While other casinos tend to pay little attention to bingo, last year the Gold Coast added several big tournaments, held in conjunction with sister casinos Suncoast and Sam's Town.

POKER ARIA
Aria's working hard and building a following with a good mix of games, lots of tournaments, and a strong comp structure where players earn $2 per hour at all game levels. There's also a good "poker rate" on rooms for players.

RACE AND SPORTS BETTING M RESORT
Cantor Gaming is Las Vegas's new big dog in sports wagering, offering bettors new technologically driven betting options, including "In-Running" wagering (betting while a game is in progress) and "Inside Wagers" (a structure that cuts the "juice" you lay when betting in half). Cantor's flagship is at the M, but it also has books at Hard Rock, Tropicana, and the Cosmopolitan of Las Vegas.

LET IT RIDE O'SHEA'S
Little separates one Let It Ride game from another, so a low-minimum-bet requirement is a good feature. O'Shea's usually has games going at $5 minimums.

CARIBBEAN STUD VENETIAN
Caribbean Stud is getting harder to find. Of the dozen or so casinos that still deal it, only two have more than a single table. Wynn Las Vegas deals two, but the pick in this category is the Venetian, which runs four, making it likely that you'll always be able to find a game.

PAI GOW POKER GOLD COAST
A favorite casino of local pai gow players, so there's constant action and low minimums.

video symbols line up on each play, and a coin tray or machine-ticket dispenser out of which you hope some winnings will come. Today, almost all slot machines are essentially computers attached to a monitor. Gone are the mechanical reels, replaced by an electronic depiction of reels or other symbols illustrated on the monitor.

While slot machines used to have three mechanical reels, most today have been replaced by either three or four electronic reels or video screens with up to 12 depictions of reels. Each reel has some number of "stops," positions where the reel can come to rest. On each reel at each stop (or resting position) is a single slot symbol (a cherry, bar, themed symbol, etc.). What you hope will happen (when the video reels stop spinning) is that paying symbols will line up. If this happens, you win some number of coins or credits based on the bet and particular symbols. With the old slot machines things were pretty simple. There was one coin slot, one handle to pull, and a display with one pay line. Symbols either lined up or they didn't. The newer machines are much more complex. All modern machines accept more than one coin per play (usually three to five but up to 250). No matter how many coins the machine will take, it requires only one to play.

If you put in additional coins (bet more), you will buy one of the following benefits:

1. **Payoff schedules** On some slot machines, the payoff schedule is posted on the glass above the screen; on others, you have to press the See Pays button to determine the winning combinations. If you study these schedules you will notice that by playing extra coins you can increase your payoff should you win the grand jackpot. Usually there is a straightforward increase. If you play two coins, you will win twice as much as if you play one coin. If you play three coins, you will win three times as much as if you play one coin, and so on. Some machines, however, have a jackpot that will pay off only if you have played the maximum number of coins. If you line up the symbols for the jackpot but have not played the maximum number of coins, you will not win the maximum amount possible. The machines with three or four reels, such as the venerable Red, White, and Blue; Double Diamonds; and Blazing Sevens, are easy to understand, with the payout schedules posted prominently on the glass screen above the reels. Video (also known as Australian) slots, on the other hand, which come in hundreds of different themes from oil wells to polar bears, are much more complicated. You can press the Help button at the bottom of the screen to bring up three or four additional screens that explain the machine. But most slot players don't bother, and it's not necessary to comprehend all the ins and outs. Just slip your money into the bill acceptor, press the button with the number of coins you want to play, and spin the reels; the machine does the rest.

   Though most casino slot machines are kept in good working order, watch to make sure the machine credits you for every coin you play and for all the winnings due to you.

2. **Multiple pay lines** When you play your first coin, you buy the usual pay line, right in the center of the display. By playing more coins, you can buy additional pay lines.

   Each pay line you purchase gives you another way of winning. Instead of being limited to the center line, the machine will pay off on the top, center, or bottom lines, and five-coin machines will pay winners on diagonal lines. Australian machines pay off on a dozen lines or more, criss-crossing symbols all over the screen. If you play machines

with multiple pay lines, make sure that each pay line you buy is acknowl-
edged by a light before you push the button.

An irritating feature of many multiple-line machines are "blanks" or
"ghosts." A blank is nothing more than an empty stop on the reel—a
place where you would expect a symbol to be but where there is nothing. As you probably know, you cannot hit a winner by lining up blanks.

NONPROGRESSIVE VERSUS PROGRESSIVE SLOT MACHINES Nonprogressive slot machines have fixed payoffs. You can read the payoff schedules
posted on the machine and determine exactly how much you will get for
each winning combination for any number of coins played.

A second type of machine, known as a progressive, has a top jackpot
that grows and grows until it's hit. After the top prize has been won, the
jackpot is reset and starts to grow. While individual machines can offer
modest progressive jackpots, the really big jackpots (up to tens of millions of dollars) are possible only on machines linked in a system to
other machines. Sometimes an "island," "carousel," or "bank" of machines in a given casino is hooked up to create a progressive system. The
more these machines are played, the faster the progressive jackpot
grows. The largest progressive jackpots come from huge multicasino
systems that sometimes cover the entire state. Players have won more
than $30 million by hitting these jackpots.

While nothing is certain in slot play, it is generally accepted that
nonprogressives pay more small jackpots. Progressives, on the other
hand, offer an opportunity to strike it really rich, but they give up
fewer interim wins.

The nonprogressive machine is for the player who likes
plenty of action, who gets bored when credits aren't rising on
the meter every four or five spins. The progressive machine is for the
player who is willing to forgo frequent small payouts for the chance
of hitting a really big one.

How Slot Machines Work

Almost all slot machines used in casinos today are controlled by micro-
processors. This means the machines can be programmed and are more
like computers than mechanical boxes composed of gears and wheels.
During the evolution of the modern slot machine, manufacturers eliminated the traditional spinning reels in favor of a video display, and replaced the pull handle with a spin button. Inside the newer machines,
there is a device that computer people call a "random number generator" and that we refer to as a "black box." What the black box does is
spit out hundreds of numbers each second, selected randomly (that is,
in no predetermined sequence). The black box has about four billion
different numbers to choose from, so it's very unusual (but not impossible) for the same number to come up twice in a short time.

The numbers the black box selects are programmed to trigger a certain
set of symbols on the display, determining where the reels stop. What most
players don't realize, however, is that the black box pumps out numbers

Slot-Machine Pay Lines

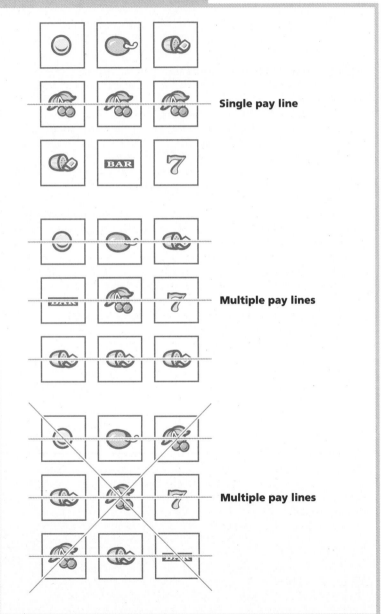

Single pay line

Multiple pay lines

Multiple pay lines

continuously, regardless of whether the machine is being played or not. If you are playing a machine, the black box will call up hundreds or thousands of numbers in the few seconds between plays while you sip your drink, put some money in the slot, and push the button.

Why is this important? Try this scenario: Mary has played the same quarter machine for hours, pumping an untold amount of money into it. She cashes out and gets up to stretch her legs for a few minutes, thinking she'll come back afterwards and keep playing. In the meantime, a man walks up to Mary's machine and hits the jackpot. Mary is livid. "That's my jackpot!" she screams. Not so. While Mary took her walk, thousands of numbers and possible symbol combinations were generated by the black box. The only way Mary could have hit the jackpot (even if the man had not come along) would have been to activate the machine at that same exact moment in time, right down to a fraction of a millisecond.

Another slot myth is that a machine is "overdue to hit." Each spin of the reels on a slot machine is an independent event, just like flipping a coin. The only way to hit a jackpot is to activate the machine at the exact moment that the black box randomly coughs up a winning number. If you play a slot machine as fast as you can, pushing the spin button like a maniac, the black box will still spew out more numbers (and possible jackpots) between each try than you will have spins in a whole day of playing.

CHERRY, CHERRY, ORANGE The house advantage is known for every casino game except slots. With slot machines, the house advantage is whatever the casino programs it to be. In Atlantic City the maximum legal house advantage is 17%. Nevada's limit for slot machines is a hold of 75%. This means that Nevada slot machines can have a house advantage of up to 25%. Interviews with ex–casino employees suggest, however, that the house advantage on casino slots in Las Vegas ranges from about 2.5% to 25%, with most machines giving the house an edge of between 4% and 14%.

Casinos advertise their slots in terms of payout or return rate. If a casino states that its slots return up to 97%, that's another way of saying that the house has a 3% advantage. Some casinos advertise machines that pay up to 98%, and on special-promotion occasions, a casino might advertise slots that pay more than 100%.

SLOT QUEST A slot machine that withholds only a small percentage of the money played is referred to as "loose," while a machine that retains closer to the maximum allowable percentage is called "tight." "Loose" and "tight" are figurative descriptions and have nothing to do with the condition of the machine. Because return rates vary from casino to casino, and because machines in a given casino are programmed to withhold vastly differing percentages of the money played, some slot players devote much time and energy to finding the best casinos and the loosest machines. Exactly how to go about this is the subject of much discussion.

In terms of choosing a casino, several theories have at least a marginal ring of truth. Competition among casinos is often a general indicator for finding loose slots. Some say that smaller casinos, which compete against large neighbors, must program their slots to provide a higher return. Alternatively, some folks will play slots only in casinos patronized predominantly by locals (Gold Coast, Palace Station, Boulder Station, Fiesta, Suncoast, Orleans, Texas Station, El Cortez, Gold Spike, Sam's Town, Arizona Charlie's, and Santa Fe Station, among others). The reasoning here is that these casinos vie for regular customers on a continuing basis and must therefore offer extremely competitive win rates. Downtown Las Vegas is likewise cast in the "we try harder" role, because smaller downtown casinos must go head-to-head with the Strip to attract patrons.

Extending the logic, machines located in supermarkets, restaurants, convenience stores, airports, and lounges are purported to be very tight. In these places, some argue, there is little incentive for management to provide good returns, because the patrons will play regardless (out of boredom or compulsion or simply because the machine is there).

Veteran slot players have many theories when it comes to finding the loose machines in a particular casino. Some will tell you to play the machines by the door or in the waiting area outside the showroom. By placing the loose machines in these locations, the theory goes, the casino can demonstrate to passersby and show patrons that the house has loose slots. Perhaps the most accurate way to judge the relative looseness of reel slots is to monitor the payouts for video poker. As explained in the next section, knowledgeable players who know how to interpret video poker pay schedules can determine the payback percentage to thousandths of percentage points. It's safe to assume (as safe as it is to assume anything) that a casino with loose video poker machines will have loose slots as well.

I have had a slot manager admit to me that his quarter machines are looser than his nickel machines and that his dollar and five-dollar machines are the loosest of all. Tight or loose, however, all slots are programmed to give the casino a certain profit over the long run. It is very unlikely, in any event, that you will play a machine long enough to experience the theoretical payoff rate. What you are concerned about is the short run. In the short run anything can happen, including winning.

MAXIMIZING YOUR CHANCES OF WINNING ON THE SLOTS If you play less than the maximum number of coins on a progressive, you are simply contributing to a jackpot that you have no chance of winning. If you don't want to place a maximum bet, play a nonprogressive machine.

Slot Machine Etiquette and Common Sense

Regardless of whether you are playing a one-armed bandit, a video-poker machine, or any other type of coin-operated gambling device, there are some things you need to know:

1. Realize that avid slot players sometimes play more than one machine at a time. Do not assume that a machine is not in use simply because nobody is standing or sitting in front of it. Slot players can be fanatically territorial.

2. Before you start to play, check out the people around you. Do you feel safe and comfortable among them?

3. Read the payout schedule of any machine you play; if you don't understand it completely, don't worry.

4. Almost all machines have credit meters; be sure to cash out your credits before you abandon the machine.

5. If the casino has a players club, join (this usually takes less than five minutes on-site, but can be accomplished through the mail or online prior to your trip). Use the club card whenever you play. When you quit, don't forget to take your club card with you.

6. Never play more machines than you can watch carefully. Be particularly vigilant when playing machines near exits and corridors. If you're asleep at the switch, you're vulnerable to victimization by thieves and scam artists, who have plenty of nefarious tricks up their sleeves to relieve you of your lucre. They even have ways of absconding with payout tickets issued from the machine while you're playing!

7. Keep your purse and your money in sight at all times. Never put your purse on the floor behind you or to the side.

8. If you line up a big winner and nothing happens, don't panic. Slot machines lock up when a jackpot exceeds the tax-reporting requirement. Any winning combination of more than $1,200 on a slot or video poker machine must be "hand paid" directly by a slot floorperson. If you're lucky and hit a big enough jackpot that tax paperwork needs to be filled out, the "candle" (light fixture) atop the machine will blink, summoning a slot attendant. Don't wander off to look for one; sit patiently and one will show up shortly.

9. If the appropriate payout sections or pay lines fail to illuminate when playing multiple coins, do not leave or activate the machine (push the button) until you have consulted an attendant.

Players Clubs

Most Las Vegas casinos now have frequent-player clubs, known as players clubs. The purpose of these clubs is to foster increased customer loyalty among gambling patrons by providing incentives.

You can join a club by signing up at the casino or (at most casinos) by applying through the mail or online. There is neither a direct cost associated with joining nor any dues. You are given a plastic membership card that resembles a credit card. This card can be inserted into a special slot on any gambling machine in the casino. As long as your card is in the slot, you are credited for the amount of action you put through that machine. Programs at different casinos vary, but in general, you are awarded "points" based on how long you play and how much you wager. All clubs award points for slot play; some also use the card at the tables to input hours played and average bets into the player-tracking database. As in an airline frequent-flyer program, accumulated points can ultimately be redeemed for awards. Awards range from casino logo apparel to discounts and comps on meals, shows, and rooms.

The good thing about players clubs is that they provide a mechanism for slot players to obtain some of the comps, perks, and extras that have always been available to table players. The bad thing about a players club is that it confines your play. In other words, you must give most of your business to one or two casinos in order to accumulate enough points to reap rewards. If you are a footloose player and enjoy gambling all around town, you may never accrue enough points in any one casino to redeem a comp.

Even if you never redeem any points, however, it's still a good idea to join. If you travel to Las Vegas regularly on business, join your favorite casinos' players clubs. Membership might make you eligible for deals on rooms and food that would otherwise not be available to you.

Join a players club so you can be identified as a gambler on the hotel-casino's mailing list. Just for joining, and without gambling that first quarter, you will be offered discounts on rooms and a variety of other special deals.

The Future of Slot Machines

The bandits have always been stand-alone machines with individual controls, from mechanical cogs and gears in the early days to central-processing units in the electronic age. So in order to change a slot's games, denominations, or payback percentages, a slot technician has had to manipulate the circuitry of the machine itself. However, a new generation of slots, known as "server-based" machines, will all be networked to a central back-office computer system; the machines on the floor will essentially become dumb monitors dressed up in slot cabinets, into which (with the click of a back-room mouse) different games, denominations, payback percentages, bonuses, promotions, and so on can be downloaded.

From the casino's point of view, server-based slots allow managers, with a few keystrokes, to tailor their games to player preferences. Perhaps the casino needs more slots during the day and more video poker at night. Or maybe weekday crowds prefer penny games and free spins, while weekend players like quarter games and second-screen bonuses. Operators could also increase denominations, say from nickels to quarters and quarters to dollars, at prime time on Saturday nights. In short, casinos will be able to adapt to changing conditions on the fly.

In addition, with the use of the player-tracking system, managers could record a player's preferred game, then offer those games on a machine as soon as a player inserts the card. The casino could also contact players right at the machine in real time. For example, a message that you've earned a free buffet or discounted show tickets could be sent to the display terminal on the machine.

From the player's perspective, server-based slots will have to overcome a long-cherished myth: that casinos can change the payback of a machine at the flip of a switch, tightening games during busy times, then loosening them again when the crowds go home. Downloadable slots will certainly have that capability. Thus, the onus will be on the casinos and gaming regulators to make the process as transparent as possible, so that when a player suddenly goes from hot to cold, he won't suspect that a computer has just changed the payback percentage from 98% to 82%. For example, the machine's screen might display a "modification-in-progress" message, followed by, say, five minutes of down time.

Early adopters of server-based slots in Las Vegas include Aria and the Cosmopolitan. Stay tuned.

VIDEO POKER

NEVER IN THE HISTORY OF CASINO GAMBLING has a game become so popular so quickly. What's the allure of video poker? More people are familiar with poker than with any other casino game. The video version affords average folks an opportunity to play a game of chance and skill without going up against professional gamblers. Also, like slot machines, video poker is fast; you can play 300, 400, 500 hands per hour. And like blackjack, it's skilled, so you can study and become an expert player and gain an edge over the house. Finally, it's hypnotic; many people find it hard to get up from a video poker machine (if that's you, you might think twice about playing too much and becoming compulsive).

In video poker you play against a machine. The object is to make the best possible five-card-draw poker hand. In the most common rendition, you insert your money and push a button marked "deal." Your original five cards are displayed on the screen. Below the screen and under each of the cards pictured are "hold" buttons. After evaluating your hand and planning your strategy, designate the cards you want to keep by pressing the appropriate hold button(s). If you hit the wrong button or change your mind, simply "unhold" your choices by pushing the buttons again. If you do not want to draw any cards (you like your hand as dealt), press all five hold buttons. When you press the hold button for a particular card, the word "hold" will appear over that card on the display. Always double-check the screen to make certain the cards you intend to hold are marked before proceeding to the draw.

When you are ready, press the button marked "draw" (on many machines it is the same button as the deal button). Any cards you have not designated to be held will be replaced. As in live draw poker, the five cards in your possession after the draw are your final hand. If the hand is a winner (a pair of jacks or better on most non-wild-card machines), you will be credited the appropriate winnings on the credit meter on the video display. These are actual winnings that can be retrieved, mostly via a machine ticket, by pressing the "cash-out" button. If you choose to leave your winnings on the credit meter, you may use them to bet, eliminating the need to physically insert more money into the machine. When you are ready to quit, simply press the cash-out button and collect your coins from the tray or a ticket from the dispenser.

As with other slot machines, you can increase your payoffs and become eligible for bonus jackpots by playing the maximum number of coins. Note that some machines have jackpots listed in dollars, while others are specified in coins. Obviously, there is a big difference between $4,000 and 4,000 nickels.

Playing video poker is vastly different from playing live poker. There's no psychology involved. You can't bluff the machine. You can show all the emotion you want. In most games, you don't hold kickers. All you need to know to play is the hierarchy of winning poker hands (pair, two-pair, three-of-a-kind, straight, and so on). All the winning hands with their respective payoffs are enumerated on or above the video display.

But to play video poker well, you need two additional skills: selecting the right machine and playing the proper strategy. The first skill requires the ability to decipher the pay schedules posted prominently on the faceplates of every machine. Some machines have a high payback percentage, even higher than 100%, while others pay less. You're looking for the highest paying schedules within each variation of video poker—and there are dozens of variations, but you have to know only a few of them.

Two of these are Jacks or Better (JoB) and Double Bonus. The highest paying version of JoB is called 9/6, meaning it pays 9-for-1 per coin played when you hit a full house, and 6-for-1 when you hit a flush. When you check the payout schedule for a single coin played, it could read 8 for a full house and 5 for a flush, even 7 or 6 for a full house. But unless you're returned 9 for the full house and 6 for the flush, you might as well play any random slot machine. The payback percentage for 9/6 JoB is 99.5%, almost break-even.

The other schedule to look for is 10/7 Double Bonus. Again, this means 10-for-1 on a full house and 7-for-1 on a flush. You'll see lower paybacks, but it's only 10/7 that we play, which pays back 100.7%, a positive game.

Other payback schedules are also playable, such as Deuces Wild and Joker Wild. But you have to recognize the highest-paying versions, which you can learn easily and quickly. Read a few pages of a good gambling primer, such as *The Frugal Gambler, More Frugal Gambling,* or *Frugal Video Poker* by Jean Scott, and you'll be locating the beatable machines like a pro.

Learning the proper playing strategies requires a bit more work. Luckily, the tools are readily available, inexpensive, easy to use, and completely effective. In fact, the first tool, the computer tutorial, is also fun. These software programs, such as *Frugal Video Poker* and *Video Poker for Winners,* teach you "computer-perfect strategy" by alerting you to and correcting strategy mistakes as you play on your home or office computer. Programming yourself with the proper plays takes only four or five enjoyable hours; this is time extremely well spent for preparing to take on the casino with real money.

Problem is, you can't take the computer into the casino. That's where strategy cards come into play—the best video-poker aids of all. These $6.95 handy-dandy trifold pocket-size color-coded laminated cards use a sort of shorthand to list every decision by which you can possibly be confronted at a machine; they pay for themselves in one playing session with the saving gained by avoiding costly mistakes. And the best thing is, other than spending a few minutes deciphering the code when you first receive them, you don't have to do anything with them, except remember to put them in your pocket and refer to them while you play.

 The edge at video poker ranges from more than 10% on the worst schedules up to positive 1% (a player advantage) on the best.

A computer tutorial and handy strategy cards will give you an edge in video poker.

An Example of Video-poker Strategy

Each hand in a video-poker game is dealt from a fresh 52-card deck. Each hand consists of ten cards, with a random number generator or "black box" selecting the cards dealt. When you hit the deal button, the first five cards are displayed face up on the screen. Cards six through ten are held in reserve to be dealt as replacements for cards you discard when you draw. Each replacement card is dealt in order off the top of the electronic deck. The microprocessor "shuffles" the deck for each new game. Thus on the next play, you will be dealt five new and randomly selected initial cards, and five new and randomly selected draw cards to back them up. In other words, you will not be dealt any unused cards from the previous hand.

THE POWER OF THE ROYAL FLUSH In video poker, the biggest payout is usually for a royal flush. This fact influences strategy for playing the game. Simply put, you play differently than you would in a live poker game. If in Jacks or Better video poker you are dealt

A ♣ Q ♣ 10 ♣ A ♠ J ♣,

you would discard the ace of spades (giving up a paying pair) to go for the royal flush. Likewise, if you are dealt

5 ♠ A ♠ K ♠ Q ♠ J ♠,

you would discard the 5 of spades (sacrificing a sure spade flush) in an attempt to make the royal by drawing the 10 of spades. If you are dealt

J ♥ Q ♥ K ♥ 4 ♥ 6 ♣,

draw two cards for the royal flush as opposed to one card for the flush.

The payoff for the royal flush is so great that it is worth risking a sure winning hand. The payoff for a straight flush, however, does not warrant risking a pat flush or straight.

OTHER SITUATIONS If you are dealt

Q ♦   A ♣   4 ♥   J ♠   4 ♣,

hold the small pair. But if you are dealt

K ♦   A ♣   4 ♥   J ♣   3 ♠,

hold the ace of clubs and the jack of clubs to give yourself a long shot at a royal flush. Similarly, if you are dealt

K ♣   A ♣   4 ♥   J ♣   3 ♠,

hold the ace of clubs, king of clubs, and jack of clubs.

DRAW POKER If you are playing draw poker (no wild cards), with a pair of jacks or better required to win, observe the following:

1. Hold a jacks-or-better pair, even if you pass up the chance of drawing to an open-end straight or to a flush. If you have

    Q ♣   4 ♠   6 ♠   2 ♠   Q ♠

    or

    Q ♥   9 ♦   10 ♣   J ♠   Q ♣,

    in each case keep the pair of queens and draw three cards.

2. Split a low pair to go for a flush. If you are dealt

    2 ♦   4 ♣   4 ♦   8 ♦   10 ♦,

    discard the 4 of clubs and draw one card to try and make the flush.

3. Hold a low pair rather than drawing to an inside or open-end straight.

4. A "kicker" is a face card or an ace you might be tempted to hang onto along with a high pair, low pair, or three-of-a-kind. If you are dealt, for example,

    5 ♣   5 ♦   8 ♠   10 ♠   A ♥

    or

    5 ♣   5 ♦   8 ♠   10 ♠   A ♥

    or

    2 ♣   2 ♣   2 ♥   8 ♠   A ♥,

    hold the pair or the three-of-a-kind, but discard the kicker (the ace).

BLACKJACK

MANY BOOKS HAVE BEEN PUBLISHED about the game of blackjack. The serious gamblers who write these books will tell you that blackjack is a game of skill and chance in which a player's ability can actually turn the odds of winning in his favor. While that is true, we also know the casinos wouldn't keep the tables open if they were taking a beating.

BASIC STRATEGY*

The dealer is showing:		2	3	4	5	6	7	8	9	10	Ace
Your total is:	4–11	H	H	H	H	H	H	H	H	H	H
	12	H	H	S	S	S	H	H	H	H	H
	13	S	S	S	S	S	H	H	H	H	H
	14	S	S	S	S	S	H	H	H	H	H
	15	S	S	S	S	S	H	H	H	H	H
	16	S	S	S	S	S	H	H	H	H	H

S=Stand H=Hit

*The correct term for the spots on playing cards is "pips."

The methods of playing blackjack skillfully involve being able to count all the cards played and flawlessly manage your own hand, while mentally blocking the bustle and distraction of the casino. The ability to master the prerequisite tactics and to play under casino conditions is so far beyond the average (never mind beginning) player that any attempt to track cards is, except for a talented and disciplined few, exhausting and futile.

This doesn't mean that you should not try blackjack. It is a fun, fast-paced game that is easy to understand, and you can play at low-minimum-wager tables without feeling intimidated by the level of play. Moreover, most people already have an understanding of the game from playing "21" at home. The casino version is largely the same, only with more bells and whistles.

In a game of blackjack, the number cards are worth their spots (a 2 of clubs is worth two). All face cards are worth ten. The ace, on the other hand, is worth either 1 point or 11, whichever you choose. In this manner, an ace and a 5 could be worth 6 (hard count) or 16 (soft count). The object of the game is to get as close to 21 as you can without going over (called "busting"). You play only against the dealer, and the hand closest to 21 wins the game.

The dealer will deal you a two-card hand, then give you the option of taking another card (called a "hit") or stopping with the two cards you have been dealt (called "standing"). For example, if your first two cards are a 10 and a 3, your total would be 13, and you would normally ask for another card to get closer to 21. If the next card dealt to you was a 7, you would have a total of 20 points and you would "stand" with 20 (that is, not ask for another card).

It makes no difference what the other players are dealt, or what they choose to do with their hands. Your hand will win or lose only in comparison to the hand that the dealer holds.

The dealer plays his hand last. This is his biggest advantage. All the players that go over 21 points, or bust, will immediately lose their cards and their bet before the dealer's turn to play. What this means

The Blackjack Table

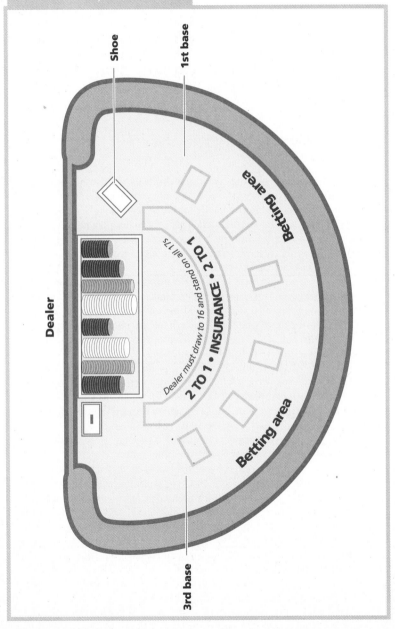

Shoe

1st base

Dealer

Betting area

2 TO 1 • INSURANCE • 2 TO 1

Dealer must draw to 16 and stand on all 17s

Betting area

3rd base

in terms of casino advantage is that while the player has to play to win, the only thing the dealer has to do is not lose. Every time you bust, the casino wins. This sequence of play ensures a profit for the casino from the blackjack tables.

Take time to observe a few hands before you play blackjack. This will give you the opportunity to find a friendly, personable dealer and to check out the minimum-bet signs posted at each table.

Be sure to check out the minimum-bet signs posted at each table. They will say something like: "Minimum bet $2 to $500." This means that the minimum wager is $2, and the maximum wager is $500. If you sit down at a blackjack table and begin to bet with insufficient cash or the wrong denomination chip, the dealer will inform you of the correct minimum wager, whereupon you may either conform or excuse yourself.

A blackjack table is shaped like a half circle, with the dealer inside the circle and room for five to seven players around the outside. Facing the dealer, the chair on the far right is called "first base." The chair on the far left is called "third base." The dealer deals the cards from first base to third, and each player plays out his hand in the same order.

If you can, try to sit at third base or as close to it as you can get. This gives you the advantage of watching the other players play out their hands before you play.

To buy in, find an empty seat at a table with an agreeable minimum wager and wait until the hand in progress is concluded. Though you can bet cash, most players prefer to convert their currency to chips. This is done by placing your money on the table *above* the bettor's box. Because blackjack is one of the many games in the casino in which the dealer is allowed to accept cash bets, he will assume that any money placed in the bettor's box is a wager.

Your dealer will take the cash, count out your chips, and push the money through a slot cut in the top of the table. Because he cannot give you change in cash, the total amount you place on the table will be converted to chips. You may at any time, however, redeem your chips for cash from the casino cashier. Once you have been given chips and have bet, you will be included in the next deal.

To confound a player attempting to count cards, many casinos deal blackjack with four to eight (two-hand held) decks shuffled together. This huge stack of cards is rendered manageable by dealing from a special container known as a shoe.

The dealer will shuffle the decks and may offer the cards to you to cut. The dealer offers you a plastic card stop. Place the card stop halfway or so into the deck, leaving the stop sticking out. The dealer will cut the deck at that point and put it into the shoe.

After he cuts a single deck, or puts the multiple deck into the shoe, the dealer will "burn" one or more cards by taking them off the top and putting them into the discard pile. This is yet another tactic to inhibit players from keeping track of cards dealt. Also to the advantage of the casino is the dealer's right to shuffle the cards whenever

SOFT-HAND STRATEGY*		2	3	4	5	6	7	8	9	10	Ace
The dealer is showing:											
You have:	Ace, 9	S	S	S	S	S	S	S	S	S	S, H
	Ace, 8	S	S	S	S	S	S	S	S	S	S
	Ace, 7	S	D	D	D	D	S	S	H	H	S
	Ace, 6	H	D	D	D	D	S	H	H	H	H
	Ace, 5	H	H	D	D	D	H	H	H	H	H
	Ace, 4	H	H	D	D	D	H	H	H	H	H
	Ace, 3	H	H	H	D	D	H	H	H	H	H
	Ace, 2	H	H	H	D	D	H	H	H	H	H

S = Stand H = Hit D = Double down

*The charts reflect basic strategy for multiple-deck games. For single-deck games, a slightly different strategy prevails for doubling and splitting.

he pleases. Usually the dealer will deal from the shoe until he reaches the plastic stop card and then he will "break the deck," which means reshuffle and recut before dealing the next hand. In a single-deck game, the dealer will usually reshuffle about three-quarters through the deck.

Because the dealer always plays his hand last, you must develop your strategy by comparing your card count to what you assume (based on his visible card) the dealer has. The rule of thumb for most situations is to play your hand as if the dealer's down card has a value of ten. The principles governing when or when not to take a hit are known as "basic strategy" (see charts on pages 323, 326, and 329). If you elect to take a hit and go over 21 (bust), you lose. If you stand with your original two cards or take a number of hits without going over 21, you can relax for a few seconds while the dealer continues on around the table, repeating the same process with the other players. When the other players finish, the dealer exposes his "down" card and plays out his hand according to strict rules. He must take a hit on any total of 16 or less and must stand on any total of 17 or more. When he finishes his hand, the dealer goes from third base to first, paying off each winning player and collecting chips from the losers who didn't bust.

If you're closer to 21 than the dealer, you win. If he is closer (or if you busted), he wins. If there is a tie, neither hand wins. When you tie, the dealer will knock on the table above your bet to indicate that the hand is a tie, or a "push." You may leave your bet on the table for the next hand, or change it.

There is a way for you to win automatically, and that is to be dealt exactly 21 in the first two cards. This can be done with an ace and any ten-value card. Called a blackjack, or a natural, this hand is an automatic winner, and you should turn your cards face up immediately.

The dealer will look to see if he ties you with a blackjack of his own; this is one of the only times a dealer will look at his cards before all the players have played. If the dealer does not have a blackjack, he will pay you immediately at three-to-two odds (or a punitive six-to-five payoff in most Strip single-deck or Super Fun 21 games), so your $5 bet pays off $7.50 and you keep your original wager. If the dealer has a blackjack too, then only you and any other players at the table with a natural will tie him. The rest lose their bets, and the next round will begin.

Nothing beats a natural. If the dealer has a 4 and a 6, then draws an ace, his 21 will not beat your blackjack. A blackjack wins over everything and pays the highest of any bet in the game. Just as you can win automatically, you may lose just as fast. When your count goes over 21 and you bust, you must turn your cards over. The dealer will collect your cards and your bet before moving on to the next player.

Hitting and Standing

When dealing, whether from the shoe or from a single deck in his hand, the dealer will give two cards to each player. Most casinos will deal both cards facedown, though some casinos, especially those that use large multiple decks, will deal both cards faceup. There is no advantage to either method. Most players are more comfortable with the secrecy of the facedown deal, but the outcome will not be affected either way. Starting with the player at first base, the dealer will give you cards to play out your hand. After the initial deal, you have two basic options: either stand or take a hit. If you are satisfied with your deal, then you elect to stand. If your cards were dealt facedown, slide them under the chips in the bettor's box with one hand, being careful not to touch your chips or conceal them from the dealer. If the cards were dealt faceup, wave your hand over the top, palm down, in a negative fashion, to signal the dealer not to give you another card.

Sometimes you will improve your hand by asking for another card. You signal for a hit by scratching the bottom of your cards toward you on the felt surface of the table. In a faceup game, scratch your fingers toward you in the same fashion. You may say, "Hit me," or "I'll take a hit," depending on the mood at your table, but use the hand gestures also. Because of noise and distractions, the dealer may misinterpret your verbal request.

The card you request will be dealt faceup, and you may take as many hits as you like. When you want to show that you do not want another card, use the signals for standing. If you bust, turn your cards faceup right away so the dealer can collect your cards and chips. He will then go to the next player. There are times when the dealer stands a good chance of busting. At these times, it is a good idea to stand on your first two cards even though your total count may seem very low. The accompanying basic strategy chart shows when to stand and when to take a hit. It is easy to follow and simple to memorize. The decision to stand or take a hit is made on the value of your hand and, once again, the dealer's up card, and is based on the probability of his busting. Although following basic strategy won't win every hand, it will improve your odds and take the guesswork out of some confusing situations.

Basic strategy is effective because the dealer is bound by the rules of the game. He must take a hit on 16 and stand on 17. These rules are printed right on the table so that there can be no misunderstanding. Even if you are the only player at the table and stand with a total of 14 points, the dealer with what would be a winning hand of 16 points *must* take another card.

There is one exception to the rule: Some casinos require a dealer to take a hit on a hand with an ace and a 6 (called a "soft 17"). Since the ace can become a 1, it is to the casino's advantage for the dealer to be allowed to hit a soft 17.

Bells and Whistles

Now that you understand the basic game, let's look at a few rules in the casino version of blackjack that are probably different from the way you play at home.

DOUBLING DOWN When you have received two cards and think that they will win with the addition of one and *only* one more card, then double your bet. This "doubling down" bet should be made if your two-card total is 11, since drawing the highest possible card, a 10, will not push your total over 21. In some casinos you may double down on ten, and some places will let you double down on any two-card hand.

To show the dealer that you want to double down, place your two cards touching each other faceup on the dealer's side of the betting box. Then place chips in the box that equal your original bet. Now, as at all other times, don't touch your chips once the bet is made.

DOUBLING DOWN

The dealer is showing:		2	3	4	5	6	7	8	9	10	Ace
Your total is:	11	D	D	D	D	D	D	D	D	D	H
	10	D	D	D	D	D	D	D	D	H	H
	9	H	D	D	D	D	H	H	H	H	H

H = Hit D = Double down

SPLITTING Any time you are dealt two cards of the same value, you may split the cards and start two separate hands. Even aces may be split, though when you play them, they will each be dealt only one additional card. If you should happen to get a blackjack after splitting aces, it will be treated as 21; that is, paid off at one to one and not three to two or six to five.

Any other pair is played exactly as you would if you were playing two consecutive hands, and all the rules will apply. Place the two cards

SPLITTING STRATEGY

The dealer is showing:		2	3	4	5	6	7	8	9	10	Ace
You have:	2, 2	H	H	SP	SP	SP	SP	H	H	H	H
	3, 3	H	H	SP	SP	SP	SP	H	H	H	H
	4, 4	H	H	H	H	H	H	H	H	H	H
	5, 5	D	D	D	D	D	D	D	D	H	H
	6, 6	H	SP	SP	SP	SP	H	H	H	H	H
	7, 7	SP	SP	SP	SP	SP	SP	H	H	H	H
	8, 8	SP	SP	SP	SP	SP	SP	SP	SP	SP	SP
	9, 9	SP	SP	SP	SP	SP	S	SP	SP	S	S
	10, 10	S	S	S	S	S	S	S	S	S	S
	Ace, Ace	SP	SP	SP	SP	SP	SP	SP	SP	SP	SP

S = Stand   H = Hit   SP = Split   D = Double down

apart from each other and above the betting box, so the dealer won't confuse this with doubling down. Then add a stack of chips equal to the original bet to cover the additional hand. Your two hands will be played out one at a time, cards dealt faceup.

You will be allowed to split a third card if it is the same as the first two, but not if it shows up as a later hit. Always split a pair of eights, since they total 16 points, the worst total. *Never* split two face cards or tens, since they total 20 and are probably a winning hand.

Some casinos will let you double down after splitting a hand, but if you're unsure, ask the dealer. Not all blackjack rules are posted, and they can vary from casino to casino, and even from table to table in the same casino.

INSURANCE When the dealer deals himself an ace as his second, faceup card, he will stop play and ask, "Insurance, anyone?" Don't be fooled. You're not insuring anything. All he's asking for is a side bet that he has a natural. He must make the insurance bets before he can look at his cards, so he doesn't know if he has won or not when he asks for your insurance bets.

The insurance wager can be up to half the amount of your original bet. Place the chips in the large semicircle marked "insurance." As it says, it pays off two to one. If your original bet was $10 and you bet $5 that the dealer had a natural, you would be paid $10 if he actually did. Depending on your cards, you would probably lose your original $10 bet, but break even on the hand. If the dealer does not have a ten-value card, you lose your $5 insurance bet, but your $10 bet still can win.

This sounds deceptively easy, but you will lose this bet more often than you will win it, though the dealer may suggest it to you as a smart move. The dealer might also tell you to insure your own blackjack, though this should never be done. The odds are always against the insurance bet.

When you insure your blackjack, you can be paid off for it at one to one, as if it were 21, instead of the three to two or six to five that you would normally be paid for the blackjack. Even though you may occasionally tie with the dealer, you will more than make up for it with the three-to-two or six-to-five payoffs on the blackjacks you don't insure.

Insurance is a bad move for the basic-strategy player, because the odds are against the dealer actually having a natural.

Avoiding Common Pitfalls

1. Always check the minimum bets allowed at your table before you sit down. Flipping a $5 chip into a $25-minimum game can be humiliating. If you make this mistake, simply excuse yourself and leave. It happens all the time.

2. Keep your bet in a neat stack, with the largest value chips on the bottom and the smallest on top. A mess of chips can be confusing should you want to double down, and your dealer will get huffy if he has to ask you to stack your chips.

3. Never touch the chips once the bet is down. Cheaters do this, and your dealer may assume you're cheating. It's too easy for a player to secretly up his bet once he's seen his cards or lower it if the cards are bad. Do not stack a double-down bet or split bets on top of the original bet. Place them beside the original bet and then keep your hands away.

4. Along the same lines, don't touch a hand if the cards are dealt faceup. Use the hand signals to tell the dealer that you stand or that you want a hit. Never move your cards below the level of the table, where the dealer can't see them. When you brush your cards for a hit, do so lightly so that the dealer won't think that you are trying to mark them by bending them.

5. Take your time and count your cards correctly. The pace of the game in the casino can pick up to a speed that is difficult for a beginner. It's perfectly all right to take your time and recount after a hit. One hint: count aces as 1 first, then add 10 to your total. An ace and a 4 is equal to 5 or 15. Once you have this notion in your head, you won't make a mistake and refrain from hitting a soft hand. If you throw down an ace, a 10, and a 9 in disgust, for example, many dealers will simply pick up your cards and your bet, even though your 20 might have been a winning hand. If you are confused about your total, do not be embarrassed to ask for help.

6. Know the denomination of the chips that you are betting. Stack them according to denomination, and read the face value every play until you know for sure which chips are which color. Otherwise you might think you are betting $5 when you are actually throwing out a $25 chip on every hand.

7. Be obvious with your hand signals to the dealer. The casinos are loud and busy, and the dealer may be distracted with another player. Don't leave any room for misinterpretation. If some problem does arise, stop the game immediately; the dealer will summon a boss to mediate.

8. If cards fly off the table during the deal, pick them up slowly using two fingers. See number four, above.

The Craps Table

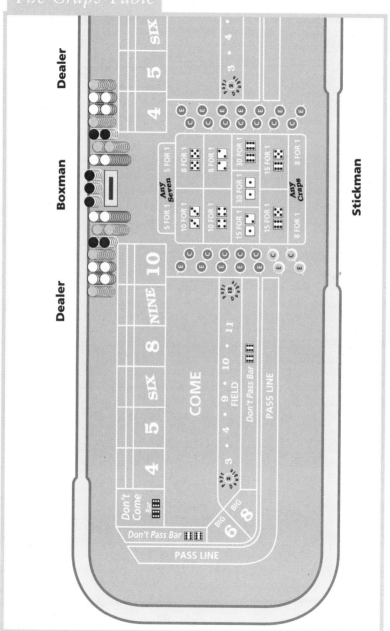

9. Tip the dealer at your discretion if he or she has been friendly and help-ful. One of the better ways to tip the dealer is to bet a chip for him on your next hand and say, "This one is for you." If you win, so does he. Never tip when a dealer has been rude or cost you money by being un-cooperative. Then you should finish your hand and leave. Period.

CRAPS

OF ALL THE GAMES OFFERED IN CASINOS, craps is by far the fastest and, to many, the most exciting. It is a game in which large amounts of money can be won or lost in a short amount of time. The craps table is a circus of sound and movement. Yelling and screaming are allowed—even encouraged—here, and the frenetic betting is bewildering to the uninitiated. Don't be intimidated, however; the basic game of craps is easy to understand. The confusion and insanity of craps have more to do with the pace of the game and the amazing number of betting pos-sibilities than with the complexity of the game itself.

The Basic Game

Because it is so easy to become confused at a crowded and noisy craps table, we highly recommend that beginning players study this section, read a more detailed book, and take advantage of the free lessons offered by most of the casinos. Once you understand the game, you will be able to make the most favorable bets and ignore the rest.

In craps, one player at a time controls the dice, but all players will eventually have an opportunity to roll or refuse the dice. Players take turns in a clockwise rotation. If you don't want the dice, shake your head, and the dealer will offer them to the next player.

All the players around the table are wagering either with or against the shooter, so the numbers he throws will determine the amount won or lost by every other player. The casino is covering all bets, and the players are not allowed to bet among themselves. Four

---

HOW NOT TO SHOOT CRAPS

On a recent visit to a downtown casino, one *Unofficial Guide* researcher pleaded with a Las Vegas friend to teach her how to play craps. Our Vegas friend not only outlined the basics, he also rattled off descriptions of all the various side bets and offered advice on when each was appropriate. By the time the lady was handed the dice, she was so apprehensive about remembering the rules that she forgot to pay attention to her throw. She hurled the dice with all her might right into a stack of chips in front of the boxman, scattering the house chips all over the table. The boxman and dealers sighed in annoyance but didn't complain as they put the table back in order. The other players were not pleased, however. And it only got worse when the flustered lady threw again, this time so worried about the boxman that she overthrew the table entirely, striking another player in the chest with the dice. Shortly after that, it was decided that she'd best stick with slot machines.

ACTUAL-ODDS CHART		
Number	Ways to roll	Odds against repeat
4	3	2–1
5	4	3–2
6	5	6–5
8	5	6–5
9	4	3–2
10	3	2–1

casino employees run the craps table. The boxman in the middle is in charge of the game. His job is to oversee the other dealers, monitor the play, and examine the dice if they are thrown off the table.

There are two dealers, one placed on each side of the boxman. They pay off the winners and collect the chips from the losers. Each dealer is in charge of half of the table.

The fourth employee is the stickman, so called because of a flexible stick he uses after each roll to retrieve the dice. His job, among other things, is to supply dice to the shooter and to regulate the pace of the game. When all bets are down, the stickman pushes several sets of dice toward the shooter. The shooter selects two dice, and the stickman removes the others from the table. Occasionally the stickman and boxman check the dice for signs of tampering.

The shooter then throws the dice hard enough to cause them to bounce off the wall at the far end of the table. This bounce ensures that each number on each die has an equal probability of coming up.

THE PLAY When it is your turn to throw the dice, pick out two and return the other to the stickman. After making a bet (required), you may throw the dice. You retain control of the dice until you throw a 7 ("seven out") or relinquish the dice voluntarily.

Your first roll, called the come-out roll, is the most important. If you roll a 7 or an 11 on your come-out roll, you are an immediate winner. In this case, you collect your winnings and retain possession of the dice. If your come-out roll is a 4, 5, 6, 8, 9, or 10, that number becomes "the point." A marker (called a puck or buck) is placed in the correspondingly numbered box on the layout to identify the point for all players at the table. In order to win the game, this number (the point) will have to be rolled again before you roll a 7.

Thus, if you roll a 5 on your first roll, the number five becomes your point. It doesn't matter how long it takes you to roll another 5, as long as you don't roll a 7 first. As soon as you roll a 7, you lose, and the dice are passed to another player.

Let's say 5 is your point, and your second roll is a 4, your third roll is a 9, and then you roll another 5. You win because you rolled a 5 again without rolling a 7. Because you have not yet rolled a 7, you retain possession of the dice, and after making a bet, you may initiate a new game.

Your next roll is, once again, a come-out roll. Just as 7 or 11 are immediate winners on a come-out roll, there are immediate losers, too. A roll of 2, 3, or 12 (all called "craps") will lose. You lose your chips, but you keep the dice because you have not yet rolled a 7.

If your first roll is 2, for example, it's craps, and you lose your bet. You place another bet and roll to come-out again. This time you roll a 5, so 5 becomes your point. Your second roll is a 4, your third is a 9, and then you roll a 7. The roll of 7 means that you lose and the dice will be passed to the next player.

This is the basic game of craps. The confounding blur of activity is nothing more than players placing various types of bets with or against the shooter, or betting that a certain number will or will not come up on the next roll of the dice.

THE BETTING Of the dozens of bets that can be made at a dice table, only two or three should even be considered by a novice crap player. Keeping your bets simple makes it easier to understand what's going on, while at the same time minimizing the house advantage. Exotic, long-shot bets, offering payoffs as high as 30 to 1, are sucker bets and should be avoided.

The line bets: pass and don't pass Pass and don't pass bets combine simplicity with one of the smallest house advantages of any casino game, about 1.4%. If you bet pass, you are betting that the first roll will be a 7 or 11 or a point number, and that the shooter will make the point again before he rolls a 7. If you bet don't pass, you are betting that the first roll will be a 2, 3, or 12, or, if a point is established, that the shooter will seven out and throw a 7 before he rolls his point number again. The 2 and 3 are immediate losers, and the casino will collect the chips of anyone betting pass. A roll of 12, however, is considered a standoff ("push") where the shooter "craps out" but no chips change hands for the "don't" bettor. Almost 90% of casino crap players confine their betting to the pass and don't-pass line.

Come and don't come Come and don't-come bets are just like pass and don't-pass bets, except that they are placed *after* the point has been established on the come-out roll. Pass and don't-pass bets must be placed before the first roll of the dice, but come and don't-come bets may be placed before any roll of the dice *except* come-out rolls. On his come-out roll, let's say, the shooter rolls a 9. Nine becomes the shooter's point. If at this time you place your chips in the come box on the table, the next roll of the dice will determine your "come number." If the shooter throws a 6, for example, your chips are placed in the box marked with the large 6. The dealer will move your chips and will keep track of your bet. If the shooter rolls another 6 before he rolls a 7, your bet pays off. If the shooter sevens out before he rolls a 6, then you lose. If the shooter makes his point (that is, rolls another 9), your come bet is retained on the layout.

If you win a come bet, the dealer will place your chips from the numbered box back into the come space and set your winnings beside it. You may leave your chips there for the next roll or you may remove them entirely. If you fail to remove your winnings before the next roll, they may become a bet that you didn't want to make.

Don't-come bets are the opposite of come bets. A 7 or 11 loses, and a 2 or 3 wins. The 12 is again a push. The don't-come bettor puts his chips in the don't-come space on the table and waits for the next roll to determine his number. His chips are placed *above* the numbered box to differentiate it from a come bet. If the shooter rolls his point number before he rolls your number, your don't-come bet is retained on the layout. You are betting against the shooter; that is, that he will roll a 7 first. When he rolls 7, you win. If he rolls your don't-come number before he sevens out, you lose.

The come and don't-come bets have a house advantage of about 1.4% and are among the better bets in craps once you understand them.

Odds bets When you bet the pass/don't pass or the come/don't come, you may place an odds bet *in addition* to your original bet.

Once it is established that the come-out roll is not a 7 or 11, or craps, the bettor may place a bet that will be paid off according to the actual odds of a particular number being thrown.

Note that the Actual-odds Chart shows the chances against a number made by two dice being thrown. For example, the odds of making a 9 are three to two. If you place an odds bet (in addition to your original bet) on a come number of 9, your original come bet will pay off at even money, but your odds bet will pay off at three to two.

Because this would make a $7.50 payoff for a $5 bet, and the tables don't carry 50-cent chips, you are allowed to place a $6 bet as an odds bet. This is a very good bet to make, and betting the extra dollar is to your advantage.

To place an odds bet on a line bet, bet the pass line. When (and if) the point is established, put your additional bet behind the pass line and say, "Odds."

To place an odds bet on a come bet, wait for the dealer to move your chips to the come number box, then hand him more chips and say, "Odds." He will set these chips half on and half off the other pile so that he can see at a glance that it's an odds bet.

Etiquette of Craps

When you arrive at a table, find an open space and put your cash down in front of you. When the dealer sees it, he will pick it up and hand it to the boxman. The boxman will count out the correct chips and give them to the dealer, who will pass them to you.

A craps table holds from 12 to 20 players and can get very crowded. Keep your place at the table. Your chips are in front of you, in the rail and on the table, and it is your responsibility to watch them.

After you place your bets, your hands must come off the table. It is bad form to leave your hands on the table when the dice are rolling.

Stick to the good bets listed here, and don't be tempted by bets that you don't understand. The box in the middle of the layout, for example, offers a number of sucker bets.

BACCARAT

ORIGINALLY AN ITALIAN CARD GAME, baccarat (bah-kah-rah) is the French pronunciation of the Italian word for "zero," which refers to the value of all the face cards in the game.

Because baccarat involves no player decisions, it is an easy game to play, yet a very difficult game to understand. Each player must decide to make a bet on either the bank or the player. That's it. There are no more decisions until the next hand is dealt. The rules of playing out the hands are ridiculously intricate, but beginning players need not concern themselves with them, because all plays are predetermined by the rules, and the dealer will tell you exactly what happened.

All cards, ace through 9, are worth their spots (the 3 of clubs is worth three). The 10, jack, queen, and king are worth zero. The easiest way to count at baccarat is to add all card totals in the hand, then take only the number in the ones column.

If you have been dealt a 6 and a 5, then your total is 11, and taking only the ones column, your hand is worth 1 point. If you hold a 10 and a king, your hand is worth zero. If you have an 8 and a 7, your point total is 15, and taking the ones column, your hand is worth 5. It doesn't get any simpler than this.

In baccarat, regardless of the number of bettors at the table, only two hands are dealt: one to the player and one to the bank. The object

BACCARAT RULES

Player

When first two cards total

1, 2, 3, 4, 5, or 10	*Draws a card*
6 or 7	*Stands*
8 or 9	*A natural—stands*

Banker

Having	*Draws when player's third card is*	*Does not draw when player's third card is*
3	1, 2, 3, 4, 5, 6, 7, 9, 10	8
4	2, 3, 4, 5, 6, 7	1, 8, 9, 10
5	4, 5, 6, 7	1, 2, 3, 8, 9, 10
6	6, 7	1, 2, 3, 4, 5, 8, 9, 10
7	*Stands*	*Stands*
8 or 9	*Stands*	*Stands*

The Baccarat Table

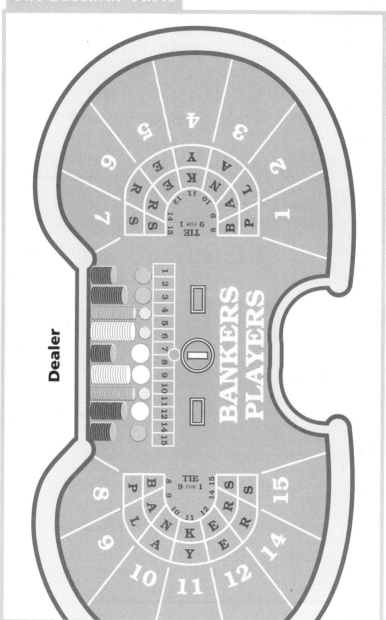

of the game is to be dealt or draw a hand closest to nine without going over. If the first two cards dealt equal nine (a 5 and a 4, for example), then you have a natural and an automatic winner. Two cards worth eight are the second best hand and will also be called a natural. If the other hand is not equal to or higher than eight, this hand wins automatically. Ties are pushes, and neither bank nor player wins, though a longshot bet on the tie (the third wager at baccarat) does.

If the hands equal any total except nine or eight, the rules are consulted. These rules are printed and available at the baccarat table. The hands will be played out by the dealer whether you understand the rules or not.

The rules for the player's hand are simple. If a natural is not dealt to either hand, and if the player holds one, two, three, four, five, or ten (zero), he will always draw a card. He will stand on a total of six or seven. A total of eight or nine, of course, will be a natural.

The bank hand is more complicated and is partially determined by the third card drawn by the player's hand. Though the rules don't say so, the bank will always draw on zero, one, or two. When the hand is worth three or more, it is subject to the printed rules.

If you study a few hands, the method of play will be clear:

FIRST HAND The player's hand is worth three, and the bank's is worth four. The player always goes first. Looking at the rules for the player, we see that a hand worth three points draws a card. This time he draws a 9, for a new total of 12 points, which has a value of two. The bank, having four points, must stand when a player draws a 9. The bank wins four to two.

SECOND HAND The player's hand is worth six points, and the bank has two queens, for a total of zero. The player must stand with six points, while the bank must draw with zero. The bank gets another card, a 4. Player wins, six to four.

The Atmosphere

The casinos try to attract players by making baccarat seem sophisticated. The section is roped off from the main casino, and the dealers are often dressed in tuxedos instead of the usual dealer's uniforms. Don't be put off by glamorous airs; everyone is welcome to play.

Because the house wants baccarat to be appealing to what they consider to be their upper-crust clientele, the table minimums are usually very high in baccarat—usually $100 to $15,000. This means that the minimum bet is $100, and the maximum bet is $15,000.

Even the shuffle and deal of the deck is designed to perpetuate an exotic feeling. Elaborately cut and mixed by all three dealers, the cards are cut by one player and marked with the plastic card stop. The dealer will then separate the cards at the stop, turn the top card over, and discard, or burn, the number of cards equal to the face value of the upturned card. The cards are then placed in a large holder called the shoe.

THE PLAY If the game has just begun, the shoe will be passed to the player in seat number one, who is then called the bank. Thereafter, whenever the bank hand loses, the shoe is passed counterclockwise to the next player, until it reaches seat number 15, where it is passed to seat number one again.

When all bets are down, one of the three dealers will nod to the holder of the shoe, who will then deal out four cards in alternating fashion—two for the player and two for the bank.

The player's hand is passed (still facedown) to the bettor who has wagered the most money on the player's hand. He looks at the cards and passes them back to the dealer. The dealer then turns both hands faceup and plays out the game according to the rules.

THE BETTING In baccarat, you must back either the player or the bank. You do this by putting your chips in the box in front of you marked "player" or "bank." Once the bets are down, the deal will begin.

The house advantage on baccarat is quite low: 1.36% on player wagers and 1.17% on bank bets. Because the bank bet has such an obvious advantage, the house extracts a commission when you win a bank bet. This is not collected with each hand, but must be paid before you leave the table.

MINIBACCARAT Some casinos offer a version of baccarat in the main pit, usually near the blackjack games. The tables are smaller and lower than normal baccarat tables, with each table seating seven players. The dealers dress in the standard casino floor uniform and the table minimums (and maximums) are much lower than the more common high stakes version. It's the same game with the same house advantage, except that in minibaccarat, the shoe is never passed. In fact, the dealer places the cards right-side-up on the table and the players never touch them at all. Also, the dealer is always the banker.

All of the rules of baccarat apply to the mini version: eight decks are used; face cards and 10s count as zero and aces count as one; the casino collects a 5% commission on a winning banker hand (when the player is ready to leave). The minimum bet is $10, though sometimes you can find $5 minimums. However, since there's much less ritual and fewer players, the speed of the game is very fast, so often more is bet at a $10 minibaccarat table than a $25 baccarat table.

Some experts believe that because minibaccarat lacks the atmosphere of the big table, the game loses its charm and becomes redundant and boring. That could explain why minibaccarat is one of the least popular table games in the casino.

TEXAS HOLD 'EM

POKER IS TAKING THE GAMBLING WORLD by storm, and Texas Hold 'Em is the favorite game, both in ring games (a "live" poker game where actual money is in play) and tournaments (buy-ins for tournament chips). The combination of procedures, strategy and tactics, and psychology can take a lifetime to perfect, but the rules of the game can be learned from an hour of study and another hour of practice.

We recommend studying the game, then playing the free games on-line at poker sites such as **partypoker.com** and **ultimatebet.com.** You should also take a lesson offered by most casino poker rooms where you play with free chips. Then, when you're ready for a live game, look for one with the lowest betting limits, such as $1 to $2 and $2 to $4. As your skills improve, you can move up in denomination, all the way to no-limit hold 'em and $25,000 buy-in tournaments. If you're just playing for fun, you'll have little to worry about in low-limit games.

The following are the basic steps in a round of Texas Hold 'Em:

There are two types of bets: blinds and antes. Antes are rare in hold 'em ring games, but they're usually imposed in the later rounds of tournaments. Blinds, a forced bet that one or more players, typi-cally to the left of the dealer, make before any cards are dealt are always used. This starts the action on the first round of betting.

The game starts when the two players to the left of the dealer make initial bets, also known as "posting the blinds." The player to the immediate left of the dealer is the small blind; he puts up a bet equal to half the minimum limit. The player two to the left of the dealer is the big blind; his bet is equal to the lower limit. If it's a $10–$20 game, the small blind bets $5 and the big blind bets $10.

Each player is dealt two cards facedown, known as hole (or pocket) cards. The first round of betting, "pre-flop," begins with the player to the left of the big blind. The betting structures can get a bit complicated, but to keep it simple, in our $10–$20 game, you'll bet $10 at a time pre-flop. You can bet four times *per betting round*: the initial bet can be "raised" by $10 three times. So if you initially bet $10, to stay in the pre-flop round, you might have to put up $30 more. "Checking" means you don't bet, but keep open your options of "calling" (betting an equal amount; not raising), raising, or folding later in the betting round. You can also "fold," which means throw-ing in your cards and ending your participation in the round.

At the end of the pre-flop betting rounds, the dealer "burns" (dis-cards) the top card, then deals three cards face up on the table: "the flop." These three cards are combined with each player's two hole cards to form the initial five-card poker hand. Then there's another round of betting, starting with the player to the left of the dealer.

At the end of the post-flop betting, the dealer burns the top card, then deals one card face up on the table: "the turn." Players can now use this sixth card to improve their five-card poker hand. Another round of betting ensues. Often, this is where the betting limit dou-bles. So in our $10–$20 game, initial bets can be $20.

At the end of the turn betting, the dealer burns the top card, then deals one card face up on the table: "the river." Players can now combine any of the five community cards with his two pocket cards to make the best five-card hand. One more round of betting ensues, again beginning with the player to the left of the dealer.

Finally, the "showdown" occurs, when players reveal their hands. The player with the best hand wins the pot. The dealer rakes the house's cut (in a ring game), collects the cards, and another round begins.

It might sound simple, like a cousin of 7-Card Stud, but there's a lot of protocol and jargon to poker. Again, we highly recommend reading up on the game, then participating in the free tournaments at poker websites, before taking a lesson in a casino poker room. These steps can (and probably will) save you a certain amount of grief when you start playing for real money, even in the lowest-limit games.

KENO

KENO IS AN ANCIENT CHINESE GAME. It was used to raise money for national defense, including, some say, building the Great Wall. Keno was brought to America by the thousands of workers who came from the Far East to work on the railroads during the 1800s. It is one of the most popular games in the Nevada casinos, though it is outlawed in Atlantic City.

This game has a house advantage between 15% and 35% or more, depending on the casino—higher than any other game in Las Vegas. Too high, in fact, for serious gamblers. If you're down to your last dollar and you have to bet to save the ranch, don't go to the keno lounge.

While keno is similar to bingo, the betting options are reminiscent of exacta horse-race betting. It is like bingo in that a ticket, called a blank, is marked off and numbers are randomly selected to determine a winner. And it is similar to exacta betting because any number of fascinating betting combinations can be played in each game. The biggest difference between keno and bingo and exactas is that in the latter two, there's always a winner. In keno, hours can go by before anyone wins a substantial amount. The main excitement in keno lies in the possibility that large amounts of money can be won on a small bet.

Playing the Game

In each casino there is a keno lounge that usually resembles a college lecture hall. The casino staff sit in front while players relax in chairs with writing tables built into the arms. It is not necessary to sit in the keno lounge to play. In fact, one of the best things about keno is that it can be played almost anywhere in the casino, including the bars and restaurants. As in bingo, it is acceptable to strike up a conversation with your neighbor during a game, and because the winning numbers are posted all over the place, keno also offers the opportunity to gamble while absent from the casino floor.

Keno is one of the easiest games to understand. The keno blank can be picked up almost anywhere in any Nevada casino. On the blank are two large boxes containing 80 numbers: the top box with 1 to 40, and the bottom box with 41 to 80. Simply use one of the crayons provided with the blanks to mark between 1 and 15 (sometimes 20) numbers on the blank, decide how much you want to bet, and turn the blank in to a keno writer. The keno writer records your wager, keeping your original, and gives you a duplicate, which you are responsible for checking. The keno writer can be found at the front of the keno lounge. The keno runner is even easier to spot: she is usually a woman in a short skirt with a hand full of blanks and crayons. She will place your bets, cash in your blanks, and bring you your winnings. Of course, you are expected to tip her for this service.

The drawing of the winning numbers takes place in the keno lounge. When the keno caller has determined that the bets are in for the current round, he will close the betting just like the steward does at the race-track. Then the caller uses a machine similar to those employed by state lotteries: a blower with numbered Ping-Pong balls. Ten balls are blown into each of two tubes. These 20 balls bear the numbers that will be called for the current round. The numbers, as called out, are posted on electronic keno boards around the casino. If any of the lighted numbers are numbers that you marked on your card, you "caught" those num-bers. Catching four or more numbers will usually win something, de-pending on how many numbers you marked on your card. The payoffs are complicated, but the more numbers you guess correctly and the more money you bet, the greater your jackpot. Suffice it to say, however, that you are not paid at anything even approaching true odds.

If by some amazing quirk of fate you win in keno, you must claim your winnings before the next round starts, or forfeit.

THE ODDS A "straight" or basic ticket is one where the player simply selects and marks a minimum of one number to a maximum of 8 to 15 numbers, depending on the casino. The ways to combine keno bets are endless and understandable only to astrophysicists. Any number can be played with any other number, making "combination" tickets. Groups of numbers can be combined with other groups of numbers, making "way" tickets. Individual numbers can be combined with groups of numbers, making "king" tickets. Then there is the "house" ticket, called different things at each casino, which offers a shot at the big jack-pot for a smaller investment, though the odds won't be any better.

All of these options and the amounts that you are allowed to bet (usually from 70 cents up per ticket) are listed in the keno brochures, which are almost as ubiquitous as the blanks. The payoffs are listed for each type of bet and for the amount wagered. Keno runners and keno lounge personnel will show you how to mark your ticket if you are confused, but they cannot mark it for you.

If you want to play keno for fun (and that is the only rational reason to play), then understand that one bet is about as bad as another. Filling out a complicated combination ticket won't increase your chances of winning. If by some miracle you do win, accept the congratulations and the winnings, and then run, do not walk, to the nearest exit. The best strategy for winning at keno is to avoid it since the house has an unbeatable advantage.

ROULETTE

A QUIET GAME WHERE WINNERS MERELY SMILE over a big win and losers suffer in silence, roulette is very easy to understand. The dealer spins the wheel, drops the ball, and waits for it to fall into one of the numbered slots on the wheel. The numbers run from zero to 36, with a zero and double zero thrown in for good measure. You may bet on each individual number, on combinations of numbers, on all black numbers, all red numbers, and many more. All possible bets are laid out on the table. (see illustration on next page)

Special chips are used for roulette, with each bettor at the table playing a different color. To buy in, convert cash or the casino's house chips to roulette chips. When you are ready to cash out, the dealer will convert your special roulette chips back to house chips. If you want cash, you must then take your house chips to a casino cashier.

To place a bet, put your chips inside a numbered square or choose one of the squares off to the side. A chip placed in "1st 12," for example, will pay off if the ball drops into any number from 1 to 12. The box marked "odd" is not for eccentrics—it pays when the ball drops into an odd-numbered slot.

Roulette is fun to play, but expect to pay! The house advantage on most bets is a whopping 5.26%, and on some wagers it can be 7%.

ROULETTE BET AND PAYOFF CHART

Bet	Payoff	Bet	Payoff
Single number	35 to 1	12 numbers (column)	2 to 1
Two numbers	17 to 1	1st 12, 2nd 12, 3rd 12	2 to 1
Three numbers	11 to 1	1–18 or 19–36	1 to 1
Four numbers	8 to 1	Odd or even	1 to 1
Five numbers	6 to 1	Red or black	1 to 1
Six numbers	5 to 1		

The Roulette Table

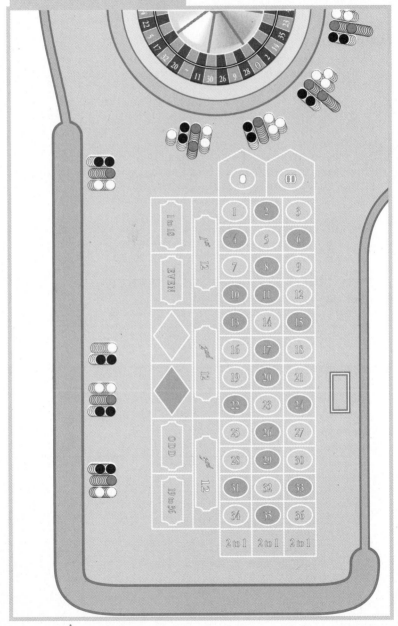

PART FOUR

DINING *and* RESTAURANTS

DINING *in* LAS VEGAS

OVER THE LAST 12 MONTHS, we've seen a mild recovery in the economy, and thus also in hotel occupancy, which means tables are at a premium in top Strip restaurants once again. However, Echelon, a multibillion-dollar casino project from Boyd Gaming, remains a half-built skeleton on the northern part of the Strip; plans for a Charlie Palmer Hotel near the World Market Center downtown have been shelved, perhaps permanently; and Trump Tower, which had such a promising start, remains virtually unknown to most visitors.

The good news is the food scene has been lively away from the Strip and all around the city, with many new and exciting restaurant openings; gourmet supermarkets, such as Resnick's in Downtown and Glazier's in Westside, opening; and a flurry of tapas bars that are fairly flourishing with locals.

On the Strip, the opening of the Cosmopolitan, likely to be the last major casino opening on the Strip for several years to come, got most of the attention, and deservedly so. The hotel has brought with it a new generation of restaurants, which set new standards of excellence for Las Vegas. It's truly an exciting destination and not to be missed.

Much credit for this goes to Cosmopolitan CEO John Unwin, whose vision for restaurants in his casino has proven to be, after just a short interval, a game-changer. For instance, his hotel's three-meal buffet, named **The Wicked Spoon,** presents an array of dishes in individual serving vessels—a radical idea, and a far more appealing one than a steam-table format. Furthermore, the scope, eclecticism, and quality of this buffet has, in the opinion of this guide, no peer on the Strip for value and enjoyableness.

Then there are the individual restaurants Unwin recruited, such as **Milos, Scarpetta, Jaleo, China Poblano, Blue Ribbon Sushi, Comme Ça,** and others, many of which are so good we've profiled them in this

Celebrity Chefs

CHEF	ORIGINAL RESTAURANT	VEGAS RESTAURANT(S)
José Andrés	Jaleo, Minibar, Café Atlantico (Washington D.C.)	Jaleo and China Poblano (Cosmopolitan)
Paul Bartolotta	Ristorante Bartolotta (Milwaukee)	Bartolotta Ristorante di Mare (Wynn)
Mario Batali	Po, Babbo Ristorante e Enoteca (New York)	B & B Ristorante (Venetian) Carnevino (Palazzo) Pizzeria Otto (Venetian)
Tom Colicchio	Craft (New York)	Craftsteak (MGM Grand)
Scott Conant	Scarpetta (New York)	Scarpetta (Cosmopolitan)
Alain Ducasse	Louis XV (Monte Carlo, Paris)	MIX in Las Vegas (Mandalay Bay)
Todd English	Olives (Charlestown, MA)	Olives (Bellagio) Todd English P.U.B. (Crystals)
Susan Feniger	Border Grill (Los Angeles)	Border Grill (Mandalay Bay)
Bobby Flay	Mesa Grill (New York)	Mesa Grill (Caesars Palace)
Pierre Gagnaire	Pierre Gagnaire (Paris)	Twist (Mandarin Oriental)
Hubert Keller	Fleur de Lys (San Francisco)	Fleur, Burger Bar (Mandalay Bay)
Thomas Keller	French Laundry (Yountville, CA) Per Se (New York)	Bouchon (Venetian)
Emeril Lagasse	Emeril's (New Orleans)	Delmonico (Venetian) Emeril's New Orleans Fish House (MGM Grand) Table 10 (Palazzo)
Nobu Matsuhisa	Matsuhisa (Beverly Hills)	Nobu (Hard Rock)
Shawn McClain	Spring (Chicago)	Sage (Aria)
Mary Sue Milliken	Border Grill (Los Angeles)	Border Grill (Mandalay Bay)
Michael Mina	Aqua (San Francisco)	Michael Mina (Bellagio) Nobhill Tavern (MGM Grand) SeaBlue (MGM Grand)

guide. What's more, the restaurants are brilliantly located in a dedicated area on the hotel's second and third floors and reached by special elevators, meaning restaurant patrons don't have to be subjected to the casino floor. With this arrangement, the Cosmopolitan is now home to what some people are calling "the ultimate food court." Unwin and his team have made it possible for those who choose to avoid the cacophony of a casino to do so and still dine in style in his building.

CHEF	ORIGINAL RESTAURANT	VEGAS RESTAURANT(S)
Bradley Ogden	The Lark Creek Inn (*Marin County*)	Bradley Ogden (*Caesars Palace*)
Charlie Palmer	Aureole (*New York*)	Aureole (*Mandalay Bay*) Charlie Palmer Steak (*Four Seasons*)
Francois Payard	Payard Patisserie & Bistro (*New York*)	Payard Patisserie & Bistro (*Caesars Palace*)
Carla Pellegrino	Baldoria (*New York*)	Bratalian (*Caesars Palace*)
Wolfgang Puck	Spago (*Los Angeles*)	Chinois, Spago (*Forum Shops*) CUT (*Palazzo*) Lupo (*Mandalay Bay*) Postrio (*Grand Canal Shoppes, Venetian*) Wolfgang Puck Bar & Grill (*MGM Grand*) Wolfgang Puck Pizzeria &Cucina (*Crystals at CityCenter*)
Joël Robuchon	Jamin, Joël Robuchon (*Paris*)	L'Atelier de Joël Robuchon, Joël Robuchon (*MGM Grand*)
Guy Savoy	Restaurant Guy Savoy (*Paris*)	Restaurant Guy Savoy (*Caesars Palace*)
Julian Serrano	Masa (*San Francisco*)	Picasso (*Bellagio*) Julian Serrano (*Aria*)
Kerry Simon	Blue Star (*Miami*)	Simon at Palms Place (*Palms*)
Joachim Splichal	Patina, Pinot (*Los Angeles*)	Pinot Brasserie (*Venetian*)
Alex Stratta	Mary Elaine's (*Scottsdale*)	Stratta (*Wynn*)
Masa Takayama	Masa (*New York City*)	Bar Masa (*Aria*)
Jean-Georges Vongerichten	JoJo (*New York*)	Prime (*Bellagio*) Jean Georges Steakhouse (*Aria*)
David Walzog	Strip House (*New York*)	SW Steakhouse (*Wynn*)
Roy Yamaguchi	Roy's (*Hawaii*)	Roy's (*Flamingo*)

There has been action and winds of change in other areas of the Strip as well. It seems that fine dining is taking quite a hit. If you talk to local chefs, such as Theo Schoenigger of **Sinatra** and Rene Lenger of **Switch** at Wynn Encore, they will tell you that people no longer clamor for fancy dishes. They have scaled back their menus somewhat to offer more conventional favorites, and other big-name chefs are doing the same.

Many chefs are re-conceptualizing their restaurants to reflect the current rash of small plates and tapas restaurants, not to mention lower prices. Chef Hubert Keller closed his landmark fine-dining establishment Fleur de Lys at Mandalay Bay and redesigned it as a more casual venue, simplifying the name to **Fleur** and using it to showcase small plates and tapas, which he considers more fun than the grand dishes.

Notable closings included the rather shocking one at Alex, the Two-Star Michelin fine-dining venue at Wynn Las Vegas. It seems the hotel is moving away from fine dining, even though restaurants there such as **Bartolotta Ristorante di Mare** and **Sinatra** continue to perform well. And at CityCenter, the daring—perhaps too much so—Silk Road has now permanently closed, dashing the hopes of talented chef Martin Heierling, who remains Food and Beverage Director at Vdara and chef at his Bellagio restaurant, **Sensi.**

There has been movement among chefs as well. Celebrity chef Carla Pellegrino has left **Rao's** at Caesars Palace and struck out on her own at **Bratalian,** where she is serving both the classics she prepared at Rao's as well as dishes from her native Brazil on her bountiful weekend brunch.

As the French say, though, *plus ça change*—the more things change, the more they remain the same. Many interesting new restaurants are now on the scene. One is **P.J. Clarke's,** a branch of the legendary New York City watering hole, now open at The Forum Shops. Iconic chef Larry Forgione consulted on the amazing upscale bar menu, which includes wonderful chicken pot pie, bread pudding, and steaks from Meyer Ranch in Montana.

DW Bistro, a wacky blend of Jamaica and New Mexico, is one of the more exciting new off-Strip restaurants—don't miss the jerk chicken or red chili—while **Forte,** even more unlikely, serves, get this, a menu of both Spanish and Bulgarian tapas.

Another story that can't be ignored is the burger craze. It seems Hubert Keller started something when he opened **Burger Bar** in 2003. Now there are too many made-to-order upscale burger joints to count. Just three of the newer ones on the Strip are **Holsteins** at the Cosmo, **KGB** by Kerry Simon at Harrah's, and **I ♥ Burgers** at the Palazzo. Off-Strip, there is the Midwestern chain **Steak & Shake,** which often has lines out the door, at South Point Casino and the new **Five Guys Burgers and Fries** in Henderson. Five Guys is the northern Virginia chain with more than 800 locations nationally that was popularized by President Obama. Beef is still what's for dinner in Vegas.

Vegas, which has a proven ability to ceaselessly reinvent itself, has shown once again that it can keep pace with any other destination to remain in the dining vanguard.

THE TOP 25

WE KNOW THAT NOT EVERYONE HAS THE DESIRE or can afford to drop $500 on a meal while visiting Las Vegas, so we present a broad range of restaurants for all tastes and price points. But we would be remiss not to recognize the finest dining experiences and celebrity chefs who have restaurants here. On pages 350–351 is a chart rating and ranking the top 25 restaurants in town, if price is no object.

THE COSMOPOLITAN

THERE IS NO DOUBT THAT AT THE MOMENT the impressive lineup at this new resort is the city's most interesting. The third floor alone is a dedicated area that houses such terrific restaurants as **Milos, Scarpetta, STK, Jaleo, Blue Ribbon Sushi, D.O.C.G., Comme Ça,** and even a secret pizza parlor that you'll have to ask about to find. The second floor has a new burger joint, **Holsteins,** and **China Poblano.** It's one fabulous place to dine.

CITYCENTER

CityCenter has 16 notable restaurants in all, most in the expensive to very expensive range for dinner. Ones open for lunch, such as **Lemongrass, MOzen Bistro,** and **Julian Serrano,** can be experienced in the moderate price range with careful ordering. Here is a quick rundown of the top spots there:

At Aria

AMERICAN FISH Michael Mina's newest concept offers fresh fish cooked in four different styles, as well as creative appetizers by chef Sven Meade.

BAR MASA The most expensive restaurant in Vegas is an airplane hangar–sized sushi restaurant from chef Masa Takayama.

BLOSSOM Traditional Cantonese food is proffered in this brilliantly designed, Asian-themed room composed of wood, bamboo, stone, and glass.

JEAN-GEORGES STEAKHOUSE This is more than just a retread of the chef's famous Prime at the Bellagio; try the Australian A300 beef or the Comte cheese fritters.

JULIAN SERRANO Tapas, paella, and Spanish wines galore are the ticket at this busy restaurant, the first high-quality Spanish restaurant to open in Las Vegas.

LEMONGRASS In this elegant room, you'll find a modern take on Thai cooking by young Thai native Krairit Krairavee, recruited from the Mandarin Oriental Bangkok.

SAGE Chicago's Shawn McClain serves what he calls "refined American cuisine" at his new aerie and bar, featuring some of the most unusual cocktails in the city.

SIRIO Pater familias Sirio Maccioni, of New York's famed Le Cirque, has opened a mezzanine-level Italian restaurant serving a compilation of his greatest hits. Adam Tihany did the design.

Top 25 Las Vegas Restaurants

RANK/NAME	CHEF	OVERALL RATING
1. Joël Robuchon	Claude LeTohic	★★★★★
2. Restaurant Guy Savoy	Eric Bost	★★★★★
3. Estiatorio Milos	Costas Spiliadis	★★★★★
4. Twist	Pascal Sanchez	★★★★★
5. Bar Masa	Masa Takayama	★★★★★
6. L'Atelier de Joël Robuchon	Steve Benjamin	★★★★★
7. Jaleo	José Andrés	★★★★½
8. Picasso	Julian Serrano	★★★★½
9. Sage	Shawn McClain	★★★★½
10. Bartolotta Ristorante di Mare	Paul Bartolotta	★★★★½
11. Aureole	Vincent Poussel	★★★★½
12. RM Seafood	Rick Moonen	★★★★
13. Valentino	Luciano Pellegrini	★★★★
14. Le Cirque	Gregory Pugin	★★★★
15. Michael Mina	Mark St. Jacques	★★★★
16. Osteria del Circo	Massimiliano Campanari	★★★★
17. CUT	Matthew Hurley	★★★★
18. Craftsteak	Matt Seeber	★★★★
19. Nobu	Joel Versola	★★★★
20. Scarpetta	Scott Conant	★★★★
21. Sensi	Martin Heierling	★★★½
22. Mix in Las Vegas	Bruno Davaillon	★★★½
23. Bouchon	Mark Hopper	★★★½
24. Spago	Eric Klein	★★★½
25. B&B Ristorante	Mario Batali	★★★

UNION The Light Group's newest steak house will remind you of Bellagio's Fix, Stack at the Mirage, and Brand in the Monte Carlo, all directed by chef Brian Massie.

At Mandarin Oriental

MOZEN BISTRO The hotel's three-meal restaurant has an eclectic menu of Chinese, Japanese, Indian, and American specialties, done under the watchful eye of chef Shawn Armstrong.

TWIST Paris superstar Pierre Gagnaire's 23rd-floor gourmet restaurant makes it possible to dine à la carte and still experience the chef's greatness without emptying your wallet.

PRICE RATING	HOST HOTEL	PROFILED
Very Expensive	MGM Grand	Yes
Very Expensive	Caesars Palace	Yes
Very Expensive	Cosmopolitan	Yes
Very Expensive	Mandarin Oriental	Yes
Very Expensive	Aria	Yes
Very Expensive	MGM Grand	Yes
Moderate	Cosmopolitan	Yes
Very Expensive	Bellagio	Yes
Very Expensive	Aria	Yes
Very Expensive	Wynn Las Vegas	Yes
Very Expensive	Mandalay Bay	Yes
Expensive	Mandalay Bay	No
Very Expensive	Venetian	Yes
Very Expensive	Bellagio	No
Very Expensive	Bellagio	No
Very Expensive	Bellagio	No
Expensive	Palazzo	No
Expensive	MGM Grand	Yes
Very Expensive	Hard Rock Hotel	Yes
Expensive	Cosmopolitan	Yes
Expensive	Bellagio	No
Very Expensive	Mandalay Bay	No
Moderate	Venetian	Yes
Moderate/Expensive	Forum Shops, Caesars Palace	Yes
Very Expensive	Venetian	Yes

BUFFETS

BUFFETS, USED BY THE CASINOS TO LURE CUSTOMERS, remain the most popular dining venues with Las Vegas visitors. Like everything else, they come, go, and are upgraded and remodeled, but on average they do not change that much. Some casinos operate their buffets at close to cost or at a slight loss. A few, those with captive clientele (Las Vegas Hilton and Red Rock Resort), are profitable, as are the upscale spreads (Bellagio, Cosmopolitan, or Wynn Las Vegas).

LAS VEGAS'S TEN BEST BUFFETS

RANK	BUFFET	QUALITY RATING	LAST YEAR'S RATING
1.	Cosmopolitan Wicked Spoon Buffet	99	–
2.	Wynn Buffet	98	1
3.	Bellagio Buffet	97	2
4.	M Studio B Buffet	96	3
5.	Planet Hollywood Spice Market Buffet	95	4
6.	Mirage Cravings	94	5
7.	Aria Buffet	93	6
8.	Buffet at T. I.	92	7
9.	Red Rock Feast	90	8
10.	Rio Carnival World	87	10

Almost all of the buffets serve breakfast, lunch, and dinner, changing their menus to some extent every day. Prices for breakfast range from $6.50 (Sam's Town) to $19 (Wynn). Lunch goes for $7.50 (Fremont) to $23 (Wynn), with dinner ranging between $10 (Terrible's) and $39 (Rio seafood buffet). Because most buffets operate as an extension of sales and marketing, there is not necessarily any relationship between price and quality.

At breakfast, relatively speaking, there is not much difference between one buffet and the next (exceptions are the standout breakfast buffets at the **Aria, Cosmopolitan, Orleans, Rio, Bellagio, The Mirage,** and **Wynn Las Vegas**). If your hotel has a breakfast buffet, it is probably not worth the effort to go somewhere else. When it comes to lunch and dinner, however, some buffets do a significantly better job than others.

If you are looking for upscale gourmet-quality food and a large variety to choose from, head straight to our top four buffets. If you're hankering for well-seasoned meats and vegetables, ethnic variety, and culinary activity, the other six will suffice nicely.

Leading the way in the buffet parade is **The Wicked Spoon** at the

Buffet-speak

Action format	Food cooked to order in full view of the patrons
Gluttony	A Las Vegas buffet tradition that carries no moral stigma
Groaning board	Synonym for a buffet; a table so full that it groans
Island	Individual serving area for a particular cuisine or specialty (salad island, dessert island, Mexican island, and so on)
Shovelizer	Diner who prefers quantity over quality
Fork lift	A device used to remove shovelizers
Sneeze guards	The plastic barriers between you and the food

Cosmopolitan. CEO and foodie John Unwin has let his and his designers' collective imaginations run wild. The result is a $20-million, 21st-century iteration of the buffet—a sprawling space filled with amber and gold floor-to-ceiling glass panels and hanging sculptures that recall otherworldly jellyfish. There is ample space between the tables and a few smaller rooms for semiprivate dining. What makes this buffet unique is that foods are often done in small individual vessels as opposed to plucking everything from the steam table. Enjoy pint-sized Benedicts with pulled pork, pancakes made with Guinness, and perfectly browned chicken apple sausages that look like British bangers at breakfast. Lunch and dinner feature an action sushi station, beef and pork sliders, and 18 bins of ice cream, gelato, and sorbet. The selection is mind-boggling; it's literally a task just to choose where to start. Prices are a bit less than the other buffets in the neighborhood, at $15 for breakfast, $19 for lunch, and $27 for dinner.

Our second choice of Las Vegas buffets is The Buffet at **Wynn Las Vegas.** The Wynn is also the most expensive, at $19 for breakfast, $23 for lunch, and $35 for dinner ($39 Friday and Saturday). The dining area is expansive and separated into alcoves, so it's quiet, unlike the din at most buffets. Food is as fresh as possible, with upscale selections such as tuna poke, octopus, pasta with Kobe meatballs, big bowls of berries, a crepe station, rack of lamb, lamb risotto, king crab, and steaks.

The **Bellagio** is our third pick and also pricey—but it's worth every penny. Seafood galore, bread warm from the oven, creative salads, gourmet entrées, perfect vegetables—this joint has it all. Even at $16 for breakfast, $20 for lunch, and $30 for dinner ($37 Saturday and Sunday), the Bellagio buffet barely breaks even. For the money, we like lunch here better than dinner.

M Resort's buffet, **Studio B,** is the most impressive off-Strip choice for quality, variety, and creativity. This could be Las Vegas's top buffet for value, for the all-you-can-drink beer and wine alone, though the quality is slightly less than at the Cosmo, Wynn, and Bellagio. The Thai station has five curries, the carving station has four meats, the salad selection seems endless, the sushi is the best of any Vegas buffet, and the dessert freezer is full of ice cream, frozen yogurt, and sherbet. It's worth the long drive south to M to experience this buffet.

Spice Market Buffet at Planet Hollywood blends quality, variety, and a surprisingly attractive and cozy setting. There are Italian, Mexican, American, Middle Eastern (grape leaves, hummus, couscous, and carved lamb), and seafood (cold king crab is the specialty) serving stations, plus salads, desserts, and breads. Everything is fresh, tasty, and well stocked. The Planet Hollywood buffet is the same price and of slightly lesser quality as the Bellagio buffet (see above).

Cravings, at the Mirage, was designed by Adam Tihany. Charlie Palmers' Aureole at Mandalay Bay, with its four-story wine tower, and Bouchon at the Venetian were also designed by him. Cravings has marble counters, an abundance of large TV screens, and stations that are self-contained "mini-restaurants," where chefs cook food to order. Prices are in the low end of the upper range. **The Buffet** at T. I. is similar, both in layout and price.

The Buffet at **Aria** has impressive cooking, and the prices—$16 for breakfast, $20 for lunch, and $28 for dinner ($37 on weekends)—aren't bad for this neck of the Strip. Hotel Executive Chef Bernard Ybarra, who came over from the Mirage, has added an Indian food station to complement the Chinese, Italian, and abundantly stocked carving stations, and the quality of products more than makes up for its lack of variety compared to the heavyweights. Some consider the room a bit sterile, but ask for a seat near the dessert station and the big picture windows and you'll enjoy a view overlooking part of the pool area.

Offering an attractive room, action cooking, high quality, extensive selections, and frequent discounts for players club members, the **Feast buffet** at Red Rock Resort is a cut above most locals' buffets.

Rounding out our list this year, The Rio started the super-buffet craze in 1993 with **Carnival World's** huge room, action cooking, and separate serving islands for a vast variety of ethnic choices: American, Italian, Chinese, Mexican, and Mongolian barbecue, along with sushi, an Asian soup station, fish and chips, pizza, burgers, salads, and desserts.

Orleans French Market Buffet is the best of the "bargain super buffets." The room is spacious and efficient, the choices are manifold, and the prices are among the lowest in town.

Fiesta Rancho Festival Buffet has a monster rotisserie for barbecuing every kind of flesh known to man, specialty Cajun and Hawaiian selections, and the first coffee bar in a Las Vegas buffet, serving espresso, cappuccino, and latte. **Texas Station** has a small chili bar and cooked-to-order fajitas; it also has good barbecue, Chinese, Italian, and lots of pizza.

Main Street Station is the only super buffet downtown, served in one of the most aesthetically pleasing buffet rooms in town. Its cuisine has a distinct Hawaiian emphasis, which is where most of its patrons come from.

Harrah's buffet gets an A for effort, a B for quality, and a C for value. **Mandalay Bay**'s buffet is expensive and odd; it's small, congested, and slow—there's something off about it. But the buffets at **Boulder Station, Texas Station, Green Valley Ranch,** and **Sunset Station,** along with **MGM Grand** and **Luxor,** are tried-and-true; you won't go wrong at any of these.

As a footnote, **Aria, Bellagio, Cosmopolitan, Main Street Station, Paris, Planet Hollywood, Sam's Town,** the **Flamingo, Caesars Palace,** the **Mirage, Fiesta Henderson,** the **Golden Nugget, Sunset Station,** the **MGM Grand, M Resort,** and **T. I.** provide the most attractive settings for their buffets. The buffets at the **Rio, Fiesta Rancho, Arizona Charlie's Decatur,** and **Texas, Palace, Sunset,** and **Boulder Stations** are the favorites of Las Vegas locals.

Seafood Buffets

Several casinos feature seafood buffets on certain days. The best of the seafood buffets is **Rio's Village Seafood Buffet** (daily). The **Orleans**'s seafood night is Friday, the **Fremont**'s are on Tuesday and Friday, **Main Street Station**'s is on Friday, and the **Golden Nugget**'s are on Friday, Saturday, and Sunday. Two worthwhile ocean spreads include those at the **Cannery** (Thursday) and **Suncoast** (Friday).

   Rio's Village Seafood Buffet is the most expensive buffet, at $39, but the quality and variety of this piscatory repast are unbelievable, even for Las Vegas. Check it out: small lobster tails (dinner), peel-and-eat shrimp, Dungeness crab legs, Manila steamers, and oysters on the half shell; seafood salads, chowders, and Mongolian grill; plus Italian, Mexican, and Chinese dishes, along with fried, grilled, broiled, breaded, blackened, beer-battered, and barbecued preparations. And if you have even a millimeter of stomach space left after the main courses, the dessert selection is outstanding.

Buffet-line Strategy

Popular buffets develop long lines. The best way to avoid the crowds is to go Sunday through Thursday and get in line before 6 p.m. or after 9 p.m, but we recommend the early strategy, when the food is fresher. If you go to a buffet on a weekend, arrive extra early or extra late. If a large trade show or convention is in town, you will be better off any day hitting the buffets of casinos that do not do big convention business. Good choices among the highly ranked buffets include **Texas Station,** the two **Fiestas, Main Street Station, Boulder Station, Gold Coast, Orleans, Suncoast,** and the **Fremont.**

   Some restaurants now use pagers to let diners know when their table is available. This gives you a bit more freedom to roam around while you wait, but many pagers have a fairly small range.

CHAMPAGNE BRUNCHES

UPSCALE, EXPENSIVE SUNDAY CHAMPAGNE BRUNCHES with reserved tables, imported Champagne, sushi, and seafood are making an impact on the local brunch scene. Although there are a plethora of value-priced Champagne brunches, the big-ticket feasts attract diners who are happy to pay a higher tab for fancy food and service at a place that takes reservations so they can avoid a wait. In general, the higher the price of the brunch, the better the Champagne served. **Bally's, Bellagio,** the **MGM,** and **Wynn Las Vegas** serve decent French Champagne; California sparkling wine is the norm at the others. Reservations are accepted at all of the following:

- **Cookin' with Jazz Brunch** Country Club Grill, Wynn LV; ☎ 702-770-7000
  New Orleans native Carlos Guia, formerly with the sorely missed Commander's Palace, has taken over this clubby steak house overlooking the Wynn golf course. During the week, he sticks to a fairly standard steak-house menu, but on weekends, the hotel allows him to

riff on the dishes he grew up with—shrimp remoulade, gumbo, various house-made sausages, grits, southern soups, even bread pudding. Add a jazz trio, and the result is one of the most indulgent, enjoyable brunches in town. $59. Weekends only, 10 a.m.–2 p.m.

- **Gospel Brunch** House of Blues, Mandalay Bay; ☎ 702-632-7777
'Praise the Lord and pass the biscuits!' This is the most raucous and joyous Sunday brunch in town. A five-member group belts out gospel tunes, and the food is soulful as well: fried chicken, skillet cornbread, jambalaya, turnip greens, made-to-order omelets, ham and prime rib, bagels and lox, smoked salmon, and banana-bread pudding. Purchase tickets at The House of Blues box office: adults, $37; children ages 3 to 11, $17. Seatings at 10 a.m. and 1 p.m.

- **Jasmine** Bellagio; ☎ 702-693-7111
Except on weekends, this space houses an elegant Chinese restaurant, notable for Cantonese cuisine and views of the Bellagio fountains. But on weekends, the room is transformed into Las Vegas's second most expensive brunch, with canapes, king crab, a seafood bar, and great desserts. There are Chinese dim sum from the Jasmine kitchen as well. $65. Weekends only, 11 a.m.–2:30 p.m.

- **Simon Brunch** Palms Place; ☎ 702-944-3292
Come as you are (pajamas included, if you dare) to celebrity-chef Kerry Simon's typically imaginative take on the Sunday brunch. Buffet offerings include sushi, panini, chicken and waffles, meatloaf, smoothies, jars full of candy, and a junk-food dessert platter (cotton candy, Twinkies, etc.); order eggs Benedict, crab omelet, pizza, and fried chicken off the accompanying menu. Adults $40 (add $11 for a do-it-yourself Bloody Mary bar or $17 for Champagne), children (age 11 and under) $12. Available 10 a.m.–4 p.m.

- **Sterling Brunch** Bally's Steakhouse; ☎ 702-967-7999
The Sterling Brunch pioneered this trend. At $85 per person, plus tax (children ages 3 to 8, $30 plus tax; under age 3 free), it's still the big ticket, but there's no shortage of diners who love it. The lavish selection includes smoked salmon, freshly made sushi, real lobster salad, seafood, caviar, and French Champagne. Pheasant and rack of lamb appear regularly. The dessert selection is awesome. Entrée selections change weekly. Available 9:30 a.m.–2:30 p.m.; reservations required.

Bally's Sterling Brunch, though quite expensive, is the most extensive brunch in town, but at $85 it's running close to pricing itself out of the market. Other good brunches can be found at **Aria, Bellagio, Mirage, Planet Hollywood,** and **Main Street Station** (the best bargain brunch at $12).

MEAL DEALS

IN ADDITION TO BUFFETS, MANY CASINOS OFFER special dining deals, including New York strip, T-bone, and porterhouse steaks, prime rib, crab legs, lobster, and combinations of the foregoing, all available at giveaway prices. There are also breakfast specials, burgers, hot dogs, and shrimp cocktails.

While the meal deals generally deliver what they promise in the way of an entrée, many of the extras that contribute to a quality dining experience are missing. With a couple of notable exceptions, the specials are served in big, bustling restaurants with the atmosphere of a high-school cafeteria. Eating at closely packed Formica tables under lighting bright enough for brain surgery, it's difficult to pretend that you're engaged in fine dining.

Our biggest complaint, however, concerns the lack of attention paid to the meal as a whole. We have had nice pieces of meat served with tired, droopy salads, stale bread, mealy microwaved potatoes, and unseasoned canned vegetables. How can you get excited about your prime rib when it is surrounded by the ruins of Pompeii?

Deke Castleman, contributor to this book and editor of the *Las Vegas Advisor,* doesn't believe that discount dining is about food at all. He writes:

Of course you're entitled to your opinion, and I'll fight to the death for your right to express it. But 'quality dining experience' is not really what Las Vegas visitors are looking for, in my humble opinion, when they pursue an $8 steak, $12 prime rib, or $24 lobster. To me what they're after is twofold: A very cheap steak, prime rib, or lobster, and damn the salad, vegetable, and Formica; and to take home a cool story about all the rock-bottom prices they paid for food.

Finally, it's hard to take advantage of many of the specials. They are offered only in the middle of the night, or alternatively you must stand in line for an hour waiting for a table, or eat your evening meal at 3:30 in the afternoon. In restaurants all over town, in and out of the casinos, there is plenty of good food served in pleasant surroundings at extremely reasonable prices. In our opinion, saving $5 on a meal is not worth all the hassle.

Because Las Vegas meal deals often come and go, it is impossible to cover them adequately in a book that is revised annually. If you want to stay abreast of special dinner offerings, your best bet is to subscribe to the *Las Vegas Advisor,* a monthly newsletter that provides independent, critical evaluations of meal deals, buffets, brunches, and drink specials. The *Las Vegas Advisor* can be purchased by calling ☎ 800-244-2224 or visiting **lvahotels.com.** If you are already in town and want to pick up the latest edition, single copies are available at the **Gamblers Book Club** at 5473 South Eastern Avenue, ☎ 702-382-7555 or 800-522-1777; **gamblersbook.com.**

STEAK Though specials constantly change, there are a few that have weathered the test of time. Our favorite is the 16-ounce porterhouse steak dinner at the **Redwood Bar & Grill** in the California, ☎ 702-385-1222. A complete dinner, including soup or salad and steak with excellent accompanying potatoes and vegetables, can be had for about $20, excluding taxes and tips. What's more, it is served in an attractive dining room. The porterhouse special, incidentally, does not appear on the menu. You must ask for it.

Ellis Island, attached to the Super 8 motel on Koval Lane near East Flamingo Road, serves an excellent $8 New York strip dinner complete with salad, baked potato, green beans, and a microbrewed beer or root beer. It's available 24 hours, but it's not on the menu, so you have to ask for it. **The Hard Rock** (☎ 702-693-5000) has a steak-and-shrimp "Gambler's Special," served 24 hours a day in the coffee shop for about $8, though it's not on the menu.

PRIME RIB One of the best prime-rib specials in a town full of prime-rib specials is available at the **Market Street Cafe** in the California downtown, where you can get a good cut of meat between 4 p.m. and 11 p.m. for $8.95; it comes with an all-you-can eat salad bar and cherries jubilee for dessert.

Mr. Lucky's, the coffee shop at the Hard Rock Hotel, offers an exquisite all-you-can-eat prime rib special for $9.99. Served daily from 4 p.m. to 4 a.m., the cooked-to-order prime rib comes with soup or salad, baked potato, and veggies.

South Point, at the far south end of the Strip, serves a big slab of prime rib prepared to order, with soup or salad, potato, rolls, au jus, and biting horseradish if you ask. It's available 24 hours a day in the coffee shop for $14.95–$19.95; ☎ 702-796-7111. For $2 more, you can enjoy the same dinner at the upscale **Primarily Prime Rib** restaurant on the second floor, where salads are mixed tableside and there's always a featured wine on sale for a bargain price. Primarily Prime Rib is open Wednesday through Sunday for dinner only. For reservations call ☎ 702-797-8075.

LOBSTER AND CRAB LEGS Lobster-and-steak (surf-and-turf) combos and crab-leg deals no longer appear as regularly as they once did on casino marquees around Las Vegas. **Pasta Pirate** at the California serves the best all-around shellfish specials, ☎ 702-385-1222. Unfortunately, they are on-again, off-again. When on, they alternately feature a steak-and-lobster combo, a lobster dinner, or a king crab dinner, all from $15 to $38, not including tax or gratuity. Entrées are served with soup or salad, pasta, veggies, garlic bread, and wine. The setting is relaxed and pleasant. Reservations are accepted. **The Flame** at El Cortez (☎ 702-385-5200) often promotes good deals on Alaskan king crab legs ($30) and double lobster tails ($40).

The best place for king crab legs is at the gourmet buffets. **Aria, M Resort, Planet Hollywood, Wynn Las Vegas,** and **Bellagio** serve all-you-can-eat cold king crab nightly; at Bellagio and Planet Hollywood you can make up a plate and ask a server to heat up the legs in a warmer in the kitchen.

Beware of lobster deals, though. You get what you pay for.

SHRIMP COCKTAILS Shrimp cocktails at nominal prices are frequently used to lure gamblers into the casinos. The shrimp are the tiny bay shrimp variety, usually drowned in cocktail sauce. The best and cheapest shrimp cocktail can be found at the **Golden Gate,** a small downtown casino, which has been serving this special for nearly 50 years. The cocktail costs $1.99, raised a dollar in early 2010 after costing 99 cents for nearly 20 years. Other contenders are the **Four Queens** and **Palace Station** (coffee shop).

PASTA AND PIZZA Pasta Pirate at the California offers some of the best designer pasta dishes in town. A good pizza play is to hit up "satellite" outlets (fast-food counters attached to the Italian restaurants) at Boulder Station and Sunset Station for a quickie slice. You can also get a good slice of New York–style pizza at **Sports Deli** at the Rio. **Metro Pizza** at Ellis Island wins the local-media popularity contests. The Red Rock and Green Valley Ranch food courts have **Villa Pizza,** a local chain. The best pizza on the Strip is now found at the no-name "hidden" pizza place on the third floor of the Cosmopolitan.

BREAKFAST SPECIALS The best ham-and-eggs specials are found at the **Gold Coast, Arizona Charlie's Decatur,** and **Boulder Station.** All offer terrific prices, usually around $3.99. Arizona Charlie's Decatur also has a decent steak-and-eggs for $3.99. Other worthwhile breakfast deals include the buffets at **Sam's Town,** the **Orleans,** and the **Rio.**

The RESTAURANTS

OUR FAVORITE LAS VEGAS RESTAURANTS

WE HAVE DEVELOPED DETAILED PROFILES for the best restaurants (in our opinion) in town. Each profile features an easily scanned heading that allows you, in just a second, to check out the restaurant's name, cuisine, overall rating, cost category, quality rating, and value rating.

OVERALL RATING The overall rating encompasses the entire dining experience, including style, service, and ambiance, in addition to taste, presentation, and food quality. Five stars is the highest rating possible and connotes the best of everything. Four-star restaurants are exceptional, and three-star restaurants are well above average. Two-star restaurants are good. One star is used to denote an average restaurant that demonstrates an unusual capability in some area of specialization—for example, an otherwise unmemorable place that has great barbecued chicken.

COST Our expense description provides a comparative sense of how much a complete meal will cost. A complete meal for our purposes consists of an entrée with vegetable or side dish, and choice of soup or salad. Appetizers, desserts, drinks, and tips are excluded.

Inexpensive	$14 or less per person
Moderate	$15–$30 per person
Expensive	$30–$45 per person
Very expensive	$46 or more per person

QUALITY RATING Beneath each heading appear a quality rating and a value rating. The quality rating is based expressly on the taste, freshness of ingredients, preparation, presentation, and creativity of food served. There is no consideration of price. If you are a person who wants the best food available, and cost is not an issue, you need look no further than the quality rating. The quality ratings are defined as:

★★★★★	Exceptional quality
★★★★	Good quality
★★★	Fair quality
★★	Somewhat-subpar quality
★	Subpar quality

VALUE RATING If, on the other hand, you are looking for both quality and value, then you should check the value rating. Value ratings are a function of the overall rating, price rating, and quality rating:

★★★★★	Exceptional value, a real bargain
★★★★	Good value
★★★	Fair value, you get exactly what you pay for
★★	Somewhat overpriced
★	Significantly overpriced

LOCATION Beneath the value rating is an area designation. This designation will give you an idea of where the restaurant described is located. For ease of use, we divide Las Vegas into seven geographic areas:

South Strip and Environs	Mid-Strip and Environs
North Strip and Environs	East of Strip
West of Strip	Downtown
Southeast Las Vegas–Henderson	

OUR PICKS OF THE BEST LAS VEGAS RESTAURANTS

BECAUSE RESTAURANTS ARE OPENING AND CLOSING all the time in Las Vegas, we have tried to confine our list to establishments with a proven track record over a fairly long period of time. Newer restaurants (and older restaurants under new management) are listed but not profiled. Those newer or changed establishments that demonstrate staying power and consistency will be profiled in subsequent editions. Also, the list is highly selective. Exclusion of a particular place does not necessarily indicate that the restaurant is not good, only that it was not ranked among the best in its genre. Note that some restaurants appear in more than one category.

MORE RECOMMENDATIONS

The Best Bagels

* **Harrie's Bagelmania** 855 East Twain Avenue (at Swenson);
  ☎ 702-369-3322. Baked on the premises. Locals' hangout.

The Best Bakeries

* **Albina's Italian Bakery** 3035 East Tropicana Avenue in the Wal-Mart
  Center; ☎ 702-433-5400. Classic Italian pastries; wide variety of cookies.

* **Great Buns** 3270 East Tropicana Avenue; ☎ 702-898-0311. Commercial
  and retail; fragrant rosemary bread, sticky buns, and apple loaf are good
  choices. More than 400 varieties of breads and pastries.

* **Tintoretto** Grand Canal Shoppes at The Venetian; ☎ 702-414-3400.
  International breads, cakes, and cookies. Charming European design and a
  patio perfect for people-watching.

The Best Brewpubs

* **Gordon Biersch Brewery Restaurant** 3987 Paradise Road (Hughes Center);
  ☎ 702-312-5247. Upbeat brewery restaurant with contemporary menu
  and surprisingly good food at reasonable prices.

* **Monte Carlo Pub** Monte Carlo; ☎ 702-730-7777. Located adjacent to the
  pool area in a faux-warehouse setting, this brewpub offers six different beers
  and affordable food options. The beer is brewed on the premises.

* **Triple Seven Brewpub** 200 North Main Street (Main Street Station); ☎ 702-
  387-1896. Late-night happy hour with bargain brews and food specials.

The Best Burgers

* **Burger Bar** Mandalay Bay Place, 3930 Las Vegas Boulevard;
  ☎ 702-632-9364. Burgers of every description, some outrageous.

* **Champagnes Cafe** 3557 South Maryland Parkway; ☎ 702-737-1699.
  Classic half-pounder with creative toppings.

* **KGB (Kerry's Gourmet Burgers)** Harrah's; ☎ 702-369-5065.
  Creative burgers and sides from celebrity chef Kerry Simon.

The Best Delis

* **Bagel Café** 301 North Buffalo Drive; ☎ 702-255-3444. They actually slice
  the lox by hand at this popular local deli. The pastry case is filled with traditional Jewish bakery faves, such as Black and White cookies and
  hamentashen.

* **Carnegie Deli at Mirage** 3400 South Las Vegas Boulevard; ☎ 702-791-
  7371. This outpost of the famous New York deli has the best pastrami and
  corned beef sandwiches in town—so big, you can barely pick them up with
  one hand. The cheesecake is shipped in from a commissary in New Jersey.

* **Harrie's Bagelmania** 855 East Twain (at Swenson); ☎ 702-369-3322.
  Breakfast and lunch only. Full-service bagel bakery and deli. The best bagels
  in the city are baked in this down at the heels cafe, the only bagels in town
  with an actual crust. Tuesdays, buy bagels by the dozen at half price.

continued on page 366

The Best Las Vegas Restaurants

NAME	OVERALL RATING	PRICE RATING	QUALITY RATING	VALUE RATING
AMERICAN				
Sage	★★★★½	Very Exp	★★★★½	★★★★
Aureole	★★★★½	Very Exp	★★★★½	★★½
Bradley Ogden	★★★★½	Very Exp	★★★★½	★★½
Botero	★★★★	Very Exp	★★★★½	★★★★
Craftsteak	★★★★	Very Exp	★★★★½	★★★
Wolfgang Puck Bar & Grill	★★★★	Mod/Exp	★★★★	★★★★½
Top of the World	★★★★	Expensive	★★★★	★★★½
Rosemary's Restaurant	★★★★	Expensive	★★★★	★★½
Spago	★★★½	Mod/Exp	★★★★½	★★½
Olives	★★★½	Mod/Exp	★★★★	★★★½
Wolfgang Puck Pizzeria & Cucina	★★★½	Expensive	★★★★	★★★½
Todd English P.U.B.	★★★½	Mod/Exp	★★★½	★★★★
P.J. Clarke's	★★★½	Moderate	★★★½	★★★½
Table 34	★★★½	Moderate	★★★½	★★★½
Nobhill Tavern	★★★	Expensive	★★★★	★★★★
Hugo's Cellar	★★★	Expensive	★★★	★★★
ASIAN/PACIFIC RIM				
Noodles	★★★	Moderate	★★★★	★★★½
Monta	★★	Inexpensive	★★★★	★★★★
BARBECUE				
Sam Woo Bar-B-Q	★★★	Inexp/Mod	★★★	★★★★★
BURGERS				
BLT Burger	★★★	Expensive	★★★★	★★
CHINESE				
Pearl	★★★★	Expensive	★★★★	★★½
Ping Pang Pong	★★★½	Moderate	★★★½	★★★½
China Mama	★★★	Inexpensive	★★★★	★★★★
China Poblano	★★★	Moderate	★★★★	★★★★
Noodles	★★★	Moderate	★★★★	★★★½
Noodle Palace	★★★	Inexpensive	★★★	★★★

NAME	OVERALL RATING	PRICE RATING	QUALITY RATING	VALUE RATING
CONTINENTAL/FRENCH				
Twist	★★★★★	Very Exp	★★★★★	★★★★★
L'Atelier de Joël Robuchon	★★★★★	Very Exp	★★★★★	★★★
Joël Robuchon	★★★★★	Very Exp	★★★★★	★★★
Restaurant Guy Savoy	★★★★★	Very Exp	★★★★★	★★★
Picasso	★★★★½	Very Exp	★★★★	★★½
Marché Bacchus: French Bistro and Wine Shop	★★★★	Moderate	★★★★	★★★★
Bouchon	★★★½	Moderate	★★★★	★★★★
Fleur	★★★½	Moderate	★★★★	★★★½
Mon Ami Gabi	★★★½	Mod/Exp	★★★★	★★★½
Michael's	★★★½	Very Exp	★★★★	★★½
CUBAN				
Florida Café	★★★	Inexpensive	★★★½	★★★★½
GERMAN				
Hofbräuhaus	★★★	Moderate	★★★½	★★★★½
GREEK				
Estiatorio Milos	★★★★★	Very Exp	★★★★★	★★★★
ENGLISH				
Todd English P.U.B.	★★★½	Mod/Exp	★★★½	★★★★
ITALIAN				
Bartolotta Ristorante Di Mare	★★★★½	Very Exp	★★★★½	★★★★
Circo	★★★★	Mod/Exp	★★★★½	★★½
Nove Italiano	★★★★	Expensive	★★★★	★★★★
Fiamma Trattoria & Bar	★★★★	Mod/Exp	★★★★	★★★½
Scarpetta	★★★★	Expensive	★★★★	★★★½
Valentino	★★★★	Expensive	★★★★	★★★
Piero's	★★★★	Expensive	★★★★	★★½
Panevino Ristorante & Gourmet Deli	★★★½	Mod/Exp	★★★★½	★★★½
B&B Ristorante	★★★	Very Exp	★★★★	★★★
Rao's	★★★	Expensive	★★★★	★★
Sinatra	★★★	Expensive	★★★	★★

The Best Las Vegas Restaurants (cont'd)

NAME	OVERALL RATING	PRICE RATING	QUALITY RATING	VALUE RATING
JAMAICAN/NEW MEXICAN				
DW Bistro	★★★	Moderate	★★★½	★★★★
JAPANESE (SEE ALSO SUSHI)				
Bar Masa	★★★★★	Very Exp	★★★★★	★★
Nobu	★★★★	Very Exp	★★★★★	★★
Raku	★★★★	Moderate	★★★★	★★★★
Noodles	★★★	Moderate	★★★★	★★★½
MEDITERRANEAN				
Olives	★★★½	Mod/Exp	★★★★	★★★½
MEXICAN				
Isla	★★★★½	Moderate	★★★★	★★★★½
Lindo Michoacan	★★★½	Inexp/Mod	★★★★	★★★★
China Poblano	★★★	Moderate	★★★★	★★★★
Garduño's	★★★	Inexp/Mod	★★★½	★★★½
T&T Tacos & Tequila	★★	Moderate	★★★★	★★
PIZZA				
Settebello	★★★½	Moderate	★★★★	★★★
SEAFOOD				
Bartolotta Ristorante Di Mare	★★★★½	Very Exp	★★★★½	★★★★
Joe's Seafood, Prime Steak & Stone Crab	★★★★½	Expensive	★★★★½	★★★½
Todd's Unique Dining	★★★★	Moderate	★★★★	★★★★
SeaBlue	★★★★	Mod/Exp	★★★★	★★★½
Kokomo's	★★★½	Expensive	★★★★	★★½
Emeril's New Orleans Fish House	★★★½	Expensive	★★★	★★★
SPANISH				
Jaleo	★★★★½	Moderate	★★★★	★★★★
Picasso	★★★★½	Very Exp	★★★★	★★½
Julian Serrano	★★★★	Expensive	★★★★	★★★★

NAME	OVERALL RATING	PRICE RATING	QUALITY RATING	VALUE RATING
STEAK				
Joe's Seafood, Prime Steak & Stone Crab	★★★★½	Expensive	★★★★½	★★★½
Craftsteak	★★★★	Very Exp	★★★★½	★★★
Prime	★★★★	Expensive	★★★★½	★★½
Todd's Unique Dining	★★★★	Moderate	★★★★	★★★★
Kokomo's	★★★½	Expensive	★★★★	★★½
The Steak House	★★★½	Expensive	★★★½	★★★½
Morels	★★★	Expensive	★★★★	★★
SUSHI (SEE ALSO JAPANESE)				
Bar Masa	★★★★★	Very Exp	★★★★★	★★
Nobu	★★★★	Very Exp	★★★★★	★★
Sen of Japan	★★★★	Mod/Exp	★★★★	★★★½
THAI				
Lotus of Siam	★★★★	Moderate	★★★★	★★½
Noodles	★★★	Moderate	★★★★	★★★½
VIETNAMESE				
Noodles	★★★	Moderate	★★★★	★★★½
Bosa 1	★★★	Inexpensive	★★★	★★★★½
Hue Thai	★★	Inexpensive	★★★	★★★
ROOMS WITH A VIEW				
Top of the World	★★★★	Expensive	★★★★	★★★½

continued from page 361

- **Siena Deli** 9500 West Sahara Avenue; ☎ 702-736-8424.
  Italian spoken here: everything is Italian and homemade. Excellent bread
  baked every morning. Siena bakes bread for many of the area's Italian restaurants. For the home cook, the selection of olive oils, tinned tomatoes,
  and balsamic vinegars is extensive and worthwhile.
- **Weiss Family Deli** 2744 North Green Valley Parkway, Henderson;
  ☎ 702-454-0565. Full-service deli, bakery, and restaurant. Home cooking
  by chef Michael Weiss is just like your Yiddish mama made, including terrific meat loaf, giant matzo balls, and rye bread baked on the premises.

The Best Espresso and Dessert

- **Coffee Bean and Tea Leaf** 4550 South Maryland Parkway; ☎ 702-944-
  5029. Many more locations around the city. California-based chain of
  specialty coffeehouses.
- **Coffee Pub** 2800 West Sahara Avenue, Suite 2A; ☎ 702-367-1913.
  Great breakfast and lunch location, plus an imaginative menu.
- **Cypress Street Marketplace** Caesars Palace; ☎ 702-731-7110. Caesars'
  bakers create pies, cakes, and cookies.
- **Palio** Bellagio; ☎ 702-693-8160. Cafeteria-style coffeehouse with pastries
  and casual eats—quiche, salads, and sandwiches, plus ice creams by the
  award-winning dessert chef Jean-Philippe Maury, who also has separate
  concessions here and at Aria.
- **Spago** The Forum Shops at Caesars; ☎ 702-369-6300. Wolfgang Puck's
  pastry chef crafts imaginative and sinful creations. Available all day in the
  café and at dinner in the dining room.
- **Starbucks Coffeehouses** Dozens of area locations.

The Best Oyster and Clam Bars

- **Bouchon** Venetian; ☎ 702-414-6200. French Laundry chef Thomas Keller
  sources the highest quality seafood possible.
- **Emeril's New Orleans Fish House** MGM Grand; ☎ 702-891-7374.
  Don't miss the banana cream pie, after you've had your oysters and gumbo.
- **SeaBlue** MGM Grand; ☎ 702-891-3486. Great tuna tartare with pine nuts.

The Best Pizza

- **Balboa Pizza** District at Green Valley Ranch; ☎ 702-407-5273.
  Good value, great pizzas and salads. Kids love it.
- **Due Forni** 3555 Town Center Drive; ☎ 702-586-6500. Carlos Buscaglia,
  former chef at Fiamma in the MGM Grand, is cooking delicious pizzas in a
  pair of Cirigliano ovens imported from Naples. Try the thin Roman-style
  crust.
- **Metro Pizza** 1395 East Tropicana Avenue; ☎ 702-736-1955. Fast service
  and generous with the cheese. Try the Old New York with thick-sliced mozzarella, plum tomatoes, and basil. Thick ragu-style tomato sauce.

- **Settebello** 140 South Green Valley Parkway, Henderson; ☎ 702-222-3556. Real Neapolitan-style pizzas cooked in a wood-fired stone oven. Toppings are from Mario Batali's father's salumeria in Seattle. Flat out the city's best pizza.
- **Spago** The Forum Shops at Caesars; ☎ 702-369-6300. Wolfgang Puck's duck sausage and smoked salmon with dill cream pizzas are legendary.

The Best Soup and Salad Bar

- **Souper Salad** 2051 North Rainbow Boulevard; ☎ 702-631-2604. 4022 South Maryland Parkway; ☎ 702-792-8555. Moderate prices, many combinations, shiny clean, and inexpensive.

Restaurants with a View

- **Alizé** Palms; ☎ 702-951-7000. At the top of the Palms, Alizé's panoramic view includes portions of the Strip.
- **Circo** Bellagio; ☎ 702-693-8150. Circo (full name Osteria Del Circo) is adjacent to its pricier sister, Le Cirque. Tuscan fare with a view of Lake Como and Paris's Eiffel Tower.
- **Eiffel Tower Restaurant** Paris; ☎ 702-948-6937. Fancy French food in a drop-dead gorgeous setting that towers over the Strip. This is one spectacular view that encompasses the fountains at Bellagio.
- **Picasso** Bellagio; ☎ 702-693-7223. Highly original food and glorious original artwork by Picasso. As good as it gets, unless you eat at Grand Vefour in the Louvre.
- **Top of the World Restaurant** Stratosphere; ☎ 702-380-7711. 360-degree revolving restaurant with excellent food and the highest and best views of any of the restaurants listed.
- **VooDoo Steak & Lounge** Rio Hotel and Casino; ☎ 702-777-7800. At the top of the Masquerade tower, VooDoo offers a complete view of the city, steak and French-Creole dishes, and a late-night lounge.

▌ RESTAURANT PROFILES

L'Atelier de Joël Robuchon   ★★★★★

FRENCH   **VERY EXPENSIVE**   **QUALITY ★★★★★**   **VALUE ★★★**

MGM Grand, 3799 South Las Vegas Boulevard; South Strip and Environs; ☎ 702-891-7358; mgmgrand.com

Customers Visitors, locals. **Reservations** A must. **When to go** Anytime. **Entrée range** $70–$230. **Payment** All major credit cards. **Service rating** ★★★★★. **Friendliness rating** ★★★. **Parking** Valet, garage. **Bar** Full service. **Wine selection** Excellent. **Dress** Upscale casual. **Disabled access** Yes. **Hours** Daily, 5:30–10:30 p.m.

SETTING AND ATMOSPHERE Chef Joël Robuchon's casual concept offers guests a view into his culinary workshop, thanks to an open-air kitchen that dissolves the boundaries between kitchen and dining room. Chic and contemporary with shades of black and red, L'Atelier is more laid-back than his fine-dining Robuchon next door, and more interactive with the staff if you sit at the bar around the open kitchen.

HOUSE SPECIALTIES *Caille au foie gras:* tender roasted quail stuffed with foie gras and served with Robuchon's famous mashed potatoes, equal parts butter and potato.

OTHER RECOMMENDATIONS To get the full experience, opt for the five-course tasting menu that changes seasonally and offers their best dishes in a thoughtful progression. Those with theater tickets will find an early-bird three-course tasting menu for $39 served in less than 20 minutes.

SUMMARY AND COMMENTS L'Atelier is fun—a less buttoned-up way to enjoy fine dining. Dining aficionados will appreciate watching the silent orchestra of chefs and cooks in their element, and the care it takes to create one of Robuchon's masterful dishes.

Aureole ★★★★½

AMERICAN	VERY EXPENSIVE	QUALITY ★★★★½	VALUE ★★½

Mandalay Bay, 3950 South Las Vegas Boulevard; South Strip and Environs; ☎ 702-632-7401; aureolelv.com

Customers Visitors, locals. Reservations Required. When to go Anytime. Entrée range $30–$40; 7-course tasting menu, $95 (main dining room) or $105 (Swan Court). Payment All major credit cards. Service rating ★★★★½. Friendliness rating ★★★★½. Parking Valet, garage. Bar Full service. Wine selection Outstanding. Dress Upscale casual. Disabled access Elevator. Hours Daily, 6–10 p.m.

SETTING AND ATMOSPHERE A one-of-a-kind, four-story wine tower dominates the entrance to this exceptional restaurant. There are three dining rooms and the separate Swan Court with just 14 tables—all have a view of the waterfall and live swans.

HOUSE SPECIALTIES Honey-spiced marinated duck; roasted rack of lamb with sweet garlic; lobster chowder with grilled prawns; citrus-basted chicken; potato gnocchi with black truffles. (Some dishes are seasonal and may not be available.)

OTHER RECOMMENDATIONS Thyme-roasted filet mignon; curry nut–crusted ahi tuna. Scrumptious desserts; homemade chocolates served with coffee.

SUMMARY AND COMMENTS The wine tower is unique—bottles are accessed by black-clad females who hoist themselves up to the various levels to remove bottles. It's quite a show and a great photo op. Another wine first is Aureole's wine e-book, which enables patrons to order their favorite dinner wines in advance. All dining rooms offer prix-fixe menus only, with an à la carte menu available in the lounge and bar area. Several multicourse tasting menus are available.

B&B Ristorante ★★★

ITALIAN	VERY EXPENSIVE	QUALITY ★★★★	VALUE ★★★

Venetian, 3355 Las Vegas Boulevard; Mid-Strip and Environs; ☎ 702-266-9977; bandbristorante.com

Customers Visitors, locals. **Reservations** Suggested. **When to go** Anytime. **Entrée range** $29–$60. **Payment** All major credit cards. **Service rating** ★★★. **Friendliness rating** ★★★. **Parking** Valet, garage. **Bar** Full service. **Wine selection** Comprehensive, with wines from every region in Italy. **Dress** Upscale casual. **Disabled access** Yes. **Hours** Daily, 5–11 p.m.; bar open until midnight.

SETTING AND ATMOSPHERE Dark woods and white tablecloths make this Italian restaurant feel like a classic supper club.

HOUSE SPECIALTIES Rustic Italian, of course. Cured meats are made in-house by Executive Chef Zach Allen or from Salumi, Batali's father's Seattle store. Pastas are wonderful, such as *bucatini all' Amatriciana* (hollow spaghetti-like pasta flavored with cured *guanciale* or marbled hog jowl) or a seasonal offering like tiny ravioli stuffed with tomato confit and sauced with pork innards.

OTHER RECOMMENDATIONS Calamari Sicilian Lifeguard-Style, rings of delicate calamari with a subtly spicy tomato sauce, and an amazing beef *brasato*. A sumptuous five-course pasta tasting menu is available paired with wines, selected by Batali's partner, Joe Bastianich. (Hence B&B.)

SUMMARY AND COMMENTS For a more casual experience, check out the other Batali outpost within the Grand Canal Shoppes at the Venetian, Enoteca Otto Pizzeria, which offers more of a wine-bar experience and great people-watching, plus that great salumi from Batali's father.

Bar Masa ★★★★

JAPANESE	VERY EXPENSIVE	QUALITY ★★★★★	VALUE ★★

Aria at CityCenter, 3730 South Las Vegas Boulevard; Mid-Strip and Environs; ☎702-590-7111; arialasvegas.com

Customers Visitors. **Reservations** Essential. **When to go** Anytime. **Entrée range** $18–$240. **Payment** All major credit cards. **Service rating** ★★★★★. **Friendliness rating** ★★★★★. **Parking** Valet, lot. **Bar** Sake, wine, beer. **Wine selection** Excellent. **Dress** Upscale. **Disabled access** Yes. **Hours** Wednesday–Sunday, 5–11 p.m.

SETTING AND ATMOSPHERE Unlike chef Masa Takayama's intimate bar at the Time Warner Center, this is a huge, high-ceilinged room the size of an airplane hangar. The ultramodern design came from a series of sketches done by the chef himself.

HOUSE SPECIALTIES There is much more than the exquisite nigiri-style sushi, made from fish flown in daily from Tokyo's Tsukiji Fish Market. Broiled skewers of Kobe beef and sizzling octopus salad are just a few of the non-sushi items gracing this eclectic menu. The otoro, fatty tuna belly said to be the world's best, is softer than butter. It is also $240 for an à la carte order.

OTHER RECOMMENDATIONS For the extremely well heeled, or those on a liberal expense budget, the private dining room Shaboo offers a multicourse meal at roughly $500 per person. There is also omakase, chef's choice dinners, starting at around $150 per person and priced on up.

SUMMARY AND COMMENTS No one can deny the impeccable quality of the products here, the wonderful service, or the stunning design. This is the

Dining and Nightlife on the South Strip

RESTAURANTS
1. L'Atelier de Joël Robuchon
2. Aureole
3. Craftsteak
4. Emeril's New Orleans Fish House
5. Fiamma Trattoria
6. Fleur
7. Jöel Robuchon
8. Michael's
9. Nobhill Tavern
10. Panevino Ristorante & Gourmet Deli
11. Pearl

12. SeaBlue
13. T&T Tacos & Tequila
14. Wolfgang Puck Bar & Grill

Buffets:
15. Luxor's MORE Buffet
16. Mandalay Bay's Bayside Buffet
17. MGM Grand Buffet
18. Orleans French Market

NIGHTLIFE
19. Aurora
20. Blue Martini Lounge
21. Coyote Ugly
22. Diablo's Cantina
23. House of Blues
24. Mix Lounge
25. Pete's Dueling Piano Bar
26. Posh Boutique Nightclub
27. Rí Rá Las Vegas
28. Stoney's Rockin' Country
29. Studio 54
30. Tabu
31. Yard House

most expensive restaurant in Vegas, so if you plan on spending less than $200 per person, chances are you will leave hungry.

Bartolotta Ristorante Di Mare ★★★★½

ITALIAN/SEAFOOD   VERY EXPENSIVE   QUALITY ★★★★½   VALUE ★★★★

Wynn Las Vegas, 3131 South Las Vegas Boulevard; Mid-Strip and Environs; ☎ 702-770-7000; wynnlasvegas.com

Customers Visitors, locals. **Reservations** Recommended. **When to go** Anytime. **Entrée range** $24–$130. **Payment** All major credit cards. **Service rating** ★★★★½. **Friendliness rating** ★★★★. **Parking** Valet, lot. **Bar** Full service. **Wine selection** Excellent. **Dress** Upscale. **Disabled access** Yes. **Hours** Daily, 5:30–10:30 p.m.

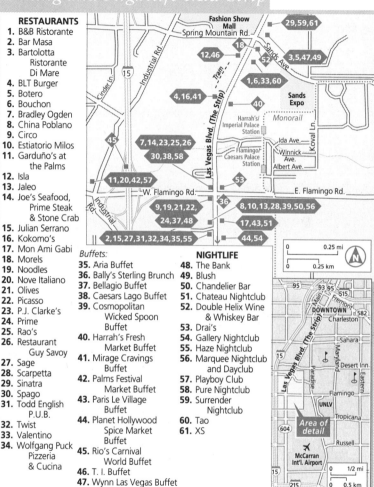

Dining and Nightlife Mid-Strip

RESTAURANTS
1. B&B Ristorante
2. Bar Masa
3. Bartolotta Ristorante Di Mare
4. BLT Burger
5. Botero
6. Bouchon
7. Bradley Ogden
8. China Poblano
9. Circo
10. Estiatorio Milos
11. Garduño's at the Palms
12. Isla
13. Jaleo
14. Joe's Seafood, Prime Steak & Stone Crab
15. Julian Serrano
16. Kokomo's
17. Mon Ami Gabi
18. Morels
19. Noodles
20. Nove Italiano
21. Olives
22. Picasso
23. P.J. Clarke's
24. Prime
25. Rao's
26. Restaurant Guy Savoy
27. Sage
28. Scarpetta
29. Sinatra
30. Spago
31. Todd English P.U.B.
32. Twist
33. Valentino
34. Wolfgang Puck Pizzeria & Cucina

Buffets:
35. Aria Buffet
36. Bally's Sterling Brunch
37. Bellagio Buffet
38. Caesars Lago Buffet
39. Cosmopolitan Wicked Spoon Buffet
40. Harrah's Fresh Market Buffet
41. Mirage Cravings Buffet
42. Palms Festival Market Buffet
43. Paris Le Village Buffet
44. Planet Hollywood Spice Market Buffet
45. Rio's Carnival World Buffet
46. T. I. Buffet
47. Wynn Las Vegas Buffet

NIGHTLIFE
48. The Bank
49. Blush
50. Chandelier Bar
51. Chateau Nightclub
52. Double Helix Wine & Whiskey Bar
53. Drai's
54. Gallery Nightclub
55. Haze Nightclub
56. Marquee Nightclub and Dayclub
57. Playboy Club
58. Pure Nightclub
59. Surrender Nightclub
60. Tao
61. XS

SETTING AND ATMOSPHERE Bartolotta is a two-level restaurant done with elegant Italian appointments. The upstairs, just off a corridor of the Wynn shopping arcade, is slightly less ornate and well suited for business dinners. Downstairs, there is a pool with private tables by a cabana perfect for a romantic tryst, and tables inside close to the action in the kitchen.

HOUSE SPECIALTIES Chef Paul Bartolotta does what no other American restaurant chef dares to do: He flies to Italy regularly to procure fresh Mediterranean fish, which he has flown in three or four times a week. Spiny lobster, rockfish, big eye, and sea bream are just a few of the fish

Dining on the North Strip

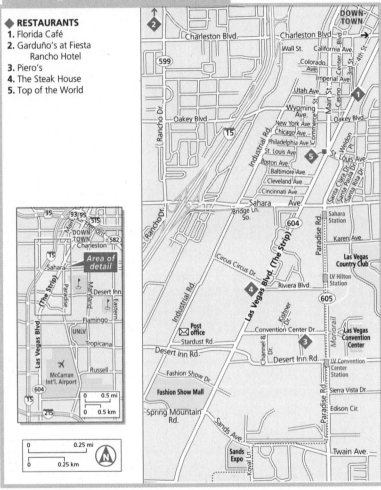

◆ **RESTAURANTS**
1. Florida Café
2. Garduño's at Fiesta
   Rancho Hotel
3. Piero's
4. The Steak House
5. Top of the World

that he or a server will present on a silver tray. You can have them a variety of ways, such as grilled, encased in salt, or a la Palermitana, Sicilian style with capers, olives, and tomatoes. Appetizers to remember include *scampi a la Diavolo* and *agnolotti del plin,* tiny stuffed pastas.

SUMMARY AND COMMENTS: This can be quite expensive, especially if you tell the chef to cook for you. It's not his fault, though, since he must have the highest food costs in Vegas, thanks to Mr. Steve Wynn, the indulgent casino owner who lets the chef travel and spend money as if it were going out of style. Nonetheless, it's an experience you can't get anywhere else in this country.

Dining and Nightlife East of Strip

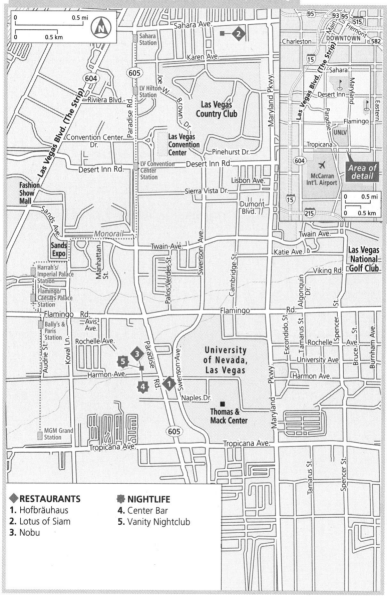

◆ **RESTAURANTS**
1. Hofbräuhaus
2. Lotus of Siam
3. Nobu

■ **NIGHTLIFE**
4. Center Bar
5. Vanity Nightclub

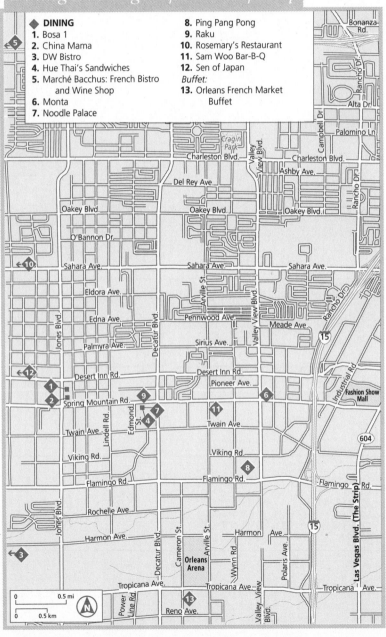

Dining and Nightlife West of Strip

◆ **DINING**
1. Bosa 1
2. China Mama
3. DW Bistro
4. Hue Thai's Sandwiches
5. Marché Bacchus: French Bistro and Wine Shop
6. Monta
7. Noodle Palace
8. Ping Pang Pong
9. Raku
10. Rosemary's Restaurant
11. Sam Woo Bar-B-Q
12. Sen of Japan
Buffet:
13. Orleans French Market Buffet

Dining and Nightlife Downtown

◆ **RESTAURANTS**
1. Hugo's Cellar

⬛ **NIGHTLIFE**
2. Downtown
Cocktail Room

BLT Burger ★★★

BURGERS	EXPENSIVE	QUALITY ★★★★	VALUE ★★

Mirage, 3400 South Las Vegas Boulevard; Mid-Strip and Environs;
☎ **702-792-7888; mirage.com**

Customers Visitors, locals. **Reservations** Not necessary. **When to go** Anytime.
Entrée range $10–$17. **Payment** All major credit cards. **Service rating** ★★★★.
Friendliness rating ★★★★. **Parking** Valet, lot. **Bar** Full service. **Wine selection**
Fair. **Dress** Casual. **Disabled access** Yes. **Hours** Sunday–Thursday, 11 a.m.–2 a.m.;
Friday and Saturday, 11 a.m.–4 a.m.

SETTING AND ATMOSPHERE BLT Burger usually has a line outside, but the wait is
never long. Feeling like a 1950s diner that has been brought into the 21st
century, the room surrounds an open-air kitchen where chefs make the
burgers for all to see. Music is cool, beers are cold, and the crowd is hot.

HOUSE SPECIALTIES Burgers, naturally. But don't expect giant stacks of meat
from BLT. Their hamburgers weigh in at around seven ounces each, but

Dining in Southeast Las Vegas–Henderson

Las Vegas Downtown

E. Sahara Blvd.

Winchester

Desert Inn Rd.

■ Boulevard Mall

Flamingo Rd.

UNLV

Paradise Valley

Tropicana Ave.

Russell Rd.

McCarran International Airport

Patrick Ln.

Sunset Rd.

Civic Center

To ← 15

Warm Springs Rd.

Green Valley

Windmill Ln.

E. Fremont St.

E. Sahara Ave.

Harmon Ave.

Vegas Valley Dr.

East Las Vegas

Tropicana Ave.

Hacienda Ave.

Whitney

Sunset Rd.

Sunset Rd.

Warm Springs Rd.

W. Lake Mead Dr.

Horizon Ridge Pkwy.

To Hoover Dam

| 0 | 1 mi |
| 0 | 1 km |

◆ **RESTAURANTS**
1. Lindo Michoacan
2. Settebello
3. Table 34
4. Todd's Unique Dining

Buffets:
5. Boulder Station Buffet
6. Green Valley Ranch Feast Buffet

that's all you need, especially when these ultra-flavorful burgers are made of lamb, American Kobe, or turkey. Appetizers such as deep-fried pickles and jalapeño poppers are made fresh in-house, never frozen. Milkshakes are mandatory as well, but go for the gusto with one of the creamy concoctions spiked with booze.

SUMMARY AND COMMENTS   If you're going to have a burger in Vegas, it might as well be a masterpiece by a renowned French chef, in this case Laurent Tourondel (famous for his restaurant BLT Steak in New York). BLT Burger is a casual spot to have an haute burger. It's popular with hungry late-night crowds coming from neighboring Jet nightclub, but during the day you'll find tourists and locals of all ages clamoring for a table.

Bosa 1 ★★★

VIETNAMESE	INEXPENSIVE	QUALITY ★★★	VALUE ★★★★½

3400 South Jones Boulevard; West of Strip; ☎ 702-418-1931

Customers Locals. **Reservations** Not necessary. **When to go** Anytime. **Entrée range** $6–$9. **Payment** Cash only. **Service rating** ★★½. **Friendliness rating** ★★★½. **Parking** Lot. **Bar** None. **Dress** Casual. **Disabled access** No. **Hours** Friday–Wednesday, 10:30 a.m.–9:30 p.m.

SETTING AND ATMOSPHERE Bosa 1 is a narrow little box with four booths and seven tables. Walls are draped in bamboo, and there are a few watercolor prints depicting life in the old country.

HOUSE SPECIALTIES Unlike the city's other Vietnamese restaurants, nearly all of which specialize in *pho* (the meal-in-a-bowl beef-and-rice noodle dish), this restaurant doesn't serve it at all, sort of like a Japanese restaurant that doesn't serve sushi. Instead, the dish to order here is a broken rice plate, piled high with steamed grains of rice that have been shattered in dry form. The rice is accompanied by a number of glorious grilled and marinated meats.

OTHER RECOMMENDATIONS *Nem nuong cuon,* four to an order, are cigar-shaped cylinders stuffed with shrimp forcemeat and grilled vegetables, plus a long, crunchy pastry for an added textural snap. There is also *bun bo Hue*, a central Vietnamese spicy pork soup that one can order either with or without the tiny cubes of jellied pork blood that most Vietnamese insist upon.

SUMMARY AND COMMENTS This is not only the most authentic Vietnamese restaurant in Las Vegas, but also the best. For a good bowl of *pho*, we suggest you head for Bolsa Avenue in the city of Westminster, California. Bosa, incidentally, is a corruption of that street name.

Botero ★★★★

NEW AMERICAN	VERY EXPENSIVE	QUALITY ★★★★½	VALUE ★★★★

Wynn Las Vegas, 3131 South Las Vegas Boulevard;
Mid-Strip and Environs; ☎ 702-770-7000; wynnlasvegas.com

Customers Visitors. **Reservations** Recommended. **When to go** Anytime. **Entrée range** $33–$75. **Payment** All major credit cards. **Service rating** ★★★★. **Friendliness rating** ★★★★. **Parking** Valet, lot. **Bar** Full service. **Wine selection** Excellent. **Dress** Upscale. **Disabled access** Yes. **Hours** Sunday–Thursday, 5:30–10:30 p.m.; Friday and Saturday, 5:30–11 p.m.

SETTING AND ATMOSPHERE The restaurant is named for a South American sculptor, Botero, who has a $2.3-million piece smack in the middle of the dining room. As if that were not special enough, the best tables front the Wynn pool visible through panoramic floor-to-ceiling windows.

HOUSE SPECIALTIES Crispy frog legs and *hamachi tartare* are two of the appetizers on chef Mark LoRusso's menu. The chef is a Michael Mina product, which means he is adept at seafood, and his Mediterranean sea bass, olive oil–poached Atlantic cod, and wild salmon are menu highlights.

OTHER RECOMMENDATIONS LoRusso, who is almost always in the kitchen, along with his talented sous chef Wren Caceres, is a star with meats as well. Bone-in rib eye and filet mignon are accompanied by a choice of mouth-watering sauces such as *chimichurri* or pepper sauces. Kobe short rib and brioche-crusted Colorado lamb rack stand out as well.

SUMMARY AND COMMENTS This is a restaurant for grown-ups. Genteel, atmospheric, and accomplished, it's one of the best restaurants at Wynn Encore. Wynn wine director Danielle Price has stocked her cellars with some of the best wines in town. Prices are commensurate.

Bouchon ★★★½

FRENCH BISTRO   MODERATE   QUALITY ★★★★   VALUE ★★★★

Venetian, 3355 South Las Vegas Boulevard, Venezia Tower;
Mid-Strip and Environs; ☎ 702-414-6200; bouchonbistro.com

Customers Visitors, locals. **Reservations** A must on weekends. **When to go** Anytime. **Entrée range** $18–$37. **Payment** All major credit cards. **Service rating** ★★★★½. **Friendliness rating** ★★★★½. **Parking** Valet, garage. **Bar** Full service. **Wine selection** Very good. **Dress** Upscale casual. **Disabled access** Yes (elevator). **Hours** Daily, 7–10:30 a.m. and 5–10 p.m.; Saturday and Sunday brunch, 8 a.m.– 2 p.m.; Oyster Bar & Lounge, 3–10 p.m.

SETTING AND ATMOSPHERE Designed to be the ultimate bistro, Bouchon is beautiful. Owner-chef Thomas Keller and renowned restaurant and hotel designer Adam Tihany have designed a Belle Epoque room filled with ornate floor tiles and brass. You could easily be on a Paris boulevard.

HOUSE SPECIALTIES Fresh seafood plateaus, grand plates with an assortment of freshly shucked raw items and shrimp and lobster; superb oysters (selection changes with the season); country pâté served with cornichons and radishes; roasted leg of lamb with flageolet beans in thyme jus.

OTHER RECOMMENDATIONS Salmon rillettes in a glass jar; leeks with chopped egg, steak frites, a pan-seared flat-iron steak with French fries; endive salad with Roquefort, apples, walnuts, and walnut vinaigrette; blood sausage with potato puree and caramelized apples.

SUMMARY AND COMMENTS The most requested tables are on the outdoor terrace. They're difficult to get, but worth a try. There are many à la carte options at a moderate cost.

Bradley Ogden ★★★★½

AMERICAN   VERY EXPENSIVE   QUALITY ★★★★½   VALUE ★★½

Caesars Palace, 3570 South Las Vegas Boulevard; Mid-Strip and Environs;
☎ 702-731-7410; caesarspalace.com

Customers Visitors, locals. **Reservations** Suggested. **When to go** Anytime. **Entrée range** $31–$65 (changes daily with menu); 3-course prix-fixe tasting menu, $59. **Payment** All major credit cards. **Service rating** ★★★★½. **Friendliness rating** ★★★★½. **Parking** Valet, garage. **Bar** Full service. **Wine selection** Very good. **Dress** Upscale casual. **Disabled access** Yes (ground floor). **Hours** Wednesday–Sunday, 5–11 p.m.; lounge menu, daily, 5–11 p.m.

SETTING AND ATMOSPHERE Elegance and simplicity. Soft lighting, beautiful table appointments, and comfortable seating in the restaurant and the adjacent bar and lounge. Relaxed and inviting surroundings.

HOUSE SPECIALTIES Menus change daily, but such signatures as foie gras, Summerfield Farms New York steak, seasonal oysters, blue-cheese–soufflé appetizer (not to be missed), and a selection of artisan American cheeses are noteworthy. Chef Bradley Ogden calls this cooking "Farm Fresh American cuisine." All products are sourced from American farmers.

OTHER RECOMMENDATIONS Fish and seafood dishes. Selection varies with the season—always exciting. Wood-grilled yellowtail with Dungeness crab leg and green-onion pancake, roasted monkfish with mussels, and clay-pot Guinea hen with Kara Kara orange sauce are three of his more successful creations. Great ice creams. The breads, especially the complimentary blue-corn muffins, are alone worth the visit.

SUMMARY AND COMMENTS The restaurant is soon to change lanes and become Bradley Ogden Steak House. Look for the same fine boutique products, but more emphasis on red meat.

China Mama   ★★★

CHINESE	INEXPENSIVE	QUALITY ★★★★	VALUE ★★★★

3420 South Jones Boulevard; West of Strip; ☎ 702-873-1977

Customers Locals. Reservations Accepted. When to go Anytime. Entrée range $7–$25. Payment All major credit cards. Service rating ★★★. Friendliness rating ★★★★. Parking Lot. Bar None. Wine selection None. Dress Casual. Disabled access Yes. Hours Daily, 10:30 a.m.–10:30 p.m.

SETTING AND ATMOSPHERE Located just off the main drag of Las Vegas's Chinatown, China Mama is bright and welcoming.

HOUSE SPECIALTIES Shanghai soup dumplings (called "juicy pork dumplings" on the menu) are steamed pockets of meat with steaming soup in the middle. Carefully bite off the top, slurp out the delicious, savory soup, and then add a bit of the Chinese black vinegar and ginger that accompanies the dish. Pot stickers are also done very well.

OTHER RECOMMENDATIONS The beef roll, a giant wheat wrapper filled with lean beef and scallions; fish filet poached in a fiery red chili oil and served in a giant clay pot—perfect with a bowl of rice.

SUMMARY AND COMMENTS Most dishes here have authentic flavors you won't find in most other American-Chinese restaurants. The Shanghai soup dumplings—ubiquitous in Asia—are finally done right here.

China Poblano   ★★★

CHINESE/MEXICAN	MODERATE	QUALITY ★★★★	VALUE ★★★★

Cosmopolitan, 3708 South Las Vegas Boulevard;
Mid-Strip and Environs; ☎ 702-698-7000; cosmopolitanlasvegas.com

Customers Locals, hotel guests, conventioneers. Reservations Accepted. When to go Anytime. Entrée range $3.95-$20.95. Payment All major credit cards.

Service rating ★★★★. **Friendliness rating** ★★★★. **Parking** Valet, garage. **Bar** Full service. **Wine selection** Fair **Dress** Casual. **Disabled access** Yes. **Hours** Daily, 11 a.m.–11 p.m.

SETTING AND ATMOSPHERE   Ultra-modern, almost wacky décor features communal benches, conceptual art with Asian themes, LCD wall-mounted panels streaming head shots of famous Asians. There are separate noodle and tortilla bars.

HOUSE SPECIALTIES   hand-rolled noodles with dan dan sauce; made-to-order dim sum; crispy quail; street tacos with various fillings such as pastor and carne asada; various rice plates; seaweed salad; conceptual desserts such as chocolate enrobed statues representing the warriors at Xian, China, filled with peanut butter chocolate mousse.

OTHER RECOMMENDATIONS   Don't miss any of the specials made by Beijing-born chef Shirley, a real charmer. The rolled pancakes with beef and onions are wonderful, and so are a number of oddball China-meets-Mexico dishes that you'll have to see to understand.

SUMMARY AND COMMENTS   This is a groundbreaking restaurant in terms of creativity, a concept new to the planet. Chef José Andrés is a wonder, and so are these prices. This has to be the least expensive place to eat in the entire Cosmopolitan.

Circo   ★★★★

ITALIAN	MODERATE/EXPENSIVE	QUALITY ★★★★½	VALUE ★★½

**Bellagio, 3600 South Las Vegas Boulevard; Mid-Strip and Environs;
☎ 702-693-8150; bellagio.com**

Customers Visitors, locals. **Reservations** Recommended. **When to go** Anytime. **Entrée range** $25–$52. **Payment** All major credit cards. **Service rating** ★★★½. **Friendliness rating** ★★★½. **Parking** Valet, garage. **Bar** Full service. **Wine selection** Excellent. **Dress** Upscale casual. **Disabled access** Yes (through casino). **Hours** Nightly, 5:30–10:30 p.m.

SETTING AND ATMOSPHERE   Circo is a delight. At once whimsical and vibrant, the circus décor is pure fun. Booths, tables, and hideaway corners with a view of the fountains are wonderful. Linger over an espresso and enjoy the action in this homespun-yet-chic haven.

HOUSE SPECIALTIES   Pizzas and homemade focaccia breads; home-style Tuscan food inspired by Egidiana Maccioni, matriarch of the New York family that owns the adjacent popular Le Cirque; grilled filet mignon with pancetta; seared chicken breast stuffed with foie gras; Tuscan octopus and calamari stew. Half orders are a good starter.

OTHER RECOMMENDATIONS   Rack of lamb crusted in herbs and potatoes; marinated wild boar chops in red wine. Sensational desserts.

SUMMARY AND COMMENTS   This elegant Italian restaurant is not as grand as the adjacent Le Cirque, but it's every bit as inviting, thanks to super views of the Bellagio fountain from most tables. Mario Maccioni, son of the owner, directs both restaurants. Menus change seasonally.

Craftsteak ★★★★

AMERICAN/STEAK   VERY EXPENSIVE   QUALITY ★★★★½   VALUE ★★★

**MGM Grand Studio Walk, 3799 South Las Vegas Boulevard;
South Strip and Environs; ☎ 702-891-7318;
craftrestaurant.com or mgmgrand.com**

Customers Visitors, locals. Reservations Recommended. When to go Anytime.
Entrée range $36–$70; tasting menu, $110–$295. Payment All major credit
cards. Service rating ★★★★½. Friendliness rating ★★★★½. Parking Valet,
garage. Bar Full service. Wine selection Excellent. Dress Business casual.
Disabled access Yes (ground floor). Hours Daily, 5:30–10:30 p.m.

SETTING AND ATMOSPHERE Smashing décor, almost a clone to chef-owner
Tom Colicchio's acclaimed Craft eatery in New York City, but larger.
Colicchio strives for simplicity and quality and can describe the reason
for every design component, from the exotic-wood floor to the bronze-
and-wood tables with butcher-block elements.

HOUSE SPECIALTIES Braised, roasted, and grilled foods; a terrific selection of
seasonal side dishes; roasted or smoked sweetbreads; grain-fed and
grass-fed New York strip steaks; lobster braised in butter.

OTHER RECOMMENDATIONS Roasted lamb loin; beef porterhouse for two;
grilled veal T-bone; quail for an appetizer or main course; Kobe beef
tartare. Any of the nostalgic desserts, especially the liquid chocolate
cake. The roasted peaches are divine and so are the B52 parfait and
flourless chocolate Napoleons.

SUMMARY AND COMMENTS Menus change seasonally, so some of the dishes
mentioned above may not be available. Valet service for Studio Walk
restaurants is available near the MGM Grand Arena. If you are expecting to see the TV-star chef, Colicchio, don't hold your breath.

DW Bistro ★★★

JAMAICAN/NEW MEXICAN   MODERATE   QUALITY ★★★½   VALUE ★★★★

6115 S. Fort Apache Road; West of Strip; ☎ 702-527-5201; dwbistro.com

Customers Locals. Reservations Recommended for weekend brunch. When to go
Anytime. Entrée range $14–$23. Payment All major credit cards. Service rating
★★★. Friendliness rating ★★★★. Parking Lot. Bar Full service. Wine selection
Average. Disabled access Yes. Dress Casual. Hours Tuesday–Thursday, 11 a.m.–3
p.m.; Friday, 11 a.m.–11 p.m.; Saturday, 10 a.m.–11 p.m.; Sunday, 10 a.m.–2 p.m.

SETTING AND ATMOSPHERE This is a nicely renovated space with a front bar
decorated with starry chandeliers and more intimate tables in a white
brick alcove. Contemporary art fills the restaurant, which can best be
described as cheery and comfortable.

HOUSE SPECIALTIES Two separate cuisines, those of Jamaica and New Mexico, are done expertly here, but it would be wrong to think of this as a
fusion restaurant. A bowl of killer red New Mexican slow-cooked pork
contrasts with a terrific Jamaican chicken curry soup, which brims with
chopped chicken.

OTHER RECOMMENDATIONS Come for weekend brunch; the jerk pork hash is one of the most compelling dishes in the city. Start with a Jamaican hot chocolate, so rich, thick, and seductive that you'll swoon when you bite in. From the more upscale dinner menu, try an irresistible plate of the jerk lamb chops.

SUMMARY AND COMMENTS This improbable place has already become a de facto club for locals, who gather at the bar several times a week. The chef, Ricardo Santana, has the knack for both cuisines. His desserts, incidentally, such as a Jamaican carrot cake, are the bomb.

Emeril's New Orleans Fish House ★★★½

SEAFOOD/NEW ORLEANS   EXPENSIVE   QUALITY ★★★   VALUE ★★★

MGM Grand, 3799 South Las Vegas Boulevard; South Strip and Environs;
☎ **702-891-7374; emerils.com or mgmgrand.com**

Customers Visitors, locals. Reservations Always. When to go Avoid convention times. Entrée range $26–$45. Payment All major credit cards. Service rating ★★★★½. Friendliness rating ★★★★½. Parking Valet, lot, garage. Bar Full service. Wine selection Excellent. Dress Upscale casual; no sleeveless shirts for men. Disabled access Yes (through casino). Hours Daily, 11:30 a.m.–2:30 p.m. and 5–10 p.m.; café and bar: daily, 11:30 a.m.–10 p.m.

SETTING AND ATMOSPHERE "A bit of New Orleans" is how award-winning chef-owner Emeril Lagasse describes his beautiful restaurant. The main room is comfortable and handsome, with fine appointments and accessories. A separate courtyard dining room is French Quarter pretty, with a faux balcony and louvered shutters. Real plants and a stone floor complete the illusion.

HOUSE SPECIALTIES Five- to eight-course tasting dinners are a fine way to sample small portions of many dishes; some are special recipes being considered for the menu. Emeril's New Orleans–barbecue shrimp is delicious, and so is the grilled-and-roasted pork chop with caramelized sweet potatoes. You can rely on the good gumbos, the fresh Gulf oysters, and the banana cream pie, which is the best anywhere. Emeril's homemade Worcestershire sauce is addictively good.

SUMMARY AND COMMENTS Emeril's trades heavily on the celebrity of the chef, but the food can be slapdash and over-conceived. The faithful don't seem to care. You have about a one in one hundred chance of seeing Emeril.

Estiatorio Milos ★★★★★

GREEK   VERY EXPENSIVE   QUALITY ★★★★★   VALUE ★★★★

Cosmopolitan, 3708 South Las Vegas Boulevard;
Mid-Strip and Environs; ☎ 702-698-7000; cosmopolitanlasvegas.com

Customers Visitors, locals. Reservations Always. When to go Avoid convention times. Entrée range $22–$75. Payment All major credit cards. Service rating ★★★★½. Friendliness rating ★★★★½. Parking Valet, lot, garage. Bar Full service. Wine selection Excellent. Dress Upscale casual. Disabled access Yes. Hours Monday–Friday, noon–2:30 p.m. and 5:30 p.m.–midnight; Saturday and Sunday, 5:30 p.m.–midnight.

SETTING AND ATMOSPHERE A dramatic, classically designed room filled with Greek urns and stonework. There is a classy bar area toward the front and a patio with Strip-facing views in the rear. Diners visit the "fish market" next to the open kitchen, where they choose the fresh, live seafood they will eat for dinner.

HOUSE SPECIALTIES Milos is doing something no other American restaurant does at the moment: flying in fresh seafood daily from the Aegean, as do sister Milos restaurants in New York City and Montreal. Standouts include octopus, red mullet, Aegean seabass, and a host of other fish. Fish are prepared simply and impeccably in the classic Greek manner.

OTHER RECOMMENDATIONS If you've never tasted a proper avgolemono, Greece's egg lemon soup, this one is a must, made with Jasmine rice, organic eggs, Meyer lemon, and broth from capons. Meat dishes are also superb, such as lamb chops grilled with oregano and garlic. Desserts are simple but satisfying, such as the Greek yogurt with walnuts and thyme honey or the textbook baklava.

SUMMARY AND COMMENTS Milos has instantly rocketed to cult status in Vegas; it's the first high-end Greek restaurant in town, and one of the best in the country. Owner Costas Spiliadis is proud of his product, and rightly so. This is a not-to-be-missed experience, but it's not for anyone on a budget.

Fiamma Trattoria & Bar   ★★★★

ITALIAN	MODERATE/EXPENSIVE	QUALITY ★★★★	VALUE ★★★½

MGM Grand, 3799 South Las Vegas Boulevard; South Strip and Environs; ☎ 702-891-7600; mgmgrand.com

Customers Visitors, locals. Reservations A must on weekends and holidays. When to go Avoid convention times. Entrée range $18–$54. Payment All major credit cards. Service rating ★★★½. Friendliness rating ★★★★½. Parking Valet, garage. Bar Full service. Wine selection Very good. Dress Upscale casual. Disabled access Main valet, garage. Hours Sunday and Monday, 5:30–10 p.m.; Tuesday–Thursday, 5:30–10:30 p.m.; Friday and Saturday, 5:30–11 p.m.

SETTING AND ATMOSPHERE This first Las Vegas venture for New York restaurateur Stephen Hanson is a casual version of Fiamma New York. A cheerful fireplace near the bar adds a comforting touch. Separate dining rooms that flow together make this sizable Italian restaurant more intimate.

HOUSE SPECIALTIES Sage-roasted chicken with white-truffle potatoes; braised short rib–filled ravioli with just enough meat and a drizzle of wine sauce; thin-sliced cured beef tenderloin with black truffle, arugula, and Parmesan cheese; wild king salmon with sweet-corn ragu; mozzarella with tomatoes, yellow-pepper crema, and basil oil.

OTHER RECOMMENDATIONS Any of the creamy risottos that change each day; the citrus-grilled octopus appetizer; seared diver scallops with pistachio; wonderful house-made pastas; irresistible pastries, especially the hot-from-the-fryer amaretti doughnuts served with dipping sauces.

SUMMARY AND COMMENTS Adventurers can order a multicourse tasting dinner. Pricey but wonderful.

Fleur   ★★★½

| TAPAS FRENCH | MODERATE | QUALITY ★★★★ | VALUE ★★★½ |

**Mandalay Bay, 3950 South Las Vegas Boulevard;
South Strip and Environs; ☎ 702-362-9400; mandalaybay.com**

Customers Tourists, conventioneers. **Reservations** Essential. **When to go** Anytime. **Entrée range** $6–$35. **Payment** All major credit cards. **Service rating** ★★★★. **Friendliness rating** ★★★½. **Parking** Valet, lot. **Bar** Full service. **Wine selection** Excellent, eclectic list. **Dress** Casual. **Disabled access** Yes. **Hours** Daily, 11 a.m.–11 p.m.

SETTING AND ATMOSPHERE Celebrity chef Hubert Keller has redone his once-formal dining room and made it more casual. A large bar area with patio tables protrudes out onto the Mandalay Bay pedestrian walkway area. The sparse new design features lamps that look like sea anemones.

HOUSE SPECIALTIES Keller is a creative force. He's serving small plates such as PEI mussels in a cast-iron pot, Parmesan-paprika popcorn, spicy Thai chicken wings, and maple-glazed pork ribs on a menu filled with more than 40 dishes.

OTHER RECOMMENDATIONS Tarte flambée; a bacon-and–white cheese flat-bread from the chef's native Alsace; and a Prime tomahawk ribeye steak, a 40-ounce monster served with a shallot au jus, show off the scope of this menu. For dessert, a good bet is affogato, an ice cream made at the table using liquid nitrogen. It's gimmicky, but it works.

SUMMARY AND COMMENTS Keller's through doing fancy schmancy food in Vegas. He wants his new incarnation to be fun. This is the man who launched the burger craze with Burger Bar, and in spite of his classical French training, he remains terminally hip.

Florida Café   ★★★

| CUBAN | INEXPENSIVE | QUALITY ★★★½ | VALUE ★★★★½ |

Howard Johnson Hotel, 1401 South Las Vegas Boulevard; North Strip and Environs; ☎ 702-385-3013; floridacafecuban.com

Customers Cuban community, locals, HoJo guests. **Reservations** Not necessary. **When to go** Anytime. **Entrée range** $6–$20. **Payment** All major credit cards. **Service rating** ★★★. **Friendliness rating** ★★★½. **Parking** Lot. **Bar** Wine and beer. **Wine selection** Small. **Dress** Casual. **Disabled access** Yes. **Hours** Daily, 7 a.m.–10 p.m.

SETTING AND ATMOSPHERE Colorful Cuban paintings adorn the walls, but it's still a coffee shop at heart.

HOUSE SPECIALTIES Cuban-American food at value prices; Cuban breakfast eggs, stuffed potatoes, sweet plantains, and toast; croquettes; corn tamales; fresh seafood; real Cuban sandwiches, pressed thin on a special grill. All entrées include side dishes.

OTHER RECOMMENDATIONS Arroz con pollo, chicken with yellow rice; marinated leg of pork with burnt orange; ropa vieja, a shredded beef dish traditionally eaten with rice and beans; *tres leches* cake.

SUMMARY AND COMMENTS Little English is spoken here, but the staff is accommodating, and menu descriptions are clear. Expect a crowd during the noon hour.

Garduño's ★★★

MEXICAN	INEXPENSIVE/MODERATE	QUALITY ★★★½	VALUE ★★★½

Palms, 4321 West Flamingo Road; Mid-Strip and Environs;
☎ **702-942-7777; palms.com**
Fiesta Rancho Hotel, 2400 North Rancho Drive; North Strip and Environs;
☎ **702-631-7000; fiestarancholasvegas.com**

Customers Visitors, locals. **Reservations** Not accepted. **When to go** Anytime. **Entrée range** $6–$23. **Payment** All major credit cards. **Service rating** ★★★½. **Friendliness rating** ★★★½. **Parking** Valet, lot, garage. **Bar** Full service. **Wine selection** Good. **Dress** Casual. **Disabled access** Yes. **Hours** *Palms:* Monday, 11 a.m.–9:30 p.m.; Tuesday–Thursday 11 a.m.–10 p.m.; Friday and Saturday, 11 a.m.–11 p.m.; Sunday, 10:30 a.m.–3 p.m. (margarita brunch, $17) and 4–9 p.m. *Fiesta:* Sunday–Thursday, 4–9 p.m.; Friday and Saturday, 4–10 p.m.

SETTING AND ATMOSPHERE Colorful, appealing Mexican décor with many plants and beautiful artifacts. Two patios for outdoor dining and dining rooms with views on two levels at the Palms.

HOUSE SPECIALTIES The sizzling fajitas, including a vegetarian version; pastas with Mexican flair (green-chile Alfredo); award-winning Blue Agave pan roasts with king crab, lobster, scallops, or shrimp; house roast with lobster, crab, or shrimp.

OTHER RECOMMENDATIONS Homemade tamales; the relleno combo; green-chile Caesar salad; steak enchiladas; chunky burritos and chimichangas. The zesty guacamole is prepared tableside—each server has a unique version; diners can add their own touches or eliminate any ingredient they don't want. Fun to watch and delicious.

SUMMARY AND COMMENTS Garduño's offers more than tasty food. There's a seemingly endless selection of margaritas, tequilas, and mockaritas. Have the fried ice cream for dessert. The Sunday margarita brunch at the Palms location is a fine value and a good way to get to know the Garduño style of Mexican cooking. Daily lunch specials are large enough to be an early dinner.

Hofbräuhaus ★★★

GERMAN	MODERATE	QUALITY ★★★½	VALUE ★★★★½

4510 Paradise Road; East of Strip; ☎ **702-853-2337;**
hofbrauhauslasvegas.com

Customers Visitors, local German community, beer enthusiasts. **Reservations** Requested for main dining room. **When to go** Anytime. **Entrée range** $13–$20. **Payment** All major credit cards. **Service rating** ★★★½. **Friendliness rating** ★★★½. **Parking** Valet, large lot. **Bar** Limited. **Wine selection** Small. **Dress** Casual. **Disabled access** Ramp. **Hours** Sunday–Thursday, 11 a.m.–11 p.m.; Friday and Saturday, 11 a.m.–midnight; lunch specials served until 4 p.m. Monday–Friday.

SETTING AND ATMOSPHERE A mini-replica of Munich's Hofbräuhaus that required permission from the German government. The main dining room is where the action is. Communal tables and oompah bands flown in monthly put the din in dinner, yet the crowds love it. Comely frauleins dressed in dirndls hoist as many as eight steins without a tray.

HOUSE SPECIALTIES Tennis ball–sized dumplings that accompany the pork stew and a few other braised dishes; sauerbraten that can be on the dry side—the beer makes it go down easier; roasted chicken and potato pancakes; pretzels baked throughout the day—the dough is shipped in containers from Germany, then shaped and baked in the kitchen.

OTHER RECOMMENDATIONS Crisp apple strudel, not too sweet, just delicious.

SUMMARY AND COMMENTS Hofbräuhaus serves the best beer in Las Vegas, and they have let go the notion that you shouldn't drink it cold. Take advantage of the discount coupons available in most hotels and taxis. Request to sit in the faux gardens behind the main dining room.

Hue Thai's Sandwiches   ★★

VIETNAMESE	INEXPENSIVE	QUALITY ★★★	VALUE ★★★

5115 Spring Mountain Road; West of Strip; ☎ 702-943-8872

Customers Locals. **Reservations** Not necessary. **When to go** Anytime. **Entrée range** $7–$15. **Payment** All major credit cards. **Service rating** ★★. **Friendliness rating** ★★★. **Parking** Lot. **Bar** None. **Wine selection** None. **Dress** Casual. **Disabled access** Yes. **Hours** Daily, 8:30 a.m.–11 p.m.

SETTING AND ATMOSPHERE The spacious dining room offers both table seating and a walk-up counter. The room is decorated in an underwater motif, with a beautiful fish tank in the middle of the space.

HOUSE SPECIALTIES *Banh mi* (Vietnamese sandwiches of grilled meats or pâté topped with pickled vegetables and jalapeños) are served on baguettes baked in-house. They're so good that often when you order, the person at the register says "Just one?" Other Vietnamese specialties such as *pho*, bun, and *shabu shabu* hot pots are popular here as well.

OTHER RECOMMENDATIONS Since the menu is comprised entirely of photos, it's easy to pick dishes you might not be familiar with at Hue Thai. There is also an entire vegetarian section of the regular meat-filled dishes made with faux meats (even meat eaters have been surprised!).

SUMMARY AND COMMENTS Despite the large number of Vietnamese restaurants in Las Vegas's Chinatown, very few actually serve *banh mi*. These sandwiches are what bring customers into Hue Thai in the first place, especially as most of the hearty sandwiches cost less than $4. At those prices, you should have plenty left over to try their other authentic Vietnamese dishes.

Hugo's Cellar   ★★★

AMERICAN	EXPENSIVE	QUALITY ★★★	VALUE ★★★

Four Queens Hotel, 202 Fremont Street; Downtown; ☎ 702-385-4011; hugoscellar.com

Customers Visitors, locals. **Reservations** Strongly recommended. **When to go** Anytime but Friday and Saturday. **Entrée range** $35–$80. **Payment** All major credit cards. **Service rating** ★★★½. **Friendliness rating** ★★★★½. **Parking** Garage, valet. **Bar** Full service. **Wine selection** Very good. **Dress** Casually elegant, tie and jacket suggested. **Disabled access** Elevator to cellar. **Hours** Daily, 5:30–11 p.m.

SETTING AND ATMOSPHERE Unique cellar location, comfortable lounge, warm bar, and gracious welcome. Booths provide privacy; noise is minimal. Cozy cocktail lounge serves pâté, cheese, crackers, and large drinks.

HOUSE SPECIALTIES Variety of breads, including lavash crackers. Waiter creates salad of your choice from selection on the cart wheeled to your table. Steaks and prime rib; duck flambé anise; snapper en papillote with shallots and white wine; medallions of lobster with white wine, crushed red pepper, sun-dried tomatoes, and mushrooms.

OTHER RECOMMENDATIONS Appetizer for two of beef-tenderloin medallions, marinated swordfish, breast of chicken, and jumbo shrimp cooked at the table on a sizzling granite slab, accompanied by a selection of herbs, seasonings, and special sauces. Imaginative preparations of veal and chicken; rack of lamb Indonesian.

SUMMARY AND COMMENTS Perhaps the most popular downtown restaurant, Hugo's is always packed on weekends, in spite of the high check averages. Some may find the old-style food here tired. They haven't changed the menu in thirty years—and sorely need to.

Isla ★★★★½

CONTEMPORARY MEXICAN	MODERATE	QUALITY ★★★★	VALUE ★★★★½

T. I., 3300 South Las Vegas Boulevard; Mid-Strip and Environs;
☎ **702-894-7223; treasureisland.com**

Customers Visitors, locals. **Reservations** Suggested for weekends. **When to go** Anytime. **Entrée range** $8–$30. **Payment** All major credit cards. **Service rating** ★★★★½. **Friendliness rating** ★★★★½. **Parking** Valet, garage. **Bar** Full service; excellent tequila list. **Wine selection** Interesting and good. **Dress** Upscale casual. **Disabled access** Valet or elevator. **Hours** Daily, 4–10 p.m.

SETTING AND ATMOSPHERE Isla is a comfort zone just off the casino floor. The stylish décor has little pretense. A patio bar is designed for those who wish to combine people-watching with their cocktails and hors d'oeuvres.

HOUSE SPECIALTIES Tableside guacamole, including one studded with bits of lobster, achiote, passion fruit, and serrano chile; pulled-pork tamale with sweet-and-spicy chipotle sauce; the Sandoval family dish of roast-pork pipian—lean pork tenderloin marinated in tamarind sauce arranged on a bed of crushed sweet corn and a rich pumpkin seed puree.

OTHER RECOMMENDATIONS Crispy empanadas filled with shredded beef, toasted pine nuts, and dried cherries; trio of corn masa cakes with various toppings; crispy rock-shrimp tacos laced with chipotle rouille, a garlicky mayonnaise; *huitlacoche* dumplings with spiced chicken breast.

SUMMARY AND COMMENTS Isla is, perhaps, the best Mexican restaurant in Vegas; it is certainly the best Mexican on the Strip. A statuesque tequila goddess serves the brew in flights, and tells you everything you always wanted to know about the origins. Isla's selection of Mexican dishes is creative and interesting. Chef Richard Sandoval knows his native cooking. The kitchen can be slow, but the food is worth the wait.

Jaleo ★★★★½

SPANISH/TAPAS	MODERATE	QUALITY ★★★★	VALUE ★★★★

**Cosmopolitan, 3708 South Las Vegas Boulevard;
Mid-Strip and Environs; ☎ 702-698-7000; cosmopolitanlasvegas.com**

Customers Visitors, locals. **Reservations** A must. **When to go** Anytime. **Entrée range** $8–$45. **Payment** All major credit cards. **Service rating** ★★★. **Friendliness rating** ★★★. **Parking** Valet, garage. **Bar** Full service. **Wine selection** Very good. **Dress** Informal. **Disabled access** Yes. **Hours** Sunday–Thursday, 5–11 p.m.; Friday and Saturday, 5 p.m.–midnight.

SETTING AND ATMOSPHERE Colorful, open restaurant filled with contemporary art from Spanish painters and sculptors. Seating is at small tables on one side of the room and at communal wooden tables that seat more than one party.

HOUSE SPECIALTIES Creative tapas from chef José Andrés, the man who imported this genre from his native Spain. Excellent ham and chicken croquetas. Catalan sausage stew with braised onion and mushrooms is not to be missed. There is an excellent selection of Iberian hams and boutique cheeses. Imaginative desserts.

OTHER RECOMMENDATIONS Don't miss the paellas, cooked over olive-and-orange wood-burning fires in an open cooking area. The best choice is probably Valenciana, which has rabbit and chicken, but the seafood paella is also quite wonderful. Avant-garde Spanish cuisine is served in a small private room in the rear, by prior arrangement only.

SUMMARY AND COMMENTS José Andrés once cooked with Ferran Adria at elBulli in Roses, Spain, so he's comfortable with both traditional and avant-garde Spanish cuisine. The patatas bravas—small, blistered potatoes served with a salt crust—come with a pair of exotic sauces from the Canary Islands. This is a most memorable experience.

Joël Robuchon ★★★★★

FRENCH	VERY EXPENSIVE	QUALITY ★★★★★	VALUE ★★★

MGM Grand, 3799 South Las Vegas Boulevard; South Strip and Environs; ☎ 702-891-7925; mgmgrand.com

Customers Visitors, locals. **Reservations** A must. **When to go** Special occasion. **Entrée range** Prix-fixe menus, $120–$240. **Payment** All major credit cards. **Service rating** ★★★★. **Friendliness rating** ★★★. **Parking** Valet, garage. **Bar** Full service. **Wine selection** Excellent. **Dress** Formal. **Disabled access** Yes. **Hours** Daily, 5:30–10:30 p.m.

SETTING AND ATMOSPHERE Small and intimate, this dining room whisks guests out of the Vegas experience and into a regal one. Adorned in hues of plush purple and gold, the room is elegant yet warm and inviting.

HOUSE SPECIALTIES Expect high-quality gourmet ingredients and treatments.

Les crustaces (truffled langoustine ravioli) is luxurious and divine. La truffe noire (shaved black truffles and potatoes topped with foie gras) has been known to make diners shed a tear or two from its pure decadence.

OTHER RECOMMENDATIONS For the full experience, opt for the 16-course tasting menu ($395 per person). There are also less-expensive and more-accessible abbreviated menus, starting at $120 per person.

SUMMARY AND COMMENTS Joël Robuchon has the distinction of being one of the most innovative chefs in the world (he was named "Chef of the Century" by *Gault Millau*), and a meal here is no small feat. It's the first and only three-star *Michelin Guide* winner in Las Vegas. Next door, L'Atelier de Joël Robuchon features a slightly more casual atmosphere where guests can watch chefs prepare their meals in an open-kitchen setting.

Joe's Seafood, Prime Steak & Stone Crab ★★★★½

SEAFOOD/STEAK   EXPENSIVE   QUALITY ★★★★½   VALUE ★★★½

The Forum Shops at Caesars Palace, 3500 South Las Vegas Boulevard; Mid-Strip and Environs; ☎ 702-792-9222; joes.net

Customers Visitors and locals. **Reservations** A must for dinner. **When to go** Avoid conventions and holidays. **Entrée range** $15–market price. **Payment** All major credit cards. **Service rating** ★★★½. **Friendliness rating** ★★★★½. **Parking** Self, valet. **Bar** Bar and lounge. **Wine selection** Very good. **Dress** Business or upscale casual. **Disabled access** Yes (Forum Shops valet). **Hours** Sunday–Thursday, 11:30 a.m.–10 p.m.; Friday and Saturday, 11:30 a.m.–11 p.m.

SETTING AND ATMOSPHERE Handsome Chicago-style décor that is a far cry from the original Miami Beach Joe's Stone Crab. The history of Joe's is chronicled in the artfully arranged photos that cover the dining-room walls. Joe's at The Forum Shops is fashioned after the Chicago Joe's.

HOUSE SPECIALTIES Stone crab as an appetizer or entrée is available year-round. The-always-in-demand claws are shipped frozen when the season ends, yet are always wonderful. Jumbo lump-crabmeat cakes; chilled or warm seafood platters priced per person; glazed black cod; prime steaks and chops.

OTHER RECOMMENDATIONS Signature bone-in steaks—the 22-ounce porterhouse is a terrific slab of beef. It's sliced in the kitchen and is perfect for sharing. Calf's liver with onions; superb hash-brown potatoes, crusty and golden brown with a creamy interior; outstanding side dishes—don't miss the fried green tomatoes or the signature grilled tomatoes with spinach and a cheddar-cheese topping.

SUMMARY AND COMMENTS Be prepared for noise—not overwhelming, but sometimes intrusive. Early dining is wise. Management prefers online reservations made well in advance. Walk-ins are not turned away but often have a wait at the bar.

Julian Serrano ★★★★

SPANISH/TAPAS   EXPENSIVE   QUALITY ★★★★   VALUE ★★★★

Aria at CityCenter, 3730 South Las Vegas Boulevard; Mid-Strip and Environs; ☎ 702-590-7111; arialasvegas.com

Customers Visitors, locals. **Reservations** Recommended. **When to go** Anytime.
Entrée range $8–$50. **Payment** All major credit cards. **Service rating** ★★★★.
Friendliness rating ★★★★. **Parking** Valet, lot. **Bar** Full Service. **Wine selection**
Excellent. **Dress** Casual. **Disabled access** Yes. **Hours** Daily, 11 a.m.–11 p.m.

SETTING AND ATMOSPHERE Contemporary Spanish décor with large open
spaces and abundant pastel colors and earth tones. Some guests prefer
to sit at the long tapas bar, where they can watch the chefs putting
together the small plates.

HOUSE SPECIALTIES Chicken croquettes; stuffed peppers; *albondigas* (Spanish meatballs); *jamon* Iberico; Serrano ham; paella Valenciana; crema
Catalana.

OTHER RECOMMENDATIONS: Many of the small plates are irresistible, but the
star dish is the paella, a rice casserole cooked in an iron pan. The Valenciana, stocked with chorizo, chicken, and rabbit, redolent of saffron, is
simply sensational.

SUMMARY AND COMMENTS Serrano is a native of Madrid, French-trained, and
chef of Picasso in the neighboring Bellagio, but his native cuisine is his
first love. Vegas has several tapas bars, but Serrano and Jaleo are really
the Spanish restaurants the city has been waiting for.

Kokomo's ★★★½

SEAFOOD/STEAK	EXPENSIVE	QUALITY ★★★★	VALUE ★★½

The Mirage, 3400 South Las Vegas Boulevard; Mid-Strip and Environs;
☎ **702-791-7111; mirage.com**

Customers Visitors. **Reservations** Recommended; high rollers and hotel guests
get preference. **When to go** Anytime. **Entrée range** $27–market price. **Payment**
All major credit cards. **Service rating** ★★★★½. **Friendliness rating** ★★★½.
Parking Lot (long walk), valet. **Bar** Full service. **Wine selection** Good. **Dress**
Casual. **Disabled access** Yes. **Hours** Daily, 5–10:30 p.m.

SETTING AND ATMOSPHERE Magnificent tropical décor—waterfalls, streams,
lush foliage, orchids, and other exotic flowers—brings the South Pacific
to the Strip. Tables are well spaced for privacy.

HOUSE SPECIALTIES Three-onion soup with Monterey Jack and Parmesan
cheeses; mashed sweet potatoes; steaks; chops and ribs; grilled rib eye
with sauteed red onions and tricolor-pepper sauce; desserts.

OTHER RECOMMENDATIONS Blackened–Kansas City steak with spicy shrimp;
veal-and-shrimp combo; double-rib lamb chops; Kobe steak; crab cakes;
oven-roasted, ginger-soy–marinated Chilean sea bass; grilled mahimahi;
wood-smoked Atlantic salmon.

SUMMARY AND COMMENTS Imaginative chefs and décor combine to create a
memorable lunch or dinner in this romantic room. Peaceful and romantic, Kokomo's is a sleeper. One of the best-kept secrets in town.

Lindo Michoacan ★★★½

MEXICAN	INEXPENSIVE/MODERATE	QUALITY ★★★★	VALUE ★★★★

2655 East Desert Inn Road; Southeast Las Vegas; ☎ **702-735-6828;**
lindomichoacan.com

Customers Locals and visitors. Reservations Suggested for dinner. When to go Anytime. Entrée range $10–$39. Payment All major credit cards. Service rating ★★★½. Friendliness rating ★★★★. Parking Large lot. Bar Beer, cocktails, tequila. Wine selection None. Dress Casual. Disabled access Yes. Hours Monday–Thursday, 10:30 a.m.–11 p.m.; Friday, 10:30 a.m.–midnight; Saturday, 9 a.m.–midnight; Sunday, 9 a.m.–11 p.m.

SETTING AND ATMOSPHERE Big and noisy with flamboyant, colorful décor.

HOUSE SPECIALTIES Lunch specials served from 11 a.m. to 5 p.m. Prices include a beverage and one refill, rice and beans, and, with most choices, thin flour tortillas. À la carte tacos, enchiladas, and burritos smothered with salsa and Monterey cheese are worth a try; so are tortas, Mexican sandwiches, and *birria*, stewed goat meat. On Saturdays and Sundays, Michoacan-style menudo (tripe soup) is served.

OTHER RECOMMENDATIONS *Flan t'o raul*, traditional Mexican caramel custard; delicate sopaipillas drizzled with honey. Also try the sopitos, six hand-made gorditas topped with beef, chicken, or chorizo, plus lettuce, cheese, and tomatoes.

SUMMARY AND COMMENTS Lindo Michoacan is a popular party place. The din is deafening when the staff salutes the celebrants by beating on drums. Enjoy a late lunch if noise is not your thing. The food is slightly toned down for the American palate. Mexicans prefer smaller, more authentic places in North Las Vegas. Lunch is served until 5 p.m. and is a super value. Service is better and the room quiets down in the evening.

Lotus of Siam ★★★★

THAI	MODERATE	QUALITY ★★★★	VALUE ★★½

Commercial Center, 953 East Sahara Avenue; East of Strip;
☎ **702-735-3033; saipinchutima.com**

Customers Locals, visitors. Reservations Recommended. When to go Anytime. Entrée range $9–$21; lunch buffet, $10. Payment All major credit cards. Service rating ★★½. Friendliness rating ★★★★½. Parking Lot. Bar No. Wine selection Excellent. Dress Casually elegant. Disabled access Yes (ground floor). Hours Monday–Thursday, 11:30 a.m.–2 p.m. and 5:30–9:30 p.m.; Friday, 11:30 a.m.–2 p.m. and 5:30–10 p.m.; Saturday and Sunday, 5:30–10 p.m.

SETTING AND ATMOSPHERE Attractive, though modest, décor; teak tables and comfortable chairs. Thai paintings and accessories.

HOUSE SPECIALTIES Beef jerky, I-saan-style—crisp yet tender marinated beef served in a spicy sauce; *som tam*, green papaya salad with salted crab; salmon Panang—charbroiled fresh salmon, served Thai-style in a thick, creamy sauce laced with curry.

OTHER RECOMMENDATIONS Sticky rice steamed in a bamboo basket; crispy rice salad; sausages made in-house. Ask the staff to show you the Northern Thai menu, specialties from the chef's hometown, Chaing Mai. *Khao soi*, Burmese-inspired noodles, and *nam prik noon*, a fiery green chile dip, are just two of them.

SUMMARY AND COMMENTS The I-saan specialties featured here come from the northeastern corner of Thailand, bordering Cambodia and Laos.

These dishes are both hotter and more highly seasoned than most Thai food, but the chef-owner will temper the heat to suit your taste. Gentle, caring service and one of the best lists of Austrian and German wines in this country are bonuses.

Marché Bacchus: French Bistro and Wine Shop ★★★★

FRENCH BISTRO	MODERATE	QUALITY ★★★★	VALUE ★★★★

2620 Regatta Drive, # 106; West of Strip; ☎ 702-804-8008; marchebacchus.com

Customers Locals. **Reservations** Suggested weekends. **When to go** Anytime. **Entrée range** $17–$40. **Payment** All major credit cards. **Service rating** ★★★★½. **Friendliness rating** ★★★★½. **Parking** Large lot. **Bar** Full service. **Wine selection** Extensive. **Dress** Casual. **Disabled access** Yes (wheelchair access on lower level). **Hours** Monday–Saturday, 11 a.m.–4:30 p.m.; Monday–Thursday, 5:30–9:30 p.m.; Friday and Saturday, 5:30–10 p.m.; Sunday brunch, 10 a.m.–4:30 p.m.

SETTING AND ATMOSPHERE Walk through the wine shop to the adjacent bistro or dine on the terrace with its gorgeous view of man-made Regatta Lake. Simply furnished, this neighborhood eatery is an escape from the cares of the day. After one visit, you're welcomed by owners Rhonda and Jeff Wyatt as if you're members of the family.

HOUSE SPECIALTIES Chef Jean-Paul Labadie came from the kitchen of Emeril Lagasse, so in addition to French bistro classics, such as escargot in garlic butter and mussels in white wine, you'll find flavorful Andouille sausage gumbo.

OTHER RECOMMENDATIONS The adjoining wine shop is dazzling. Any wine can be purchased to enjoy with dinner for only $10 over the retail price.

SUMMARY AND COMMENTS Wines by the glass are terrific here, as is the charcuterie, made on premises. The terrace is favored by local sommeliers who bring visiting winemakers and chefs to relax here, making it a great place for networking.

Michael's ★★★½

CONTINENTAL	VERY EXPENSIVE	QUALITY ★★★★	VALUE ★★½

South Point Hotel, 9777 South Las Vegas Boulevard; South Strip and Environs; ☎ 702-796-7111; southpointcasino.com

Customers Visitors, locals. **Reservations** Difficult to obtain; starts taking reservations at 3:30 p.m. **When to go** Whenever you can get a reservation. **Entrée range** $56–$105, à la carte. **Payment** All major credit cards. **Service rating** ★★★★½. **Friendliness rating** ★★★★½. **Parking** Garage, valet. **Bar** Full service. **Wine selection** Excellent. **Dress** Sport coat, dressy. **Disabled access** Access ramp at side entrance. **Hours** Daily, 5:30–10 p.m.

SETTING AND ATMOSPHERE Comfortable chairs in intimate table settings. Deep carpeting and romantic lighting create a luxurious room in the rococo style of early Las Vegas.

HOUSE SPECIALTIES Rack of lamb bouquetiére for two; live Maine lobster; veal saltimbocca, sauteed and topped with prosciutto; fresh Dover sole;

complimentary relish plate with humongous green and black olives.

OTHER RECOMMENDATIONS Shrimp cocktail served atop an igloo of ice, illuminated from within; bananas Foster for two. All meats are prime.

SUMMARY AND COMMENTS Early diners have a better chance of securing a table than those who like to dine at prime time. Complimentary petits fours, chocolate-dipped fruits, and fancy fresh fruits are presented after dinner. The menu (strictly à la carte) is a high-priced view of the Las Vegas of yesteryear.

Mon Ami Gabi ★★★½

CONTINENTAL/FRENCH	MOD/EXP	QUALITY ★★★★	VALUE ★★★½

Paris, 3655 South Las Vegas Boulevard; Mid-Strip and Environs;
☎ **702-944-4224; parislasvegas.com or monamigabi.com**

Customers Visitors, locals. **Reservations** Requested for dining room, not accepted for patio. **When to go** Anytime. **Entrée range** $13–40. **Payment** All major credit cards. **Service rating** ★★★½. **Friendliness rating** ★★★½. **Parking** Garage, valet. **Bar** Full service. **Wine selection** All French. **Dress** Upscale casual. **Disabled access** Yes. **Hours** Brunch: Saturday and Sunday, 11 a.m.–4 p.m.; breakfast: daily, 7–11 a.m.; lunch: Monday–Friday, 11:30 a.m.–4 p.m.; Saturday and Sunday, 11 a.m.–4 p.m.; dinner: Monday–Friday, 4–11 p.m.; Saturday and Sunday, 4 p.m.–midnight.

SETTING AND ATMOSPHERE Handsome brasserie with black-leather booths and tables. The main dining room leads to a wonderful, plant-filled patio and a marvelous sidewalk café with a view of the Strip.

HOUSE SPECIALTIES Steak frites, thin-sliced steak and French fries; an excellent selection of seafood and hors d'oeuvres; many hot seafood appetizers; the daily special listed on the blackboard; filet mignon and New York strip are among the regular steak selections.

OTHER RECOMMENDATIONS Crêpes; omelets and sandwiches served at lunch; plates of seafood; *mussels gribiche* (mussels with caper mayonnaise).

SUMMARY AND COMMENTS Mon Ami is a charming dining place. Everyone wants to dine at the sidewalk café, but you'll have to come early to get a table (no reservations). The *frites* are curly fries, not steak fries, but they're crisp and good: so what if they're not authentic? Everything else is right on the mark. And for those whose dinner isn't complete without a good bottle of wine, there's a separate list of fine reserve wines.

Monta ★★

RAMEN	INEXPENSIVE	QUALITY ★★★★	VALUE ★★★★★

3600 W. Spring Mountain Road; West of Strip; ☎ **702-367-4600**

Customers Local Japanese. **Reservations** Not accepted. **When to go** Lunch or late dinner. **Entrée range** $7–$10. **Payment** Cash only. **Service rating** ★★★. **Friendliness rating** ★★. **Parking** Lot. **Bar** Beer and wine. **Dress** Casual. **Disabled access** No. **Hours** Daily, 11 a.m.–midnight.

SETTING AND ATMOSPHERE A rabbit warren–sized ramen bar where the chefs toil behind a counter. Seating is cramped, on wooden chairs, with tables crowded closely together. A mostly Japanese-speaking clientele predominates.

HOUSE SPECIALTIES The specialty here is ramen—long, wheat-based noodles slurped from giant bowls of broth. There are essentially two types: miso ramen, in a piquant broth made from fermented soy beans, and shoyu ramen, based on soy sauce. The flavorful broth is slow-cooked and tastes it, and the noodles are perfectly al dente.

OTHER RECOMMENDATIONS Toppings are to ramen as they are to pizza. Don't miss the melt-in-your-mouth, thinly sliced pork—slices so light they literally float up to the top of the broth. Corn, egg, and several other toppings enhance the ramen experience. There are also bowls of fried rice and several types of house-made Japanese pickles.

SUMMARY AND COMMENTS This place ain't fancy, but it's the most authentic Japanese food in town, even more so than the so-called sushi palaces. Be prepared to wait in line. It is always in demand, and the restaurant just doesn't seat too many people.

Morels ★★★

STEAK	EXPENSIVE	QUALITY ★★★★	VALUE ★★

**Palazzo, 3325 South Las Vegas Boulevard; Mid-Strip and Environs;
☎ 702-607-6333; palazzolasvegas.com**

Customers Visitors, locals. **Reservations** Accepted. **When to go** Anytime. **Entrée range** $26–$67. **Payment** All major credit cards. **Service rating** ★★★★. **Friendliness rating** ★★★. **Parking** Valet, garage. **Bar** Full service. **Wine selection** Very good. **Dress** Upscale. **Disabled access** Yes. **Hours** Monday–Thursday, 8 a.m.–11 p.m.; Friday and Saturday, 8 a.m.–midnight; Sunday, 8 a.m.–10 p.m. Brunch: Saturday and Sunday, 8 a.m.–3 p.m.

SETTING AND ATMOSPHERE Guests are greeted with tasteful erotic paintings adorning the foyer wall, then once you get past staring at that, enter the plush lounge, complete with white-leather couches and a beautiful dark wood bar. An iced seafood bar and a fresh cheese and charcuterie bar offer an up-close look at the quality of products on the menu. Be prepared for occasional explosions and booms from the Sirens of T. I. show across the Strip.

HOUSE SPECIALTIES Steaks are stellar. Paired with homey sides, such as the earthy porcini macaroni and cheese and the pleasantly spicy roasted jalapeño creamed corn, and sauces such as the classic Bearnaise and verdant chimichurri, this is one steak dinner that outshines the rest.

SUMMARY AND COMMENTS Yes, every hotel has a steak house (Palazzo has three), but very rarely do they stand out amongst their peers. Morels does that with their steaks alone, as their 32-day dry-aged cuts carry incredibly intense flavor. Combined with their classic steak-house service and dark ambiance, a meal here is a true steak-dinner experience.

Nobhill Tavern ★★★

AMERICAN	EXPENSIVE	QUALITY ★★★★	VALUE ★★★★

**MGM Grand, 3799 South Las Vegas Boulevard; South Strip and Environs;
☎ 702-891-7337; mgmgrand.com**

Customers Visitors. **Reservations** Recommended. **When to go** Anytime. **Entrée range** $30–$85. **Payment** All major credit cards. **Service rating** ★★★★. **Friendliness rating** ★★★★. **Parking** Valet, garage. **Bar** Full service. **Wine selection** Good. **Dress** Business casual. **Disabled access** Yes. **Hours** Sunday–Thursday, 5:30–10 p.m.; Friday and Saturday, 5:30–10:30 p.m.

SETTING AND ATMOSPHERE Meant to evoke the feel and vibe of a cool San Francisco eatery, Nobhill Tavern is sophisticated and sexy. The bar is a great place to start the night with a few of Nobhill's signature cocktails. The restaurant is elegant yet casual at the same time.

HOUSE SPECIALTIES Specials such as meat loaf, fish and chips, and prime rib evoke a feeling of familiarity with diners who are pleasantly surprised at their upscale execution. Mina's signature San Francisco cioppino, chock full of shellfish in a tomato-pepper broth, is always a hit.

OTHER RECOMMENDATIONS Anything under the Snacks & Finger Foods portion of the menu, which is small plates served family style, including a cheese fondue, sliders, and mini oyster po' boy sandwiches.

SUMMARY AND COMMENTS Chef Michael Mina's Nobhill Tavern has flown low under the radar the past couple of years, but in 2009 it underwent a complete branding change. The word 'Tavern' itself appeared on the sign, and the menu has been revamped to reflect a comfortable yet upscale bar-food experience. Gone are Mina's signature tasting trios, replaced with small plates of comfort food meant to share.

Nobu ★★★★

JAPANESE/SUSHI   VERY EXPENSIVE   QUALITY ★★★★★   VALUE ★★

Hard Rock Hotel, 4455 Paradise Road; East of Strip; ☎ 702-693-5090; hardrockhotel.com

Customers Visitors, locals. **Reservations** Recommended. **When to go** Anytime. **Entrée range** Sushi and sashimi, $7–$15; sushi dinners, $50 and $75; hot and cold dishes, $15–$50. **Payment** All major credit cards. **Service rating** ★★★★. **Friendliness rating** ★★★. **Parking** Lot, garage, valet. **Bar** Full service. **Wine selection** Good. **Dress** Upscale casual. **Disabled access** Yes. **Hours** Daily, 6–11 p.m.

SETTING AND ATMOSPHERE Zen-like décor, juxtaposing contemporary modern elements, from willowy bamboo to black lacquer, throughout. The room can get rather loud when the restaurant is full of hipsters and scenesters from the Hard Rock crowd.

HOUSE SPECIALTIES The menu is a reflection of Japanese technique and precision with South American ingredients and influence. Signature dishes include black cod with miso glaze and expertly sliced yellowtail sashimi with slivers of jalapeño.

OTHER RECOMMENDATIONS Sushi and sashimi, of course. *Tiraditos*, a South American play on ceviche and sashimi, are served on a brick of beautiful pink Himalayan salt, which gently seasons the raw offerings atop it.

SUMMARY AND COMMENTS Chef Nobu Matsuhisa is considered one of the pioneers of modern Japanese cuisine. His spot at the Hard Rock is a nightly gathering of the beautiful people who often stick to ordering plain sushi and maki. While these are exceptional, we find that the chef's specials and more creative offerings are what the true Nobu experience should be all about.

Noodle Palace   ★★★

CHINESE	INEXPENSIVE	QUALITY ★★★	VALUE ★★★

5115 Spring Mountain Road, #203; West of Strip; ☎ 702-798-1113

Customers Locals. **Reservations** Not necessary. **When to go** Anytime. **Entrée range** $7–$12. **Payment** All major credit cards. **Service rating** ★★★. **Friendliness rating** ★★★. **Parking** Lot. **Bar** None. **Wine selection** None. **Dress** Casual. **Disabled access** Yes. **Hours** Daily, 11 a.m.–10 p.m.

SETTING AND ATMOSPHERE Located upstairs in one of the ubiquitous strip malls in Las Vegas's Chinatown, this bright but small restaurant draws a big lunch crowd for inexpensive midday deals. Specials posted on the walls tell diners of new and authentic dishes.

HOUSE SPECIALTIES Noodles, of course. Cantonese and Hong Kong–style noodles are dominant on the menu, as well as Hawaiian-inspired noodle dishes, such as crispy cake noodles and saimin.

OTHER RECOMMENDATIONS Szechuan chicken salad is dressed tableside according to your heat specifications and is a nice, light starter to share. Hong Kong–style lo mein noodles are dry egg noodles topped with a variety of roasted meats or dumplings, with a side of clear broth.

SUMMARY AND COMMENTS Most customers at Noodle Palace are of Asian descent, picking from plates sitting atop their ever-moving lazy Susans. This is a no-frills Asian dining experience, sort of like a true Hong Kong experience. Service is competent and friendly, and food arrives quickly.

Noodles   ★★★

ASIAN	MODERATE	QUALITY ★★★★	VALUE ★★★½

Bellagio, 3600 South Las Vegas Boulevard; Mid-Strip and Environs; ☎ 702-693-8131; bellagio.com

Customers Visitors, locals. **Reservations** No. **When to go** Anytime. **Entrée range** $12–$30, à la carte. **Payment** All major credit cards. **Service rating** ★★★½. **Friendliness rating** ★★★½. **Parking** Valet, lot. **Bar** Full service. **Wine selection** Good. **Dress** Casual. **Disabled access** Yes. **Hours** Daily, 11 a.m.–2 a.m. Dim sum: Friday–Sunday, 11 a.m.–3 p.m.

SETTING AND ATMOSPHERE Follow the marble floor with Chinese brass inlays that represent bits of Asian wisdom into this wonderful eatery. There's an open kitchen, a wall of artifacts, and the hustle and bustle of an authentic noodle kitchen.

HOUSE SPECIALTIES Oodles of slurpy, authentic noodle dishes from China, Vietnam, Thailand, and Japan and authentic Hong Kong–style barbecue dishes. There's a long list of appetizers and many different teas.

SUMMARY AND COMMENTS Noodles is small, only 88 seats, so it's tough to get in at prime times, but it's open long hours so you're bound to get in sometime. This is a favorite stop for Bellagio's Asian clientele. Find the baccarat bar, and you'll find Noodles.

Nove Italiano ★★★★

ITALIAN	EXPENSIVE	QUALITY ★★★★	VALUE ★★★★

Palms, Fantasy Tower, 4321 West Flamingo Boulevard; West of Strip;
☎**702-942-6800; palms.com**

Customers Visitors. **Reservations** Recommended. **When to go** Anytime. **Entrée range** $40–$75. **Payment** All major credit cards. **Service rating** ★★★½. **Friendliness rating** ★★★★. **Parking** Valet, lot. **Bar** Full service. **Wine selection** Extensive list of boutique Italian wines. **Dress** Casual. **Disabled access** By special elevator. **Hours** Daily, 6 p.m. until last seating, which varies according to number of reservations.

SETTING AND ATMOSPHERE Located on the 52nd floor in the Palms Fantasy Tower, Nove offers a commanding view of the Vegas Valley. It's a large, noisy room. One of the more interesting design features are interactive plasma screens that display rotating tableaux by various European masters such as Rembrandt, Van Gogh, and Modigliani.

HOUSE SPECIALTIES Creative cocktails; *crudo* (raw seafood, Italian-style, rather like Japanese sashimi); white clam pizza; steaks.

OTHER RECOMMENDATIONS Tell the server that you want the talented chef, Geno Bernardo, to cook for you, and the result will be one of the best Italian meals you will ever have. He might do grilled fresh sea bass with Mediterranean herbs, his own ravioli with tomato confit, or cuttlefish with cannellini beans.

SUMMARY AND COMMENTS In spite of the young, exuberant crowd at the Palms (the owners, the Maloof family, also own the Sacramento Kings in the NBA), the cooking is serious here. Locals tend to overlook Nove, but Bernardo may be the most underrated chef in Las Vegas.

Olives ★★★½

AMERICAN/MEDITERRANEAN	MOD/EXP	QUALITY ★★★★	VALUE ★★★½

Bellagio, 3600 South Las Vegas Boulevard; Mid-Strip and Environs;
☎ **702-693-7223; bellagio.com**

Customers Visitors, locals. **Reservations** Accepted. **When to go** Anytime. **Entrée range** $27–$53. **Payment** All major credit cards. **Service rating** ★★★½. **Friendliness rating** ★★★★½. **Parking** Valet, garage. **Bar** Full service. **Wine selection** Eclectic. **Dress** Casual. **Disabled access** Ground floor. **Hours** Daily, 11 a.m.–2:45 p.m. and 5–10:30 p.m.

SETTING AND ATMOSPHERE Intricate mosaic tiling, a sculpted wood ceiling, an open kitchen, and an outdoor patio with a view of the lake.

HOUSE SPECIALTIES The menu changes regularly but always includes a lobster scampi; signature butternut-squash tortellini with brown butter, sage, and Parmesan cheese; savory spit-roasted chicken on a crisp mashed-potato cake; grilled pork chop in clam-chorizo broth. Typical of the daily specials is the slow-braised lamb chops.

OTHER RECOMMENDATIONS Beef carpaccio; grilled squid and octopus; pan-seared salmon; chocolate falling cake; roasted-banana tiramisu; any of the wonderful sandwiches served only at lunch.

SUMMARY AND COMMENTS Recently remodeled, Olives is a sleeker version of the Boston original and has the same warmth and expert staff; many are from the Boston Olives. These Olives veterans have re-created the essence and spirit of the original. Everyone wants a terrace table, but the terrace seating cannot be reserved.

Panevino Ristorante & Gourmet Deli ★★★½

| ITALIAN | MODERATE/EXPENSIVE | QUALITY ★★★★½ | VALUE ★★★½ |

246 Via Antonio, east of Las Vegas Boulevard at Sunset Road; South Strip and Environs; ☎ 702-222-2400; panevinolasvegas.com

Customers Visitors, locals. **Reservations** Recommended. **When to go** Anytime. **Entrée range** $14–$43. **Payment** All major credit cards. **Service rating** ★★★★½. **Friendliness rating** ★★★★½. **Parking** Large lot. **Bar** Full service. **Wine selection** Excellent Italian. **Dress** Business casual. **Disabled access** Yes. **Hours** Monday–Friday, 11 a.m.–3 p.m.; Dinner Monday–Saturday, 5–10 p.m.

SETTING AND ATMOSPHERE Designed by owner Anthony Marnell, Panevino's red travertine walls were custom-quarried in Italy. A spectacular curved glass wall shapes the view of the Las Vegas skyline. Italy's finest artisans contributed their best to this gorgeous restaurant.

HOUSE SPECIALTIES Pastas, breads, and pastries baked daily. Gnocchi al pesto, homemade potato dumplings with fresh pesto sauce and shaved, aged ricotta cheese; risotto porcini, arborio rice slowly cooked with mushrooms, sausage, and cheese; *pollo alla brace,* grilled boneless chicken breast prepared with olive oil, garlic, red pepper, and rosemary and served with roasted potatoes; *filetto di Manzo,* a ten-ounce filet mignon with shallots, corn-mashed potatoes, and porcini-mushroom sauce.

OTHER RECOMMENDATIONS Pear-and-gorgonzola-cheese salad; pappardelle pasta with lamb ragu, tomato, and mushroom sauce.

SUMMARY AND COMMENTS Panevino is located in Marnell's corporate office business complex. There is plenty of signage on Sunset Road, but the entrance is easy to miss, so stay alert. Adjacent to Panevino Ristorante is a delightful gourmet deli featuring homemade soups, sandwiches, salads, and other casual Italian eats. Eat in or take out. Prices are reasonable, the staff is congenial, and this is the prettiest deli outside of Italy.

Pearl ★★★★

| CHINESE | EXPENSIVE | QUALITY ★★★★ | VALUE ★★½ |

MGM Grand, 3799 South Las Vegas Boulevard; South Strip and Environs; ☎ 702-891-7380; mgmgrand.com

Customers Visitors, locals. **Reservations** Recommended. **When to go** Anytime. **Entrée range** $22 and up. **Payment** All major credit cards. **Service rating** ★★★★½. **Friendliness rating** ★★★★½. **Parking** Valet, parking garage. **Bar** Full service. **Wine selection** Very good. **Dress** Business attire, casual chic. **Disabled access** Ramp. **Hours** Sunday–Thursday, 5:30–10 p.m.; Friday and Saturday, 5:30–10:30 p.m.

SETTING AND ATMOSPHERE Sleek and inviting, tall booths offer privacy and a view of the dining room. A private dining area adjacent to the wine cellar is in great demand. Expert lighting and gorgeous appointments.

HOUSE SPECIALTIES The three-course tasting menu is worth it. Pearl's family-style menus for two or more—six or more courses for a fixed price. Spider-prawn dumplings, minced tiger prawns and pine nuts in lettuce petals; deep-fried shiitake mushrooms glazed with spicy black vinegar; live fish and seafood selection; Dungeness crabmeat baked in the shell; Cantonese-style wok-fried filet of venison and asparagus.

OTHER RECOMMENDATIONS The signature Asian bouillabaisse; spiced king crab legs with chili and garlic; the steamed Maine and Australian lobster tasting; Maine lobster fried rice; braised Thai eggplant with chili-plum sauce; star-anise lamb chops with string beans; tableside tea service.

SUMMARY AND COMMENTS Dining at Pearl is relaxing and satisfying. It's elegant and inviting.

Picasso ★★★★½

| FRENCH/SPANISH | VERY EXPENSIVE | QUALITY ★★★★ | VALUE ★★½ |

Bellagio, 3600 South Las Vegas Boulevard; Mid-Strip and Environs;
☎ **702-693-7223; bellagio.com**

Customers Visitors, locals. Reservations A must. When to go Anytime you can get a reservation. Entrée range Prix fixe only, $90 or $100. Payment All major credit cards. Service rating ★★★★½. Friendliness rating ★★★★½. Parking Valet, self. Bar Full service. Wine selection Excellent. Dress Casually elegant, jackets recommended. Disabled access Elevator. Hours Wednesday–Monday, 6–9:30 p.m.

SETTING AND ATMOSPHERE Arguably the most beautiful dining room in Las Vegas, with original Picasso artworks adorning the walls. The flower displays throughout the restaurant are exquisite. A wall of windows gives most tables a full view of the dancing fountains.

HOUSE SPECIALTIES Selections on both the five-course degustation and the four-course prix-fixe menus change regularly according to the whim of the chef. The warm lobster salad, sauteed foie gras, sauteed medallions of swordfish, and aged lamb roti with truffle crust appear often. The roasted pigeon (squab) is outstanding. Chef Julian Serrano, formerly of Masa's in San Francisco, sometimes offers a sensational *amuse-bouche,* a tiny potato pancake topped with crème fraîche and osetra caviar.

SUMMARY AND COMMENTS This exceptional restaurant is grand yet unpretentious. Allow enough time to enjoy the experience. After dinner have a drink on the terrace. Where else but in Las Vegas can you have a view of Lake Como as well as one of the Eiffel Tower?

Piero's ★★★★

| ITALIAN | EXPENSIVE | QUALITY ★★★★ | VALUE ★★½ |

355 Convention Center Drive; North Strip and Environs;
☎ **702-369-2305; pieroscuisine.com**

Customers Visitors, locals, conventioneers. Reservations Required. When to go Anytime. Entrée range $26–$47 (higher for lobster). Payment All major credit cards. Service rating ★★★★. Friendliness rating ★★★★. Parking Valet, lot. Bar

Full service. **Wine selection** Excellent. **Dress** Business casual. **Disabled access** Yes (ground floor). **Hours** Daily, 5:30–10 p.m.

SETTING AND ATMOSPHERE Many softly lit booths and alcoves for guests desiring privacy. There are two private dining rooms for 12–20 people, a banquet room that can accommodate up to 250, a piano bar, and a much larger kitchen.

HOUSE SPECIALTIES Osso buco Piero; scaloppine Parmigiana; *verde e legumi inbrodo* (soup of fresh vegetables and pasta in broth); whole roasted kosher chicken as good or better than Mama used to make; any dish with Provimi veal; Italian pastas with French-influenced sauces; 25-ounce New York steak; stone crab claws or cakes of Maryland blue crab, in season.

SUMMARY AND COMMENTS Celebrities and sports figures always make their way to Piero's, as do Las Vegas power brokers, who consistently dine here. Dom Perignon, Cristal, Grand Cordon Champagnes and pricey bottles of Montrachet are the norm at Piero's.

Ping Pang Pong ★★★½

| CHINESE | MODERATE | QUALITY ★★★½ | VALUE ★★★½ |

Gold Coast Casino, 4000 West Flamingo Road; West of Strip;
☎ **702-367-7111; goldcoastcasino.com**

Customers Locals. **Reservations** Unnecessary. **When to go** Avoid Saturday and Sunday lunch hour. **Entrée range** $9–$29. **Payment** All major credit cards. **Service rating** ★★★. **Friendliness rating** ★★★★. **Bar** Beer and wine. **Wine selection** Limited. **Dress** Casual. **Disabled access** Yes. **Hours** Lunch, featuring dim sum: daily, 10 a.m.–3 p.m.; dinner: daily, 5 p.m.–3 a.m.

SETTING AND ATMOSPHERE A roomy space decorated with Chinese red and gold banners and tables fronting slot machines on the casino floor. Servers hawk their wares from rolling carts that they push through the dining room, just as they do in Hong Kong or Canton, China.

HOUSE SPECIALTIES Dim sum (literally 'touch the heart' in Cantonese) are sweet and savory pastries, meats, and vegetable dishes that are consumed with tea, generally slowly, so Chinese people can socialize over them. Just a few to try are Chiu Chow Fun Gor, a type of dumpling, a shark's fin soup dumpling, and crispy shrimp rolls.

OTHER RECOMMENDATIONS Night market fried rice, a huge platter of spicy rice mixed with beef, onions, tomatoes, and hot chilies, will make you rethink the chicken fried rice you take from the supermarket Panda Express. There are also wonderful soups here, like hot and sour, or a very Chinese West Lake beef soup.

SUMMARY AND COMMENTS Ping Pang Pong is owned by Karrie and Kevin Wu, who also have the very good Noodle Asia just down the hall. The staff, mostly Chinese speaking, will guide you through the experience. This is the only dim sum parlor in Vegas that can stand up to ones in L.A. or San Francisco.

P.J. Clarke's   ★★★½

| AMERICAN | MODERATE | QUALITY ★★★½ | VALUE ★★★½ |

The Forum Shops at Caesars Palace, 3500 South Las Vegas Boulevard; Mid-Strip and Environs; ☎ **702-434-7900; pjclarkes.com**

Customers Visitors, locals. **Reservations** Recommended. **When to go** Anytime. **Entrée range** $13–$36. **Payment** All major credit cards. **Service rating** ★★★½. **Friendliness rating** ★★★★. **Parking** Lot. **Bar** Full service. **Wine selection** Very Good. **Dress** Casual. **Disabled access** Yes. **Hours** Daily, 11:30 a.m.–11 p.m.

SETTING AND ATMOSPHERE P.J. Clarke's Vegas is a careful re-creation of the legendary New York City watering hole–restaurant, with framed, black-and-white shots of turn-of-the-century New York City and Deco stylings.

HOUSE SPECIALTIES Iconic chef Larry Forgione consulted on the menu here, which includes a terrific New England lobster roll, a rich chicken pot pie, and one of the best burgers on the Strip.

OTHER RECOMMENDATIONS Forgione has sourced Meyer Ranch organic beef from a Montana ranch, and the steaks are first-rate. You wouldn't come to a place like this expecting desserts, but both the apple cobbler and bread pudding rival any in the city.

SUMMARY AND COMMENTS This is both a great place to drink and eat, but it's relatively undiscovered because of a hard-to-spot location behind a fountain that separates it from the better-known Joe's Stone Crab, a few doors away.

Prime   ★★★★

| STEAK | EXPENSIVE | QUALITY ★★★★½ | VALUE ★★½ |

Bellagio, 3600 South Las Vegas Boulevard; Mid-Strip and Environs; ☎ **702-693-7223; bellagio.com**

Customers Visitors, locals. **Reservations** Requested. **When to go** Avoid convention times. **Entrée range** $25–$48. **Payment** All major credit cards. **Service rating** ★★★★½. **Friendliness rating** ★★★★½. **Parking** Valet, self. **Bar** Full service. **Wine selection** Excellent. **Dress** Casually elegant, jackets preferred. **Disabled access** Elevator. **Hours** Daily, 5:30–10 p.m.

SETTING AND ATMOSPHERE Dazzling powder-blue and chocolate carpets and wall hangings in a setting seldom seen for a steak house—it's gorgeous. In keeping with Bellagio's fine-arts policy, there's plenty of original art to view here. Have a drink at the elegant bar and take it all in.

HOUSE SPECIALTIES Prime, aged steaks and seafood; lamb chops in balsamic syrup; filet mignon with tomatoes; veal chop in pineapple chutney. A choice of a variety of sauces and excellent side dishes.

SUMMARY AND COMMENTS Prime is on the lower level of the shopping corridor beside Picasso, with which an outdoor patio is shared. Both restaurants get their share of lookers, but the staff keeps them from disturbing diners. Service here rarely misses a beat.

Raku ★★★★

| JAPANESE | MODERATE | QUALITY ★★★★ | VALUE ★★★★ |

5030 Spring Mountain Road; West of Strip; ☎ 702-367-3511; raku-grill.com

Customers Visitors, locals. **Reservations** Recommended. **When to go** Anytime. **Entrée range** $15–$30. **Payment** All major credit cards. **Service rating** ★★★★. **Friendliness rating** ★★★★. **Parking** Lot. **Bar** Full service. **Wine selection** Fair. **Dress** Casual. **Disabled access** Yes. **Hours** Monday–Saturday, 6 p.m.–3 a.m.

SETTING AND ATMOSPHERE This newly enlarged space now seats 60 people, including the bar.

HOUSE SPECIALTIES Don't expect sushi at this Japanese restaurant; it is a sakaba, or sake bar, where small, salty dishes meant to encourage thirst are served. A Japanese lump charcoal–fired grill is the source of the wonderfully smoky flavor imparted to meats such as pork cheek, Kobe tendon, bacon-wrapped enoki mushrooms, and whole fish. House-made tofu is silky and creamy, especially when paired with fresh tomato and seaweed, a sort of Japanese take on a caprese salad.

OTHER RECOMMENDATIONS Check a nightly specials board for seasonal additions. Traditional Japanese flavors and techniques are the ticket. Also, this is one of the few Asian restaurants that does desserts, including a creative green-tea crème brûlée and a surprisingly wonderful—though ubiquitous—molten chocolate cake.

SUMMARY AND COMMENTS Raku is an off-Strip standout, garnering the attention of critics, locals, and, most importantly, the chefs in town. Chef Mitsuo Endo finds himself cooking for some of the biggest culinary names in Vegas after they get off work, so the restaurant is open late-night. A true Japanese *izakaya* dining experience, round after round of Raku's grilled, small plates go well with beer, wine, or sake.

Rao's ★★★

| ITALIAN | EXPENSIVE | QUALITY ★★★★ | VALUE ★★ |

Caesars Palace, 3570 South Las Vegas Boulevard; Mid-Strip and Environs; ☎ 877-346-4642 (reservations); caesars.com

Customers Visitors, locals. **Reservations** Suggested. **When to go** Anytime. **Entrée range** $25–$40. **Payment** All major credit cards. **Service rating** ★★★★. **Friendliness rating** ★★★★★. **Parking** Valet, garage. **Bar** Full service. **Wine selection** Very good. **Dress** Casual. **Disabled access** Yes. **Hours** Daily, 5–11 p.m.

SETTING AND ATMOSPHERE Modeled after the original, tiny restaurant in New York, the Las Vegas outpost of Rao's is nearly three times the size, but you can still feel the heart of this family-owned business. Christmas lights and decorations hang year-round, and the walls are adorned with framed photographs of Rao's customers old and new. Dark woods along the bar and dining room evoke a classic, traditional feel. Don't be surprised if you hear Italian-American classics such as "Volare" interspersed with covers by Michael Buble from the jukebox; this restaurant is all about intermingling old and new traditions.

HOUSE SPECIALTIES Red-sauce Southern Italian classics such as meatballs, gnocchi with Bolognese sauce, and Uncle Vincent's lemon chicken have been on the menu since the original restaurant opened in 1896. You'll also find some fresh seafood dishes and lighter pastas.

SUMMARY AND COMMENTS Rao's is a family-run joint—always has been and always will be. The restaurant in New York is notorious for being the hardest reservation to get, so when they finally opened their spot in Caesars Palace, those in the know rejoiced. Owner and partner Frank Pellegrino Jr. runs the front of the house, and chances are you'll find him there with guests, including the celebrities that frequent Rao's, on any given night. Unfortunately, Bubbles, the legendary host with the gravelly voice and wise-guy demeanor, has shuffled off this mortal coil.

Restaurant Guy Savoy ★★★★★

FRENCH   VERY EXPENSIVE   QUALITY ★★★★★   VALUE ★★★

Caesars Palace, 3570 South Las Vegas Boulevard; Mid-Strip and Environs; ☎ 877-346-4642 (reservations); caesarspalace.com

Customers Visitors, locals. **Reservations** A must. **When to go** Special occasion. **Entrée range** $45–$95. Prix-fixe menus, $98–$290. **Payment** All major credit cards. **Service rating** ★★★★. **Friendliness rating** ★★★. **Parking** Valet, garage. **Bar** Full service. **Wine selection** Excellent. **Dress** Upscale. **Disabled access** Yes. **Hours** Wednesday–Sunday, 5:30–9:30 p.m.

SETTING AND ATMOSPHERE Clean lines and modern sophistication are the theme here. Guy's son, Franck, runs this outpost for his father, so you can be sure that the same elegance and refinement you would expect from the original Paris restaurant is alive and well in Las Vegas.

HOUSE SPECIALTIES The artichoke-and-black-truffle soup is one of Savoy's signature items all the way from his Paris restaurant. Served with toasted mushroom brioche and a little truffle butter, it's one of the most decadent dishes ever to be consumed.

SUMMARY AND COMMENTS To get the full experience without breaking the bank, try either the four-course TGV prix-fixe menu or grab a seat at the Bites and Bubbles Bar, which features some exquisite Champagnes by the glass as well as smaller bites of the menu's greatest hits.

Rosemary's Restaurant ★★★★

AMERICAN   EXPENSIVE   QUALITY ★★★★   VALUE ★★½

8125 West Sahara Avenue, Summerlin; West of Strip; ☎ 702-869-2251; rosemarysrestaurant.com

Customers Visitors, locals. **Reservations** Recommended. **When to go** Anytime. **Entrée range** $32–$48. **Payment** All major credit cards. **Service rating** ★★★★. **Friendliness rating** ★★★★½. **Parking** Large lot. **Bar** Full service. **Wine selection** Very good. **Dress** Upscale casual. **Disabled access** Yes. **Hours** Lunch: Friday, 11:30 a.m.–2:30 p.m.; dinner: daily, 5:30 p.m.–close.

SETTING AND ATMOSPHERE A comfortable bar separates the street side from the attractive dining room. Simple décor spotlights local artwork. A partially open kitchen affords a view of the chefs plying their trade.

HOUSE SPECIALTIES Roasted rack of lamb with black-olive mashed potatoes and arugula; crispy-skin striped bass; grilled prime flat-iron steak.

OTHER RECOMMENDATIONS Salmon tartare; creamy potato-and-sweet-onion soup; wilted spinach salad; brick chicken; seared scallops.

SUMMARY AND COMMENTS Chef-owner Michael Jordan was formerly the executive chef for Emeril's at the MGM Grand. Jordan cooks with wit and style, and he's made his restaurant the most popular off-Strip gourmet dining room in the city.

Sage ★★★★½

| AMERICAN | VERY EXPENSIVE | QUALITY ★★★★½ | VALUE ★★★★ |

Aria at CityCenter, 3730 South Las Vegas Boulevard; Mid-Strip and Environs; ☎ 877-230-2742; arialasvegas.com

Customers Visitors. **Reservations** Essential. **When to go** Anytime. **Entrée range** $20–$50. **Payment** All major credit cards. **Service rating** ★★★★★. **Friendliness rating** ★★★★½. **Parking** Valet, lot. **Bar** Full service; excellent cocktail menu. **Wine selection** Excellent. **Dress** Upscale. **Disabled access** Yes. **Hours** Monday–Saturday, 5–11 p.m.

SETTING AND ATMOSPHERE You enter through an elegant bar. The dining room is dark, clubby, and formal. The room has high ceilings, and appointments, such as fine stemware and table settings, are first-rate.

HOUSE SPECIALTIES Chicago's Shawn McClain (Spring) cooks smart American fare with hints of almost everywhere on the planet. He refers to his cooking as "refined American cuisine," and we are apt to agree. Kusshi Island oysters from Vancouver Island are topped with Tobasco sorbet and aged tequila. Don't miss the foie gras custard brûlée, the chef's signature.

OTHER RECOMMENDATIONS Main courses not to miss include roasted loin of Iberico pork, short ribs braised in Belgian ale, and roast Sonoma chicken with a maitake mushroom persillade. The chef has also added a small but imaginative vegetarian menu. Slow-poached organic farm egg or Bellwether Farm sheep's milk ricotta gnocchi are so good you would swear off meat to eat them.

SUMMARY AND COMMENTS McClain is a great addition to the local dining scene. Other than Bradley Ogden at Caesars Palace, he's the best example of a native American talent who sources the best American products.

Sam Woo Bar-B-Q ★★★

| CHINESE BARBECUE | INEXPENSIVE/MODERATE | QUALITY ★★★ | VALUE ★★★★★ |

Chinatown Mall, 4215 Spring Mountain Road; West of Strip; ☎ 702-368-7628

Customers Asian community, locals, tourists. **Reservations** No. **When to go** Anytime. **Entrée range** $10–$12. **Payment** Cash only. **Service rating** ★★★½. **Friendliness rating** ★★★½. **Parking** Large lot. **Bar** None. **Wine selection** None. **Dress** Anything goes. **Disabled access** Yes (ground floor). **Hours** Monday–Saturday, 10 a.m.–midnight; Sunday, 11 a.m.–11 p.m.

SETTING AND ATMOSPHERE Enter Sam Woo and enjoy the sights of meats and whole ducks hanging from hooks in the glass holding case. To the left is the popular take-out barbecue counter; to the right, a spacious good-sized restaurant. No frills, but pleasant.

HOUSE SPECIALTIES Any of the barbecued foods—roast pork, spare ribs, duck, and chicken; the Sam Woo combination plate is an exceptional value, heaped high with roast and barbecued pork, roast duck, and chicken. Vegetable dishes are outstanding and inexpensive.

SUMMARY AND COMMENTS Very little English is spoken here, but the menu is in English. Service is good but can be brusque when the restaurant is busy. Take it in stride. Sam Woo is one of the best values in town. Watch what other diners are eating for clues to what to order.

Scarpetta ★★★★

ITALIAN	EXPENSIVE	QUALITY ★★★★	VALUE ★★★½

**Cosmopolitan, 3708 South Las Vegas Boulevard;
Mid-Strip and Environs; ☎ 702-698-7000; cosmopolitanlasvegas.com**

Customers Locals, visitors. **Reservations** Essential. **When to go** On special occasions. **Entrée range** $23–$36. **Payment** All major credit cards. **Service rating** ★★★★★. **Friendliness rating** ★★★. **Parking** Valet, lot. **Bar** Full service. **Wine selection** Excellent. **Dress** Elegant. **Disabled access** No. **Hours** Daily, 5:30–11 p.m.

SETTING AND ATMOSPHERE In this elegant establishment diners enter through a long bar area. The dining room features unique yin-yang curving banquettes. Acoustics are intelligent, and the muted colors are relaxing. This is one of the few places at the Cosmo to have a conversation.

HOUSE SPECIALTIES Everyone is curious to try chef Scott Conant's $24 spaghetti, but there are many other dishes not to miss. *Agnolotti del plin* are tiny Piedmontese ravioli with a forcemeat of veal and pork. The red beet and smoked ricotta *casonsei,* little pasta envelopes glazed with poppy seeds, is wonderful.

OTHER RECOMMENDATIONS The real surprise here are main dishes. Most Italian restaurants soar with the starter courses and run out of steam. Entrées here are a strong suit. A black cod with crisp skin on one side and fennel and tomato is a must-try, as is the moist roasted *capretto,* a gamy goat stew. Save room for pastry chef Vita Shanley's desserts.

SUMMARY AND COMMENTS Scarpetta is a mature restaurant owned by a mature chef. This is smart, tasty food that you want to eat. What's more, the service is ministered to by a longtime Strip veteran, GM Antonello Pagnuzzi, and doesn't miss a beat.

SeaBlue ★★★★

SEAFOOD	MODERATE/EXPENSIVE	QUALITY ★★★★	VALUE ★★★½

**MGM Grand, 3799 South Las Vegas Boulevard; South Strip and Environs;
☎ 702-891-3486; mgmgrand.com or michaelmina.net**

Customers Visitors, locals. **Reservations** Suggested weekends. **When to go** Anytime. **Entrée range** $29 and up. **Payment** All major credit cards. **Service rating** ★★★½. **Friendliness rating** ★★★★½. **Parking** Valet, garage. **Bar** Full service. **Wine selection** Very good. **Dress** Upscale casual. **Disabled access** Main entrance. **Hours** Sunday–Thursday, 5:30–10 p.m.; Friday and Saturday, 5:30–10:30 p.m.

SETTING AND ATMOSPHERE A large, circular aquarium filled with glimmering small fish captivates as diners approach SeaBlue, chef-owner Michael Mina's latest concept. A sizable raw bar almost fills one side of the dining room. There is booth seating here, too. SeaBlue puts into play a new Mina concept based on seafood. With cascading water walls and other special effects, SeaBlue's décor is magic.

HOUSE SPECIALTIES Small plates that can be a meal (think tapas). There are three choices in each category, mix and match as you will, marking off what you want on the list provided. Choose up to ten. Create your own salad from a long checklist of ingredients.

OTHER RECOMMENDATIONS Tagines (Moroccan stews cooked in clay pots); no cream or butter is used in any of the dishes (excluding dessert). Apple-pomegranate cider à la mode, almond financier, cookies, ice creams, and fruits are refreshing and delicious.

SUMMARY AND COMMENTS Mina's passion for seafood was aroused when he was part of the team that developed Aqua in San Francisco. Mina is also the managing chef of Michael Mina at Bellagio, SeaBlue and Nobhill Tavern at MGM Grand, StripSteak at Mandalay Bay, and the new American Fish at Aria.

Sen of Japan ★★★★

SUSHI	MODERATE/EXPENSIVE	QUALITY ★★★★	VALUE ★★★½

8480 West Desert Inn Road; West of Strip; ☎ 702-871-7781; senofjapan.com.

Customers Locals. **Reservations** Recommended. **When to go** Anytime. **Entrée range** $7–$48. **Payment** All major cards. **Service rating** ★★★. **Friendliness rating** ★★★. **Parking** Lot. **Bar** Beer, wine, and sake. **Wine selection** Limited. **Dress** Casual. **Disabled access** No. **Hours** Monday–Saturday, 5 p.m.–2 a.m.; Sunday, 5 p.m.–midnight.

SETTING AND ATMOSPHERE A pleasant but generic room located in a mini-mall, the restaurant features a sushi bar and a comfortable dining area.

HOUSE SPECIALTIES Omakase, or chef's choice, is the way to go here. Tell the server what you want to spend, and then let chef Hiro Nakano rock and roll. The salmon skin salad is superb, and the quality of the chef's sushi rice, the ne plus ultra for a Japanese gourmet, is the best around.

OTHER RECOMMENDATIONS It doesn't just have to be sushi here. Tsukune, delicious meatballs of chicken with a soy glaze served on wooden skewers, and shishito, grilled Japanese green pepper, are wonderful, as is the tempura, served with a grated radish dipping sauce.

SUMMARY AND COMMENTS This is the best sushi restaurant in Las Vegas, and prices are about half what they would be in comparable sushi restaurants on or neaar the Strip, such as Nobu at Hard Rock or Yellowtail at Bellagio. If you are on the Westside and crave sushi, this place is a must.

Settebello ★★★½

140 Green Valley Parkway; Henderson; ☎ 702-222-3556; settebello.net

Customers Visitors, locals. **Reservations** Recommended. **When to go** Anytime. **Service rating** ★★★. **Friendliness rating** ★★★. **Entrée range** $8–$15. **Payment** All major credit cards. **Parking** Lot. **Bar** Beer and wine. **Wine selection** Good. **Dress** Casual. **Disabled access** Yes. **Hours** Daily, 11 a.m.–10 p.m.

SETTING AND ATMOSPHERE The restaurant has a decidedly neighborhood feel, but those who have discovered the joys of Settebello's pizza find themselves trekking all the way to Green Valley for a slice of their pie.

HOUSE SPECIALTIES Settebello serves quite possibly the best pizza in Las Vegas, made according to tenets of the Vera Pizza Napoletana, an Italian organization dedicated to the preservation of true Napoli-style pizza. The crust (which takes only about 45–60 seconds to cook in their 950°F beautiful, imported wood-fired oven) is crisp on the bottom from the high heat, yet somewhat soft enough to tear. Toppings, from the simplest tomatoes, mozzarella, and olive oil, are mostly imported, pure ingredients that taste fresh and wholesome.

SUMMARY AND COMMENTS Settebello has a sort of cult following in Las Vegas—those who have been there love it and have followed it faithfully to its new location across from Green Valley Ranch. Owner Brad Otton, who was trained as a pizzaiolo in Italy, oversees the place himself and greets regulars and newcomers on a daily basis.

Sinatra ★★★

Wynn Encore, 3131 South Las Vegas Boulevard; Mid-Strip and Environs; ☎ 702-248-3463; wynnlasvegas.com

Customers Visitors. **Reservations** Suggested. **When to go** Anytime. **Entrée range** $26–$52. **Payment** All major credit cards. **Service rating** ★★★★. **Friendliness rating** ★★★. **Parking** Valet, garage. **Bar** Full service. **Wine selection** Very good. **Dress** Business casual. **Disabled access** Yes. **Hours** Daily, 5:30–10 p.m.

SETTING AND ATMOSPHERE Nothing says Las Vegas quite like Frank Sinatra, and Ol' Blue Eyes finally gets his restaurant at Encore, except the restaurant interior is less Sinatra *Ocean's 11* and more Clooney *Ocean's 11*. The room itself is a blend of modern and antique, with natural hues of brown and green. Five custom-made olive green chandeliers are made of eco-friendly hemp rope and burlap. Fear not, frequent reminders of Sinatra's influence include his Oscar for *From Here to Eternity* and his Grammy for "Strangers in the Night," as well as gold albums and personal letters between him and Rat-Pack pals.

HOUSE SPECIALTIES The menu is a twist on classic Italian dishes, some of which were Sinatra's tried-and-true favorites, and some signature dishes such as *zuppa di fagioli* (made with borlotti beans); agnolotti with

ricotta, herbs, and winter truffles; and osso bucco "My Way," with can-
nelloni risotto and *gremolata*.

SUMMARY AND COMMENTS Michelin-starred chef Theo Schoenegger portrays
his Italian roots in creative, modern ways for this menu. To be fair, we'd
eat his food even if it didn't have an icon's name next to it.

Spago ★★★½

AMERICAN	MODERATE/EXPENSIVE	QUALITY ★★★★½	VALUE ★★½

**The Forum Shops at Caesars Palace; 3500 South Las Vegas Boulevard;
Mid-Strip and Environs; ☎ 702-369-6300; wolfgangpuck.com**

Customers Visitors, locals. **Reservations** Recommended for dinner. **When to go**
Anytime except during busy conventions. **Entrée range** $18–$36. **Payment** All
major credit cards. **Service rating** ★★★½. **Friendliness rating** ★★★★½. **Parking**
Garage, valet. **Bar** Full service. **Wine selection** Excellent. **Dress** Informal, casual.
Disabled access Yes. **Hours** Café and bar: Sunday–Thursday, 11:30 a.m.–11 p.m.;
Friday and Saturday, 11:30 a.m.–midnight; restaurant, daily, 5:30–10 p.m.

SETTING AND ATMOSPHERE There are two separate dining rooms. The casual
café offers a bird's-eye view of The Forum Shops from the comfort of a
European-style sidewalk setting. The restaurant inside is an eclectic mix
of modern art, wrought iron, and contemporary tables, chairs, and
booths. Each Sunday in the café from about 2:30–6:30 p.m., a jazz band
entertains. A private banquet room is available for parties of up to 100.
A small private room within the restaurant can seat up to 20.

HOUSE SPECIALTIES *Café:* Wolfgang Puck's signature pizzas; imaginative sandwiches; salads; pastas; and frequently, a super-tasty meat loaf with
port-wine sauce, grilled onions, and garlic-potato puree. *Restaurant:*
exquisite appetizers; pastas; veal wiener schnitzel with potato salad and
lemon-caper sauce; yellowfin tuna with jasmine rice, baby bok choy, and
shiitakes; and striped bass with artichoke ravioli and garlic nage. Menus in
the café and restaurant change daily. Signature dishes always available.

SUMMARY AND COMMENTS Recently refurbished and updated, Spago has a
new look. The café has been enlarged, and the bar is a busy centerpiece.
Locals, who've always considered Spago a favorite, now have their
home parties catered by the restaurant. Owner Wolfgang Puck surrounds himself with the best staff, the best ingredients, the best of
everything. One caveat—on very busy nights the dining room noise level
can make conversation difficult. But the people-watching is terrific.

The Steak House ★★★½

STEAK	EXPENSIVE	QUALITY ★★★½	VALUE ★★★½

**Circus Circus, 2880 South Las Vegas Boulevard; North Strip and Environs;
☎ 702-794-3767; circuscircus.com**

Customers Visitors, locals. **Reservations** Required. **When to go** Anytime.
Entrée range $32–$49 (add lobster, $55 or $75). **Payment** All major credit
cards. **Service rating** ★★★½. **Friendliness rating** ★★★½. **Parking** Garage, lot,
valet. **Bar** Full service. **Wine selection** Good. **Dress** Informal. **Disabled access**
Ramps. **Hours** Sunday–Friday, 5–10 p.m.; Saturday, 5–11 p.m.

SETTING AND ATMOSPHERE Wood-paneled rooms. The small dining room is decorated like a manor-house library. A mesquite-fired broiler in the center of the main room creates a cozy atmosphere. The glass refrigerator case displays more than 3,000 pounds of aging meat.

HOUSE SPECIALTIES Thick steaks; black-bean soup; giant baked potato; shrimp, crab, and lobster cocktails; Caesar salad; grilled chicken.

SUMMARY AND COMMENTS Consistently high quality and service. Don't be fooled by the children running around the lobby. Inside The Steak House, the atmosphere is adult, and the food is wonderful.

T&T Tacos & Tequila ★★

MEXICAN	MODERATE	QUALITY ★★★★	VALUE ★★

Luxor, 3900 South Las Vegas Boulevard; South Strip and Environs; ☎ 702-262-5225; luxor.com

Customers Visitors. **Reservations** Not required. **When to go** Anytime. **Entrée range** $13–$25. **Payment** All major credit cards. **Service rating** ★★★. **Friendliness rating** ★★★★. **Parking** Garage, valet. **Bar** Full service. **Wine selection** Good. **Dress** Casual. **Disabled access** Yes. **Hours** Daily, 11 a.m.–11 p.m.; Sunday brunch, 11 a.m.–3 p.m. and dinner 3–11 p.m.

SETTING AND ATMOSPHERE The sounds of rock and roll and modern Mexican artwork are kind of a disparity from the still-Egyptian interior of the Luxor, but Tacos & Tequila is part of the move toward rebranding the pyramid-shaped hotel.

HOUSE SPECIALTIES Mexican street food–inspired tacos are fresh and authentic, made with high-quality ingredients such as flavorful carne asada. Our favorite version is the *Alambre* (grilled skirt steak served with bacon, Oaxaca cheese, and poblano chilies). From the grill, check out the *pollo Sabana* (chicken breast pounded thin with sautéed onions and chilies).

OTHER RECOMMENDATIONS Tequilas and margaritas are a must from the creative cocktail list. Specialty margaritas are made from top-shelf tequilas, but if you want to go straight to the source, their Tequila Temptresses will happily guide you through the best of the best.

SUMMARY AND COMMENTS Good Mexican food in Las Vegas is hard to come by, especially on the Strip. T&T offers a fun, sexy experience while still remaining true to authentic Mexican flavors and cuisine.

Table 34 ★★★½

CONTEMPORARY AMERICAN	MODERATE	QUALITY ★★★½	VALUE ★★★½

600 East Warm Springs Road; Southeast Las Vegas; ☎ 702-263-0034

Customers Locals, visitors. **Reservations** Suggested on weekends. **When to go** Anytime. **Entrée range** $14–$31. **Payment** All major credit cards. **Service rating** ★★★★. **Friendliness rating** ★★★★. **Parking** Large lot. **Bar** Full service. **Wine selection** Good; many wines by the glass. **Dress** Casual. **Disabled access** Ground floor. **Hours** Monday, 11 a.m.–3 p.m.; Tuesday–Friday, 11 a.m.–3 p.m. and 5 p.m.–close; Saturday, 5 p.m.–close; happy hour, Tuesday–Friday, 4–6 p.m.

SETTING AND ATMOSPHERE A hip, appealing eatery with a freestanding bar and brilliant use of colors.

HOUSE SPECIALTIES Menu changes seasonally, but favorites such as chef Wes Kendrick's soups always remain. The apple–butternut squash (lunch only) is a joy, as is the cream of tomato with tarragon. Try house-smoked salmon on a crisp potato galette (pancake); grilled Maine sea scallops with braised greens and Dijon-barbecue sauce; or gratinéed macaroni and cheese with smoked ham and English peas. The all-beef meat loaf with mashed potatoes and onion gravy is like a taste of home.

OTHER RECOMMENDATIONS Grilled rack of pork with chipotle potatoes, asparagus, and hard-cider glaze; wild mushroom pizza with fresh herbs; the signature Key Lime pie. Note that menus change frequently; dishes listed here may not always be available.

SUMMARY AND COMMENTS Reasonable prices for fine bistro-style food.

Todd English P.U.B. (Public Urban Bar) ★★★½

ENGLISH/AMERICAN   MODERATE/EXPENSIVE   QUALITY ★★★½   VALUE ★★★★

Crystals at CityCenter, 3720 South Las Vegas Boulevard; Mid-Strip and Environs; ☎ 702-489-8080; toddenglishpub.com

Customers Visitors, locals. **Reservations** Not required. **When to go** Avoid large conventions. **Entrée range** $12–$48. **Payment** All major credit cards. **Service rating** ★★★½. **Friendliness rating** ★★★★½. **Parking** Valet, garage. **Bar** Full service. **Wine selection** Good. **Dress** Casual. **Disabled access** Yes. **Hours** Daily, 11 a.m.–2 a.m.

SETTING AND ATMOSPHERE The P.U.B. is a cavernous space on the outskirts of the mall facing Beso, Eva Longoria's restaurant. The décor is traditional English pub, complete with dartboards, drinking games, a high ceiling, and an open kitchen that features a huge rotisserie for carved meats.

HOUSE SPECIALTIES The Carvery features meats carved by the chefs, a wide variety of fare ranging from brisket and Long Island duck to roasted turkey breast and Greek-style leg of lamb. There are a number of sauces and breads to choose from as well.

OTHER RECOMMENDATIONS It would be a shame for anyone who likes beer to come here and not experience the super selection of microbrews, hand-crafted ales, and imported beers from the major European countries. There are dozens of beers on draft. In addition, savory pub fare such as Welsh rarebit and shepherd's pie are also done well here.

SUMMARY AND COMMENTS This restaurant is a departure for celebrity chef Todd English, and it strikes almost everyone as a good idea. Veteran operator Kelley Jones is a partner, so the place is run like a tight ship. Things get a little rowdy during major sports weekends, though.

Todd's Unique Dining ★★★★

STEAK AND SEAFOOD   MODERATE   QUALITY ★★★★   VALUE ★★★★

4350 East Sunset Road; Henderson; ☎ 702-259-8633; toddsunique.com

Customers Locals. **Reservations** Recommended. **When to go** Anytime. **Entrée range** $25–$38. **Payment** All major credit cards. **Service rating** ★★★. **Friendliness rating** ★★★★. **Parking** Lot. **Bar** Full service. **Wine selection** Small. **Dress** Casual. **Disabled access** Yes. **Hours** Monday–Saturday, 4:30–9:30 p.m. (last seating).

SETTING AND ATMOSPHERE A small storefront located among big-chain restaurants in Henderson, Todd's Unique Dining is homey, casual, and comfortable. A favorite with Green Valley residents, Chef Todd Clore, a veteran of corporate Strip restaurants, makes his mark with this neighborhood restaurant.

HOUSE SPECIALTIES Mainly a seafood restaurant, Todd's Unique definitely has some Asian influence. Standards like the goat-cheese wontons are a surprising bite of pungent goat cheese balanced with an herby raspberry-and-basil sauce. Seared ahi tuna with wasabi and mashed leeks reveals a touch of East meets West, as does the Kobe skirt steak finished with black bean–and-chili sauce.

SUMMARY AND COMMENTS Todd Clore has definitely elevated neighborhood dining for Green Valley, garnering local regulars night after night. It's solid, high-end cuisine without the prices, or pretentions, that plague many Strip restaurants.

Top of the World ★★★★

AMERICAN	EXPENSIVE	QUALITY ★★★★	VALUE ★★★½

Stratosphere Tower, 2000 South Las Vegas Boulevard; North Strip and Environs; ☎ 702-380-7711; stratospherehotel.com

Customers Visitors, locals. Reservations Required. When to go Anytime. Entrée range $40–market. Payment All major credit cards. Service rating ★★★★½. Friendliness rating ★★★½. Parking Valet, garage, lot. Bar Full service. Wine selection Excellent. Dress Upscale casual. Disabled access Elevator. Hours Lunch: daily, 11 a.m.–4:30 p.m.; dinner: Sunday–Thursday, 4:30–10:30 p.m.; Friday and Saturday, 4:30–11 p.m.

SETTING AND ATMOSPHERE Top of the World offers one of the most beautiful views of the city. The restaurant revolves as you dine, giving a panoramic spectacle of the surrounding mountains. One complete revolution takes an hour and 20 minutes. The dining room is elegant and sophisticated.

HOUSE SPECIALTIES Shrimp cocktail, beef tasting, Tater Tots with foie gras.

OTHER RECOMMENDATIONS Fresh Atlantic salmon encrusted with fresh sage and prosciutto di parma; lobster ravioli; the towering vacherin dessert; tiramisu or panna cotta.

SUMMARY AND COMMENTS The food has significantly improved here but still takes a back seat to the view. You must check in at a podium, go through security, and ride an elevator to the top. Arrive before sunset for an unforgettably romantic experience. $30 per person minimum charge.

Twist by Pierre Gagnaire ★★★★★

FRENCH	VERY EXPENSIVE	QUALITY ★★★★★	VALUE ★★★★★

Mandarin Oriental Hotel, 3752 South Las Vegas Boulevard; Mid-Strip and Environs; ☎ 702-590-8888; mandarinoriental.com

Customers Visitors. Reservations Essential. When to go Dinner. Entrée range $32–$68. Payment All major credit cards. Service rating ★★★★★. Friendliness rating ★★★★★. Parking Valet. Bar Full service. Wine selection Reasonably priced

list of upscale wines. **Dress** Upscale. **Disabled access** Yes. **Hours** Tuesday–
Saturday, 5:30–10 p.m.

SETTING AND ATMOSPHERE On the 23rd and top floor of the chi-chi Mandarin
Oriental Hotel; tables look out onto the Strip. The modern dining room
is tastefully elegant and decorated with glass globes and decorative art.

HOUSE SPECIALTIES Colorful, creative canapés, such as gelee made from Guinness, and the swank-tasting menus are a calling card. The food of Pierre
Gagnaire is among the most creative of the world's chefs. It's food you not
only haven't seen before, it's food that most have never even imagined.

OTHER RECOMMENDATIONS Langoustine five ways is one signature dish. The
chef also does tricks with fish and game, incorporating flavors you don't
expect, such as lavender or licorice, in combinations that work like
magic. Save room for the wonderful desserts by Keiko.

SUMMARY AND COMMENTS It's a feather in the proverbial cap to get this celebrated Parisian to open here, ably assisted by chef Pascal Sanchez, who
ran his restaurant in London. If you don't wish to order the tasting menus,
just order an entrée à la carte and still experience all the bells and whistles,
such as canapés and petit fours, without spending a fortune in here.

Valentino ★★★★

ITALIAN	EXPENSIVE	QUALITY ★★★★	VALUE ★★★

**Venetian, 3355 South Las Vegas Boulevard; Mid-Strip and Environs;
☎ 702-414-3000; venetian.com**

Customers Visitors, locals. **Reservations** Suggested. **When to go** Anytime.
Entrée range $18–$38. **Payment** All major credit cards. **Service rating** ★★★★.
Friendliness rating ★★★. **Parking** Valet, garage. **Bar** Full service. **Wine selection**
Good. **Dress** Upscale in dining room; more casual in grill room. **Disabled access**
Yes. **Hours** Dining room: daily, 5:30–10 p.m.; grill: daily, 11:30 a.m.–11 p.m.

SETTING AND ATMOSPHERE Valentino's opulent dining room invokes the
burnt oranges and reds of Tuscany, with six private dining rooms ideal
for romantic evenings or intimate gatherings.

HOUSE SPECIALTIES The team behind Valentino all originate from Italy, so
authenticity of flavor is paramount to their dishes. Try signature items
such as scallop saltimbocca with potato rosti and Maine lobster fra Diavolo with fresh black taglioni pasta sautéed with lobster and tomatoes.

OTHER RECOMMENDATIONS With a collection of more than 2,400 wines from
wineries in Italy, France, and California, Valentino has earned itself the
reputation of being one of the foremost spots on the Strip to enjoy amazing wines, as well as a Grand Spectator Award annually since 2002.

SUMMARY AND COMMENTS An unsung hero in Las Vegas, consistently delivering fantastic upscale food. Visitors are beginning to catch on to the
simplicity of Valentino's ambiance and cuisine, while locals make it a
definite special-occasion destination.

Wolfgang Puck Bar & Grill ★★★★

AMERICAN	MODERATE/EXPENSIVE	QUALITY ★★★★	VALUE ★★★★½

**MGM Grand, 3799 South Las Vegas Boulevard; South Strip and Environs;
☎ 702-891-3000; wolfgangpuck.com or mgmgrand.com**

Customers Visitors, locals. Reservations Recommended. When to go Anytime. Entrée range $15–$40. Payment All major credit cards. Service rating ★★★★½. Friendliness rating ★★★★½. Parking Valet, garage. Bar Full service. Wine selection Very good. Dress Casual. Disabled access Ground floor. Hours Monday–Thursday, 11:30 a.m.–10 p.m.; Friday–Sunday, 11:30 a.m.–11 p.m.; late-night dining nightly, 11 p.m.–6 a.m.

SETTING AND ATMOSPHERE A celebration of America, this restaurant takes us back to early California and its laid-back style. Relaxed and beautiful décor with a flavor reminiscent of Puck's first restaurant. It's lovely.

HOUSE SPECIALTIES The boneless rib eye, a succulent pleaser served with crushed red potatoes and onion rings; pizzas with creative toppings.

OTHER RECOMMENDATIONS Starters and salads that could be a light meal; calf's liver with leeks and pancetta; fish of the day; ricotta gnocchi with sweet fennel sausage; pork chop with goat-cheese polenta and tomato sauce.

SUMMARY AND COMMENTS Menus change all the time, but the favorites always remain. Puck's is a hipster's hangout.

Wolfgang Puck Pizzeria & Cucina ★★★½

AMERICAN	EXPENSIVE	QUALITY ★★★★	VALUE ★★★½

Crystals at CityCenter, 3720 South Las Vegas Boulevard; Mid-Strip and Environs; ☎ 702-238-1000; wolfgangpuck.com

Customers Visitors, locals. Reservations Suggested. When to go Anytime. Entrée range $21–$46. Payment All major credit cards. Service rating ★★★★. Friendliness rating ★★★★. Parking Valet. Bar Full service. Wine selection. Very good. Dress Casual. Disabled access Yes. Hours Sunday–Thursday, 11:30 a.m.–10 p.m.; Friday and Saturday, 11:30 a.m.–11 p.m.

SETTING AND ATMOSPHERE Puck's newest concept replaced Brasserie Puck in early June 2010. This beautiful dining room sits on the mezzanine level of Crystals, which is also home to Puck's new coffee-shop concept, The Pods, one level below. The best tables overlook upscale shops such as Tom Ford and give diners a chance to watch the people shopping below.

HOUSE SPECIALTIES The menu is a compilation of Italian favorites. There is a delicious board of salumi (Italian cold cuts) and terrific fried calamari. Pizzas, such as the one with Italian sausage and rapini, come on thin crusts from a wood oven. Prime beef carpaccio, a fairly classic version of the dish, comes topped with celery hearts and shaved Parmesan.

OTHER RECOMMENDATIONS Main courses are usually a letdown at casual Italian restaurants, but here they come as a major surprise. The kitchen turns out a delicious osso buco and one of the best chicken piccatas in the city, slathered with a lemon-caper butter. Pastas are excellent as well, especially ricotta gnocchi with a sausage Bolognese.

SUMMARY AND COMMENTS Corporate Chefs Lee Hefter and David Robins are masters, and the man in the kitchen, Dustin Lewandowski, who moved over from the Wolfgang Puck Bar & Grill in the MGM Grand, is talented. The original concept here, Brasserie Puck, didn't take. So Puck's management team has moved on, and now business is brisk.

PART FIVE

SHOPPING *and* SEEING *the* SIGHTS

SHOPPING *in* LAS VEGAS

THE MOST INTERESTING AND DIVERSIFIED specialty shopping in Las Vegas is centered on the Strip at the **Fashion Show Mall** (☎ 702-369-0704; thefashionshow.com), **The Forum and Appian Way Shops at Caesars Palace** (☎ 702-893-4800; caesarspalace.com), and the **Grand Canal Shoppes at the Venetian** (☎ 702-414-4500; thegrandcanalshoppes.com). These three venues, within walking distance of each other, collectively offer the

unofficial **TIP**
The Fashion Show Mall is the place to go for that new sport coat, tie, blouse, or skirt at a reasonable price.

most unusual, and arguably the most concentrated, aggregation of upscale retailers in the United States. It should be noted that The Forum Shops and the Grand Canal Shoppes are not your average shopping centers. In fact, both are attractions in their own right and should be on your must-see list even if you don't like to shop. Both feature designer shops, exclusive boutiques, and specialty retailers. Fashion Show Mall, by comparison, is plain white bread, with no discernible theme but a great lineup of big-name department stores.

At the intersection of Las Vegas Boulevard and Spring Mountain Road, the Fashion Show Mall is anchored by **Saks Fifth Avenue, Neiman Marcus, Macy's, Nordstrom, Bloomingdale's Home, Ann Taylor,** and **Dillard's,** and contains more than 100 specialty shops, including three art galleries. There is no theme here—no Roman columns or canals with gondolas. At the Fashion Show Mall, shopping is king. And although there is no shortage of boutiques or designer shops, the presence of the big department stores defines the experience for most customers. The selection is immense, and most of the retailers are familiar and well known. To underscore its name, the mall stages free fashion shows most weekend afternoons.

The Forum Shops is a *très chic (et très cher)* shopping complex situated between Caesars Palace and the Mirage. Connected to the

Las Vegas Strip Shopping and Attractions

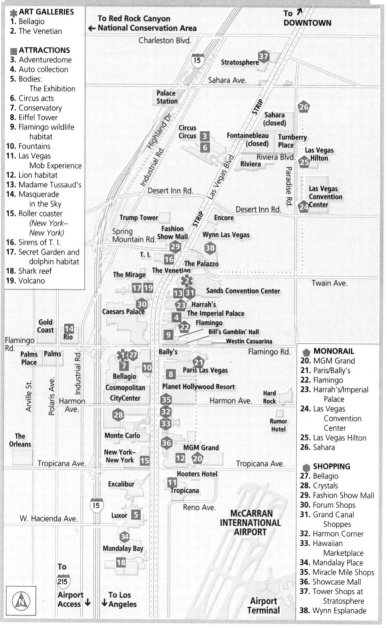

❋ ART GALLERIES
1. Bellagio
2. The Venetian

■ ATTRACTIONS
3. Adventuredome
4. Auto collection
5. Bodies:
   The Exhibition
6. Circus acts
7. Conservatory
8. Eiffel Tower
9. Flamingo wildlife
   habitat
10. Fountains
11. Las Vegas
    Mob Experience
12. Lion habitat
13. Madame Tussaud's
14. Masquerade
    in the Sky
15. Roller coaster
    *(New York–
    New York)*
16. Sirens of T. I.
17. Secret Garden and
    dolphin habitat
18. Shark reef
19. Volcano

● MONORAIL
20. MGM Grand
21. Paris/Bally's
22. Flamingo
23. Harrah's/Imperial
    Palace
24. Las Vegas
    Convention
    Center
25. Las Vegas Hilton
26. Sahara

● SHOPPING
27. Bellagio
28. Crystals
29. Fashion Show Mall
30. Forum Shops
31. Grand Canal
    Shoppes
32. Harmon Corner
33. Hawaiian
    Marketplace
34. Mandalay Place
35. Miracle Mile Shops
36. Showcase Mall
37. Tower Shops at
    Stratosphere
38. Wynn Esplanade

To Red Rock Canyon
← National Conservation Area

To ↗
DOWNTOWN

Charleston Blvd.

Stratosphere

Sahara Ave.

Palace
Station

Sahara
(closed)

Circus
Circus

Fontainebleau
(closed)

Turnberry
Place

Las Vegas
Hilton

Riviera Blvd.

Riviera

Desert Inn Rd.

Las Vegas
Convention
Center

Desert Inn Rd.

Trump Tower

Encore

Fashion
Show Mall

Wynn Las Vegas

Spring
Mountain Rd.

Twain Ave.

T. I.

The Venetian

The Palazzo

The Mirage

Sands Convention Center

Harrah's

Caesars Palace

The Imperial Palace

Flamingo

Bill's Gamblin' Hall

Westin Casuarina

Gold
Coast

Rio

Flamingo
Rd.

Bally's

Flamingo Rd.

Palms
Place

Palms

Paris Las Vegas

Bellagio

Planet Hollywood Resort

Cosmopolitan
CityCenter

Hard
Rock

Harmon
Ave.

Harmon Ave.

The
Orleans

Rumor
Hotel

Monte Carlo

Tropicana Ave.

New York–
New York

MGM Grand

Tropicana Ave.

Hooters Hotel

Excalibur

Tropicana

Reno Ave.

W. Hacienda Ave.

Luxor

**McCARRAN
INTERNATIONAL
AIRPORT**

Mandalay Bay

To
215

Airport
Access ↓

To Los
↓ Angeles

**Airport
Terminal**

Forum Casino in Caesars Palace, The Forum Shops offers a Roman market–themed shopping environment. Executed on a scale that is extraordinary even for Caesars, The Forum Shops replicates the grandeur of Rome at the height of its glory. More than 160 shops and restaurants line an ancient Roman street punctuated by plazas and fountains. Dozens of retailers and eateries populate the three-story, 175,000-square-foot Appian Way expansion. Though indoors, clouds, sky, and celestial bodies are projected on the vaulted ceilings to simulate the actual time of day outside. Statuary in The Forum is magnificent; some is even animatronic. New shops include the **Max Brenner** chocolate shop; clothing retailer **H&M; UGG,** featuring leathers, suedes, and sheepskin; luxury street apparel by **Christian Audigier; True Religion** for denim; and makeup retailer **Inglot.** New to the Forum Shops restaurant lineup is New York institution **P.J. Clarke's,** a saloon known for its signature bacon cheeseburger and home fries.

The Grand Canal Shoppes are similar to The Forum Shops in terms of the realistic theming, only this time the setting is the modern-day canals of Venice. Sixty-four shops, boutiques, restaurants, and cafes are arrayed along a quarter-mile-long Venetian street flanking a canal. A 70-foot ceiling (more than six stories high) with simulated sky enhances the openness and provides perspective. Meanwhile, gondolas navigating the canal add a heightened sense of commerce and activity. The centerpiece of the Grand Canal Shoppes is a replica of St. Mark's Square, without the pigeons.

The Grand Canal Shoppes connect to **The Shoppes at the Palazzo** (☎ 702-414-4525; **theshoppesatthepalazzo.com**), located at the Venetian's sister hotel. Anchored by **Barneys New York,** the two-story shopping arcade offers more than three dozen upscale retailers and restaurants. Unlike the Grand Canal Shoppes, The Shoppes at the Palazzo is essentially unthemed, or expressed differently, check your gondola at the door.

The new CityCenter development situated between Bellagio and the Monte Carlo adds another mega-retail venue, **Crystals** (☎ 702-590-9299 and 866-754-2489; **crystalsatcitycenter.com**), to the Strip-shopping lineup. Because Crystals is located more or less across the street from the Miracle Mile Shops (described below), the two together offer the second-largest concentration of retailers on the Strip.

Crystals, a 500,000-square-foot high-end retail and entertainment center, is tightly wedged between Veer condominium towers and The Harmon boutique hotel (opening unknown). Conceived as an urban city park, exterior landscapes have moved inside. Tall deciduous trees line the walkways, and a sculpture of horizontal wooden slats at the midpoint looks like an avant-garde tree house. Displays throughout reflect and celebrate the four seasons. Though slowed by the recession, Crystals will eventually host 71 international luxury stores, including **Louis Vuitton, Tiffany & Company, Mikimoto, Prada, Christian Dior, Hermès, Versace, Gucci, Yves Saint Laurent, Stella McCartney,** and **Harry Winston** to drop a few well-recognized names. Several are two-level flagship stores. Don't expect coupons or deep discounts. Between the Mandarin Oriental and Aria is **Crystals Place,** a 4,200-square-foot annex and collection of several art galleries displaying the artwork, designs, and furniture of the CityCenter architects and artists. Seven restaurants, a 24,000-square-foot nightclub, and a bar and entertainment venues are also onsite. The hard-to-miss main entrance into Crystals is right on the Strip between Harmon Road and CityCenter Place. There is another entry inside CityCenter near Veer Towers and the tram station. Underground parking and valet service are available. Crystals is also the intermediate stop on the tram, which carries visitors between the Bellagio Spa Tower and the Monte Carlo.

A fifth major Strip shopping venue is **Miracle Mile Shops,** a 450,000-square-foot shopping and entertainment complex at Planet Hollywood (☎ 888-800-8284; **miraclemileshops.com**). The venue re-creates street scenes from a boutique shopping concourse and stretches around the periphery of the hotel and casino. The shop facades sit beneath an arched ceiling painted and lighted to simulate the evening sky. Overall, although the replication is effective, it is bland compared to The Forum Shops and the Grand Canal Shoppes. Like the Grand Canal Shoppes, Miracle Mile Shops offers primarily upscale boutique shopping, but more of it. A new pedestrian bridge, situated mid-Strip from the north edge of CityCenter at the Cosmopolitan crossing into Planet Hollywood, makes the upgraded Miracle Mile Shops more accessible. Much of the affordable merchandise tends toward the flashy and glamorous—**Tumi, Swarovski, Sur La Table, Benetton, Herve Leger, Kafri di Mexico, Betsey Johnson,** and a **Victoria's Secret** prototype store. Spectators can enjoy the hourly indoor rainstorm and light shows at the central fountain. The complex houses three theaters offering 12–15 shows daily. Several of the mall's 15 restaurants are open after midnight beyond retail hours.

Opening in late fall 2011, the most recent addition to on-Strip shopping is sun-drenched **Harmon Corner,** a triangular tri-level wedge at the key intersection of Harmon Avenue and the Strip. Directly across from CityCenter and adjacent to Planet Hollywood and the Miracle Mile Shops, this New York Times Square–themed glass-and-steel complex is accessed via two elevated pedestrian walkways. Although the anchor is a two-story Walgreens, the 17 shops are primarily small mid-priced boutiques, and the mall includes three restaurants offering alfresco dining. Parking is limited since the mall caters to foot travelers.

At Paris is **Le Boulevard,** 31,000 square feet of upscale French boutique shopping. Modest in size by Las Vegas shopping standards, the Rue de la Paix re-creates a Paris street scene with cobblestone pavement and winding alleyways.

The Wynn Esplanade (**wynnlasvegas.com**) connecting Wynn Las Vegas and Wynn Encore is an insanely expensive array of upscale shops and boutiques, including **Brioni, Oscar de la Renta, Graff,** and **Manolo Blahnik.** Garnering the most attention is the **Penske-Wynn Ferrari Maserati** dealership, including a Ferrari merchandise store.

The **Tower Shops** at the Stratosphere (☎ 702-380-7777; **strato sphere hotel.com**) are part midway and part strip mall. Extending along a narrow passageway on the hotel's second floor, the 35 establishments and kiosks are about 50-50 retail shops and fast-food purveyors. Merchants specialize in figurines, costume jewelry, leather, men and women's clothing, hats, tattoos, magic, Asian wear and gifts, and souvenirs. An oxygen bar and a daiquiri bar are next to each other by the fitness center.

Mandalay Place (**mandalaybay.com**), a mall with more than 25 boutiques and restaurants, also serves as the pedestrian connector linking Mandalay Bay and Luxor. The retailers seem more diverse and selectively chosen than at many other venues, making the shopping interesting even for those not hooked on shopping. There are nine upscale clothing and shoe retailers, a barber spa and retail shaving emporium for men, and a chocolate shop, among many others. Among the restaurants is the **Burger Joint,** featuring a $60 hamburger dressed with truffles. Fortunately, there are also less frou-frou burgers at reasonable prices.

Another Strip shopping venue is the **Showcase,** adjacent to the MGM Grand. Although most of the 190,000-square-foot shopping and entertainment complex is devoted to theme restaurants, a Sega electronic games arcade, and an eight-plex movie theater, space remains for a number of retail specialty shops. Practically next door is the **Hawaiian Marketplace** (☎ 702-795-2247), an 80,000-square-foot mall. Though the theme is Polynesian, the mall's restaurants and retailers are an eclectic lot ranging from **Café Capri** to **Zingers,** and from **Tropical Jewelers** to the **Las Vegas Tobacco Company.**

unofficial **TIP**
For those without transportation, Las Vegas Citizen's Area Transit (CAT) operates a bus route that connects the various Strip and suburban shopping centers. Fare is $1.25 in residential areas and $2 on the Strip. Service is provided daily, 5:30 a.m.–1:30 a.m. For more information on CAT, call ☎ 702-228-7433.

Adjacent to Green Valley Ranch Resort & Spa, **The District** (☎ 702-564-8595; **thedistrict atgvr.com**) offers 60 stores and restaurants. The shops line a long pedestrian plaza with two smaller plazas intersecting. Resembling a Georgetown, Washington, D.C., commercial and residential street, The District's shopping mix includes restaurants, apparel shops, and a couple dozen specialty stores, including **REI, Williams-Sonoma,** and **Pottery Barn.**

Just south of Mandalay Bay on South Las Vegas Boulevard is **Town Square** (☎ 702-269-5000; **townsquarelasvegas.com**). Town Square is designed as a multiblock village with streets, sidewalks, and even a park. The development is comprised of almost 130 stores and businesses, large and small, including shops, restaurants, entertainment venues, beauty salons, and offices. Prominent retailers are **Borders Books, BCBG, bebe, Whole Foods Market,** and **Robb & Stucky,** among others. Town Square is a dining destination with **California Pizza**

Kitchen, Claim Jumper, The Grape, Cadillac Ranch, Tommy Bahama's Restaurant & Bar, Yard House, Texas de Brazil, Brio Tuscan Grille, Bar Louie, Blue Martini, and **Kabuki Japanese Restaurant.** All the restaurants except for California Pizza Kitchen and Claim Jumper are new to Vegas. There is metered parking streetside (bring quarters) or free parking in large lots on the periphery.

The newest shopping opportunity in Las Vegas is **Tivoli Village** at Queensridge, where 33 retailers reside in an Italianate setting. Tivoli Village is 13 miles west of the Las Vegas Strip via I-95 North and the Summerlin Parkway. The 370,000-square-foot open-air Mediterranean-style complex features eight restaurants plus shops, including **Charming Charlie, Kidville, CORSA Collections, Roc of Republic Couture, Obika Eyewear,** and **Stash.** At night, the mall's decorative cherry trees are lit with 5,000 LED bulbs, enveloping the complex in a cerise glow. Since Tivoli Village is located in a suburban neighborhood, there is plenty of above and below-ground parking. (☎ 702-570-7400; **tivolivillagelv.com**)

Downtown is **Las Vegas Premium Outlets North** (☎ 702-474-7500; **premiumoutlets.com**), an $85-million, 150-store outlet mall. A clone of other Premium Outlet malls, featured brands include **AIX Armani Exchange, Dolce & Gabbana, Ann Taylor Factory Store, Kenneth Cole, Lacoste,** and **Coach.** The mall is just west of downtown, between downtown and Interstate 15. It's a bit far from downtown to walk but is only a short cab ride away. From I-15, the mall entrance is off Charleston Boulevard.

The former Las Vegas Outlet Center has been expanded and upscaled and now calls itself **Las Vegas Premium Outlets South** (☎ 702-896-5599; **premiumoutlets.com**) and is very similar to its sister mall downtown. Located 5 miles south of Tropicana Avenue at 7400 South Las Vegas Boulevard, the remodeled discount shopping venue is near the Blue Diamond Road exit off I-15. The center added 70,000 square feet, more merchants, and a larger food court. Recent additions to its inventory of 143 stores include **Michael Kors, Coach Men's, Under Armour, Loft Outlet, and Toys R Us.** Promotional literature listing the individual shops is available in almost all hotel brochure racks. The easiest way to reach the outlets is to drive south on I-15 to Exit 33, Blue Diamond Road. Proceed east on Blue Diamond Road to the intersection with Las Vegas Boulevard. Turn left on Las Vegas Boulevard to the center.

About an hour southwest on I-15 in Primm, Nevada, is **Fashion Outlets of Las Vegas Mall** (☎ 702-874-1400; **fashionoutletlasvegas.com**), offering themed dining and 100 outlet stores. You'll find **Williams-Sonoma, American Eagle Outfitters, Fossil, Tommy Hilfiger, Kenneth Cole, DKNY, Fendi, Kate Spade, Tommy Bahama,** and **Last Call from Neiman Marcus,** among others. The mall is adjacent to the Primm Valley Resort and Casino. For $15 round-trip, the Shoppers Shuttle runs consumers 40 miles to Primm from three locations: MGM Grand, Miracle Mile Shops, and the Fashion Show Mall. (☎ 888-424-6898.)

UNIQUE SHOPPING OPPORTUNITIES

WINE AND LIQUOR Though not centrally located, **Lee's Discount Liquors** (☎ 702-269-2400; **leesdisliquor.com**) on South Las Vegas Boulevard just south of Blue Diamond Road offers the best selection of wine, liquor, and beer within easy access of the Strip. Unless your hotel is south of Tropicana, take I-15 to the Blue Diamond Road exit and then head south on South Las Vegas Boulevard. If your hotel is south of Tropicana you're just as well off taking South Las Vegas Boulevard the whole way.

ART Las Vegas is a great place to shop for contemporary and non-traditional art and sculpture, with galleries in the Fashion Show Mall, The Forum Shops, the Grand Canal Shoppes, and elsewhere around town. Do not, however, expect any bargains.

On the first Friday of every month from 6 to 10 p.m. the visual arts are celebrated in Las Vegas. In an eight-block area, generally bound on the north and south by Hoover and Wyoming streets and on the west and east by Commerce and Third streets, lies the Arts District. Eclectic and eccentric, the area is abundant with art galleries, restaurants and bars, gift emporiums, vintage couture, antiques shops, and malls of memorabilia; quality ranges from exceptional to gawd-awful. With free parking at the Clark County Government Center, complimentary trollies transport arts lovers and the curious to this venerable commercial neighborhood. The lively First Friday festival (☎ 702-384-0092) incorporates local bands, food, artist demonstrations, clairvoyants, and street performers. It's great for people-watching, and more than 60 businesses participate.

Also in the Arts District is the **Not Just Antiques Mart** at 1422 Western Avenue (☎ 702-384-4922). Along with daily estate sales, the 12,000-square-foot arcade offers treasures and kitsch in themed galleries of collectables, antiques, consignments, and whatever. You want it, they've got it (probably). Closed on Sunday.

GAMBLING STUFF As you would expect, Las Vegas is a shopping mecca when it comes to anything gambling related. If you are in the market for a roulette wheel, a blackjack table, or some personalized chips, try the **Gamblers General Store** at 800 South Main (☎ 702-382-9903 or 800-322-CHIP outside Nevada; **gamblersgeneralstore .com**). For books and periodicals on gambling, we recommend the **Gamblers Book Shop** store at 5473 South Eastern Avenue (☎ 702-382-7555 or 800-522-1777; **gamblersbook.com**).

HEAD RUGS The next time you go to a Las Vegas production show, pay attention to the showgirls' hair. You will notice that the same woman will have a different hairdo for every number. Having made this observation, you will not be surprised that the largest wig and hairpiece retailer in the United States is in Las Vegas. At 4515 West Sahara Avenue, **Serge's Showgirl Wigs** inventories more than 7,000 hairpieces and wigs, made from both synthetic materials and human hair. In addition to serving the local showgirl population, Serge's Showgirl Wigs also specializes in assisting chemotherapy patients. A catalog and additional information can be obtained by calling ☎ 702-207-7494.

ETHNIC SHOPPING At the southwest corner of Spring Mountain and Wynn roads is **Las Vegas Chinatown Plaza** with 22 outlets (☎ 702-221-8448; **lvchinatown.com**). This location offers Asian-theme shopping and Asian restaurants.

For Native American art, crafts, books, music, and attire, try the **Las Vegas Indian Center** at 2300 West Bonanza Road (☎ 702-647-5842; **lasvegasindiancenter.org**). And 25 minutes north of Las Vegas in Moapa, Nevada, you'll find the **Moapa Tribal Enterprises Casino and Gift Center** (☎ 702-864-2600). Take I-15 north to Exit 75.

COSTUMES Halloween Experience (☎ 800-811-4877 or 702-740-4224; 6230 South Decatur Boulevard, Suite 101; **halloweenmart.com**) features thousands of costumes, masks, and accessories year-round. The showroom is open Monday through Friday to the public and on weekends by special arrangement (☎ 702-740-4224). For "sex-theme" apparel and costumes, try **Bare Essentials Fantasy Fashions** at 4029 West Sahara (☎ 702-247-4711; **bareessentialsvegas.com**). You'll find everything from dresses to G-strings. There's even a large selection of "bare essentials" for men. Some merchandise would be at home in suburbia, but some is strictly XXX. And speaking of XXX, that goes for sizes, too.

SHOES If you have feet a helicopter could land on, you might want to check out **Leonard's Wide Shoes,** 4480 Paradise Road (☎ 702-895-9993; **leonardswideshoes.com**). Leonard's specializes in W-I-D-E sizes, 5 to 13EE for women, and 6 to 18 (6E) for men. If smoking stunted your growth, increase your height with custom-made platforms, boots, and high heels from **Red Shoes,** 4011 West Sahara, Unit 1 (☎ 702-889-4442). For a great selection of cowboy boots, try **Cowtown Boots,** 1080 East Flamingo (☎ 702-737-8469; **cowtownboots.com**).

WESTERN WEAR Sheplers, the world's largest Western-wear retailer, can be found at Sam's Town on Boulder Highway (☎ 702-454-5266) and 4700 West Sahara Avenue (☎ 702-258-2000); **sheplers.com.**

GUNS Want to fire a machine gun? You can blast away at **The Gun Store**'s indoor range (2900 East Tropicana; ☎ 702-454-1110; **thegunstorelas vegas.com**). Firearm brands include Uzi, Thompson, and Madsen.

SEEING *the* SIGHTS

RESIDENTS OF LAS VEGAS ARE JUSTIFIABLY PROUD of their city and are quick to point out that it has much to offer besides gambling. Quality theater, college and professional sports, dance, concerts, art shows, museums, and film festivals contribute to making Las Vegas a truly great place to live. In addition, there is a diverse and colorful natural and historical heritage. What Las Vegas residents sometimes have a difficult time understanding, however, is that the average business and leisure traveler doesn't really give a big hoot. Las Vegas differs from Orlando and Southern California in that it does not have any bona fide tourist attractions except Hoover Dam. Nobody drives all the way to Las Vegas to take their children to visit the Liberace Museum. While there have always been some great places to detox from a long trade show or too many hours at the casino, they are totally peripheral in the minds of visitors. Las Vegas needs a legitimate, nongaming tourist draw, but the strange aggregation of little museums, factory tours, and mini–theme parks is not it.

During the 1990s and through 2000, a number of Strip casinos, including Caesars Palace, Circus Circus, the Stratosphere, New York–New York, and the Las Vegas Hilton, opened new attractions. They are, by and large, imaginative, visually appealing, and high-tech. Some would stand out as headliners in any theme park in the country. Others, while not up to Disney or Universal standards, represent a giant leap forward for Las Vegas.

ADVENTUREDOME AT CIRCUS CIRCUS

TO FURTHER APPEAL TO THE FAMILY MARKET, Circus Circus opened a small but innovative amusement park in August of 1993. Situated directly behind the main hotel and casino, the park now goes by the name of Adventuredome. Architecturally compelling, the entire park is built two stories high atop the casino's parking structure and is totally enclosed by a huge glass dome. From the outside, the dome surface is reflective, mirroring its surroundings in hot tropical pink. Inside, however, the dome is transparent, allowing guests in the park to see out. Composed of a multilayer glass-and-plastic sandwich, the dome allows light in but blocks ultraviolet rays. The entire park is air-conditioned and climate-controlled 365 days a year.

Adventuredome is a fun way to escape the heat of a Vegas summer day.

The park is designed to resemble a classic Western desert canyon. From top to bottom, hand-painted artificial rock is sculpted into caverns, pinnacles, steep cliffs, and buttes. A stream runs through the stark landscape, cascading over a 90-foot falls into a rippling blue-green pool. Set among the rock structures are the attractions: a roller coaster, a flume ride, an inverter ride, and Chaos, a spinning amusement that hauls riders randomly through three dimensions. There are also some rides for small children. Embellishing the scene are several life-sized animatronic dinosaurs, a re-creation of an archeological dig, a fossil wall, and a replica of a Pueblo cliff dwelling. There is also a small theater featuring magic and illusion. Finally, and inevitably, there is an electronic games arcade.

Adventuredome's premier attractions are the **Canyon Blaster,** the only indoor, double-loop, corkscrew roller coaster in the United States; **Rim Runner,** a three-and-a-half-minute water-flume ride; **Chaos,** a vertical Tilt-A-Whirl on steroids; and **Disk'O,** which has the rocking motion of a pirate ship–type amusement ride and then spins you and about 20 other folks like a human discus. Canyon Blaster and Rim Runner wind in, around, and between the rocks and cliffs. The flume ride additionally passes under the snouts of the dinosaurs. Adventuredome also features a new Special FX Theater showing 4-D films.

Guests can reach the theme park by proceeding through the rear of the main casino to the entrance and ticket plaza situated on the mezzanine level. Circus Circus has changed the admission policy so many times we have lost track. You can choose between paying for each attraction individually ($5 to $8) or opting for an all-inclusive day pass ($26.95 adults; $16.95 juniors). For exact admission prices on the day of your visit, call ☎ 702-794-3939 or visit **adventuredome.com.**

BELLAGIO ATTRACTIONS

THE BIG DRAW AT THE BELLAGIO is the **Gallery of Fine Art,** which hosts temporary traveling exhibits. Tickets run about $15 for adults, $12 for seniors and Nevada residents, and $10 for children, teachers, and those in the military; children age 12 and under are admitted free. For information, call ☎ 702-693-7871 or visit **bellagio.com.**

A very worthwhile and free attraction is the **Bellagio Conservatory and Botanical Gardens.** Located adjacent to the hotel lobby, the display features more than 10,000 blooming flowers, a diverse variety of plants, and even trees. The flora is changed periodically to reflect the season of the year or the theme of upcoming holidays.

Bellagio's free outdoor spectacle is a choreographed **water-fountain show** presented on the lake in front of the hotel (which stretches the length of three football fields). At the bottom of the eight-acre lake over 1,000 "water expressions"—think jets—and 4,000-plus individually programmable white lights are harnessed in choreography to "dance," if you will, to classical, popular, operatic, holiday, and sacred music. The waters are capable of reaching 240 feet into the air (approaching a football field's length), undulating in graceful S-curves, or cascading open like a gigantic surrendering lotus. Realized by WetDesigns, the entire vision, including the music selections, is Steve Wynn's, who is famous for his involvement with every detail of every aspect of the properties he designs. The magical waters of the Bellagio are for all to enjoy on the half hour every Saturday, Sunday, and holidays from noon to 8 p.m. and every 15 minutes from 8 p.m. to midnight. Weekdays the schedule begins at 3 p.m. The view from the street is assuredly wonderful, but many of the rooms at Caesars across the street can also offer a visual feast.

 Bellagio's dramatic three-story, glass-domed botanical garden provides a quiet oasis.

DOWNTOWN ATTRACTIONS

DOWNTOWN LAS VEGAS IS TIED TOGETHER under the canopy of the **Fremont Street Experience** (☎ 702-678-5777; **vegasexperience .com**), a high-tech, overhead sound-and-light show. The 12.5-million-light canopy extends from Main Street to Las Vegas Boulevard, covering the five-block pedestrian concourse where most downtown casinos are situated. Canopy shows occur on the hour, with the first show at 8:30 p.m. and the last show at midnight (subject to seasonal change). The canopy show is free, as are nightly concerts on the **3rd Street Stage,** located outdoors between Four Queens and Fitzgerald's. Across Las Vegas Boulevard beyond the canopied pedestrian plaza is the **Fremont East District,** a burgeoning nightlife and dining venue.

Flightlinez at Fremont Street offers the intrepid and newly brave the thrill of hurtling 850 feet under the 12.5 million LEDs of the Fremont Street Experience. This hard-to-miss new overhead ride begins 65 feet atop scaffolding at 425 Fremont Street next to Walgreens, zips over the traffic on 4th Street, scoots under the LED canopy, and ends two blocks to the west by the Four Queens. Riders are strapped into a harness, take a flying leap, and zoom down a steel line, controlling the rate of descent by tilting their bodies at various angles. Speeds can reach 35 mph. There are four parallel lines, so flyers can race. The ride is open daily, 2 p.m.– midnight (or later); cost is $15 until 6 p.m. and $20 after. There is no age or height restriction, but participants must weigh between 60 and 250 pounds. Pending higher approval, future plans include a longer plunge from a loftier platform (☎ 702-410-7999 or **bcflights.com**).

Entertainment aside, Fremont Street's most renowned attraction is the flashing neon marquees of the downtown casinos, the reason Fremont Street is called "Glitter Gulch." Augmenting the neon of the casinos are vintage Las Vegas neon signs dating back to the 1940s. The **Neon Museum,** located at 821 North Las Vegas Boulevard, is a three-acre outdoor collection of more than 150 vintage neon signs celebrating Las Vegas's small-town, bright-lights era. Signs are stacked along pathways winding through a maze of metal sculpture, huge panels of light bulbs, and yards of glass tubing. Among huge classic structures are Sassy Sally's facade of lights, Debbie Reynolds' autograph, Aladdin's lamp, and the graceful green and yellow flowering plant designating the Yucca Motel. Each recalls the era when hotels and motels outdid each other with extravagant signage. The glory days of the now-departed Dunes, Landmark, Stardust, Frontier, Sahara, and Desert Inn are also remembered by their signature marquees, which are prominently exhibited. Even the museum's name is spelled in capital letters from the famous hotels. The guide's commentary about these treasures is intertwined with the history of Las Vegas. One-hour tours of the boneyard are conducted Tuesday through Friday at noon and 2 p.m., Saturday at 9:30 a.m. and 1 p.m., and earlier during the summer months. Be sure to wear close-toed shoes to avoid stepping on metal and glass, the detritus of disintegrating signs. A camera is the only photographic equipment allowed. Cost of the tour is a $15 donation. For reservations or more information, call ☎ 702-387-NEON (6366) or visit **neonmuseum.org.**

Icons such as the Horseshoe's "H"; the Hacienda's horse and rider; and the silver slipper, bow and arrow, and Indian chief from their namesake properties have been reconditioned and highlight the nearby median of Las Vegas Boulevard heading north from Fremont

Street. Seven more refurbished historic signs are positioned at the Fremont Street Experience, including the Flame restaurant, The Red Barn lounge, Wedding Information, and the Nevada Motel.

LUXOR ATTRACTIONS

THE LUXOR OFFERS TWO CONTINUOUSLY RUNNING gated (paid admission) attractions inside the pyramid on the level above the casino. **Bodies...The Exhibition** (☎ 702-262-4000; **bodiestheexhibition.com**) is an extraordinary introduction to human anatomy through authentic, preserved human bodies. Though somewhat grisly sounding, the exhibit is extremely tasteful and respectful. Arranged sequentially, Bodies takes you through every part of the human body, explaining its many systems. Though most of the exhibit deals with the anatomy of healthy people, there is some discussion of disease. One of the more arresting displays is that of a normal lung side-by-side with the lung of a smoker. The second Luxor attraction is **Titanic: The Artifact Exhibition,** which takes guests on a chronological odyssey from the design and building of the ocean liner to life on board to its sinking (☎ 702-262-4400 or 800-557-7428; **luxor .com** or **titanictix.com**). Allow a minimum of two hours to see Bodies and 90 minutes to take in Titanic. General admission is $31 adults, $23 children (ages 4 to 12) for Bodies; $28 adults, $21 children for Titanic.

MANDALAY BAY ATTRACTION

THE BIG DRAW AT MANDALAY BAY is the **Shark Reef** aquarium featuring sharks, rays, sea turtles, venomous stonefish, and dozens of other denizens of the deep playing house in a 1.3-million-gallon tank. If you don't like fish, separate exhibits showcase rare golden crocodiles and pythons. The Shark Reef audio tour is open Sunday–Thursday 10 a.m.–8 p.m. and Friday and Saturday 10 a.m.–10 p.m. (last admission is one hour prior to close). Admission is about $18 for adults, $12 for children age 12 and under, and those age 4 and under are free. Additional information is available at ☎ 702-632-4555 or **sharkreef.com.**

MGM GRAND ATTRACTIONS

MGM GRAND HOSTS a **tri-story 5,000-square-foot lion habitat** that houses up to five big cats. Lions are on duty from 11 a.m. until 7 p.m. daily; admission is free. There is also, of course, an MGM Lion logo shop and the opportunity (for $20) to be photographed with a lion.

   CSI: The Experience (**csitheexperience.org**) exhibit is the first new major attraction to open on the Strip in some time. Originally developed by the Fort Worth Museum of Science and History with a grant from The National Science Foundation (NSF), CSI: The Experience gives you the opportunity to play the role of a crime-scene investigator, learning scientific principles and real investigative techniques as you try to solve the case. Two state-of-the-art crime labs will help you piece together the evidence. Hands-on science combines with special effects to create an exciting, realistic, and educational experience. There are three different crime scenes to investigate (pick one), following which "new recruits" (yes, that would be you Gladys) take their observations and hunches to the crime lab. With video input from investigators from the television show, you formulate a hypothesis, validate your findings, and then present your solution in a re-creation of the office of Gil Grissom—the enigmatic *CSI* head investigator. Of the three crime scenes to choose from, we thought the most interesting was Crime Scene 2: Who Got Served? It involves the discovery of a woman's body in an alley near a dumpster. Once you select your crime scene, you're issued a clipboard with an evidence form that has a diagram of the crime scene with space to record your observations. Each scene contains all sorts of evidence, from insects and latent fingerprints to vehicle tracks and various litter. Part of the challenge is discerning what at the crime scene is relevant and what is not. CSI: The Experience is self-guided and takes about an hour for most people.

The MGM Grand doesn't put much promotional oomph behind CSI, nor are there any signs in the casino to help you find it (follow the signs to the monorail). There's a box office next to CSI, but unfortunately it sells tickets to all MGM Grand shows. We waited a half hour to buy our CSI admission behind folks picking out their seats for the *Ka* and *Crazy Horse* shows. CSI is open daily, 10 a.m.–10 p.m. Tickets are $30 for adults and $23 for children ages 4–11. From our observation, it's pretty much a waste of money to take children younger than 11.

MIRAGE AND T. I. ATTRACTIONS

NOT ONLY ARE THE MIRAGE AND T. I. attractions of top quality, they are also free. The two biggies are the **Sirens of Treasure Island** and the **exploding volcano at the Mirage.** The disco naval battle takes place every 90 minutes, weather permitting, beginning at 7 p.m. (5:30 p.m. in winter), with the last performance at 10 p.m. (11:30 p.m. during warm-weather months) nightly. As part of an image makeover, T. I. wrote the British out of the script (they always lost anyway) and replaced them with "a group of sexy women" called the Sirens of T. I., who now fight the pirates. In the new production, the pirates are apparently so disconcerted by all the leg and cleavage that they do not put up a very robust fight. The best vantage points are along the rope rail on the entrance bridge to the casino. On weekdays, claim your spot 15 to 20 minutes before showtime. On weekends, make that 35 to 45 minutes. If you do not insist on having a *perfect* vantage point, you can see most everything just by joining the crowd at the last minute. If you are short, or have children in your party, it's probably worth the effort to arrive early and nail down a position by the rail.

The volcano at the Mirage goes off about every hour from 7 p.m. until 11 p.m., if the weather is good and winds are light. In the winter, when it gets dark earlier, the volcano starts popping off at 6 p.m. The volcano was souped-up in 2009. The new volcano boasts new fire effects and an exclusive soundtrack composed by Grateful Dead drummer and Rock and Roll Hall of Fame member Mickey Hart and

Indian tabla virtuoso Zakir Hussain. Massive fireballs are fired more than 12 feet into the air, and eruptions of fiery "lava" flow down the mountain's fissures. Usually, because of the frequency of performances (eruptions?), getting a good railside vantage point is not too difficult. If you want to combine the volcano with a meal, grab a window table at the second-floor restaurant in the Casino Royale across the street. Dinner here costs $10 to $20, though, so these are not cheap seats.

The Mirage has some of *Siegfried and Roy*'s white tigers on display in a well-executed, natural habitat exhibit. In addition to the tigers, the Mirage has a nice dolphin exhibit. Both are open weekdays 11 a.m.–5:30 p.m. and weekends and holidays 10 a.m.–5:30 p.m. The exhibit costs $17 for adults and $12 for children ages 4 to 12. (Children age 3 and under get in free.) For the price of admission you can also take in the **Secret Garden** next to the dolphin habitat, a small zoo with Siegfried and Roy's white and Bengal tigers, white lions, an Indian elephant, and more. For more information about Mirage, call ☎ 702-791-7111 or visit **mirage.com.** For more information about T. I., call ☎ 702-894-7111 or visit **treasureisland.com.**

PARIS LAS VEGAS ATTRACTION

THE BIG DRAW AT PARIS IS, OF COURSE, the 540-foot-tall replica of the **Eiffel Tower.** Requiring 10 million pounds of steel and more than two years to erect, the Las Vegas version is a little more than half the size of the original. Just below the top (at 460 feet) is an observation deck accessible via two ten-passenger glass elevators. It costs a stiff $10.50 to ride ($15.50—or an express pass for $22—starting at 7:30 p.m.), but that's just the beginning of the story. You must first line up to buy tickets. Your ticket will show a designated time to report to the escalator (that's right: *escalator*. You must take an escalator to reach the elevators). If you're late you'll be turned away, and there are no refunds. The escalator will deposit you in yet another line where you'll wait for the elevator. The elevators run from 9:30 a.m. until 12:30 a.m., except when it's raining.

unofficial TIP
If accessing Paris's observation platform seems like too much work, take the separate elevator that serves the restaurant and bar on the 11th floor of the tower. You don't need reservations to patronize the bar, but you must be nicely dressed (absolutely no jeans, T-shirts, tank tops, or sandals). The bar is open 11:30 a.m.–midnight and serves lunch.

Though all this hopping from line to line is supposed to take 5 to 20 minutes, we found 40 to 60 minutes more the norm. Here's the rub. The observation deck holds fewer than 100 persons, and once people get up there, they can stay as long as they want. Hence, when the observation deck is at max capacity, nobody can go up unless someone comes down. Because the tower affords such a great view of the Bellagio across the street, gridlock ensues several times nightly while people squeeze on the observation deck overlong to watch Bellagio's dancing-waters show.

STRATOSPHERE ATTRACTIONS

THE STRATOSPHERE TOWER STANDS 1,149 feet tall and offers an unparalleled view of Las Vegas. You can watch aircraft take off simultaneously from McCarran International Airport and Nellis Air Force Base. To the south, the entire Las Vegas Strip is visible. To the west, Red Rock Canyon seems practically within spitting distance. North of the Tower, downtown glitters beneath the canopy of the Fremont Street Experience. By day, the rich geology of the Colorado Basin and Spring Mountains merge in an earth-tone and evergreen tapestry. At night, the dark desert circumscribes a blazing strand of twinkling neon.

A 12-level pod crowns the futuristic contours of three immense buttresses that form the Tower's base. Level 12, the highest level, serves as the boarding area for **X-Scream,** a dangle-daddy; **Insanity,** a sort of Tilt-A-Whirl in the sky; and the **Big Shot,** an acceleration–free-fall thrill ride. Latest to join the lineup is **SkyJump,** a parachute ride with an 855-foot "controlled" free-fall descent. Oh, did we forget to mention that there's no parachute? Instead you're hooked up to a zip line on the 108th floor of the tower where you heave yourself over the side of a platform. Happily, after reaching speeds of 40 miles per hour, you'll be slowed to a comfortable landing. The price to jump off a perfectly good building instead of taking the elevator is $99 and up. It's said the views on the descent are stupendous if you happen to open your eyes.

Levels 11 and 10 are not open to the public. An outdoor observation deck is Level 9, with an indoor observation deck directly beneath it on Level 8. Level 7 features a 220-seat lounge, and Level 6 houses an upscale revolving restaurant. Levels 4 and 3 contain meeting rooms, and the remaining levels—1, 2, and 5—are not open to the public.

 The view from the Tower is so magnificent that we recommend experiencing it at different times of the day and night. Sunset is particularly stunning, and a storm system rolling in over the mountains is a sight you won't quickly forget. Be sure to try both the indoor and outdoor observation decks.

The rides are a mixed bag. The Big Shot is cardiac arrest. Sixteen people at a time are seated at the base of the skyward-projecting needle that tops the pod. You are blasted 160 feet straight up in the air at 45 miles per hour and then allowed to partially free-fall back down. At the apex of the ascent, it feels as if your seat belt and restraint have mysteriously evaporated, leaving you momentarily hovering 100-plus stories up in the air. The ride lasts only about a half minute, but unless you're accustomed to being shot from a cannon, that's more than enough.

If you're having difficulty forming a mental image of the Big Shot, picture the carnival game where macho guys swing a sledgehammer, propelling a metal sphere up a vertical shaft. At the top of the shaft is a bell. If the macho man drives the sphere high enough to ring the bell, he wins a prize. Got the picture? OK, on the Big Shot, you are the metal sphere.

In X-Scream, you ride in a large gondola attached to a huge steel arm. The arm dangles the gondola over the edge of the Tower, then releases it to slide forward a few feet as if the gondola is coming unglued from the arm. All and all, it's pretty dull.

The third ride, Insanity, is a little harder to describe. It consists of an arm that extends 64 feet over the edge of the Tower. Passengers are suspended from the arm in beefed-up swing seats and spun at up to three g's. As the ride spins faster and faster, the riders are propelled up to an angle of 70 degrees, at which point they're pretty much looking straight down. The Stratosphere touts the ride as providing "a great view of historic Downtown Las Vegas."

The elevators to the Tower are at the end of the shopping arcade on the second floor of the Stratosphere, above the casino. Get tickets for the Tower at the ticket center in the elevator lobby on the second floor or at various places in the casino. Tower tickets cost about $16 for adults and $10 for children. Packages including the Tower and the rides run $22–$34, depending on the number of rides included. You can purchase individual tickets for the rides at a cost of $12, in addition to your Tower admission.

Expect big crowds at the Tower on weekends. Once up top, the observation levels are congested, as are the lounge, snack bar, restrooms, and gift shops. If you want to try the rides, expect to wait an additional 20 to 40 minutes for each on weekends. When you've had your fill of the Tower and

unofficial **TIP**
If you must see the Tower on a weekend, go in the morning as soon as it opens.

are ready to descend, you'll have another long wait before boarding the elevator. However, if you walk down to the restaurant (you'll take the emergency staircase; ask an attendant where to find it), you can catch the down elevator with virtually no wait at all.

Another way to see the Tower without a long wait is to make a reservation for the **Top of the World** restaurant. To be safe, make reservations at least two weeks in advance. When you arrive, inform the greeter in the elevator lobby that you have a dinner reservation and give him your confirmation number. You will be ushered immediately into an express elevator. The restaurant is pricey, but the food is good and the view is a knockout, and you do not have to pay the Tower admission. If you want to try the Big Shot or the High Roller, purchase ride tickets before taking the elevator to the restaurant. Finally, be aware that most folks dress up to eat at Top of the World.

On weekdays, it is much easier to visit the Stratosphere Tower. Monday through Thursday, except at sunset, the wait to ascend is usually short. Waits for the rides are also short. Tower hours are daily, 10 a.m.–1 a.m. For more information, call ☎ 702-380-7711 or visit **stratospherehotel.com.**

VENETIAN ATTRACTIONS

LIKE NEW YORK–NEW YORK DOWN THE STRIP, it can be argued that the entire Venetian is an attraction, and there's a lot to gawk at even if you limit your inspection to the streetside Italian icons and the

Grand Canal Shoppes. But there's more. The Venetian is host to the first **Madame Tussaud's Wax Museum** in the United States. Covering two floors and 28,000 square feet, the museum is about half the size of the original London exhibit (☎ 702-862-7800; **mtvegas.com**). More than 100 wax figures are displayed in theme settings. Some, like Frank Sinatra and Tom Jones, were central to the development of the entertainment scene in Las Vegas. The museum opens daily at 10 a.m. Admission is $25 per adult and $15 per child.

TROPICANA ATTRACTION

THE LAS VEGAS MOB EXPERIENCE (☎ 702-739-2662; **lvme.com**) inside the Tropicana Resort is a 26,000-square-foot, high-tech immersive attraction and museum that takes visitors through the life of a Mob member. From arrival at Ellis Island through being made to don-like success, witness protection, or getting whacked, participants become part of the story and make choices along the way based on various scenarios and role-playing with actors posing as gangsters, cops, or casino owners. Movie stars in 3-D video clips from Mob-themed films provide commentary and advice. On display are personal artifacts, family photos, vehicles, and home movies humanizing notorious wise guys, including Lucky Luciano, Bugsy Siegel, and Meyer Lansky. Admission is $39.95. If you're interested in learning more about the history of the Mob, see our coverage of the new Mob Museum on pages 432–433.

A WORD ABOUT STRIP ROLLER COASTERS

THERE ARE TWO ROLLER COASTERS on the Strip. After careful sampling, we have decided that, although shorter, the **Canyon Blaster** at **Adventuredome** offers a better ride than the more visually appealing **Manhattan Express** at **New York–New York.** The Canyon Blaster is tight and oh-so-smooth. The Manhattan Express, on the other hand, goes along in fits and starts, all of which are jerky and rough. It does, however, provide a great view of the Strip as it zips in and out of the various New York–New York buildings.

The Canyon Blaster at Adventuredome is the *Unofficial* favorite of the Vegas Strip coasters.

QUIRKY TOURS

AMONG MANY GUIDED TOURS of various ilk available in Las Vegas are the **Vegas Mob Tour** and **Haunted Vegas Tour,** both bus tours and both running two and a half hours. The Mob Tour traces organized crime's history in Las Vegas and visits the sites of various murders, suicides, and celebrity deaths. The Haunted Vegas Tour features haunted casinos, Elvis hauntings, and the antics of Bugsy Siegel's ghost among other imponderables. Both tours, in addition to being great fun, serve up large doses of little-known Vegas history and are quite substantive. For tickets and information call ☎ 866-218-4935 or visit **vegasmobtour.com** and **hauntedvegastours.com.** Tickets run $66.25

plus tax. Look for discount coupons in *What's On* and other Las Vegas visitor magazines.

OTHER ATTRACTIONS

THERE ARE A GOODLY NUMBER of Las Vegas attractions, ranging from go-cart tracks to planetariums and aviation museums, that we don't have space to cover in the *Unofficial Guide.* All of them are listed and described at **vegas.com/attractions.** If you provide your name and address they'll mail you a free brochure. The site is sponsored by Museums and Attractions in Nevada (MAIN) in partnership with the Nevada Commission on Tourism.

MORE FREE STUFF

TWO FREE "ATTRACTIONS" worthy of your consideration are the Rio's **Show in the Sky** and a **water-and-laser show** at The Forum Shops. The show at the Rio is an edgy, PG-13 Las Vegas production show complete with floats, acrobats, musicians, and dancers, circling the casino suspended from a track on the ceiling (who thinks this stuff up?). The water-and-laser show at Caesars Palace at The Forum Shops, staged daily on the hour beginning at 10 a.m., combines animatronic statues as well as fire and laser effects. Outdoor productions at Bellagio, T. I., and the Mirage (all described earlier) are also free.

REALLY EXPENSIVE THRILLS

FOR $109 TO MORE THAN $3,000, YOU CAN FLY a foot off the ground at the **Richard Petty Driving Experience.** Here you can get behind the wheel of a 600-horsepower NASCAR Winston Cup–style stock car. The Driving Experience is located at Las Vegas Motor Speedway. Call ☎ 702-643-4343 or visit **drivepetty.com** for additional information.

▌ OTHER AREA ATTRACTIONS

THE LOCAL VISITOR GUIDES DESCRIBE nearby attractions and sites pretty honestly. If you have children, try the **Lied Discovery Children's Museum,** ☎ 702-382-3445, for a truly rewarding afternoon of exploration and enjoyable education. Right across the street from the Lied is the **Las Vegas Natural History Museum,** ☎ 702-384-3466.

Near scenic Red Rock, a side trip just outside of Las Vegas is **Bonnie Springs Old Nevada.** This rustic re-creation of an Old West town features trinket stores, a saloon, two museums, a restaurant, a petting zoo, and guided horse rides. The hoot that goes with this holler is the low-budget melodrama. The kicker is the real, live Western hanging that takes place at noon, 2, and 4 p.m. "You can't hang me, sheriff!" "Why not?!" "Cause yer wife'll miss me!" Cost to get in—$20 per carload; ☎ 702-875-4191; **bonniesprings.com.** Real rope, real fun.

Adults who wax nostalgic over vintage automobiles should check out the **Auto Collection at the Imperial Palace,** ☎ 702-794-3174, where more than 250 antique and historically significant vehicles are on display. The collection is well worth the admission price of $8.95, $5 for seniors and children under age 12, though discount coupons are readily available in the local visitor guides, and you can even print out a free admission pass at **autocollections.com.**

Unique to Las Vegas is the **Atomic Testing Museum,** which chronicles through exhibits and film the history of the Nevada Test Site, where atomic bombs were detonated only 65 miles from Las Vegas. When a vital sense of place, artifacts, and good storytelling come together, the result should be a powerful museum experience. This is the case at the Atomic Testing Museum, which presents the story of the development of nuclear weapons. In particular, the Nevada Test Site located just north of Las Vegas is featured, where as one Nevada governor put it, "atoms bloom(ed) in the desert."

This museum is cerebral, instructive, and entertaining. Laden with artifacts, there is much to look at (and much to read for a full encounter). The strength of the experience is greatly enhanced by the overall design that re-creates settings with fine attention to materials. For example, the entrance to the 8,000 square feet of exhibit space is a replica of the stainless-steel facade of the Wackenhut guard station located at the Nevada Test Site. A good balance of videos and interactive stations can engage anyone with a passing interest in this seemingly and sadly ever-important topic. Although varied, with metal and concrete dominating, in sum the exhibit spaces convey the sense of a bunker. This scheme sounds oppressive, but it deftly supports the power and secrecy of the nuclear program. In one of two small theaters, the brief, overpowering experience of a nuclear test explosion is alone nearly worth the price of admission. Near the end of the technology-based interpretations, a room of Native American artifacts and perspectives restores a balance to the mechanistic themes. It also provokes thought about the power of the earth, the deathly horrors of humankind, and the need for nuclear weapons in an age of terrorism.

If you are looking for some brain stimulation to escape the midway atmosphere of the casinos, you can't do better than the Atomic Testing Museum, created in association with the Smithsonian Institution. Furthermore, the museum store might be a good place to look for a stimulating present for that eggheaded child you left at home. Open daily, the museum is located at 755 East Flamingo Road. Admission is $12 adults and $9 children. Call ☎ 702-794-5161 for more information, or see **atomictestingmuseum.org.**

Opening in December 2012, the **Las Vegas Museum of Organized Crime and Law Enforcement** or **Mob Museum** (☎ 702-229-6581; **mobmuseum.org**) commemorates the extensive nationwide history of the Mob and its influence on Las Vegas. The interactive exhibits on three floors provide diverse viewpoints about the impact of organized crime and the feds who worked to crush the gangs. The museum is in the city's former federal courthouse (300 Stewart Avenue), the only Las Vegas building listed in the National Register of Historic Places. It houses the courtroom where the Kefauver Hearings on Organized Crime were conducted in 1950. Among the exhibits are the barber's chair where Albert Anastasia was shot and the bullet-strewn garage wall from Chicago's 1929 St. Valentine's Day Massacre. Admission is $12–$17 with discounts for seniors, locals, and groups. For an interactive Mob experience, see our description of the Las Vegas Mob Experience on page 430.

Las Vegas's entertainment ambassador Wayne Newton is opening his prodigious estate to visitors. Projected to open in early 2012, the **Wayne Newton Museum and Shenandoah Ranch Tour** (☎ 702-450-2272) will provide a look at Newton's classic cars, private jet, and mansion appointed with exotic antique furniture and fixtures. Outside, the gardens house the acclaimed Arabian Horse–training compound plus a wildlife center with penguins, wallabies, exotic birds, and more. The visitors center showcases Newton's memorabilia collection, shows a documentary detailing his life and extensive career, and includes a gift shop. The estate is located in southeast Las Vegas at Sunset and Pecos roads and open during daylight hours. A shuttle service is available from the Strip.

NATURAL ATTRACTIONS NEAR LAS VEGAS

IN THE MEXICAN PAVILION OF EPCOT at Walt Disney World, tourists rush obliviously past some of the rarest and most valuable artifacts of the Spanish colonial period in order to take a short, uninspired boat ride. Many Las Vegas visitors, likewise, never look beyond the Strip. Like the Epcot tourists, they are missing something pretty special.

Las Vegas's geological and topographical diversity, in combination with its stellar outdoor resources, provides the best opportunities for worthwhile sightseeing. So different and varied are the flora, fauna, and geology at each distinct level of elevation that traveling from the banks of Lake Mead to the high, ponderosa pine forests of Mount Charleston encompasses (in 90 minutes) as much environmental change as driving from Mexico to Alaska.

Red Rock Canyon, the **Valley of Fire,** the **Mojave Desert,** and the **Black Canyon of the Colorado River** are world-class scenic attractions. In combination with the summits of the **Spring Mountains,** they compose one of the most dramatically diversified natural areas on the North American continent. So excuse us if we leave coverage of the Guinness World of Records Museum to the local visitor's guides.

Springs Preserve

If you like your outdoor experience with a healthy dose of history, Springs Preserve is the place for you. This 180-acre natural oasis, approximately 3 miles west of downtown Las Vegas, is filled with museums, galleries, an interpretive trail system, botanical gardens, and plenty of wildlife. The **Origen Museum** is the preserve's focal point for history, geology, and wildlife and features three galleries with more

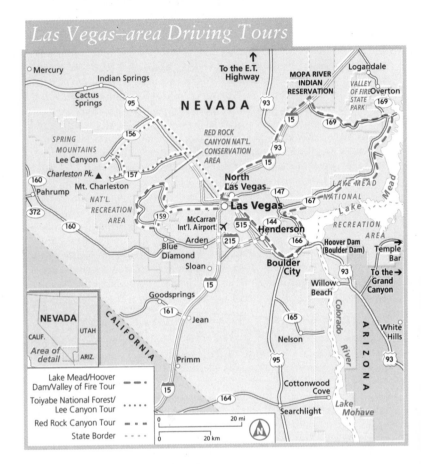

Las Vegas–area Driving Tours

than 75 exhibits. The preserve also features a 25-acre, re-created desert wetland with more than 35 species of wildlife and an 1,800-seat amphitheater. If you need a bite to eat after your hike, visit Wolfgang Puck's **Springs Cafe** for healthy American cuisine. The preserve is open daily, from 10 a.m. to 6 p.m. (trails close at dusk). Admission to museums and exhibits is $18.95 adults and $10.95 children (ages 5 to 17). Admission to trails is free. For more information, visit **springspreserve.org.**

Driving Tours

If you wish to sample the natural diversity of the Las Vegas area, we recommend the following driving tours. The trips begin and end in Las Vegas and take from two hours to all day, depending on the number of stops and side trips. The driving tours can conveniently be combined with picnicking, hiking, horseback riding, and sightseeing. If you have the bucks, we also recommend taking one of the air/ground tours of the Grand Canyon.

1. MOUNT CHARLESTON, KYLE CANYON, LEE CANYON, AND THE TOIYABE NATIONAL FOREST 4 to 6 hours   If you have had more than enough desert, this is the drive for you. Head north out of Las Vegas on US 95 and turn left on NV 157. Leave the desert and head into the pine and fir forest of the Spring Mountains. Continue up Kyle Canyon to the Mount Charleston Inn (a good place for lunch) and from there to the end of the canyon. Backtracking a few miles, take NV 158 over Robbers Roost and into Lee Canyon. When you hit NV 156, turn left and proceed to the Lee Canyon Ski Area. For the return trip, simply take NV 156 out of the mountains until it intersects US 95. Turn south (right) on US 95 to return to Las Vegas. If you start feeling your oats once you get into the mountains, there are some nice short hikes (less than a mile) to especially scenic overlooks. If you are so inclined, there is also horseback riding, and there are some great places for picnics.

2. RED ROCK CANYON SCENIC LOOP 1½ to 3 hours   Red Rock Canyon is a stunningly beautiful desert canyonland only 20 minutes from Las Vegas. A scenic loop winds among imposing, rust-red Aztec sandstone towers. There is a visitor center, as well as hiking trails and picnic areas. With very little effort you can walk to popular rockclimbing sites and watch the action. From Las Vegas, head west on Charleston Boulevard (NV 159) directly to Red Rock Canyon. The scenic loop is 13 miles (all one-way), with numerous places to stop and enjoy the rugged vistas. The loop road brings you back to NV 159. Turn left and return to town via Charleston Boulevard.

3. LAKE MEAD AND THE VALLEY OF FIRE 5 to 8 hours   This drive takes you to the Lake Mead National Recreation Area and Valley of Fire State Park. How long the drive takes depends on how many side trips you make. If you plan to visit Hoover Dam during your visit, it will be convenient to work it into this itinerary. The same is true if you wish to tour the Ethel M (as in Mars bars) Chocolate Factory and Cactus Garden.

Head south out of Las Vegas on US 95/93 (detour west on Sunset Road to visit the Chocolate Factory and Cactus Garden), continuing straight on US 93 to Boulder City. From Boulder City continue to the Hoover Dam on US 93 (if desired) or turn left on the Lakeshore Scenic Drive (NV 166) to continue the drive. Travel through the washes and canyons above the lake until you reach the Northshore Scenic Drive (NV 147 and NV 167). Turn right, continuing to the right on NV 167 when the routes split. If you wish, you can descend to the lake at Callville Bay, Echo Bay, or Overton Beach. If you are hungry, Callville Bay and Echo Bay have restaurants and lounges. Overton Beach has a snack bar, but Echo Bay has the best beach.

Near Overton Beach, turn left to NV 169 and follow signs for Valley of Fire State Park. Bear left on NV 169 away from Overton. Valley of Fire features exceptional desert canyon scenery, panoramic vistas, unusual and colorful sandstone formations, and Indian petroglyphs. A short two-mile scenic loop makes it easy to see many of the valley's most interesting formations. If you have time, take the road past the visitor center and climb to the Rainbow Vista overlook. From here a new highway accesses some of the most extraordinary terrain in the American Southwest. After the loop (and any other detours that interest you), continue west on NV 169 until it intersects I-15. Head south to return to Las Vegas.

Eldorado Canyon

When you've covered Las Vegas for as long as we have it's really an event to bump into something totally new and different. Actually, to be precise, we stumbled onto something *old* and different. About a 40-minute drive from the Strip via US 95 and NV 165, is Eldorado Canyon, so named by the Spanish circa 1776 when gold and silver were discovered there.

Gold was rediscovered, along with nickel and lead, in 1859, leading to the establishment of the Techatticup Mine, which operated until 1945. A place of rough-and-tumble life with little order and much violence, the town of Nelson attracted a number of deserters from both the Union and Confederate armies during the Civil War. Lawlessness was so commonplace in the mine's heyday (the nearest sheriff was a one-week ride away on horseback) that a company of infantrymen was stationed nearby to discourage the killings and disputes among the miners themselves and with Native Americans.

At the bottom of the canyon was Nelson's Landing on the Colorado River, where the gold was loaded on riverboats to Yuma, Arizona, and sent downstream to California. The landing and a small village surrounding it were destroyed by a flash flood in 1974. By then, however, several dams had long since rendered the Colorado unusable for commercial purposes.

If you've ever wanted to drive from the canyon rim to the bottom of the Grand Canyon, the drive from the top of Eldorado Canyon to the Colorado River is a good facsimile. The road is good, and the vistas are glorious as you descend. At the bottom, there is a recreational area alongside the river, and the river itself, on a sunny day, is the darkest shade of blue imaginable. Be sure to top off your gas tank before leaving Las Vegas.

Eldorado Canyon is a recreational treasure trove. Mine tours, as well as guided kayak, mountain bike, hiking, ATV, and horseback tours, are available. Outfitters for guided trips include **Awesome Adventures** (☎ 800-519-2243, **awesomeadventuretv.com**); **Adventure Las Vegas** (☎ 888-867-6259, **adventurelasvegas.com**); and **Desert Adventures** (☎ 702-293-5026, **kayaklasvegas.com**). Of course, you can also do all of this on your own using your own or rented equipment. For mine tours, try **Eldorado Canyon Mine Tours** (☎ 702-291-0026, **eldoradocanyonminetours.com**).

Pink Jeep Tours offers guided off-road experiences to Eldorado Canyon, Red Rock Canyon, and Valley of Fire in the Las Vegas area. Excursions farther afield include Death Valley, the Grand Canyon north, south, and west rims, and Zion National Park. Jeeps seat ten persons and are pretty plushy. Guides are certified by the National

Association for Interpretation. Lunch is included on most outings. For additional information and prices call ☎ 888-900-4480 or visit **pinkjeep.com/jeep-tours/lasvegas/.**

Hoover Dam

Hoover Dam is definitely worth seeing. There is a film, a guided tour, and a theater presentation on the Colorado River drainage, as well as some static exhibits. Try to go on a Monday, Thursday, or Friday. Arrive no later than 9 a.m., when the visitor area opens, and do the tour first ($11, $9 seniors and children ages 4–16). After 9:30 a.m. or so, long lines form for the tour, especially on Tuesdays, Wednesdays, Saturdays, and Sundays. The dam is closed to visitors at 6 p.m. (tickets sold until 5:15 p.m.—4:15 p.m. in winter). A ban on visitors inside the dam, initiated following 9/11, was subsequently lifted, but there are security checkpoints on US 93 leading to the dam.

Other than chauffeured transportation, there is no advantage in going to Hoover Dam on a bus tour. You will still have to wait in line for the tour of the dam and to see the other presentations. If you are the sort of person who tours quickly, you probably will have a lot of time to kill waiting for the rest of the folks to return to the bus.

With the opening of the new bridge, those few miles of US Highway 93, which traverse the historic dam and pass by the visitors center, will no longer accommodate through traffic. Now the only access to the dam is from the Nevada side. An upgraded interchange on Highway 93 is under construction just east of the Hacienda Hotel and Casino on the outskirts of Boulder City. It is still possible to drive across the dam for a sweeping view of Lake Mead and the lower Colorado, but the existing road terminates on the Arizona side just above the last parking lot at the top of the hill. Keep an eye out for elusive desert bighorn sheep, as this is their primary migration route. For more information, call ☎ 702-494-2517.

HOOVER DAM BYPASS BRIDGE   The long-awaited and long-delayed $114-million Hoover Dam bypass bridge opened in 2010, saving travelers minutes to hours of driving time between Nevada and Arizona.

The old two-lane road, US Highway 93, which links the two states, incorporated hairpin turns and twisted down rocky canyons from both sides to cross the top of the dam. Traffic congestion mingled sightseers, commuters, truckers, and film crews, much to the frustration of all.

Officially named the Mike O'Callaghan–Pat Tillman Memorial Bridge after a former Nevada governor and an Arizona football player/US Army Ranger killed in Afghanistan, the structure features two enormous cable-less arches projecting from the sheer cliffs above the waterway to buttress the road. Intrepid visitors can walk across the one-third-mile, four-lane bypass rising 850 feet above the choppy Colorado River. A sidewalk begins on the Nevada side and stretches the length of the span. The view of the canyon, the river, and the bridge's remarkable engineering is stunning. An information plaza, hiking trail, and parking area will be completed by the end of 2010.

The Canyons of the Southwest

Las Vegas tourist magazines claim **Bryce Canyon** (400 miles round-trip; ☎ 435-834-5322) and **Zion Canyon, Utah** (350 miles round-trip; ☎ 435-772-3256), as well as the **Grand Canyon, Arizona** (☎ 928-638-7888) as local attractions. We recommend all of the canyons if you are on an extended drive through the Southwest. If your time is limited, however, you might consider taking one of the air day-tours that visit the canyons from Las Vegas. Running roughly between $100 and $400 per passenger, the excursions follow one of two basic formats: air only, or air and ground combined. Some tour companies offer discounted fares for a second person if the first person pays full fare. Also, discount coupons are regularly available in *What's On* and *Today in Las Vegas,* distributed free of charge in most hotels.

Almost all canyon tours include a pass over **Lake Mead** and **Hoover Dam.** The trip involving the least commitment of time and money is a round-trip flyover of one or more of the canyons. A Grand Canyon flyover, for example, takeoff to touchdown, takes about two hours. While flying over any of the canyons is an exhilarating experience, air traffic restrictions concerning the Grand Canyon severely limit what air passengers can see. Flying over the other canyons is somewhat less restricted.

 If you want to get a real feel for the Grand Canyon particularly, go with one of the air/ground excursions. The Grand Canyon is many times more impressive from the ground than from the air.

The air/ground trips fly over the Grand Canyon and then land. Passengers are transferred to a bus that motors them along the rim of the canyon, stopping en route for lunch. Excursions sometimes additionally include boat and helicopter rides. These multifaceted tours last from seven to ten hours. Many flights offer multilingual translations of the tour narrative.

All of the aircraft used will feel very small to anyone accustomed to flying on big commercial jets. Most of the planes carry between 8 and 20 passengers. The captain often performs the duties of both flight attendant and pilot. Each passenger usually has a window, though some of the windows are pretty small. Cabin conditions for the most part are spartan, and there is usually no toilet on board.

Because small aircraft sometimes get bounced around and buffeted by air currents, we recommend taking an over-the-counter motion-sickness medication if you think you might be adversely affected. The other thing you want to do for sure is to relieve your bladder *immediately* before boarding.

Following are descriptions of the tours we consider to be the cream of the crop. Because they offer the most extensive introduction to the Grand Canyon, they rank among the most expensive (see the chart on the following page).

Grand Canyon Tours

Grand Canyon West Rim Voyager
☎ 702-851-8436; grandcanyonfuntrips.com

TRANSPORTATION	BUS, BOAT, HELICOPTER
SIGHTSEEING	BOULDER CITY, HOOVER DAM, LAKE MEAD, WEST RIM, COLORADO RIVER
LENGTH	11 HOURS*
COST	$229

Grand Canyon 4 in 1 Best Adventures
☎ 702-851-8436; grandcanyonfuntrips.com

TRANSPORTATION	AIRPLANE, HELICOPTER, BOAT
SIGHTSEEING	BOULDER CITY, HOOVER DAM, LAKE MEAD, WEST RIM, COLORADO RIVER
LENGTH	7½ HOURS*
COST	$295

Grand Canyon Helicopter below the Rim and Sunset Ranch Adventure
☎ 800-359-8727; heliusa.com

TRANSPORTATION	HELICOPTER, WAGON, BUS, HORSEBACK
SIGHTSEEING	HOOVER DAM, LAKE MEAD, CANYON WEST RIM, RANCH
LENGTH	9 HOURS*
COST	$349

Grand Canyon Picnic
☎ 800-653-1881; sundancehelicopters.com

TRANSPORTATION	HELICOPTER, WAGON, BUS, HORSEBACK (ADDITIONAL CHARGE)
SIGHTSEEING	HOOVER DAM, LAKE MEAD, EXTINCT VOLCANOES, LAVA FLOWS, CANYON WEST RIM
LENGTH	3½ HOURS*
COST	$429 (DISCOUNTS AT **looktours.com**)

Length includes hotel pickups and drop-offs.

BEST TOURS The **Grand Canyon West Rim Voyager** and **Grand Canyon 4 in 1 Best Adventures Airplane, Copter, and Boat Tours** carry the best bang for your buck from Best Tours. The only difference between the two tours is the transportation used to see Boulder City, Lake Mead, and the Hoover Dam, and to reach the Grand Canyon.

If you would prefer an aerial view of Boulder City, Lake Mead, and the Hoover Dam, then Grand Canyon #1 is your tour. All airplanes are high wing, and helicopters sport extra-large vista windows, allowing all passengers to have a spectacular view. If you wish for a more up-close and personal look at the attractions, and have an extra three and a half hours to allocate, the Grand Canyon West Rim Voyage tour incorporates the aforementioned sights into a three-hour relaxing motorcoach ride en route to the Canyon.

The tours are identical once you reach the Grand Canyon. You take a chopper to the Canyon floor (15 minutes), and shuffle onto a pontoon boat for a 25-minute ride down a flatwater section of the Colorado River. After the ride, you are airlifted back up to the West Canyon Rim to enjoy a barbecue lunch. Following lunch, you reboard the coach or plane and head back to Vegas.

GRAND CANYON HELICOPTER FLIGHTS Grand Canyon Helicopter below the Rim and Sunset Ranch Adventure is the best package we reviewed for those wanting to combine a lengthy helicopter tour with other activities. Leaving from Las Vegas, the tour consists of a 45-minute helicopter flight with views of the Hoover Dam and Lake Mead, and flying through the Canyon at 1,500 feet below the rim.

Upon arrival at the Grand Canyon West Ranch, about 12 miles from the West Rim, you are shuttled in about ten minutes from the landing pad to the ranch in a horse-drawn wagon. At the ranch, horseback riding is available for an additional charge of $49 for a half hour. A Western-style dinner along with songs and stories around a campfire complete the ranch experience. Alcohol is available at an additional charge, and the ranch buildings are air-conditioned. The return bus trip to Las Vegas takes about two and a half hours.

SUNDANCE HELICOPTERS If all you seek is a helicopter ride without the added bells and whistles of additional activities, then go with the Sundance Grand Canyon Picnic Tour. You will arrive at the launch pad in style by a ride in the complimentary limousine.

The helicopter tour is a round-trip one and a half hours spent in the air, viewing the Hoover Dam, Lake Mead, extinct volcanoes, lava formations, and the West Rim of the Grand Canyon. A maximum number of six people can fit in the helicopter. However, if a guest weighs over 275 pounds, he or she will have to purchase two seats. All guests have unobstructed views.

The helicopter lands on a plateau between the river and the ridge. A box lunch and Champagne are provided, and there is time to do a little exploring on foot before jumping back in the helicopter for the ride back to the Strip. Reserve the flight through **looktours.com** and save over $100 per person as opposed to reserving through the Sundance company directly.

IF YOU GO Grand Canyon tours are a perfect respite from the glitz and frenetic activity of the Strip. Whether you're looking for a flyby, great photo ops, or a cowboy ranch experience, it can be found with one of the tours we describe.

All tours described here are geared toward families and people of all ages. The tours involving a boat ride use craft that guests of all ages can easily board, and the gentle, scenic section of the river featured contains no rapids.

SKYWALK Located 121 miles from Las Vegas over some primitive roads, Skywalk is a horseshoe-shaped observation platform projecting from the remote western edge of the Grand Canyon on the Hualapai reservation. The ends of the horseshoe are anchored to the rim of the canyon while the rounded section, the observation platform, cantilevers into space 4,000 feet above the canyon floor. Both the sides and the floor of the platform are transparent. The flexible Skywalk is designed to withstand 100-mile-per-hour winds and

8.0-magnitude earthquakes and to support 71 million pounds—it wobbles and vibrates a little. The sensation is a bit like walking on a cruise ship—not unpleasant at sea but disconcerting when you're hanging over the Grand Canyon. Add the fact that the walls are only about mid–chest high and Skywalk begins to seem as much a thrill ride as a spectacular viewing spot.

Speaking of the view, it's magnificent. From Skywalk you can see standing waves on the Colorado River to the left (they look like tiny ripples from this height) and Eagle Point to the right, where the configuration of the canyon looks like the outstretched wings of a bird.

To walk on Skywalk you must purchase a Legacy Gold package, which also includes a visit to the Hualapai Ranch, Guano Point, and Eagle Point, a Native American cultural performance, and an all-you-can-eat meal among other things (see **destinationgrandcanyon.com** or call ☎ 702-878-9378). The package runs $86 (including taxes and fees) for adults and $72 for children ages 4–11. A wheelchair ramp is available. There's no limit to the time you can spend on Skywalk and no maximum weight for visitors. You are not allowed to bring cameras or any personal belongings onto Skywalk. For additional information see **grandcanyonskywalk.com.**

If you drive from Las Vegas but don't want to drive the final 14-mile graded but unpaved road to the reservation, make a reservation to use the Park & Ride service by calling ☎ 702-260-6506. The service costs $15 per person. Because the drive is a little more than three hours one-way from Las Vegas, you'll have to leave early to take advantage of all the elements of the tour package. If you want to drive over prior to your tour, you can spend the night at the Hualapai Lodge in the hardscrabble town of Peach Springs (49 miles away), the center of the Hualapai Tribe; call ☎ 928-769-2230 or visit **hualapaitourism.com** for reservations.

If you don't want to drive, these companies will fly you there:

Vision Holidays **visionholidays.com** | ☎ 800-256-8767

Maverick Helicopters **maverickhelicopter.com** | ☎ 888-261-4414

Sundance Helicopters **helicoptour.com** | ☎ 800-653-1881

Fares range from $250 to over $500 round-trip, although sometimes a discount can be found on the Internet.

PART SIX

EXERCISE *and* RECREATION

WORKING OUT

MOST OF THE FOLKS ON OUR *UNOFFICIAL GUIDE* research team work out routinely. Some bike; some run; some lift weights or do yoga. Staying in hotels on the Strip and downtown, they realized that working out in Las Vegas presents its own peculiar challenges.

The best months for outdoor exercise are October through April. The rest of the year it is extremely hot, though mornings and evenings are generally pleasant in September and May. During the scorching summer, particularly for visitors, we recommend working out indoors or, for bikers and runners, very early in the morning.

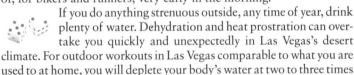 If you do anything strenuous outside, any time of year, drink plenty of water. Dehydration and heat prostration can overtake you quickly and unexpectedly in Las Vegas's desert climate. For outdoor workouts in Las Vegas comparable to what you are used to at home, you will deplete your body's water at two to three times the usual rate.

WALKING

PRIMARILY FLAT, LAS VEGAS IS MADE FOR WALKING and great people-watching. Security is very good both downtown and on the Strip, making for a safe walking environment at practically all hours of the day and night. Downtown, everything is concentrated in such a small area that you might be inclined to venture away from the casino center. While this is no more perilous than walking in any other city, the areas surrounding downtown are not particularly interesting or aesthetically compelling. If the downtown casino center is not large enough to accommodate your exercise needs, you are better off busing or cabbing to the Strip and doing your walking there.

If you are walking the Strip, it is about four miles from Mandalay Bay on the south end to the Stratosphere on the north end. Because the topography is so flat, however, it does not look that far. We met a

Las Vegas Strip Walking Map

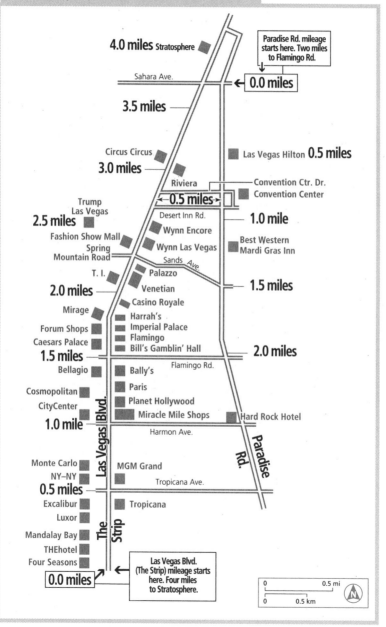

4.0 miles Stratosphere

Paradise Rd. mileage
starts here. Two miles
to Flamingo Rd.

0.0 miles

Sahara Ave.

3.5 miles

Las Vegas Hilton **0.5 miles**

Circus Circus
3.0 miles

Riviera

Convention Ctr. Dr.
Convention Center

0.5 miles

Trump
Las Vegas
2.5 miles

Desert Inn Rd.   **1.0 mile**

Fashion Show Mall

Wynn Encore

Best Western
Mardi Gras Inn

Spring
Mountain Road

Wynn Las Vegas

Sands   Ave.

T. I.

Palazzo

2.0 miles

Venetian

1.5 miles

Casino Royale

Mirage

Harrah's

Forum Shops

Imperial Palace

Caesars Palace

Flamingo

1.5 miles

Bill's Gamblin' Hall

2.0 miles

Bellagio

Bally's

Flamingo Rd.

Cosmopolitan

Paris

CityCenter

Planet Hollywood

1.0 mile

Miracle Mile Shops

Hard Rock Hotel

Harmon Ave.

Paradise
Rd.

Monte Carlo

MGM Grand

NY–NY

0.5 miles

Tropicana Ave.

Excalibur

Tropicana

Luxor

Mandalay Bay

THEhotel

Four Seasons

0.0 miles

Las Vegas Blvd.
(The Strip) mileage starts
here. Four miles
to Stratosphere.

Las Vegas Blvd.

The Strip

0   0.5 mi
0   0.5 km

number of people who set out on foot along the Strip and managed to overextend themselves. Check out our Strip walking distance map on the previous page before you go, and bear in mind that even without hills, marching in the arid desert climate will take a lot out of you.

 When walking the Strip, carry enough money to buy refreshments en route and to take a cab or bus back to your hotel if you poop out or develop a blister.

RUNNING

IF YOU STAY ON THE STRIP, you will have more options than if you stay downtown. Those of us who are used to running on pavement ran on the broad sidewalks of South Las Vegas Boulevard. These runs are great for people-watching also, but are frequently interrupted by long minutes of jogging in place at intersections, waiting for traffic lights to change. Our early risers would often run before 7:30 a.m. on a golf course. This was the best (and safest) running in town, with good footing, beautiful scenery, and no traffic. Suffice it to say, however, that course managers were less than overjoyed to see a small platoon of travel writers trotting off the 18th fairway. If you run on a golf course, stay off the greens and try to complete your run by 7:30 a.m. In addition to area golf courses, the Las Vegas Hilton and Mandalay Bay each have a jogging circuit.

If you stay downtown, you must either run on the sidewalks or drive to a more suitable venue. Sidewalks downtown are more congested than those on the Strip, and there are more intersections and traffic lights with which to contend. If you want to run downtown, particularly on Fremont Street, try to get your workout in before 10 a.m.

For those who dislike pounding the blacktop, sneaking onto golf courses, or exercising early in the morning, a convenient option is to run on the track at the University of Nevada, Las Vegas. Located about two miles east of the Strip on Harmon Avenue, **UNLV** offers both a regulation track and some large, grassy athletic fields. Park in the dirt lot near the tennis courts if you do not have a university parking sticker. For more information, call ☎ 702-895-4729.

If you have a car and a little time, two of the better off-road runs in the area are at **Red Rock Canyon,** out Charleston Boulevard, 35 minutes west of town. Red Rock Canyon Conservation Area, managed by the U.S. Bureau of Land Management, is Western desert and canyon scenery at its best. Spectacular geology combined with the unique desert flora and fauna make Red Rock Canyon a truly memorable place. Maps and information can be obtained at the visitor center, on-site.

A two-mile round-trip, **Moenkopi Loop,** begins and ends at the visitor center. A three-mile circuit, **Willow Springs Trail,** begins at Willow Springs Picnic Area and circles around to Lost Creek Canyon. Both routes are moderately hilly, with pretty good footing. Moenkopi Loop is characterized by open desert and expansive vistas, while the Willow Springs Trail ventures into the canyons. The Willow Springs Trail is also distinguished by numerous Indian petroglyphs and other artifacts. Both trails, of course, are great for hiking as well as for running.

Finally, if you want to hook up with local runners, join the Las Vegas Track Club for a weekly run to **Tule Springs** (north of downtown on US 95) or many other area locations. For a current schedule or additional information, call the Village Runner at ☎ 702-898-7866 or visit **villagerunner.com.**

SWIMMING AND SUNBATHING

SWIMMING, DURING WARM-WEATHER MONTHS, is the most dependable and generally accessible form of exercise in Las Vegas. Most of the Strip hotels and a couple of the downtown hotels have nice pools. Sometimes the pools are too congested for swimming laps, but usually it is possible to stake out a lane.

If the pool at your hotel is a funny shape or too crowded for a workout, there are pools more conducive to serious swimming at the **Las Vegas Athletic Club** on Flamingo Road and in the **McDermott Physical Education Complex** of UNLV.

For those who want to work on their tans in style, the **Mirage, Tropicana, Wynn Las Vegas, Wynn Encore, M Resort, Mandalay Bay, Venetian, Palazzo, Aria, Paris, Monte Carlo, MGM Grand, T. I., Caesars Palace, Rio, Las Vegas Hilton, Flamingo, Palms, Green Valley Ranch, Hard Rock Hotel, Bellagio, Planet Hollywood,** and **JW Marriott Las Vegas,** among others, have particularly elegant facilities. Hotels with above-average pools include the **Luxor, Riviera,** and **Harrah's.**

Be forewarned that sunbathing in Las Vegas can be dangerous. The climate is so arid that you will not feel yourself perspiring: perspiration evaporates as soon as it surfaces on your skin. If there is a breeze, particularly on a pleasant fall or spring day, you may never feel hot, sticky, or in any way uncomfortable until you come out of the sun and discover that you have been fried.

 You can get sunburned quickly if you do not protect yourself properly. Even those with a tan should be careful. See our sidebar on the following page for sun-protection tips.

HEALTH CLUBS

IF YOU CAN GET BY WITH A LIFECYCLE, a StairMaster, or a rowing machine, the fitness rooms of most major hotels should serve your needs. Fortunately, local health clubs welcome visitors for a daily ($15 to $20) or weekly ($30 to $50) fee. All of the clubs described here are coed.

The **Las Vegas Athletic Clubs,** with six locations, offer racquetball, tennis, basketball, exercise equipment, and aerobics, though not all features are provided at each location. These clubs depend more on local patronage than on visitors; their facilities are commodious but not luxurious, and fees are at the lower end of the range. While reasonably convenient to the Strip, only the West Sahara club is within walking distance. For rates and additional info visit **lvac.com** or call:

Respect for the Sun

Newsweek health and science writer **Avery Hurt** sheds some light on the often confusing products and methods for avoiding sunburn. Here's the basic advice from the medical experts.

Choose a sunscreen that is convenient for you to use. Some prefer sprays, others lotions. The form of sunscreen doesn't matter as much as the technique of applying it.

Apply sunscreen a half hour before going out, and be sure to get enough on you. One ounce per application is recommended—that means a full shot glass worth each time you apply. The one-ounce amount was calculated for average adults in swimsuits; an average 7-year-old will probably take two-thirds of an ounce (20 cc). It's a good idea to measure that ounce in your hands at home so you will be familiar with what an ounce looks in your palms. It really is far more sunscreen than you tend to think.

Be sure and get a generous covering on all exposed skin. Then reapply (another full shot glass) every two hours or after swimming or sweating. No matter what it says on the label, no sunscreen is waterproof, and water resistance is limited. And none of them last all day.

There is very little difference in protection between 15 or so SPF and 45 or 50 or greater. There is no need to spend more for higher SPF numbers. In fact, it is much safer to choose a lower (and typically less expensive) SPF (as long as it is at least 15) and apply it more often. However, do be sure to choose a product that has broad-spectrum coverage, meaning that it filters out both UVA and UVB rays. As long as the SPF is at least 15 and offers broad-spectrum protection, one brand can serve the whole family. There's no need to pay extra for special formulas made for children.

It is best to keep babies under 6 months old covered and out of the sun. However, the AAP condones a small amount of sunscreen on vulnerable areas, such as the nose and chin, when you have your baby out. Be very careful to monitor your baby even if he is wearing a hat and sitting under an umbrella.

Use a lipgloss with an SPF of 15 and reapply often to your own lips and those of your kids. Again, the brand is less important than choosing something that you will use—and remembering to use it.

Sunglasses are also a must. Too much sun exposure can contribute to age-related macular degeneration (among other things). Not all sunglasses filter out damaging rays. Be sure to choose shades (for adults and kids) that have 99% UV protection. Large lenses and wraparound styles might not look as cool, but they offer much better protection. You may have to spend a little more to be sure you are getting adequate protection, but you don't want to skimp on this.

If you do slip up and get a burn, cool baths, aloe gels, and ibuprofen (or for adults, aspirin) usually help ease the suffering. Occasionally sunburns can be as dangerous in the short term as they are in the long term. If you or your child experience nausea, vomiting, high fever, severe pain, confusion, or fainting, seek medical care immediately.

5200 W. Sahara Ave.	9065 S. Eastern Ave.	3830 E. Flamingo Rd.
☎ 702-364-5822	☎ 702-853-5822	☎ 702-898-5822
2655 S. Maryland Pkwy.	1725 N. Rainbow Blvd.	9615 W. Flamingo Rd.
☎ 702-734-5822	☎ 702-835-5822	☎ 702-798-5822

The **24 Hour Fitness** centers, with two locations, run an excellent aerobics program and have an extensive weight and exercise facility. While the facilities are good and the use fees midrange, locations are a little remote for most visitors staying on the Strip or downtown.

S. Eastern near Sahara	Cheyenne and Rainbow
☎ 702-641-2222	☎ 702-656-7777

FREE WEIGHTS AND MACHINES

ALMOST ALL OF THE MAJOR HOTELS have a spa or fitness room with weight-lifting equipment. Some properties have a single Universal machine, while others offer a wide range of free-weight and Nautilus/Cybex equipment. Hotels with above-average facilities for pumping iron are the **Las Vegas Hilton, Bellagio, Venetian, Caesars Palace, Aria, Golden Nugget, Mirage, Paris, Wynn Las Vegas, Wynn Encore, M Resort, Mandalay Bay, Monte Carlo, MGM Grand, Luxor,** and **T. I.**

For hard-core power lifters and bodybuilders, try **Gold's Gym.** Gold's is coed and offers daily and monthly rates ($15 and $70, respectively) for use of its Nautilus equipment and free weights. Contact them at any one of their six locations: East, ☎ 702-451-4222; South, ☎ 702-914-5885; Southeast, ☎ 702-269-0828; Summerlin, ☎ 702-360-8205; Centennial, ☎ 702-657-0171; and Aliante, ☎ 702-396-0800.

GOLF

PEAK SEASON FOR GOLF IN LAS VEGAS is October through May. The other four months are considered prohibitively warm for most golfers, but greens fees are reduced substantially at most courses during summer. Certain courses also have reduced rates for locals and for guests staying at hotels affiliated with the golf course. Also, almost all Las Vegas–area courses offer discounted twilight rates, which, depending on time of year, often start as early as noon. In general, morning tee times are more difficult to arrange than afternoons. Call the pro shop at least one day before you wish to play. Same-day phone calls are discouraged. Due to the sharp drop in Las Vegas golf and tourism activity two years ago, most courses are now boldly advertising discounts and specials at almost all times, so check the course's website before booking. In summer most courses and driving ranges stay open until at least 7:30 p.m. A well-established company called **Stand-By Golf,** now in its 20th year, offers unsold tee times from some courses in Las Vegas and now Mesquite up to 14

GOLF COURSE RATINGS	
QUALITY RATING	**VALUE RATING**
★★★ Championship, challenging	1 A good bargain
★★ Playable, suitable for all caliber golfers	2 A fair price
★ Preferred by beginners and casual golfers	3 Not a good bargain

Note: Quality and value ratings are abbreviated as QV rating in the following listings.

days in advance at discounts of 20 to 60% (☎ 866-711-2665, **stand bygolflv.com**). In winter and early spring, temperatures drop rapidly near sundown, so always bring a sweater or jacket. It can also be very windy. Las Vegas has an elevation of 2,000 feet and is considered high desert. Take this into account when making club selections.

IMPORTANT NOTES Many top Las Vegas courses are private clubs that do not allow outside access, and thus are not listed. In addition, Las Vegas has created a unique sort of golf course that could be called "almost private." This started with **Shadow Creek Country Club,** which was built specifically for the highest of high rollers and originally had neither members nor allowed paying guests. Now privately owned by MGM Resorts International, the course is open to guests of its hotels, but on a very limited basis. Only a handful of "public" tee times are available each day (Monday through Thursday only) at a cost of $500 per person, which along with the similar course Cascata, constitute the nation's highest greens fees. In this sense Vegas has created its own category of courses that are open only to a handful of guests from specific hotels at extremely high prices. Not quite so extravagant is **The Tournament Players Club,** which is now open to the general public, but guests of JW Marriott Las Vegas at Summerlin receive preferred tee times and personalized service. Prices are high but not sky-high. This is where Tiger Woods won his very first PGA Tour event back in 1996. The Summerlin course was designed by architect Bobby Weed with assistance from player-consultant Fuzzy Zoeller and has been rated by both *Golf Digest* and *Golfweek* magazines as the second-best course in Nevada, behind Shadow Creek. The opulent Wynn course once fell into the "almost private" category, but feeling the pressure of Vegas's economic downturn has now opened its course to fully public outside play.

Despite the number of golf courses in the Las Vegas area, for serious golf travel fans there are only three choices that could accurately be called golf resorts—and that is still a bit of a stretch. **Lake Las Vegas,** about half an hour from the Strip, was once one of the top self-contained golf resorts in the nation. However, recently it has become an economic victim of over-leveraging, losing both its resort courses and the Ritz-Carlton hotel, which abruptly closed its doors in early 2010. The now-defunct flagship layout, Reflection Bay, was arguably the best in town. The good news is that the resort's fortunes are looking up, with well-regarded golf resort management company Dolce reviving the Ritz property as the Ravella in late 2010, and both the Ravella and Loews Lake Las Vegas hotels are partnering with the formerly private, resident-only country club course at Lake Las Vegas, the Jack Nicklaus–designed South Shore Golf Club. For the time being, Lake Las Vegas is hanging on and still offering both very good golf and lodging, and there are rumors that the awesome Reflection Bay course, which has been modestly maintained throughout the bankruptcy resolution, will again reopen. In **Summerlin,** about 25 minutes from the Strip, the JW Marriott is surrounded by nine courses within ten minutes and offers preferred tee times and free shuttles to several of them, making it a true destination golf resort. In the city, the **Wynn** is the only hotel with an on-site course, making it an urban golf resort of sorts, though a very pricey one. All three properties have lavish spas, pools, activities, multiple restaurants, bars, and casinos.

Nationwide, more golf courses have closed than opened in the past three years, reflecting the economic realities, and boom-or-bust Las Vegas is no exception. The Falls and Reflection Bay at Lake Las Vegas were the first two high-profile layouts to shutter, and they will soon be joined by Bali Hai, one of only two courses with enviable Strip locations; the other is Wynn Golf Club. Bali Hai, which was always overrated and overpriced but certainly ultra-convenient, is slated to be paved under for a 2-million-square-foot commercial center as soon as final permitting is done, almost certainly in 2011.

Angel Park Golf Club

ESTABLISHED 1989 | STATUS MUNICIPAL | QV RATING ★★ 2

100 South Rampart Boulevard, Las Vegas, NV 89145; ☎ 702-254-4653; angelpark.com

Tees PALM COURSE
- **Professional: 6,500 yards, par 70, USGA 70.3, slope 124**
- **Championship: 5,857 yards, par 70, USGA 67.1, slope 115**
- **Forward: 4,578 yards, par 70, USGA 66.8, slope 110**

MOUNTAIN COURSE
- **Professional: 6,722 yards, par 71, USGA 71.1, slope 130**
- **Championship: 6,223 yards, par 71, USGA 68.8, slope 125**
- **Forward: 5,150 yards, par 71, USGA 69.1, slope 114**

Fees Nonresidents: $75–$135; Residents: $40–$49

Facilities Pro shop, night-lit driving range, 12-hole par-3 course and 9-hole putting course, putting green, restaurant, snack bar, bar, tennis courts, golf club and shoe rentals.

Comments Angel Park, a good, functional golf complex, is rapidly becoming one of the most successful public golf facilities in the United States. Its courses are well designed—by Arnold Palmer, no less—and the sophisticated 18-hole putting course, complete with night lighting, sand traps, rough, and water hazards, is a popular attraction even for nongolfers. Its "Cloud Nine" short course is unique and great for golfers needing a quick fix, with reproductions of 12 famous par-3 holes from around the world, 9 of which are lit for night play. There is also a lighted natural-grass putting course—think fancy mini-golf. Both courses are crowded year-round, as the facility is close to the Strip and popular with locals.

Bear's Best

ESTABLISHED 2002 | STATUS PUBLIC | QV RATING ★★★ 2

11111 West Flamingo Road, Las Vegas, NV 89135; ☎ 866-385-8500; clubcorp.com

Tees • **Gold:** 7,194 yards, par 72, USGA 74.0, slope 147
• **Blue:** 6,628 yards, par 72, USGA 71.3, slope 130
• **White:** 6,043 yards, par 72, USGA 68.3, slope 122
• **Red:** 5,043 yards, par 72, USGA 68.7, slope 116

Fees $59–$250, depending on time of day; see website for details. Club rentals, $50.

Facilities Pro shop, driving range, putting green, restaurant, full locker facilities, caddies, fore-caddies, club and shoe rentals.

Comments One of only two Bear's Best courses (the other is in Atlanta), this is a tribute by Jack Nicklaus, aka the Golden Bear, to himself. Here Nicklaus has re-created holes from his favorite original designs, but unlike most tribute or replica courses, including Vegas's Royal Links, the holes were specifically chosen to fit the desert setting. As a result, this is one of the best of these gimmicky layouts in the world. Fans have the opportunity to play holes from Nicklaus's most acclaimed public courses, such as Cabo del Sol, Palmilla, and Castle Pines, along with very private ones from Desert Mountain, Desert Highlands, and PGA West. Since opening it has been ranked among the city's best courses. It is also a classy operation and one of the few golf clubs anywhere to boast top-quality rental sets, sparing no expense right down to Scotty Cameron putters and choice of shaft stiffness. Since the demise of Reflection Bay, this is the best public course in the Vegas area other than the barely public Shadow Creek.

Black Mountain Golf and Country Club

ESTABLISHED 1959 | STATUS SEMIPRIVATE | QV RATING ★ 1

500 Greenway Road, Henderson, NV 89015; ☎ 702-565-7933; golfblackmountain.com

Tees • **Championship:** 6,556–6,613 yards, par 72, USGA 70.6–71.1, slope 124–129
• **Men's:** 6,148–6,279 yards, par 72, USGA 69.0–69.6, slope 121–128
• **Ladies':** 5,148–5,319 yards, par 72, USGA 69.4–70.2, slope 111–114

Fees Nonresidents: high season, $95 (carts included on weekends only); low season, $75. Residents: high season, $48; low season, $45.

Facilities Pro shop, clubhouse, driving range, putting green, restaurant, club rentals, snack bar, bar.

Comments 27-hole Black Mountain is set amidst the Henderson hills, 20 minutes from the Strip. Many who prefer walking to riding play here, as it's one of the few area courses that doesn't require electric carts during the week. Many bunkers and unimproved areas off fairways make for tough recovery shots. A good course for beginning and intermediate golfers and juniors—and a good value year-round. The course wrapped up a $2-million renovation in late 2008 and is uniquely semi-public, fully owned by members but wide-open and welcoming to visitors.

Cascata

ESTABLISHED 2000 | STATUS PUBLIC | QV RATING ★★★ 3

1 Cascata Drive, Boulder City, NV 89142; ☎ 702-294-2005; cascatagolf.com

Tees • **Black: 7,137 yards, par 72, USGA 74.6, slope 143**
• **Blue: 6,664 yards, par 72, USGA 71.7, slope 138**
• **Gold: 6,206 yards, par 72, USGA 69.9, slope 135**
• **Red: 5,591 yards, par 72, USGA 67.2, slope 117**

Fees $325–$375. Closed Tuesdays. Fees include round-trip limo transfer from hotel and caddie (recommended tip $50). Discounted golf and lodging packages are available with Caesars properties. Primarily reserved for guests of Caesars (Harrah's) properties, with limited availability for the general public.

Facilities Pro shop, driving range, putting green, restaurant, full locker facilities, caddies.

Comments After the runaway success of Shadow Creek, another casino group built the even more expensive Cascata, said to have the highest golf course construction price tag ever, for its high rollers. Now owned by Caesars Entertainment, it is a truly unique design in golf. Acclaimed designer Rees Jones blasted the course out of a rocky mountain. The holes are built in a series of narrow, parallel finger canyons radiating from the summit and running up and down the rocky slopes. Sitting in the canyons, the lush green fairways are completely isolated from one another by sloped canyon walls. The par-3s are especially dramatic, often backed by amphitheater cliffs and waterfalls. Because its name is Italian for "waterfall," Jones built one 40 stories high that pours through the center of the marble Italian palazzo–style clubhouse. Among the three $500 Vegas courses, Cascata was the first to blink in the recession and has been offering rates of "only" $325–$375, 7 days a week, in prime times.

Desert Pines Golf Club

ESTABLISHED 1997 | STATUS PUBLIC | QV RATING ★ 2

3415 East Bonanza Road, Las Vegas, NV 89101; ☎ 702-388-4400; desertpinesgolfclub.com

Tees • **Championship: 6,810 yards, par 71, USGA 70.6, slope 125**
• **Men's: 6,494 yards, par 71, USGA 67.9, slope 118**
• **Ladies': 5,873 yards, par 71, USGA 69.4, slope 116**

Fees Peak Season: $149 Sunday–Thursday, $179 Friday–Sunday ($99 twilight). Rates vary widely by time, even in peak season. Walters Golf's new website (**waltersgolf.com**) offers a low-rate guarantee and up-to-date deals for same- and next-day bookings.

Facilities Pro shop, driving range, putting green, snack bar, restaurant.

Comments Desert Pines is a 6,810-yard course on Bonanza Road between Mojave and Pecos roads. Inspired by the Pinehurst courses in North Carolina, its fairways and greens are flanked by trees, some already as tall as 40 feet. Instead of rough, developer Bill Walters laid down 45,000 bales of red-pine needles imported from South Carolina, making it hard to lose a ball here. Its very low off-season rates make it one of the best hot-weather choices in the region. The course recently renovated its fairways and putting surfaces and is in its best shape in years. Owner Walters Golf partnered with the now independent T. I. resort-casino and now offers some excellent stay-and-play packages.

Highland Falls Golf Club

ESTABLISHED 1992 | STATUS SEMIPRIVATE | QV RATING ★★★ 2

10201 Sun City Boulevard, Las Vegas, NV 89134; ☎ 702-254-7010; golfsummerlin.com

Tees • **Championship: 6,512 yards, par 72, USGA 70.1, slope 119**
• **Men's: 6,017 yards, par 72, USGA 68.1, slope 118**
• **Gold: 5,579 yards, par 72, USGA 71.4, slope 122**
• **Ladies': 5,099 yards, par 72, USGA 68.4, slope 112**

Fees Nonresidents: $95 daily; $75 twilight. Residents: $55 daily; $45 twilight.

Facilities Pro shop, driving range, putting green, restaurant, luncheon area, patio for outside dining, bar.

Comments In a local shocker, readers of the *Review Journal* voted this the best golf in Las Vegas for 2011. It's hard to fathom, but the course is good, a testing layout designed by Hall of Famer Billy Casper's company, Casper-Nash Associates. The unique design sits in the mountains at over 3,000 feet, and the cooler weather allows it to use superior quality bentgrass greens, unusual in this climate, and Bermuda fairways to combine the best of both worlds. More undulations than most desert courses, with several demanding holes. No one broke par for the first six months after opening. Schedule tee times at least seven days in advance. The course now offers specials to its Twitter followers.

Lake Las Vegas

ESTABLISHED 1998 | STATUS RESORT, PUBLIC | QV RATING ★★★ 2

101 Montelago Boulevard, Henderson, NV 89011; ☎ 702-567-6000; loewshotels.com/lakelasvegas

Tees • **Black: 6,917 yards, par 72, USGA 72.6, slope 135**
• **White: 6,524 yards, par 71, USGA 70.7, slope 130**
• **Blue: 6,254 yards, par 71, USGA 70.4, slope 130**
• **Gold: 6,204 yards, par 71, USGA 66.5, slope 123**
• **Red: 4,852 yards, par 71, USGA 67.9, slope 115**

Fees Weekday $190, weekend $210, resort guests only. Lodging and golf packages available from $299 per night.

Facilities Pro shop, driving range, putting green, snack bar, restaurant, full locker facilities.

Comments Expensive but worth it. Replacing the shuttered Reflection Bay and The Falls courses is access to the private South Shore Golf Club—but only for guests of Loews Lake Las Vegas and the new Dolce resort, Ravella (formerly Ritz-Carlton). With sweeping views of Lake Las Vegas, the waterfront signature design by Jack Nicklaus was named one of the "Top 10 Private Golf Courses in America" by *Golf Digest* when it opened in 1996 and has hosted the Wendy's 3-Tour Championship. The course is both beautiful and challenging, with numerous forced carries over canyons and water and substantial elevation changes, plus high-quality bentgrass greens. We'll hope the rumors are true and the excellent Reflection Bay course here will reopen within the next year.

Las Vegas Golf Club

ESTABLISHED 1949 | STATUS PUBLIC | QV RATING   ★   2

4300 West Washington Avenue, Las Vegas, NV 89107;
☎ **702-646-3003; lasvegasgc.com**

Tees • **Championship: 6,290 yards, par 72, USGA 69.8, slope 121**
• **Men's: 5,917 yards, par 72, USGA 68.2, slope 116**
• **Ladies': 5,260 yards, par 72, USGA 69.9, slope 113**

Fees Nonresidents: weekdays $59, $49 twilight; weekends $69.

Facilities Pro shop, night-lit driving range, putting green, restaurant, snack bar, bar, and beverage-cart girls who patrol the course.

Comments The past two years have seen $5 million in renovations and improvements pumped into the first and oldest golf course in Las Vegas, laid out by the legendary William Bell in 1938. It has remained a popular public course and a site of many local amateur tournaments. Formerly owned and managed by Senior PGA star Jim Colbert, then American Golf, it again changed hands and is now operated by Eagle Golf. A good choice for recreational golfers, with fairly wide-open fairways and little trouble, so play should move briskly.

Las Vegas National

ESTABLISHED 1961 | STATUS PUBLIC (PRIVATELY OWNED) | QV RATING   ★★   2

1911 East Desert Inn Road, Las Vegas NV 89109; ☎ **866-731-4658 or 702-734-1796 (tee-time service and other reservations); lasvegasnational.com**

Tees • **Championship: 6,773 yards, par 72, USGA 73.5, slope 137**
• **Men's: 6,260 yards, par 71, USGA 71.6, slope 133**
• **Ladies': 5,640 yards, par 72, USGA 68.8, slope 130**

Fees Before 11 a.m., $99; 11 a.m.–1 p.m., $69; 1 p.m. on, $40.

Facilities Pro shop, night-lit driving range, putting green, restaurant, bar.

Comments New lower rates, usually less than $99, make this one of the best and most convenient buys in town. A championship course that has at one time cohosted the Tournament of Champions, the Sahara Invitational, and the Ladies' Sahara Classic. Tiger Woods is a past champion here (he shot 70 to win). The course is convenient to the Strip ($10 cab ride) and offers an excellent variety of holes, with good bunkering and elevation changes uncharacteristic of a desert course. Better for intermediate and advanced golfers.

Las Vegas Paiute Resort

EST. 1995 | STATUS PUBLIC | QV RATING ★★ 2 (SNOW/SUN) ★★★ 2 (WOLF)

10325 Nu-Wav Kaiv Boulevard, Las Vegas, NV 89124 (US 95 between Kyle Canyon and Lee Canyon turn-off to Mount Charleston); ☎ 702-658-1400 or 800-711-2833; lvpaiutegolf.com

Tees SNOW MOUNTAIN
- **Tournament: 7,146 yards, par 72, USGA 73.3, slope 125**
- **Championship: 6,645 yards, par 72, USGA 71.2, slope 120**
- **Regular: 6,035 yards, par 72, USGA 68.6, slope 112**
- **Forward: 5,341 yards, par 72, USGA 70.4, slope 117**

SUN MOUNTAIN
- **Tournament: 7,112 yards, par 72, USGA 73.3, slope 130**
- **Championship: 6,631 yards, par 72, USGA 70.9, slope 124**
- **Regular: 6,074 yards, par 72, USGA 68.8, slope 116**
- **Forward: 5,465 yards, par 72, USGA 71.0, slope 123**

WOLF
- **Tournament: 7,604 yards, par 72, USGA 76.3, slope 149**
- **Black: 7,009 yards, par 72, USGA 73.5, slope 134**
- **Yellow: 6,483 yards, par 72, USGA 71.4, slope 130**
- **White: 5,910 yards, par 72, USGA 76.5, slope 125**
- **Red: 5,130 yards, par 72, USGA 68.5, slope 116**

Fees March 1–May 30: $139; twilight (seasonal), $89. June 1–August 31: $89; twilight, $69. There is always a $20–$30 surcharge to play the Wolf course. They offer discounts on multiday play and for military.

Facilities Pro shop, driving range, 2 putting greens, restaurant, snack bar, bar with gaming.

Comments The region's only 54-hole resort golf complex, all three courses are Pete Dye designs. Dye is infamous for creating difficult tests, but the original two layouts, Snow and Sun Mountain, are comfortable desert courses, beauty without brawn, and have remained among the public favorites in the region since opening. Not so for the newer Wolf, which is one of, if not the most, difficult courses in Las Vegas. From the tips it is 500 yards longer than any course most golfers have played, and strewn with hazards of the wet and dry variety. Still, it is as well conditioned and thought out as its tamer siblings and has a near re-creation of Dye's famous island hole par-3 he pioneered at the TPC Sawgrass. Despite its stiff challenge, it has quickly become the most demanded course here and is accordingly priced higher. In keeping with Las Vegas's recent aggressive discounting, the Paiute Resort now offers "Golfapalooza" packages all the time, which include lunch, 50% off rentals, and a free replay round from just $159.

Legacy Golf Club

ESTABLISHED 1989 | STATUS PUBLIC (PRIVATELY OWNED) | QV RATING ★★ 2

130 Par Excellence Drive, Henderson, NV 89014; ☎ 702-897-2187; thelegacygc.com

Tees
- **Championship: 7,233 yards, par 72, USGA 74.5, slope 137**
- **Men's: 6,744 yards, par 72, USGA 71.5, slope 128**
- **Ladies': 5,340 yards, par 72, USGA 71.5, slope 128**
- **Resort: 6,211 yards, par 72, USGA 69.3, slope 119**

Fees January 1–May 31: weekdays, $135; weekends, $155. June 1–October 1: $75. Twilight rates vary ($75–$85). All greens fees include mandatory carts. Club rentals, $50 ($35 twilight).

Facilities Clubhouse, pro shop, driving range, chipping facility, putting green, restaurant, snack bar, bar.

Comments A long course by Arthur Hills, the Legacy is a mixture of rolling fairways and target golf. It is also one of the most photographed courses in Vegas because its tees are shaped like playing card suits. Championship tees require a long carry on the tee-ball to clear desert mounding. Located at the southeastern tip of Las Vegas, Legacy has quickly become a favorite of intermediate and advanced golfers.

Painted Desert

ESTABLISHED 1987 | STATUS PUBLIC | QV RATING ★★ 2

5555 Painted Mirage Drive, Las Vegas, NV 89149; ☎ 702-645-2570; painteddesertgc.com

Tees
- **Championship: 6,781 yards, par 72, USGA 71.8, slope 129**
- **Men's: 6,269 yards, par 72, USGA 69.9, slope 125**
- **Ladies': 5,647 yards, par 72, USGA 72.2, slope 126**

Fees Peak season: Monday–Thursday, $89; twilight rate, $69; Friday–Sunday, $99; twilight rate, $79. Off-peak: Monday–Thursday, $69; Friday–Sunday, $79. Club rentals, $45 (includes 2 sleeves of golf balls).

Facilities Pro shop, driving range, putting green, restaurant, bar.

Comments Target course designed by renowned architect Jay Morrish, Tom Weiskopf's partner. Lush fairway landing pads and well-manicured greens, but make certain you're on target. The rough is pure waste-area. Now operated by Eagle Golf, the course offers numerous discounts seasonally.

PGA Golf Club at Coyote Springs

ESTABLISHED 2008 | STATUS SEMIPRIVATE | QV RATING ★★★ 2

3100 State Route 168, Coyote Springs, NV 89037; ☎ 702-422-1438; coyotesprings.com

Tees
- **Black: 7,471 yards, par 72, USGA 75.8, slope 141**
- **Blue: 6,807 yards, par 72, USGA 72, slope 137**
- **White: 6,215 yards, par 72, USGA 69.3, slope 132**
- **Red: 5,288 yards, par 72, USGA 70.5, slope 127**

Fees Peak: daily, $175 ($145 after 11 a.m.); off-peak (after June 1): daily, $105 ($90 after 11 a.m.).

Facilities Pro shop, driving range, putting green, snack bar, restaurant, full locker facilities.

Comments The biggest recent addition to the Las Vegas golf scene, the Chase at Coyote Springs anchors a new residential community 50 minutes north of downtown. Developed by the PGA of America, the Chase opened in May 2008 to rave reviews—named "Best New U.S. Public Course" in 2009 by *Links* and in the top ten new courses by *Golf Magazine* and *Golf Digest*. It is just the first of several Jack Nicklaus Signature courses planned for the community, with the same designer who has had so much success locally with Reflection Bay and Bear's Best. The Chase is reminiscent of Reflection Bay with elaborate rock-lined water features—11 lakes in all—but has more dramatic fairways and pronounced undulations, and the desert hazards are sandier and more landscaped, less wild, than many area courses. Nicklaus is famed for his dramatic waterfront finishes, and this course is no exception, with the last four holes curving around lakes. Prices are in line with the more expensive Vegas-area courses, but the quality is better than most. However, it's not as good a value as the equally far-flung courses of Primm and Mesquite, Nevada. In an interesting homage to the setting, each hole is named for Vegas slang, such as "On Tilt" and "Shooter." Free replay and stay-and-play specials with the Golden Nugget are offered.

The Revere at Anthem

ESTABLISHED 1999 | STATUS PUBLIC | QV RATING ★★ 2

2600 Hampton Road, Henderson, NV 89052; ☎ 702-259-GOLF or 877-273-8373; reveregolf.com

Tees LEXINGTON

- **Black: 7,143 yards, par 72,** USGA **73.5, slope 138**
- **Gold: 6,590 yards, par 72,** USGA **70.8, slope 131**
- **Silver (Ladies'): 5,941 yards, par 72,** USGA **73.3, slope 127**
- **Bronze (Ladies'): 5,216 yards, par 72,** USGA **69.9, slope 118**

CONCORD

- **Black: 7,069 yards, par 72,** USGA **72.8, slope 126**
- **Gold: 6,546 yards, par 72,** USGA **69.8, slope 121**
- **Silver: 6,094 yards, par 72,** USGA **67.6, slope 119**
- **Bronze (Ladies'): 5,171 yards, par 72,** USGA **69.7, slope 118**

Fees $90–$199; rates are seasonal—visit their website for the most current information. Club rentals, $65.

Facilities Fully stocked clubhouse and snack bar, golf shop, restaurant.

Comments This 36-hole facility was named the nation's best facility operated by Troon Golf, a highly respected management company. Both courses were designed by Billy Casper and Greg Nash, and the club is consistently rated among the city's top ten. About 20 minutes from the Strip in the southeast Las Vegas Valley, Revere is built in a natural canyon, with a feel that is secluded and intimate. Lexington is the longer and more challenging layout, with numerous risk–reward opportunities, while the slightly shorter and newer Concord features wider fairways and larger greens. Much of the year, 36-hole specials are offered for playing both courses in the same day.

Rio Secco Golf Club

ESTABLISHED 1997 | STATUS RESORT, PUBLIC | QV RATING ★★ 3

2851 Grand Hills Drive, Henderson, NV 89052; ☎ 888-867-3226; riosecco.net

Tees • **Championship: 7,313 yards, par 72, USGA 75.0, slope 153**
• **Blue: 6,927 yards, par 72, USGA 73.0, slope 149**
• **Middle: 6,375 yards, par 72, USGA 70.7, slope 136**
• **Forward: 5,758 yards, par 72, USGA 70.7, slope 127**

Fees $60–$285; rates vary—visit their website for the most current information. Club rentals, $75 (includes 2 sleeves of balls).

Facilities Pro shop, driving range, putting green, snack bar, restaurant, full locker facilities, Butch Harmon Golf School.

Comments The best and closest of Las Vegas's pure desert-style courses, Rio Secco is set amid 240 acres of dramatic canyons just 12 minutes from the Strip. Variety, beauty, and strategic design highlighted by 88 bunkers make this a challenging but beautiful course. However, its perimeter is heavily lined with homes, negating some of the desert feel. It is also golf-school headquarters for celebrity instructor Butch Harmon, whose former pupil, Tiger Woods, holds the course record with a stunning 63. Like Cascata, the course is owned by Caesars and recently added a T-Mates program, a combination of Las Vegas showgirls with (scantily clad) forecaddies.

Royal Links

ESTABLISHED 1999 | STATUS PUBLIC | QV RATING ★★ 3

5995 East Vegas Valley Road, Las Vegas, NV 89142; ☎ 888-427-6678; royallinksgolfclub.com

Tees • **Royal: 7,029 yards, par 72, USGA 73.7, slope 135**
• **Gold: 6,602 yards, par 72, USGA 71.2, slope 131**
• **Ruby: 5,864 yards, par 72, USGA 68.4, slope 125**
• **Emerald: 5,142 yards, par 72, USGA 69.8, slope 115**

Fees September–April: weekdays $175, weekends $199; twilight $150 daily; super-twilight (after 3:30 p.m.) weekdays $75, weekends $95. Summer rates: $99–$135; $59–$90 twilight. Club rentals, $70. Walters Golf's new website (**waltersgolf.com**) offers a low-rate guarantee and up-to-date deals for same- and next-day bookings.

Facilities Pro shop, driving range, putting green, restaurant, English pub, full locker facilities, fore-caddies.

Comments Royal Links sets out to emulate 18 holes from British Open venues in England and Scotland. In many ways the course succeeds, with excellent representations of links bunkering, exposure to fierce winds, and authentic rough and gorse. But nearly every course represented is on the ocean, something that cannot be replicated in the desert, and the re-creations are far from exact. As a result, the course is more fun the less you know about the real thing. For instance, the famous Postage Stamp hole from Royal

Troon, the shortest hole on the British Open rota, is copied here, but for some reason the elevation is way off, the bunkering is different, and architect Perry Dye saw fit to add a pond to the famously dry hole. Once very expensive among Vegas courses, the layout is now middle-of-the-pack and worth playing, especially as a novelty if you've never been to the English courses. The course offers the very Vegas "Parmates" program—a female caddie staff of beautiful women hired to sex up the golf experience.

Shadow Creek Golf Club

ESTABLISHED 1990 | STATUS RESORT | QV RATING   ★★   3

3 Shadow Creek Drive, Las Vegas, NV 89030; ☎ 866-260-0069; shadowcreek.com

Tees • **Championship: 7,560 yards, par 72, USGA 71.0, slope 115**
• **Regular: 7,102 yards, par 72, USGA 68.9, slope 113**

Fees Monday–Thursday $500, includes caddie and round-trip limo transportation; must be a guest of an MGM Resorts International hotel to play, but weekends it's invited guests only.

Facilities Pro shop, driving range, putting green, restaurant, full locker facilities, caddies.

Comments Shadow Creek is widely rated as not just the best course in Las Vegas, but among the best in the country. It is ranked 57th in the nation, including privates, by *Golf Magazine,* and in the top ten among public courses, deservedly. Shadow Creek is better considered barely "near public," with the nation's highest greens fees (tied), and those allowed only Monday through Thursday, with weekends reserved for VIPs and high-rolling gamblers. Nonetheless, when the required lodging and dining are thrown in, Shadow Creek falls in the same price range as Pebble Beach and Pinehurst Number Two and offers a far more luxurious experience than either. The course is always empty and meticulously maintained, the caddies are excellent, and the layout is both gorgeous and fun to play. Despite the high level of conditioning, Shadow Creek closed for nearly seven months in 2008 for extensive improvements, including all new tees and greens and the addition of a comprehensive short-game practice area to further enhance the already royal treatment—it is now better than ever. An engineering marvel that transported a classic, heavily wooded Carolina-style parkland layout to the desert, it is rumored to be one of the most expensive courses ever built, having cost about $38 million in the 1980s. The finishing three holes are as memorable and dramatic a close as you will find in the golf world.

Siena Golf Club

ESTABLISHED 2000 | STATUS SEMIPRIVATE | QV RATING   ★★   1

10575 Siena Monte Avenue, Las Vegas, NV 89135; ☎ 888-689-6469; golf shop ☎ 702-341-9200; sienagolfclub.com

Tees • **Gold: 6,843 yards, par 72, USGA 71.7, slope 131**
• **Black: 6,538 yards, par 72, USGA 70.4, slope 129**
• **Blue: 6,146 yards, par 72, USGA 68.6, slope 125**

- **White: 5,639 yards, par 72, USGA 66.4, slope 114**
- **Green: 4,978 yards, par 72, USGA 68.0, slope 112**

Fees $99–$189; rates are seasonal—visit their website for the most current information; special twilight rates available.

Facilities Pro shop, driving range, putting green, snack bar, restaurant, full locker facilities.

Comments A sleeper course in the Summerlin residential community, Siena welcomes outside play and is one of the region's best buys. The bargain replay option is a good deal, and other special promotions are occasionally offered. The course showcases extensive rock outcroppings and water features, including cascading waterfalls around the 18th green. All four par-3s are unique and notable, including "sunken treasure," a gorgeous island green. Well-separated tees offer the right challenge for every player.

TPC Las Vegas

ESTABLISHED 1996 | STATUS PUBLIC | QV RATING   ★★★   3

9851 Canyon Run Drive, Las Vegas, NV 89145; ☎ 702-256-2000; tpc.com

Tees
- **TPC: 7,081 yards, par 71, USGA 73.4, slope 136**
- **Blue: 6,769 yards, par 71, USGA 71.0, slope 128**
- **White: 6,047 yards, par 71, USGA 68.0, slope 127**
- **Red: 4,963 yards, par 71, USGA 67.8, slope 117**

Fees $59–$229; rates are seasonal—visit their website for the most current information.

Facilities Pro shop, driving range, putting green, snack bar, restaurant, full locker facilities.

Comments Long known as TPC Canyons, this course by any name is one of the few public offerings among the Tournament Players Clubs, or the TPC network, so-called "stadium courses," designed specifically to host and showcase tournaments and owned by the PGA Tour. Designed by Bobby Weed and Ray Floyd, it hosts the Las Vegas Invitational and has hosted the Michelob Championship. This is a tough desert course, with plenty of opportunities to lose balls in the dry wash and cacti, but is well designed and appealing to the better player. The facilities are first-rate, but they should be at this price. The course has packages with the adjacent JW Marriott Summerlin resort and Red Rock Casino Resort.

Wynn Golf Club

ESTABLISHED 2005 | STATUS PRIVATE | QV RATING   ★★   3

3131 South Las Vegas Boulevard, Las Vegas, NV 89109; ☎ 702-770-GOLF; wynnlasvegas.com

Tees
- **Back: 7,042 yards, par 70, USGA 73.9, slope 124**
- **Black: 6,464 yards, par 70, USGA 72.5, slope 120**

Fees $500 ($300–$375 in summer). Fees include caddie.

Facilities Pro shop, driving net, putting green, restaurant, full locker facilities, caddies.

Comments Steve Wynn collaborated with Tom Fazio, widely considered the top golf architect in the world, to build Shadow Creek when Wynn owned Mirage Resorts. The duo got together again for this course on the former site of the Desert Inn Country Club. Nothing of the old layout is recognizable, as Fazio moved 800,000 cubic yards of earth and changed the flat course to one with rolling elevation changes, boulder-strewn creeks, a huge four-story waterfall you drive carts behind, and endless flowerbeds. The fairways and greens are immaculate, and the devotion to maintenance and aesthetics are obvious, making Wynn GC a very attractive and playable course, but frankly it is not on par with its $500 brethren, Cascata and Shadow Creek, as once-in-a-lifetime experiences. Anywhere else this course would be lucky to command $250, but as the old real estate adage goes, location is everything, and this is the only hotel course on the Strip where guests can walk to the first tee rather than face daunting cab rides, and with the impending demise of Bali Hai, it will soon be the only course on the Strip period. Still, the location comes at a cost: the new Las Vegas Monorail runs along the perimeter, and instead of majestic trees, skyline views are of the Eiffel Tower, Stratosphere, and myriad new condo high-rises. Lack of space explains the par-70 design, and even at that length it remains a bit crowded. In a big change of direction, Wynn GC recently opened to the public, and you no longer need to stay here to play.

OUTDOOR RECREATION

LAS VEGAS AND THE SURROUNDING AREA offer a host of outdoor and adventure activities. The following section provides information on the activities available.

BICYCLING

ASK ANY CYCLIST IN LAS VEGAS about the on- and off-road riding nearby and you'll probably hear two kinds of comments. First, why pedaling in the desert is such a treat: excellent surface conditions; the option of pancake-flat or hilly riding; starkly beautiful scenery any time of year, and cactus blossoms in March and April; the possibility of spying raptors or jack rabbits or wild burros as you pedal; the unbelievably colorful limestone and sandstone formations.

Unfortunately, newcomers to desert and high-elevation biking often recall only these comments and not the "Be sure to carry—" warnings, which fellow riders usually provide after they've gotten you all revved up. So read the following and remember that bikers are subject to those very same conditions—heat and aridity—that make the desert so breathtaking.

Biking Essentials

1. TIME OF DAY Desert biking in late spring, summer, and early fall is best done early or late in the day. Know your seasons, listen to weather reports, and don't overestimate your speed and ability.

2. CLOTHING Ever see someone perched on a camel? What was he wearing? Right, it wasn't a tank top and Lycra shorts. The point is protection—from the sun during the day, from the cold in the morning and evening. And if you don't use a helmet, wear a hat.

3. SUNSCREEN In the desert, even well-tanned riders need this stuff.

4. SUNGLASSES The glare will blind you without them.

5. WATER The first time we rode in the desert, we carried as much water as we would have used on a ride of comparable distance in the eastern United States. Big mistake. Our need for water was at least twice what it normally would be in New York or Alabama. We were thirsty the entire trip and might have gotten into serious trouble had we not cut our ride short.

You already know that you will need extra water, but how much? Well, a human working hard in 90°F temperature requires ten quarts of fluid replenishment every day. Ten *quarts.* That's two and a half gallons—12 large water bottles, or 16 small ones. And with water weighing in at eight pounds per gallon, a one-day supply comes to a whopping 20 pounds.

 Pack along two or three bottles even for the shortest rides. For longer rides, we carry a large Camelbak water carrier along with two bottles of water on the bike frame and a third stuffed inside the mesh of the Camelbak.

In the desert, the heat is dry, and you do not notice much perspiration because your sweat evaporates as quickly as it surfaces. Combine the dry heat with a little wind, and you can become extremely dehydrated before realizing it. Folks from the East (like us) tend to regard sweating as a barometer of our level of exertion (if you are not sweating much, in other words, you must not be exercising very hard). In the desert, it doesn't work that way. You may never notice that you are sweating. In the desert you need to stay ahead of dehydration by drinking more frequently and more regularly and by consuming much more than the same amount of exercise would warrant in other climates. Desert days literally suck the water right out of you, even during the cooler times of the year.

6. TOOLS Each rider has a personal "absolute minimum list," which usually includes most of the following:

tire levers	spoke wrench
chain rivet tool	allen wrenches (3, 4, 5, and 6 mm)
spare tube and patch kit	6-inch crescent (adjustable-end)
spare chain link	wrench
air pump or CO_2 cartridges	small flat-blade screwdriver

7. FIRST-AID KIT This, too, is a personal matter, usually including those items a rider has needed due to past mishaps. So, with the desert in mind, add a pair of tweezers (for close encounters of the cactus kind) and a snakebite kit. Most Las Vegas bikers have only seen snakes at the zoo or squashed on the highway, but you'll feel better if you pack one (the kit, that is) along.

Road Biking

Road biking on the Strip, downtown, or in any of Las Vegas's high-traffic areas is suicidal. Each year an astoundingly high number of bikers are injured or killed playing Russian roulette with Las Vegas motorists. If you want to bike, either confine yourself to sleepy subdivisions or get way out of town on a road with wide shoulders and little traffic.

There are a number of superb rides within a 30- to 40-minute drive from downtown or the Strip. The best is the **Red Rock Canyon Scenic Loop ride,** due west of town, which carves a 15.4-mile circuit through the canyon's massive, rust-colored, sandstone cliffs. The route is arduous, with a 1,000-foot elevation gain in the first six miles, followed by eight miles of downhill and flats with one more steep hill. One-way traffic on the scenic loop applies to cyclists and motorists alike. Although there is a fair amount of traffic on weekends, the road is wide and the speed limit is a conservative 35 miles per hour. If you park your car at the Red Rock Canyon Visitor Center, take careful note of when the area closes. If you are delayed on your ride and get back late, your car might be trapped behind locked gates.

A second ride in the same area follows NV 159 from the town of Blue Diamond to the entrance of Red Rock Canyon Scenic Loop Drive and back again, approximately eight miles. From Blue Diamond the highway traverses undulating hills, with a net elevation gain of 193 feet on the outbound leg. In general, the ride offers gentle, long grades alternating with relatively flat stretches. Cliff walls and desert flora provide stunning vistas throughout. Traffic on NV 159 is a little heavy on weekends, but the road is plenty wide, with a good surface and wide shoulders. In the village of Blue Diamond there is a small store.

Another good out-and-back begins at Overton Beach on Lake Mead, northeast of Las Vegas, and ascends 867 feet in eight miles to the visitor center at the Valley of Fire State Park. (You can, of course, begin your round-trip at the visitor center, but we always prefer to tackle the uphill leg first.) Geology in the park is spectacular, with the same red sandstone found in the cliffs and formations of the Grand Canyon. There are no shoulders, but traffic is light and the road surface is good. Since the route runs pretty much east–west, we like to schedule our ride in the afternoon so that we will have the setting sun at our back as we coast down to the lake on the return leg. Another good option is an early-morning ride with the sun at your back as you ascend and high in the sky as you return.

Dressing for a bike ride in the canyons and high country around Las Vegas is a challenge. In early December, when we rode the Red Rock loop, it was about 62°F in town and about 10°F cooler in the canyon. We started out in Lycra bike shorts and polypro long-sleeve wind-breakers. By the time we completed the six-mile uphill, we were about to die of heat prostration. On the long, fast downhill, we froze. Our recommendation is to layer on cooler days so that you can add or shuck clothing as conditions warrant. On warm days, try to bike early in the morning or late in the afternoon and wear light clothing. Always wear a helmet and always, always carry lots of water.

There is no place on any of these routes to get help with a broken bike. You should bring an extra tube and a pump and know how to fix flats and make other necessary repairs. Water is available at Blue Diamond and at the Red Rock and Valley of Fire visitor centers, but no place else. Always replenish when you have the opportunity.

Mountain Biking

Las Vegas, most unexpectedly, has become a mountain-biking destination. Southwest of Las Vegas on NV 160 is Cottonwood Valley, with more than 200 miles of single track and double track for all skill levels. There are five named loop trails, two named out-and-backs, and miles of unnamed trails and unpaved roads. Trail surface is mostly packed sand (good traction) with loose rock and a little soft sand. Trails on the north side of NV 160 are mellower in general, though there's some advanced riding below the east face of Wilson Cliffs. If it's your first time in the area, start with the figure-eight Mustang Trail. Almost all single track on good surface, this trail over rolling high desert offers moderate climbs, gradual descents, and great views of the Red Rock cliffs and valleys. A number of trails branch off Mustang if you want to lengthen your ride or opt for more advanced terrain.

On the south side of NV 160, the rides require more climbing. The showcase trail is the Dead Horse Loop, 14 miles of intermediate to advanced single track. Site of NORBA races, the route climbs to an overlook, with a stunning view of Las Vegas in the distance, and then drops off the mountain in a blue-cruiser known locally as the three-mile smile. Out-and-backs and additional loops connecting to Dead Horse serve up more technical climbs and descents.

There are two ways to reach Cottonwood Valley. The fastest is to go south on I-15, exit onto NV 160, and head west 16 miles to the Mustang Trailhead parking lot (on the right) or 17 miles to the Cottonwood Valley Trailhead on the left. You can also go west out of town on Charleston Boulevard, which becomes NV 159. Take NV 159 until it intersects NV 160 south of Blue Diamond. Turn right on NV 160 for five to six miles to the parking lots.

Try riding Cottonwood Valley first. If Cottonwood doesn't offer enough challenge, try Bootleg Canyon.

Southeast of Las Vegas near Boulder City, Hoover Dam, and Lake Mead is Bootleg Canyon, primarily an advanced-skill-level mountain-bike park, though it does offer some trails for all skill levels. While mostly known for its full-body-armor downhills and jumps, the park also serves up some technical cross-country, great views of Boulder City, and, on the backside, Lake Mead. Though hard to get really lost, the layout, with lots of crisscrossing trails, is confusing to many bikers riding there for the first time. A lot, if not most, of the riding is hard core, as are the riders who hang here. Surface is packed dirt or sand and a lot of rock, much of it loose. Trails, carved into the side of the hill, are frequently off-camber. To get there from Las Vegas, take NV 93 to Boulder City. Turn left at the light onto Buchanan Boulevard, and then left onto Canyon Road. Continue beyond where the pavement gives way to dirt to the Bootleg Canyon parking lot situated between two hills. Usually there are freebie maps of the park in a box at the parking lot, but if possible, team up with locals who know the area and terrain.

If you're not used to riding in the high desert, you won't believe how much water you consume. We recommend a full Camelbak plus as many water bottles as you can carry on the frame. Rental bikes, unfortunately, generally come with only one water holder (if that). If you can jam an extra water bottle into the deep pouch on your Camelbak, you'll be glad you did. Wind, almost always howling out of the west, is a factor at both biking destinations, so much so that trails are generally laid out on a north–south axis with as little east–west as possible. Even so, tackling a tough climb into a headwind will probably be part of your Nevada biking baptism. Finally, almost all of the riding is exposed. If you want shade, bring an umbrella.

Other area rides include the Bristlecone Pine Trail in Lee Canyon on Mount Charleston, about an hour northwest of Las Vegas. Though just under six miles in length, this loop trail is at altitude (above 7,500 feet) with a 700-foot rise and fall in elevation. Take US 95 north and then follow NV 157 for 17 miles up into the mountains until you see a dirt road where you can turn off and park.

Good bikes are available for rent at **Escape Adventures,** 8221 West Charleston Boulevard (☎ 702-596-2953 or **escapeadventures.com**). Helmets, bike racks, water bottles, Cottonwood Valley trail maps, and other gear are likewise available for rent or sale. Escape also offers guided mountain-bike tours daily, with trails chosen based on the skill level of the group. If you book a tour, Escape will pick you up at your hotel or one close by.

Another option is to rent a bike from **McGhie's Bike Outpost** (☎ 702-875-4820 or **mcghies.com**), in the little desert town of Blue Diamond. Blue Diamond is off NV 159 about three miles north of the intersection with NV 160. Located on the east end of Cottonwood Valley, you can actually get on the trail outside the back door of the shop. That said, you have to bike quite a way uphill and west to access the popular loop trails.

In addition to the foregoing, many mountain bikers ride the paved scenic loop at Red Rock Canyon (described under "Road Biking," page 462). Visit **redrockcanyonlv.org** for more information.

HIKING AND BACKPACKING

HIKING OR BACKPACKING IN THE DESERT can be a very enjoyable experience. It can also be a hazardous adventure if you travel unprepared. Lake Mead ranger Debbie Savage suggests the following:

The best months for hiking are the cooler months of November through March. Hiking is not recommended in the summer, when temperatures reach 120°F in the shade. Never hike alone and always tell someone where you are going and when you plan to return. Carry plenty of water (at least a half gallon per person) and drink often.

Know your limits. Hiking the canyons and washes in the desert often means traveling over rough, steep terrain with frequent elevation changes. Try to pick a route that best suits your abilities. Distances in the desert are often deceiving. Be sure to check the weather forecast before departure. Sudden storms can cause flash flooding. Seek higher ground if thunderstorms threaten.

Essential equipment includes sturdy walking shoes and proper clothing. Long pants are suggested for protection from rocks and cacti. A hat, sunscreen, and sunglasses are also recommended. Carry a small daypack to hold items such as a first-aid kit, lunch, water, a light jacket, and a flashlight.

Canyons and washes often contain an impressive diversity of plant life, most easily observed during the spring wildflower season. Desert springs are located in some of the canyons and support a unique community of plants and animals. They are often the only source of water for many miles around. Take care not to contaminate them with trash or other human wastes. Along similar lines, understand that desert soils are often very fragile and take a long time to recover if disturbed. These surfaces are recognizable by their comparatively darker appearance and should be avoided whenever possible.

Poisonous animals such as snakes, spiders, and scorpions are most active after dark and are not often seen during daylight hours by hikers. Speckled rattlesnakes are common but are not aggressive. Scorpion stings are no more harmful than a bee sting, unless you are allergic. Black widow spiders are shy and secretive and are most often found around man-made structures. Watch where you place your hands and feet and don't disturb obvious hiding places.

The Las Vegas area offers quite a diversity of hiking options. Trips that include a choice of canyons, lakes, desert, mountains, or ponderosa pine forest can be found within an hour's drive of Las Vegas.

The Lake Mead National Recreation Area, an hour southeast of Las Vegas, offers a wide variety of hiking experiences, although there are few designated trails. Included within the NRA are Lakes Mead and Mohave, and part of the Mojave Desert. Ranger-guided hikes are offered during the winter months. The outings cover six to eight miles and are moderate to strenuous in difficulty. If you prefer to explore on your own, detailed maps and instructions to the most popular areas are available at the visitor centers. An admission fee of $10 per vehicle ($5 on foot or bike) is good for seven days. For information, call ☎ 702-293-8990 or visit **nps.gov/lame.**

The Red Rock Canyon National Conservation Area contains some of the most rugged rock formations in the West. Only 40 minutes from Las Vegas, Red Rock Canyon offers loop as well as out-and-back trails of varying lengths. (See map on next page.) The short Moenkopi Loop originates at the visitor center, and it takes a little more than an hour to walk over undulating terrain in a broad desert valley. Other popular short hikes include out-and-backs to Lost Creek (three-tenths of a mile, one-way), Icebox Canyon (one and three-tenths miles, one-way), and Pine Creek Canyon (one mile, one-way), leading to the ruins of a historic homestead near a running creek surrounded by large ponderosa pine trees. Our favorite trail, and certainly one of the most scenic, is the out-and-back Calico Tanks Trail (two and a half miles, round-trip), which winds up through a narrow canyon to a *tinaja,* a circular canyon, or "tank," that forms a natural lake. The hike is a stunner, even in hot dry months when there's little or no water in the tank, and ends at the top of the canyon with a knockout view of Las Vegas on the distant valley floor.

Altogether there are 19 trails: 4 rated easy, 5 rated easy to moderate, 9 rated moderate, and 1 classified as difficult. Distances range from three-fourths of a mile to six miles. Estimated hiking times are one to two hours for most trails (30 minutes for the shortest and three hours for the longest). Most of the easy and easy-to-moderate trails are pretty level. Elevation gain for moderate and difficult trails is 300–1,700 feet. Maps and hiking information are available free when you pay your entrance fee and for sale in the visitor center. For more information about Red Rock trails, see **sunsetcities.com/redrock.html.** If you'd like to spend a few days here and camp, Red Rock offers a good campground (see profile below). For more information, call ☎ 702-515-5350, or check out **desertusa.com/redrock.**

Red Rock Canyon Campground

RV ★★★   TENT ★★   BEAUTY ★★★   SITE PRIVACY ★   QUIET ★★★½
SPACIOUSNESS ★★½   SECURITY ★★   CLEANLINESS ★★★   INSECT CONTROL ★★★

**Red Rock Canyon National Conservation Area, HCR 33, Box 5500,
Las Vegas, NV 89124; ☎ 702-515-5350; nv.blm.gov/redrockcanyon**

FACILITIES
Acres 60. **Number of RV sites** 5. **Number of tent-only sites** 71. **Number of multi-purpose sites** 52. **Site to acreage ratio** 1:0.8. **Hookups** None. **Each site** Table, fire pit. **Dump station** No. **Laundry** No. **Pay phone** No. **Restrooms and showers** Restrooms, no showers. **Fuel** No. **Propane** No. **Internal roads** Dirt. **RV service** No. **Market** No. **Restaurant** No. **General store** No. **Vending** No. **Swimming** No. **Playground** No. **Nearby attractions** Red Rock Canyon National Conservation Area.

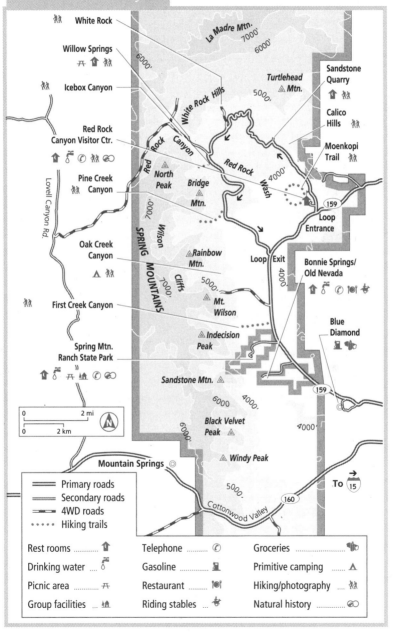

Red Rock Canyon

White Rock 🚶

Willow Springs
🛏 🏠 🚶

Icebox Canyon 🚶

Red Rock
Canyon Visitor Ctr.
🏠 🚰 ✆ 🚶 🔭

Pine Creek 🚶
Canyon

Oak Creek
Canyon
⛺ 🚶

First Creek Canyon 🚶

Spring Mtn.
Ranch State Park
🏠 🚰 🛏 🏛 ✆ 🔭

La Madre Mtn.
7000'
6000'

6000'

White Rock Hills

Red Rock Canyon

North
Peak

Bridge
△ Mtn.

Wilson

SPRING MOUNTAINS

7000'

7000'

Cliffs

△ Rainbow
Mtn.

5000'

△ Mt.
Wilson

△ Indecision
Peak

Sandstone Mtn. △

6000'

6000'

△ Black Velvet
Peak

△ Windy Peak

Mountain Springs ◎

5000'

Turtlehead
△ Mtn.

5000'

Red Rock Wash

4000'

Loop
Entrance

Loop Exit

4000'

4000'

4000'

Sandstone
Quarry
🏠 🚶

Calico
Hills 🚶

Moenkopi
Trail 🚶

(159)

Bonnie Springs/
Old Nevada
🏠 🚰 ✆ 🍴 🐴 🚶

Blue
Diamond
⛽ 🍺

(159)

To → (15)

Cottonwood Valley

(160)

Lovell Canyon Rd.

0		2 mi
0	2 km	

N

═══ Primary roads
─── Secondary roads
══▪ 4WD roads
••••• Hiking trails

Rest rooms .... 🏠	Telephone ...... ✆	Groceries .... 🛒
Drinking water .... 🚰	Gasoline .... ⛽	Primitive camping ...... ⛺
Picnic area .... 🛏	Restaurant ...... 🍴	Hiking/photography ... 🚶
Group facilities ... 🏛	Riding stables ... 🐴	Natural history .... 🔭

KEY INFORMATION

Operated by Bureau of Land Management. **Open** September–May. **Site assignment** First come, first served. **Registration** At ranger station. **Fee** $15 per day per site. **Parking** Maximum 2 vehicles per site.

RESTRICTIONS

Pets On leash only. **Fires** Allowed; sites have fire pits, and firewood is available for purchase from campground hosts September 1–May 31. **Alcoholic beverages** Not allowed. **Vehicle maximum length** 16 feet.

TO GET THERE   From Las Vegas, drive west on Charleston Boulevard/NV 159 for six miles. Two miles before the Red Rock Canyon scenic drive, turn left on Moenkopi Drive. Pass the fire station on the right, the group campground on the left, then drive down the hill to the campground.

DESCRIPTION   It's the desert, and nothing but. Set in a low hollow just below the Calico Hills, Red Rock Canyon Campground offers the bare minimum: a place to pitch your tent, and little else. The campground's compact main loop is bisected by two spoke roads, with sites feathering off at regular angles. Pit toilets are set at the corners. There's no foliage to screen your site from neighbors, who are not that far off in any case. A small RV loop and a similar-sized walk-in tent-only loop dangle off to the south, near the campground host. Five large group sites are set out near the entrance. The low setting makes views of the hills problematic, but it's extremely serene and quiet—and even with the lights of the Strip a few miles away, the clear night sky makes for great stargazing.

The Humboldt-Toiyabe National Forest, high in the mountains 40 minutes northwest of Las Vegas, provides a totally different outdoor experience. The air is cool, and the trails run among stately forests of ponderosa pine, quaking aspen, white fir, and mountain mahogany. Hikes range in distance from one-tenth of a mile to 21 miles, and in difficulty from easy to very difficult. Most popular are the Cathedral Rock Trail (two miles round-trip), which climbs 900 feet to a stark summit overlooking Kyle Canyon, and Bristlecone, a five-mile loop that traverses the ridges above the Lee Canyon Ski Area. Though the distances of these loops are not great, the terrain is exceedingly rugged, and the hikes are not recommended for one-day outings unless you begin very early in the morning and are used to strenuous exercise at high elevations. For more information, call ☎ 775-331-6444.

The Valley of Fire State Park, 45 minutes northeast of Las Vegas, rounds out the hiking picture. This park features rock formations similar to those found in the Grand Canyon, as well as a number of Indian petroglyphs. The *Las Vegas Advisor* compares hiking the Valley of Fire with being "beamed" onto another planet. Trails traverse desert terrain and vary from a half mile to seven miles in length. Visitors should check in at the visitor center before they begin hiking. The park fee is $10 ($8 for locals); for more information, call ☎ 702-397-2088 or visit **http://parks.nv.gov/vf.htm.**

Guided Hikes and Tours

Rocky Trails (☎ 888-892-5380 or **rockytrails.com**) offers guided tours to the natural sites described above as well as to Death Valley, the Grand Canyon, Bryce Canyon, and Zion National Park. Guests are picked up at their hotel and transported in modern Suburbans or vans. Lunch or dinner is included. Expeditions to the Valley of Fire, Red Rock Canyon, Death Valley, and the Grand Canyon last six to ten hours and cost $99 to $539 per adult.

ROCK CLIMBING AND BOULDERING

THE RED ROCK CANYON NATIONAL CONSERVATION AREA is one of the top rock-climbing resources in the United States. With more than 1,000 routes, abundant holds, and approaches ranging from roadside to remote wilderness, the area rivals Yosemite in scope and variety for climbers. Offering amazing diversity for every skill level amidst desert canyon scenery second to none, the area is less than a 40-minute drive from Las Vegas.

Though there is some granite and limestone, almost all of the climbing is done on sandstone. Overall, the rock is pretty solid, although there are some places where the sandstone gets a little crumbly, especially after a rain. Bolting is allowed but discouraged (local climbers have been systematically replacing bolts on some of the older routes with more modern bolts that blend with the rock). There are some great spots for bouldering, some of the best top-roping in the United States, a lifetime supply of big walls, and even some bivouac routes. Climbs range in difficulty from nonbelayed scrambles to 5.13 big-wall overhangs. You can climb year-round at Red Rock. Wind can be a problem, as can most of the other conditions that make a desert environment challenging. Having enough water can be a logistical nightmare on a long climb.

The Red Rocks of Southern Nevada by Joanne Urioste describes a number of the older routes. Newer route descriptions can be obtained from **Desert Rock Sports** in Las Vegas (☎ 702-254-1143; **desert rocksportslv.com**). Desert Rock Sports can also help you find camping and showers and tell you where the loose rock is. Offering climbing-shoe rentals, the store is at 8221 West Charleston, conveniently on the way to the canyon from Las Vegas. The **Red Rock Climbing Center** (☎ 702-254-5604; **redrockclimbingcenter.com**) is next to Desert Rock Sports and offers excellent indoor climbing and showers. Guides and/or instruction are available from Desert Rock Sports.

RIVER RUNNING

THE BLACK CANYON OF THE COLORADO RIVER can be run year-round below Hoover Dam. The most popular trip is from the tailwaters of the dam to Willow Beach. In this 11-mile section, canyon walls rise almost vertically from the water's edge, with scenery and wildlife very similar to that of the Colorado River in the Grand Canyon above Lake Mead. There are numerous warm springs and waterfalls on feeder streams, presenting the opportunity for good side-trip hikes. Small beaches provide good rest and lunch sites. Bighorn sheep roam the bluffs, and wild burros can often be seen up the canyons. The water in the river, about 53°F year-round, is drawn from the bottom of Lake Mead and released downstream through the Hoover Dam hydroelectric generators.

Under normal conditions, the Black Canyon is a nice flatwater float trip with a steady current to help you along. There are places along the river such as Ringbolt Rapids and the Chute that are named for falls and rapids long since covered up and flattened out by the voluminous discharge of water from the dam. There is nothing remaining on the run in the way of paddling challenges beyond a few swells and ripples. The Black Canyon is suitable for canoes, kayaks, and rafts. Motorized craft cannot be launched below the dam but can come upstream to the dam from Willow Beach or from other marinas farther downstream. The trip takes about six hours, including side trips and lunch, for a canoe or kayak, and about three and one half hours for a commercial motorized raft.

There are several ways you can get into serious trouble. The put-in below the dam is rocky and slippery. More than a few boaters have accidentally launched their boat before they climbed aboard, while others have managed to arrive in the river ahead of their boat. Once you're under way, it's important to keep your group close together. With the water temperature at 53°F, you want to pluck people out of the river posthaste in the event of a capsize. When you go ashore to explore, pull your boat way up out of the water and tie it to something sturdy. If at the dam they happen to crank up an extra generator or two while you're off hiking in a side canyon, it's possible for the river to rise several feet, sweeping any unsecured boats and equipment downstream.

 If the weather service predicts headwinds in excess of 18 miles an hour, cancel your paddling trip, even if it means losing your permit fee.

For the most part, the 11-mile run from the dam to Willow Beach does not require any prior paddling experience. On most days, you could practically float to the takeout, with breaks for lunch and exploring, in five hours. The exception, and it's a big one, is when headwinds blow up the canyon from the west. Though headwinds of less than ten miles an hour won't affect the paddling situation much, winds of 10 to 18 miles an hour require more experience and advanced boat-handling skills. When the wind is high, it can blow you upstream, making forward progress grueling or impossible, and can whip up crosscurrents as well as waves up to three feet high. Chances of capsizing grow exponentially with wind speed, and rescue efforts become correspondingly more difficult.

Private parties must obtain a launch permit from:

Black Canyon/Willow Beach River Adventures
☎ 702-294-1414
fax 702-294-4464
blackcanyonadventures.com

The launch permit costs $10 per person and is required to launch from below Hoover Dam. A $3 per person National Park Service entrance fee is also required for those age 16 and older. Only 30 boats are allowed to launch from below the dam each day, so weekends sell out well in advance. On weekdays, it's sometimes possible to get a permit on short notice. Permits can be obtained on a first-come, first-serve basis six months in advance. The permits and fees apply to a specific date and are nonrefundable, though if there's space available, the permitting authority will try to assign you an alternate date in the event of bad weather, high winds, or other mitigating circumstances.

The application can be downloaded from the website; alternatively, you can phone and request that the application be faxed or mailed to you. Completed applications can be submitted by e-mail or fax. When your permit is approved, it will be e-mailed, faxed, or mailed to you along with directions, put-in/take-out instructions, and salient information about the river. Also included is information on canoe and kayak rentals, transportation of rented boats, and shuttle arrangements.

The best time to run the Canyon is in the fall through December. The spring is prettiest, with new green foliage seen on the beaches and in the side canyons. The spring, along with January and February, tend to be the windiest times of year, however. Summers are hot, and the canyons tend to hold the heat. The water, however, provides some natural cooling. Canoeists and kayakers can make the run in one day or alternatively camp overnight in the canyon en route. Commercial raft trips are one-day affairs.

If you don't have your own equipment, you can rent canoes as well as one- and two-person kayaks from **Down River Outfitters** in nearby Boulder City (☎ 702-293-1190 or **bouldercityoutfitters.com**). The kayaks are the preferred craft but unfortunately don't come with spray skirts. This means essentially that every time you take a paddle stroke, 53°F water drips off the paddle into your lap. Canoes are drier, but slower, and more affected by wind. In addition to providing equipment, Down River Outfitters also transports you and your boat to the river. At the end of the run, they pick you up at Willow Beach and drive you back to your car. Canoe and two-person kayaks run $50 per person for one-day trips; one-person kayaks, $55. Call or visit the outfitter's website for booking procedures and rates for multiday trips. In addition to granting permits, Black Canyon/Willow Beach River Adventures also operates guided, motorized raft trips, with guest transportation provided from the Strip and downtown. No permit is required for these trips.

The raft outing is unlike most commercial river trips. First, the rafts are huge, accommodating more than two dozen guests. Secondly, the trip is entirely passive—no paddling or anything else required. The rafts motor up from Willow Beach in the morning and pick up their passengers at the put-in below the dam. From there, it's a scenic, narrated three-hour or so float back to Willow Beach, where guests are loaded up and transported back to their cars or delivered to their Las Vegas hotel. The trips run $86 for adults, $83 for children ages 13 to 15, and $54 for children ages 5 to 12. For transportation from your Las Vegas hotel, add $44.

 There is little protection from the sun in the Black Canyon, and temperatures can surpass 110°F in the warmer months. Long-sleeve shirts, long pants, tennis shoes, and a hat are recommended minimum attire year-round. Be sure to take sunscreen and lots of drinking water.

SNOW SKIING

THE LAS VEGAS SKI AND SNOWBOARD RESORT at Lee Canyon is a 45-minute drive from Las Vegas. Situated in a granite canyon in the Spring Mountain range, the resort provides three double chairlifts servicing ten runs. Though the mountain is small and the runs short by Western standards, the skiing is solid intermediate. Of the ten runs, seven are blue, two are black, and there is one short green. Base elevation of 8,510 feet notwithstanding, snow conditions are usually dependable only during January. Because of its southerly location and the proximity of the hot, arid desert, there is a lot of thawing and refreezing in Lee Canyon, and hence, frequently icy skiing conditions. If the snow is good, a day at Lee Canyon is a great outing. If the mountain is icy, do something else.

Snowmaking equipment allows the resort to operate from Thanksgiving to Easter. There is no lodging on-site and only a modest coffee shop and lounge. Parking is a fairly good hike from the base facility.

Skis can be rented at the ski area. For information on lift tickets or snow conditions, call the ski area office at ☎ 702-385-2754 or see **skilasvegas.com.** For summer event info at Lee Canyon, call ☎ 702-593-9500.

HORSEBACK RIDING

THE CLOSEST HORSEBACK-RIDING OUTFITTERS are in the Red Rock Canyon area half an hour west of Las Vegas. Riding is allowed on only a couple of trails in the Red Rock National Conservation Area, but there's a lot of riding to be found just outside the Conservation Area. **Bonnie Springs** (☎ 702-875-4191; **bonniesprings.com**) and **Cowboy Trail Rides** (☎ 702-387-2457; **cowboytrailrides.com**) are both located within a four- to ten-minute drive from Red Rock Canyon.

FISHING

LAKE MEAD BAIT AND TACKLE, BOAT RENTAL, FUEL, AND SUPPLIES

Callville Bay Resort	☎ 702-565-8958
Cottonwood Cove Resort	☎ 702-297-1464
Echo Bay Marina	☎ 702-394-4000
Lake Mohave Resort (AZ)	☎ 928-754-3245
Temple Bar Resort (AZ)	☎ 928-767-3211

THE LAKE MEAD NATIONAL RECREATION AREA offers some of the best fishing in the United States. Lake Mead is the largest lake, with Lake Mohave, downstream on the Colorado River, offering the most diverse fishery. Largemouth bass, striped bass, channel catfish, crappie, and bluegill are found in both lakes. Rainbow and cutthroat trout are present only in Lake Mohave. Remote and beautiful in its upmost reaches, Lake Mohave is farther from Las Vegas but provides truly exceptional fishing. Bass and trout often run three pounds, and some trout weigh ten pounds or more. Willow Beach, near where the Colorado River enters the pool waters of Lake Mohave, is where many of the larger trout are taken.

Lake Mead, broader, more open, and much closer to Las Vegas, has become famous for its stripers, with an occasional catch weighing in at over 40 pounds. Bass fishing is consistently good throughout Lake Mead. The Overton Arm (accessed from Echo Bay or Overton Beach) offers the best panfish and catfish action.

Because lakes Mead and Mohave form the Arizona/Nevada state line, fishing license regulations are a little strange. If you are bank fishing, all you need is a license from the state you are in. If you fish from a boat, however, you need a fishing license from one state and a special-use stamp from the other. All required stamps and licenses can be obtained from marinas and local bait and tackle shops in either state.

Nonresidents have the option of purchasing one- to ten-day fishing permits in lieu of a license. Permits are $18 for one day (with a $7 charge per additional consecutive days) and $69 for annual, and apply to the entire state of Nevada. In addition to the permit, a special-use stamp costing $3 is required for those fishing from a boat. Plus, a $10 trout stamp is necessary to take trout if you buy the annual permit; the trout stamp is included in the price of the daily permit. In addition, a $10 stamp is available for fishing with two rods. Youngsters age 14 years and under in the company of a properly licensed, permitted, and stamped adult can fish without any sort of documentation.

Sixteen-foot, aluminum fishing boats (that seat five) can be rented on both lakes by the hour (about $40 with a two-hour minimum), by the half day (four hours for about $50), or by the day (about $100). Bass boats, houseboats, and pontoon craft are also available. Rods and reels rent for about $5 for four hours or less and about $12 a day.

PLEASURE BOATING, SAILING, WATER SKIING, AND JET SKIING

LAKE MEAD AND LAKE MOHAVE are both excellent sites for pleasure boating, water skiing, and other activities. Both lakes are so large that it is easy to find a secluded spot for your favorite boating or swimming activity. Rock formations on the lakes are spectacular, and boaters can visit scenic canyons and coves that are inaccessible to those traveling by car. Boats, for example, can travel into the narrow, steep-walled gorge of Iceberg Canyon in Lake Mead or upstream into the Black Canyon from Lake Mohave.

First-timers, particularly on Lake Mead, frequently underestimate its vast size. It is not difficult to get lost on the open waters of Lake Mead or to get caught in bad weather. Winds can be severe on the lake, and waves of six feet sometimes arise during storms. In general, there is no shade on the lakes, and the steep rock formations along the shore do not make very hospitable emergency landing sites. When you boat on either lake, take plenty of water, be properly dressed and equipped, and be sure to tell someone where you are going and when you expect to return.

Most of the resorts listed under "Fishing" rent various types of pleasure craft and water-skiing equipment, and the Callville Bay Resort also rents personal watercraft. In addition, at Callville Bay on Lake Mead and Cottonwood Cove on Lake Mohave, luxury houseboats are available for rental. The boats sleep up to 12 adults and have fully equipped galleys and heads. For rates and other information concerning houseboats, call ☎ 800-255-5561 or 800-752-9669 or visit **callvillebay.com** or **cottonwoodcoveresort.com**.

SPA 101

GETTING THE INSIDE TRACK ON SPA KNOW-HOW

LET'S FACE IT. MOST PEOPLE SPEND MORE TIME AND MONEY on preventive maintenance for their cars than on themselves. After all, changing the oil and checking tire pressure go a long way in extending the life of a car, let alone ensuring a smoother ride along the way. Believe it or not, this analogy fits for why we should participate in spa experiences. Call it preventative or maintenance medicine of your chassis, and a whole lot more.

SPA LINGO

ACUPRESSURE AND ACUPUNCTURE Acupressure, or fingertip massage, frees the body's energy channels, or "meridians," for a relaxing and energizing treatment. Acupuncture uses ultrafine needles for more specific and chronic ailments.

AROMATHERAPY A full-body massage using scented essential oils and light, smoothing movements. Different oils are used for different therapeutic benefits.

AYURVEDA The ancient system of traditional Indian medicine and science that incorporates nutrition, herbal medicine, aromatherapy, massage, and meditation.

BODY SCRUB A light massage and exfoliation that stimulates blood circulation and prepares the skin for mineralization and moisturizing.

BODY WRAP Cotton sheets or strips of cloth, steeped in a variety of aromatic herbs and/or sea enzymes, are wrapped around the body, which is then covered with blankets or towels to prevent the moist heat from escaping. Body wrap is a relaxing treatment to soothe soreness, soften skin, and detoxify the body.

HOT STONE MASSAGE This type of massage—also known as La Stone Therapy—uses smooth, dark, heated stones to relieve stiffness and soreness and to restore energy.

HYDROTHERAPY This relaxing and detoxifying therapy includes underwater jet massage, showers, jet sprays, and mineral baths.

MASSAGE THERAPY Massaging skin, muscles, and joints relieves muscle spasms and tension, and improves flexibility and circulation. Various types of massage range from gentle aromatherapy to a sports massage directed at specific muscles used in athletic activities to deep-tissue Swedish massage, which kneads and separates muscle groups while stretching connective tissue to help realign the body.

MINERAL WATERS Originating from natural springs and wells, these waters contain high concentrations of rare or biologically active elements and are known to improve circulation, detoxify the body, and ease ailments such as rheumatism and arthritis.

REFLEXOLOGY A Chinese-based massage of the feet and hands that includes pressure points to areas said to correspond with organs and tissues throughout the body. Treats a wide range of ailments.

SALT GLOW A mixture of salt, oils, and water is used to scrub the body to remove dead skin, clean pores, and stimulate circulation.

SHIATSU A Japanese massage therapy during which practitioners apply rhythmic finger pressure at specific points on the body in order to relieve pain, and release and balance blocked energy.

THAI MASSAGE In this form of massage a therapist manipulates the body using passive, yoga-like stretching and applies gentle pressure with his or her hands and feet along "energy lines" in the body.

Las Vegas Health Spas

SPAS OPEN TO THE PUBLIC

Aria	The Spa at Aria	☎ 877-312-2742
Bellagio	Spa Bellagio	☎ 702-693-7111
Caesars Palace	Qua Baths and Spa	☎ 702-731-7266
Excalibur	Royal Treatment Spa	☎ 702-597-7772
Flamingo	The Spa at Flamingo	☎ 702-733-3535
Four Seasons	The Spa at Four Seasons	☎ 702-632-5302
Golden Nugget	The Spa at Golden Nugget	☎ 702-386-8186
Green Valley Ranch Resort and Spa	The Spa at Green Valley Ranch	☎ 702-617-7570
Hard Rock Hotel	The Rock Spa	☎ 702-693-5554
Harrah's	The Spa at Harrah's	☎ 702-369-5189
Hyatt Regency at Lake Las Vegas	Spa Moulay	☎ 702-567-6049
Imperial Palace	The Spa at I. P.	☎ 702-794-3242
Las Vegas Hilton	The Spa at the Las Vegas Hilton	☎ 702-732-5648
Luxor	Nurture Spa	☎ 702-730-5721
MGM Grand	MGM Grand Spa	☎ 702-891-1111
Mirage	The Spa at the Mirage	☎ 702-791-7472
Monte Carlo	The Spa at Monte Carlo	☎ 702-730-7590
New York–New York	The Spa at New York–New York	☎ 702-740-6955
Paris Las Vegas	Spa by Mandara	☎ 702-946-4366
Planet Hollywood	Mandara Spa	☎ 702-785-5772
Red Rock Resort	The Spa at Red Rock (Mon.-Fri.)	☎ 702-797-7878
Rio	Rio Spa	☎ 702-777-7779
Riviera	Executive Fitness at the Riviera	☎ 702-794-9441
T. I.	Salon & Spa at T. I.	☎ 702-894-7472
The Venetian	Canyon Ranch SpaClub	☎ 702-414-3610
Wynn Encore	The Spa at Wynn Encore (Sun.-Thurs.)	☎ 702-770-8000

SPAS FOR HOTEL GUESTS ONLY

Mandalay Bay	Spa Mandalay	☎ 702-632-7220
Red Rock Resort	The Spa at Red Rock (Sat. and Sun.)	☎ 702-797-7878
Wynn Encore	Spa at Wynn Encore (Fri. and Sat.)	☎ 702-770-8000
Wynn Las Vegas	Spa at Wynn Las Vegas	☎ 702-770-8000

THALASSOTHERAPY A full-body exfoliation and detoxification treatment that uses nutrient-rich marine elements along with other skin-conditioning agents.

VICHY SHOWER MASSAGE This relaxing massage is performed under sprinklers to improve the body's circulation; water is heated to body temperature.

THE 21ST-CENTURY SPA

TODAY, SPAS HAVE REINVENTED THEMSELVES into exotic environments, where professional practitioners trained in a variety of traditional and alternative approaches to wellness offer pampered luxury. Look beyond everyone's favorite, the relaxation massage, and you're likely to find more spa-treatment options than there are flavors of Baskin-Robbins ice cream.

The competition for your spa dollar is so fierce that resort spas in particular are constantly upping the ante for your spa experience. More than ever, with basic spa treatments, resorts are including value-added services such as the complimentary use of mineral pools, waterfall massages, and detoxifying steam rooms and saunas—amenities that can turn a manicure or facial into an all-out getaway. In addition, spa-ing has become a valuable adjunct to other activities from golf to eco-safaris.

GETTING DOWN TO SPA BASICS

A GOOD SPA IS DEFINED BY the purity of experience it provides and how it makes you feel the moment you enter it. A spa needs to engage and soothe all five senses and provide an ambience that removes you from the outside world. Often you can't put into words the nurturing wave of care that envelops you, yet the feeling is instant and palpable.

Five things to watch for in a spa:

- The hair salon should be well separated from the spa—the noise of dryers and smell of perm solution fly in the face of serenity and jasmine-scented air.
- The gym should be considered a part of the spa in name only; sharing locker space with treadmill enthusiasts isn't conducive to the spa ethos.
- Retail sales should be physically a part of the reception and transaction area rather than any transition zone.
- There should be RMTs (registered massage therapists) on staff, in addition to body-care workers.
- Skin-care products should be eco-friendly and free from animal testing.

SPA NEOPHYTE: THE NAKED TRUTH

ALL SPAS CATER TO THE FIRST-TIME VISITOR—and ease anxiety about those nagging questions regarding nudity and massage. Don't worry. Treatments are usually explained to you prior to the start of any session, and therapists use professional draping techniques to ensure privacy; there's no need to mentally race ahead of the treatment process with niggling doubts as to what's coming next. For example, when you're having a full-body massage and are asked to turn over, your therapist will raise the covering sheet so high that no one gets a boo at your privates, and the sheet will be settled over your body only when the therapist notes that your feet are facing in the right direction. Always let the spa know if you have a preference for either a male or female therapist.

Most people strip to the buff for full-body massages and wraps, but if modesty is a concern, disrobe to your level of comfort, keep your undies on, or ask the spa if they have disposable panties. If you and your teen are venturing into a side-by-side massage, spas usually ask that your child wear a swimsuit so that they (and you) have a sense of comfort about being touched. If you are having any form of body treatment or men's facial, don't shave for at least four hours prior to your service. And let the spa know in advance of any special conditions such as pregnancy, high blood pressure, heart ailments, or any condition where certain heat therapies, massage, or skin care might not be appropriate. If waxing services are on your agenda, a pre-steam or sauna is not recommended, and, please, don't eat a full meal just before any spa visit. Lastly, remove your contact lenses before heading into a eucalyptus steam as its astringent qualities may cause your eyes to sting.

During your treatment, your therapist will take their lead from you and be as silent or as talkative as you wish. Some will talk you through the process, especially during a facial, so that you know what sensations to expect as the therapist cleanses, tones, steams, and applies a mask. The choice is always yours.

THE "SHOULDS" TO NOTE

THERAPISTS SHOULD ALWAYS CHECK IN on your comfort with and preference for lighting (too bright?), music (too loud or not loud enough?), warmth (we love spas with heated bed pads), and pressure of massage touch.

On the latter, be aware that an RMT is highly skilled at finding those stubborn knots, and kneading their release might cause minor discomfort; that's why you warm muscles up in a steam or sauna first. Still, RMTs are not there to hurt you. Breathe, moan, whimper, exhale dramatically—these are all great ways to help your therapist help you relieve tension.

Don't think you have to buy into the spa silence, although if your treatment involves a shower, please don't practice your operatic arias, however good you feel.

And don't think you have to buy into product sales pitches. Estheticians are well versed to share the benefits of the products they use, and experienced practitioners should share comparisons between these and others you might know. Conversation should be informational only.

THE "SHOULD NOTS" TO NOTE

YOUR THERAPIST SHOULD NOT LEAVE THE ROOM without informing you. After all, when you're cocooned in a cellophane wrap, you feel pretty helpless. And if you're having a sensitive beauty or refinement service like an eyelash tint, sudden light, sound, and chatter can cause your eyelids to flicker involuntarily; tint in your eyes is no fun.

During your treatment, therapists should not move around the room in search of products, water, and equipment. Everything should have been preset for easy access. For full-body work, they should have warmed their hands before contact, "tuned" into your space by noting the rhythm of your breathing, and never should they lose contact with you for more than a split second. An unexpected touch, however gentle, can awaken the senses very abruptly. At the conclusion of your session, therapists shouldn't flick on the lights or slap you on the backside and say "go bucko, go." Bedside manner is everything.

SPA BELLS AND WHISTLES

UNLESS YOU'RE VISITING A SMALL DAY SPA where space limits facilities, here are some complimentary amenities you can expect.

- Same-sex changing rooms with personal lockers, spa sandals, robes, and towels.

- Some spas will have either same-sex (swimsuit-optional) steam rooms, saunas, and mineral pools, or will provide direct access to similar coed facilities (swimsuit mandatory).

- A grooming bar with hairstyling products, body moisturizers, and sundry personal items.

- Easy or direct access to either a same-sex or coed relaxation area for pre- and posttreatment "integration" time. This is an opportunity to snooze, bask in your newly acquired mellow mood, and read. Popular magazines and inspirational texts are usually on hand.

- The relaxation area should also provide healthy grazing foods like nuts and fresh fruit as well as tea infusions and other refreshments. Don't expect coffee.

- When you have a body scrub, it is customary for the spa staff to offer you the loofah brush or mitten to take home.

- When you receive a manicure or pedicure, some spas provide mini-bottles of polish for touch-ups, as well as the emery board used during the treatment.

- When you enjoy a facial, ask for free samples (see A Word about Retail below) of the products used or recommended. Enough samples from enough spa treatments and you'll always have a travel-sized supply at hand for that overnight getaway.

- Spas that are really on the ball will offer value-added services to every treatment, at no additional cost. Examples include a hand, foot, or scalp massage with every facial; a paraffin-wax treatment with every manicure; or a complimentary brow shape. The idea is to engage as many of the five senses as possible with every treatment.

TO TIP OR NOT TO TIP?

GRATUITIES ARE USUALLY LEFT to a guest's discretion and are similar to that given for hair-salon services, that is, 15–20% of the price of the service provided. At all-inclusive resorts, verify the spa's tipping policy upon arrival. Unlike a hair salon where you sometimes have to track down your stylist and slip a little gratitude into their pocket, spas operate with gratuity envelopes, which are administered by the reception staff. Tips can also be charged to your debit or credit card.

BE THERE OR BE SQUARE

TREATMENTS ARE BLOCKED BY TIME, and synchronized with Swiss efficiency so that rooms can be quickly flipped. As a courtesy, arrive early (especially if you want to take advantage of a spa's amenities) and leave your treatment room promptly. You can take all the "zone-out" time you wish in the relaxation lounge. Be aware that if you arrive late, your treatment will still end at the appointed time since there's another client scheduled right behind you. Be sure to check the spa's cancellation policy when you make your reservation; no-shows are generally charged at least 50% of the full treatment fee. Remember to silence your cell phone and pager before entering the spa.

A WORD ABOUT RETAIL

ALTHOUGH SPA-INDUSTRY EXPERTS CLAIM that retail sales should make up some 30% of a spa's revenues, most spas generate about half that figure, largely because, inexplicably, they haven't caught up with the very world they have created in terms of maximizing retail opportunities. Consequently, there's pressure on frontline staff to sell, and estheticians especially walk a fine line of wanting to be genuinely helpful and needing to meet commission quotas. There is absolutely no obligation to buy, however nicely the product is presented (often in a basket at the end of your treatment alongside a customized treatment regimen for you to take home).

A Few Words to the Wise

If you honestly like a product and feel its results, then why not buy it? Ask for travel samples as well. After all, you have just spent good money for an excellent treatment, and manufacturer's samples cost the spa nothing but goodwill.

If the product is indigenous to the region (for example, seaweed from Vancouver Island or Tahitian balm from Polynesia), consider it an indulgence in the same way as you would a specialty soap or hand-crafted wine. Treat a spa's own signature line in the same vein; items are usually just repackaged versions of a well-to-do product line that could well be sitting on the same shelf.

Lastly, if the product you like is widely available, it might be less expensive at home and even cheaper on eBay.

Skincare products aside, it seems that individual spas are beginning to catch on to their own success. Those that are shop-savvy showcase fashion, jewelry, music, housewares, self-help materials, and other spa-empowering products and gift ideas designed to re-create the spa experience back home. After all, that's the bottom line. That's what the industry wants of you: to have the concept of a spa as a can't-live-without, fun part of your everyday life. Besides, spa-ing really does lead to better health, so why not give it a go?

UNOFFICIAL OVERVIEW OF SIN CITY SPAS

IN A CITY THAT REINVENTS ITSELF at least every decade, it comes as no surprise that its spas do the same. With more than 45 luxury resort spas, Las Vegas spas have transformed themselves from being simply sidekicks that offer guests beauty amenities to lucrative mind-body-soul profit centers of Disneyesque proportions.

In the competition to entertain an increasingly aware spa crowd, destinations are constantly trying to out-spa one another in design, therapies, products, and promises. Like everything in Las Vegas, most spas present larger-than-life experiences within vast expanses of square footage with lots of service add-ons such as steam rooms and saunas, thus turning a simple pedicure into an all-day retreat. However, the trip from changing room to treatment area can be a hike unto itself, and although the walk is usually more like a shuffle in disposable slippers, without an escort or a trail of bread crumbs, you could be hard-pressed to find your way from one area to the next.

Surprisingly, in spite of the spa scene's meteoric growth, the overall quality and professionalism of practitioners are high. The desire to be a part of "the next big idea" sees therapists move from one spa to the next. Consequently, many of them not only maintain a hyper, Red-Bull enthusiasm (sometimes rather counterintuitive to the spa experience) but also a diverse knowledge of different products and competitive brands. If products are your thing, then therapists are a resource worth plumbing. Most staff members are equally polished at delivering pampering services with efficiency. Sometimes that's notice-able, but when you're able to languish laconically, the concept of time simply dissolves and all is forgiven.

Our advice is to take full advantage of a spa's facilities. Get a day pass so you can pop back in later for a relaxing steam—trust us, the moisture will feel delicious after traipsing around in the desert heat. Ask the spa if they'll spring for a pass for your partner; it only costs them laundry pennies to extend this privilege. Be aware, though, that their answer may depend on whether your service is a multisensory package or just a quick polish change. If you're a hotel guest, however, negotiate a pass for the hotel's on-site spa regardless. Tough times have humbled Vegas, and spa inducements are proving a valuable marketing tool to boost hotel occupancies.

Las Vegas's keep-up-with-the-Joneses climate means that spas are constantly catching, or creating, the newest wave. In recent years **Caesars Palace, Mandalay Bay, Bellagio,** and the **Venetian** have all undergone multimillion-dollar expansions for an updated look and service standard while the **Wynn** and **Trump** (owned by the two most competitive egos in town) hotels have countered the city's penchant for splashy with more intimate spa surroundings. New concepts such as **WET at Treasure Island, Nurture at Luxor,** and **Mio at M Resort** just south of the Strip have yet to find their stride, while traditionalists like the **Four Seasons** hotel have stayed the course with pricey, elegant refinement.

Although a crushing economy seems far removed when enjoying the excesses of any Las Vegas spa, the fallout is evident. Projects such as Fontainebleau have fallen by the wayside, and several spa expansions are on hold, most noticeably at **Canyon Ranch** (read its review below) and the **Mandara Spa at Paris,** where brand confusion has created a mediocre experience. Mandara has done a better job over at **Planet Hollywood.**

MGM has a large enough presence here that it was able to finish off its gargantuan $8.6-billion CityCenter development, including **The Spa at Aria,** as well as the city's first **Mandarin Oriental.** Then there's **ELEVEN,** a new day spa that opened its doors with gusto. Located in Town Square, this day spa stands independent of any resort and like its sister location in South Florida is quickly establishing itself as a hip and happening gathering spot.

The spa scene in Las Vegas might be large-scale, confusing, and generic, but the individual Strip spas are opulent, accessible, diverse, and pay-through-the-nose fun. Spa snobs need to chill out and enjoy. Sin City spas counter where the overall spa industry is heading (think personalized, focused, indigenous, holistic well-being, multidimensional, and spiritual), but isn't that the story of Las Vegas? So, for *Unofficial* purposes, we're staying on the Strip (Trump is the exception) with what we consider the spas that best epitomize Las Vegas's sizzle and audacity.

Bathhouse ★★★★
THEhotel, 3950 South Las Vegas Boulevard; ☎ 877-632-9636; mandalaybay.com

---

Customer service ★★★★. Facilities ★★★★. Amenities ★★★★. Sales pressure Low. **Price range** $65–$265, spa services; $45–$130, nail and refinement services. **Spa amenities** Complimentary with spa services for hotel guests; complimentary for non-hotel guests with spa services over $60; spa pass $30 per day for hotel guests only.

SUMMARY AND COMMENTS Although part of the Mandalay complex, THE-hotel is a separate entity with its own ultra-trendy spa, The Bathhouse, which pioneered communal spa-ing on the Strip. With its granite and suede-covered walls, stylish fixtures, and brightly colored furniture, including orange-fur benches, it retains a quasi-nightclub atmosphere, only rock and rhythm is replaced with sounds of trickling water at every turn. This is in-your-face, modern-bat-cave relaxation with soaring, monolithic black-slate walls and floors inset with a narrow, softly lit soaking pool. The whole deal is unexpected. With only 12 treatment rooms, this spa is small by Las Vegas standards, but because every room has a private shower, they feel like mini-suites. The Scents-of-You service is a fun way to customize your service. Arrive early to fill out a body-mind-soul personality questionnaire, have your answers punched into the computer, and, presto, it calculates a blend of essential oils for your massage, custom-tailored to your needs. Granted, certain oils do have relaxing or detoxifying properties, but don't take the process too seriously. The actual service, though, is excellent—a hybrid massage of hot stones, aromatherapy, and Swedish techniques. Add an express facial with an oxygen spray for a "wow" youthful glow.

RECOMMEND The Bathhouse Sampler combines a customized Scents-of-You bath, a Swedish massage, a refresher facial, and classic pedicure.

LOVE The contrasting exotica (no, not erotica) environment of Mandalay Spa. Its more traditional Zen environment is almost a sigh of relief to the Bathhouse.

THE ULTIMATE It may be an illusion (Las Vegas has the most magicians in the world), but the Mocha Java Sculpting Wrap really does seem to dissolve some of those cellulite dimples, at least for a while.

DISLIKE A private cabana is nice, but Mandalay would do well to have a spa-only area on the Beach to keep moods mellow.

TIP Organize a spa treatment for every day of your stay to enjoy daily access to the spa and fitness amenities for free; includes breakfast muffins at the spa bar.

Canyon Ranch Spa Club ★★★½
Venetian/Palazzo, 3355 South Las Vegas Boulevard; ☎ 702-414-3600; canyonranchspaclub.com

Customer service ★★. **Facilities** ★★★★★. **Amenities** ★★★★★. **Sales pressure** Medium. **Price range** $150–$355, spa services; $25–$155, nail and refinement services. **Spa and fitness center amenities** $20 with the purchase of any service; $40 per day without spa services; SpaClubPassport includes access to fitness center.

SUMMARY AND COMMENTS Covering a staggering 134,000 square feet of treatment areas, this is the mother of all spas, complete with a separate gym filled with treadmills, moving stairs, arm flexors, and weight machines. There's even a climbing wall that rises 40 feet in the middle of the cavernous reception area. If you enter from The Palazzo side, bring along a GPS. It's a long walk down faceless corridors through expansion space that the economic downturn has halted mid-plan. Don't be dissuaded, though. This is a top-notch spa that exemplifies the venerable and much-heralded Canyon Ranch ethos of promoting lifestyle wellness. It's also the spa that forced the other casino resorts to get serious about their facials. The rather aloof front desk staff doesn't always convey the care you'll receive once you're in the spa's inner sanctum. Canyon Ranch is often described as an upmarket (read: celebrity) spa, and because there are no easy-to-buy packages, spa-ing here can add up to a chunk of change when stringing together different services, which include everything from 18-carat facials and Aghyanga massage from India to vibrational therapy. If money's tight, buy a SpaClubPassport that lets you into the fitness center and all its classes and wellness presentations, as well as enjoy the spa's extensive amenities that are nothing short of fabulous. Aquavana is a myriad of high-tech water experiences, including clothing-optional experiential rains that mimic a Caribbean storm, a tropical downpour, or a cool fog. There's even a cool-down igloo. Coed environments (bring your swimsuit) include a salt grotto and a multisensory wave room that simulates the look and feel of breaking waves under a domed canopy.

RECOMMEND Rasul Ceremony. Slather your skin, or your partner's, with purifying mud and relax for 50 minutes in a gently warmed, tiled chair in a private, ornately tiled steam chamber.

LOVE Canyon Ranch's skin care products—Pro-NAD—which deliver time-released vitamin-B complex, as well as Goji juice, one of nature's most powerful antioxidants derived from the wolfberry.

THE ULTIMATE Canyon Ranch has the most "shared-experience" spa space on the Strip, so share this spa with your honey.

DISLIKE Services such as a jet-lag-relief scalp massage that come as add-on expenses rather than easy-to-incorporate value-added inclusions.

TIP Pretreatment, mix your oils, scrubs, and body butters at the spa's Living Essentials boutique.

Qua Baths and Spa ★★★★½
Caesars Palace, 3570 South Las Vegas Boulevard; ☎ 866-782-0655; harrahs.com/qua/caesars-palace

Customer service ★★★★. Facilities ★★★★★. Amenities ★★★★★. Sales pressure Medium. Price range $90–$325, with specialty treatments up to $1,200; $45–$150, nail and refinement services. Spa amenities Complimentary with all spa treatments; $25-per-day pass without services or $45 with Qua baths.

SUMMARY AND COMMENTS Qua Baths and Spa is top-class branding and Las Vegas showmanship—a 21st-century Roman-inspired pleasure that has set the standard for "gathering-space" spas. Innovation makes this a must-try spa, especially since prices are comparatively reasonable. The Roman baths consist of three distinct pools of varying temperatures: the Tepidarium, a warm mineral-enriched bath; the hotter Caldarium; and the much cooler Frigidarium. You can also languish in the coed, circular Laconium sauna, where the climate is kept at a constant 140°F and 35-percent humidity—the optimum conditions for relaxation. The Laconium is also quite the hot spot for get-togethers. The Arctic room is a real treat. The floor and benches are heated even though the room temperature is a crisp 55°F—cold enough to have snow fall from the ceiling and melt on your hot skin. Qua's menu of services runs the gamut of wet rooms with Vichy showers to a crystal–body-art room where, you've guessed it, a body scrub and massage is combined with a style of Swarovski body art. Is this why spa practitioners are called artisans? It might sound somewhat anomalous, but if you're serious about energy-related treatments, Qua has some of the better ones available.

RECOMMEND Chakra Balancing Treatment—a combination of energy and massage that balances your energy centers, after which your body artist will gift you a special stone-charm chakra necklace.

LOVE The in-house tea sommelier who pairs various teas with spa treatments as wine is matched to fine food. The dream-interpretation coach runs a close second.

THE ULTIMATE The personal hydrotherapy tub with its changing pulsating rhythms and colored lights.

DISLIKE Shopaholics might think this is a real bonus, but Qua has retail down to an art; a plethora of spa stuff bombards you coming and going.

TIP Remember your swimsuit.

The Spa at Aria ★★★★
Aria, 3730 South Las Vegas Boulevard; ☎ 702-590-9600; arialasvegas.com

Customer service ★★★★. Facilities ★★★★. Amenities ★★★★. Sales pressure Low. **Price range** $90–$540 spa services; $13–$195 nail and refinement services. **Spa amenities** Complimentary with treatment; spa and fitness center pass $30 a day without treatment.

SUMMARY AND COMMENTS The Spa at Aria synchronizes beauty and progressive luxury with a conscious respect and preservation of nature's elements. Natural stone, wood, and metal mingle together like a melodic dance inside the 80,000-square-foot, bi-level total wellness sanctuary. Inspired by the East, from the freestanding petrified wood from Thailand that greets salon customers to Japanese water gardens adorned with sacred Aji stones, the spa is distinctively warm and tranquil. The Spa at Aria features a full complement of services to promote peace and harmony, with such offerings as ashiatsu, couples' massage, Thai massage, hydrotherapy, and vichy. The Japanese Ganbanyoku stone-bed relaxation area—the only one in the country—provides guests with heated black mineral stone beds that emit negative ions, helping to improve circulation and increase metabolism. Two steps away is the Shio Salt Room lined entirely with illuminated amber-colored salt blocks, providing dewy, marine-rich salt-infused air. The Spa at Aria also boasts a full-service salon, which includes one barber station for gents who want to receive more than the classic shave and haircut. An advanced fitness center showcases top-of-the-line equipment to kick anyone into high gear. It also features a semiprivate stretch area, one-on-one training sessions, and movement classes, including kettle bells and body sculpt, among a range of others. Finally, for those who enjoy a unique hiking experience, the spa offers the Indoor Hike. While carrying a stretch mat on their backs, guests are guided through the most scenic areas of the resort and challenged with an exhilarating and heart-pumping workout that focuses on the whole body. The Spa at Aria is a complete wellness center that elevates guests to a meditative state for introspection, relaxation, and inspiration.

RECOMMEND The Thai Poultice Massage, a signature service, is based on a century-old healing practice that soothes away tension with a set of warm poultices infused with lemongrass, ginger, and prai extract.

LOVE The Spa is loaded with coed spaces, such as the fitness center, the Ganbanyoku heated-stone beds, Shio Salt Room, an outdoor balcony, a therapy pool, and a fire lounge.

THE ULTIMATE A "spa within a spa" private suite—complete with a personal spa attendant and amenities such as a three-person hydrotherapy tub, relaxation area, and flat-screen television—can be requested for a couple or small group celebrating a special occasion.

DISLIKE The spa offers far too many "add-on" services, when in fact some of them should be included in their signature offerings.

TIP Don't forget your swimsuit to experience the outdoor infinity-edge therapy pool. Take in the view and experience the social vibe.

The Spa at Bellagio ★★★
Bellagio, 3600 South Las Vegas Boulevard; ☎ 702-693-7472; bellagio.com

Customer service ★★★★. Facilities ★★★. Amenities ★★★. Sales pressure Low. **Price range** $130–$285, spa services; $25–$100, nail and refinement services. **Spa amenities** Complimentary with any spa service over $50; spa pass $29 per day without services; $70 3-day and $100 5-day passes also available.

SUMMARY AND COMMENTS No sooner had Bellagio opened its exclusive spa, than its popularity initiated plans to double its size. As a result, what started as a guest-only amenity is now a 56-room classic spa. While the bright and airy entrance bespeaks "spa," the rest of the decor misses the mark. Because it doesn't have the techno-wizardry of some of its competitors, it would have done well to employ some of Dale Chihuly's glass art that has made the Bellagio lobby such a landmark; instead, the long corridors are rather nondescript and dimly lit, so the water wall and illuminated aqua-colored glass features lose their impact. The elemental theme needs more than granite walls and votive candles, though for many guests, this very simplicity exudes peace. Overall, this is a classy spa with an exceptionally high standard of treatments, especially in skin care. In-the-know spa-goers would choose nowhere else for their facials. In fact, the service menu does a better job than most in delivering what Bellagio terms as world treatments—therapies from different continents that appeal to Bellagio's international guest set. Thai Yoga Massage, Indian Head Massage, and Ashiatsu Oriental Bar Therapy run alongside energy experiences such as a Chakra Balancing Treatment, a combination of energy and massage after which your body artist will gift you a special stone-charm chakra necklace. It's a nice touch and reflective of the attention to detail this spa delivers, with value-added extras that make every treatment a five-sensory affair.

RECOMMEND Bellagio's signature Watsu® Massage, an aquatic experience in which you float, cradled in the arms of a therapist who combines gentle Shiatsu stretches with movements in, out, under, and over the 94°F warm water. The sensations are almost sensual.

LOVE Hot Toe Bliss, a warm-stone tootsies massage (with elements of reflexology) that truly works wonders after walking the Strip.

THE ULTIMATE Ultimate HydraFacial. Unlike its competitors, Bellagio includes all five specialty-treatment steps in the service, including a crystal-free microdermabrasion. It's pricey but it works.

DISLIKE Decor doesn't reflect the elegance of the Bellagio name.

TIP This place has a great range of product samples, and they're unrelated to any sales pitch.

The Spa at Trump ★★★★
Trump International Hotel, 2000 Fashion Show Drive;
☎ **702-476-8000; trumplasvegashotel.com**

Customer service ★★★★★. **Facilities** ★★★★. **Amenities** ★★★. **Sales pressure** Low. **Price range** $35–$275, spa services; $35–$125, nail and refinement services. **Spa amenities** Complimentary with any spa service over $95; $12 hotel guests; pass includes access to fitness center.

SUMMARY AND COMMENTS With only nine treatment rooms, this refreshingly small spa emanates a modern elegance, as in grape-colored suede walls and lounge furniture, with quiet finesse. *New York* magazine voted it the best hotel spa in Las Vegas, and it's already made *Condé Nast*'s hot list. Spa treatments embrace the philosophy described in the best-selling *The Secret*—each blends your personal intention with oils and lotions that are mixed to embody balance, healing, revitalization, calm, and purity. These words reverberate throughout the spa industry, but here, they're cleverly packaged. Rooms, too, are named for the healing intentions of various gemstones, as are many oils. Choose Ruby to fire enthusiasm and detoxify the body, blood, and lymph systems. Opt for Emerald to overcome misfortunes, or go for rebalancing Diamond. The personal spa attaché is what really sets this spa apart, though others are sure to follow.

RECOMMEND Royal Lulur Ritual, created in 17th-century Indonesia for royal brides who were lavished with this ritual for 40 consecutive days prior to her wedding. It involves a body scrub, bath, and moisturizing massage with jasmine- and frangipani-infused products.

LOVE The morning-after eye cure, a 30-minute makeover for tired eyes.

THE ULTIMATE Trump Luxury, a seven-hour package for $1,120.

DISLIKE Twenty-percent service charge that's automatically charged to your bill, even though it's a discretionary gratuity.

TIP Spa-goers have direct access to the hotel's sundeck and outdoor pool. Have your personal spa attaché organize lunch in a shaded cabana.

The Spas at Wynn ★★★½
3131 South Las Vegas Boulevard; ☎ 702-770-8000; wynnlasvegas.com

Customer service ★★★★. Facilities ★★★★. Amenities ★★★★. Sales pressure Medium. Price range $135–$370, spa services; $35–$120, nail and refinement services. Spa amenities Complimentary with treatment of $75 and above; spa and fitness center pass $30 per day without treatment.

SUMMARY AND COMMENTS Wynn is all about over-the-top indulgence, so the spas at Wynn and Encore radiate lavish elegance that appeals to the heavy-wallet brigade and honeymooners. At Wynn, hoteliers obviously designed the layout with its 36 treatment rooms running off either side of the proverbial long corridor. At least you're walking on a handcrafted rug to give your feet a pampered touch, and sounds of trickling water and high-octane soothing music accompany you en route to your service. The full spa experience is as much about anticipation as it is delivery and on this, in both spas, Wynn scores top marks. Encore's spa, however, raises the bar even higher with an opulent Zen-inspired tropical environment; Buddha statues dominate the setting, as well as a number of natural-light garden suites (think lush foliage), which for Vegas is pretty radical. The staff is excellent. Not only have they been drilled in customer service (they seem to mind-read your name), the spa practitioners are knowledgeable, professional, and top of their form. Wynn has a good number of male estheticians, so be sure to specify if you have a gender preference. In terms of services, the menus may appear different in treatment descriptions between the two spas, but, in reality, a number of therapies are quite similar. If you have the time, enjoy a treatment in both. If not, go for Encore. It has an atmosphere of tranquil glitz, which is an oxymoron only possible in a place like Las Vegas.

RECOMMEND The signature Good Luck Ritual Massage is based on the five elements of feng shui: health, wealth, prosperity, happiness, and harmony. It's a yummy head-to-toe event with a heated, Thai herbal-body massage, a lemon verbena-and-peppermint foot treatment, an ultra-moisturizing hand therapy, and a wild-lime–botanical scalp service.

LOVE A massage in a private poolside cabana, or even in-room.

THE ULTIMATE A couple's stone massage in one of the four oversized couples suites—the nicest on the Strip.

DISLIKE Like most casino resorts, getting to anywhere is a marathon through a maze of slot machines (in Encore especially); directional signs need improvement.

TIP Spa is exclusive to hotel guests Friday and Saturday.

INDEX

Unofficial Guide Reader Survey

If you would like to express your opinion in writing about Las Vegas or this guidebook, complete the following survey and mail it to:

> *Unofficial Guides* Reader Survey
> P.O. Box 43673
> Birmingham, AL 35243

Inclusive dates of your visit:_____

Members of your party:

	Person 1	Person 2	Person 3	Person 4	Person 5
Gender:	M F	M F	M F	M F	M F
Age:					

How many times have you been to Las Vegas? _____
On your most recent trip, where did you stay?_____

Concerning your accommodations, on a scale of 100 as best and 0 as worst, how would you rate:

The quality of your room?   The value of your room?
The quietness of your room?   Check-in/check-out efficiency?
Shuttle service to the airport?   Swimming pool facilities?

Did you rent a car?_____   From whom?_____

Concerning your rental car, on a scale of 100 as best and 0 as worst, how would you rate:

Pick-up processing efficiency?_____ Return processing efficiency?___
Condition of the car?_____   Cleanliness of the car?_____
Airport shuttle efficiency?_____

Concerning your dining experiences:

Estimate your meals in restaurants per day? _____
Approximately how much did your party spend on meals per day? _____
_____

Favorite restaurants in Las Vegas:_____
_____

Did you buy this guide before leaving? _____ While on your trip?_____

How did you hear about this guide? (check all that apply)

Loaned or recommended by a friend ☐   Radio or TV ☐
Newspaper or magazine ☐   Bookstore salesperson ☐
Just picked it out on my own ☐   Library ☐
Internet ☐

What other guidebooks did you use on this trip?_____

_____

_____

_____

On a scale of 100 as best and 0 as worst, how would you rate them?

_____

_____

_____

Using the same scale, how would you rate the _Unofficial Guides_(s)?

_____

Are _Unofficial Guides_ readily available at bookstores in your area?_____

Have you used other _Unofficial Guides_? _____

Which one(s)? _____

_____

_____

Comments about your Las Vegas trip or the _Unofficial Guides_(s):

_____

_____

_____

_____

_____

_____

_____

_____

_____

_____

_____

_____

_____

_____

_____

_____

_____

_____

_____

_____